RENAISSANCE
DECORATIVE PAINTING
IN SCOTLAND

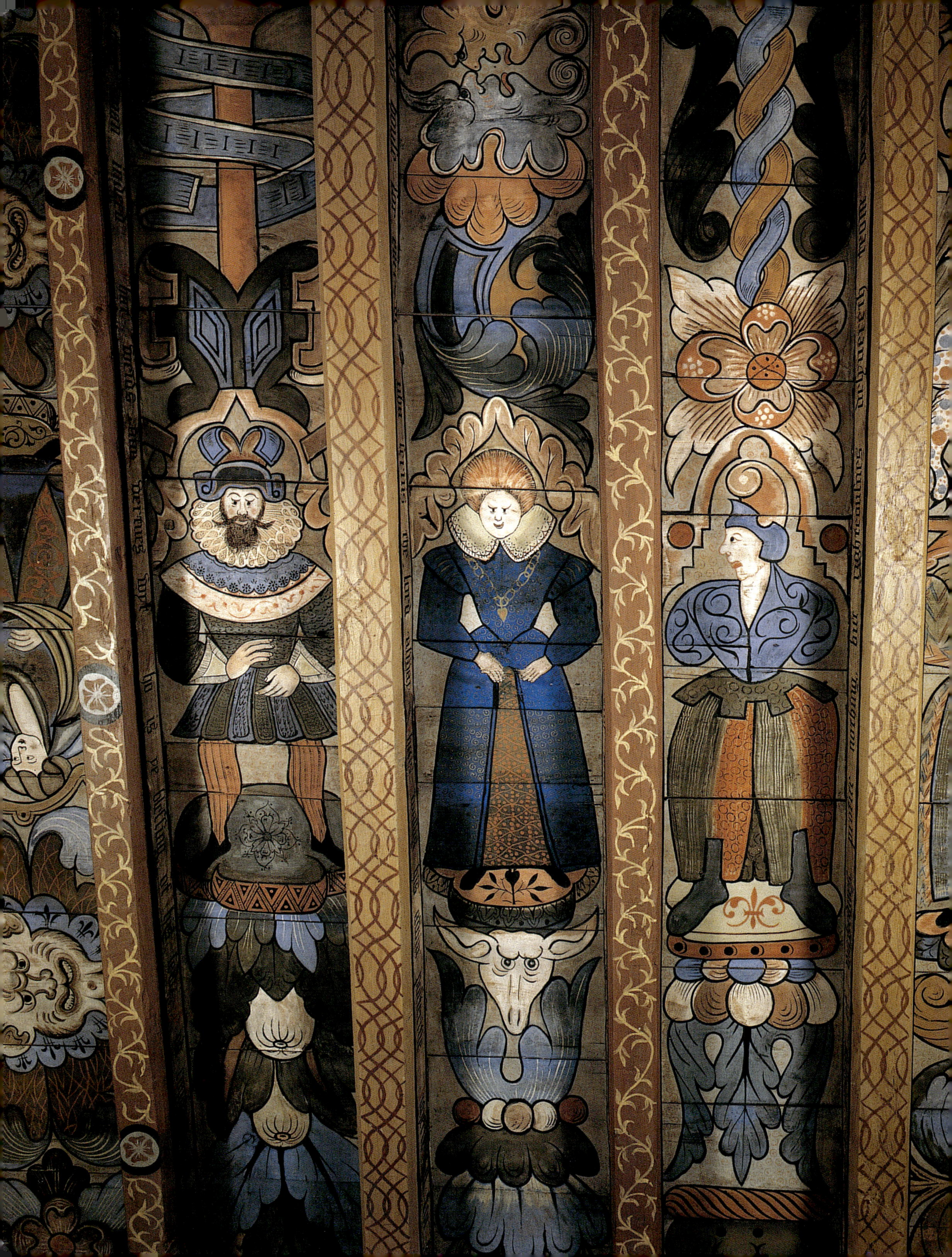

RENAISSANCE DECORATIVE PAINTING IN SCOTLAND

MICHAEL BATH

National Museums of Scotland Publishing

Cover: *Detail from* The sense of Hearing *panel from Dean House, Edinburgh, now NMS.* NMS

Frontispiece: *Detail from the ceiling painting in the Green Lady's Room at Crathes Castle.* D MACGREGOR, NTS

Published by
NMS Publishing
a division of NMS Enterprises Limited
National Museums of Scotland
Chambers Street
Edinburgh EH1 1JF

British Library Cataloguing in Publication Data
A catalogue record for this book is available from the British Library.

ISBN 1 901663 60 4

Project management and design by Elizabeth Robertson of NMS Publishing.

Printed and bound by Craftprint International plc, Singapore.

CONTENTS

Abbreviations and references

Historic Scotland	Branch of the Government Department of the Environment, with special responsibility for the listing and maintenance of historic buildings. Its Conservation Centre holds many examples removed from buildings in its stores; it also holds important conservation files and photographs.
NMS	The National Museums of Scotland.
NTS	The National Trust for Scotland, a charitable trust which purchases and conserves important heritage and environmental sites, most of which are open to the public.
RCAHMS	The Royal Commission on the Ancient and Historical Monuments of Scotland (includes National Monuments Record of Scotland).

Locations open to the public

Many buildings containing decorative painting are open to the public, although others, including some of the more important sites, are privately owned. Some, including those owned by the National Trust for Scotland, are only open during the summer months; local Tourist Information Centres will normally have information on opening hours and access.

Historic Scotland	Aberdour Castle; Argyll's Lodging; Dunfermline Abbey; Queen Mary's Room, Edinburgh Castle; Grandtully Chapel; Huntingtower Castle; Kinneil House (access by arrangement); Skelmorlie Aisle; Chapel Royal, Stirling Castle.
NMS	Painted ceilings on display from: Craig Castle; Dean House; Herdmanstone; Rossend Castle; Wester Livilands.
NTS	Crathes Castle; Culross Palace; Gladstone's Land; Falkland Palace; and Sailor's Walk (access by arrangement).
Other properties	Old Bridge Tavern; Delgaty Castle; Abbot House; Old Gala House; Holyrood Palace; Huntly House Museum (contains part of ceiling from Pinkie House); Innerpeffray Chapel; John Knox's House; Newark Castle; Provost Skene's House; Traquair Castle.

PREFACE

DECORATIVE paintings ('painted ceilings') of the sixteenth and seventeenth centuries are preserved in many buildings throughout Scotland, including quite a number that are open to the public – at the National Trust, Historic Scotland, or at other properties which are listed in the Inventory at the end of this book. Yet visitors wanting to know more about the meaning, artistry or history of such painting get very little help from existing guidebooks, and the only book ever to have been written on the subject was published many years ago and is long out of print. This distinctive Scottish tradition is not a mere tourist attraction, however, but an important addition to the corpus of Renaissance painting and European applied arts. It certainly requires careful art-historical study if we are to understand what we are looking at when we visit such places as Crathes Castle, Culross Palace, Gladstone's Land, Grandtully Chapel, Provost Skene's House or Skelmorlie Aisle – to name only a few of the more familiar examples. Understanding what these paintings mean, and how they might be functioning in the buildings which they decorate, will tell us quite a lot about the history and culture of Scotland at this period and, particularly, about its Renaissance pretensions and European connections. That is to say, this artistic heritage is not just a local antiquarian curiosity but an important body of work which requires the attention of academic art historians, media and cultural studies, students of the applied arts, iconology and semiotics. Hence what I have written is, necessarily, an 'academic' book; I hope and believe, however, that it will also be accessible and informative to non-specialist readers who want to know more about this neglected and little understood area of our Scottish heritage.

My own interest in this painting arose out of work on the multifarious applications of Renaissance emblem books. That may explain why a major preoccupation in the chapters that follow is with the problem of what these images mean – questions of emblematics, iconology, iconography. However, I have tried also to address questions of their architectural function, their style, and the way they participate in the wider systems of representation, the visual economies, and grammars of ornament that were current at this period throughout Europe. I have, I believe, been able to show how deeply indebted they were to commercial prints and pattern books, many of them published on the continent.

Nicolas Barker's magnificent edition of Thomas Trevilian's *Great Book* appeared only as my own book was going to press. Containing more than 1000 pages of coloured designs for embroidery and other patterns, Trevilian's manuscript of 1616, together with the earlier manuscript of 1606 in the Folger Shakespeare Library, must now be recognised as key documents for any research into the decorative arts in Britain at this period. I have to thank my long-suffering editor for allowing me at the very last minute to give some account of Trevilian's work in chapter one, and to signal its particular connections with Scottish decorative painting in the pages that follow. I would, indeed, like to record my gratitude for the trouble which Cara Shanley and Elizabeth Robertson of NMS Publishing have taken to realise its author's intentions in the design and production of this book.

I have been lucky to secure the help over the years of many people whose own knowledge and expertise has helped to cover the gaps in my own. I wish to acknowledge the kindness of Alison Adams, Harry Adams, John Astington, Peter Davidson, Milad Doueihi, Alastair Fowler, Antony Griffiths and Sheila O'Connell of the British Museum Department of Prints and Drawings, Malcolm Jones, Kit Martin, Jean Michel Massing, Aonghus McKechnie, Charles McKean, and Stephen Rawles. I am particularly grateful to Fiona Allardyce of Historic Scotland Conservation for much help and advice, Robert Wilmot for allowing me access to HS Conservation files, Alec Colthart, also of HS Conservation, for laying out innumerable painted boards and sharing his knowledge of what they contained. Staff at the Royal Commission on the Ancient and Historical Monuments of Scotland have been helpful beyond the call of duty, and I wish to acknowledge particularly the kindness of Neil Cameron and Clare Sorenson in identifying and supplying illustrations from the National Monuments Record. Those who have opened doors include Joseph Chandler at Loretto School, Father Raymond at Nunraw, Mr and Mrs David Baxter and, more recently, Mr and Mrs Paul Veenheijzen at Earlshall, Mrs J V Robinson of Beldorney, the late Capt. Hay and Mrs J Johnson at Delgaty, the Earl of Perth at Stobhall, Alison Butler at Gladstone's Land (and all the way down the Royal Mile in Edinburgh!), Grace Murray with invaluable help at Culross, Laura Norris at Moubray House and in Kirkcaldy, the Earl of Crawford at Balcarres, and Lady Grant at Monymusk. Several years ago I learned that Elizabeth Bracegirdle was working on a thesis on this subject for the University of Aberdeen. Since we both felt that there was no point in competing for results, duplicating research effort, or harassing the owners of historic buildings to open them up for our separate visits, we agreed on a policy of mutual collaboration of which this book is the major beneficiary. Particular debts are her identification of an engraving from Vredeman de Vries's *Perspectiva* as the pattern for the *trompe l'oeil* cupola at Pinkie House and of other print sources for religious painting at Provost Skene's House, but I have also gained in less immediately identifiable ways from her insights and approaches to the material we have both been studying. Finally, my wife Penny spent precious time checking 'final' drafts, insisting all along that what I write should make sense to the non-specialist reader.

My work was greatly facilitated by a research grant from the British Academy that allowed me to take time out from teaching in 1996, and this book is published with the aid of a generous publications grant from the Paul Mellon Centre for Studies in British Art. I would like through this work to repay some of my manifold debts to Scotland, my adoptive *patria*, and I dedicate the book to my daughter Annabel, *hereditatis custos optima.*

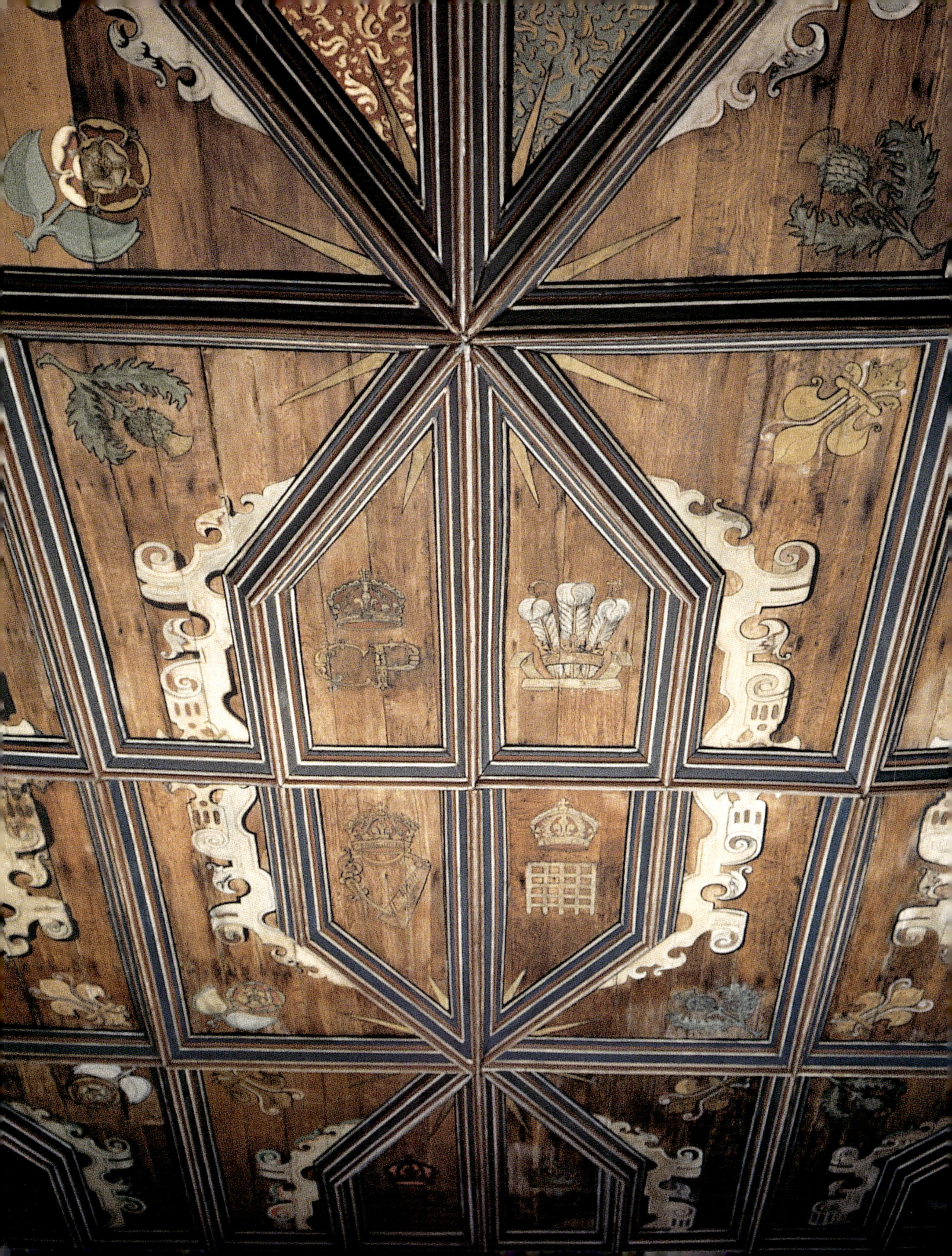
CP

1

A NATIONAL STYLE

IN his standard history of *Scottish Art* (1990) Duncan Macmillan writes, 'The decorative painting of the reign of James VI and the early years of his son would, by its very quantity alone, be a striking feature of Scottish culture, but it also seems to be quite specific to Scotland' (p.56). Such painting survives, or is recorded, in more than one hundred different buildings throughout Scotland, ranging from royal palaces and the castles of the nobility to modest burgess houses of the increasingly affluent middle class. Nor is such painting confined to domestic buildings since, despite the wholesale destruction of Scotland's medieval inheritance of religious painting following the Reformation, new schemes of decoration were executed in a number of churches and chapels. Indeed, perhaps the most surprising thing about this tradition of decorative painting is that it should have coincided with a period of such intense religious iconoclasm. In 1559 the Reformation breaking of images was described by a witness as follows: 'The manner of reformation is this – they pull down abbeys, cleanse parishes of all images – and prohibit all masses.' In the following year the *First Book of Discipline*, which laid down the law on the regulation of the reformed church in Scotland, required 'all idolatry ... to be utterly suppressed'. Yet the new style of decorative painting uses images which are far from being simply decorative; more often its subjects – secular and religious, classical, emblematic, historical, or heraldic – are iconographically significant, full of meaning; speaking pictures. Understanding what they were saying and how they were functioning in this Scottish climate of Renaissance iconology and Reformation iconoclasm would seem to be a task worth pursuing.

As Macmillan says, 'The sheer quantity of such painting and the social range of those for whom it was executed clearly reflect the establishment of a new standard of civil life' (p.56). It therefore has to be understood as part of a wider development in Scottish culture that includes the architectural revival of the late sixteenth and early seventeenth centuries. What a contemporary observer describes as the 'fair new fabric and stately edifices' (cited Howard 1995, p.48) which had arisen out of monastic properties, not only served to define their owners' social status but were also designed to express a new sense of national identity. It is now more widely accepted

Opposite: *Regal iconography for a royal palace, the Chapel Royal at Falkland Palace.* HS

than it used to be that the castellated style of building, and particularly the use of a native style of flamboyant bartizans, skewputs, and corbels, represents a conscious stylistic choice, rather than any kind of defensive necessity. These Renaissance castles and tower houses are making stylistic statements before they are doing anything else, and their internal decoration has to be seen as contributing to such statements.

Much of this painting was carried out for the class of person described by William Lithgow in 1628: 'as for the nobility and gentry of the kingdom, certainly, as they are generous, manly and full of courage; so are they courteous, discreet, learned scholars well read in the best histories, delicate linguists, the most part of them being brought up in France or Italy' (cited Howard 1995, p.49). We shall certainly see that much of this painting assumes a certain level of literacy, both verbal and visual, in its viewer, which undoubtedly reflects not only the humanism of the court of James VI but also the level of general education that was available to virtually all social classes who had access to the Scottish universities. Moreover, many graduates of Scottish universities in the late sixteenth and early seventeenth centuries went on to further study abroad, in the Netherlands, France, Italy and as far afield as Poland. There they would have had direct access to buildings that exhibited the latest trends in the European decorative arts. Scottish connections with continental Europe had, of course, been much closer throughout the sixteenth century than England's, and we should not make the mistake of regarding this northern tradition as some kind of regional extension of an English fashion. It is, rather, a fully independent national tradition with its own European connections. Its failure to attract the kind of scholarly attention it manifestly deserves is a symptom of the marginalisation of Scottish culture in a British context and the traditional neglect of the applied arts by conventional 'fine art' historians.

Painted decoration in royal palaces was the responsibility of successive Masters of the King's Works, who were periodically charged with restoring or refurbishing one or other of the five palaces between which the royal household regularly migrated. After the Union of the Crowns in 1603 such redecoration was most likely to be required in anticipation of projected royal visits, which James and his successor made to their northern kingdom in 1617 and 1633. Undoubtedly royal tastes influenced architectural styles in the houses of the nobility, and some of the most outstanding examples of decorative painting are to be found in the houses of noble families whose names figure in the history of Scotland – the Gordons, Hamiltons, Ruthvens, Hays, Setons, Stewarts, Kerrs, Drummonds, Lindsays. Both the ancient members of the Scottish nobility, and the more recent 'lords of erection' who played such a significant part in the increasingly competent administration of James VI, had taken over the estates of the Catholic Church (which had owned about a third of the land in Scotland before the Reformation). Younger sons of the nobility were regularly appointed as lay 'commendators' to ancient abbeys, thus securing their family's title to the property and income of the ecclesiastical estates which they tried to consolidate by affirming the antiquity of their lineage and titles through the heraldic and dynastic iconography that often predominates on both the external sculptured stonework and internal painting of their houses. Often this dynastic iconography, however, is intent not so much on establishing the particular lineage and antiquity of the owner's own family – though it may be doing so – as on defining a more extended scheme of European monarchy and/or Scottish nobility, which normally includes direct or implied statements of loyalty to the Scottish crown. Such heraldic schemes help to define the relation of the Scottish nobility to its monarchy, and it seems likely that important reconstructions of the nation's relation to its history were also at play in these architectural and iconographic programmes, reconstructions which have at least some similarities with the revival of medieval chivalry (in the work of Edmund Spenser and Philip Sidney, for instance) which took place at this period in Elizabethan England.

The architectural context in which this painting flourished does not consist, however, solely of this exploitation of a native style, for its vocabulary includes some elements, or some developments, which one can only describe as classical. The rebuilding of the Chapel Royal at Stirling in 1594 saw one of the earliest Scottish examples of a purely classical design, with its entrance portal based on continental models illustrated by Serlio (Howard 1995, pp.31-3). Its interior was treated to an elaborate programme of decoration, including the surviving decorative painting. The paintings executed for Alexander Seton at Pinkie House, Musselburgh, are similarly contained in a building that insistently declares its aspiration towards an ideal of classical humanism. We need to beware, however, of assuming that 'classicism' is a matter of unswerving commitment to Vitruvian models. Historians sometimes write as though architecture in Britain at this time was holding its breath for the belated arrival of Inigo Jones, but the visual arts in both England and Scotland employed more diverse classical elements long before any strict adherence to classical models became de rigueur. As Lucy Gent argues, 'twentieth-century perceptions of the classicism embodied in the Italian Renaissance are inappropriate to sixteenth- and seventeenth-century Britain' (Gent 1995, p.3, and see Christy Anderson, 'Learning to Read Architecture ...' in Gent, pp.239-86). Even before the arrival of a thoroughgoing neoclassical revival, which in Scotland means the period of William Bruce or of William Adam, Scottish buildings will be found to be signalling, however sporadically and indistinctly, their aspiration towards those standards of taste and cultivation which traditionally adhered to the classical. Those signals represent an international dimension which complements the more vernacular vocabulary of the castellated Scottish baronial style, a style which itself turns out to have more continental analogues than was sometimes thought. Both are essential, and complementary rather than opposed, elements of a local renaissance.

Scottish decorative painting conforms to this pattern in its inclusion of both vernacular and more cosmopolitan elements. While Duncan Macmillan's claim that it was 'specific to Scotland' has much to be said for it, decorative painting of various kinds can be found throughout Europe in buildings of this

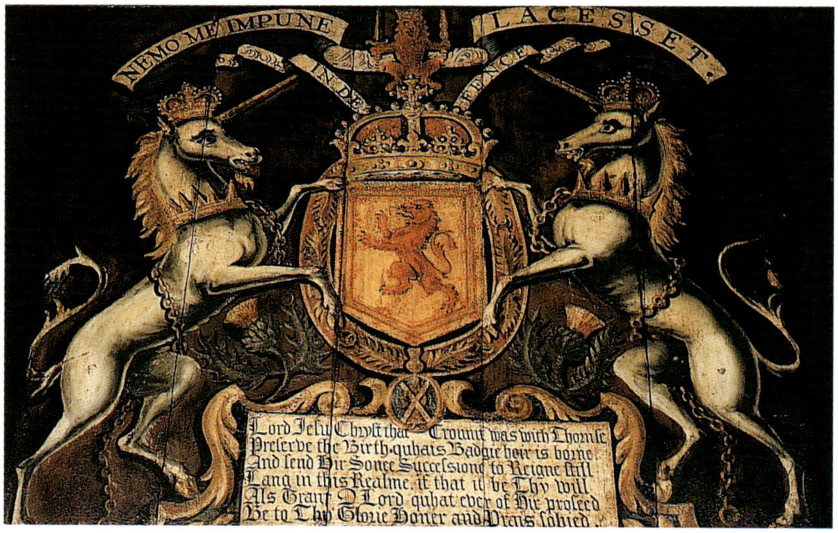

Royal arms of Scotland and inscription in the birthroom of James VI in Edinburgh Castle, painting executed by John Anderson for the royal visit of 1617.

period, and the Scottish school demonstrably draws on a decorative vocabulary of wider provenance. The identification of some of its analogues and antecedents will, perhaps, help us to define the international context within which it was working. A national style need not be parochial.

The question of how far this style of painting was regionally or geographically distinctive is closely linked to the related question of its historical termini. There are good reasons for claiming that it is both geographically and historically distinct, with the Reformation as a clear enough starting point, and the Civil Wars of the 1640s signalling its close. A near-contemporary description of the work of a painter called Andrew Bairhum, who was working at Kinloss Abbey as early as 1538, describes some of his work as in 'the lighter style of painting which is now customary throughout Scotland' (Ferrerius, *Historia Abbatum de Kinloss*, cited Macmillan 1990, p.35), and this highly suggestive comment has been taken as an indication that 'the fashion for painted interiors, that we know from surviving painted ceilings, was already established in the reign of James V' (ibid., p.36). The earliest paintings we can identify as belonging to the new tradition, however, are those executed for the Earl of Arran at Kinneil, which date from the 1650s. Arran was Regent of Scotland from 1542-54, and these are predominantly religious subjects, but the next-earliest datable example, the remarkable scheme of grotesque painting executed for Mark Kerr at Prestongrange, is dated 1581 and could certainly be described as 'in the lighter style', including, as it does, Priapic figures copied from a book ascribed to Rabelais. The majority of its grotesque motifs are copied directly from the *Grottesco: in diversche manieren* (c.1565-71) of Jan Vredeman de Vries, and the style of this ceiling has to be seen as the earliest Scottish example of that Renaissance ornamental vocabulary which began to spread across northern Europe from its Flemish sources in the second half of the sixteenth century. The painted ceilings at Delgaty Castle record their own dates as 1592, 1593 and 1597, whilst those at Crathes similarly have the dates 1599 and 1602 painted on the beams. We know that the painting in the Chapel Royal, Stirling, was executed for the baptism of Prince Henry in 1594, the painting in James VI's birthroom in Edinburgh Castle was of 1617, and the redecoration at Falkland Palace was ordered for the royal visit of 1633. Painted ceilings at Gladstone's Land bear the date 1620; at The Dean, Edinburgh, 1627; at Ballachastell, 1634; at Gala House,

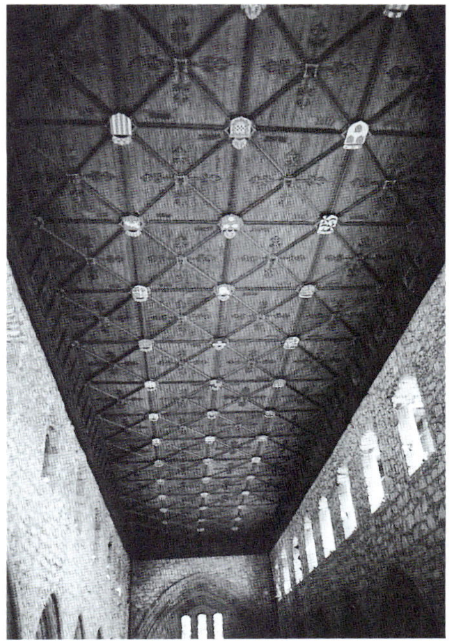

Galashiels, 1635; and at Skelmorlie Aisle, 1638. The dating of other examples depends on what we know about the history of the building, or may be inferred from dates carved on lintels, from owners' initials, or from armorial bearings elsewhere in the building. It seems likely that most of the painting at Culross, for instance, was executed for George Bruce shortly after one or other of the dates, 1579 and 1611, carved on the respective wings of his house, the latter being the date when he was knighted.

Some examples, however, have been included which fall outside these historical boundaries. Around 1520 Gavin Dunbar, Bishop of Aberdeen, had the nave of St Machar's Cathedral decorated with a series of carved and painted coats of arms which includes the shields of the Scottish bishops, of the nobility of Scotland, and of the European (or terrestrial) monarchies. This scheme is unlike anything else to be found in British churches, and its connections are almost certainly with an armorial tradition that descends from the later Middle Ages and was taken up by a number of the armorial ceilings of the later period. The St Machar's decoration therefore constitutes an important precursor of a type of painting that concerns us in this book. There are also at least a few examples of more traditional painting in Scottish churches that escaped the destruction of the image breakers. Two of the best known examples are the paintings at Foulis Easter, near Dundee, and at Guthrie Aisle, near Brechin, which repre-

Nave of St Machars Cathedral, Aberdeen, pre-Reformation painting showing the heraldic arms of the terrestrial monarchies, the Scottish bishops, and the Scottish nobility.

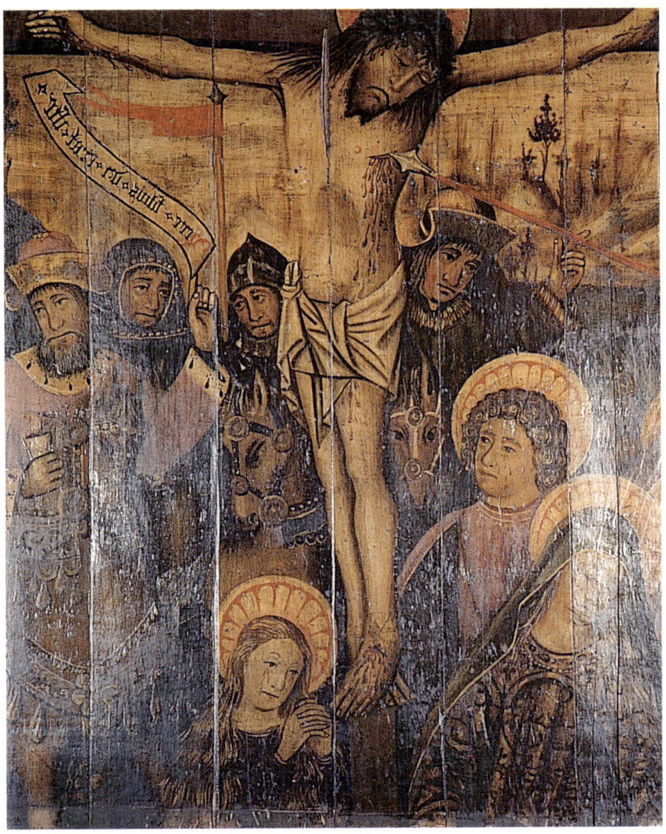

Pre-Reformation Scottish painting, part of the late fifteenth-century rood screen at Foulis Easter, Angus. HS

sent clear survivals, dating as they probably do from the late fifteenth century. Other ecclesiastical painting which is more difficult to date, such as that in the cathedrals at Elgin and Dunkeld, and in the abbey at Dunfermline, may well represent a survival of pre-Reformation art in Scotland and should not be included in the Renaissance decorative tradition which is our subject. But it is not easy to supply a precise date for most of these, and it seems worth giving some account of them for the sake of completeness.

A few examples, likewise, can be assigned dates which might seem to call into question Duncan Macmillan's statement that this type of painting 'stopped abruptly with the Civil War' (p.52). The painted gallery at Cullen, for instance, includes not only the royal arms of Scotland on the wall at one end but also the arms of Charles II, clearly ascribed in the painted initials 'CR2', forcing us to assign both coats of arms to the Restoration period. The stellar painting, with its planetary and other deities on the soffit of the same ceiling, appears to have been executed by the same hand and is almost certainly of the same date, unlike the classical subjects – the Sack of Troy, the Calydonian Boar-Hunt, and Diana and Actaeon – painted on the two side panels, which are evidently earlier work. Such later work would include a barrel-vaulted ceiling in the remains of the town house of General Thomas Dalziel, commander of the forces of Charles II, persecutor of the Covenanters, and victor in the Battle of Pentland, 1666. According to Daniel Wilson in his *Memorials of Edinburgh* (1848, vol. ii, p.70), 'The chief apartment was a hall of unusually large dimensions, with an arched or waggon-shaped ceiling adorned with a painting of the sun in the centre, surrounded by gilded rays on an azure ground. The remainder of the ceiling was painted to represent sky and clouds and spangled over with a series of silvered stars in relief.' It would appear that this was similar to the type of stellar ceiling we find at Innerpeffray Chapel, at Liberton House (Edinburgh), and in Linlithgow. The nineteen *trompe l'oeil* Corinthian pilasters in Argyll's Lodging in Stirling were executed as late as 1675 – these are one of the few commissions for which a surviving contract enables us not only to date the work but also to identify the artist, namely the painter David McBeath, who had been apprenticed to Joseph Stanefield in Edinburgh in 1671. Though there may be a few such precursors or remnants of this decorative tradition, all its major examples nevertheless belong in the reins of James VI and Charles I. The tradition is, we may claim, both geographically and historically discrete.

It has sometimes been said that the demise of decorative painting coincides with and, by implication, was a consequence of, the development of a taste for decorative plasterwork in the later seventeenth century. We should, however, beware of assuming a clear break between the fashion for tempera painting on boards and the new taste for decorative plasterwork that undoubtedly spread north from England. Some of the decorative plasterwork in Scotland is quite early and is associated with the same patrons, families, and buildings where painted decoration is found. The plasterwork at Muchalls, Aberdeenshire, for instance, was carried out for Thomas Burnett, whose main residence was just

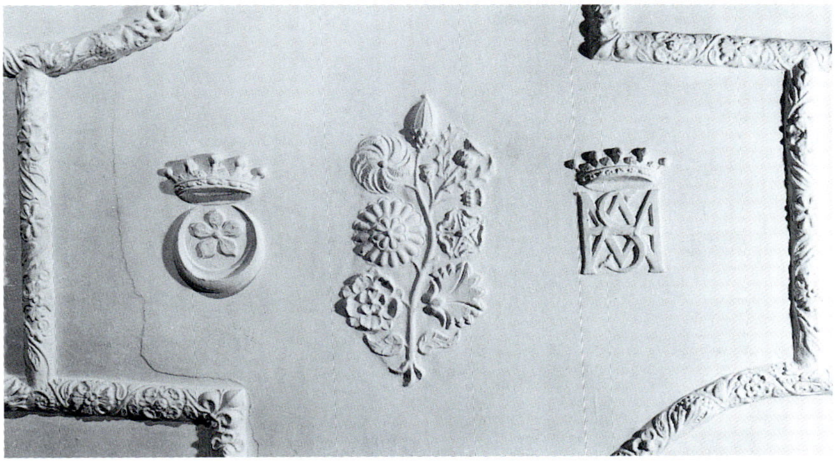

Plasterwork from Pinkie House, using motifs – cinquefoil, crescent, and coronet with monogram of Alexander Seton and Margaret Hamilton – which also features in the decorative painting. HS

twenty miles away at Crathes, where his father Alexander had executed the most extensive programme of painted decoration to be found anywhere in Scotland only twenty years previously. The early plasterwork at Pinkie House is almost certainly contemporary with the decoration of the painted long gallery, using the same personal devices of Alexander Seton that we find in his decorative painting. Seton was a cousin and close friend of Alexander Burnett, as it happens. The delicate mouldings at Pinkie are copied at Winton Castle, East Lothian, where documents record 'John Quytte' as the plasterer. The English plasterers Richard Cob and Ralph Rawlinson travelled to Scotland to do plasterwork, and almost certainly a taste for decorative plasterwork was acquired by the large number of Scots who migrated to London in the years immediately following the Union of Crowns. Moulds used in England were also employed in Scotland; the cycle of heads of the nine Worthies which is found at Merchiston, Edinburgh, and at Balcarres, Fife, for instance, has been shown to use the same moulds as the heads from Bromley-by-Bow in London (1606), now in the Victoria and Albert Museum.

Decorative painting is found on plaster, stonework, the walls of houses, window embrasures, overmantels and vaulting, but by far the greater part of this work is painted on wooden boards on the ceiling; indeed decorative painting in Scotland is commonly described in the phrase 'painted ceilings'. This alone makes the Scottish tradition somewhat exceptional. Sometimes, it is true, the painting is carried onto the plaster to create a decorative frieze, as at Gladstone's Land, Earlshall, or Crathes, but the rest of the walls tended to be left bare. This was probably because they would normally be covered with tapestry or painted cloths. The ceilings themselves tend to be of two kinds. Most common is the type we call open *board-and-beam* ceilings. In these the supporting beams are likely to be painted on all three sides and between them are the undersides of the floorboards of the room above. Such a surface places severe constraints on design possibilities, consisting as it does of a series of long, narrow compartments between beams. It favours linear, repetitive, or elongated images: rows of heraldic shields, flower and plant forms, winged cherubs, and animals and grotesque figures in fixed or, more often, in seemingly random sequences. That there were several such compartments lying side by side occasionally suggested its suitability for such fixed and conventional sequences as the nine Worthies or the Cardinal Virtues (both at Crathes), one per section. The beams themselves are generally given a purely decorative treatment, though their sides may be covered in writing, usually texts from the Bible or proverbial sayings, sometimes versified. These images often assume a viewing angle that changes as one moves about the room. Sometimes it is not easy to make much sense of the way such viewing angles articulate the spaces which the decoration fills, though much may depend on the position of doors, windows, or fireplace, and the uses to which the chamber was put.

These problems of articulation become, if anything, greater in the second type, the *barrel-vaulted* or *coved* ceiling, whose surface is entirely covered with wooden boards suspended from the roof, creating an unbroken surface upon which the painter has a free hand. Nothing much can be done on such a surface, however, until it has been divided up into sections – until it has been articulated. Often the solution is to treat it to some false architecture, divide it up with *trompe l'oeil* coffering, with the illusion of moulded rib-work or with false vaulting. Such divisions of the surface space create a number of smaller compartments that can be filled with images.

The medium for most of this painting is tempera colour. The painting was normally executed *in situ*, with the artist working above his head. The surface was first prepared by laying on a white ground, made up of a mixture of chalk and size, and the design was drawn onto this in a black outline, which was then filled in with colour. The black outlining remains visible and should not be seen as the sign of crude and unskilful work; in cases where the colour has since decayed or faded it remains our only clue as to what was represented. As Schomberg Scott says, 'The drawing of the outline and the infilling of colour were not necessarily done by the same hand. There are indications in certain instances that when more than one room in a house was being done at the same time, the master would draw in all the outline designs and then, in the less important places, leave the infilling of colour to his assistants' (Scott 1971, pp.33-4). There are two places, Aberdour and Northfield, where the ground is not white but black, and at Prestongrange the grotesque designs are all executed on a ground that was originally a bright red.

Glue tempera is a type of water-based distemper, in which the pigment is suspended in a glue-based size. The pigments used are natural materials: lamp-black, chalk, lead- or iron-oxide for red, copper verdigris for green and a crushed azurite for blue. Though subject to discolouration as a result of damp or dirt, such pigments do not fade appreciably on exposure to light, but because they are water-based are badly damaged by water penetration. Many of the vanished examples fell victim to leaking roofs and gutters, and many survivors show signs of such damage. Several of the ceilings, including some of the more important ones, only survived as a result of last-minute rescue operations. Since the 1950s, however, there has been a growing body of technical expertise devoted to their conservation and restoration at the Stenhouse Conservation Centre (now Historic Scotland Conservation) in Edinburgh. Many of the original ceilings were later plastered over; perhaps the best thing that could have happened to them since it afforded protection until paintings came to light during more recent alterations. As Schomberg Scott notes, 'No protective coat

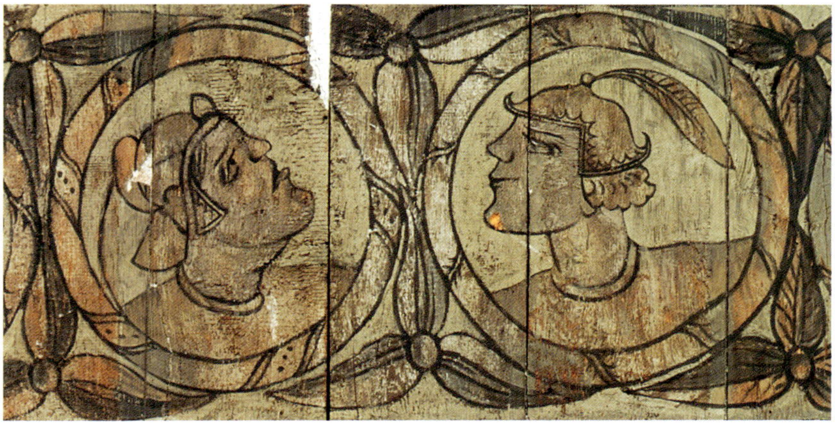

Vigorously drawn roundels from Craig Castle, Montrose, now on display in NMS. NMS

of varnish was ever applied by the original artists so that the finished surface should be absolutely matt, almost chrystalline. Where this has survived it can be appreciated how important it is to the general character. Unfortunately there are cases where varnish has been applied in the present century in a mistaken attempt at preservation and it has always proved wholly disastrous'. With some examples, particularly those that came to light in the nineteenth century, restoration consisted largely of heavy overpainting, so that much of the paint one sees at Crathes, at Stobhall, and at Gala House, for instance, is not original. Conservation techniques applied to the earliest property to come into the safe-keeping of the National Trust for Scotland, Culross, in 1937, turned out to be inappropriate to the tempera medium and, rather than conserving the paint, have destroyed most of it. Early pre-conservation sketches and photographs now represent the best record we have of some of this decoration. These include the colour sketches by the nineteenth-century architect, Thomas Bonnar, who drew a number of the schemes in the 1840s and 1850s as patterns or precedents for some of his own designs for the decoration of Victorian neo-baronial interiors. Bonnar's drawings, now conserved in the National Monuments Record in Edinburgh, not only offer a record of some of the surviving ceilings before more recent restoration or overpainting, but also represent the unique record of a number of examples, such as Dalcross and Borthwick castles and Pitcairn Church, which have since been destroyed. Early restorers did not scruple to supply missing detail or missing letters from an inscription, even managing in some cases to get the Latin grammar wrong. In looking at these paintings, therefore, we need to bear in mind that what we are looking at is not always what was originally painted or, at least, may not be the original paint. In the concluding Inventory of this book I have tried to supply details not only of the non-extant examples but also of the conservation history of the surviving painting wherever this could be important.

Oil paint is sometimes used rather than tempera – for instance at Skelmorlie Aisle, or the panels from The Dean, Edinburgh – but was normally reserved for external use; indeed the accounts written in 1628-9 by the Master of the King's Works, James Murray, specify oil for external and tempera for internal surfaces at Stirling Castle, 'the window brodis to be layit over without with oyle cullour and within in Temper cullour and the articles weill set af' (*Maitland Club Miscellany* 1843, p.372). These instructions, and payments, are recorded specifically to the painter Valentine Jenkin, and they allow us a rare chance of identifying the actual painter responsible for the work. Valentine Jenkin also worked

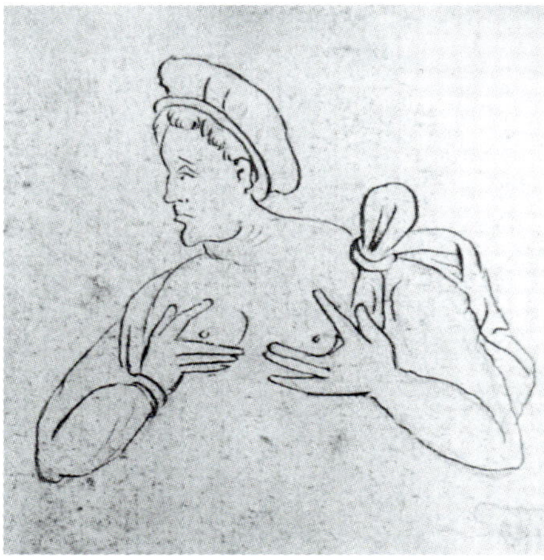

Sketch from Lyon Court's Forman Armorial of an unidentified figure; if this was intended for decorative use it suggests the close connections between decorative and heraldic painting.

in Glasgow at this time, where he gilded the cock and painted the civic and royal arms above the Tolbooth, and in 1629 he was also being paid for work at Falkland Palace. In 1634 the accounts of Lady Hamilton record payments to the same artist for work at Hamilton and at Kinneil, allowing us almost certainly to ascribe the surviving painting of this period at Kinneil to him. It is seldom possible, however, to identify the artist who carried out the painting in specific buildings. We do know that in preparation for King James's return to Scotland in 1617 John Anderson (fl.1599-1649) was summoned from Huntly Castle to carry out work at Falkland Palace, and at Edinburgh Castle, where he painted the room in which the king had been born fifty years earlier. George Jamesone, afterwards to become the most celebrated Scottish portrait painter of the seventeenth century, was Anderson's apprentice in 1612. Sir John Grant of Freuchie regarded Anderson as the only artist good enough to paint the ceiling of his gallery at Ballachastell. The only paintings to be signed by the artist are at Delgaty, where the initials 'JM' have been taken to be those of John Melville (or Mellin), who worked in Aberdeen, and the Skelmorlie Aisle at Largs, where one of the compartments is signed 'J Stalker fecit 1638'. This has to be the James Stalker who was registered apprentice to John Sawers in Edinburgh in 1632. Sawers, his master, was appointed Snowdon Herald in 1643 and compiled a manuscript armorial (Nat Lib Scot Adv MS 31.4.4) and it may be Sawers and not his pupil who was responsible for the fine heraldic painting in the aisle at Largs. Other herald painters are worth recording, since they are very likely to have been responsible for decorative painting. Perhaps the most interesting of these is James Workman (fl.1587-1633) who was appointed Marchmont Herald in 1597, and has left us an illustrated armorial manuscript which contains what look like sketches of biblical scenes for decorative use. We know that he, too, was paid for work at royal palaces, Edinburgh, Holyrood, Linlithgow, at various times between 1616 and 1633. Since he owned a house in Burntisland, Fife, it seems not unlikely that he was responsible for the two surviving painted ceilings at Burntisland, at Rossend Castle and at Mary Somerville's House.

There were no Painter-Stainers Guilds in Scotland as there were in England, and painters belonged to the same trade guild as the Wrights and Masons. Payment accounts confirm that they were normally expected to carry out not only artwork in the form of figure and scene paintings, but a whole variety of other types of work: John Sawers, for instance, was paid in 1618 for colours 'for painting of his majesties bed that wes sent up to London'; James Workman was paid for work on the ship that took the king to Denmark to bring home his queen in 1589, and for gilding and painting of the decorations that greeted Queen Anne on her ceremonial entry into Edinburgh (Apted and Hannabuss 1978, p.108). Use of the English term 'limners' is unknown in Scotland before the late seventeenth century and there seems to have been no distinction between what we would think of as 'art' painting and routine decoration. The painting we are looking at in this study is all the work of tradesmen; journeymen artists.

The surviving corpus of painting from the sixteenth and seventeenth centuries in Britain, though not exactly meagre, should nevertheless be regarded as small enough for us to want to preserve and document the whole surviving corpus. A primary aim of this study has been, therefore, to offer as exhaustive an account of Renaissance decorative painting in Scotland as possible, and the Inventory at the end of the book aims to provide an inclusive catalogue of all known examples, both surviving instances and records of those which have disappeared. Only a sufficiently inclusive Inventory will allow us to draw reliable conclusions, for instance, about the distribution and extent of such painting in Scotland.

Even before we have established the corpus, however, we need to ask various questions of these paintings, questions which we might distinguish under the separate headings of content and context. Under content, I assume that we want to know what the painting represents. In many cases that may seem obvious enough, though accurate description will often reveal significant details even in images that appear to be self-evident. But some of this painting represents subjects by no means obvious or commonplace and which have remained unidentified, or sometimes misidentified, by previous viewers. Allegorical and emblematic images, for instance, draw on the iconological systems of their day and can only be properly explicated once their iconology has been recognised. Such description and explication is fundamental; before we do anything else with this painting we need to know what we are looking at and what it represents.

Iconology is largely a matter of identifying sources and analogues for particular images. The best book on the decorative arts of this period in England, Anthony Wells-Cole's *Art and Decoration in Tudor and Jacobean England* (1997), concentrates on identifying sources in contemporary English and continental prints. Wells-Cole's pioneering study has shown just how derivative the decorative arts were at this period; very little appears to be original work. That sets it apart from many of our modern assumptions about 'creative' design and artistic originality – instead we probably need to bear in mind those much older Renaissance doctrines which saw the close connection between imitation and invention. Scottish decorative painting can be shown to be equally indebted to continental prints, and much of the discussion that follows will be taken up with an exploration of the relationship between specific paintings and particular prints which supplied their patterns.

Woodcuts and copperplate engravings circulated both in printed books – illustrated Bibles, natural histories, fable and emblem books – and as commercial prints which might be sold either in single sheets or in 'sets' which could be bound up. The printing of multiple copies from woodcuts developed in the late fourteenth century and the use of intaglio prints, where the ink lies in the grooves scraped out of a copper plate, developed in the late fifteenth. This technology helped to secure the circulation of multiple copies of the same image with consequences for the visual arts that were, arguably, almost as momentous as the invention of movable type was for the printed book. In the early sixteenth century there were still a few artists – of whom Dürer is probably best known – who excelled both in the art of painting and as engravers, but by the mid-sixteenth century a gap had opened between the artist who drew the pictures and the engraver who executed the print. That gap helped to foster the growth of a separate trade of professional craftsmen who made their living from the production of commercial prints. By the mid-sixteenth century there were leading European centres for printmaking in Italy (Rome, Florence, Venice, Bologna); France (Paris, Lyon); Germany (Augsburg, Frankfurt, Nuremberg);

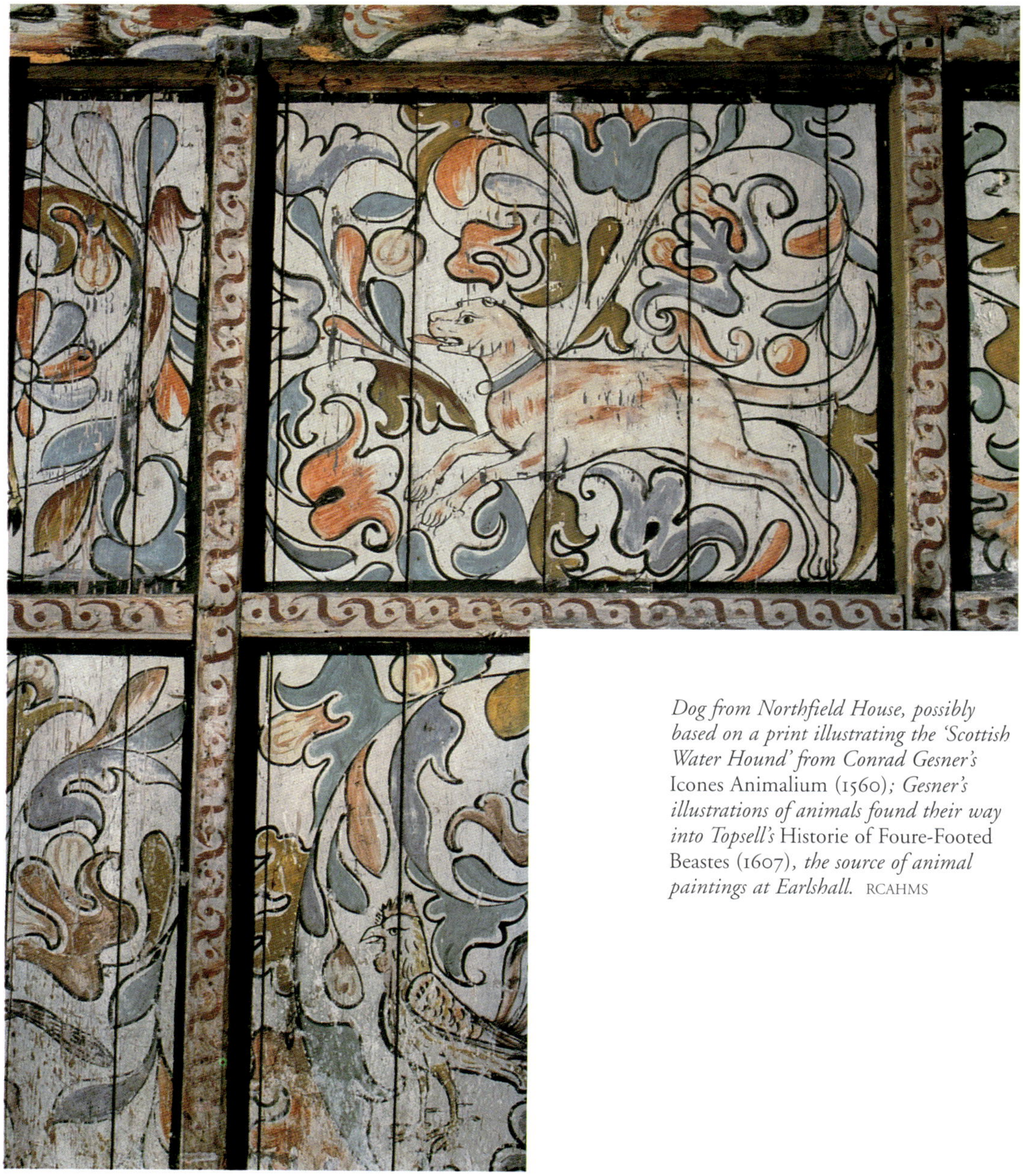

Dog from Northfield House, possibly based on a print illustrating the 'Scottish Water Hound' from Conrad Gesner's Icones Animalium (1560)*; Gesner's illustrations of animals found their way into Topsell's* Historie of Foure-Footed Beastes (1607), *the source of animal paintings at Earlshall.* RCAHMS

and the Netherlands (Antwerp, Rotterdam). As Wells-Cole says, 'It would be virtually impossible to list all the types of prints being produced by the middle of the sixteenth century. The range was vast, from illustrations to the Bible, Classical and modern literature, scientific discoveries, through title pages and page borders, printers' devices and emblems, to a whole range of popular printed ballads and broadsheets' (p.5). They include subject prints and a specific genre, or genres, of ornament prints designed as patterns for the use of craftsmen in the design of jewellery, ceramics, needlework, armour, woodcarving, and interior decoration.

There were few printmakers in Britain before the late seventeenth century and fewer, if any, in Scotland, but continental prints are known to have been imported by merchants or purchased abroad by travellers. The cheapest single-leaf woodcuts would be sold by itinerant pedlars, and such prints have been shown to have been used for decoration by quite modest householders in England (Watt 1991), but they are among the most ephemeral of such sources and there does not appear to be any place in Scotland that corresponded to the area of London, around St Paul's and Blackfriars, which became the recognised centre for London booksellers. Scholars such as Lucy Gent have begun the difficult work of trying to identify copies of particular prints in the inventories of English households at this period, so that we can begin to understand how popular they were among different social classes, but this work has hardly begun in Scotland. Nevertheless, the sheer number of different sources identified in the following chapters leaves no room for doubt that Scottish householders, or their painters, owned or had access to a large number of continental prints and regularly used them as patterns for decorative painting. It is not my purpose in this book to provide an exhaustive list of such print sources – I have not scoured the major European prints collections for unknown sources and the extent of Scottish painting's indebtedness to early decorative prints remains to be fully researched.

Such source hunting helps us to define the context within which such images circulated and allows us to place national traditions in their international context. Source identification can also help us with problems of interpretation. Commercial prints and engravings in books of this period tend to identify their subject and comment on its significance. Emblematic decoration in buildings can be impenetrably obscure until one discovers its source in particular emblem books; then the accompanying epigram or commentary will generally explain what it is and what it means. The same is often true of biblical, classical, and more loosely allegorical images.

However, as with all source studies, it is important not only to identify the patterns that are used by decorative artists, but also to show exactly how they are used. This was, after all, a period when *imitatio* occupied a central place in the process of *inventio*. In some cases, certainly, we shall find the pattern functioning simply as a cartoon, to be copied exactly, but more often we shall find the Scottish patron, or his artist, adapting his source, changing significant details, or combining different sources to produce a new synthesis. This would suggest that some, at least, of this painting is engaging in an inventive process of original composition. Such composition at this period always used received materials.

Those materials constitute the pictorial vocabulary within which painting and the visual arts operated and it would seem to be worth documenting this corpus if only to clarify the different systems of representation, the particular visual economies, which were available to people living in Scotland at this time. They were, we shall discover, quite rich, diverse, and complex. They have both native roots, in such areas as proverbial wisdom or national heraldry for instance, and specific lines of connection with foreign fashions such as European grotesque or 'antique' painting, continental Mannerism, and Renaissance emblematics. I shall spend some time documenting Scottish debts to all these traditions.

The appropriation of foreign styles and received images to a specifically Scottish tradition needs to be read in context. Better knowledge of how an image functioned in its source may clarify how it was understood in its Scottish application, but we also need to recognise that it may function differently in its new context from the way it functions in its source. Emblems were symbolic pictures teaching a generalised moral, applicable to any observer. They were often distinguished from personal devices, or *imprese,* which signalled the moral and political aspirations of their bearer. These more personal devices had been adopted – like the heraldic badge, which they closely resemble – by individual courtiers, nobles, churchmen and scholars from the later middle ages onwards, and in the sixteenth century they were often collected in printed anthologies that closely resemble the illustrated emblem books. When a painter takes images from Claude Paradin's *Devises heroïques*, however, to decorate ceilings at Rossend, at Nunraw, at Blyth's Close or the outside of houses in Edinburgh, it is by no means certain that they retain their original function as personal *imprese.* A lot depends on the way they are used, and on how they relate to the overall decorative programme and to the larger architectural statements made by the building of which they are now a part. The meaning of an image is likely to involve not only its received iconology but also the specific purpose it has in its new setting. The attempt to reconstruct a patron's or artist's motives for the selection of particular subjects and images is always likely to be speculative, however. It helps to find out as much as we can about the religious beliefs and social standing of the patron and, sometimes, the occasion of the original commission. We know, for instance, that the chapel of Stirling Castle was rebuilt and decorated to celebrate the baptism of Prince Henry in August 1594, at a cost of £100,000, and that it brought together 'the greatest number of artificers in the whole country'. But in many cases information on the occasion and motivation for the painting has disappeared without trace.

Much may depend on where the decoration was located in the actual building. The work of modern scholars such as Mark Girouard or Maurice Howard has improved our understanding of the way buildings of this period were designed, where their main offices were located and how they were used. The changing architectural functions of the great hall and of the 'great chamber', the 'withdrawing chamber', closets, saloons, and galleries are increasingly well understood, at least in England. Some of the outstanding examples of decorative painting in Scotland – at Pinkie House, at Earlshall, at Cullen – are, indeed, to be found in that most characteristic of Renaissance apartments, the long gallery. The decorated long gallery in Scotland can tell us a lot about the way this well-known and much-studied feature of the early modern country house was designed and used. Hitherto, however, these impressive Scottish painted galleries have remained largely unknown to architectural historians.

We need to bear in mind that the buildings that were decorated with painting in Scotland were of many different kinds, ranging from royal palaces and fortified tower houses to modest town houses, merchant and burgess houses, private chapels and funerary aisles. Even when we know what kind of building contained the painted decoration, we do not always know what kind of apartment it decorated or what the apartment was used for. It has been suggested, for instance, that the wing of the Earl of Arran's house at Kinneil containing painted decoration was for the use of his wife and that its religious and heraldic iconography was designed to suit the needs of Lady Hamilton. If this were true it might be interesting evidence of the importance of gender in the choice of decorative subjects at this period, but I believe the assumption that this wing of the building was for her exclusive use is not as well established as it needs to be before embarking on a gendered reading of its iconography. In some cases where painted boards have been removed from their original locations for conservation it is no longer easy to establish which rooms in a house they originally came from – records have not always been as scrupulously kept as they ought to have been, and even where the painting remains in its original setting, subsequent alterations to buildings can make their original layout difficult to reconstruct.

A potentially useful distinction might be between public and private apartments. The decoration of public apartments is often seen as making statements about the social status, doctrinal or ethical values of the owner. Alexander Seton's painted gallery, I shall argue, is

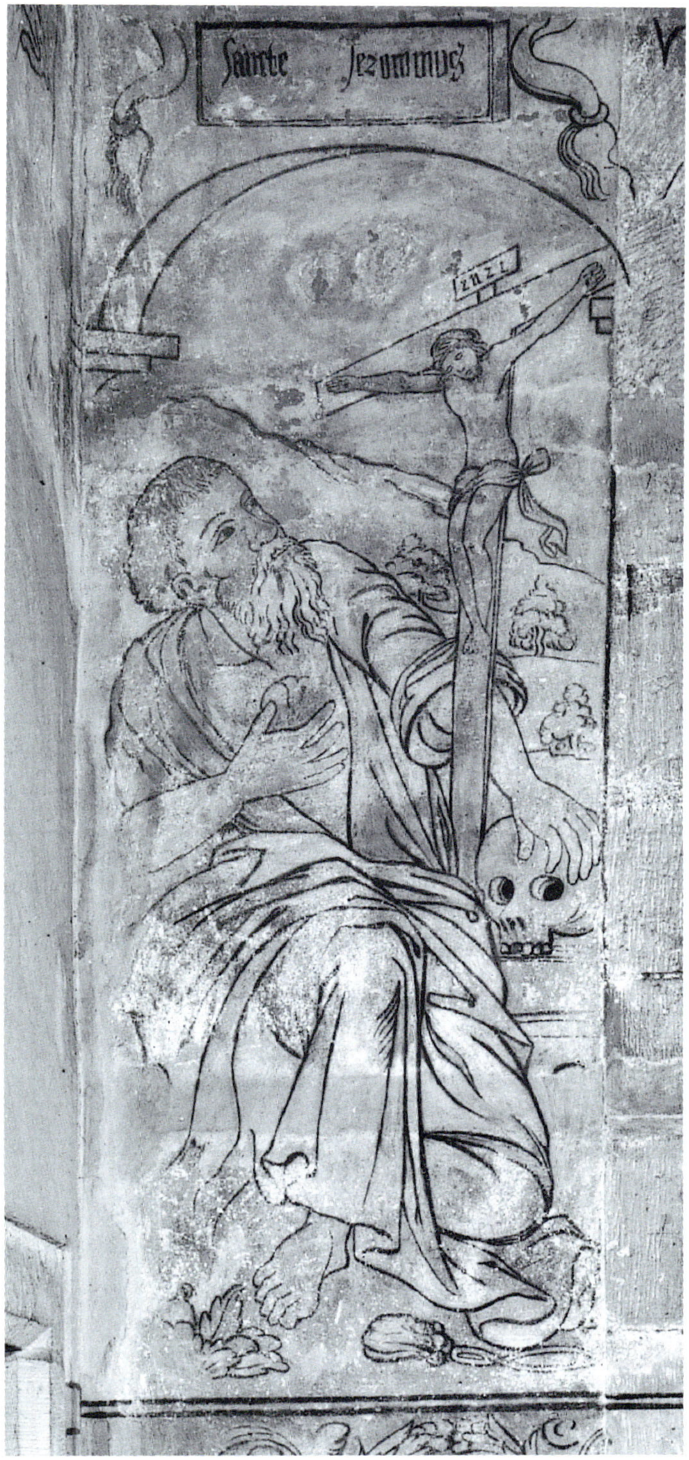

Kinneil House, Saint Jerome, mural painting on plaster dating from c.1560.
HS

an extended exercise in public self-fashioning, depicting its owner (literally, since it includes a rather remarkable portrait of him) as a neo-Stoic. Its programme of classical apophthegms and emblems, discussed in some detail in Chapter 4, lays great stress on modesty, moderation, friendship, and fortitude in adversity. Those values, so strongly exemplified in the long gallery, extend to the neoclassicism of the house as a whole, with its claim to be viewed as a Scottish *villa suburbana.* It is, indeed, surprising how many of the inscriptions that Seton placed on his house at Pinkie, both inside and out, talk about the building of which they are a part. Here is a house which keeps telling us what it means, a building that, quite literally, speaks.

Other decoration is more private, located in rooms seldom, if ever, open to visitors. Private oratories, bedrooms, or withdrawing chambers used only by the occupants and their immediate family are more likely to offer texts and images for private devotion. The programme of emblems from Hawstead Hall in Suffolk, traditionally known as 'Lady Drury's Oratory', has now been shown to realise some of the emblematic images that are strongly implied in the *Occasional* and other meditations of her chaplain at Hawstead, Joseph Hall. Though we do not know exactly where these painted panels were located in the house, it is beyond doubt that they were designed to serve as emblems for private meditation (Mantz, Gardner and Ramsden 1997). There is nothing quite so specific or original of this kind in Scotland, and although the room decorated with Sibyls from Wester Livilands in Stirling has been described as an 'oratory', it is difficult to be sure what this small, very narrow room, subsequently converted into a stairway and cupboard, was really for, or how such images would have been used in any kind of spiritual exercise.

Painted images, particularly of a striking and memorable kind, were often recommended as suitable vehicles for use in the construction of a private memory theatre. As we shall see in Chapter 8, the traditional *ars memorativa* was taught and practised in Scotland in the sixteenth and seventeenth centuries; indeed the Art of Memory became one of the skills to be mastered by craftsmen in the new Masonic lodges instituted and regulated by the architect and Master of the King's Works, William Schaw (Stevenson 1988). But though some of the cycles of imagery found in Scottish decorative painting at this period would have been well adapted for such use, I have found no evidence that they were actually designed for such purposes, and such memory schemes did not have to be located in a private apartment, they simply had to be committed to memory.

Traditional memory theatres not only made use of the types of imagery we find in Scottish houses but were often used to help memorise precisely the type of sententious wisdom frequently inscribed along the beams and elsewhere in their schemes of decoration. Any attempt to understand the function, or functions, of such schemes needs to come to terms with the conventions that influenced the manifold combinations of word and image in the art and culture of this period. The use of proverbial or sententious inscriptions in the decorative arts at this time is by no means unique to Scotland; indeed Tessa Watt has

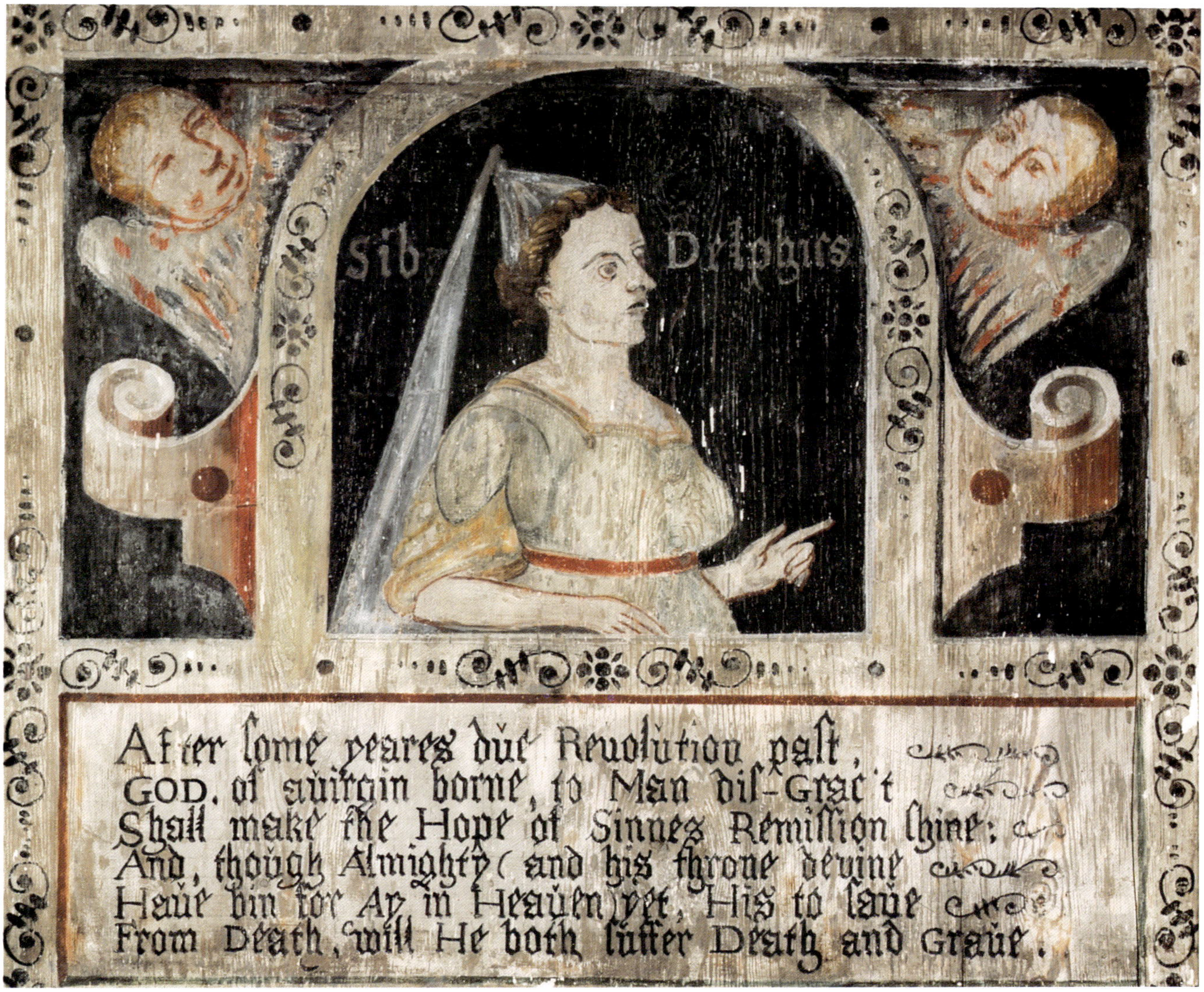

Sibyl from Wester Livilands, Stirling, now on display in NMS*; though painted in a narrow closet it is uncertain if this was a 'prayer closet', or how such an image would have been used in private devotions. The same verses are recorded from a house, Cheyney Court, in Herefordshire, and in the* Great Book *of Thomas Trevilian.* NMS

shown how prevalent was the use of 'Stories for Walls' among the applications of popular prints in England during the seventeenth century (Watt 1991, ch. 5). But the sheer volume of writing inscribed on ceilings and murals from an early date in Scottish houses does seem to be something of a special phenomenon.

Such inscriptions take a variety of forms, in Scots and Latin. They vary from strict biblical quotations, often taken from the Geneva Bible (though the King James version is also used), through versified Scots proverbs, to Latin *adagia* and learned *sententiae*. Sometimes they have a discernible connection with adjacent images, as with the inscriptions voiced by the nine Worthies or the nine Muses at Crathes, but often seem to have no relationship at all with the surrounding iconography, as with the verse proverbs from the 'Green Lady's Room' at Crathes. Some of these Scottish cycles of proverbial inscriptions have the appearance of a private commonplace book writ large, and they were almost certainly influenced by some of the rhetorical functions which commonplace books traditionally served – they were compiled by students in order to master and memorise a number of classical or moral apophthegms, out of which written exercises could be composed. We need to be on our guard against the modern assumption that popular proverbs are an unsophisticated commodity whose natural home would have been the kitchen. Proverbial wisdom was collected, and memorised, by both the learned – students of rhetoric – and the unschooled at this period. Hence it probably makes no sense to insist on a clear break between vernacular proverbs, so often set out for us in spelling that suggests their native Scots pronunciation, and the kind of Latin learning represented by the *Adagia* of Erasmus, that great collection of Latin proverbs which spawned innumerable similar anthologies used as textbooks for Latin composition in schools. When George Bruce used the English epigrams to Geffrey Whitney's *Choice of Emblems* (1586) on his ceiling at Culross, he adapted their spelling to reflect his Scots pronunciation, making them sound like bits of native proverbial wisdom indistinguishable from the versified Scots proverbs we read on beam after beam, for instance at Delgaty. However, the mottoes to these same emblems at Culross are all in Latin. We cannot make anything of the choice of language in our, probably misguided, attempts to make hard and fast distinctions between popular and learned styles of decoration; this is not kitchen wisdom. Nevertheless, the Renaissance tradition of commonplace rhetoric is closely involved, as Walter Ong has shown, with a 'residual orality' which long outlasted the growing dominance of the print medium (Ong 1974, p.94), while the readiness of Scottish householders such as George Bruce or Alexander Hay to adapt the spelling of the (English) printed commonplace or emblem books to reflect Scots pronunciation almost certainly reflects the assumption that proverbial sayings are predominantly a spoken form. Whatever their printed sources, these painted inscriptions are strongly voiced.

Emblems, or emblem books, represent probably the most important vehicle through which the connections between word and image were regulated in Renaissance culture, which is why their prevalence in Scottish decorative painting needs to be acknowledged and accounted for. Although Scotland produced no emblem books or emblem writers of its own (with one or two possible exceptions), Scottish culture was deeply infused with an emblematic mentality, and its material culture, as we shall see, was deeply impregnated with applied emblematics. This whole context needs to be explored in order to understand how these emblems may be functioning in decorative painting in Scotland. Emblem books combine word and image in a closely regulated format that normally assumes their interdependence – the words explain the picture, the picture illustrates the words. However, we shall find not only schemes of decoration combining word and image in formats that preserve the tripartite combination of *inscriptio* (motto), *pictura* (image), and *subscriptio* (verse), but also schemes which simply appropriate emblematic images without accompanying text. Moreover, we shall find at least one example – Gardyne's House at Dundee – which appears to have used lines taken from Francis Quarles's *Emblemes* (1635) with no accompanying pictures.

Emblems are by definition speaking pictures: ideographic images which call for interpretation, but the question of how much significance was retained once they were adapted to 'decorative' schemes is one to which I shall keep returning. Indeed, whether they had any significance once they had been stripped, as at Nunraw or at Rossend, of their accompanying texts, has to be open to doubt. Much depends on how familiar we can assume their viewers to have been with the received iconography. There are grounds fo thinking that at least some of the patrons who commissioned the schemes were familiar with their sources and that, just as a biblical quotation would have called to mind for its early readers its biblical context, so at least a few of these emblems would have recalled their contexts. Some of the emblems of Paradin certainly became part of the stock-in-trade of the artisans who carried out the painting and sculpture that adorns these buildings; the reduplication of one or two of the more familiar designs at several different places (Paradin's *Spes altera vitae* device, for instance, which shows corn stalks growing out of a heap of bones) suggests that such emblems had become part of the painters' acquired design vocabulary with a received meaning that would have been easily understood by contemporary viewers.

That there was such an acquired vocabulary is beyond doubt. We shall find decorative schemes that were drawn on at site after site, where the patron evidently commissioned established styles of decoration used in buildings owned by his friends and neighbours. The garlands of fruits and flowers, with occasional animals, at Gladstone's Land are typical of a style of ornamental painting found in burgess houses of this period all down the Royal Mile in Edinburgh. Versions of it are found elsewhere too – at Galashiels, Stobhall, Aberdour, Northfield House and in St Andrews. The sides of beams are often divided into rectangular framed sections, each of which is filled with a stencil-like arabesque motif. The underside of the beams is sometimes decorated by a repeated motif which is difficult to characterise, but which I propose to call 'trailing tassel' since it takes the form of a tassel or pan-shaped object that diminishes or fades into its successor all along the beam. Vine scrolls with swags of other fruit, gourds, flowers and foliage can be elaborated at random or in repetitive sequences. Though close similarities sometimes suggest the work of a single painter (at Northfield House and Gladstone's Land, for instance), this was a design vocabulary easily taught to apprentice craftsmen and, once learned, could be applied by the yard.

It will become clear that heraldic painting was also of this type, part of the stock-in-trade of more than a few of the artists responsible for this decorative work, several of whom (James Workman, or John Sawers, for instance) were either official Heralds or had close connections with the Court of the Lyon King of Arms in Edinburgh, whose job it is to regulate the award of coats of arms (Scotland has no need of the English College of Arms; heraldry is a legal rather than academic discipline in Scotland). In some places (Kinneil, Collairnie and Pinkie, for example) herald painters were required to execute armorial schemes which had specific relevance to the dynastic connections of the owner; but elsewhere (at Balbegno, Nunraw and Linlithgow) they were called upon to execute extended armorials which could include the arms of the Scottish nobility, of royalty, of the nine Worthies, or of the 'Kings of Collene' (the

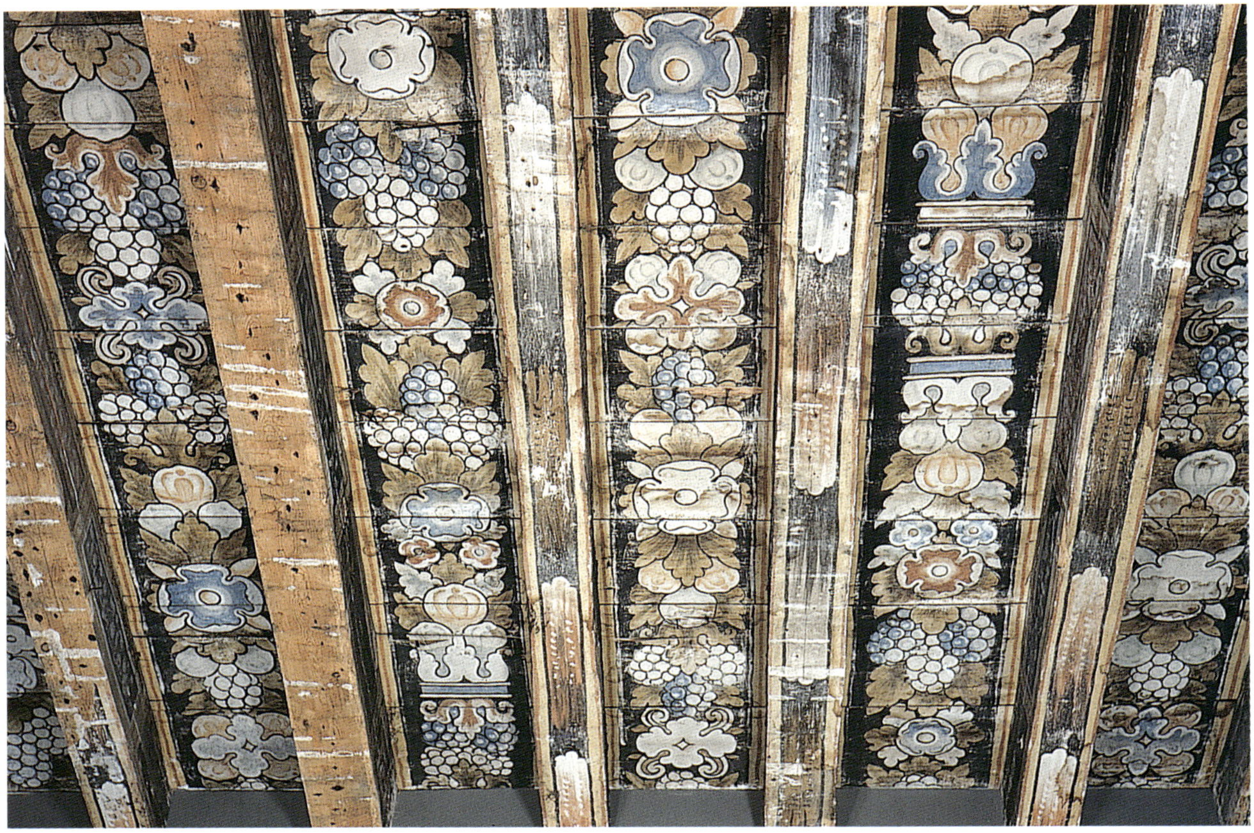

Fruit and flowers from Gladstone's Land, perhaps the most popular type of decoration on Scottish board-and-beam ceilings. HS

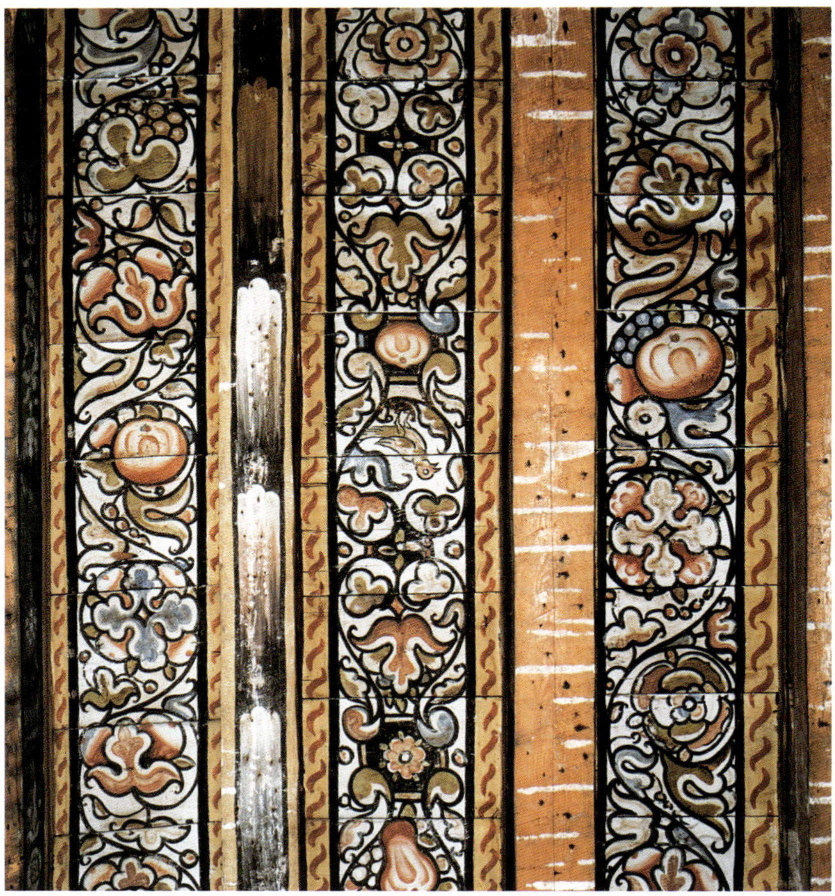

Fruit and flowers from Northfield House, here also using the type of ornamental leaf-scroll typical of 'arabesque' ornament; the scrollwork is balanced and symmetrical in the centre compartment of this illustration, but the leafy scrolls in the two outer compartments branch alternately to right and left in a pattern known as rinceau ornament. RCAHMS

Magi); arms which make no reference to the family connections of the patron. Clearly, the execution of such a scheme called upon the artist's own mastery of the science of arms and of the specific heraldic achievements of the Scottish nobility. Such mastery must have been acquired through prior study at the Lyon Court, and what we find painted on such ceilings is very close to the extended armorial manuscripts, sometimes by the same painters, that have survived at the Lyon Court and elsewhere. Sometimes they made mistakes, and at least one, James Workman, compiled a manuscript (Nat Lib Scot Adv MS 31.3.5) which a later Lyon King took to task for the frequency of its errors. When we examine some of these schemes of heraldic decoration it will be instructive to put them alongside the illustrated armorial manuscripts they so closely resemble.

However, although the artists brought with them their own repertoire of styles and subjects on which a house-owner could draw, it will become clear that in many cases the patron had a major input into the design of the programme and the detail of its execution. It is inconceivable that Alexander Seton's gallery at Pinkie does not call upon a depth of classical erudition way beyond the competence of a journeyman artist. Its emblems and inscriptions are demonstrably indebted to rhetorical skills its patron would have mastered in the course of his education by the Jesuits in Rome. Other schemes may well be informed by the humanistic tastes their patrons had developed as part of their education in the Scottish universities. The illustration of scenes from classical literature and mythology – at Cullen House and Monymusk, and in the Abbot House, Dunfermline – is likely to owe at least something to the educated tastes of their owners. The inclusion of the nine Muses and the nine Worthies at Crathes, and of other commonplace schemes such as the Cardinal Virtues at Crathes and also at Earlshall, may owe something to the popularity

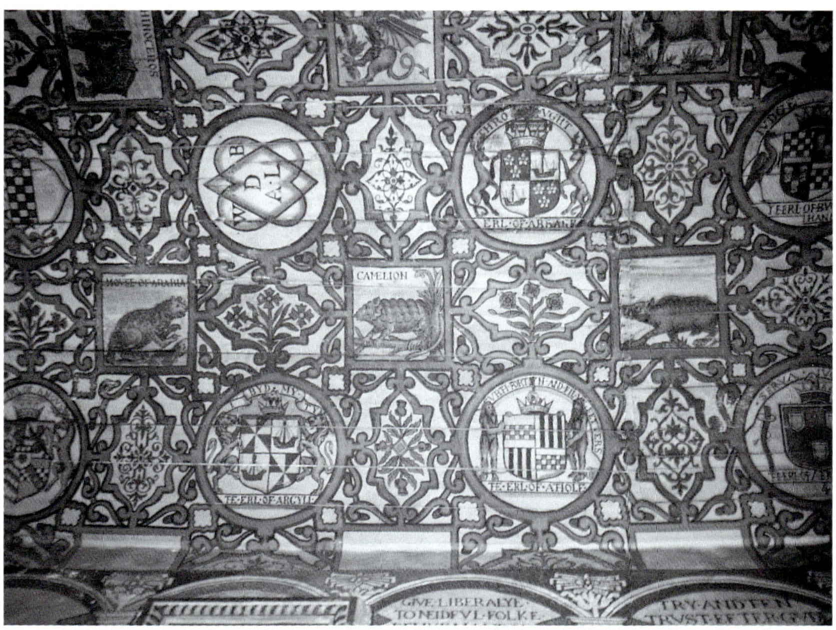

Heraldry at Earlshall; the initials of William Bruce and Dame Agnes Lyndsay identify the house's owners but the surrounding coats of arms do not signal kinship. The painting also includes animals, intricately scrolled frames and proverbial texts.

such schemes gained from their depiction in prints and other familiar sources, but it is also likely to have been a deliberate choice on the part of the patron rather than simply part of the stock-in-trade of the artist.

Religious subjects, such as the Old Testament scenes at The Dean, the Passion cycle at Provost Skene's House, the *Veritas et Vita* panel from Blyth's Close, Edinburgh, the Good Samaritan cycle at Kinneil, or the Last Judgement and four Evangelists at Grandtully, also have to be seen as decisions which were too important, not to say too controversial at a time of widespread religious iconoclasm, to have been left to the choice of the artist. Such choices can be assumed to reflect the particular doctrinal and sectarian convictions of the patron. It has often been claimed that the Reformation purged Christian iconography of representations of the Passion, the Virgin, and the saints, but we find instances of all of these in Scottish decorative painting of this period. For example, the merchant John Watson (or possibly his son Andrew) included not just the pagan Sibyls on his ceiling at Burntisland ('Mary Somerville's House'), but also images of the Agnus Dei and of the Virgin Mary with her name 'MARIA' inscribed on a label. Around 1620 Matthew Lumsden decorated the ceiling of his house in the centre of Aberdeen with scenes illustrating the Annunciation, Nativity, Crucifixion and Entombment of Christ, together with the instruments of the Passion and the Stigmata. Lumsden belonged to an Aberdeen family several times persecuted for its recusancy; in 1629 the Register of the Privy Council records a complaint against Dr William Lumsden 'for hearing mass and resetting Jesuits', and in 1650 he was imprisoned; in 1656 his son, Patrick, was 'excommunicate for poperie' (Forbes Leith 1909, III, p.369).

The remarkable range of styles and types of subject matter that were available to decorative artists in England at this period is suggested by two extraordinary manuscripts executed in 1606 and in 1616 by Thomas Trevilian (or Trevelyon). Long known, at least by repute, to English art historians, their actual contents were familiar, until quite recently, only to scholars able to consult the originals, of which the 1606 volume is in the Folger Shakespeare Library at Harvard, Washington DC. The larger 1616 version, which duplicates nearly all of the material from its predecessor, can now be consulted in Nicolas Barker's exhaustively researched edition (Barker, 2000). A glance at its contents will immediately suggest how much of the subject matter which we have already identified in Scottish decorative painting corresponds to the decorative vocabulary which was also favoured by English designers at this period. Consisting of 531 leaves comprising 1014 numbered pages, the *Great Book* includes a variety of material. The two hundred pages of what Barker identifies as 'the central part of the work' (Barker, vol. i, p.10) include the twelve degrees of the world, the twelve tribes of Israel, the twelve apostles, the prophecies of the twelve Sibyls, the nine Muses, nine Worthies, seven Deadly Sins, seven Cardinal Virtues, seven Liberal Arts, seven points of humanity and inhumanity, five senses, four Ages of Man, and four continents. Then there are Old Testament subjects, moral tags and wise saws, and New Testament subjects which provide what Barker rightly describes as 'some unexpected images' – including the Annunciation, Nativity,

Circumcision, Temptation, Crucifixion and Ascension, and the martyrdom of St Sebastian (although Trevilian makes his own anti-Catholicism quite clear elsewhere in the manuscript). Many of these images, which Trevilian depicts in vivid watercolour sketches, often with explanatory texts, have now been shown to copy woodcuts and engravings, including a number of the very same prints which – as we shall see – are also used by the decorative painters in Scotland.

Almost everything we know about Trevilian derives from what he tells us, or what he shows us, in these two manuscripts. Born in 1545, probably in Cornwall or the West Country, he almost certainly worked as an embroiderer or as a draughtsman for embroiderers, probably in London. The large number of embroidery patterns were for many years the only part of these books to have been reproduced (Nevinson 1966-8); and until recently scholarly attention has largely been preoccupied with attempts to identify actual embroideries of the period which use Trevilian's patterns. These identifications have had only modest success, and it remains the case that very few surviving artefacts in the material culture show any direct relationship with Trevilian's pattern books; indeed the very status of the books as pattern books is open to doubt and their function and purpose remains one of the greatest mysteries about them. They are, as Barker stresses, utterly unique: 'No other picture book of the period, manuscript or printed, is so large, in either the size or number of pages; none provides so large and diverse a profusion of visual imagery .... What purpose the two books served, and why he made them, are questions to which there is no obvious answer' (p.4). Subjects which we shall find both in Trevilian's books and in Scottish decorative painting include: the Sacrifices of Cain and Abel, copying the same print by Johannes Sadeler after Maarten de Vos that was used at Dean House, Edinburgh; the five Senses as depicted also by Sadeler after de Vos at Dean House; Judith and Holofernes at Dean House; the badges of the tribes of Israel at Skelmorlie Aisle; the nine Worthies at Crathes; the Cardinal Virtues at Earlshall; the parable of the Good Samaritan at Kinneil; and caryatids from Vredeman de Vries, also used at Prestongrange. Trevilian also has a fifty-page section of animals copied from Topsell's *Foure-Footed Beastes,* source of many of the animals at Earlshall (and widely used in decorative arts elsewhere in Britain at this time). Perhaps the most telling overlap between Trevilian's designs and Scottish painting is the set of pagan Sibyls which Trevilian has copied from a set of prints by de Passe which, as we shall see, is also copied at Mary Somerville's House at Burntisland; but the verses which Trevilian has inscribed below the half-length portraits of the Sibyls in the *Great Book* are not found in any known print series; however they do correspond, word for word, to the sets of verses we find inscribed beneath another set of Sibyls from the house known as Wester Livilands, Stirling. This overlap confirms the case, which Barker and others have argued persuasively, for the widespread indebtedness of the decorative arts in Britain to ephemeral, popular prints, of which no copies may have survived. As it is very unlikely that Trevilian's books were the actual source or pattern for any of these Scottish examples, it must be the case that they go back to a common source.

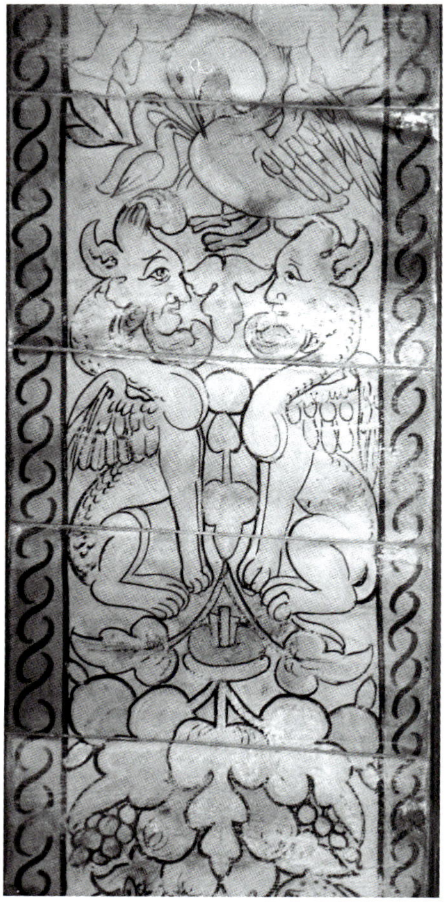

Grotesque painting at Nunraw. The creation of monstrous hybrid creatures is characteristic of this style of 'antique' decoration.

Although I shall identify all of these particular examples in due course, what we perhaps need to recognise at the moment is the more general evidence they provide of a shared vocabulary of styles and subjects between the decorative arts in both England and Scotland at this time. Although we can certainly make a strong case for the distinctiveness of the Scottish tradition, we need to recognise that there was at the same time a strong community of taste between the two countries.

Grotesque painting represents a style that certainly became part of the stock-in-trade of practising decorative artists. Originating in the antiquarian excavations of Nero's *Domus Aurea* in Rome in the late fifteenth century, it was adopted by Raphael for the decoration of the Vatican Loggia, and by imitators at major sites like the Escorial, Fontainebleau and the Doge's Palace, so that by the later sixteenth century it had become recognised across Europe as the authentic style for decorative painting *à l'antique*. Subsequent artists acquired their knowledge of the style both directly from actual buildings, some of them very famous, and from the growing body of prints and pattern books which supplied them with models, in particular the work of such Netherlands engravers as Cornelis Bos, Nicholas de Bruyn and Jan Vredeman de Vries. Their engravings supplied the patterns for decoration in several English houses of the sixteenth and seventeenth centuries (Wells-Cole 1997) and were also known in Scotland. The style is characterised by the fantastic transformation of images into monstrous and imaginary shapes, challenging that principle of truth to nature generally seen as the test of Renaissance art. Metamorphosis – of plants into humanoid or monstrous figures, of the animate into the inanimate, of the familiar into the strange – is fundamental to the style. Decorative painters quickly learned to elaborate their leaf scrolls into grotesque faces and to incorporate hybrid shapes of fantastic beasts – a woman with a fish's tail, a man's head upon a horse's neck (as Horace satirises in the opening lines of his *Ars Poetica*), so that we should not always assume that such designs copy a printed pattern, however often they do so. The narrow boarded sections of Scottish board-and-beam ceilings lent themselves to the transformation of one object into another in a continuing interplay of animate and inanimate shapes; we find some notable examples on the ceilings at Delgaty, at Nunraw, at Prestongrange, at Rossend, and at John Knox's House in Edinburgh. Though some of the most accomplished of these copy continental prints, others appear to be original compositions.

By the mid to late seventeenth century such a style had become *démodé*, dismissed in 1658 in a telling comment by an English writer as 'ale-house' painting, but it always appears to have retained something of the prestige which attached to all manifestations of the antique in many of the highly prestigious buildings (castles and palaces, not ale-houses); this re-established its position in modern European architecture. What we may need to recover in a Scottish context is, indeed, some sense of precisely what status it held – what its recognised antecedents and associations were – for those who were redesigning and redecorating their houses, baronial or otherwise, in the remarkable flowering of Scottish domestic architecture of the late sixteenth and early seventeenth centuries.

Antique, or grotesque, painting had strong links with the wider development of European Mannerism in the visual arts. 'False architecture' is an expression that usefully describes the tendency of so much of this painting to reinterpret the architectural spaces it fills. Time and again we shall see how such painting remodels the surfaces and spaces it occupies in order to make them look like something they are not. The Montgomery Aisle at Skelmorlie, for instance, suspends a barrel-vaulted ceiling from its sloping roof, which it covers in boards painted with ribs, rising from false corbels, to imitate a stone-built vault; it then carries this rib-work across the soffit of the ceiling to divide the surface into panels in a kind of false coffering. Seton's long gallery at Pinkie does something similar. None of these buildings uses such *trompe l'oeil* conventions with anything like the assurance of such places as Fontainebleau, but the questions we need to ask have less to do with the relative sophistication of this false architecture in comparison with acknowledged masterpieces than with what such practices imply about the cultural aspirations of builders and owners in a Scottish context. That they imply some kind of aspiration towards European models of architectural sophistication seems more than likely. Such aspiration does not depend wholly on the relative skill or finesse of their execution.

Trompe l'oeil effects are certainly omnipresent in the decorative painting we shall be looking at, whether in the use of *trompe* pilasters to break up and articulate architectural spaces (Provost Skene's House, Argyll's Lodgings), false corbelling, false coffering, or the extraordinary *trompe* lantern at Pinkie which, it can now be shown, copies a print from one of the most influential books of its time on the theory and practice of perspective, Jan Vredeman de Vries' *Artis perspectivae* (1st edn, Antwerp, 1568). The tendency to decorate ceilings with deities, radiant suns, angels, putti, moon and stars, may seem to be nothing more than naive painting that never attains anything resembling the splendour of the European baroque, but the taste for ornamental strapwork, in which the painted surface is richly elaborated in outward-curving and receding segmented forms resembling leather-work (hence the name), clearly appealed to a decorative taste in which two-dimensional surfaces are interpreted as three-dimensional. Such strapwork is widely used in the ornamental cartouches that frame both texts and images on these surfaces, where the boundaries between frame and image may easily be rendered ambiguous. The design of such cartouches was, evidently, something on which an artist could exercise his inventive skills, which is why cartouche patterns were printed and sold by the same engravers who devoted their energies to grotesque patterns and caryatids.

Scottish use of continental engravings as patterns is evidence of its close connection with continental tastes and fashions. More work needs to be done before we can claim to have identified all the commercial prints which Scottish decorative painting copies, but enough sources have now been identified to

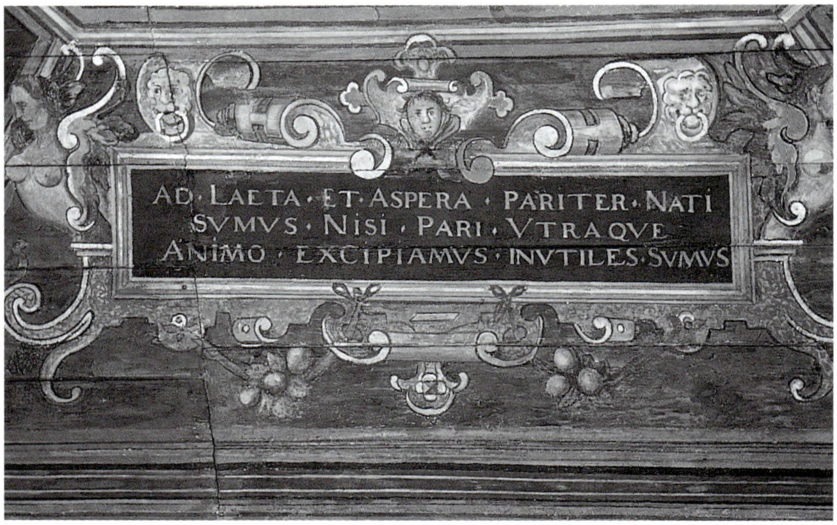

Strapwork cartouche, used here to frame an inscription in the long gallery at Pinkie House.

leave no doubt that decorative prints and engravings circulated widely in Scotland at this period and constituted a major resource for decorative artists. Grotesque patterns from Vredeman de Vries were not only copied at Rossend and Prestongrange but incorporated in embroideries by Bess of Hardwick; prints by Etienne Delaune supplied the patterns for Mannerist decoration at Skelmorlie Aisle. Much of the stencil-like scrollwork that is everywhere painted along the beams of these Scottish ceilings closely resembles the type of 'arabesque' ornament marketed in numerous decorative pattern books by artists such as Virgil Solis, Jost Amman, Pierre Flötner and Theodore de Bry in Germany; by Androuet Ducerceau and Etienne Delaune in France; and by Frans, Jacob and Cornelis Floris, the Collaerts and de Vries in the Netherlands, though no particular sources have yet been identified.

Decorative painters did not confine themselves to such purely ornamental prints and patterns, for many of the classical, biblical and allegorical subjects

Arabesques from 302 Lawnmarket, Edinburgh. Unlike strapwork, arabesque designs are one-dimensional; the repeated design on the soffit of the beam shown here is common though difficult to characterise – I shall call it 'trailing tassel'.

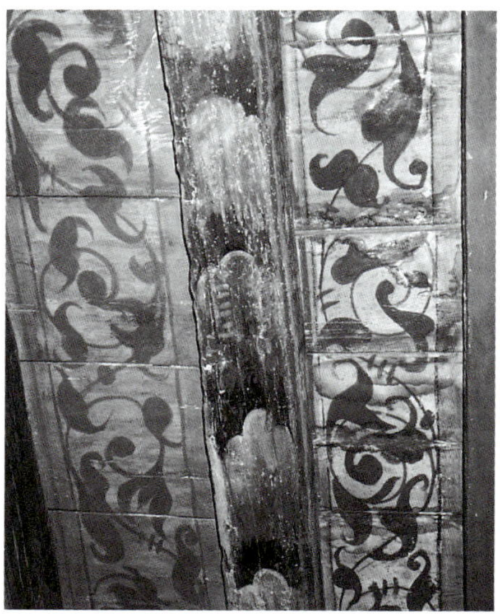

Framed arabesques of a type very common on beams; these examples are from Edinburgh, Abbey Strand.

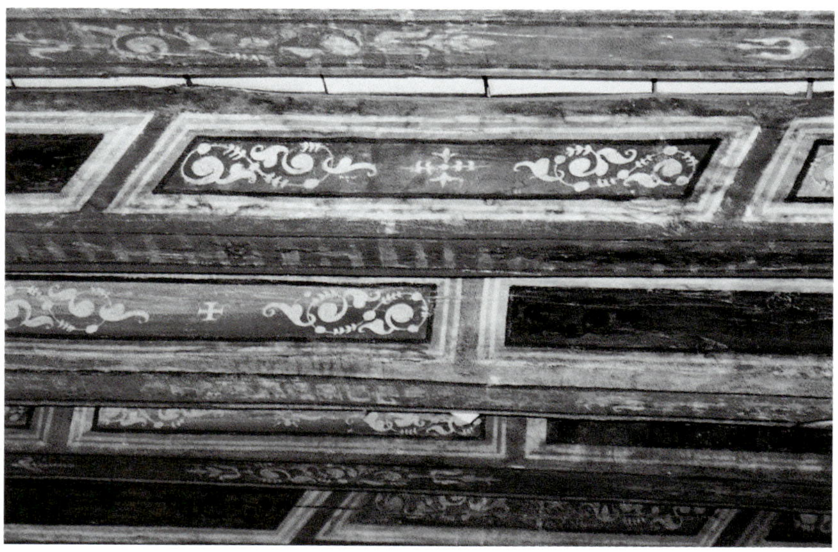

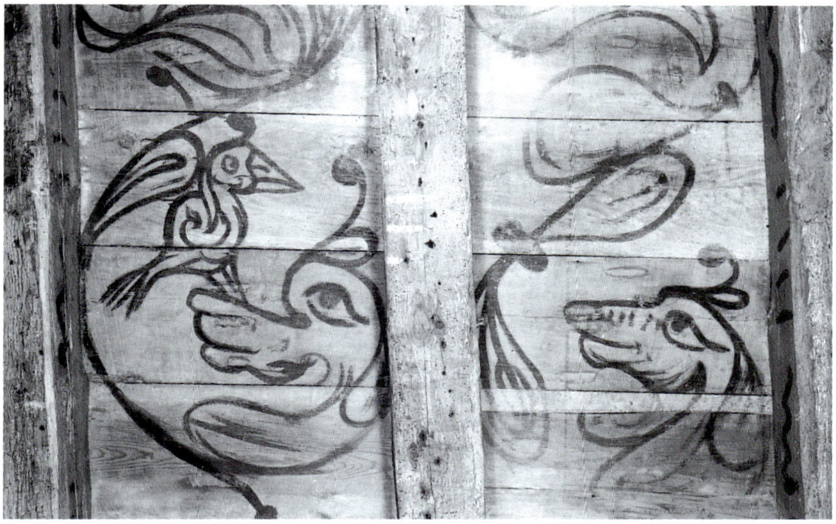

Grotesque doodles from Sailor's Walk, Kirkcaldy. The grotesque shape on which the bird perches in the left-hand section parodies the canine head to its right. HS

depicted on these ceilings also go back to continental engravings. Often these are treated, as we shall see, with some freedom. The Old Testament scenes from The Dean, for instance, rework engravings by Philips Galle after Maerten van Heemskerk (Judith and Holofernes), by Wierix and by Johannes Sadeler after Maarten de Vos (Abraham and Isaac, Cain and Abel), whilst its personifications of the five Senses owe something to engravings of the same subject after designs by Maarten de Vos. The Provost Skene's House Annunciation also has a number of details that must go back to one or other of the prints of this subject after designs by de Vos. The way each of these paintings adapts its source – whether commercial print or illustration from a printed book – will be explored in the chapters which follow or in the Inventory. Perhaps the most important of the printed books they used were the illustrated emblem books, and the way they copy, adapt, or reinvent the images from these provides us with the clearest evidence of the working methods of these artists. An examination of emblematic sources soon reveals the close relationship between imitation and invention in the decorative painting of this period in Scotland.

Arabesque designs were published in pattern books; for example this one from Ducerceau's Livre contenant passements de moresques.

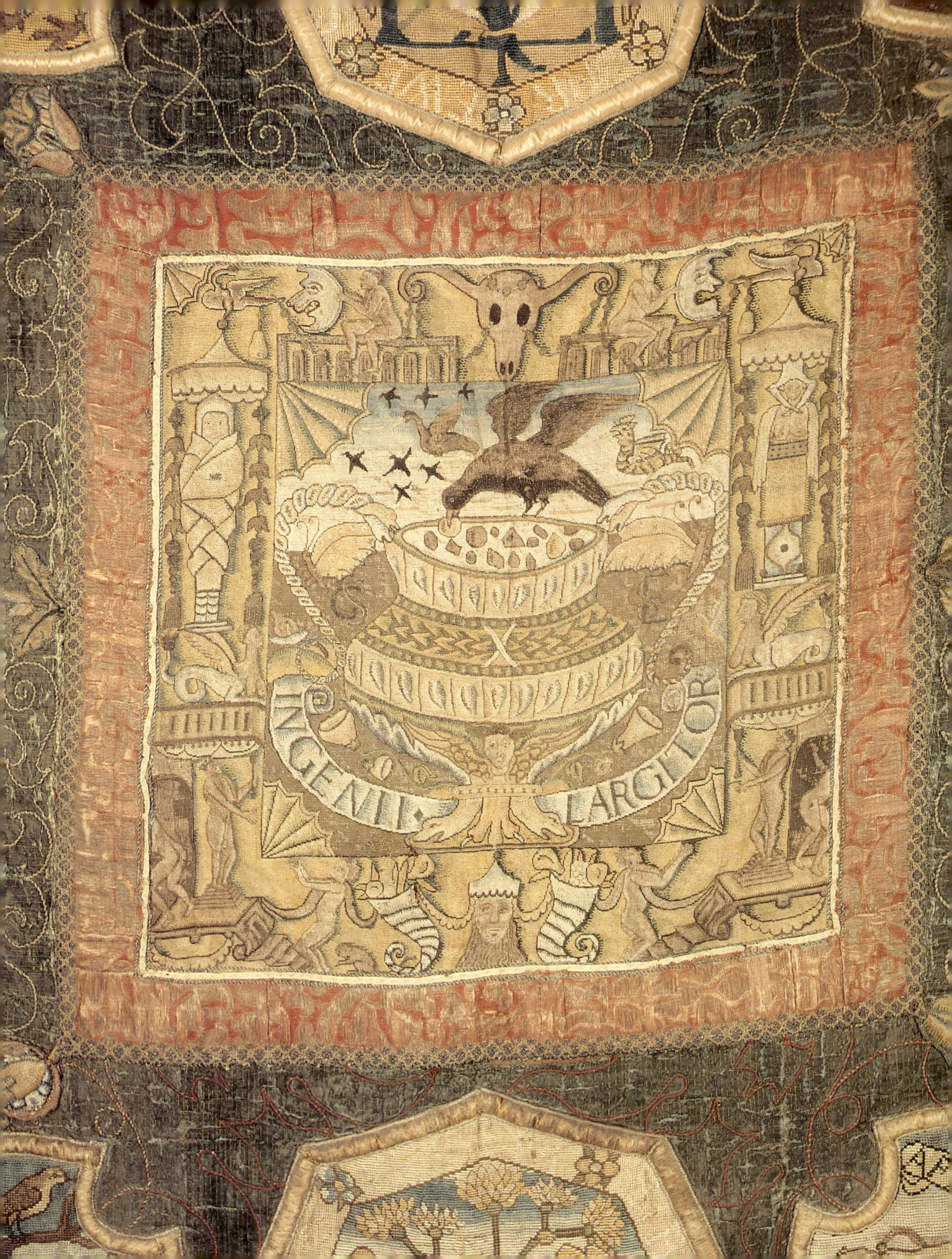
INGENII LARGITOR

2

APPLIED EMBLEMATICS

IT is evident from surviving examples that the decorative painter's professional skills included a mastery of the complex rules and conventions of the Renaissance *impresa* and emblem. Emblem books were of recent origin and Scotland produced few, if any, examples of its own during the period when decorative painting was fashionable. It is therefore surprising to discover how many houses include either complete cycles of Renaissance emblems or use images that can be shown to derive from printed emblem books. Clearly English and continental emblem books must have circulated quite widely in Scotland and must have been available for use as pattern books in the applied arts. Emblem books originated in the illustrated Latin epigrams of Andrea Alciato (*Emblematum liber*, Augsburg, 1531), which started a vogue that rapidly spread across Europe.

The emblematic content of decorative painting in Scotland is not solely a matter of decorative painters using foreign emblem books as pattern books, however, for there is plenty of evidence that an emblematic mentality was already deeply embedded in Scottish culture. To understand how these emblems work in decorative schemes in Scotland we therefore need to do two things. Firstly, examine the way emblems work in the emblem books themselves; secondly, explore some of the different applications made of emblems in the material culture of Renaissance Scotland itself. Are we to see these applied emblems as foreign imports or as native customs? I suggest that they are both.

This genre of 'speaking picture' had its origins earlier in the sixteenth century, when the Augsburg printer, Heinrich Steyner, added woodcuts to a collection of Latin epigrams by the famous Italian lawyer, Andrea Alciato. This unprepossessing little book had an extraordinary influence, inspiring imitations beginning in France in the 1540s and spreading to Italy, the Netherlands and Germany in the 1550s, and to almost every part of Europe by the turn of the century, or soon after. By the end of the seventeenth century more than two thousand different emblem books had been published (nobody has ever managed to count them all, and we still await the exhaustive bibliography). Because it normally combined picture and text in a sententious and significant format, the emblem exercised an enormous

Opposite: *Bess of Hardwick, 'Shrewsbury Hanging' using Paradin's* Ingenii largitor *device, the initials 'GS' and 'ES' are those of Elizabeth and George Shrewsbury.* V&A

influence on literature and the visual arts. Such was its influence that the very term 'emblem', literally 'mosaic-work or decorative inlay', came in most European languages to refer to any symbolic image or speaking picture of the kind that the emblem books employed.

Based on the models derived from Alciato, the emblem typically consists of a moralising motto (normally in Latin), a picture which, properly interpreted, could be seen as illustrating the motto, and a verse epigram which explains the relevance of the picture to its motto and draws the implied moral. Alciato's emblems and those of his immediate successors are full of humanistic learning, often using classical adages or exempla, but, as the genre evolved, it embraced all kinds of subject matter, including erotic, alchemical, hieroglyphic and heraldic topics, and in the seventeenth century a vigorous tradition of religious emblem books developed which had close connections with the Counter-Reformation rehabilitation of images, with Jesuit rhetoric and pedagogy, and with both Catholic and Protestant traditions of Christian meditation. The crossing of sectarian, linguistic and national boundaries seems to have been quite easy for the emblem, which was a truly international phenomenon.

Just as the first English emblem book, Whitney's *Choice of Emblemes* (1586) – the model for all Sir George Bruce's emblems at Culross – drew on continental sources (and was, indeed, published abroad, in Leiden), so the most influential of the English religious emblem books – Francis Quarles' *Emblemes* (1635) – adapted material from Jesuit emblem books produced for Catholic readers on the continent. That did not prevent it from becoming an instant success in Reformation Scotland, even at a time when the doctrinal and sectarian disputes of the 1630s, which would soon lead to the signing of the National Covenant, were fomenting. Within months of its first printing the Catholic Earl of Nithsdale used Quarles' emblems as patterns for some of the elaborately carved lintels on the new classical wing of his moated ancestral castle at Caerlaverock, Dumfriesshire (Hunwick 1993). Three years later a stonemason in Stirling was using them for the design of a carved gravestone in the yard of Holy Rude kirk, thereby initiating a distinctive style of Scottish gravestone carving which has no parallel in England. No fewer than ten seventeenth and eighteenth-century gravestones that use Quarles' emblems as their source have been identified in Scotland (Bath and Willshire 1996). The engravings that Quarles took over from his Catholic continental sources, *Pia Desideria* (1624) and *Typus Mundi* (1627), are by no means the simplest of designs for painters or stonemasons to use as patterns; they usually show the two allegorical figures, *Amor Divinus* and *Anima*, Divine Love and the human Soul, engaged in various activities whose moral significance has to be expounded in their continuing dialogue and debate. Once the engravings have been stripped of their accompanying verses it is extremely difficult to imagine how early viewers could possibly have interpreted their significance. John Service, the carver of the Stirling gravestone, accordingly adds a couple of speech balloons to the mouths of his allegorical figures. Later Quarles gravestones in Scotland tend at least to quote the scriptural text upon which Quarles' emblem is based, thus

Holy Rude churchyard, Stirling, gravestone of John Service († 1637) combining two different emblems from Quarles, encircled by a serpent biting its tail, the ancient symbol of time or eternity.

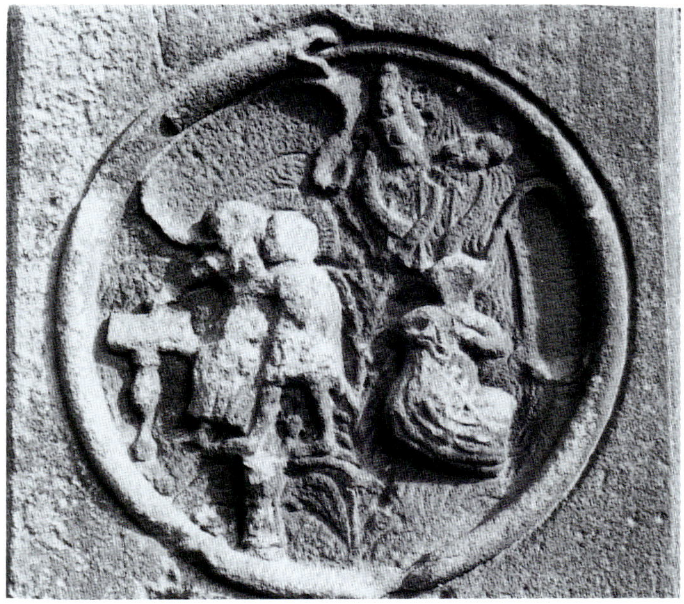

preserving the interactive elements of word and image that were fundamental to this essentially bimedial form. A merchant's house in Dundee destroyed in the nineteenth century (Gardyne's House) is recorded as having a painted ceiling decorated with emblems drawn from Quarles' collection, though this ceiling appears to have abstracted quotations from Quarles' verse epigrams and ignored the pictures. More commonly we shall find images copied from emblem books without the accompanying words. The speed with which Quarles' emblems were appropriated to the applied arts in Scotland suggests how deeply engrained the emblem

Quarles, Emblemes *(1635) p.172, source of the left-hand detail on the Service gravestone.* GUL

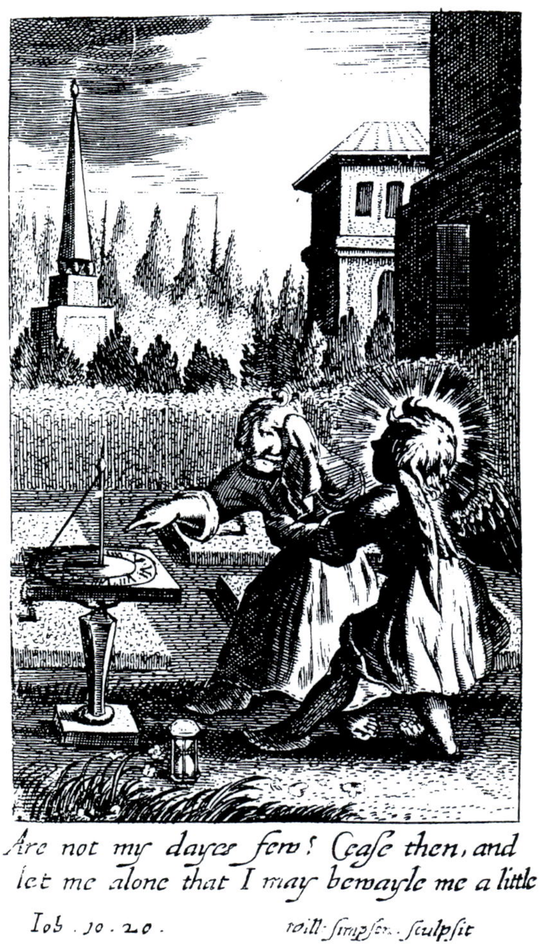

Quarles, Emblemes *(1635) p.124, source of the right-hand detail on the Service gravestone.* GUL

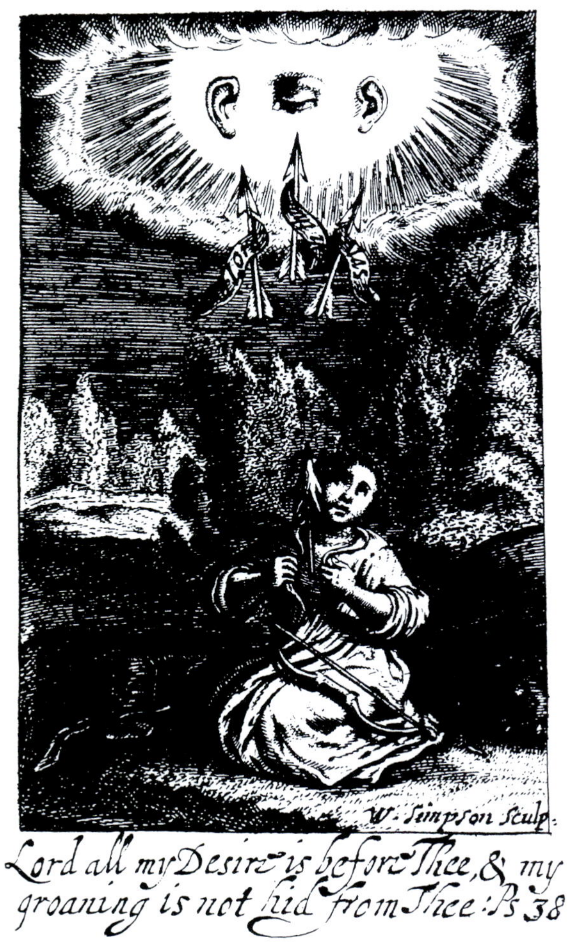

tradition had become in the material culture. We should not, therefore, be surprised to find decorative painters utilising the same emblematic sources and many of the same significant images.

That emblems were, almost by definition, suitable to be inserted on walls and ceilings, was frequently spelled out in contemporary prefaces and by the Italian *impresa* theorists. As the preface to the Rouille/Bonhomme (Lyons) editions of Alciato pointed out, the emblems were regrouped under *loci communes* headings in these editions so that the decorative artist

> may from a little book of emblems, as from an excellently-prepared handbook, have what he may be able to impress on the walls of houses, on windows of glass, on tapestry, on hangings, on tablets, vases, ensigns, seals, garments, the table, the couch, the arms, the sword, and, lastly, furniture of every kind. (Lyons 1551, p.4)

That the purpose of such applied emblems was not purely ornamental is confirmed by John Willis in his *Art of Stenographie*:

> An embleme is so called εμβλημα, which signifieth 'to place between' or 'among'. For in auncient times, the builders of princes palaces, noble men's houses, and other sumptuous edifices, used for the beautifying of their worke, to set here and there in convenient places of the walles, faire squared stones, or timber worke; wherein were curiously graven certaine images and devices, signifying some profitable instruction .... (1602, sig. E8^{v})

Willis' definition is interesting for the primacy which it gives to the emblem as an applied art and in this Willis is only repeating what all the early lexicographers had to say about the meaning of the word. They all insist that its root meaning has to do not with the kind of thing we might find in printed books, but rather with the decorative arts where it is something 'inserted' in walls or on furniture, clothing or tableware. Scotland's exclusive preoccupation with the emblem's decorative function might therefore be seen as a recognition of the strictly classical meaning and application of the word. You don't need printed emblem books in order to have an emblem tradition.

One of the clearest statements of how such applied emblems would have been used is provided by Henri Estienne in the treatise which Thomas Blount translated in 1648 as *The Art of Making Devices*:

> I know well that an author may compose devises of love, morality, or such like subjects, wherewith to adorne the chimney-peeces, closets, or galleries of his house, with intention to have them understood by his compatriots; but this reason hinders not, the mottoes being in an universall language, because strangers (that shall visit you out of a curiosity to see rarities) will take as much pleasure in contemplating the acuteness of your witt, as in beholding the magnificence of your buildings, and your countrymen will receive the same contentment, and no less profit, when they shall be entertained by you with the exposition of the words. (1650 edn, p.39)

This passage comes from that part of his treatise in which Estienne is debating the rather dry question, which had much engaged the quibbles of the Italian *impresa* theorists, of what language, classical or vernacular, should be used for the motto. His description of how visitors would be entertained through the learned and witty exposition of the emblems' meaning is almost incidental to his adjudication of this point. It is nevertheless an invaluable witness to the spirit in which such decorative schemes would have been enjoyed. Emblems are by definition speaking pictures, images which call for interpretation. They might therefore be thought of as the type of decorative imagery at the furthest remove from a purely 'decorative' function. Emblems are ideographic signs carrying an encoded message. Whenever they are associated with mottoes or inscriptions, as are those Estienne is describing, they challenge their viewer to work out the relationship of text to image. Such applied emblems are not simply offering commonplace moral counselling, though they may certainly be doing that, they are offering a hermeneutic challenge and the viewer's primary task, then as now, has to be the interpretation of their meaning. We come to them, like Estienne's visitors, as strangers, and we should welcome his statement of the spirit in which to respond to their learned enigmas.

However, the 'profitable instruction' John Willis identifies as the emblem's function when 'inserted' on walls and buildings is not confined to emblems *stricto sensu*. The decorative arts traditionally went in for a whole range of allegorical imagery or sententious inscription with a similar aim. Such arts are vividly suggested by a passage in Anthony Munday's play *The Death of Robert Earl of Huntingdon* (1601):

> About his hall and chambers if you looke,
> The morall vertues in faire effigie,
> Are lively painted: morall Philosophie
> Has not a sentence, be it great or small,
> But it is painted on his Honours wall.

Such 'effigies' may not be strictly emblematic in their function or their format, and Munday's description might call to mind the kind of decoration we see at Crathes, Delgaty and Earlshall before it suggests the emblems at Culross or Pinkie. However, the aim of 'profitable instruction' is common to both, and suggests the applied emblem's affinities with a wider range of texts and images, also used in the decorative arts. The proverbial inscriptions painted along the beams at Delgaty and at Crathes are in no sense 'emblems', but emblems were often based on the same proverbs. When Sir George Bruce abstracted two lines from the epigrams to Whitney's emblems in order to create the rhyming-couplet *subscriptio* to his own emblems at Culross, he was producing the kind of 'sentence' which is otherwise quite undistinguishable from the verse proverbs we find on the beams at Crathes and Delgaty. We can still, speaking loosely, refer to the seven Cardinal Virtues at Earlshall or at Crathes as 'emblems',

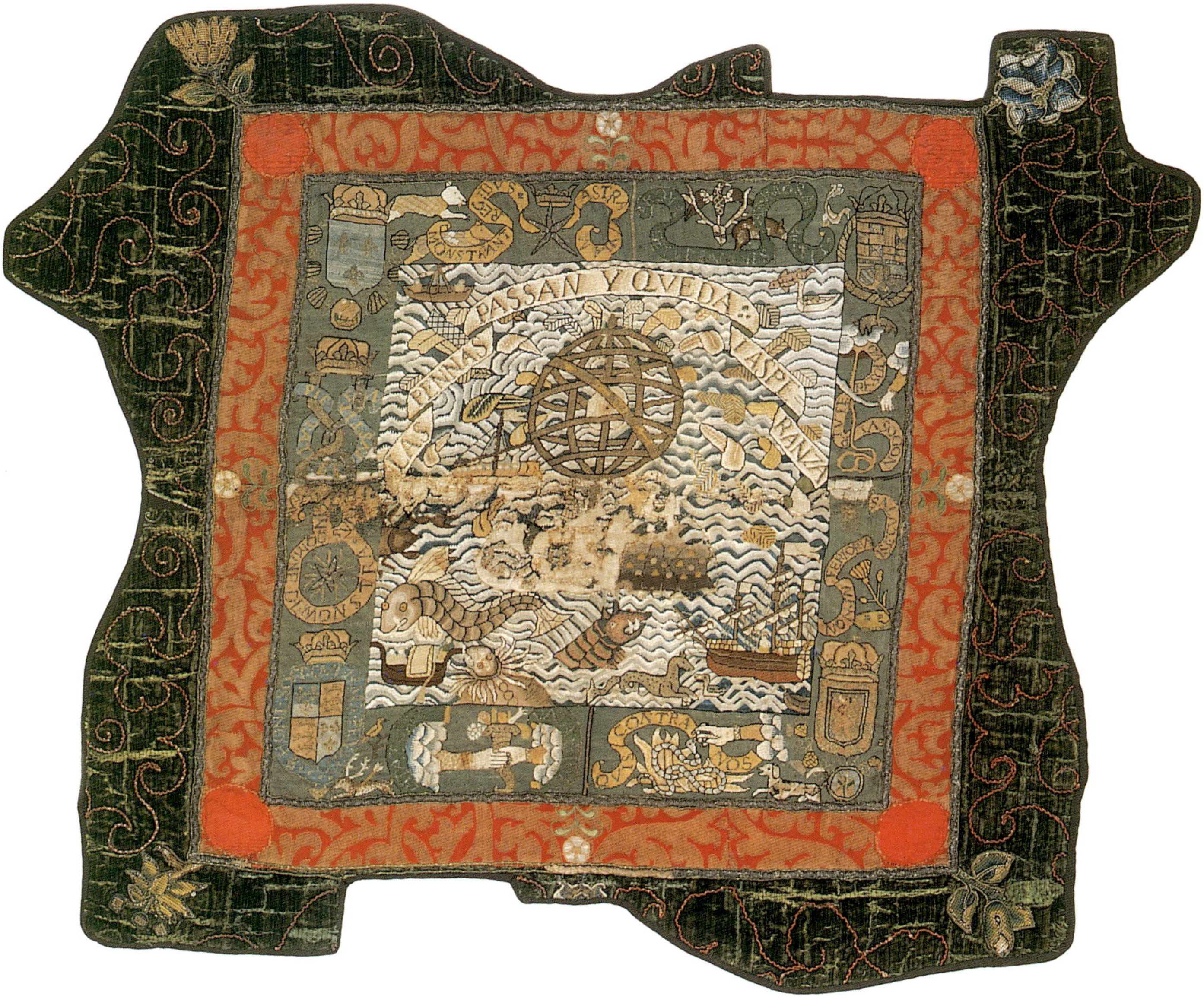

Mary, Queen of Scots' embroidery, panel Las Pennas Passan Y Queda La Speranza *('Sorrows pass but hope survives') with nine* imprese *in the inner border copied from Paradin and Simeoni.* V&A

though it would be wiser to reserve the term for strictly emblematic rather than loosely allegorical images, but clearly both types of imagery appeal to a taste for what Munday calls 'morall virtues' and 'morall Philosophie'.

Emblems in the stricter sense were well known in Scotland. In 1549 Barthélemy Aneau's French translation of Alciato's emblems was printed with a dedication to James Hamilton, son of Regent Arran, *'Duc de Chastel le herault, Prince Gouverneur du Royaume d'Escoce'*. Latin emblem books were purchased for the library of the young king James VI by his tutors, George Buchanan and Peter Young, and evidently played a part in the schooling of that monarch who famously complained that he was taught to speak Latin before he knew how to speak Scots. Both his predecessors – his mother, Mary, Queen of Scots, and Mary of Guise, widow of James V and Regent of Scotland from 1551 to 1559 – had direct knowledge of French fashions and expressed their own tastes in decorations which may well have been influenced by French models, including applied emblems. Mary of Guise occupied the so-called 'Guise Palace', at the top of Lawnmarket in Edinburgh, during her Regency. When it was pulled

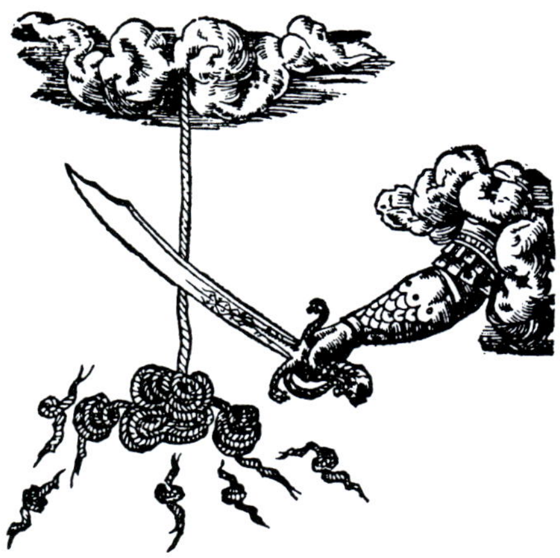

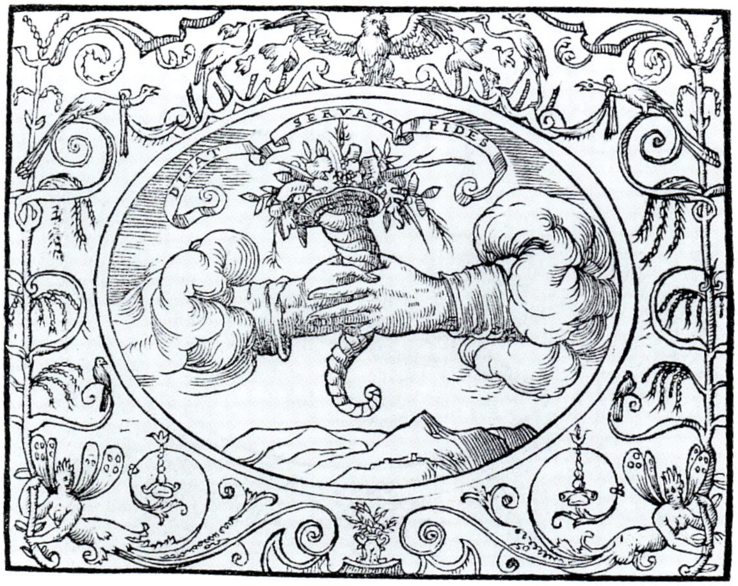

Left: *Claude Paradin,* Devises Heroïques *(1557) p.214, device of Maréchal de Saint André showing sword of Alexander the Great cutting the Gordian knot of adversity, one of the six devices from Paradin copied in Mary, Queen of Scots'* Las Pennas Passan *panel.* GUL

Right: *Gabriele Simeoni,* Le Imprese heroiche et morali *(1559) p.32,* impresa *illustrating the idea that faithful service will bring rewards,* Ditat servata fides, *copied in border of Mary, Queen of Scots'* Las Pennas Passan *panel.* GUL

down in the nineteenth century, remains of painted decoration were discovered which included six emblems copied from the *Devises heroïques* (1551) of Claude Paradin. It is by no means certain that all this decoration goes back to the time of Mary's residence, though some certainly does, but Paradin's emblems were quite widely used on buildings in Edinburgh, suggesting they were part of the acquired vocabulary of decorative artists.

Mary, Queen of Scots made use of Paradin's emblems in the embroideries which were her pastime both before and during her long exile in England. Some of those embroideries have, miraculously, survived and others are described in a letter which poet William Drummond wrote to Ben Jonson. The Oxburgh panel '*Las pennas passan*' includes a number of devices from Paradin – *Monstrat Regibus astra viam* (the star that guided the Magi); *Ardua deturbans* (the eagle that perches on the skull of a stag); *Nodos virtute resolvo* (the sword that cuts the Gordian knot of adversity); *Non inferiora secutus* (the sunflower device of Marguerite of Navarre); *Quis contra nos?* (the hand of St Paul shaking off the viper, which cannot harm those whom God protects); *Vias tuas Domine demonstra mihi* (the star surrounded with arrows which admiral Andreas Darius used as a call for divine direction on his voyage) – while the 'Marian' hanging has a version of *Latet anguis in Herba.* The two hands holding a cornucopia on the same panel copy Gabriele Simeoni's *Ditat servata fides* from his *Imprese heroiche et morali* (1559), a volume often reprinted in joint editions with Paradin. It is commonly supposed that Mary acquired her knowledge of this continental fashion during her youthful years in France when purchases of materials for needlework are recorded in her accounts. She would have had ample opportunity during the years preceding and following her marriage to François II to absorb the courtly fashion for emblem and *impresa* that flourished in the French court.

The *impresa* or personal device, with motto and picture but no verse epigram, was popular in both France and Italy, the fashion having developed during the French incursions into Italy earlier in the century. The invention of personal devices consisting of a symbolic image and an enigmatic motto signalling one's personal values, beliefs or intentions became one of the most highly regarded of courtly accomplishments. Its rules were spelled out in the elaborate treatises of Italian *impresa* theorists like Paolo Giovio and Scipione Bargagli. These devices had some connection with heraldic badges, but unlike heraldic arms were not hereditary and did not have to be registered at the Lyon Court or, in England, at the College of Arms. Henri II of France, for instance, took as his device the three crescent moons whose connection with the goddess Diana was taken as a reference to his mistress, Diane de Poitiers, whilst its Latin motto *Donec totem impleat orbem* ('Until it fills the whole world') was taken as referring to the unity and growing splendour of the universal church under his protection (Paradin 1557, pp.20-1). Mary adapted her own device of the marigold that turns its face to the sun from Henry's sister, Marguerite de Navarre, for whom the sun-turning daisy or marguerite punned on her own name, but Mary changed the motto to *Sa virtu m'atire* ('Its strength draws me'), which anagrammatises her own name, 'MARIE STVART'.

One of the better known of Mary's *imprese* is the 'Norfolk panel' with the emblem 'VIRESCIT VULNERE VIRTUS' ('Virtue flourishes from its wounds'), which shows a hand holding a pruning knife and cutting the branches of a vine, since the vine grows more fruitful through pruning. The embroidered panel was executed about 1570, when it was sent to the Duke of Norfolk, and it had specific application to her current circumstances, as Margaret Swain explains:

> It appeared to be a pious exercise on the part of the captive breathing the spirit of Christian resignation, but the panel was intended to convey a very different message. Mary sent it to Norfolk, and the message was plain for him to read: the unfruitful branch of the royal house (Elizabeth) was to be cut down; the fruitful branch (Mary) would be left to flourish and bear more fruit. When Ridolfi's plot was uncovered, Mary's ambassador, the Bishop of Ross, was imprisoned, and under threat of torture revealed that she had been in correspondence with Ridolfi, and had sent the cushion with its equivocal message to Norfolk. (1973, p.75)

It is characteristic of the *impresa* to hold a meaning that is personal to its bearer and speaks of their particular circumstances. Tournament *imprese* frequently delivered such coded messages and the Italian theorists regularly pointed to the etymological link between *impresa* and the verb *imprendere*, 'to undertake', or 'intend' – your *impresa* should signal your intention. Unlike the reverse of a medal, which celebrated things you had done, your *impresa* signified things to come.

We should pause, however, before concluding that all the *imprese* to be found on Mary's embroideries represent a foreign import into an alien Scottish environment. There is good evidence that such devices had already found their place in the Scottish system for marshalling coats of arms with the bearer's badge and motto displayed above the shield. The combination of motto and device, both of which began to be registered at the Lyon Court during the sixteenth century, offered a syntaxis of word and image closely resembling the structure of the Italian *impresa* and using some of its conventions. Italian collections of personal devices and *imprese* (Giovio, Cartari, Paradin, Simeoni)

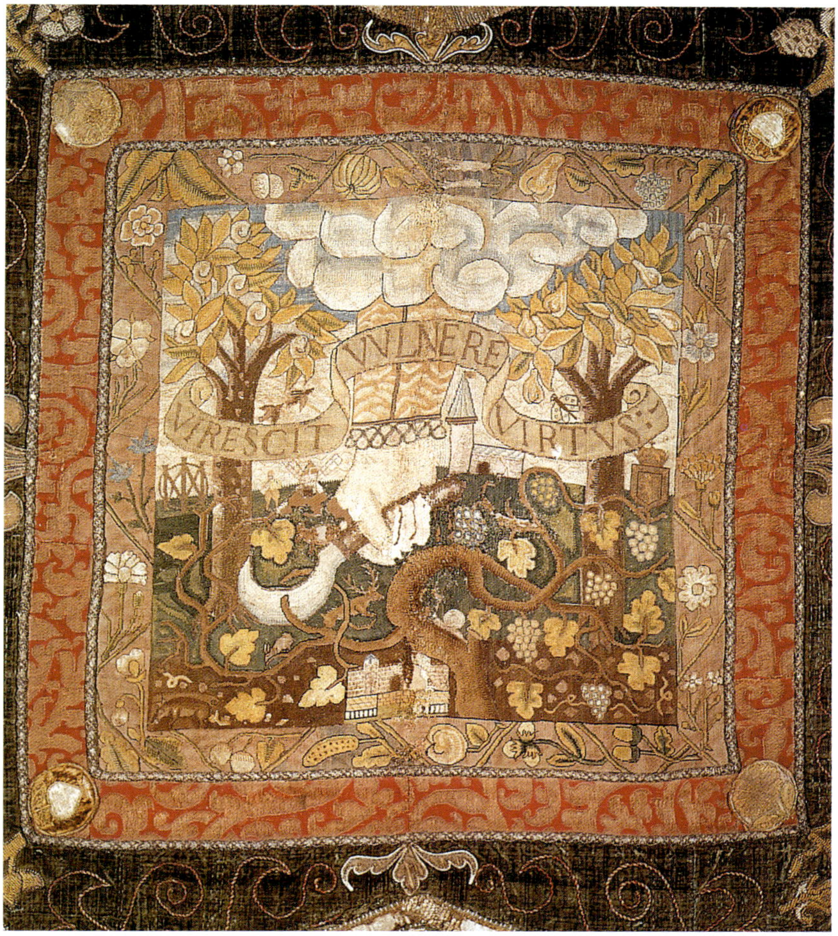

Mary, Queen of Scots' embroidery, the Norfolk panel, 'VIRESCIT VULNERE VIRTUS' ('Virtue flourishes from its wounds'). V&A

Crathes Castle, Aberdeenshire, arms of Alexander Burnett showing the same crest and motto as Mary, Queen of Scots' Norfolk panel.

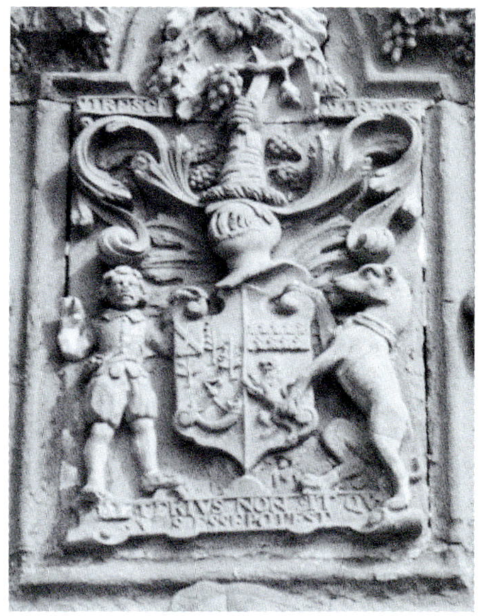

frequently included the traditional heraldic badges of the nobility. Indeed, Mary's motto figures in Scottish heraldry some time before she sent her coded message, for 'VIRESCIT VULNERE VIRTUS' was the motto of the Earls of Galloway, combined with the image of the pelican-in-her-piety, the bird that pecks its breast to feed its young with its life blood, traditionally an image of Christian sacrifice and resurrection.

Moreover, the hand holding a pruning knife over vine branches, with the same motto, was adopted as early as 1550 as the heraldic crest of two branches of the Burnett family. In 1550 a famous legal case was fought between two Burnetts over the right to this very badge and motto; Burnett of Burnetland took action in the Lyon Court against Alexander Burnett of Leys for possession of the motto 'VIRESCIT VULNERE VIRTUS'; the case was heard by Lyon King, Sir David Lindsay of the Mount, the most famous of Scotland's Renaissance poets. Three years later Alexander Burnett began building his new castle at Crathes (only completed by his great-grandson and successor some fifty years later), filling it with impressive painted ceilings and decorating its harled stonework with carved inset panels, one of which, indeed, bears the Burnett arms with its

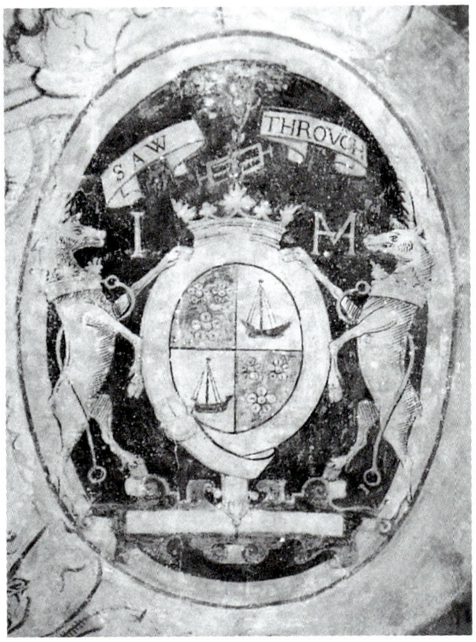

Kinneil, Bo'ness, Hamilton arms with crest and motto 'Saw through': the antelope was thought to have antlers shaped like a saw; the medieval Bestiary moralised that this signified the Christian who should cut away vices with the horns of the two Testaments.

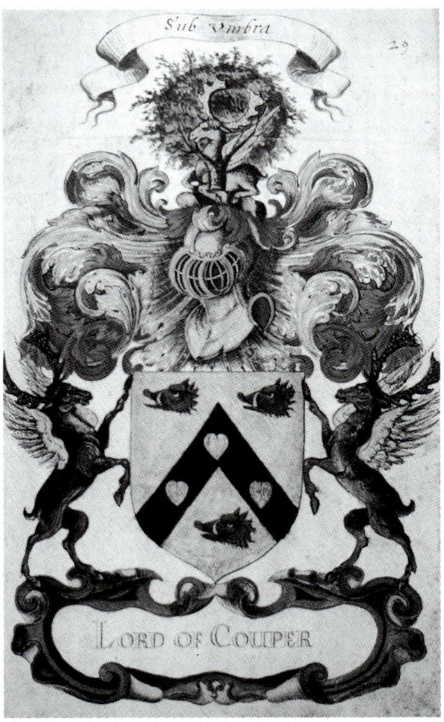

Arms of the Lord of Couper showing winged stags as supporters and on crest. Lyon Court MS21, *fol.96.*

crest showing the pruned vine and the Latin motto. The immediate precedent for Mary's 'VIRESCIT VULNERE VIRTUS' device, then, was not a continental model she had absorbed in France but a native Scottish practice of marshalling arms with a heraldic crest (or 'badge') and motto.

This heraldic practice was evidently one of the channels through which the continental *impresa* conventions had penetrated Scottish culture at a comparatively early date. It must also have made the Scottish climate particularly receptive to continental emblematics. The traditional mottoes and war cries of the Scottish clans and their leaders easily lent themselves to the *impresa* theorists' rule that one's *impresa* should signal one's intention – the Athol motto 'Furth forth and fill thy fetters', or the Earl of Bothwell's 'Keip traist', Rothes' 'Grip fast', Morton's 'Lok sicker', Huntley's 'Bydand', all warn friend or foe what they should expect. Such mottoes, however, do not always have any very clear connection with the heraldic badge. The 'badge' is quite separate from the emblazonment on the shield itself – in Scottish heraldry the personal badge is marshalled along with the motto above the helmet, crest and mantling, right at the top of the 'achievement'. Unlike a personal *impresa*, however, the Scottish badge and motto are heritable devices – once registered they were taken over, along with all the other features of your coat of arms, by your descendants.

Sometimes the connection between motto and badge may depend on the viewer's detailed knowledge, as with the Earl of Errol's motto, *Serva iugum* ('Preserve the yoke'), which refers to the legendary origins of the title when his ancestor, a ploughman, rescued Scotland from defeat by the invading Danish army by turning back the retreating Scots with no other weapon but his ox-yoke. The supporters of the Errol shield are ox-yokes but the badge is a bird whose relevance only becomes apparent once one knows the rest of the story, for the king of the Scots in gratitude for this rescue awarded the ploughman possession of all those lands contained within the circle flown by a falcon that he had released. All this iconography figures in Errol's painted ceiling at Dalgety, none of which uses emblems.

A similar link between badge and motto is in the arms of Arran which we find in the decorative painting at Kinneil and which show the motto 'Saw through' and a frame saw, sometimes shown cutting the trunk of a tree. The legend was that Sir Gilbert de Hamilton, whilst fleeing in 1323 from the court of Edward II, escaped capture when he and his servant swapped clothes with a couple of foresters and pretended to be at work felling trees. When their pursuers had passed by he cried out, 'Through!' The tree with the antelope horn was used by the first Lord Hamilton in 1477, whilst the motto first appears in 1560 on a seal of Regent Arran, created Duke of Châtelhérault, who began building Hamilton Palace and Kinneil with their extensive painted ceilings and who was the first to bear the arms with this achievement: first and fourth three cinquefoils, second and third a lymphad; crest and oak tree traversed by a frame saw; supporters two antelopes; motto 'Through' or 'Saw through' (*cf* Harvey Johnston 1909). In this case the heraldic supporters confirm the symbolism since they are antelopes – a creature traditionally thought to have large antlers

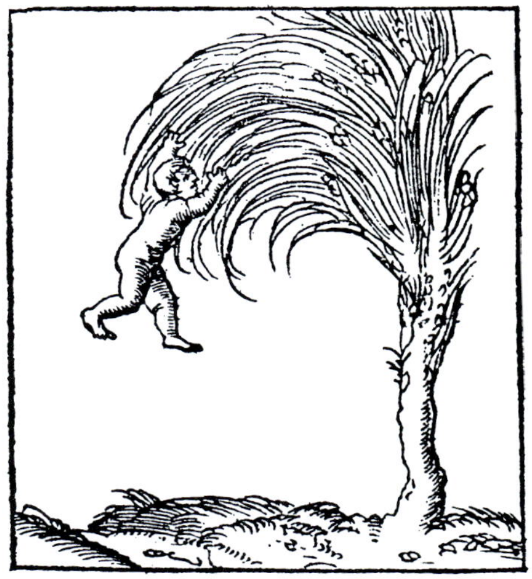

Andrea Alciato, Emblematum libellus *(Paris: Wechel, 1534) p.28, emblem showing the palm tree which only yields its fruits to those who persevere.* GUL

'made like a saw' (as Edward Topsell puts it) with which they can cut through the branches of trees.

None of these looks particularly emblematic but in the later sixteenth century awards of arms are recorded in which the bearer appears to have taken greater cognisance of the continental demand for wit, erudition and rhetorical skill in the composition of one's personal device. The Lord of Couper, for instance, has a crest that features a winged stag couchant beneath a tree, with the motto 'SUB UMBRA' ('In the shade'). Just how close the Scottish armorial badge or crest could come to the emblem is suggested by the arms of the Lord of Holyroodhouse, whose badge shows a boy clinging to the branches of a date palm, with the motto 'OBDURANDUM ADVERSIS URGENTIA' ('One must be steadfast under pressure'); a crest and motto copied directly from Alciato's *Emblemata* that moralise the commonplace of the palm tree, which traditionally grows stronger under pressure and whose fruits can only be gathered by those who persevere in a difficult task. The Holyroodhouse title and coat of arms were granted to John Bothwell son of Adam, Bishop of Orkney, who officiated at the marriage of Queen Mary with the Earl of Bothwell in 1567. Adam Bothwell had been Commendator of Holyroodhouse and when his eldest son was created a Lord of Parliament he took the title Lord Holyroodhouse, adopting this crest and motto.

The close connection between the Scottish heraldic crest and the emblematic *device* is, indeed, recognised in one of the authoritative Scottish guides to the science of heraldry. Alexander Nisbet's *System of Heraldry,* printed in Edinburgh in 1722, has a chapter 'Of Mottoes, Cries of War, and Devices' which shows unmistakable debts to the discourse and arguments of *impresa* theorists such as Giovio, Bargagli, Camden, Estienne or Menestrier. Nisbet has no hesitation in taking the whole science of armoury back to the same ancient sources that had regularly been identified by Renaissance emblem theorists.

> Devices which consists [sic] of figures without words are the same with the hieroglyphics and emblems used by the ancients of old to dignify their minds, conceptions and intentions; and from such came originally crests, and other armorial figures placed on the shield above or at the side of it. (vol. ii, p.26)

Nisbet is clearly suggesting that not only the armorial crest but also the supporters and charges on the actual shield could function as emblematic devices. Italian *impresa* theorists, as we have already noted, insist that the personal *impresa* or device expresses its bearer's mind or intention, and it was the same theorists of Renaissance emblematics who laid down those strict rules governing the relation of motto to picture which Nisbet is drawing on.

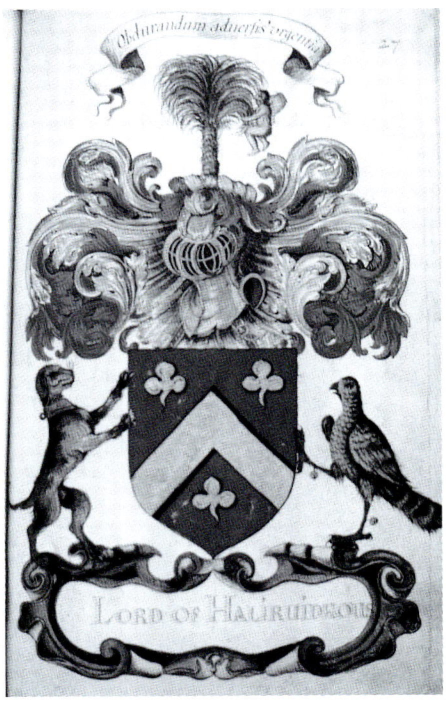

Arms of the Lord of Holyroodhouse with crest copied from Alciato's emblem of the oppressed palm tree. Lyon Court MS21, *fol.94.*

> Mottoes and Cries of War consist of a word or words without any figure; and the device here mentioned is a figure without a word, being a representation, and emblem or heroglyphic [sic] painted, to express something that is to be kept in mind; and these were much in use among the Egyptians, and other ancient

> nations. The word without a figure, and the figure without a word, are lookt upon as imperfect devices; but when the word and figure are joined together, making an allusion, to show the inclination and humours of the assurance, or of something done, or to be done, tho' they be not easily understood by the vulgar, are perfect devices, consisting of a body (the figure) and soul (the word) as heralds say ... Camden for motto says *Inscriptio* ....
>
> However mottos for the most part are relative to some part of the achievement, and especially to the crest; and from them arises a comparison, the one explaining the other, and so make a proper device; as by these following instances. The ancient motto of the Earls of Sutherland, *Without Fear*, speaks to the crest, *a wild cat sitting*. *Virescit vulnere virtus*, the motto or ditton of Steuart Earl of Galloway is relative to the crest, a *Pelican vulnered* feeding her young in a *nest* proper, which figure is an emblem of our Saviour .... (1722, vol. ii, pp. 21-2)

The tenor of Nisbet's argument here is quite simply that Scottish heraldic crests with their mottoes are capable of fulfilling the established rules for the fashioning of a perfect *impresa*. Clearly he was familiar with William Camden's *Remains Concerning Britain*, which had discussed some of these issues in its chapter on 'Impresses' and had first appeared in 1605 (though it had been reprinted as late as 1674). Nisbet's familiarity with Camden's work should not surprise us since Camden had been Clarenceux King of Arms in his day, but Nisbet also knows the work of the great French theorist of symbolic images, Claude-François Menestrier, whom he repeatedly cites. By the time Menestrier wrote his encyclopaedic *summae*, in the later seventeenth century, of the art of the emblem and the philosophy of images, the emblematic vogue was already past its prime and we might think that the early eighteenth century was a bit late in the day for Nisbet to be offering us this theory of the heraldic crest based on Renaissance *impresa* theory. Nevertheless it seems likely that Nisbet is only summarising assumptions that had long informed heraldic practices in Scotland. Heraldry is not the same as emblematics, but the two things had many points of contact.

Something similar seems to have been the case with inscriptions on buildings. Houses of this period in Scotland appear to have been covered with writing, carved on door lintels or on panels inserted on walls, often with the owner's monogram, coat of arms, or date. They range from the pious commonplace to the erudite adage, in Scots or in Latin – sometimes both on the same building. 'Excep the lord build in wane builds man' wrote Joseph Marjoribanks above the door of his house at Northfield, East Lothian. 'Blissit be ye Lord for all his giftis 1578' wrote the Archbishop of St Andrews above his Edinburgh lodgings. Such texts declare their owner's piety and probity rather than demonstrating any particular epigraphic skill, but others have a lapidary point: *Sedes manet optima caelo* ('Home is better than heaven') was the inscription above a door in Sempil's Close, Edinburgh; *Angusta ad usum augusta* ('A strait gate to admit the great') wrote William Fowler, whose son was a poet and secretary to Anne of Denmark and whose sister was mother of the poet William

Drummond. 'This house loves peace, hates knaves, crimes punisheth, preserves the laws, and good men honoureth' was the inscription above the courthouse in Perth, which may look more righteous than elegant, but the version inscribed above the Tolbooth in Glasgow turns the same saying into a competent example of *versus rapportati*:

> Haec domus odit, amat, punit, conservat, honorat,
> Nequitiam, pacem, crimina, jura, probos.

No doubt that would deter the criminal classes! Such inscriptions should not be seen simply as the claims to moral rectitude of straitlaced Protestant Scotland, they also reflect an educated interest in classical epigraphy. Humanist and antiquarian scholars from the late fifteenth century onwards – including the emblematist Alciato himself – had spent a lot of their time collecting and publishing the inscriptions they found on the ruins or remains of classical buildings. Such inscriptions have to be seen as sending clear neoclassical signals.

None of these inscriptions seems much like an emblem, but there are examples where much the same type of inscription is associated with an image. Cullen House has carvings of the three theological Virtues on the triangular lintels to the attic windows, with the legends 'Faith ye grund of al', 'Hope ye anker of faith', 'Charitie covereth manie sins'. These are not what we could properly describe as fully fledged emblems, but on Huntly House in Edinburgh's Canongate we have the mottoes 'HODIE MIHI CRAS TIBI CVR IGITVR CVRAS 1570' ('Today is mine, tomorrow yours, so why worry?'); 'VT TV LINGVAE TVAE SIC EGO MEARVM AVRIVM DOMINVS SVM' ('As you are master of your tongue, so I am master of my ears'); 'CONSTANTI PECTORI RES MORTALIVM VMBRA' ('To the firm hearted, mortal things are a shadow'). None of these inscriptions has a sculpted image but the last panel, at the western end of the front, reads 'SPES ALTERA VITAE' ('Another hope of life') and this inscription is accompanied by the image of stalks of grain rising from a heap of bones. This is the final emblem in Paradin's *Devises heroïques*, and Huntly House is not the only place where it is used as a lapidary emblem, for in 1588 John Gourlay, son of a wealthy Edinburgh burgess, built a house with the same device on its front. Daniel Wilson records a ceiling in Blyth's Close, now destroyed, which used further devices from Paradin, including the ape that crushes its offspring in its embrace with the motto 'CAECUS AMOR PROLIS' (Paradin 1557, p.226); the serpent among strawberry plants, 'LATET ANGUIS IN HERBA' (ibid., p.70); the hedgehog with grapes on its quills, 'MAGNUM VECTIGAL' (p.140); and the two hands holding a sword and a trowel, 'IN UTRUMQUE PARATUS' (p.115) (Wilson 1848, vol. i, p.150). Such devices suggest that these sources had been fully absorbed into the iconographic repertoire of Scottish painters and sculptors well before the turn of the century. In 1633, the year Charles I came to Edinburgh for his Scottish coronation, Sir Archibald Acheson installed a carved pediment above his doorway, with the motto 'VIGILANTIBUS' ('To those

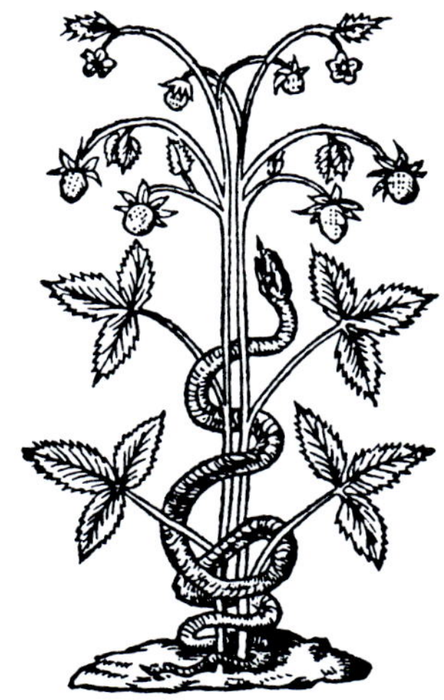

Paradin, Devises heroïques *(1557) p.70, device showing snake coiled in strawberry plant, meaning that when gathering wise fruits from books we must beware of dangerous opinions lurking amongst them.* GUL

Paradin, Devises heroïques *(1557),* Spes altera vitae, *p.258.* GUL

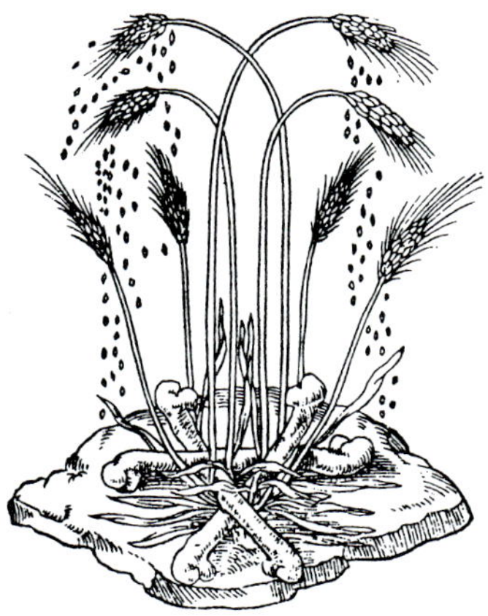

Huntly House in Canongate, Edinburgh, carving on façade copying Paradin's device.

The same device from Paradin on the painted ceiling from Rossend, Fife.

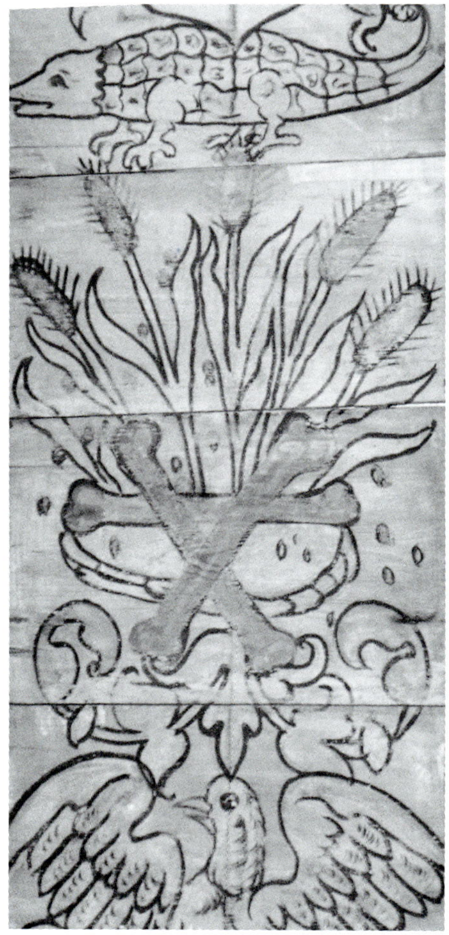

who are vigilant'), together with the image of a cock standing on a trumpet. This was evidently modelled on Paradin's *Pacis & armorum vigiles,* a device which, Paradin explains, symbolises the difference between peace and war: the cock-crow awakes us in times of peace whereas the trumpet's reveille does so in time of war.

Although this is clearly functioning as an emblem, it has also once again to be identified as a heraldic badge, which is probably why the initials 'AMH' are also carved into the design, standing for Acheson and his wife Margaret Hamilton. We find the same image of the vigilant cock on the painted ceiling at Nunraw together with Paradin's emblem of the salamander lying in its flames, the device of François I. The Nunraw ceiling also has a dittany-eating stag that has been pierced by an arrow, almost certainly copied from Gabriele Simeoni's *Imprese heroiche.* On the Nunraw ceiling these emblematic devices are all assimilated to a variety of other images, grotesques, coats of arms, birds and beasts, which have no emblematic significance. It is difficult to believe that here the images from Paradin retain anything of the function they had in their source as 'speaking pictures'. The boundaries between these different systems of signification

Paradin, Devises heroïques *(1557) p.209, 'Be ready for peace or war'.* GUL

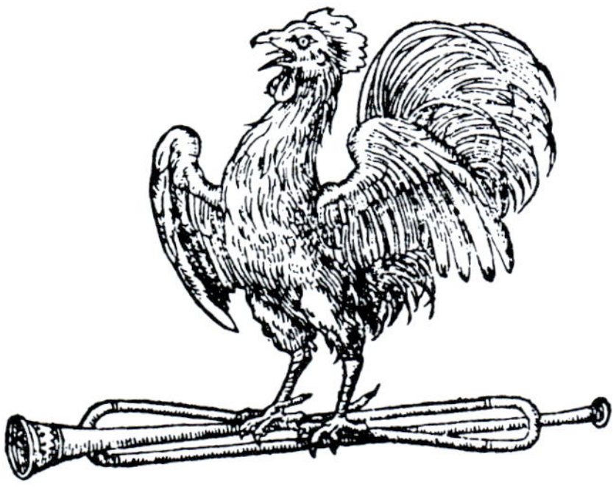

Pediment over doorway of Sir Archibald Acheson's house in Edinburgh. Acheson was Secretary of State for Scotland; from the sketch by James Riddel illustrating Robert Chambers Traditions of Edinburgh *(1868, repr. 1931, p.315).*

Nunraw, detail of painted ceiling showing a version of Paradin's Pacis & armorum vigiles *device.* HS

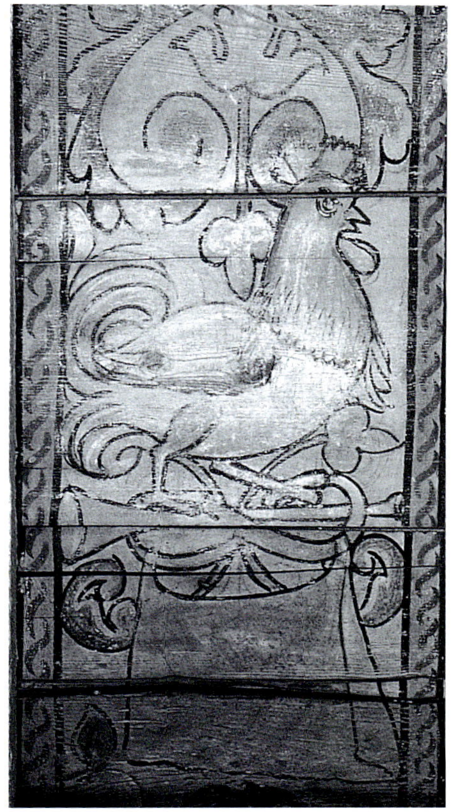

are not at all clear – there was some overlap. We are talking of a pictorial vocabulary that brings together and merges different dialects.

The ceiling from Rossend preserves one of the richest gatherings of emblematic images to be found on any of these ceilings, including as it does fifteen or more devices from Paradin, a couple more from Simeoni, and another that copies an emblem from Alciato. The style is very close to Nunraw and to John Knox's House in Edinburgh and all three ceilings may be by the same hand; however, the fact that these images snatched out of emblem books are mixed up in a random sequence, with similar motifs which go back to other sources, calls into question any idea that, stripped of their supporting *scriptura*, these devices retain any emblematic meaning in their new decorative surroundings. The two hands, one holding a sword and the other a trowel, are certainly always likely to have suggested Paradin's *In utrumque paratus* motto to any informed viewer, but we cannot know how far Sir Robert Melville expected this image on his ceiling to call to mind the readiness of the people of Israel to build and defend the walls of Jerusalem, or the 'ministers of Christ' who, in the words of Paradin's English translator, 'are bound to instruct the ignorant & to fight manfully with the sword of God's word against the enemies thereof' (London

Paradin, Devises heroïques *(1557) p.16, salamander device of François I.* GUL

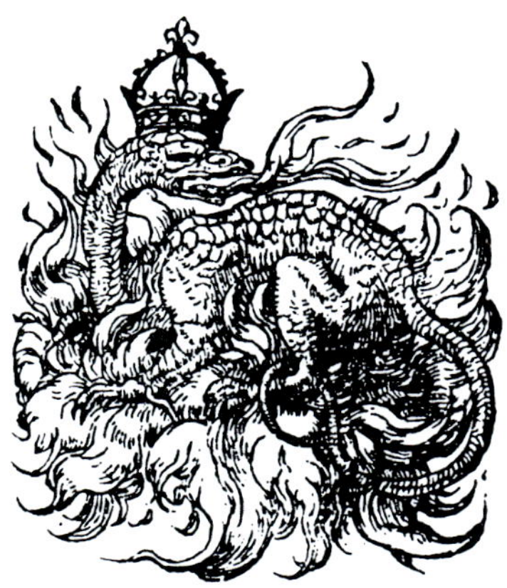

Nunraw, detail of painted ceiling showing salamander lying amidst flames.

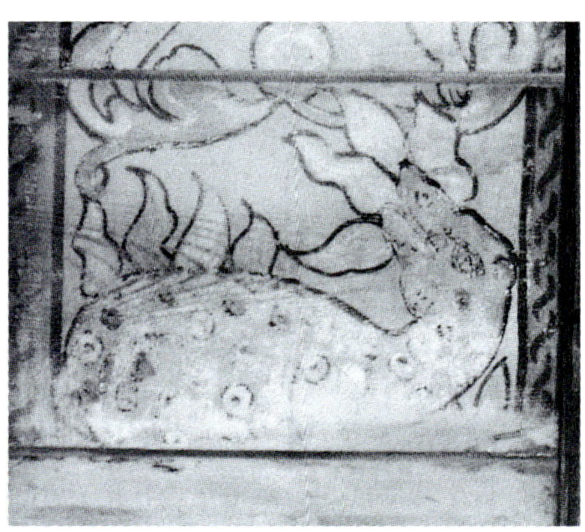

Nunraw, detail of painted ceiling showing arrow-pierced stag with the herb dittany in its mouth.

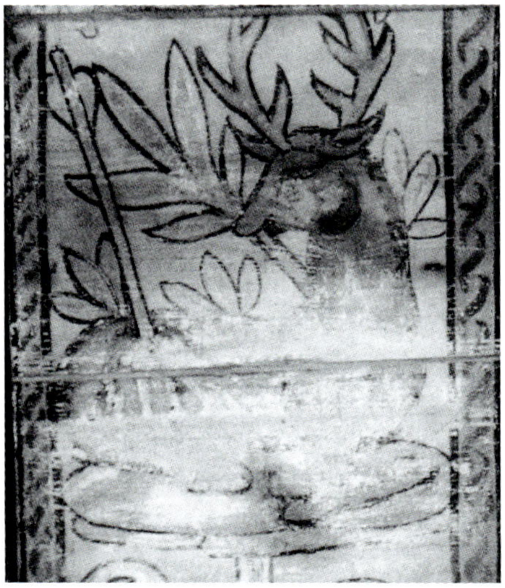

Simeoni, Imprese heroiche et morali *(1559) p.34, device illustrating the plight of lovers for whom there is no remedy for love's wounds, unlike the stag which traditionally ate medicinal herbs to expell arrows.* GUL

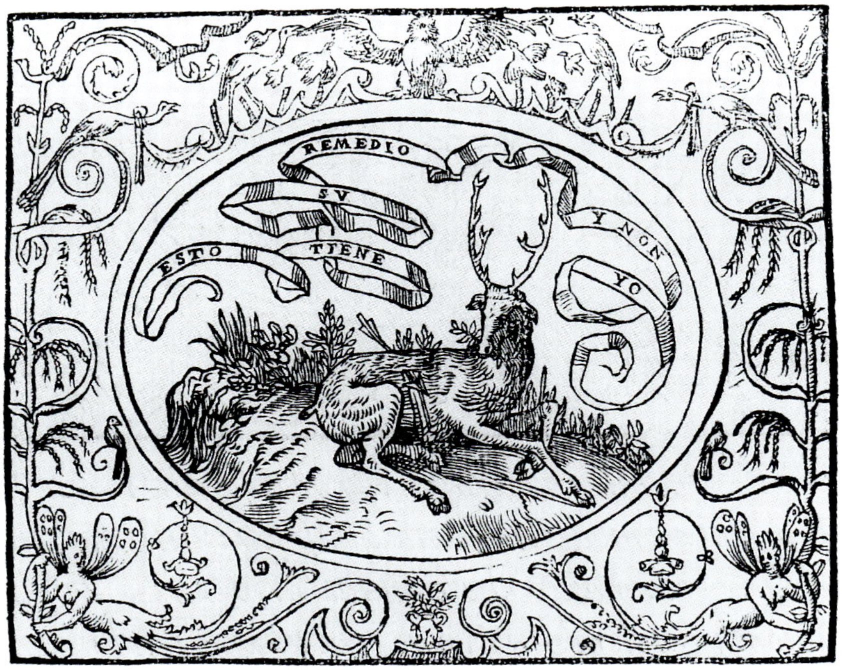

1591, p.145). This device was also used on the Paradin ceiling at Blyth's Close, in the house known as Bay Horse Inn at Dysart, and – heavily adapted – in the Skelmorlie Aisle at Largs. At Rossend the image of the raven perched on top of a large water vessel that it is filling with stones in order to raise the water to a level from which it can drink is the device Bess of Hardwick had borrowed from Paradin as the centrepiece of the Shrewsbury Hanging. The moral of this fable from Pliny is that necessity is the mother of invention or, as Paradin's motto puts it, *Ingenii largitor* ('Bestower of stratagems'). Two hands holding a cornucopia is Simeoni's *impresa* showing how loyalty to one's friends (the joined hands) is likely to make your fortune (the cornucopia). Mary, Queen of Scots had used this in her *Las Pennas Passan* panel; she had also used the image we find at Rossend showing a hand with a sword that cuts through the Gordian knot, Paradin's *Nodos virtute resolvo* ('It is by virtue that I untangle knots'). The horse wearing a blindfold, *Premitur, non opprimitur,* illustrates an anecdote from Suetonius, who tells how emperor Galba settled a question of disputed ownership by blindfolding the beast, and awarding it to whichever claimant it approached once its eyes were uncovered.

Though Paradin and Simeoni are the principal emblematic sources which the Rossend ceiling uses, one of its emblems, the goat suckling a wolf cub, must have been copied from Alciato (*In eum qui sibi ipsi damnum apparat*) since neither Paradin nor Simeoni have this device. Though Whitney also has this emblem, the Rossend artist can be shown to have used the woodcut which illustrated the Paris, Wechel, editions of Alciato (1534, etc) rather than the woodcut which Whitney took over from Plantin's stock in Leiden – the latter shows the wolf cub suckling from the rear between the goat's legs (reproduced in Apted 1966, p.83), whereas Rossend and the Wechel picture both show the cub squatting beneath the udder and facing the other way. It is rare to be able to identify not just the emblem but the actual edition which the decorative artist must have used. Rossend uses one further emblem from Alciato, a caduceus of two entwined snakes crowned by Mercury's winged hat with two cornucopiae. This copies Alciato, *Virtuti fortuna comes* ('Fortune, companion of virtue'), a well-known emblem on the power of wisdom and eloquence to bring good fortune or abundance. The artist evidently misinterprets or misunderstands some of its elements since he has omitted the wand (Mercury's caduceus) which the two snakes should be entwined around and has, accordingly, attached the lower pair of wings to the bases of the cornucopiae and not to the foot of the caduceus; this is iconographic nonsense since it is eloquence not abundance that is conventionally winged.

Paradin, Devises heroïques *(1557) p.115, device signifying that God's chosen people should be equally prepared both to build and to defend the Church. And below:* GUL

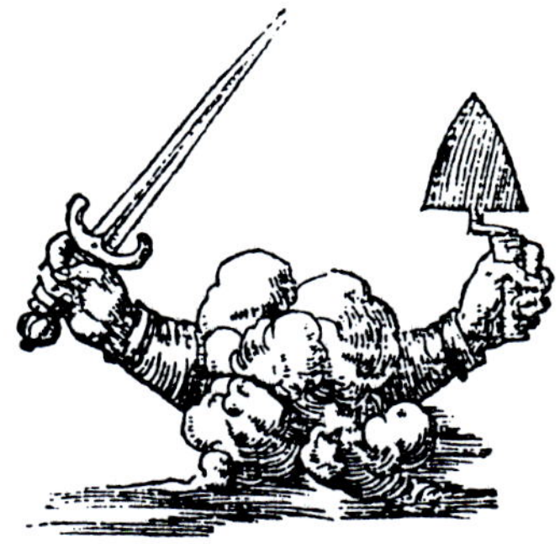

Rossend, detail of painted ceiling copying Paradin's In utrumque paratus *device.*

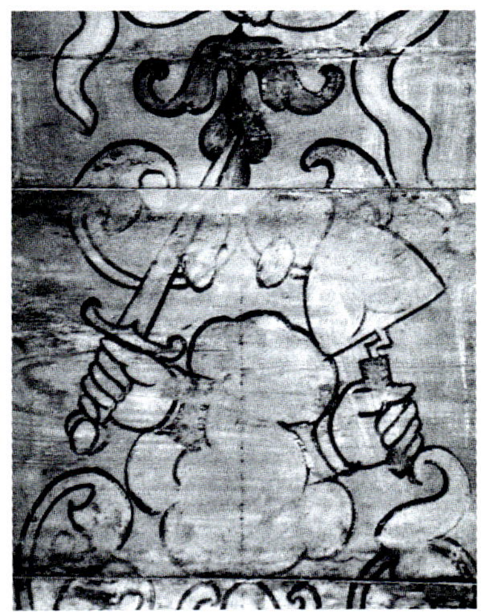

Rossend, detail copying Paradin's Ingenii largitor *device.*

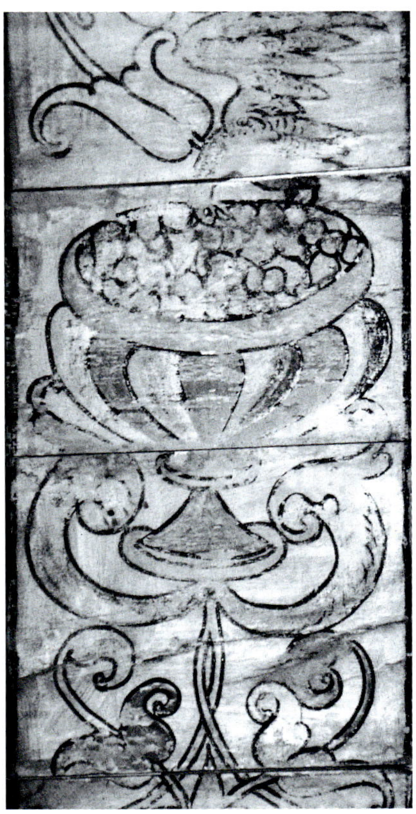

Paradin, Devises heroïques *(1557) p.141, device showing the stratagem of the ingenious raven that raises the water level in a cup by filling it with stones in order to drink – necessity is the mother of invention.* GUL

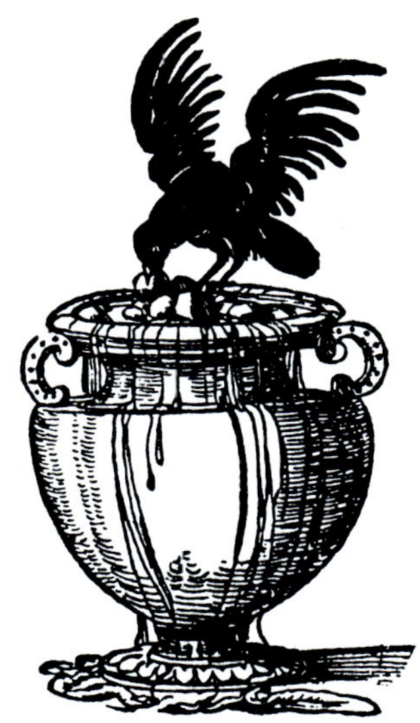

Andrea Alciato, Emblematum libellus *(Paris: Wechel, 1534) p.22, showing the Rossend winged hat as an attribute of Mercury, whose winged caduceus is also shown, an emblem on the power of wisdom and eloquence. And below:* GUL

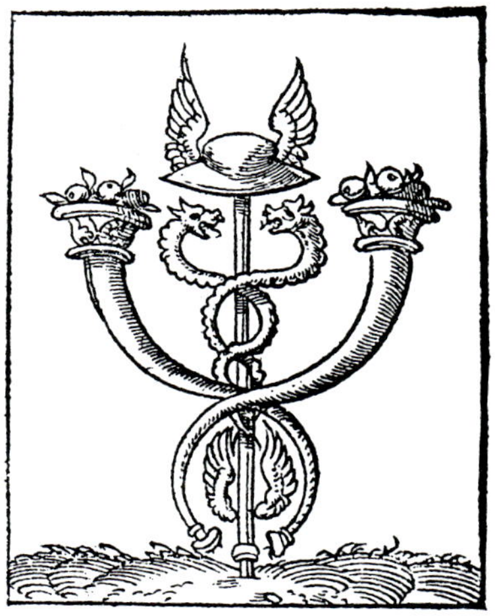

It is not impossible that such images might have recalled their received morals to an informed viewer, but it is less easy to see how viewers would have distinguished such emblematic images from the non-emblematic or quasi-emblematic images on the same ceiling. The two embracing mermen with entwined tails might just suggest friendship, and the bunch of gardening tools above them – spade, rake, basket, with wine amphora – is topped by what may be a broad-brimmed *pileus* or freedom-hat, but none of these devices is to be found in Paradin. In fact they go back to a quite different continental print source that requires separate and extensive treatment elsewhere in this study, namely the Renaissance tradition of antique or grotesque painting.

The sequence of images just described – gardening tools, brimmed hat, bucranium – is in fact one of more than half a dozen motifs on this ceiling that can be shown to copy details from a series of prints by Hans Vredeman de Vries: *Grottesco: in diversche manieren* (Antwerp: de Jode, c.1565-71). Twenty or more years earlier the same set of prints had supplied the patterns for most of the decoration on Mark Kerr's extraordinary grotesque ceiling at Prestongrange, which I shall examine in some detail in Chapter 5; indeed the Prestongrange

Rossend, detail showing entwined snakes with cornucopiae, copying Alciato's emblem Virtute fortuna comes *('Fortune, companion of virtue').*

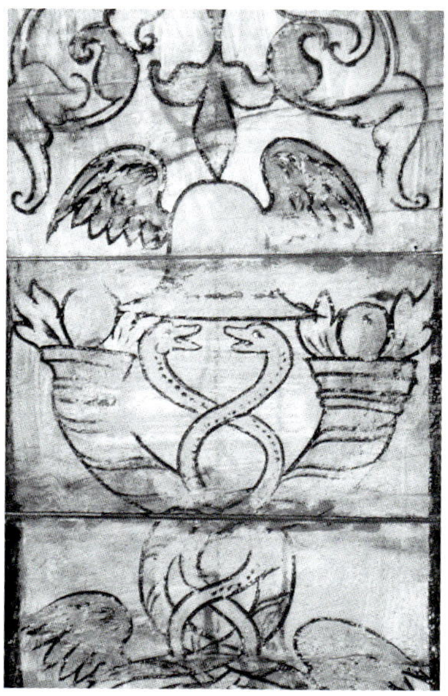

Andrea Alciato, Emblematum libellus *(Paris: Wechel, 1534) p.96, the goat that suckles the wolf-cub.* GUL

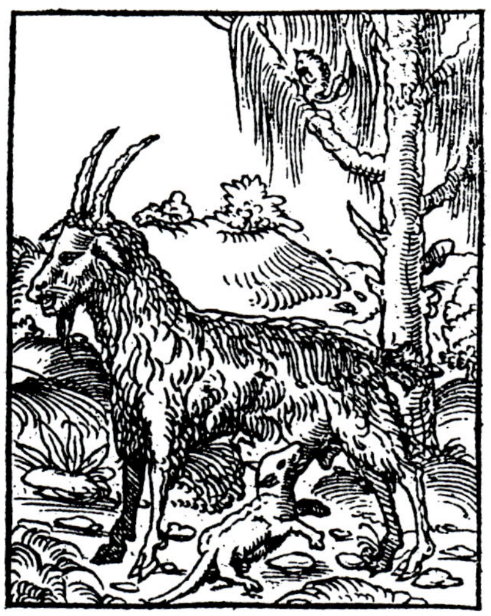

Rossend, detail showing goat suckling the wolf cub that will eventually devour it, copies from Alciato's emblem In eum qui sibi ipsi damnum apparat *('On someone who brings ruin on himself').*

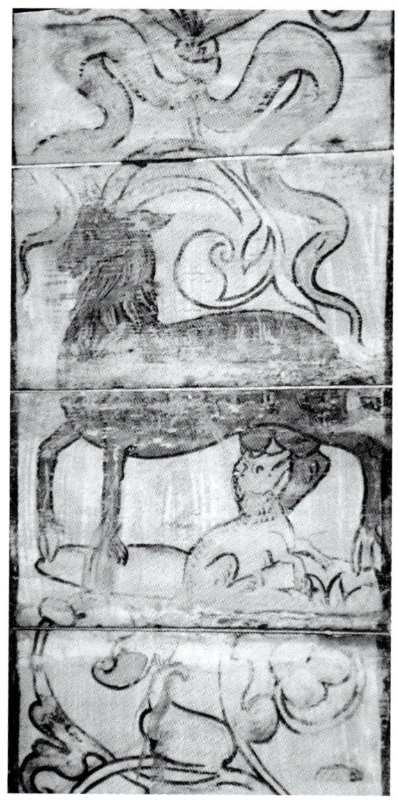

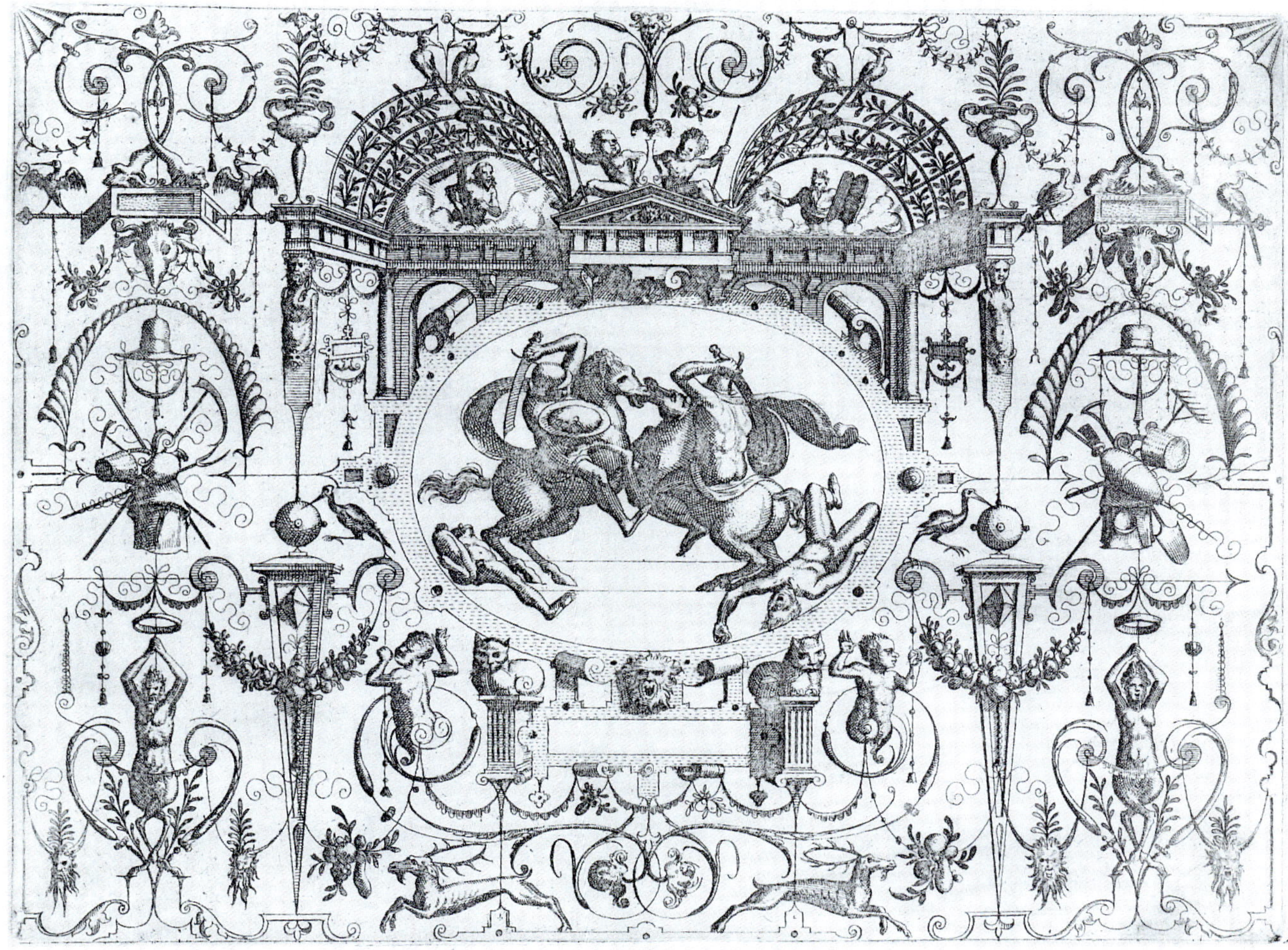

Engraving from Hans Vredeman de Vries, Grottesco: in diversche manieren *(Antwerp, c.1565-71).* V&A

ceiling uses this very same sequence of images. We can be sure, however, that the Rossend artist had independent access to these prints since other *Grottesco* details at Rossend use images not found at Prestongrange. Before looking more closely at Rossend's use of Vredeman it is worth unpacking some of the theoretical consequences of this discovery. The sources are discrepant, I suggest, because emblems are ideographic or symbolic images, pictures with some allegorical significance, whereas early writers on the grotesque tend to insist, as we shall see, that the grotesque style is devoid of meaning. As Cotgrave puts it in his *Dictionary* (1611), grotesques are 'Pictures wherein (as please the Painter) all kinds of odde things are represented without anie peculiar sence, or meaning, but only to feed the eye'. Insofar as emblems from Paradin or Simeoni are assimilated into a grotesque context on this ceiling, therefore, it follows that they have been stripped of whatever 'peculiar sence, or meaning' they may have had in their source.

Vredeman's sixteen *Grottesco* prints surround their central frames with an abundance of decorative detail and it is this detail that supplied such fertile copy for the decorative artists at Prestongrange and at Rossend. Often this succession of ornamental oddities will be strung down either side of Vredeman's page, literally strung out on beaded threads which tie together a series of anomalous details in an entirely arbitrary sequence; this is evidently what made them so readily adaptable to the restricted space which Scottish

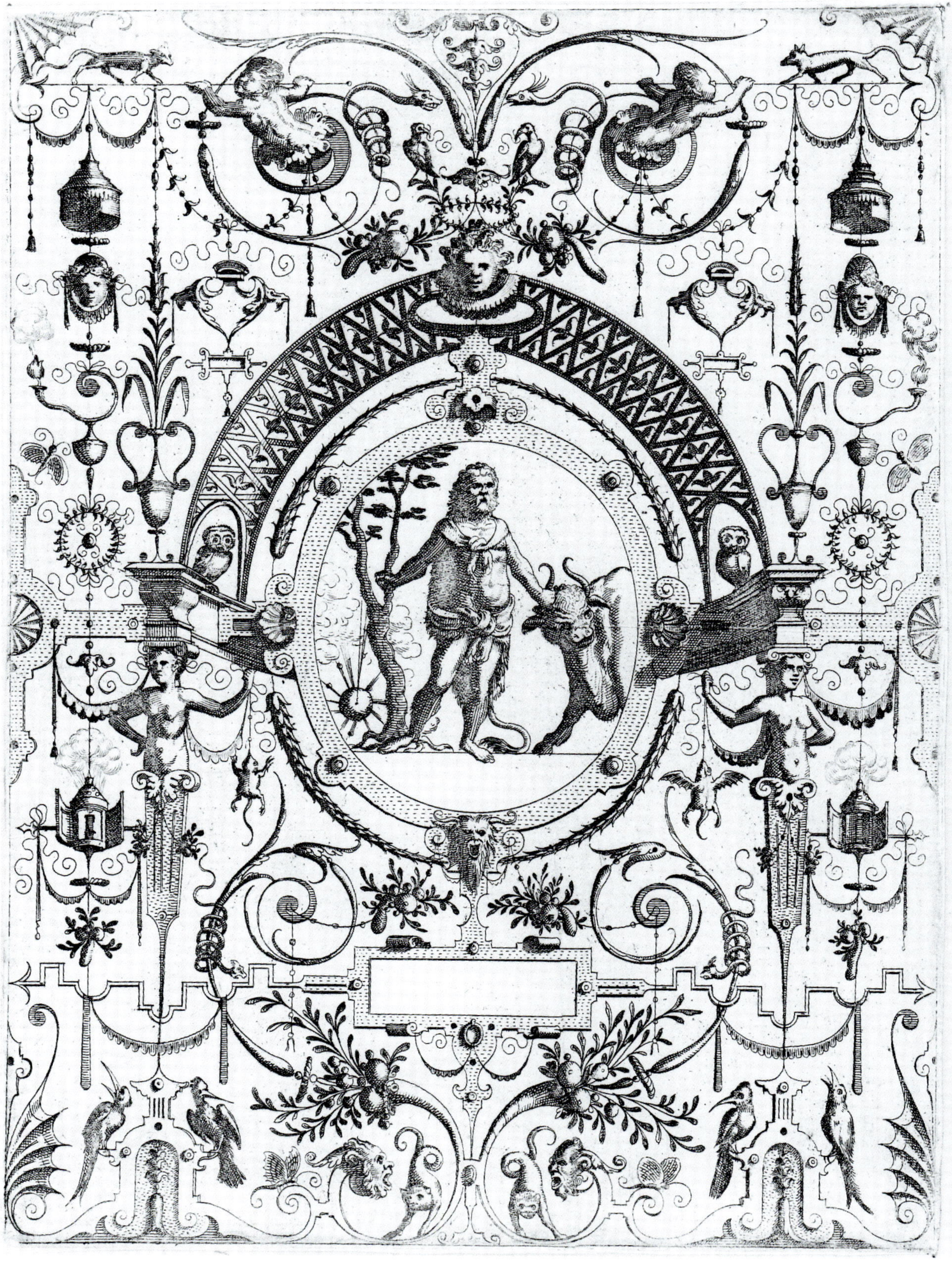

Engraving from Hans Vredeman de Vries,
Grottesco: in diversche manieren
(Antwerp, c.1565-71). V&A

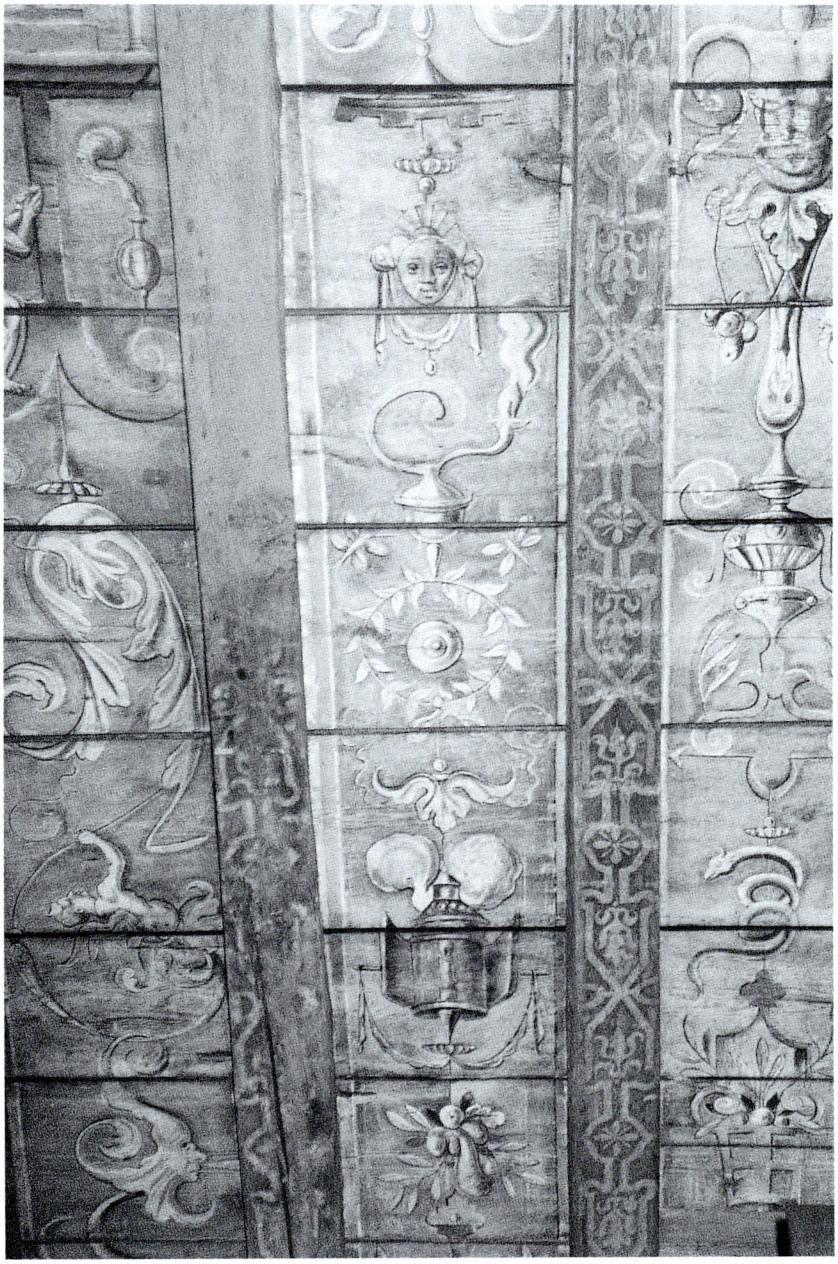

Prestongrange ceiling of 1581 showing grotesque ornament copied from Vredeman de Vries and also found, twenty years later, on the ceiling from Rossend.

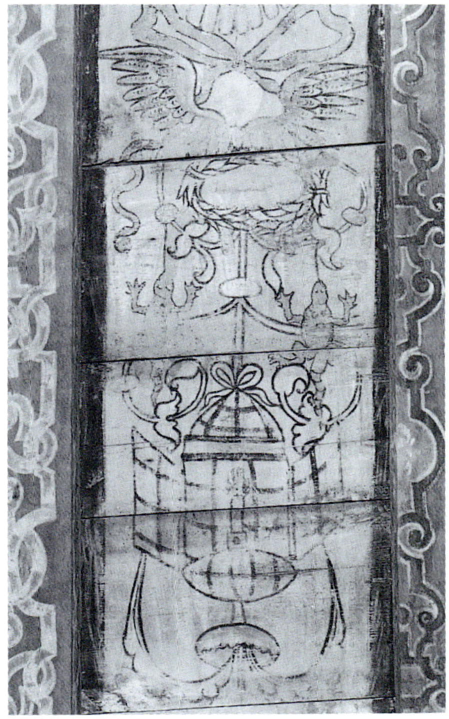

The same detail on the ceiling from Rossend. NMS

artists had to fill between the supporting beams on ceilings. Another such sequence which we find at both Prestongrange and Rossend consists of a lantern with open doors holding a lighted candle; an ornamental drape hangs below it, and above it there is a wreath of leaves encircling a button; all these hang on a beaded thread, and above them Vredeman has drawn a flaming torch and a human mask which Prestongrange includes but Rossend ignores. The Rossend artist has, however, included two new details in the shape of a couple of lizards which hang down on threads from the wreath; these are copied from lizards that hang on threads from the central cartouche in Vredeman's print and, in place of the torch and mask at the head of the series, Rossend inserts a panoply of armour consisting of a classical breastplate with spear and flag below a helmet with a face in profile. This detail is copied from a different print (Hollstein p.254) which supplied a number of further details at Rossend,

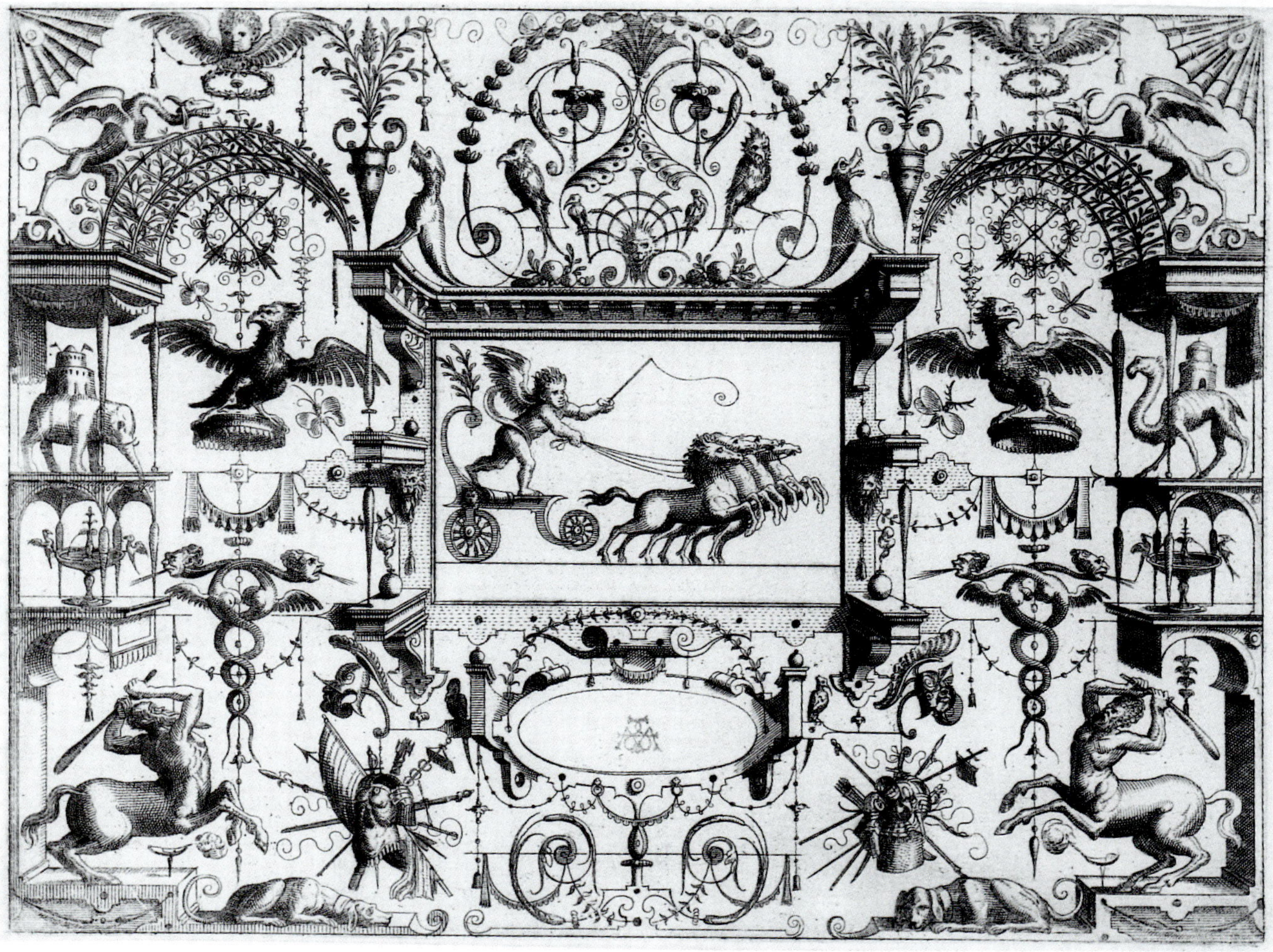

Engraving from Vredeman de Vries, Grottesco, *source both of the panoply of armour at Rossend and of the Rossend entwined snakes and bird of prey perched on a canopy.* MP-M

notably a third series of threaded motifs in which a pair of entwined winged snakes with human heads are suspended on a thread from a bar that is hung with a draped cloth; above this a bird of prey with spread wings perches on a canopy, above which is a wreath intersected by two crossed arrows. Rossend copies this sequence in exactly the way it appears in Vredeman's print. Moreover, the same print also supplied two further details on the ceiling, for at the other end of this compartment we find an elephant with a howdah. At the same end of the adjoining compartment on the ceiling is a camel with a similar howdah. These details evidently took their hint from the elephant and camel carrying howdahs on opposite sides of Vredeman's print.

The sources so far identified for the ceiling at Rossend allow us to distinguish the emblems from the grotesques, but it would be difficult if not impossible to make any such distinction unless we had identified their different print sources. Hence, although the Rossend ceiling must be recognised as one of the more important examples of applied emblems to be found in Britain, it has to be stressed that these images may no longer be functioning emblematically. Just as quite a few of the 'grotesque' images on the ceiling could be ascribed some kind of allegorical significance, if we were so inclined, so conversely many of the devices copied from Paradin seem to have been reduced to a purely decorative function. The covered vase, for instance, is just the sort of detail that antique ornament normally went in for and is surrounded by acanthus sprays

Right: *Rossend ceiling, grotesque ornament copied from Vredeman de Vries. Rossend, camel with howdah copied from Vredeman's* Grottesco. NMS

Left: *Detail, taken from the same Vredeman engraving, of the painted ceiling from Prestongrange, East Lothian.*

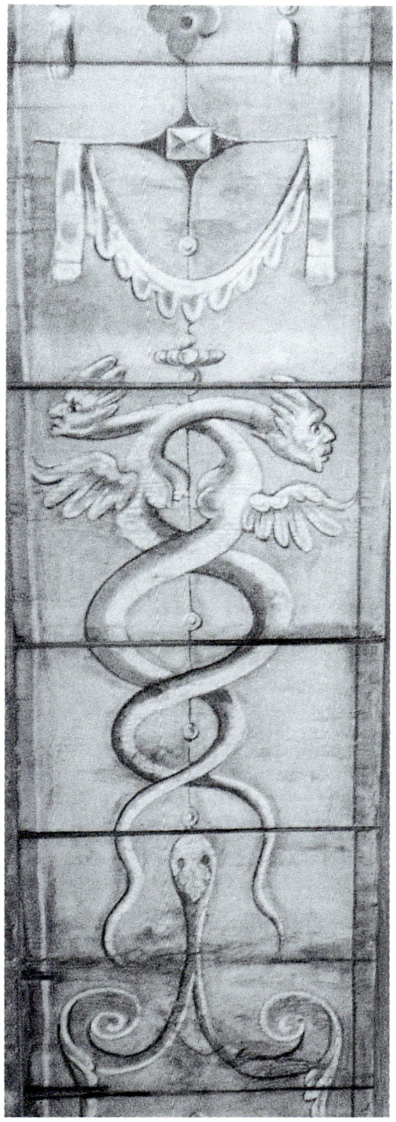

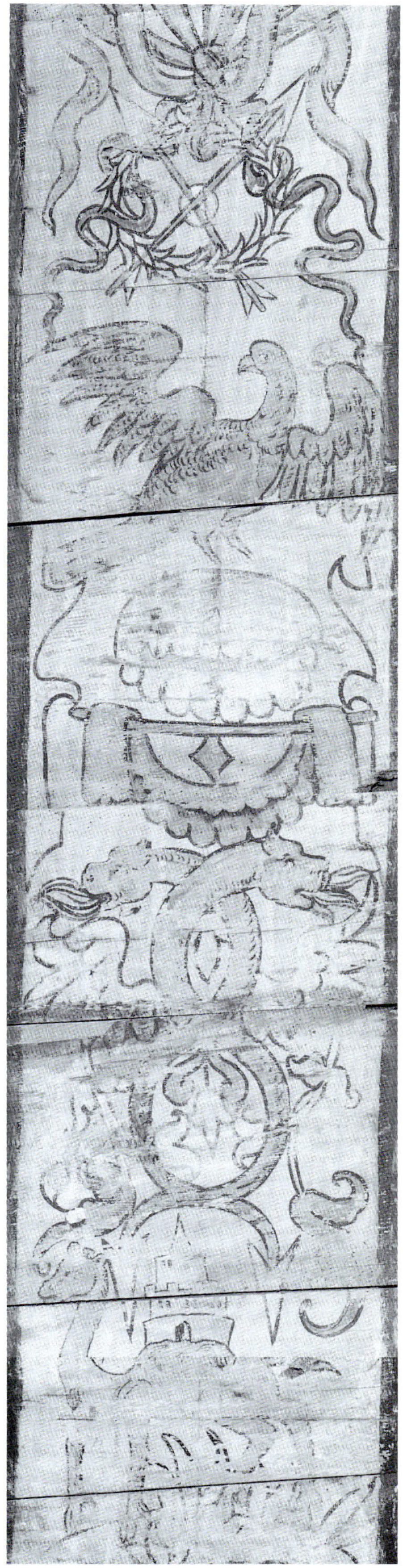

which seem to confirm this impression – ornamental prints do indeed include patterns for just such vases as this. This covered cup, however, is almost certainly copied from Paradin's *Inter eclipses exorior* ('I come forth between eclipses'), which Paradin explains as the device of the French Dauphin, whose *impresa* was taken as a reference to the constellation known as the 'Cup', associated with Apollo and thought to be visible above the horizon at times that coincided with eclipses of the sun and moon. The significance of this emblem is, indeed, excessively obscure, even if one has access to Paradin's text, and it appears to have defeated most of its early and later commentators (*cf* Daly 1993, p.62). Paradin himself says that this 'great and rich golden cup ... seems to me to represent the Crater of Apollo's crow, which (according to the poets) was transformed into a glittering heavenly sign'. What on earth, we may ask, was this '*Crater du Corbeau d'Apollo*'? The answer seems to depend on the reader's, or viewer's, knowledge of Ovid's *Fasti* (vol. ii, pp.243-66), where we are told of three constellations known as the 'Raven', the 'Snake', and the 'Bowl', which take their names from a fable in which the god Apollo sent a raven to fetch water in a golden bowl. The raven, however, stopped to satisfy its own hunger

Paradin, Devises heroïques *(1557) p.74, device of the Dauphin of France symbolising the constellation known as the 'Cup' which shines out between eclipses of the sun.* GUL

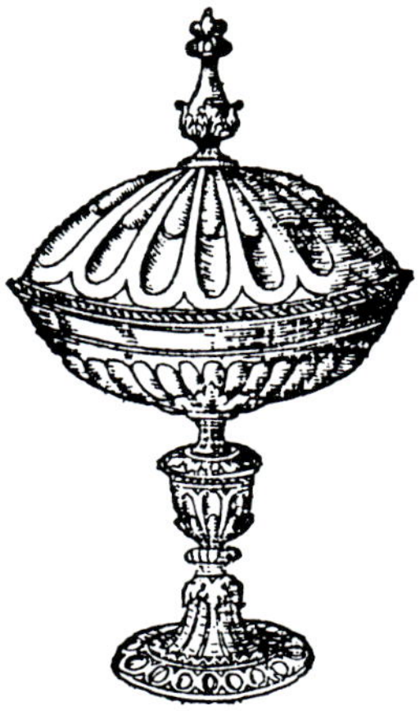

Rossend ceiling, covered cup copied from Paradin, Inter Eclipses Exorior *('I come forth between eclipses').*

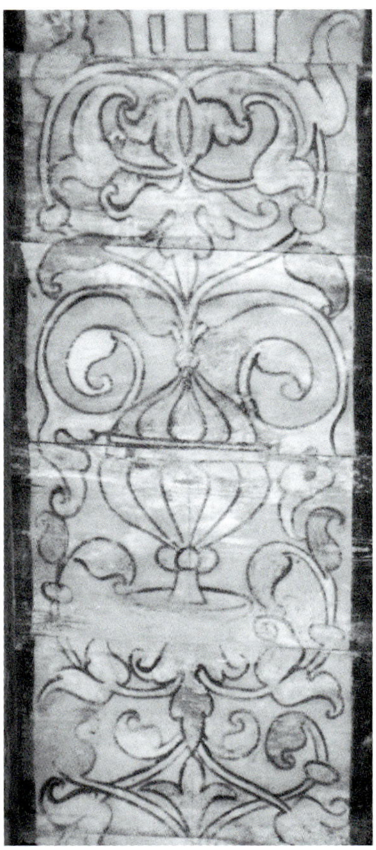

at a fig tree and neglected to fetch the water; it tried to excuse itself by blaming a snake, but the god detected its lies and set the signs of the three constellations up in the heavens as a perpetual reminder of the penalty for attempting to deceive a god. It is difficult to see what relevance this symbolism could have had for Robert Melville when he was designing his ceiling at Rossend, even if he was aware of it. Nor is it easy to see what would be gained by any viewer who recognised this as the device of the French dauphin, a device only adopted since François II was born in 1544 a few days after a solar eclipse and shortly before a partial eclipse of the moon (Palliser 1870, p.123, citing Claude Menestrier). While the discovery of an image's emblematic source is often crucial if we are to explain its iconography and explicate its meaning, we should be on our guard against assuming that early patrons or their artists necessarily had an informed and exhaustive knowledge of the iconography of their images, or that they always wanted to use that iconography in significant ways in the decorative schemes they commissioned. It is the way that emblematic images are incorporated at random into the similar non-emblematic images from Vredeman's *Grottesco* that should put us on our guard against assuming that such images on this ceiling retain an emblematic function.

The problems of decorative function raised by a ceiling such as Rossend, where we have the emblematic picture without explanatory text or motto, would hardly be lessened if we were to find a decorative scheme which quoted the text of the emblems without the symbolic picture. And yet that is just what we do find recorded in a house in Dundee. In 1887 builders were pulling down the interior of a seventeenth-century burgess house known as Gardyne's House when they noticed traces of decorative painting on the boards and beams of at least one of the rooms. Local antiquarian A C Lamb managed to salvage what had not already been destroyed, including three of the supporting beams covered in inscriptions that to his credit he recognised as copied from Quarles' emblems. He took photographs (preserved in Dundee Central Library), and in 1887 local historian Alexander Hutcheson wrote an account of this discovery in the *Dundee Advertiser* together with a transcription of the texts and a description of the decorative painting. The underside of the boards between the beams 'was richly painted in Jacobean panels and scrolls, with foliage, fruit, and flowers', but there was no sign of any accompanying emblematic pictures.

The passages excerpted on the beams are surprising choices in a number of respects, above all for the way in which they do not offer generalised moral apophthegms but rather use passages that depend on their emblematic context for any understanding of their moral point. The seven inscriptions consist of four lines either abstracted from Quarles' longer verse *subscriptio* or, in four cases, quoting the whole of his concluding four-line 'epigram' to particular emblems. How are we expected to read such inscriptions? The problem is particularly pressing if you use a source such as Quarles where the words of the English *subscriptio* are assigned to one or other of the two characters, Cupid and Anima, whose actions and interactions are dramatised in the engravings. Typically in a Quarles emblem the actions of the two agonists dramatised in the *pictura* are voiced in the *scriptura*. Quarles' pictures are dramatic and his verses are dialogic; the first thing you have to do when reading one of Quarles' emblems is to assign voices. That is a very unusual thing to do when you are looking at a painted ceiling.

The dialogic mode is illustrated by the passage quoted on the first of the beams from *Emblemes* 1.1.55-8; the context is the conclusion of a temptation-scene dialogue between Eve and the Serpent:

> 'Tis but an apple, and it is as good
> To do as to desire. Fruit's made for food;
> I'le pull and taste and tempt my Adam too
> To know the secrets of this dainty. Serp. Doe.

These lines are only intelligible if the reader recognises that the speaker is Eve; the change of voice is indicated on the beam, as it is in Quarles' verse-*subscriptio,* by the interpolated speech marker 'Serp[ent]', even though he has but one word to say: 'Doe'. The dialogic mode is continued in the verses abstracted from *Emblemes* 1.2.1-5, where the context is the speaker regretting the consequences of Eve's fall, immediately following the previous dialogue, and the speaker is Amor Divinus:

> Lament, lament; look, look what thou hast done!
> Lament the world's, lament thy own estate.
> Look, look by doing how thou art undone;
> Lament thy fall, lament thy change of State;
> Thy faith is broken and thy freedome gone.

It may have been his recognition of the problems raised by this dialogic mode that persuaded the Gardyne's House artist in no fewer than four of the seven inscriptions to quote the concluding four-line 'epigram' to the emblem rather than a passage abstracted from the longer poem that precedes it, but the difficulties of interpretation are hardly fewer when these concluding epigrams are taken out of the context of the emblem whose message they normally sum up in a spirit of irritated epigrammatic closure, as with the verses on the reverse of the first beam:

> Epigram. My soule if Ignorance puffe out this light
> Sheell doe a favour that intends a spight
> T'seems dark abroad but take this light away
> Thy windows will discover break of day.

This epigram, in which the speaker comments on the soul's longing for spiritual illumination, hardly makes sense except as a concluding comment on the image of Phosphor, the morning star whose rising is anticipated in the emblem as a whole, with its Latin motto *Phosphere redde diem* and its opening picture showing Anima sitting before a lighted candle in front of a darkened orb.

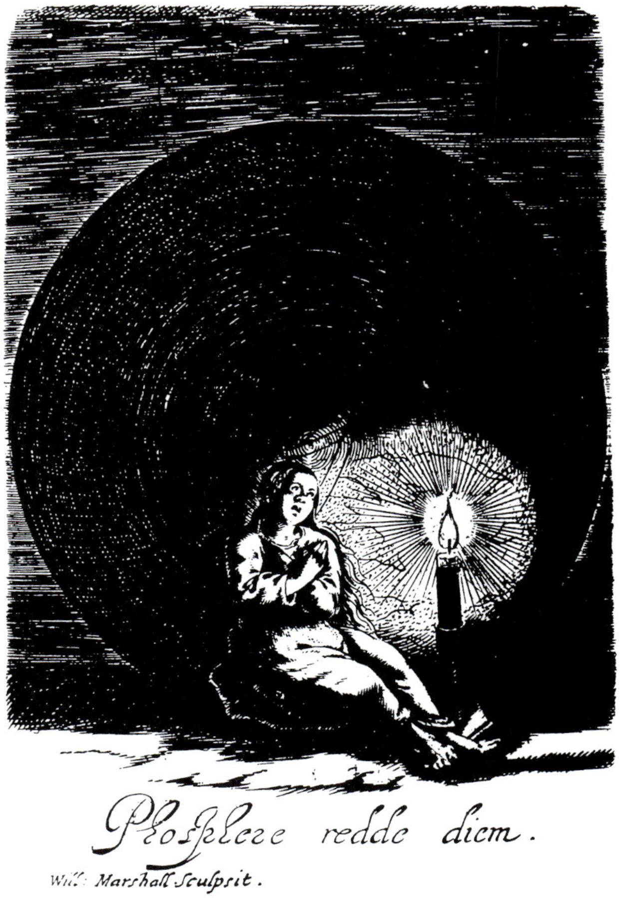

Francis Quarles, Emblemes *(1635) p.56, 'Sweet Phosphor bring the day', picture illustrating the verses inscribed on one of the beams from Gardyne's House, Dundee.* GUL

It is clear that these inscriptions would only have been intelligible to a reader who had some knowledge of the emblems from which they were abstracted. Familiarity with the Temptation scene from Genesis might be enough to allow early readers to assign voices in the first of these emblems even without the accompanying *pictura*, but it is less easy to imagine readers who would recognise the allusion to Phosphor, or to the fruit and flowers of Canticles 2.5, the subject of Beam 3a. Perhaps these inscriptions were designed to remind their readers of printed emblems with which they were already familiar. The seven inscriptions on the beams make use of only four different emblems from the two hundred that make up Quarles' book – perhaps these particular emblems had been the subject of a sermon, a collective meditation or instruction, or some other kind of spiritual exercise which the house's owner or his family had been exposed to. There is an overall consistency of register to these citations insofar as they reflect on the consequences of original sin, drawn out of discrete passages in Quarles' first two emblems, while two later citations come from a single emblem in Book 5, in which the soul's appetite for salvation, based on Canticles 2.5, is characterised as a desire for apples.

While the Rossend emblems offer us emblematic pictures without explanatory texts, the Dundee emblems supply texts without pictures. If either scheme is functioning emblematically it necessarily requires that its viewers, or readers, should have memorised the missing element since, for instance, the Rossend image of the ape killing its young with kindness will only hold that meaning for a viewer who knows what Pliny tells us about the tendency of apes to hold their young ones so tight that they crush them to death. And even if such animal lore was common knowledge, the image would only function as an emblem once the viewer 'moralised' it by applying it to the habit of parents 'to be so lavish in the nice education of their children, that with their too much cockering [pampering] of them, at the last they bring them to naught', to quote PS's English translation (1591, p.282). When emblems were based on familiar proverbs and figures of speech, it would undoubtedly have helped early viewers to supply the missing motto, or the equivalent meaning, but such proverbial familiarity is a feature of by no means all these images.

Similarly, it is difficult to imagine how the verses abstracted from Quarles in Dundee could have functioned as meditative *topoi* unless their reader recalled the relevant picture, without which it is not easy to work out who is speaking.

It will be clear that the Scottish cultural climate was highly favourable to the use of emblems, and that they represent an important part of the pictorial vocabulary available to decorative artists. However, it would also seem that the way emblems were used varies at different sites and the problem of defining their decorative function at a particular location cannot always easily be solved. The two most elaborate and interesting examples of applied emblematics in Scotland – at Culross, Fife, and at Pinkie House, Musselburgh – have yet to be described; both are quite different from anything we have yet seen, if only because they include both image and text and thus combine the two elements of this essentially bimedial form. Yet both examples make radical and significant changes to their sources and only an exhaustive analysis of those changes will allow us to draw reliable conclusions about their form and function.

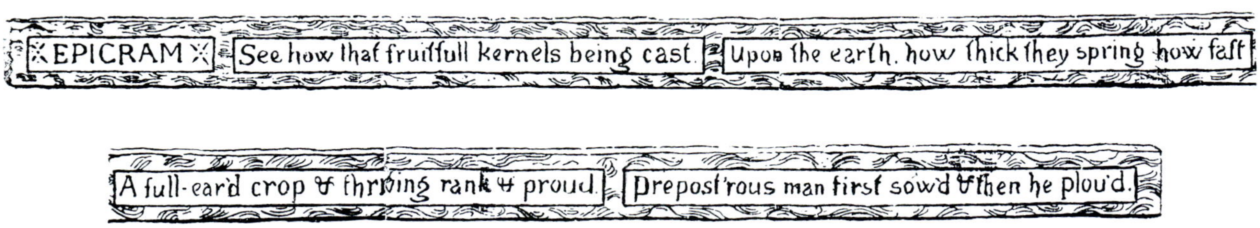

Facsimile transcript of verses from Quarles' Emblemes *painted on a beam from Gardyne's House, Dundee, as printed in a nineteenth-century newspaper report recording their discovery,* Dundee Advertiser, *21 Feb 1887.*

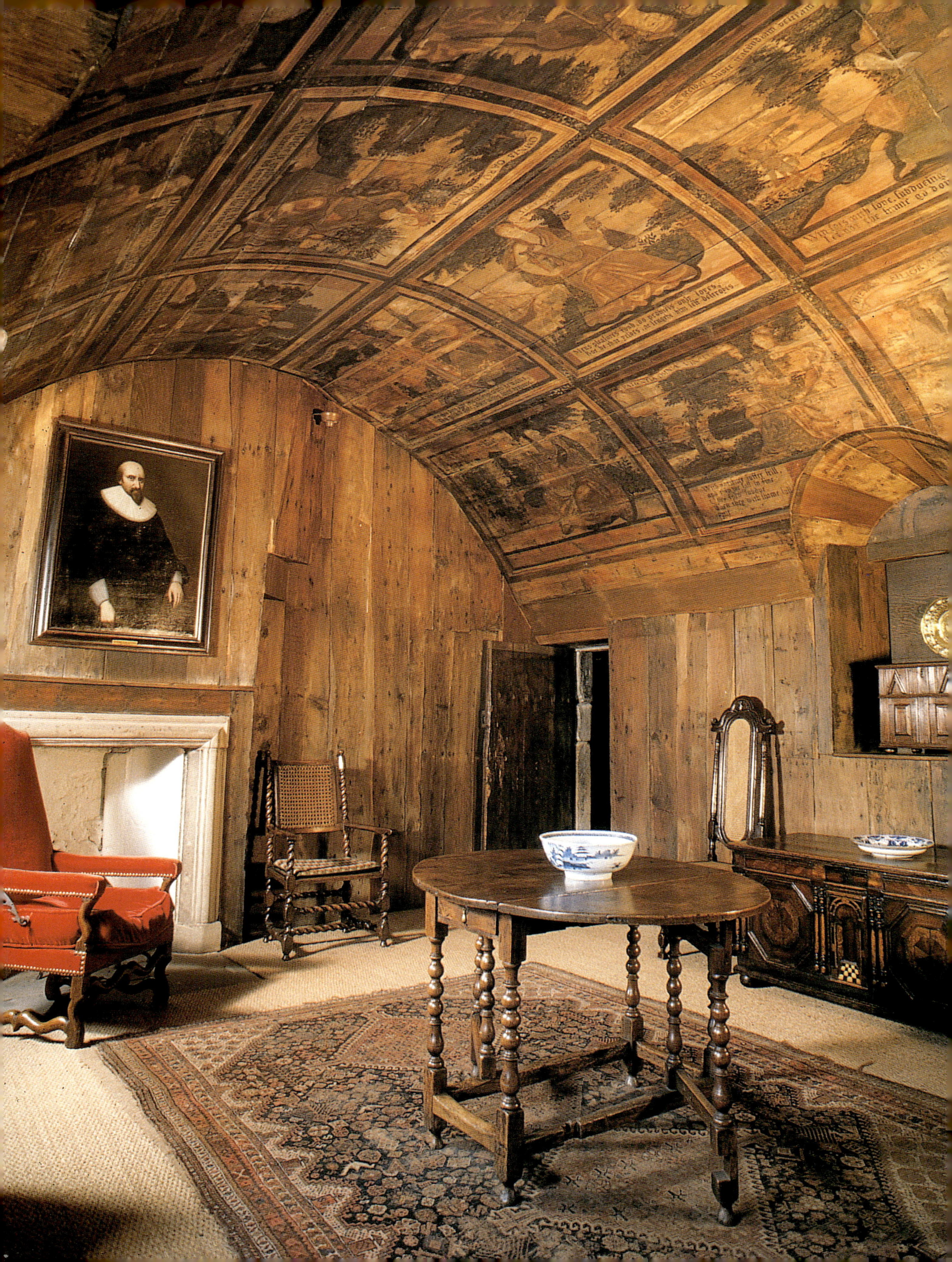

3

EMBLEMS NEWLY DEVISED

George Bruce's Palace

THE first English emblem book to be printed was Geffrey Whitney's *A Choice of Emblemes* (1586), compiled during the Earl of Leicester's campaign in the Netherlands which Whitney had joined. It was published in Leiden by Christopher Plantin's son-in-law, Francis Raphelengius, using woodcut illustrations drawn, for the most part, from the extensive stock of woodblocks the Plantin press had produced to illustrate their own editions of continental emblem books by such authors as Alciato, la Perrière, Paradin, Sambucus, and Hadrianus Junius. In taking over their woodcuts, Whitney was obliged to translate or adapt their emblems, which is why he describes his *Choice* on the title page as 'gathered out of sundrie writers', though he also states that his book contains 'divers newly devised' emblems. The first English emblem book thus made a significant portion of the existing continental emblem tradition available for the first time to English readers. Though it never ran to a second edition, Whitney's book is known to have been quite well received in England – passages were copied into several personal commonplace books, and a few were included in a printed collection of moral commonplaces, Bodenham's *Belvedere*, in 1600. Composer William Byrd turned six of Whitney's emblem verses into madrigals, and four of the woodcuts in Whitney were used as patterns for the decoration of the Vyvyan Salt in the Victoria and Albert Museum (Bath 1994, pp.86-7). By far the most extensive and inventive application of these emblems is to be found, however, not in England but in a house built by George Bruce in 1597 at Culross (Fife) in Scotland.

Bruce was the third son of Edward Bruce, who had acquired part of the Blairhall estate from William Colville, Commendator of Culross Abbey. Edward Bruce's second son, Edward, was a lawyer who became Lord of Session in 1597 and helped negotiate the Union of the Crowns, for which he received a peerage as Lord Bruce of Kinloss in 1602. He became a Privy Counsellor and Master of the Rolls, amassing a fortune, part of which he devoted to building the nearby mansion, Culross Abbey House, one of the earliest and most important of the strictly classical buildings in Scotland. His brother George's 'Palace', however, is a town house in a more modest and traditional style, which probably owes its received name to legal terminology

Opposite: *Emblem Chamber in Culross Palace, Fife. Portrait of Sir George Bruce can be seen on the far wall.* Harvey Wood, NTS

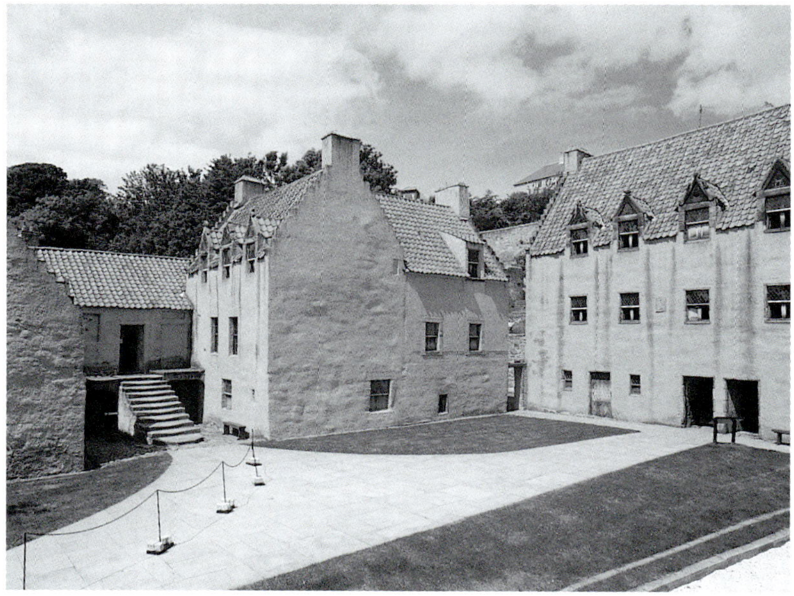

Culross Palace, south block (viewer's left) built in 1597, north block (right) 1611. Brian Chapple, NTS

where 'palatium' signifies any substantial dwelling (see MacGibbon and Ross, vol. v, p.24). The house reflects the money he made as a result of developing the neighbouring coal mine as one of the most technically advanced examples of industrial innovation in late sixteenth-century Britain, with mechanically drained and ventilated pit shafts extending under the sea. A contemporary document describes him as being 'Episcopall in his judgement and a great courtier with King James' (Beveridge 1885, p.147). James had conferred Royal Borough status on Culross in 1592, and in 1611 George Bruce was knighted. There is a probably reliable tradition that James himself visited the mine on his brief return to his Scottish kingdom in 1617, when he was taken undergound to inspect the long and surprisingly spacious galleries.

Bruce's religious opinions were sufficiently liberal for him to have defended more than one of the local inhabitants who got into trouble for their anti-episcopalianism, on one occasion sending the bishop a free cargo of coal in return for charges being dropped against a certain John Row, who had attacked episcopacy. Bruce's grandson Alexander, second Earl of Kincardine, became one of Charles II's supporters in exile and a leading member of the Royal Society after the Restoration, when he resided at Culross and further developed the coal, salt, and quarrying enterprises begun by his grandfather.

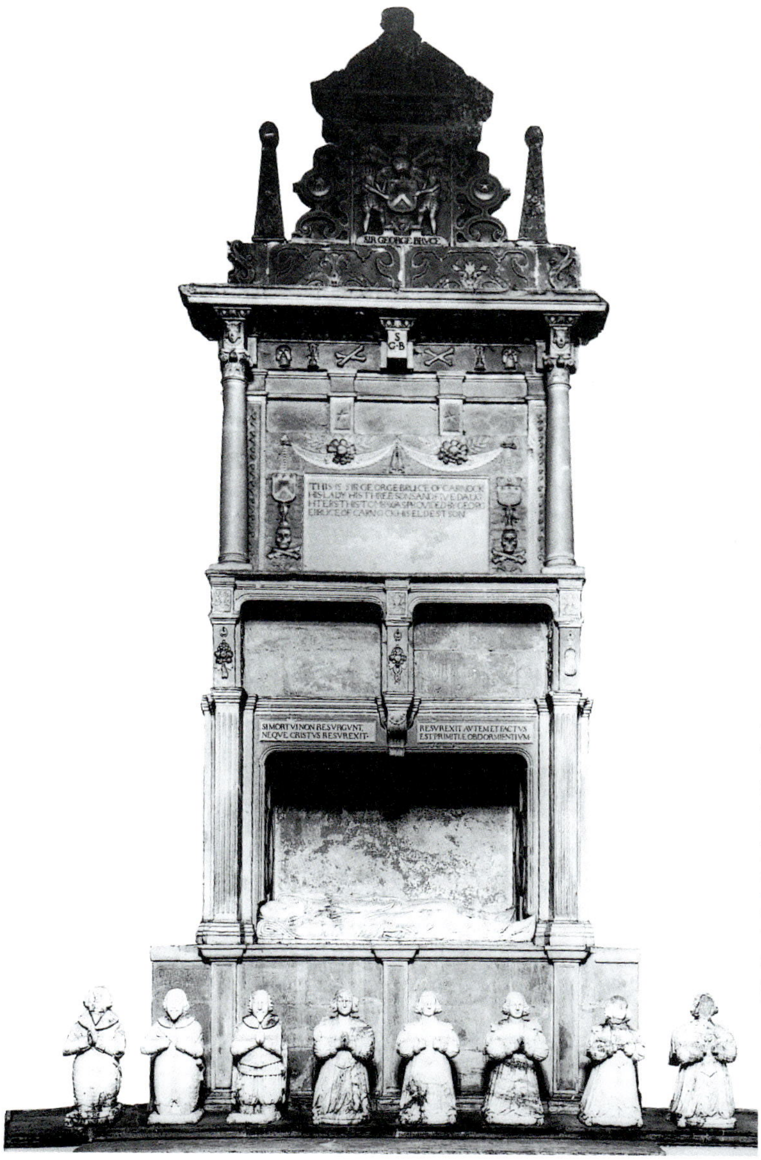

Tomb of George Bruce at Culross Abbey. RCAHMS

The impressive monument to Bruce, executed by his son, can be seen in the abbey church where he and his wife lie in effigy beneath an imposing structure of classical entablatures and columns filled with inscriptions, armorial (and possibly masonic) symbols; beneath them kneel their eight children (three sons and five daughters) in seventeenth-century costumes, finely carved in rose-veined marble. The exceptional accomplishment of this carving, of his brother Edward's abbey house, and of his enterprising grandson's interests – which included medicine, classics, mathematics and mining technology, along with divinity, horticulture and forestry – suggest the enlightened sophistication of this remarkable family as the essential context for the decorative painting Sir George Bruce executed in his 'toun mansion' at Culross. That painting fills a number of rooms in the two separate wings of the 'Palace', consisting for the most part of elaborate, purely decorative, patterns. One room, however, was decorated with a large Judgement of Solomon, and the chamber that concerns us in this chapter is wholly filled with emblems.

At first sight the sixteen allegorical paintings that fill the painted ceiling of a room on the second floor of the south block do not look like copies of Whitney. Their emblem format is, however, clear enough, consisting of a Latin motto in a scroll at the top of the picture (eg 'OMNIS CARO FOENUM', 'All flesh is grass'); a picture showing a large female figure seated in a landscape and holding various objects; and a two-line *subscriptio* consisting of a rhyming couplet of English (or, more accurately, Scots) verse (eg 'All flesche is grasse, and withereth lyk the haye,/And warneth ws how weill to live, bot not how long to waye'). Interpreting such an emblem requires the reader to make sense of the various attributes of the seated figure, which ought to signal her allegorical identity to the iconologically informed viewer. We then have to work out how this identity relates to the motto, or to the moral, of the emblem.

The introduction of the female figure is the major difference between the Culross emblems and Whitney's woodcuts. We look in vain for such a figure in most of the woodcuts that the ceiling copies. Normally emblem books were used by decorative artists as pattern books, but Whitney's woodcuts are not functioning as patterns here, but as stimulants for original exercises in emblematic composition – these emblems are 'newly devised'. Identifying their debts to Whitney will, undoubtedly, help us to see what is going on, but Whitney will not solve all the problems they pose. Examining how they relate to their source will, however, help us to show exactly what processes of adaptation and invention were involved in the composition of a decorative programme such as this.

The 'OMNIS CARO FOENUM' emblem will, indeed, expose some of the difficulties. Whitney's emblem under the same motto (1586, p.217, based on Paradin) shows no seated figure, but a bundle of hay hanging from an upright staff. Paradin explains that the bundle of hay hung from a lance was the badge of Romulus, designed to show the early Romans that they had the strength to survive all processes of corporal mutability and decay – 'The grass withereth, but Rome surviveth' is its message. The great commentator on Alciato's emblems, Claude Mignault, had also explained in his *Syntagma de Symbolis*

(1573, etc) that the ancient Romans used such a bundle of hay as their *stemma* (coat of arms), whence the legions came to be known as *manipulus*, meaning both a bundle of hay and a company of soldiers (*manipulus* in Latin means both a bundle and a squad, *cf* modern English 'bunch'). Whitney repeats none of this but returns the emblem to its biblical context, which his motto signals; indeed he attributes the motto, in a side-note, to its biblical source, Isaiah [40.6]. Whitney supplies the two-line *subscriptio* that the Culross inventor has had to adapt by selecting the first and last lines of Whitney's ten-line epigram, which happen to rhyme. He pays a price for this, however, since he has had to borrow a couple of words ('Which warneth [us]…') from the penultimate line in order to complete the syntax and supply a main verb. The result is that what should be an iambic pentameter couplet no longer scans (the second line has seven stresses). Nevertheless, this selective quotation from Whitney's verse epigram leaves no doubt that it was the Culross source.

The process of adaptation for each of these emblems at Culross, then, evidently required its inventor to abstract two lines from Whitney's epigram to sum up the moral point of the emblem. Very often this was simple enough since it was possible to find an existing couplet, usually at the end of the epigram. Clearly it would have been impractical to copy more than a few lines onto a ceiling where a longer inscription would be very difficult to read. However, this epigrammatic abbreviation makes these adaptations look very similar to the type of verse proverbs in rhyming couplets which we find inscribed along the beams on painted ceilings at Crathes or Delgaty, and the changes Culross makes to Whitney's spelling so that it reflects Scots pronunciation reinforce this impression. At first sight the rhyming couplets at Culross look just like versified Scots proverbs, which is probably why no one noticed that they are clippings from a printed English emblem book. There is one other place in Scotland where we find a similar adaptation of Whitney's emblems, for the painted ceiling of the Skelmorlie Aisle at Largs has one detail which has similarly been shown to quote Whitney's final couplet to the emblem *In utrumque paratus* (see Chapter 6).

When we look at the picture to 'OMNIS CARO FOENUM', the relationship between source and copy becomes more problematic. The Culross picture bears almost no resemblance to its source; it shows a female figure seated in a landscape holding two large urns of flowers. We might conclude that these urns symbolise fertility or abundance, though in this case we should have a somewhat paradoxical emblem illustrating the quality of decay (the withered grass) by its opposite – this substantial lady certainly does not look like the embodiment of fleshly decay. Is the motto, or the epigram, expressing irony at her expense? A solution to the identity of these allegorical figures might be sought in any of the standard Renaissance iconologies. Cesare Ripa's *Iconologia* first appeared in Rome in 1593, just about early enough for George Bruce to have used it at Culross, but Ripa's figures were not illustrated until his book was reprinted in 1603. Valeriano's *Hieroglyphica* (1556, and many subsequent editions) includes many such allegorical personifications, and there is good

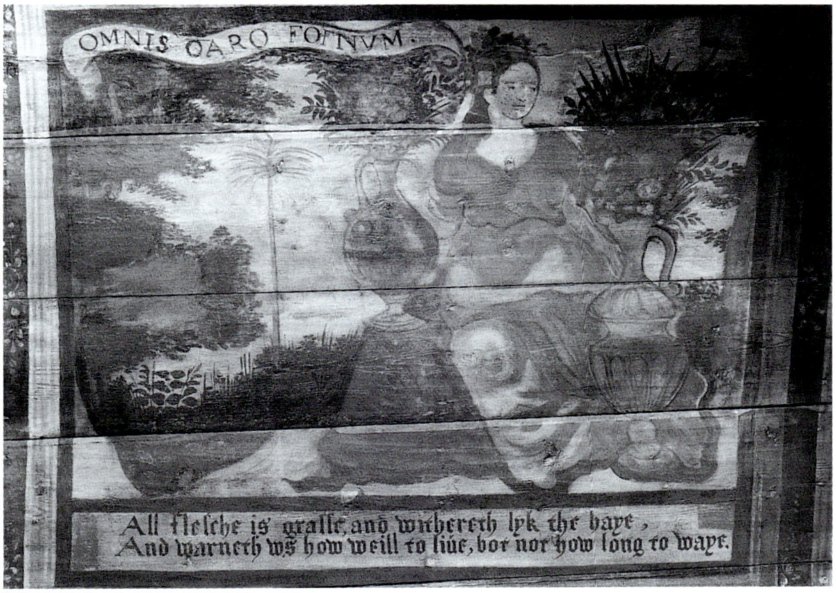

Omnis caro fœnum.

To M. Elcocke *Preacher.*

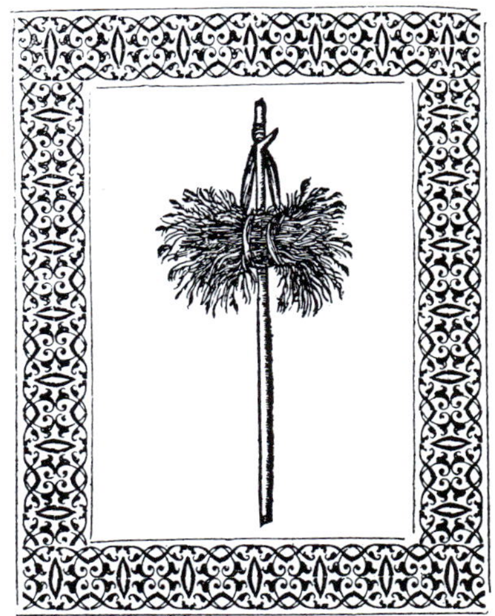

All fleſhe, is graſſe; and withereth like the haie:
To daie, man laughes, to morrowe, lies in claie.
Then, let him marke the frailtie of his kinde,
For here his tearme is like a puffe of winde,
Like bubbles ſmalle, that on the waters riſe:
Or like the flowers, whome Flora freſhlie dies.
Yet, in one daie their glorie all is gone:
So, worldlie pompe, which here we gaze vppon.
Which warneth all, that here their pageantes plaie,
Howe, well to liue: but not how longe to waie.

Inter ſpem curamq́ʒ, timores inter & iras,
Omnem crede diem tibi diluxiſſe ſupremum.
Grata ſuperueniet, quæ non ſperabitur, hora.

Left: *Culross, the Palace. Detail of painted ceiling, emblem adapted from Whitney, 'All flesh is grass'.* HS

Right: *Whitney* A Choice of Emblemes *(1586) p.217.* GUL

reason to think that the Culross artist knew his *Hieroglyphica*, but we shall look in vain for a model for the Culross lady holding her two vases of flowers in either Valeriano or Ripa. Vases of flowers were, however, used in *vanitas* still lifes as emblems of the evanescence of human life, sometimes associated with the goddess Flora (see Hall, *Dictionary of Subjects and Symbols*, p.126). This identity of the Culross figure is confirmed by an unquoted part of Whitney's epigram, for, instead of paraphrasing Paradin's ascription of this bunch of hay to the ancient device of the Roman legions, Whitney tells us that this bundle of withered grass is

> like the flowers, whome FLORA freshlie dies,
> Yet, in one daie their glory all is gone.
> (p.217, ll.6-7)

There can be no doubt, once we recognise the source, that the Culross figure represents a realisation of this image from the uncited part of Whitney's epigram, and that the picture has been redesigned so as to realise more fully part of this emblem which the artist was unable to cite in his verse *subscriptio*. The allegorical figure in this emblem on the Culross ceiling is, we may now conclude, the figure of Flora and she is shown as flourishing because, as Whitney's unintentional pun puts it, it is she who dyes the flowers before they fade, before they 'freshly die'.

There is one further detail in the picture that tells us something about the relation of this emblem to its source. The landscape details to the lady's right include what looks like a tall palm tree with a tuft of branches at the top. This was, indeed, how T Etherington Cooke – one of the few observers to have commented on these emblems to date – described it in 1885. His unpublished description dates from a time when the decorative painting at Culross had not decayed quite so badly as it has in the twentieth century, when inappropriate conservation methods have had particularly unfortunate results. Etherington Cooke's descriptions are an invaluable witness to several details of these paintings that are now invisible or in doubt. Describing the seated figure, he writes, 'On her right is a palm tree, emblematic of flourishing life, but having one of

In amore tormentum.

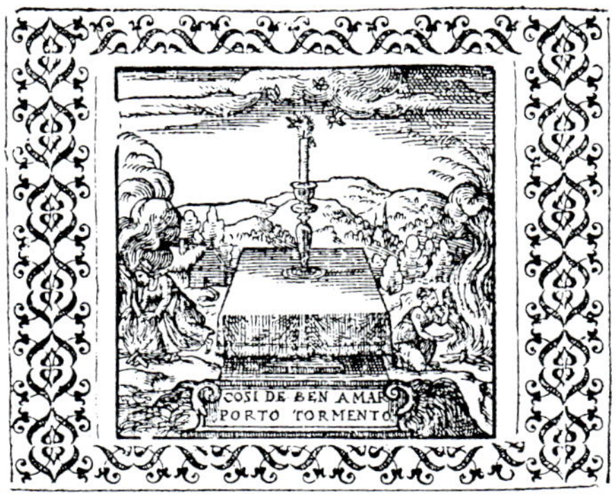

EVEN as the gnattes, that flie into the blaze,
Doe burne their winges and fall into the fire:
So, thoſe too muche on gallant ſhowes that gaze,
Are captiues caught, and burne in their deſire:
And ſuche as once doe feele this inwarde warre,
Thoughe they bee cur'de, yet ſtill appeares the ſcarre.

For wanton LOVE althoughe hee promiſe ioies,
Yet hee that yeeldes in hope to finde it true,
His pleaſures ſhalbee mated with annoyes;
And ſweetes ſuppoſ'de, bee mix'd, with bitter rue:
Bicauſe, his dartes not all alike, doe wounde:
For ſo the frendes of coye ASPASIA founde.

They lou'd, ſhee loth'de: they crau'd, ſhee ſtill deni'de.
They ſigh'd, ſhee ſonge: they ſpake, ſhee ſtopt her eare.
They walk'd, ſhee ſatte: they ſet, awaye ſhee hi'de.
Lo this their bale, which was her bliſſe, you heare.
O lóue, a plague, thoughe grac'd with gallant gloſſe,
For in thy ſeates a ſnake is in the moſſe.

Then ſtoppe your eares, and like VLISSES waulke,
The SYREENES tunes, the careleſſe often heares:
*CROCVTA killes when ſhee doth frendly taulke:
The Crocodile, hathe treaſon in her teares.
In gallant fruicte, the core is ofte decay'd;
Yea poiſon ofte in cuppe of goulde aſſay'd.

Then, in your waies let reaſon ſtrike the ſtroke,
ASPASIA ſhonne, althoughe her face doe ſhine:
But, if you like of HYMENÆVS yoke,
PENELOPE preferre, thoughe ſpinninge twine,
Yet if you like, how moſt to liue in reſt,
HIPPOLYTVS his life, ſuppoſe the beſt.

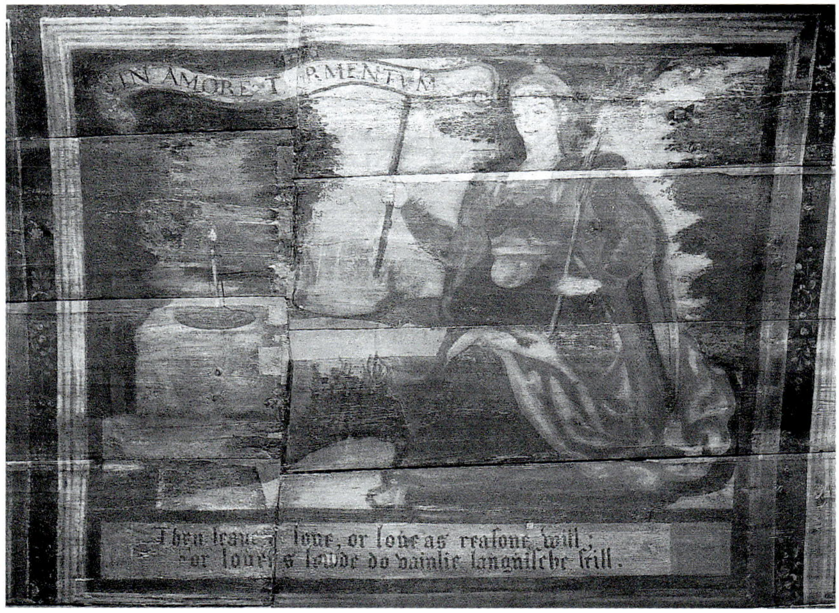

Left: *Whitney* A Choice of Emblemes *(1586) p.219.* GUL

Right: *Culross, the Palace. Emblem adapted from Whitney, 'The tortures of love'.*
Trevor Graham

its branches hanging withered'. The description corresponds to what we can still see in the picture, but it is difficult to say what the iconographic justification would be for including a palm tree in this emblem of mutability – the palm tree is an emblem of endurance under oppression or, as a pair, of mutual affection between partners (male and female trees on opposite sides of a river bend towards each other, according to Pliny, *Nat Hist*, XIII.26); it has nothing to do with mutability and bodily decay. Moreover, palm trees don't look like this, either in real life or in Renaissance pictures; they have thick trunks covered in scales or bracts – Whitney has such palm trees on pp.118, 193 and 216 of his *Choice of Emblemes* which the Culross artist could have copied if he needed a palm tree here. I am in no doubt that this 'palm tree' was originally Whitney's bundle of hay hanging from an upright staff, indeed signs of the encircling binding fillets can still just be seen. The resemblance to a palm tree is almost certainly the result of an early restorer's attempts to make sense of what he was seeing; Whitney's bundle of hay tied to a staff would have been unintelligible to such a restorer.

This inclusion of a detail based on Whitney's woodcut in the background to the new *pictura* at Culross is typical of the way most of the emblems on the painted ceiling adapt their printed source. We can see the same pattern in the adjacent emblem, 'IN AMORE TORMENTUM'. Whitney's emblem under this motto (1585, p.219) pictures a candle on a plinth, the flame surrounded by flies, which Whitney's epigram explains,

> Even as the gnattes, that flie into the blaze,
> Doe burne their winges and fall into the fire:
> So, those too muche on gallant showes that gaze,
> Are captives caught, and burne in their desire.

This is the one emblem at Culross that draws its *subscriptio* from a different emblem from that which supplied its motto and picture, for the couplet 'Then leave to love, or love as reasone will;/For lovers lewde do vainlie languische still' comes from Whitney's emblem *Qui me alit me extinguit* ('That which feeds me

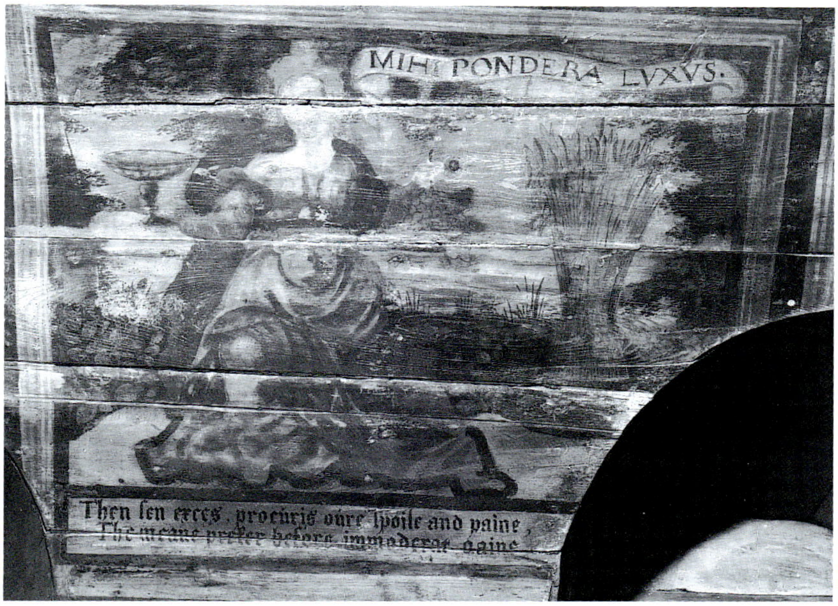

Mihi pondera, luxus.

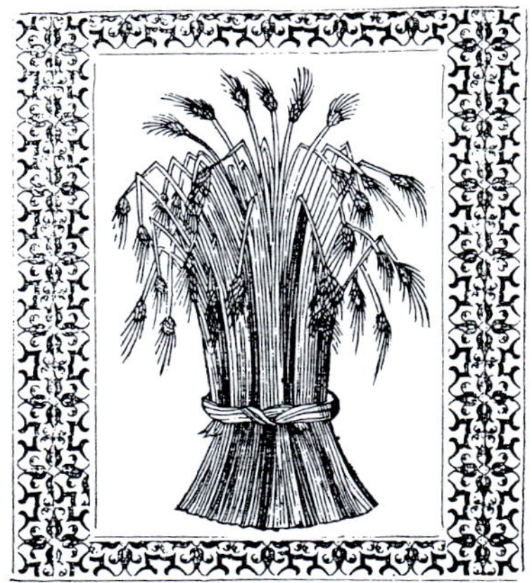

When autumne ripes, the frutefull fieldes of graine,
And Ceres doth in all her pompe appeare,
The heauie eare, doth breake the ſtalke in twaine,
Wherebie wee ſee, this by experience cleare:
Hir owne exceſſe, did cauſe her proper ſpoile,
And made her corne, to rotte vppon the ſoile.

Soe worldlie wealthe, and great aboundaunce, marres:
The ſharpenes of our ſences, and our wittes,
And oftentimes, our vnderſtanding barres,
And dulles the ſame, with manie carefull fittes:
Then ſince Exceſſe procures our ſpoile and paine,
The meane preferre, before immoderate gaine.

——— nec te iucunda fronte fefellit
Luxuries prædulce malum, quæ dedita ſemper
Corporis arbitriis, hebetat caligine ſenſus
Membraq; Circæis effeminat acrius herbis.

Left: *Culross, the Palace. Emblem adapted from Whitney, 'Excess is a burden to me'.* HS

Right: *Whitney* A Choice of Emblemes *(1586) p.23.* GUL

kills me', p.183, from Simeoni), which shows a torch turned upside down so that the melting wax quenches the flame. The Culross artist evidently despaired of finding two satisfactory lines from the emblem he was copying to sum up the emblematic moral, but was sufficiently enterprising to find two lines from a different emblem. Although Culross draws on a different emblem for its *subscriptio*, it borrows Whitney's picture, for the candle surrounded by flies is shown in the landscape to the right of the seated woman. She is holding two rods which are now impossible to interpret, but which we are fortunate to find represented in sketches of the ceiling made by John Houston which show the woman stirring the flames in a bowl with her fork; in her other hand she bears what looks like a switch, or bunch of birch twigs used for flogging children. Etherington Cooke also describes in 1885 a three-pronged fork that she is dipping into a golden dish filled with flames on a table covered with a white cloth, the same table on which the Culross artist has placed Whitney's candle surrounded by flies. The attributes of this figure clearly have something to do with the torments of love – an emblem of love's power both to stir the fires of passion and to punish its excesses, perhaps. A few years later Gabriel Rollenhagen was to show a woman holding a switch as the emblem of women's power to chastise men and boys alike (*Pueros castigo virosque* 1611, no. 81).

Similar space coding can be seen in the emblem 'MIHI PONDERA LUXUS' ('Excess is a burden to me'), another device that goes back to Paradin (1557, p.244). Whitney shows a wheatsheaf whose stalks are bent over by the weight of the ears of grain. Culross shows this image to the left (viewer's right) of the seated female figure who holds a shallow cup in her right hand, and a bunch of grapes in her left. In this instance it is possible to make sense of the allegorical attributes of the seated figure, for Valeriano identifies the vine with grapes as an attribute of Abundance, and for a precise analogue to this figure we have only to turn to the personification of 'Excess' in Spenser's description of the Bower of Bliss in *The Faerie Queene* (II.xii.56):

> In her left hand a Cup of gold she held,
> And with her right the riper fruit did reach.

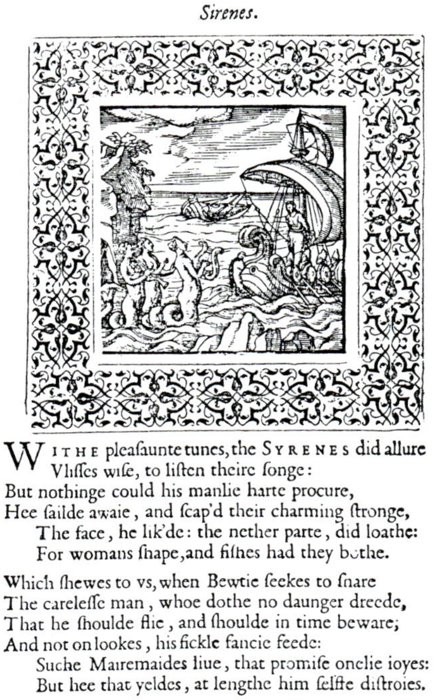
Sirenes.

WITHE pleaſaunte tunes, the SYRENES did allure
Vliſſes wiſe, to liſten theire ſonge:
But nothinge could his manlie harte procure,
Hee ſailde awaie, and ſcap'd their charming ſtronge,
The face, he lik'de: the nether parte, did loathe:
For womans ſhape, and fiſhes had they bothe.

Which ſhewes to vs, when Bewtie ſeekes to ſnare
The careleſſe man, whoe dothe no daunger dreede,
That he ſhoulde flie, and ſhoulde in time beware;
And not on lookes, his fickle fancie feede:
Suche Mairemaides liue, that promiſe onelie ioyes:
But hee that yeldes, at lengthe him ſelfe diſtroies.

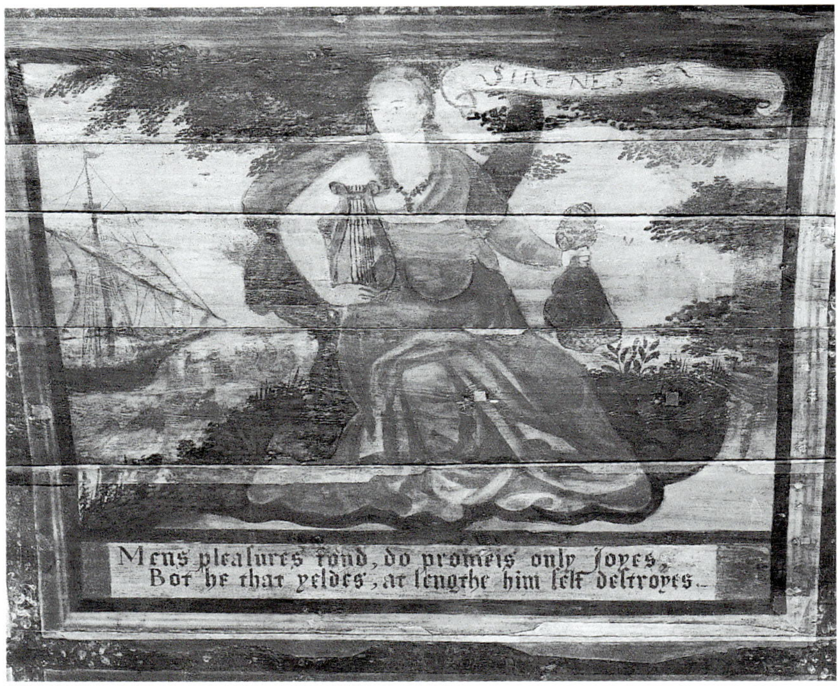

Left: *Whitney* A Choice of Emblemes *(1586) p.10.* GUL

Right: *Culross, the Palace. Emblem adapted from Whitney, 'The Sirens'.* Trevor Graham

'Excess' is, indeed, the name Culross abstracts from the last two lines of Whitney's epigram to supply the Culross emblem with its *subscriptio*:

> Then sen exces, procuris oure spoile and paine,
> The meane prefer before immoderat gaine.

Such shallow cups, Italian *tazze*, are invariably associated with secular drinking in Renaissance pictures; you drink wine out of them – they have nothing to do with communion chalices, and the corn and wine in this emblem at Culross are unlikely to have any sacramental symbolism.

The iconography of this figure appears to have influenced Culross' adaptation of Whitney's emblem *Sirenes* (1586, p.10) which goes back to Alciato, and shows the fish-tailed Sirens, with various musical instruments, wading, or swimming, out to entice Ulysses ashore from his ship. Culross's *subscriptio* paraphrases Whitney's last two lines, to draw the conventional moral:

> Mens pleasures fond, do promeis only Joyes,
> Bot he that yeldes, at lengthe him self destroyes.

Culross transfers the leading Siren's lyre to its favourite seated figure, who no longer has a mermaid's tail but wears a voluminous skirt. In her other hand she holds a dangling object, now difficult to make out, but which is almost certainly the same bunch of grapes we have seen Excess holding in the 'MIHI PONDERA LUXUS' emblem. This was certainly what Etherington Cooke thought he saw in 1885: 'In her left hand is a bunch of withered grapes, an emblem of the transient and disappointing nature of sensual pleasures.' He saw other details which are now difficult, if not impossible, to make out: 'Four sirens, one of whom is blowing a long trumpet, are wading out towards the vessel, and luring the infatuated sailors to their destruction.' This suggests that the picture was originally much closer to its source than it now appears to be, for Whitney's

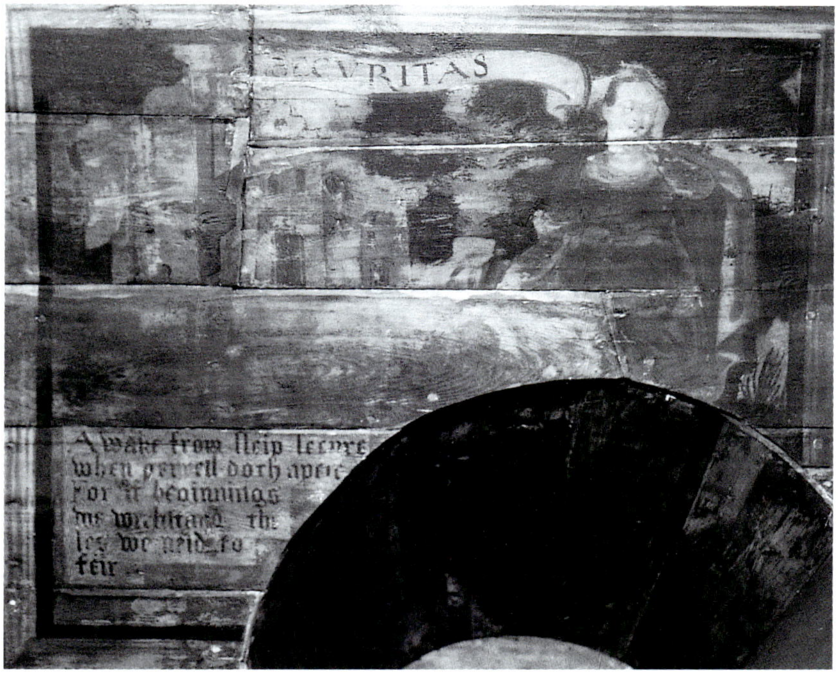

Tunc tua res agitur, paries cùm proximus ardet.

To M. THOMAS WHETELEY.

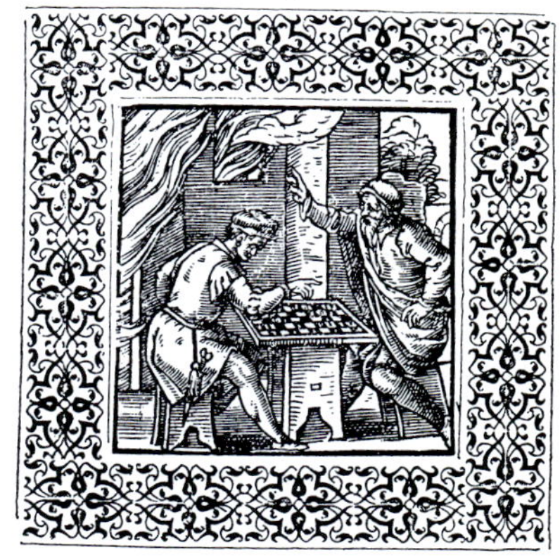

AWAKE from ſleepe ſecure, when perrill doth appeare:
No wiſedome then to take our eaſe, and not the worſt to feare.
Still ARCHIMEDES wroughte, when foes had wonne the*towne,
And woulde not leaue his worke in hande, till he was beaten downe.
No ſuretie is within, when roofe alofte doth flame:
It is a madnes then to ſtaye, till wee haue donne our game.
Yea, thoſe that helpe deferre, when neighbours houſe doth burne:
Are like with griefe, to ſee their owne, with ſpeede to cinders turne.
Then, cut of all delaies when daungers are begonne,
For if beginnings wee withſtande, the conqueſt ſooner wonne.

Left: *Culross, the Palace. Emblem adapted from Whitney, 'Safety'.* Trevor Graham

Right: *Whitney* A Choice of Emblemes *(1586) p.208, 'It's your business when your neighbour's house is on fire'.* GUL

woodcut shows a group of three Sirens doing exactly what he describes, indeed one of them blows a long trumpet. Houston's sketch confirms this description. Although Ulysses' ship is approaching the shore from a different direction, and does not resemble Whitney's ship either in the shape of its hull or its rigging, it is clear that the iconography of this picture is indebted to Whitney.

Although the Culross picture often bears only a slight resemblance to Whitney's woodcut, usually demoting Whitney's image to a secondary position to one side of its dominant seated figure, the motto and verse *subscriptio*, as we have seen, are usually copied directly from Whitney, so that in most cases the motto alone is enough to identify the emblem Culross is adapting. There is, however, one emblem that does not use Whitney's motto, headed 'SECVRITAS'; Whitney has no emblem with such a motto (or title). The Culross emblem shows a seated female figure who rests her head on her arm as if asleep. To her right there is a building, of which all one can now make out (the picture is badly damaged) is a crow-stepped gable enveloped in flames. The *subscriptio* reads, 'Awake from sleip secure when perrell doth apeir/For if beginnings we withstand, the les we neid to feir', and it is the *subscriptio* alone in this case which allows us to attribute this emblem to its source in Whitney, for these lines adapt the first and last lines of Whitney's emblem *Tunc tua res agitur, paries cum proximus ardet* ('It concerns you, when your neighbour's wall is on fire', 1586, p.208), a motto which quotes Horace's *Epist* 1.18.84 on the dangers of associating with people exposed to slander, since you are likely to be tarred with the same brush (as we would put it) – if their reputation is going up in flames, then it's time to look to your own fire extinguishers (as Horace puts it). Whitney's picture (from la Perrière) shows us what Horace's metaphor describes, namely two people playing chess while flames burst through the wall of a room adjoining the one in which they are sitting. The Culross picture shows nothing of this; instead it shows the outside of a house whose crow-stepped gable is not unlike that of George Bruce's palace itself. However, the fact that it is going up in flames clearly takes its cue from the Horatian metaphor in which this emblem has its

SECVRITAS.

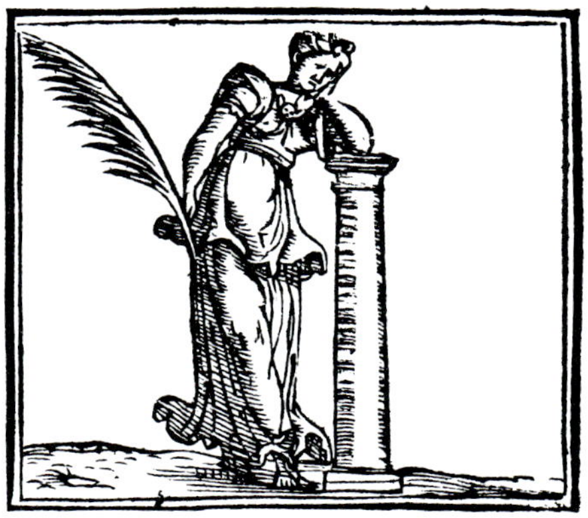

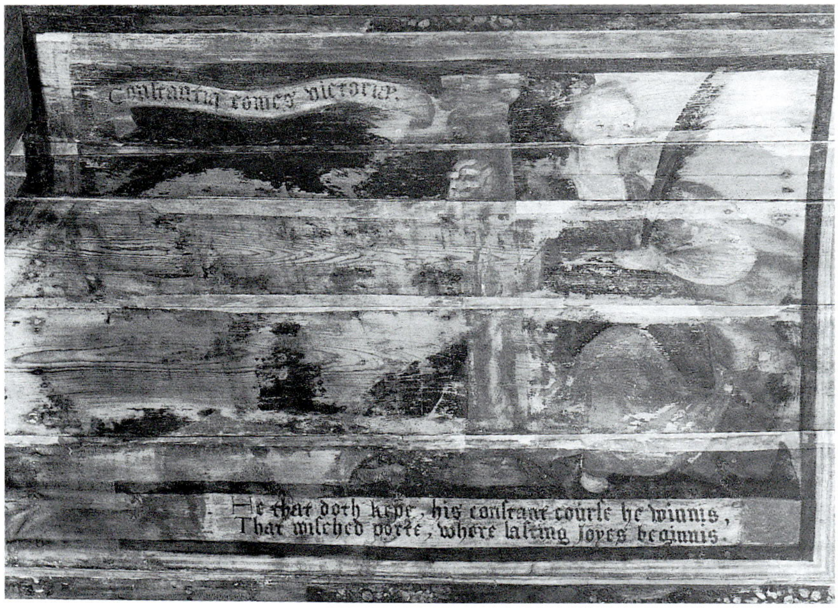

Left: *Pierio Valeriano,* Hieroglyphica *(1556) p.367.* GUL

Right: *Culross, the Palace. Emblem adapted from Whitney, 'Perseverence brings success'.*

Whitney A Choice of Emblemes *(1586) p.137.* GUL

Conſtantia comes victoriæ.
To MILES CORBET *Eſquier.*

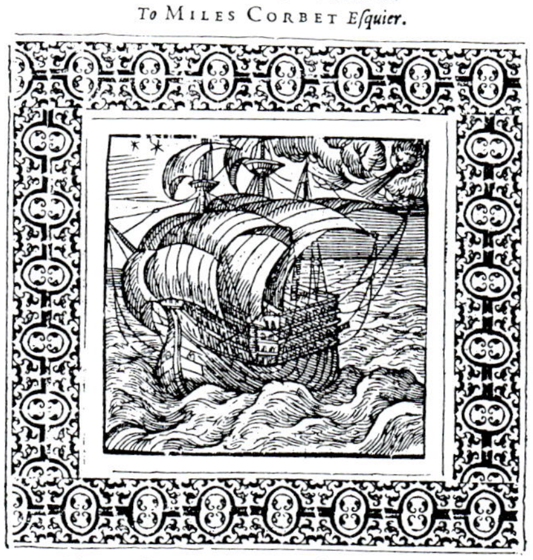

THE ſhippe, that longe vppon the ſea dothe ſaile,
And here, and there, with varrijng windes is toſte:
On rockes, and ſandes, in daunger ofte to quaile.
Yet at the lengthe, obtaines the wiſhed coaſte:
Which beinge wonne, the trompetts ratlinge blaſte,
Dothe teare the ſkie, for ioye of perills paſte.

Thoughe maſter reſte, thoughe Pilotte take his eaſe,
Yet nighte, and day, the ſhip her courſe dothe keepe:
So, whilſt that man dothe ſaile theiſe worldlie ſeas,
His voyage ſhortes: althoughe he wake, or ſleepe.
And if he keepe his courſe directe, he winnes
That wiſhed porte, where laſtinge ioye beginnes.

origins. Why should Bruce have made such a radical adaptation of his model? Possibly because he wished this emblem to refer to the value and security of his own property, in which case the new 'SECVRITAS' motto would have something of the connotations it might have for a modern house-insurance logo.

However, the choice of this new motto is interesting for other reasons, since it tells us about one of the other sources almost certainly used in the design of this ceiling. If we look up the image Securitas in Valeriano's *Hieroglyphica* we find it illustrated by a female figure holding a palm branch and leaning on a classical column. The Culross artist must have known of this image since he uses it for his seated figure, not in the 'SECVRITAS' emblem as we might expect, but in the emblem 'CONSTANTIA COMES VICTORIAE' ('Constancy is the companion of victory' or, perhaps, 'Perseverance brings success'). The fact that he not only uses the image of Securitas here but also borrows her title to supply the motto, or header, for the one and only emblem on this ceiling which does not copy its motto from Whitney leaves little doubt that the Culross artist must have had access to this source. Whitney's emblem shows a picture of a ship in full sail, whose moral is summed up in the last two lines of the epigram that Culross quotes, or adapts, thus:

> He that doth kepe, his constant course he winnis,
> That wisched porte, where lasting Joyes beginnis.

The picture at Culross is so badly damaged that it is impossible to say whether it used Whitney's image, though the metaphor in these lines would seem to require it. Etherington Cooke, however, says that this part of the picture was entirely filled with a large oak tree, which is what we see in Houston's sketch.

Another motto on the ceiling which differs, though only slightly, from Whitney's is *Vincit qui patitur* ('He who endures conquers'), which Culross adapts as 'PATIENTIA OMNIA VINCIT' ('Endurance wins through everything'), most likely as a way of foregrounding the keyword 'patience' which the Culross artist also took some trouble to include in his adaptation of the epigram

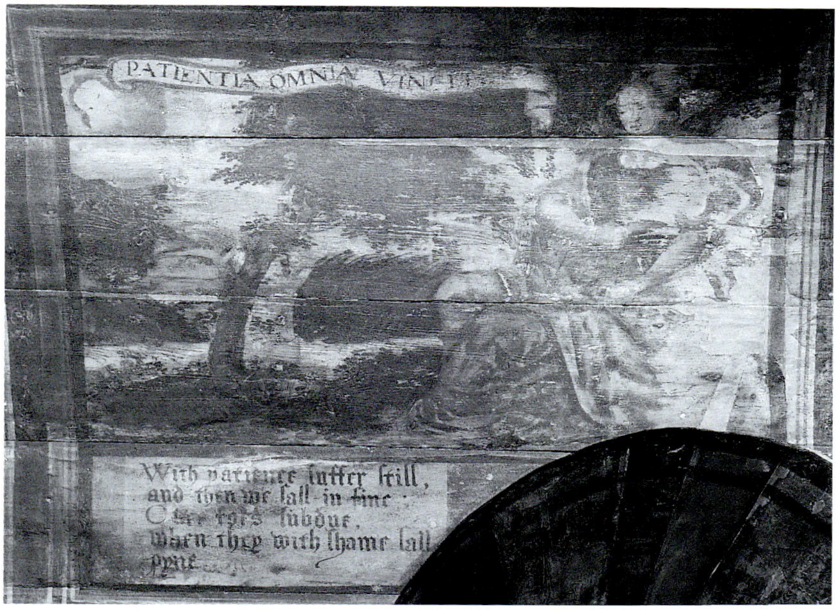

Vincit qui patitur.

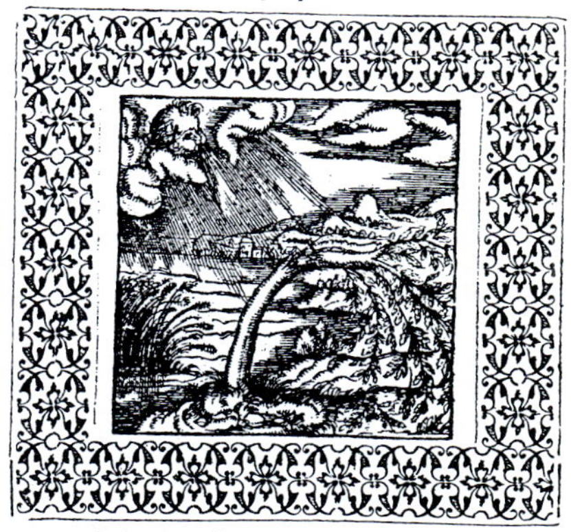

THE mightie oke, that ſhrinkes not with a blaſte,
But ſtiffie ſtandes, when Boreas moſte doth blowe,
With rage thereof, is broken downe at laſte,
When bending reedes, that couche in tempeſtes lowe
With yeelding ſtill, doe ſafe, and ſounde appeare:
And looke alofte, when that the cloudes be cleare.

When Enuie, Hate, Contempte, and Slaunder, rage:
Which are the ſtormes, and tempeſtes, of this life;
With patience then, wee muſt the combat wage,
And not with force reſiſt their deadlie ſtrife:
But ſuffer ſtill, and then wee ſhall in fine,
Our foes ſubdue, when they with ſhame ſhall pine.

Left: *Culross, the Palace. Emblem adapted from Whitney, 'Patience wins through'.* Trevor Graham

Right: *Whitney* A Choice of Emblemes *(1586) p.220, 'He who suffers wins'.* GUL

subscriptio, though it turns his line into a hexameter. The *subscriptio* copies Whitney's last two lines in all respects but this, picking up the word 'patience' from two lines earlier in Whitney's epigram:

> With patience suffer still, and then we sall in fine;
> Oure foes subdue, when they with shame sall pyne.
> (Culross)

> With patience then, wee must the combat wage,
> And not with force resist their deadlie strife:
> But suffer still, and then wee shall in fine,
> Our foes subdue, when they with shame shall pine.
> (Whitney, p.220, ll.9-12)

Whitney's emblem, from Hadrianus Junius, shows an oak tree being blown over and snapped by the blast of wind emerging from the mouth of a Zephyrus figure in the top left-hand corner; the slender reeds by the water's edge, however, bend but do not break. The Culross picture copies this quite closely, but also includes its favourite seated female figure; no attributes are now visible (the painting is quite badly damaged), though we can hardly doubt that she represents Patience who was conventionally shown as a woman with a lamb.

Another emblem where the seated figure at Culross appears to have taken its hint from an allegorical keyword in the epigram is 'RES HUMANA IN SUMMO DECLINANT' ('Mortal things decline when at their height', from Sambucus). Whitney's picture shows two images, a ship foundering in a storm, and a patch of snow on a hill slope that is melting in the sun, of which Culross copies only the foundering ship. However, the closing lines of Whitney's epigram refer to 'Fortunes wheele' and it is this detail that is reflected in the allegorical figure and the lines Culross uses for its *subscriptio*:

> This warneth all, on fortunes whele that clime
> To bear in mynd, how schort thay have there tyme.

Res humanæ in ſummo declinant.

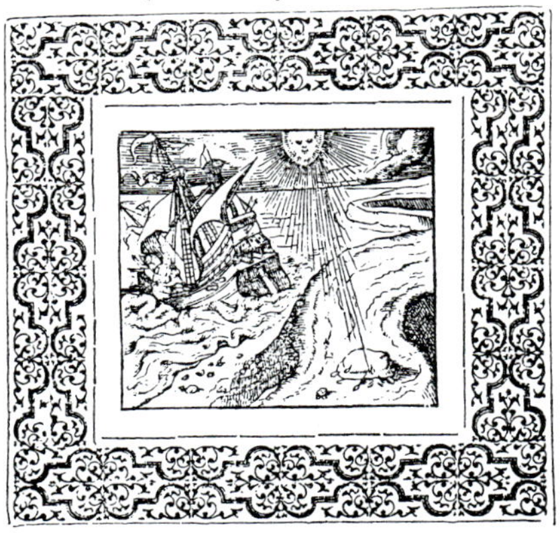

THE gallante Shipp, that cutts the azure ſurge,
And hathe both tide, and wiſhed windes, at will:
Her tackle ſure, with ſhotte her foes to vrge,
With Captaines boulde, and marriners of ſkill,
With ſtreamers, flagges, topgallantes, pendantes braue,
When Seas do rage, is ſwallowed in the waue.

The ſnowe, that falles vppon the mountaines greate,
Though on the Alpes, which ſeeme the clowdes to reache.
Can not indure the force of Phœbus heate,
But waſtes awaie, Experience doth vs teache:
Which warneth all, on Fortunes wheele that clime
To beare in minde how they haue but a time.

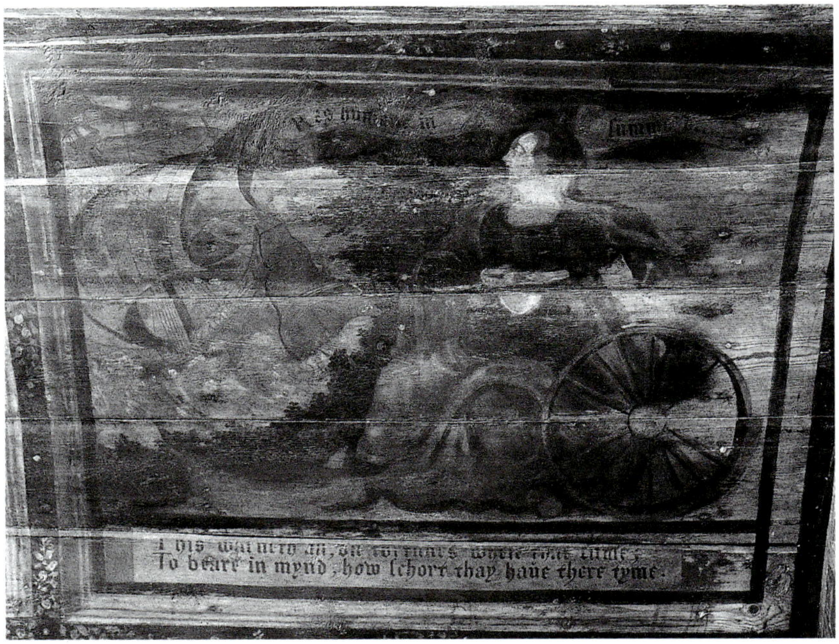

Left: *Whitney* A Choice of Emblemes *(1586) p.11.* GUL

Right: *Culross, the Palace. Emblem adapted from Whitney, 'Human affairs decline when at their height'.*
Trevor Graham

It is, accordingly, the goddess Fortuna we see here, shown not in her guise as Occasio, a blindfolded nude with her long lock of hair and standing on a globe, but in her equally traditional guise as a woman holding a wheel.

In several cases the hint for Culross' seated figure was supplied by Whitney's own picture. Whitney's *Neglecta virescunt* ('Despised things flourish', p.222, from Sambucus) shows a helmeted female figure holding a staff or lance and (possibly) a mace, who has been variously interpreted as Virtue or Athena, *scil* Minerva (Daly, *Index Emblematicus: The English Emblem Tradition*, vol. 1, p.327). Her identity and her significance in relation to the moral of this emblem are not clear but she has some connection with the similar figure who features in the only emblem at Culross which now lacks any motto, since its *subscriptio*,

> Althoghe the world, the verteous still despyse,
> Yet up aloft in spyte of them they rise.

quotes the last two lines of Whitney's epigram. The Culross figure does not wear the helmet, and instead of Whitney's mace (?) she holds a shield, but the lance she also holds resembles that held by Whitney's seated figure, and the addition of the shield ought to strengthen her identification with the conventional representation of Minerva/Pallas/Athene. The shield is clearly marked in Houston's sketch with a saltire and cross of St George, though these are highly unlikely for a painting of this date. Clear signs of falsification of the iconographic evidence through the erroneous guesswork of successive restorers can be witnessed in the difference between Houston's sketch and the modern restoration. The sketch shows the topmost board as blank, or missing, which is why his lady lacks a head, and also why it alone of all the emblems on this ceiling still lacks a motto. However, since Houston's sketch, someone has supplied the woman with a head and a top to her lance, but evidently refused the challenge of supplying her missing Latin motto. If she is Minerva, however, she needs not just a head but also a helmet such as the one Whitney's figure wears.

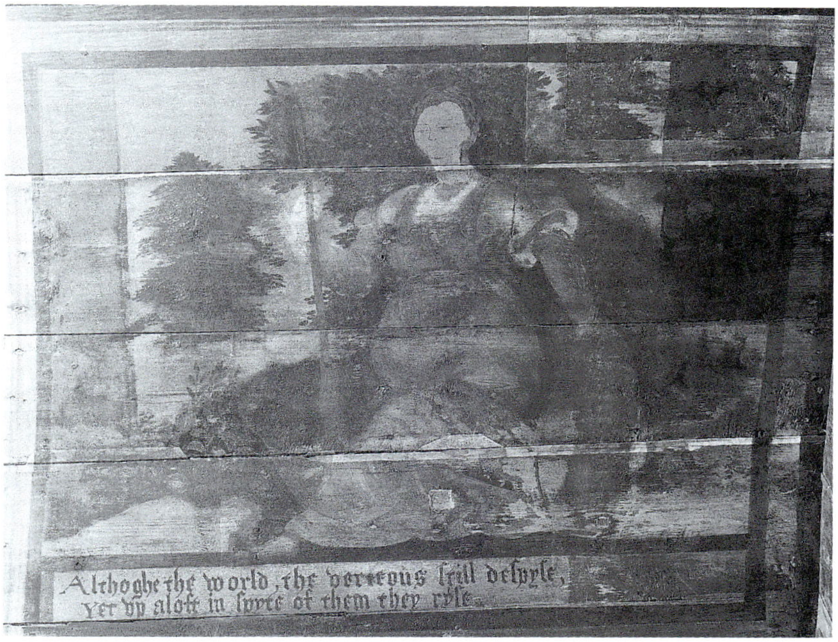

Neglecta virescunt.

To M. RAWLINS *Preacher.*

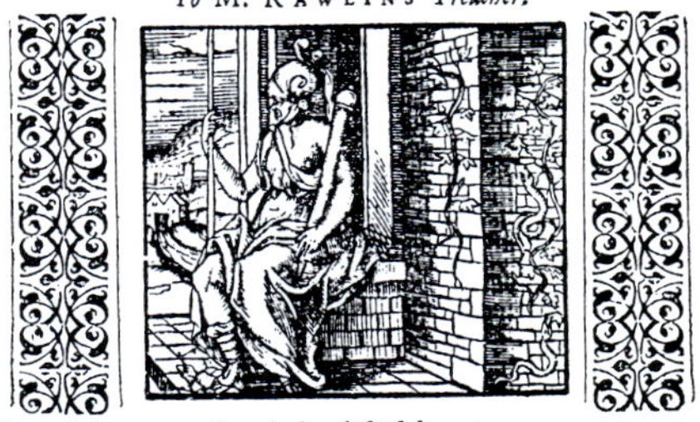

THE Iuie greene that dothe diſpiſed growe,
And none doth plante, or trimme the ſame at all,
Althoughe a while it ſpreades it ſelfe belowe,
In time it mountes, with creepinge vp the wall.
So, thoughe the worlde the vertuous men diſpiſe,
Yet vp alofte in ſpite of them they riſe.

Left: *Culross, the Palace. Emblem adapted from Whitney, seated figure possibly modelled on that of Pallas in Whitney's emblem.* Trevor Graham

Right: *Whitney* A Choice of Emblemes *(1586) p.222, 'Despised things flourish'.* GUL

Similarly, in the emblem 'MURUS AENEUS, SANA CONSCIENTIA' ('A clear conscience is like a wall of brass', Whitney p.67, from Sambucus), Whitney's woodcut shows a male figure grasping the trunk of a laurel tree for protection from the thunderbolt which Jupiter *tonans* threatens him with in the sky above (laurel trees were traditionally thought to be proof against lightning). Culross changes this to its favourite female figure, but the way she encircles the tree trunk with her right arm must go back to Whitney's figure. The branch of leaves she holds in her left hand is identified as laurel by Etherington Cooke, who also mentions clouds in the sky, now barely visible but maybe a relic of Whitney's Jupiter figure. Whitney's secondary image, a swan swimming in a pool with a laurel wreath around its neck, is repositioned to the left of the main figure. Whitney's

Left: *Culross, the Palace. Emblem adapted from Whitney, 'A clear conscience is a wall of brass'.* Trevor Graham

Right: *Whitney* A Choice of Emblemes *(1586) p.67.* GUL

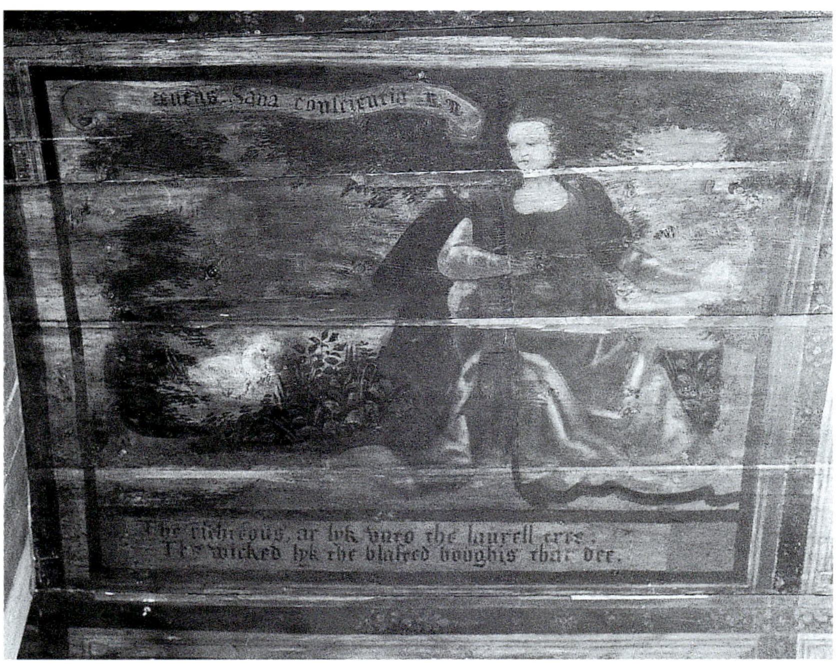

Murus aeneus, ſana conſcientia.

To MILES HOBART *Eſquier.*

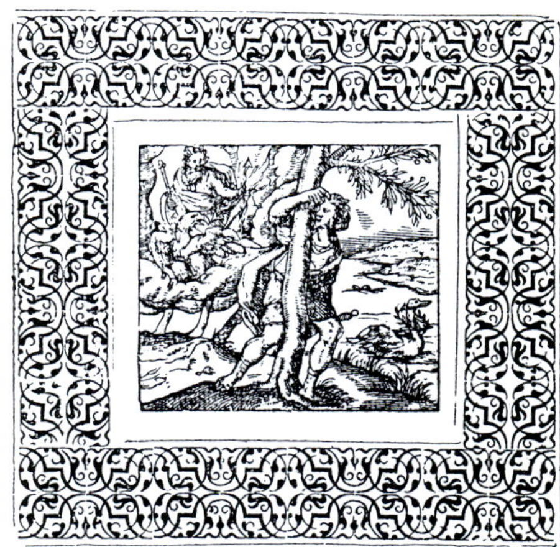

BOTHE freſhe, and greene, the Laurell ſtandeth ſounde,
Thoughe lightninges flaſſhe, and thunderboltes do flie:
Where, other trees are blaſted to the grounde,
Yet, not one leafe of it, is withered drie:
Euen ſo, the man that hathe a conſcience cleare,
When wicked men, doe quake at euerie blaſte,
Doth conſtant ſtande, and dothe no perrilles feare,
When tempeſtes rage, doe make the worlde agaſte:
Suche men are like vnto the Laurell tree,
The others, like the blaſted boughes that die.

Soli Deo gloria.
To M. HOWLTE *Preacher.*

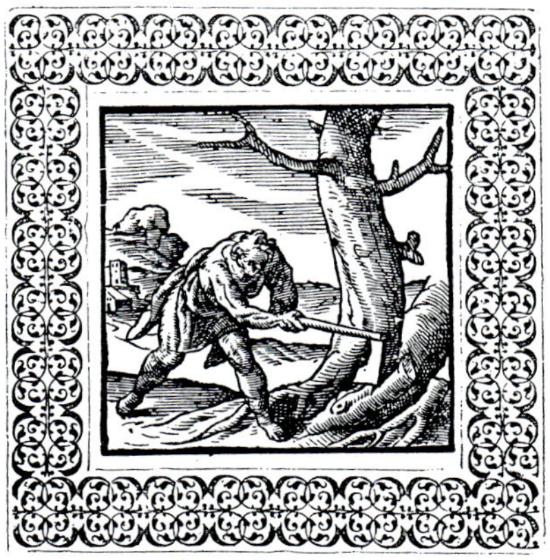

HERE, man with axe doth cut the boughe in twaine,
And without him, the axe, coulde nothing doe:
Within the toole, there doth no force remaine;
But man it is, that mighte doth put thereto:
Like to this axe, is man, in all his deeds;
Who hath no ſtrength, but what from GOD proceedes.

Then, let him not make vaunt of his deſert,
Nor bragge thereof, when hee good deedes hath donne:
For, it is GOD that worketh in his harte,
And with his grace, to good, doth make him ronne:
And of him ſelfe, hee weake theretoo, doth liue;
And GOD giues power, to whome all glorie giue.

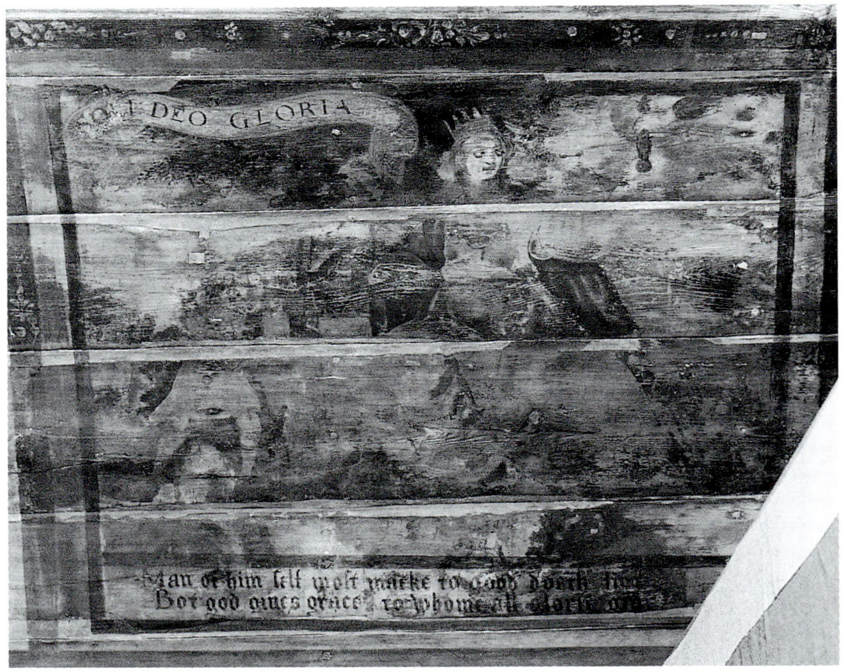

Left: *Whitney* A Choice of Emblemes *(1586) p.228.* GUL

Right: *Culross, the Palace. Emblem adapted from Whitney, 'To God alone be the glory'.* Trevor Graham

closing couplet again supplies the Culross *subscriptio.* Only Sambucus clarifies the significance of the swan to this moral (1564, p.14), explaining it as a conventional symbol of mortality since traditionally it sings before dying (hence 'swansong'). It was evidently the *subscriptio*'s reference to 'blasted boughes that die' that justified the retention of this subordinate detail in the Culross *pictura.*

Recognising the emblem from Whitney which it copies can sometimes supply details in the Culross *pictura* which are otherwise now damaged beyond recall. In the Culross emblem 'SOLI DEO GLORIA' ('To God alone be the glory') the picture is badly decayed, and virtually all that is now visible is the allegorical figure of a crowned woman, to whom a hand-of-God in the sky (top right) passes what looks like a sceptre. The left-hand half of the painting is now illegible, but the legs and skirt of a figure which has all but disappeared can still be made out. When we turn to the emblem from Whitney with the same motto, however, we see a man in precisely the attitude of this ghostly effigy at Culross. Whitney's figure is swinging an axe and cutting the branch of a substantial tree trunk. This illustrates the moral, Whitney explains, that just as no man can cut down a tree without appropriate tools (the axe), so we have no strength to achieve anything for ourselves without the power of God. The Culross *subscriptio* paraphrases Whitney's last two lines: 'Man of him self most weake to good doeth live/Bot god gives grace to whome all glory give.' The emblem, which goes back to Georgette de Montenay, is primarily an emblem of divine grace (de Montenay was a Protestant), but the Culross seated figure appears to be giving it a new slant, the crown and sceptre suggesting that it is specifically the power bestowed on kings for which God deserves all the credit. One wonders whether Bruce's good standing with King James might have influenced this iconography or even whether the whole emblem cycle at Culross might not have been executed to coincide with the royal visit in 1617. Although accounts of the visit to Culross suggest that it was unplanned and unforeseen – James simply happened to be hunting nearby – the reliability of these accounts is open to doubt.

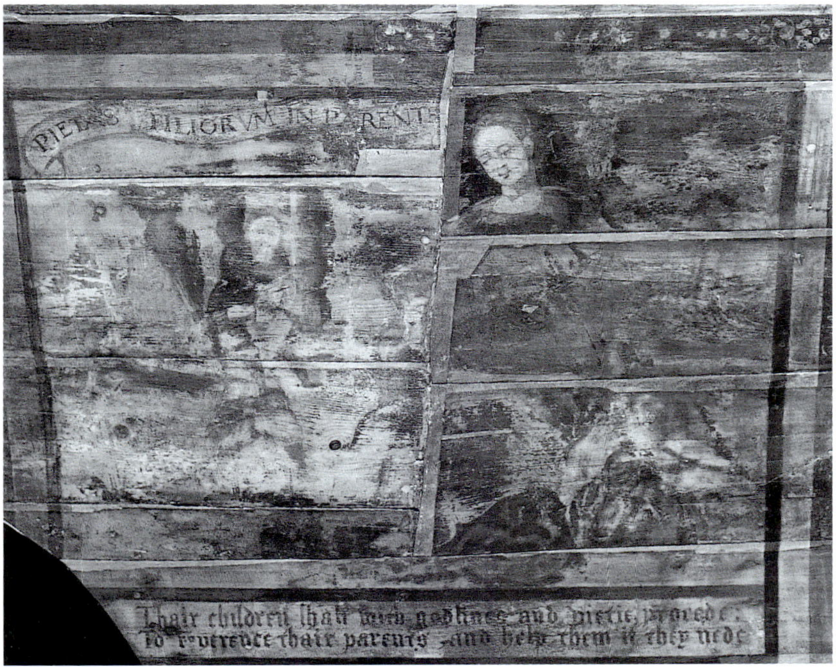

Pietas filiorum in parentes.

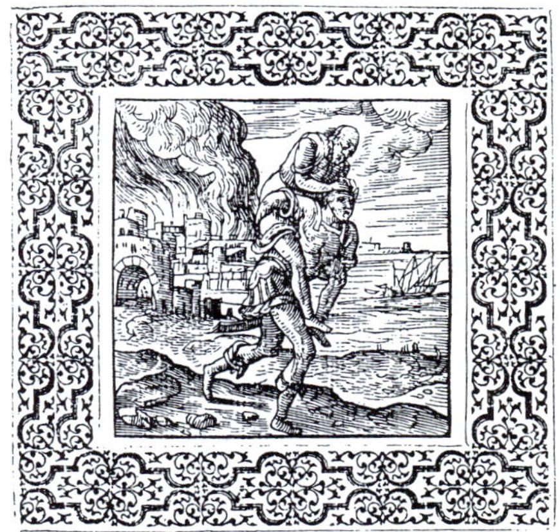

AENEAS beares his father, out of Troye,
When that the Greekes, the ſame did ſpoile, and ſacke:
His father might of ſuche a ſonne haue ioye,
Who throughe his foes, did beare him on his backe:
No fier, nor ſworde, his valiaunt harte coulde feare,
To flee awaye, without his father deare.

Which ſhowes, that ſonnes muſt carefull bee, and kinde,
For to releeue their parentes in diſtreſſe:
And duringe life, that dutie ſhoulde them binde,
To reuerence them, that God their daies maie bleſſe:
And reprehendes tenne thowſande to their ſhame,
Who ofte diſpiſe the ſtocke whereof they came.

Left: *Culross, the Palace. Emblem adapted from Whitney, 'The devotion of sons towards parents'.* Trevor Graham

Right: *Whitney* A Choice of Emblemes *(1586) p.163.* GUL

Not quite so badly damaged is the detail which goes back to Whitney in the Culross version of *Pietas filiorum in parentes* ('The devotion of sons towards parents', p.163), for the figure of Aeneas carrying his father Anchises on his back away from the burning city of Troy can still just about be made out, though the two-line *subscriptio* takes only the merest hints from its source. The seated female figure reading an open book is difficult to interpret. There is a version of this emblem, which goes back to Alciato, at Pinkie, and in the *Siege of Troy* painting at Cullen – the Homeric topos was well known to writers at this period, such as Sir Philip Sidney, who recommends to his reader,

> Onely let *Aeneas* bee worne in the Tablet of your memorie, how he governeth himself in the ruine of his Countrey, in the preserving of his old Father, and carrying away all his religious Ceremonies .... (*Defence of Poesie*, ed Fueillerat, p.25)

Sidney's is a useful reminder of how such 'speaking pictures' were used, whether in literature or in the visual arts, at this period, 'worne in the Tablet of your memorie' as examples of heroic virtue or stoic resolve,

> For as the Image of each Action stirreth and instructeth the minde, so the loftie Image of such woorthies, most inflameth the minds with desire to be woorthie: and enformes with counsaile how to be woorthie. (ibid., p.25)

The emblem 'SOL NON OCCIDAT SUPER IRACUNDIAM VESTRAM' ('Let not the sun set on your anger') takes its motto from the Bible (Ephesians 4.26*)* and goes back to de Montenay. The seated allegorical figure has no discernible identifying attributes, but the background has the remains of a detail based on Whitney's woodcut, showing two enemies who have thrown down their swords and are embracing in the light of a setting sun; they stand by a laurel tree and hold laurel branches. 'VERBUM EMISSUM NON EST REVOCABILE' ('A word once spoken cannot be called back') is indebted to Whitney's emblem (p.180, from la Perrière), but

Veritas inuicta.
To my vncle GEFFREY CARTWRIGHTE.

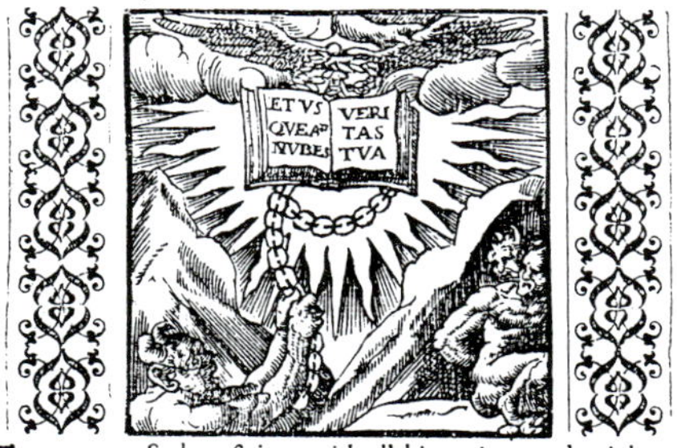

THOVGHE Sathan ſtriue, with all his maine, and mighte,
To hide the truthe, and dimme the lawe deuine:
Yet to his worde, the Lorde doth giue ſuch lighte,
That to the Eaſt, and Weſt, the ſame doth ſhine:
And thoſe, that are ſo happie for to looke,
Saluation finde, within that bleſſed booke.

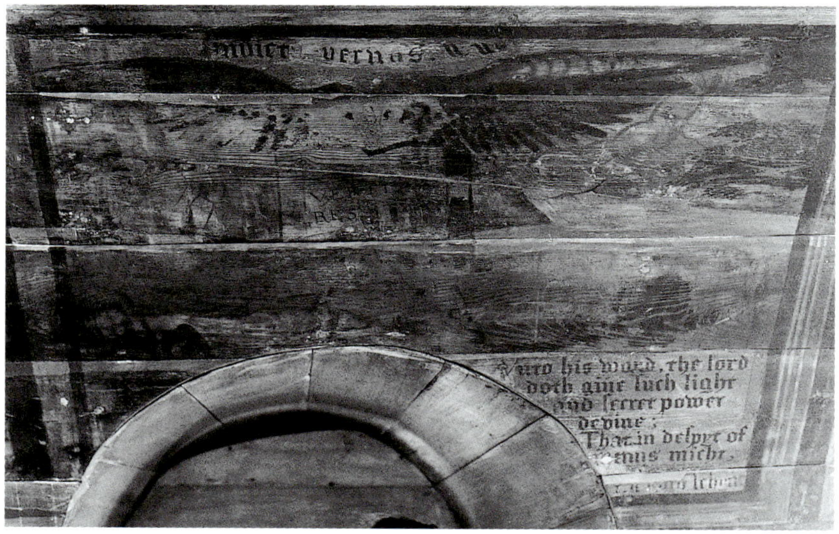

Left: *Whitney* A Choice of Emblemes *(1586) p.166.* GUL

Right: *Culross, the Palace. Emblem adapted from Whitney, 'Truth remains unconquered'.* Trevor Graham

there is now no sign of Whitney's rustic figure shown releasing a bird; all that can be seen is the usual seated female, this time holding a closed book, and with her finger at her lips in the gesture of Whitney's own *Silentium* figure (p.60); Valeriano (bk 30, ch. 14) also gives this gesture as the hieroglyphic for Silence, though it is probably too familiar to require any such source.

Knowledge of sources does help us, however, to reconstitute two remaining emblems at opposite corners of the room, both of which are badly damaged but look like the terminal emblems of any sequence into which these sixteen emblems might be ordered. '[MANET] INVICTA VERITAS' ('Truth remains unconquered') is the emblem in the south-east corner of the ceiling, furthest from the door, and evidently copied from Whitney's *Veritas invicta* ('Invincible truth'), which again goes back to de Montenay. It shows an open book below a laurel wreath suspended beneath a pair of outspread wings; in Whitney's picture the book is encircled by a chain, held by devils, in a rocky landscape, intent on dragging it down to hellmouth. There is, for once, no added allegorical figure. Whitney's book is open to show the words 'ET USQUE AD NUBES VERITAS TUA' ('And your truth will soar even up to the clouds'), which Culross shortens to 'VERITAS RESTITUA' ('Restore the truth' – the syntax is doubtful, though my reading is not in doubt; Etherington Cook made the same transcription in 1885). The *subscriptio* adapts lines 3-4 of Whitney's epigram, which it has to rejig somewhat awkwardly in order to secure a rhyme, kidnapping the rhyme word 'devine' from the previous line and tagging it on to the following line with scant regard, once again, for the metre.

In the opposite corner of the room, over the door, are the relics of an emblem which it is difficult not to think of as the terminal emblem of any sequence. Though much is damaged, the seated figure, holding a terrestrial globe and a pair of dividers, is evidently bald, evidently bearded, and evidently male, unlike the rest of his companions on the ceiling. Of the motto in its scroll the only word now fully legible is the word 'TERMINAT', but Etherington Cooke transcribed the whole motto as 'TEMPUS OMNIA TERMINAT', which corresponds with the motto to the very last emblem in Whitney's *Emblemes*. Whitney's woodcut shows three trees, in progressive states of decay, with a setting sun. The epigram quotes the ancient proverb of the Oldest Animals (on which see Bath 1992, ch. 4). It is possible that the damaged left half of the painting used

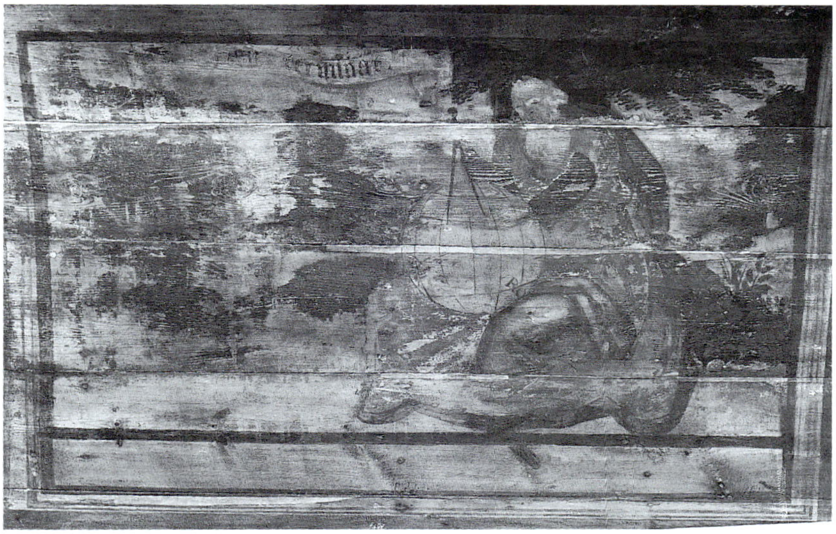

Tempus omnia terminat.

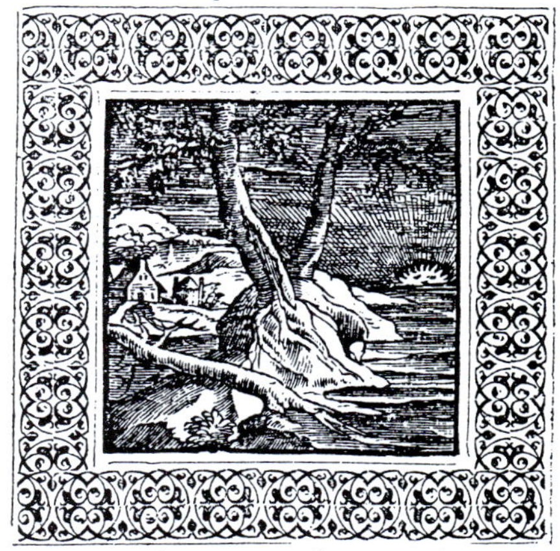

THE *longest daye, in time resignes to nighte.*
The greatest oke, in time to duste doth turne.
The Rauen dies, the Egle failes of flighte.
The Phœnix rare, in time her selfe doth burne.
The princelie stagge at lengthe his race doth ronne.
And all must ende, that euer was begonne.

Euen so, I, here doe ende this simple booke,
And offer it vnto your Lorshippes sighte:
Which, if you shall receiue with pleasinge looke,
I shall reioyce, and thinke my labour lighte.
And pray the Lorde your honour to preserue,
Our noble Queene, and countrie long to serue.

FINIS.

Left: *Culross, the Palace. Emblem adapted from Whitney, 'Time ends all things'.* Trevor Graham

Right: *Whitney* A Choice of Emblemes *(1586) p.230.* GUL

this image, and Houston's sketch certainly shows several trees, though they all appear to be in full leaf. The figure measuring a globe with a pair of compasses is normally identified as Geometria in Renaissance iconologies, where she is shown as female (as in Maarten de Vos, engraved by de Passe, Hollstein, vol. 46, no. 1516). But the bearded old man (with wings and an hour glass) who measures the globe with compasses in Enea Vico's engravings from a series of emblematic figures probably designed by Francesco Salviati (Bartsch, 15, no. 66) is certainly labelled 'TEMPVS', 'Time', and there can be little doubt that this is the identity of the Culross figure. The Culross globe has one further detail, the two letters 'RO' which can still be seen marked near the bottom. Houston's drawing shows that these are the middle letters of the continent 'EUROPA' – his sketch also shows 'ASIA' clearly marked.

Though it seems natural to think of this as some kind of terminal emblem, it is not clear whether the sixteen emblems on the Culross ceiling do in fact constitute a sequence or, if so, how such a sequence would be ordered. The way they are articulated is, in any case, complicated somewhat by the fact that these are not the only emblems to be found in this room. Whitney's usefulness in enabling us to restore decayed or damaged imagery in this decorative scheme is even more apparent when we look at one or two of the fragments which have survived on the boarded walls and window recesses. Most of these are now so fragmentary that one can hardly tell they were emblems, still less precisely what they illustrated. Boards in the arch at the east end of the room are divided into two panels, of which the left-hand panel still shows the image of a boar confronting a fox-like animal; a cartouche at the foot of the panel evidently once contained an inscription, none of which can now be read, but which Etherington Cooke in 1885 transcribed: 'Which warneth ws in peace o'mynds for weir to frame,/Whereby we aye sall subdeue, or wine ye field with fame.' This is a version of the last two lines to Whitney's *In pace de bello* ('In peace [be ready] for war', p.153), 'Which teacheth vs, in peace, our force for warres to frame:/Whereby, we either shall subdue, or loose the field with fame.' The picture, which goes back to an Aesop fable, shows a boar sharpening its tusks on the bole of a tree, and a fox who asks him what he's up to, to which the boar replies that you can never be sure what dangers might lurk behind apparently peaceful trees, so it's as well to keep your powder dry (or words to that effect).

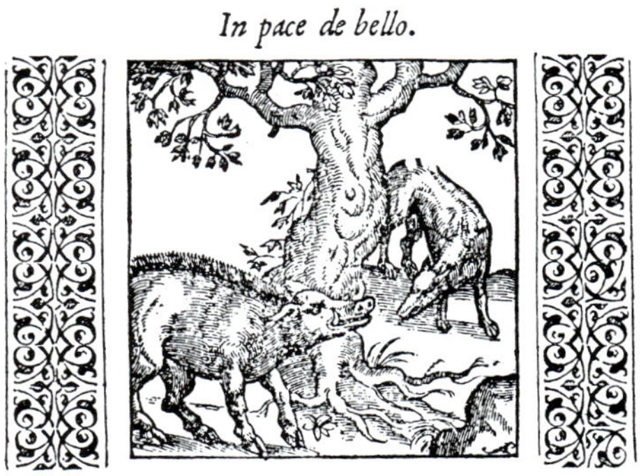

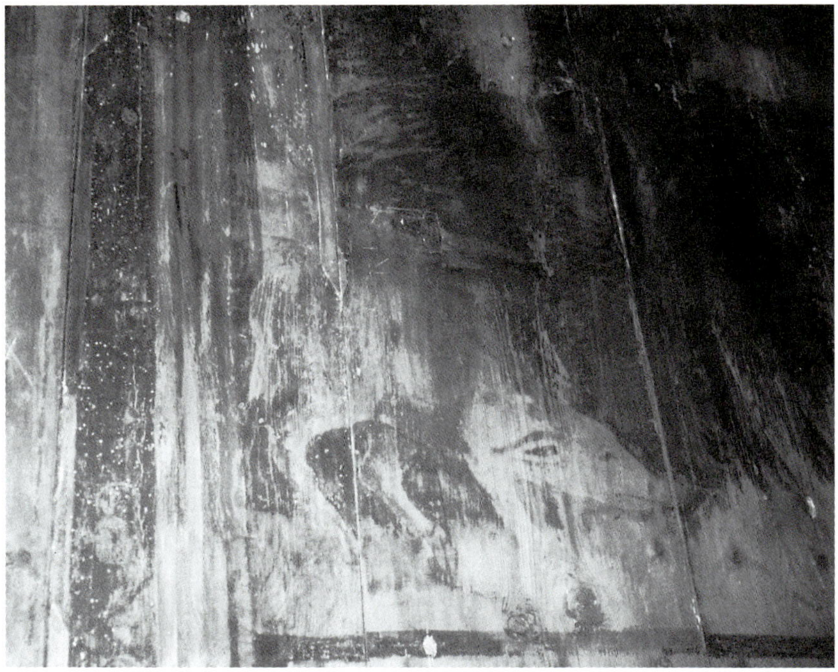

Left: *Whitney* A Choice of Emblemes *(1586) p.153.* GUL

Right: *Culross, the Palace. Emblem on the end wall, copying Whitney,* In pace de bello *('In peace be ready for war').*

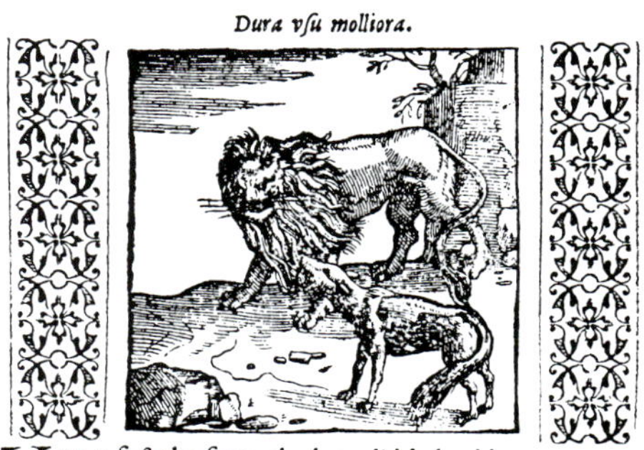

WHEN firſt the foxe, the lyon did behoulde,
Hee quak'd for feare, and almoſt dead did fall:
The ſecond time, he waxed ſomewhat boulde;
But at the third, hee had no feare at all.
Which ſhewes, that artes at firſt moſte harde to ſee,
With triall oft, both playne, and eaſie bee.

Whitney A Choice of Emblemes *(1586) p.156, 'Hard things become easier with practice'.* GUL

Opposite: *Second-floor room in Bruce's 1611 north block shows how extensive the decorative painting once was throughout his house in Culross.* Harvey Wood, NTS

The adjacent emblem on this end wall evidently also once showed two animals on either side of a tree, of which only a fox can now be made out, but which Etherington Cook describes as a lion and a squirrel. His misidentification was evidently occasioned by the fox's upreared brush, but fragments of the, now illegible, inscription that he quotes enable us to identify the source of this emblem with some confidence, for the phrases 'This schawes ye ... airts at feld .... / With ... ' must be a version of the closing lines of Whitney's emblem *Dura usu molliora* ('Hard things become easier with practice', p.156). This shows a fox and a lion, illustrating the fable of the fox which at first feared the lion but on subsequent meetings overcame its fears, 'Which shewes, that artes at first most harde to see,/ With triall oft, both playne, and easie bee'. We could now reconstruct with some confidence the subject and, I believe, the original appearance of these two badly decayed emblems on the end wall.

Etherington Cooke also describes some foliage on this east wall, with labels bearing the words 'ANGUSTA ... HERBA'. This seems likely to have been a version of the emblem *Latet anguis in herba* ('The snake lurks in the grass', Whitney p.14, from Paradin), which shows a snake climbing a branch of foliage towards the fruit at the top. Fragments of inscriptions can still be seen on two recessed window bays. That on the north wall beside the door shows a scroll which, unlike those holding the mottoes on the ceiling, is doubled into several folds suggesting that it is still in its original position. The remaining letters read, 'PAUPERTATEM [...] HANTUR'. This must be Whitney's *Paupertatem summis ingeniis obesse ne provehantur* ('Poverty obstructs the progress of the most gifted minds', p.152). Etherington Cooke, indeed, quotes the whole motto and accurately describes the picture, which evidently copied Whitney's, showing a man with winged hand who aspires to the heavens weighed down by the stone of poverty to which his other hand is bound; the emblem goes back to Alciato. Etherington Cooke also records that the central window recess showed several flowers on a single stem, with the label 'VITAE ARBOR' ('Tree of Life'). This has no known emblematic source.

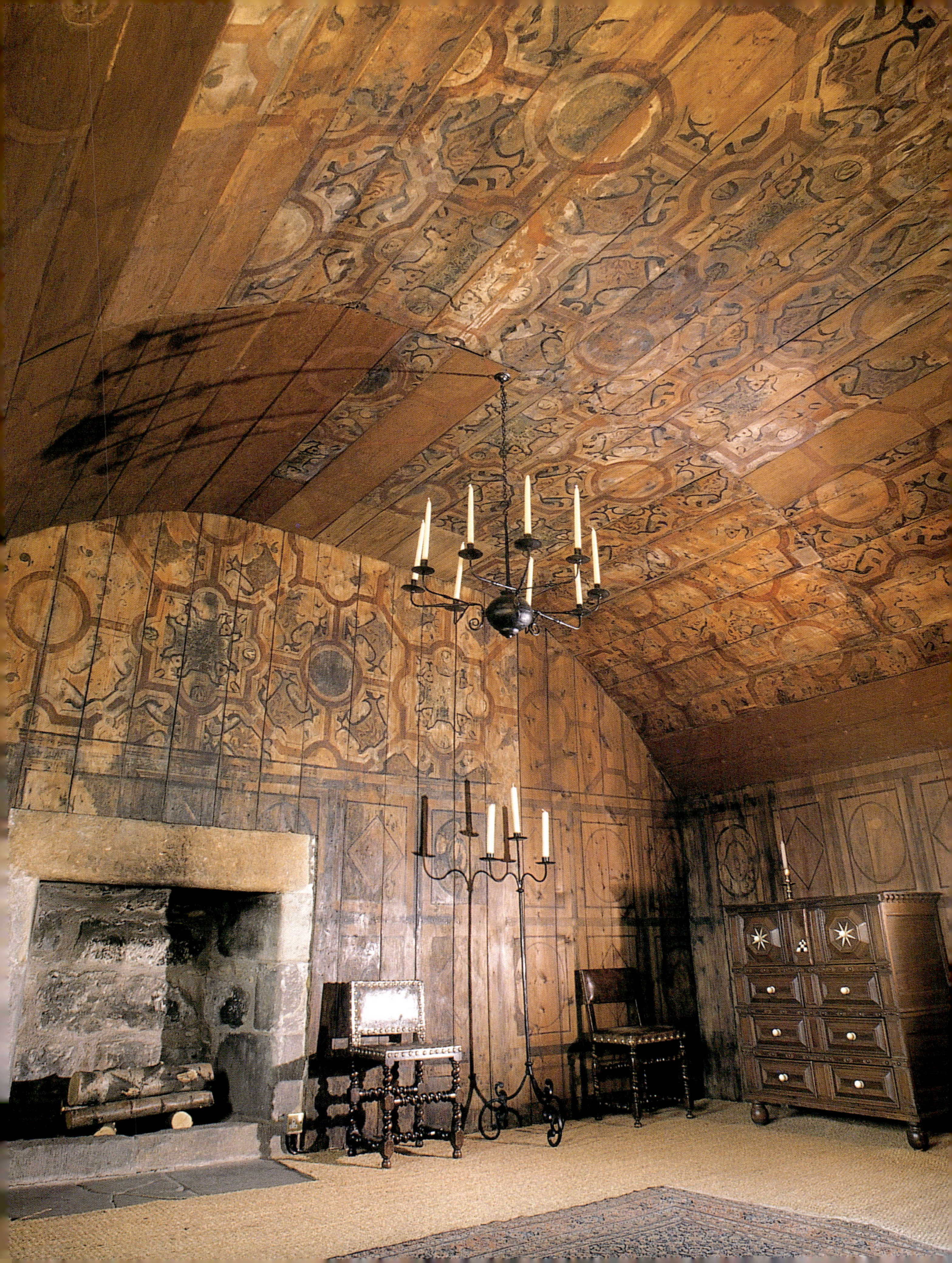

R

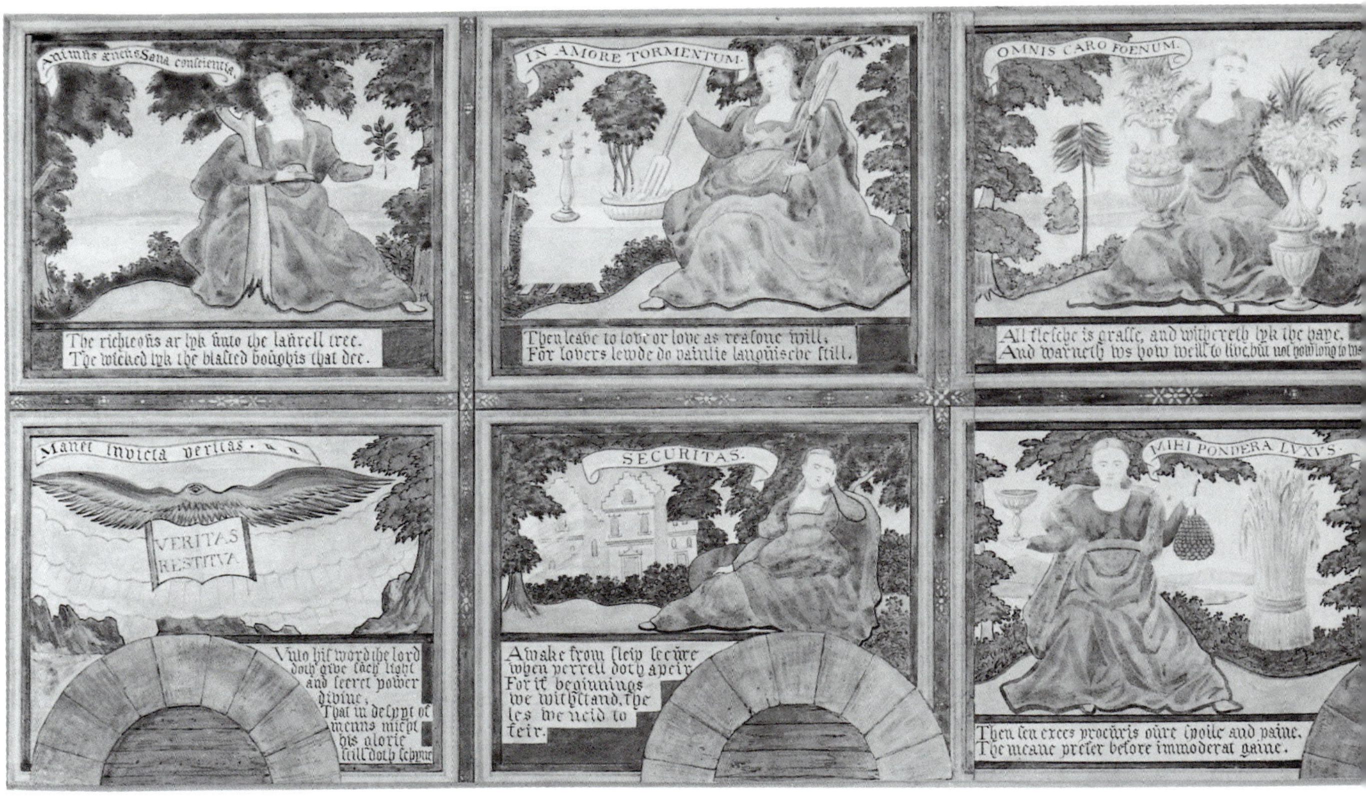
Animus æneus Sana conscientia
The richteous ar lyk unto the laurell tree.
The wicked lyk the blasted boughis that dee.
IN AMORE TORMENTUM.
Then leave to love or love as reasone will,
For lovers lewde do vainlie languische still.
OMNIS CARO FOENUM.
All flesche is grasse, and withereth lyk the haye,
Manet invicta veritas.
VERITAS RESTITVA
Unto his word the lord doth give sach light and secret power divine,
That in despyt of menns micht his glorie still doth schyne
SECURITAS.
Awake from sleip secure when perrell doth apeir
For if beginnings we withstand, the les we neid to feir.
MIHI PONDERA LVXVS.
Then sen exces procuris oure spoile and paine,
The meane prefer before immoderat gaine.

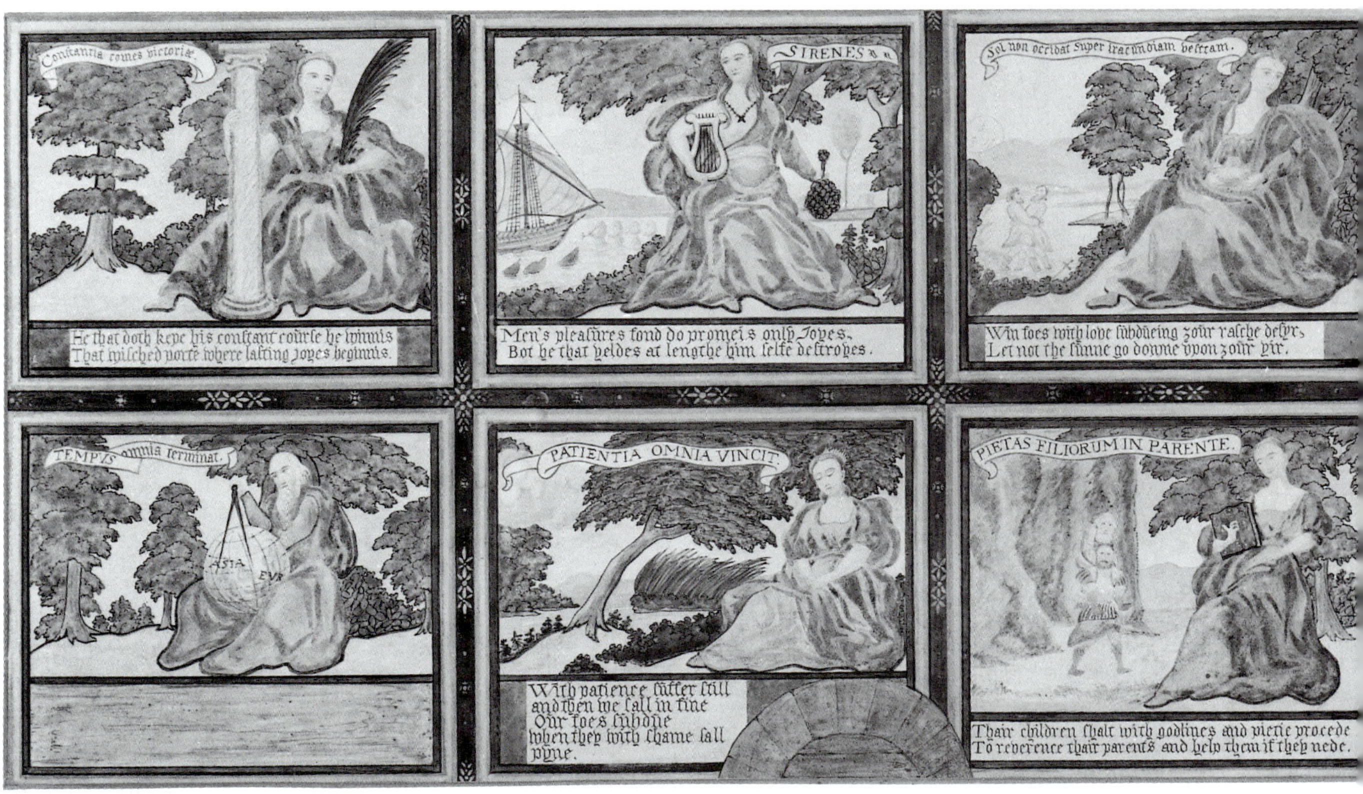
Constantia comes victoriæ.
He that doth kepe his constant course he winnis
That wisched porte where lasting Joyes beginnis.
SIRENES
Men's pleasures fond do promeis only Joyes,
Bot he that yeldes at lengthe him selfe destroyes.
Sol non occidat super iracundiam vestram.
Win foes with love subdueing zour rasche desyr,
Let not the sunne go downe upon zour yir.
TEMPVS omnia terminat.
ASIA
EVR
PATIENTIA OMNIA VINCIT.
With patience suffer still
and then we sall in fine
Our foes subdue
when they with shame sall
pyne.
PIETAS FILIORUM IN PARENTE.
Thair children shalt with godlines and pietie procede
To reverence thair parents and help them if they nede.

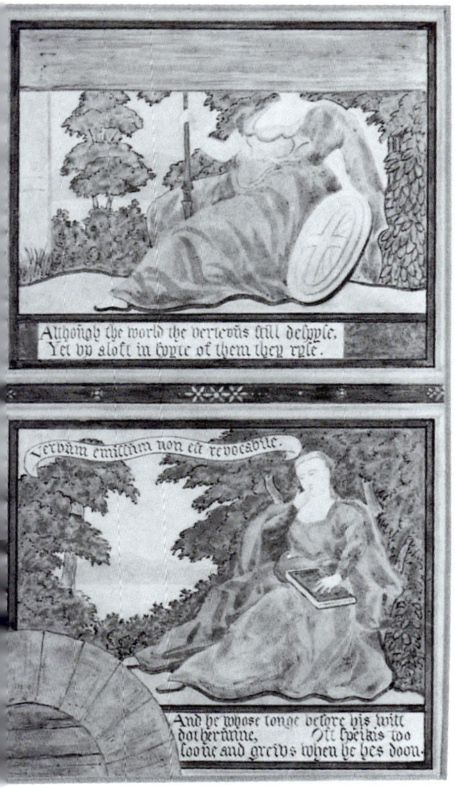

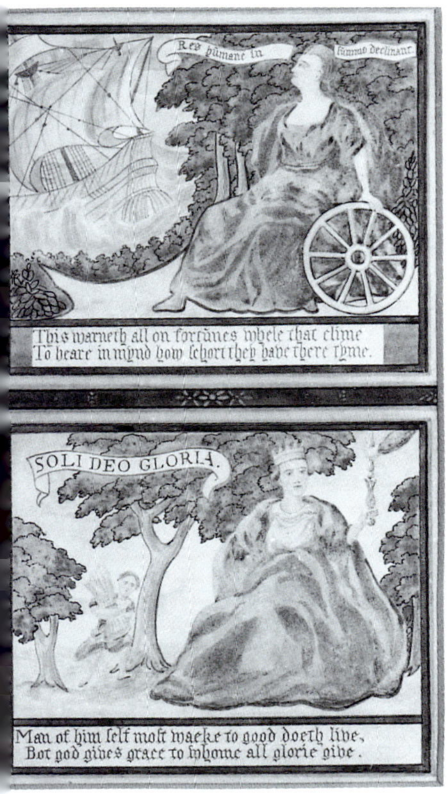

The poor quality of these paintings at Culross is not entirely a result of their inadequate conservation over the last four hundred years, though that certainly has not helped. They are not the kind of paintings likely to attract attention on grounds of artistic merit, but their neglect can only have been further encouraged by the difficulty of making sense of them. Recognising their debts to Whitney, as I have tried to show, takes us a long way towards understanding just what we are looking at – we might now be persuaded that work which may seem aesthetically naïve can nevertheless be iconographically sophisticated. The way at least some of these emblems handle their sources makes that suggestion more plausible, but in order to make such a claim we do need to know how far we can trust the iconographic evidence, and it does appear that some of that evidence has not only disappeared through the ravages of time but has also suffered from the erroneous guesses of incautious restorers. Etherington Cooke's descriptions and Houston's drawings are invaluable witnesses to the content of these emblems before more recent damage, but even these need to be treated with some scepticism. For instance Etherington Cooke describes, and Houston draws, the man who should be felling a tree in the 'SOLI DEO GLORIA' emblem as carrying a sheaf of corn. The fact that Houston could draw what Cooke describes confirms that it must have been visible at this date, but I do not believe that this is what George Bruce had painted on his ceiling. His picture, I am certain, showed the man at the foot of the tree wielding the same axe that he wields in Whitney's woodcut, the instrument of divine grace without which no achievement is possible. The sheaf of corn, like the bunch of hay – the Latin *manipulus* that has somehow turned into a palm tree – has to be the mistaken guesswork of a restorer. If we put such errors aside, we can begin to make better sense of what we see at Culross.

Culross, the palace. Pre-restoration sketches of southern and northern halves of emblem ceiling by John Houston showing details which are no longer visible. HS

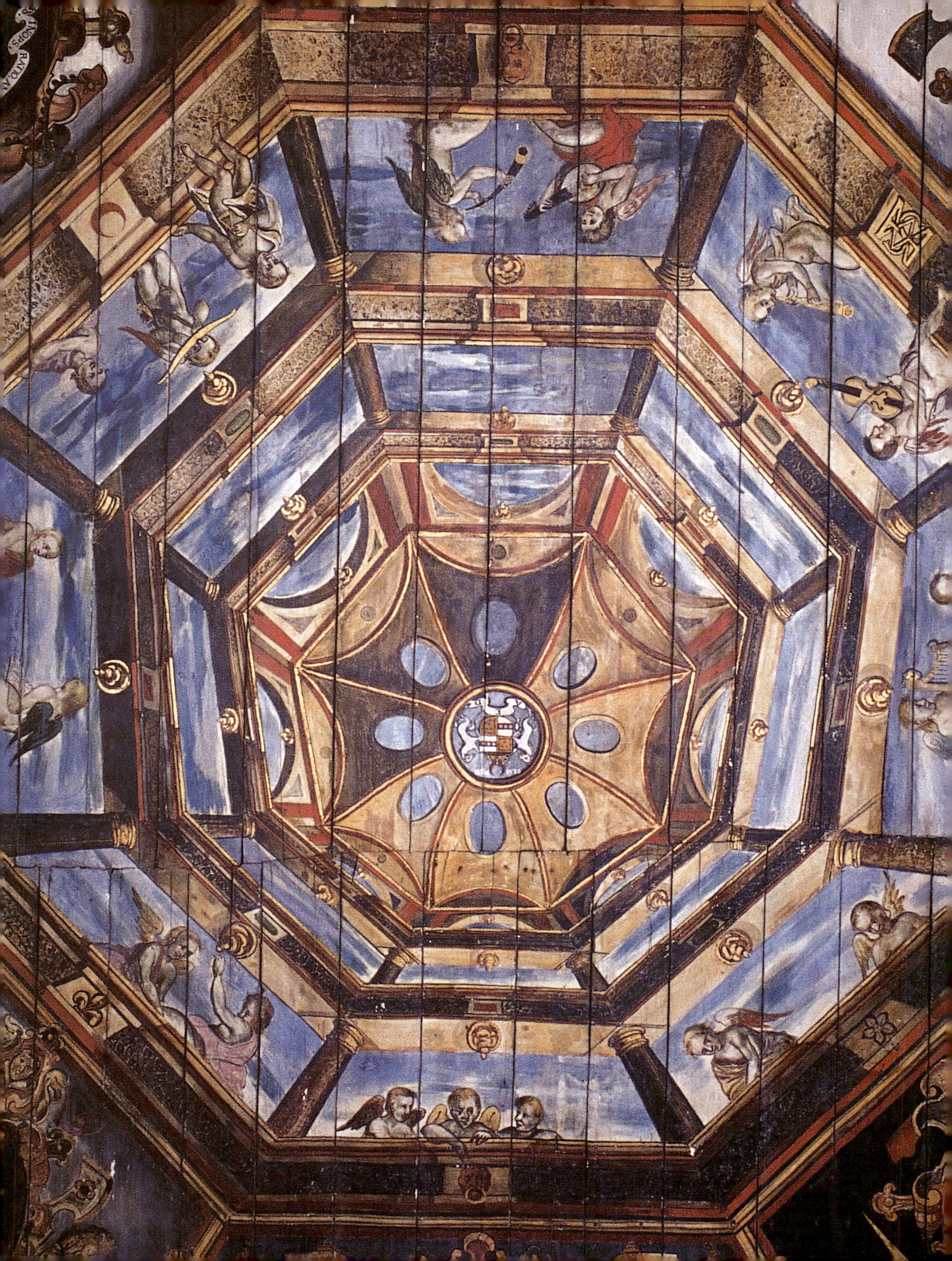

4

ALEXANDER SETON'S SUBURBAN VILLA

ALEXANDER Seton, Earl of Fyvie and first Earl of Dunfermline, was a distinguished lawyer, a Latin poet, and one of the most powerful officers of state in Scotland from around 1580 to 1622. Hailed by his contemporaries as an enlightened patron of learning and the arts, Seton's role in the development of early modern architecture in Scotland has won increasing recognition in recent times. As Deborah Howard notes, the inscription which Seton composed for the monument to William Schaw (d.1602) in Dunfermline Abbey, which describes Schaw as *architecturae peretissimus*, 'most skilled in architecture', is one of the earliest places to use the word 'architect' in something like its modern sense (Howard 1995a, p.25). The houses Seton built, or improved, at Fyvie (Aberdeenshire) and at Pinkie (East Lothian), are notable for their use of an extended vocabulary of heraldic and emblematic devices which must be seen as making claims for his own and his family's role in bringing an implicitly neoclassical *urbanitas* and *humanitas* to Renaissance Scotland.

Seton's father had been Keeper of the Household to Mary, Queen of Scots, and his aunt, Mary Seton, was one of the famous 'Four Maries' who had accompanied the queen in her years of exile. Alexander Seton had been educated by the Jesuits in Rome, where he precociously delivered, at the age of only sixteen, an oration before the Pope. His seventeenth-century biographer records that if he had remained in Rome he would probably have become a cardinal (Maitland 1829, p.63). Instead, as the Reformation took hold in Scotland, he abandoned his candidature for the priesthood in favour of legal studies, and rose to become the most eminent of Scottish lawyers, appointed Lord of Session in 1583, President of the Court in 1593, and Lord Chancellor in 1604. In 1595 the collapse of the public finances through corruption and mismanagement led King James to appoint Seton to the council of eight lawyers, known as 'Octavians', which met daily in the Edinburgh Tolbooth, without salary, in order to reform fiscal abuses, weed out corruption, and restore the public exchequer. In 1600 Seton was appointed guardian to the future Charles I, and in 1604-5 he travelled to London as newly created Chancellor and Commissioner responsible for finalising the Treaty of Union of the crowns. Seton was not only a powerful

Opposite: *Pinkie House, long gallery,* trompe l'oeil *cupola.* HS

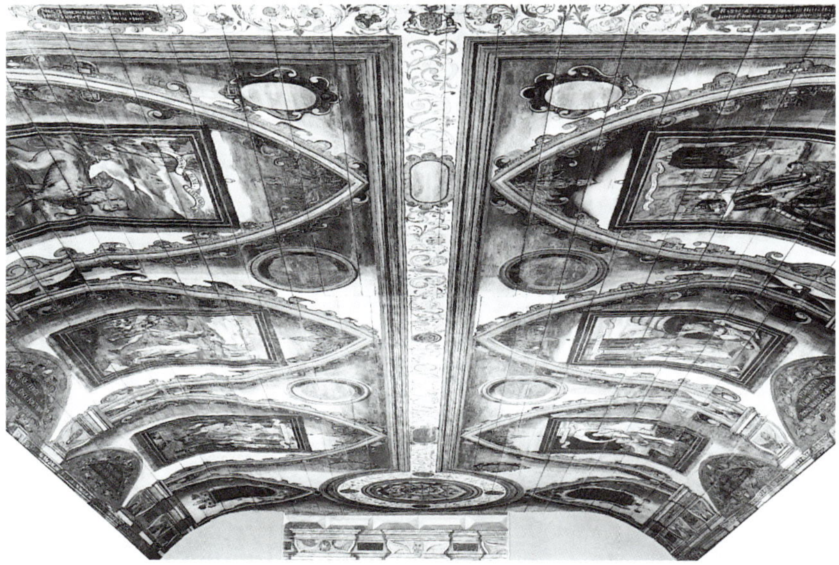

Pinkie House, Musselburgh, long gallery. HS

officer of state and King James' most trustworthy servant, but was described after his death as 'a great humanist in prose and poecie, Greek and Latine, well versed in the mathematicks and had great skill in architecture and herauldrie' (Kingston in Maitland 1829, p.63). He built two of the most outstanding and innovative buildings of this period, one of which retains painted ceilings that are among the most sophisticated examples of such work in Scotland.

In 1613 Seton made extensive additions to the house at Pinkie, Musselburgh, a few miles east of Edinburgh. The eastern block he added is chiefly notable for the long gallery, eighty-five feet in length. Its coved ceiling is filled with coats of arms, Latin inscriptions and emblematic panels of classical and mythological subjects contained in illusionistic vaulting, painted onto the boarded ceiling and dividing the whole area into arcaded partitions. At the centre of the ceiling is an extraordinary *trompe l'oeil* cupola offering the illusion of a glimpse of the sky and populated by a host of putti; two smaller cupolas at either end repeat this illusion. The Latin emblems which dominate the long gallery's ceiling are not just emblematic motifs but complete, tripartite Renaissance emblems consisting of Latin motto, allegorical *pictura*, and a further Latin *subscriptio*. Eleven of the seventeen panels of emblems go back directly to known sources in printed emblem books but at least some of the remainder are undoubtedly original exercises in emblematic composition. As with any emblem the combination of text and image demands interpretation; moreover, in this case, the emblems assume a classical knowledge on the part of their viewer that is an intrinsic part of their Renaissance *humanitas*.

The way the ceiling illustrates its classical subjects can be clearly demonstrated in the eight of its seventeen panels which illustrate texts from the poetry of Horace, texts already turned into emblems by the Dutch artist Otto van Veen ('Vaenius'), the teacher of Rubens. The *Emblemata Horatiana* of Otto Vaenius first appeared in Antwerp in 1607, two further editions, 1607 (a different edition) and 1612, having appeared by 1613 when Seton had this ceiling painted (on Vaenius, see Bath 1997). The book consists, as its title suggests, of moral emblems based on classical *sententiae* drawn out of Horace and amplified by citations from other classical writers. Eight of the panels in the long gallery are modelled closely on emblems from this source. At the end of the gallery, nearest

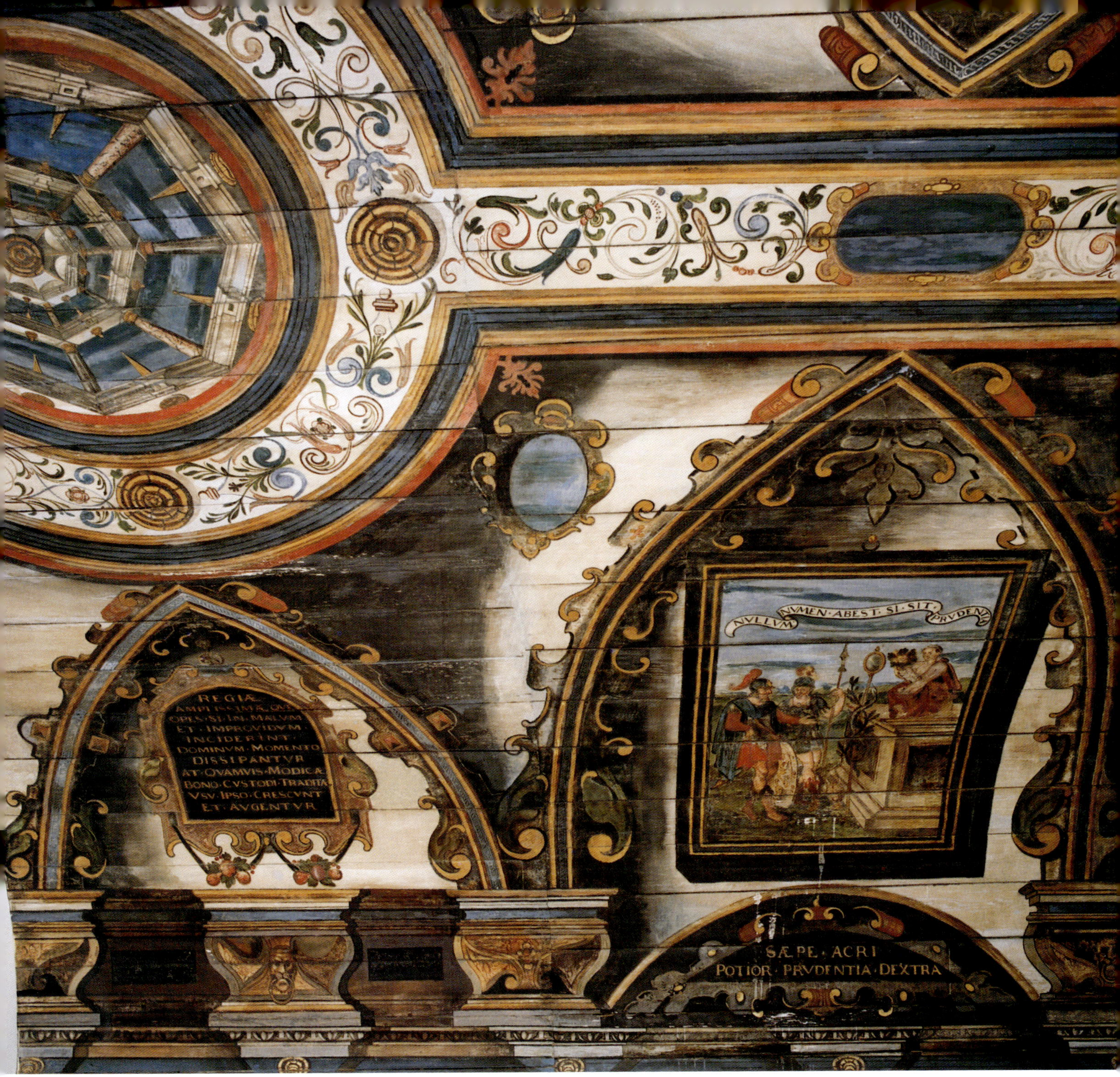

Pinkie House, detail from the long gallery. The relationship between epigraphy and emblem in the Renaissance was particularly close. RCAHMS

the oriel window, is an emblem from Vaenius illustrating Horace's motto (*Epist* I.2.46) *Nihil amplius opto* ('I choose nothing more'). The picture shows the wise man who fills his cup at the fountain, while his greedy companion thinks he can get a bigger draught from the river, but pays for his lack of moderation when he falls in and is drowned. The emblem is based on Horace's *Satire* I.I.52-8, in which the poet praises moderation and wonders at men who covet more than they need, as if a man who needed only a glass of water should risk drawing it from the River Aufidus, by which he might be swept away, rather than using a modest fountain. Vaenius draws what Horace had described, turning it more decisively into an emblem of Temperance by showing the two vessels with

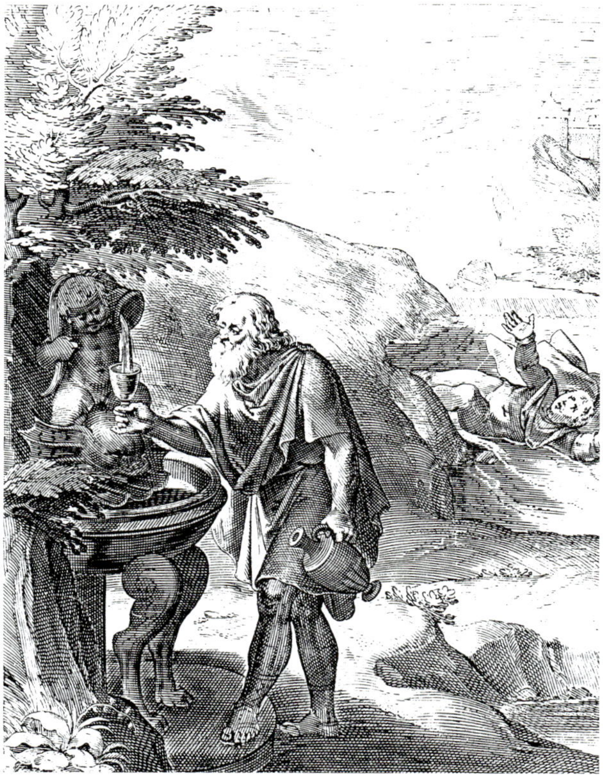

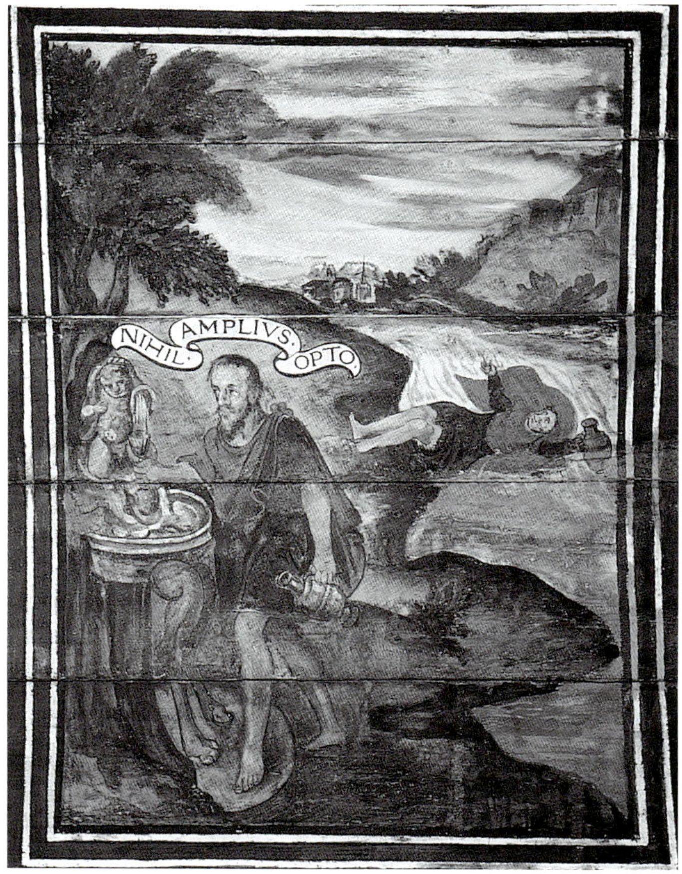

Left: *Otto Vaenius,* Emblemata Horatiana *(1607) p.113,* Nihil amplius optat. GUL

Right: *Pinkie House. Emblem copied from Otto Vaenius, 'I choose nothing more'.* HS

which Temperance is conventionally depicted – normally she pours liquid from one into the other, which the viewer is expected to understand as water being poured into wine so as to moderate its strength. The Pinkie ceiling copies Vaenius' engraving closely.

There is, however, one detail in this picture which makes a highly significant change to its source, for if we look closely at the head of the modest, bearded man who is filling his pitcher at the fountain it can be seen that the rather shaggy hair and unkempt beard of Vaenius' figure is reinterpreted to show an altogether thinner face with a pointed beard. We have only to look at the portrait of Alexander Seton which was painted by Marcus Gheerearts the Younger three years before this gallery was constructed to recognise that this detail is offering us a portrait of Seton himself. The narrow, rather ascetic face with its receding hairline and aquiline nose are distinctive and quite different from the features we see on the hirsute face in the emblem engraving. This adaptation of the source to present a portrait of the patron is unparalleled in any decorative scheme of this period in Britain. It would appear that Seton wished to identify himself with the qualities of temperance and moderation this emblem exemplifies. The shift of case ending in the motto might indeed be seen as signalling such a claim: Vaenius's *optat* is third-person, '*he* who has enough chooses nothing more', whereas the Pinkie motto is first-person *opto*, '*I* choose nothing more'. The positioning of this scroll round the figure's head clearly identifies the sentiment with the character it portrays.

Such a piece of self-fashioning is wholly consistent with what recent historians have called the 'conspicuous modesty' of Seton's architectural ambitions

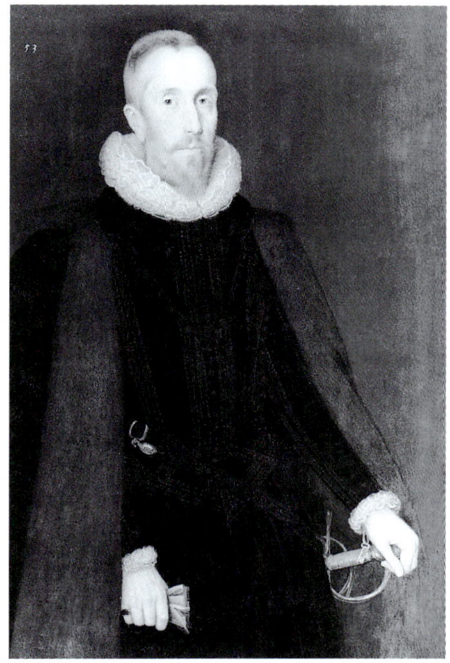

Alexander Seton, first Earl of Dunfermline, by Marcus Gheeraerts, oil on canvas, dated 1610. SNPG

(Glendinning, MacInnes and MacKechnie 1996, p.56). That modesty is signalled by some of the other Latin inscriptions about the house, such as that in the gallery itself, which advises us, 'A happy home is preferable to a large house; often toil and sorrow dwell in palaces, peace and happiness in cottages', or that on the south front which declares that 'Alexander Seton built this house in 1613, not as he would have wished, but as his fortunes and the size of the site permitted'. Such declarations define what MacKechnie calls 'Seton's theme of Augustan Stoicism' – a theme which 'was of particular relevance in the early seventeenth century context, not only to his own predicament as a Catholic government official, but to the changing *Weltanschauung* of the nation as a whole' (Glendinning, *et al* 1996, p.56). That identification with Renaissance neo-Stoicism is surely the motivation for Seton's choice of Vaenius' Horatian emblems as a source for his gallery of emblems, for Vaenius' book was both projected and received specifically as a collection of Stoic emblems, and – as I shall argue – this gallery was almost certainly designed as a version of the *stoa poikile* or 'painted gallery' in Athens in which Stoicism had its origins and from which it took its name.

Four panels further along on the same side, another emblem of moderation shows the philosopher Diogenes sitting in his tub, with his famous dog, arguing with his fellow philosopher Aristippus the Epicurean who believes that philosophers do better to live at court than to become destitute on the streets. Diogenes is claiming that Aristippus would not stay with Alexander the Great (who stands beside him) if only he had the courage to be self-reliant, to which Aristippus is replying that you don't have to drop out to do philosophy, or as Vaenius's motto puts it: 'One can be wise in any estate of life' (*In quocunque*

Left: *Vaenius,* Emblemata Horatiana *(1607).* GUL

Right: *Pinkie House. Emblem copied from Vaenius, Diogenes in his tub, 'A sensible man adapts to all ways of life'.* HS

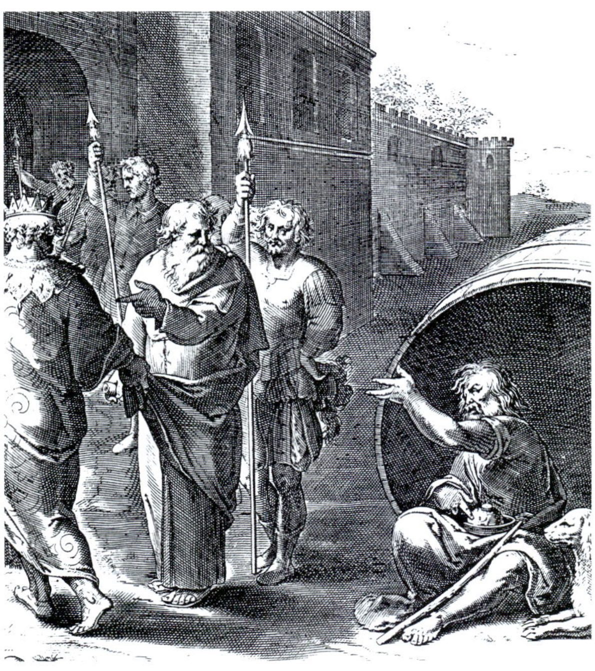

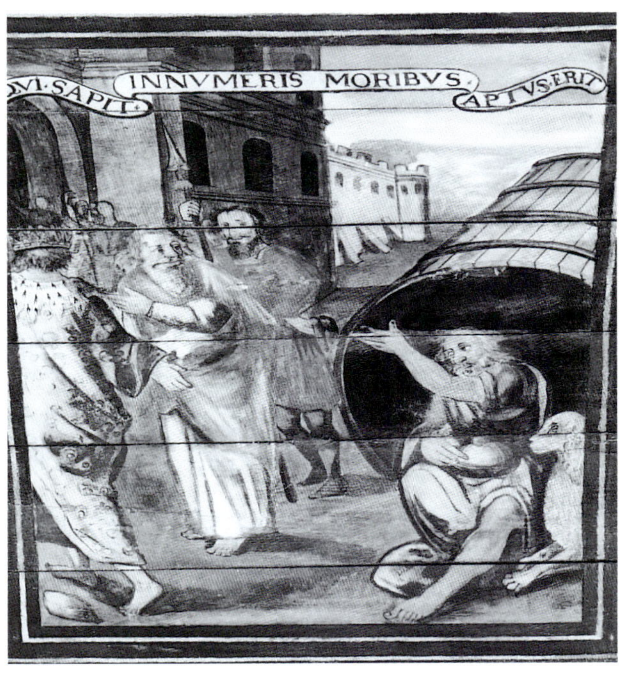

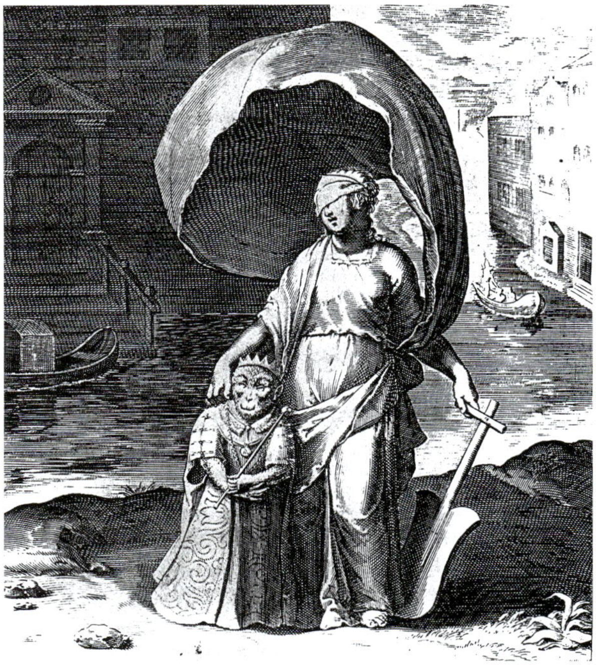

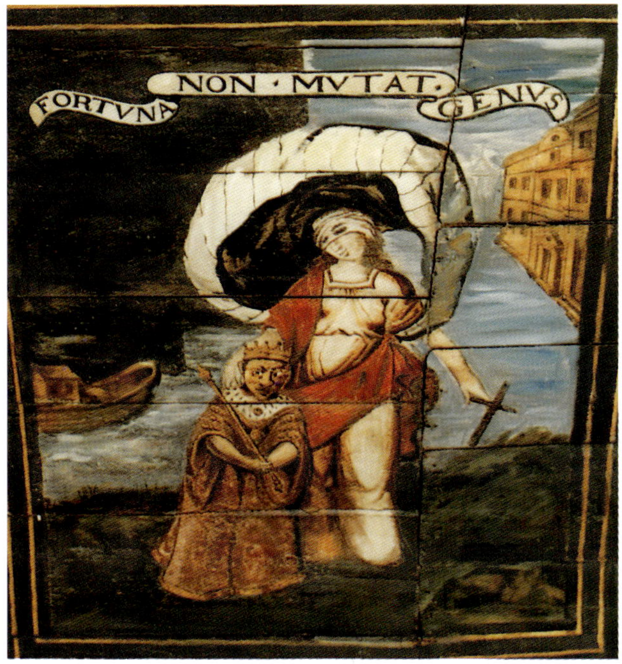

Left: *Vaenius,* Emblemata Horatiana *(1607) p.155.* GUL

Right: *Pinkie House. Emblem copied from Vaenius, 'Fortune doesn't change one's nature'.*

vitae genere philosophari licet). The Pinkie motto, *Qui sapit innumeris moribus aptus erit* (from Ovid, *Artis amat* 1.760), means much the same: 'The sensible man adapts to all ways of life.' In the next panel we see a richly dressed ape with crown and sceptre standing beside the goddess Fortuna shown, as was conventional, blindfold with her sail and rudder. The motto, *Fortuna non mutat genus*, from Horace, means 'Fortune can't change one's nature' – once an ape always an ape; you can't turn a monkey into a king.

On the opposite side we have more emblems from Vaenius' Horatian collection. *Semper avarus eget* means 'The greedy man is always in want' and shows a man suffering from dropsy; he can't stop drinking and his gouty leg is propped up towards the fire while a physician examines his urine. In Vaenius' emblem the physician held a scroll with an inscription, *Danda est hellebori multo pars maxima avaris/ Nescio an Anticyram ratio illis destinet omnem* ('By far the greatest portion of hellebore is to be administered to the covetous:/ I don't know whether reason should not consign all Anticyra to their use', Horace, *Sat* 2.3). The Pinkie artist has borrowed this inscription and made it serve as the new motto to the emblem, also from Vaenius, of the miser who sits in his cellar surrounded by barrels of wine and chests of corn (and gold, no doubt), but who is dressed in rags and eats turnips. The motto refers to the city of Anticyra, famous for producing hellebore, a herb used to cure madness; Horace suggests that misers are so mad that he would consign the whole of Anticyra's produce to their use alone. This copying of an inscription from one of Vaenius' engravings to serve as the motto for a different emblem is further evidence of the Pinkie artist's readiness to adapt his sources.

Two emblems of friendship complete Pinkie's selection from the Horatian Emblems of Otto Vaenius. *Nil ego contulerim iucundo sanus amico* means 'In my opinion, there's nothing better than a good friend'. The picture shows a man dismissing the temptations of wealth, fame, love and worldly power, all displayed on the table behind him, in favour of friendship. Beside it the emblem *Firma amicitia*, 'Firm friendship', shows us Zethus, who loved hunting, with his

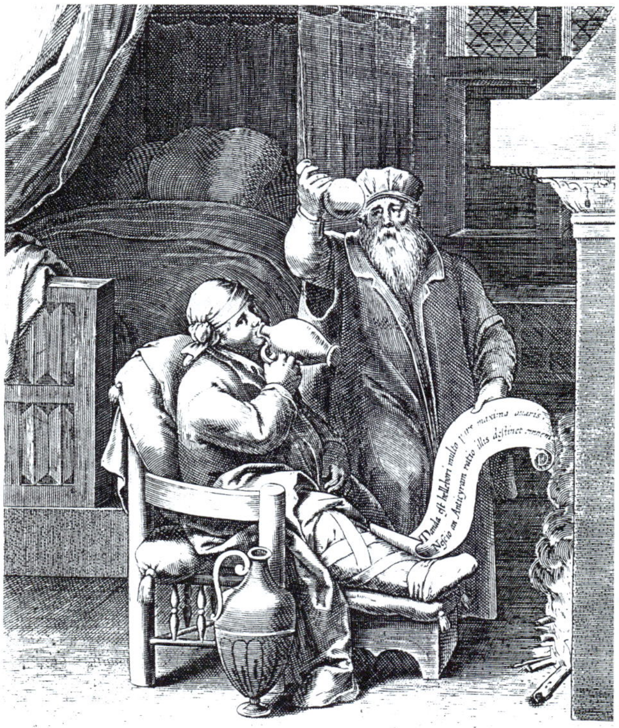

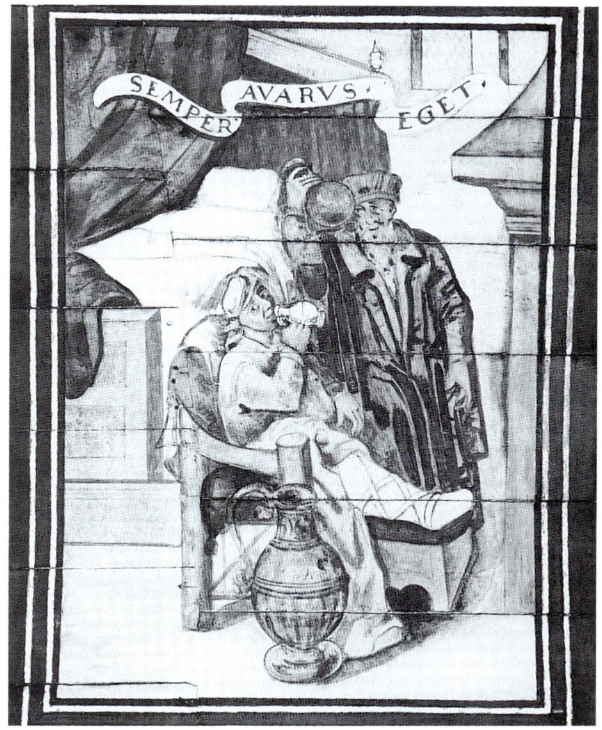

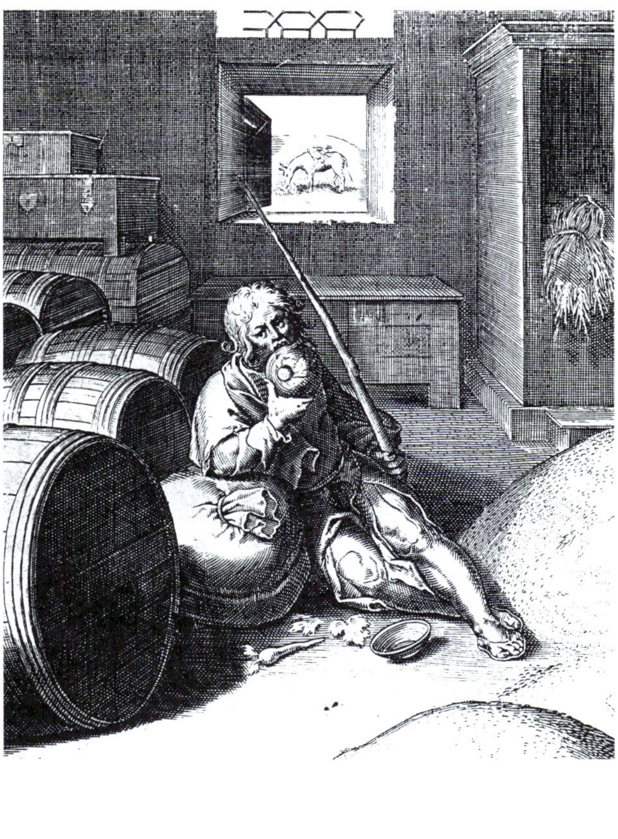

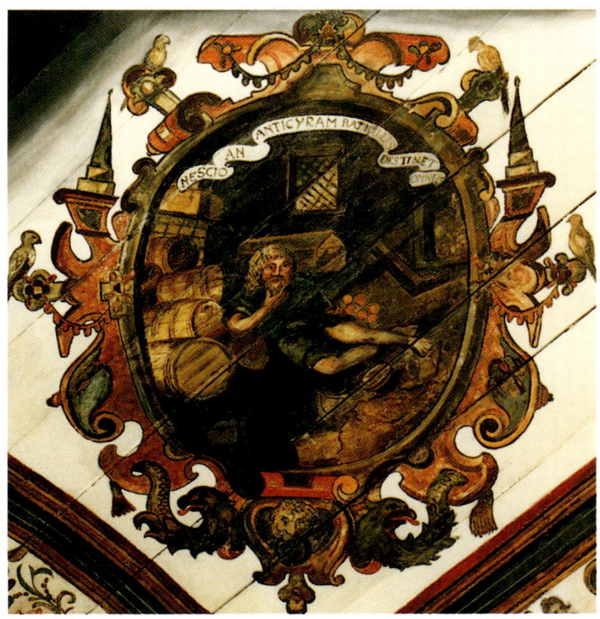

Left: *Vaenius,* Emblemata Horatiana *(1607) p.111 top, and p.131 bottom.* GUL

Top right: *Pinkie House. Emblem copied from Vaenius, 'The greedy man is always in want'.* HS

Bottom right: *Pinkie House. Emblem copied from Vaenius, 'Misers are all madmen'.*

Left: *Vaenius,* Emblemata Horatiana *(1607) p.137 top, and p.143 bottom.* GUL

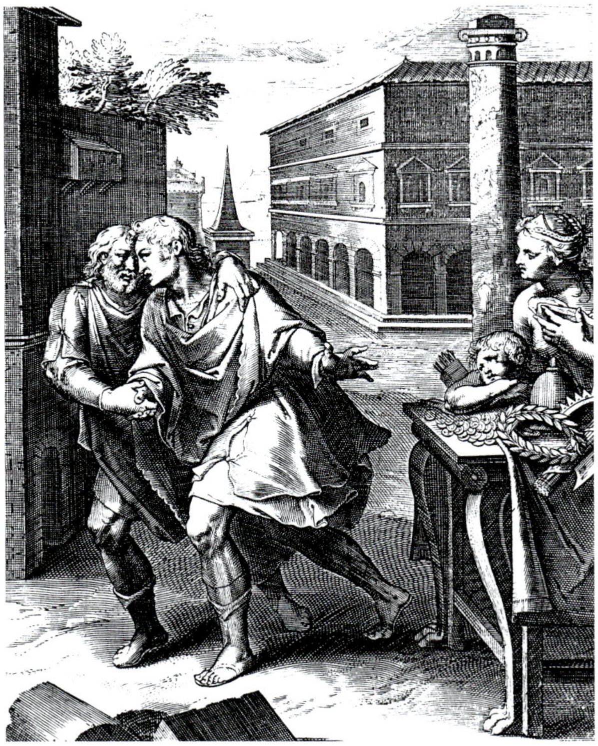

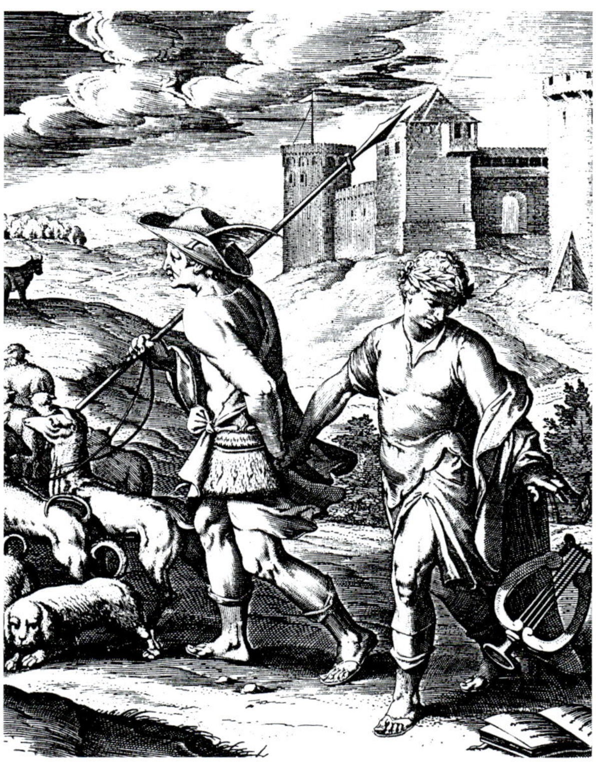

Right: *Pinkie House. Emblems copied from Vaenius, 'Nothing's better than a good friend' top, and 'Firm friendship' bottom.* HS

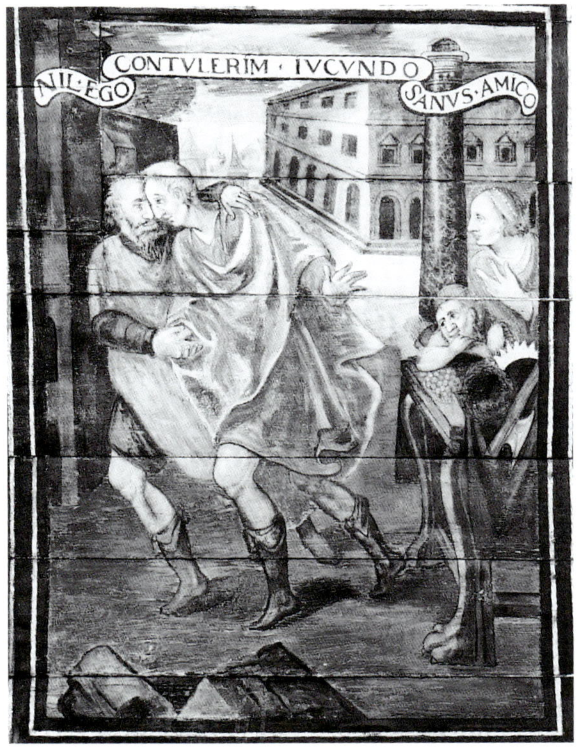

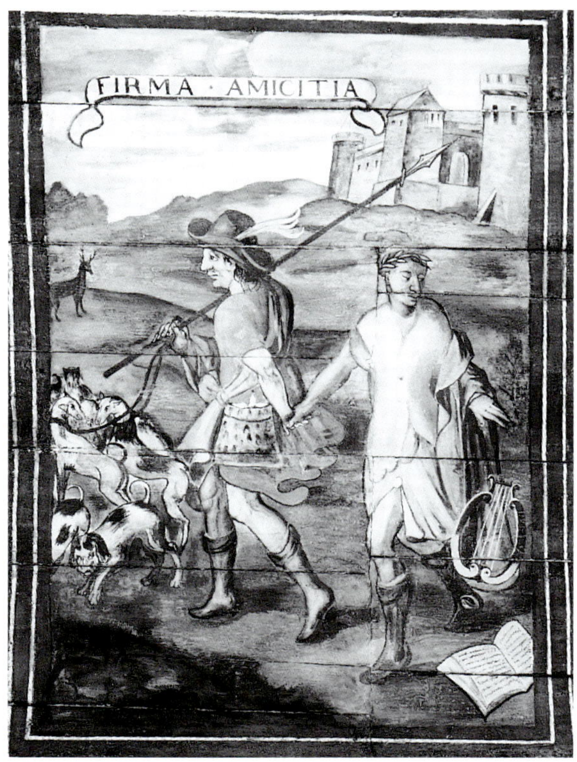

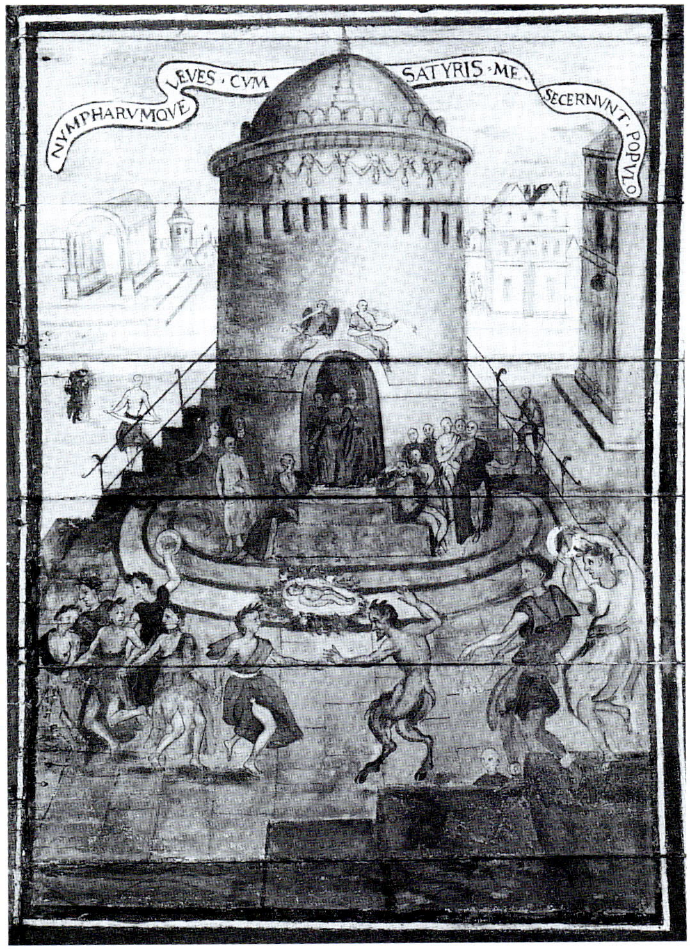

Pinkie House. Unsourced emblem illustrating Horace, 'Nymphs and satyrs entice me away from town'. HS

twin brother Amphion, who preferred music. The emblem is based on Horace's *Epist* 1.18, which recalls that Amphion gave up harping in order to humour his brother and stay friends with him – sibling rivalry abandoned for the sake of brotherly love.

Though these are the only panels that copy Otto Vaenius' Horatian emblems, there are a couple more that use quotations from Horace. *Nympharumque leves cum satyris* [*chori*] *me secernunt populo* is a quotation from *Odes* 1.1.32 and it means 'The nimble chorus of nymphs with their satyrs separate me from other people'. Horace is reflecting on the life of the poet, cut off from ordinary affairs, consorting with gods, and crowned with the ivy of Bacchus; poets are privileged to enjoy an orgy of heightened emotions. The picture at Pinkie shows nymphs and satyrs dancing round a classical temple, within which sits a group of three figures; on its steps lies a naked child. I have not discovered a source for this picture and several of its details are difficult to explain, though the *subscriptio*: *Dignum laude virum musa vetat mori*, is also from Horace (*Odes* 4.8.28) and means 'The muse confers immortality on men worthy of praise'. Maybe Seton's choice of this emblem in praise of poets reflects the fact that he was himself a poet.

The only other panels for which direct sources in printed emblem books have been identified are the roundel at the base of the central cupola with the motto *A teneris adsuesce labori*, and the panels *Pax optima rerum* and *Nullum numen abest si sit prudentia*. These are all closely copied from the *Emblemata* printed in Frankfurt (1596) with verses written by Denis Lebey de Batilly and engravings by Jean Jacques Boissard executed by Theodor de Bry. The book contains sixty-three numbered emblems consisting of engraved motto and picture, with a Latin verse epigram beneath, headed in most cases with a dedication and with a prose essay or commentary on the facing page. Because of the important roles played by artist, author, and engraver in the production of this emblem book it may be listed or catalogued under any one of the three. Lebey de Batilly is an unfamiliar name, but Boissard and de Bry are better known for their collaboration on the engravings for a book of portraits of famous men, *Icones Virorum Illustrium*, and de Bry is well known in England for his engravings in Thomas Heriot's *Report of Virginia* and

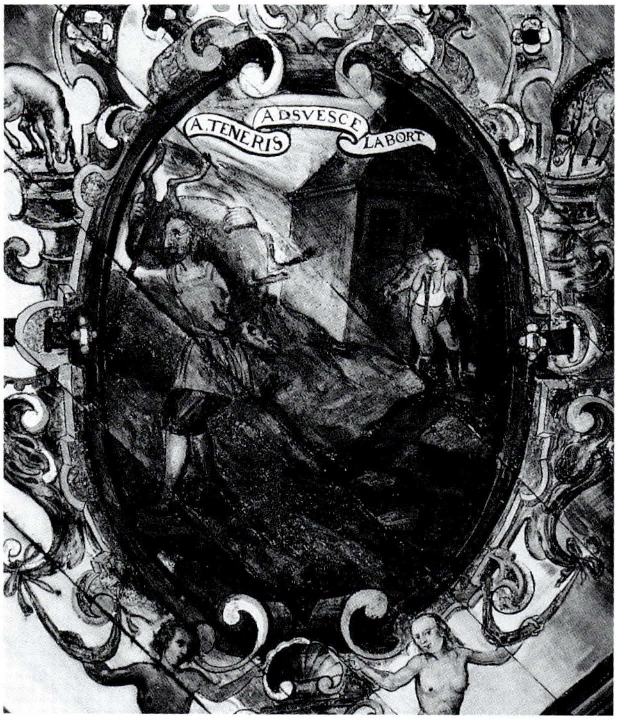

Pinkie House. Emblem from Lebey de Batilly, athlete Milo carries an ox, 'Weight training makes you fit'. HS

his 'Funeral Procession of Sir Philip Sidney'. It should not, therefore, surprise us that an emblem book by the same engraver should have attracted the attention of a man such as Alexander Seton at this date.

Of the three emblems Seton selects for use in his gallery, *A teneris adsuesce labori* means 'Get fit enough for hard work through lighter training', and it shows the classical athlete Milo who trained in his youth by carrying a young calf on his shoulders so that when he was grown up he could carry a full-grown ox. This bit of classical weight training signifies that the strength we need to live satisfactory lives has to be built up gradually. *Nullum numen abest si sit prudentia* ('If prudence is present, no divine power is missing') shows the Roman general Fabius Maximus being offered the fruits of wisdom, peace and plenty at the altar of Bacchus. Fabius Maximus was known as the 'Delayer', since he avoided direct confrontation with his enemy, Hannibal, preferring to weaken him by more prudent delaying tactics. This is what the motto beneath the picture, drawn from

Left: *Pinkie House. Emblem from Lebey de Batilly, Fabius Maximus chooses a prudent peace rather than an impetuous war from the altar of Bacchus.* HS

Right: *Denis Lebey de Batilly,* Emblemata *(1596) no. 32, engraving by J. J. Boissard.* GUL

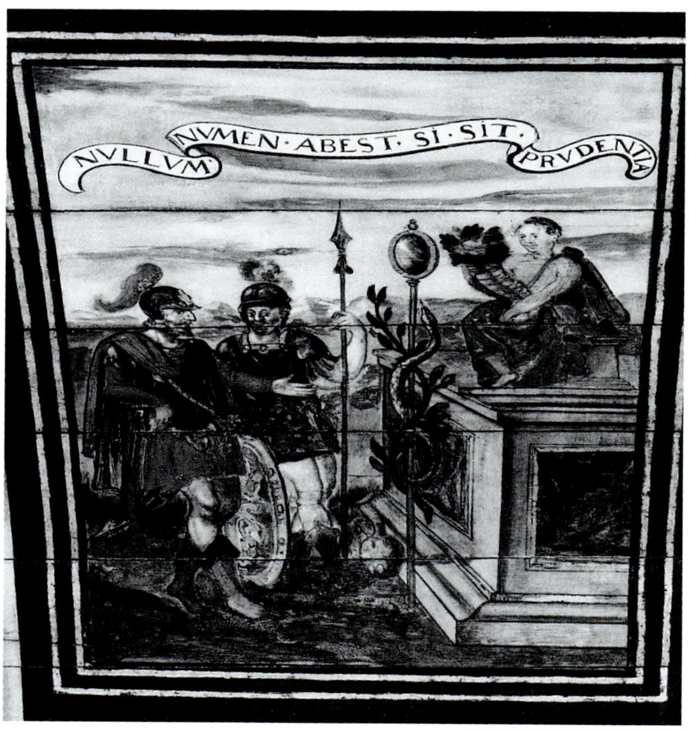

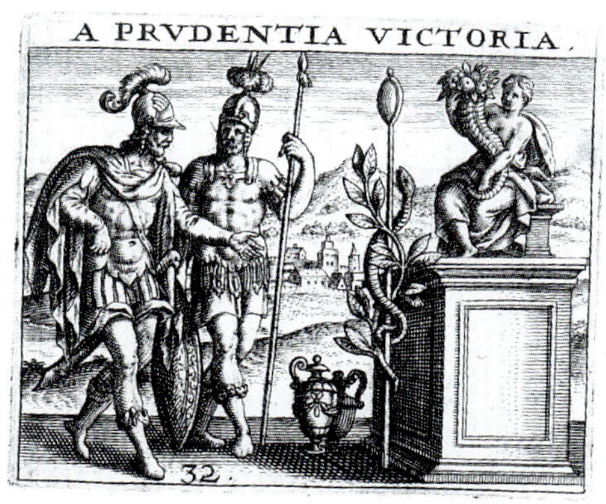

Dionysij Lebei-Batillij Emblemata.

XXXII.

AD IOACHIMVM TINTEVILLANVM.

Sæpe animis etiam in bello Prudentia, sæpe
Acri etiam dextra est, viribus & potior.
Et quæ cum dubiis victoria quæritur armis,
Consilij posita est omnis in arbitrio.

I 3 AD FRAN

Lebey de Batilly's commentary on the emblem, refers to: *Saepe acri potior prudentia dextra* ('Skilful prudence is often better than impetuous bravery'). The emblem *Pax optima rerum* ('Peace is best of all things') has a similar message, and shows us the seated figure of King Cecrops, first king and founder of Athens, who had to choose between Poseidon (shown here with his trident and horse) and Pallas Athena, patron of the arts of peace and civilisation. The gods promised Attica to whichever deity could give the more useful present to the inhabitants; Poseidon struck the ground with his trident, and a horse sprang up; Athena produced the olive tree we see beside her in the picture. Cecrops's choice of Athena as victor becomes an emblem of the superiority of the civilised arts with which the city of Athens has always been identified. As the lower motto puts it: *Pax una triumphis innumeris potior* ('One peace is better than countless victories'). Seton's picture to this emblem copies Boissard's engraving for an emblem with a different motto, *Paci studere praestat quam bello* ('Better to study peace than war'). Seton supplies two new inscriptions, both of which come from a passage cited in Lebey's commentary from Silius Italicus, whose long poem on the Punic wars was a fount of such pithy sayings as

Pax optima rerum
Quas homini novisse datum est, pax una triumphis
Innumeris potior.

Left: *Pinkie House, Musselburgh. Emblem from Lebey de Batilly, king Cecrops of Athens chooses the olives of peace rather than Poseidon's horse, peace rather than war.* HS

Right: *Denis Lebey de Batilly,* Emblemata *(1596) no.28, engraving by J. J. Boissard.* GUL

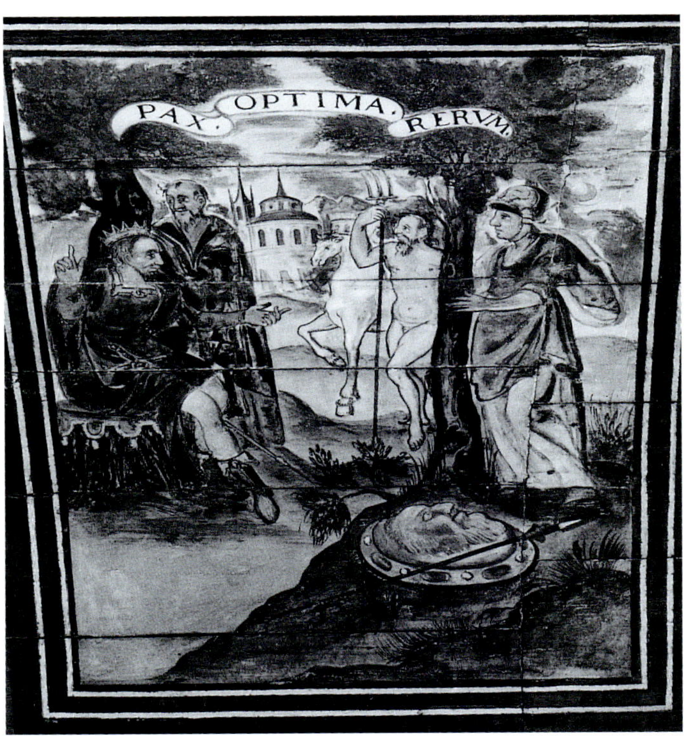

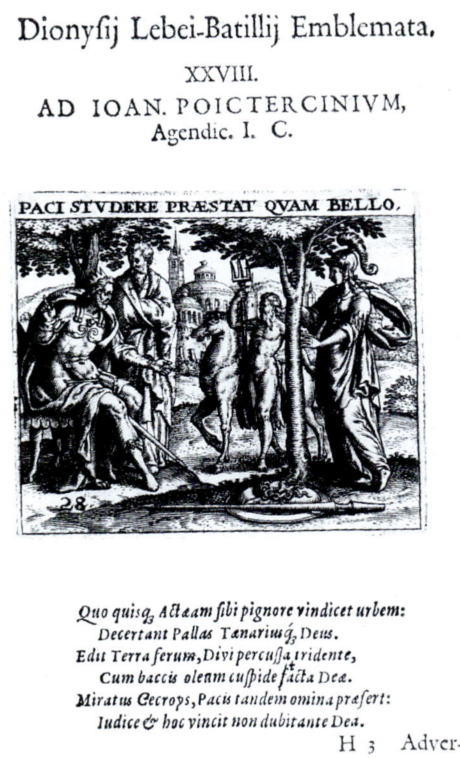
Dionysij Lebei-Batillij Emblemata.

XXVIII.

AD IOAN. POICTERCINIVM, Agendic. I. C.

PACI STVDERE PRÆSTAT QVAM BELLO.

28

Quo quisq; Actæam sibi pignore vindicet urbem:
Decertant Pallas Tænariusq; Deus.
Edit Terra ferum, Divi percussa tridente,
Cum baccis oleam cuspide facta Deæ.
Miratus Cecrops, Pacis tandem omina præfert:
Iudice & hoc vincit non dubitante Dea.

H 3 Adver-

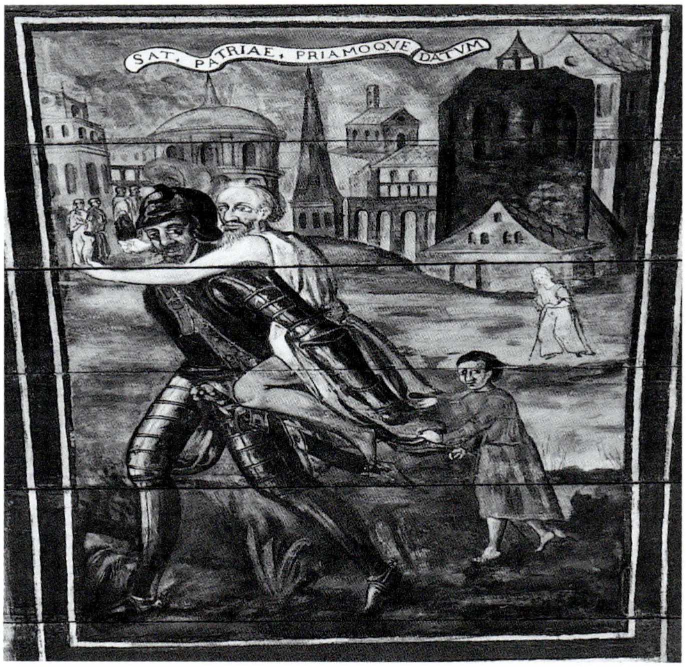

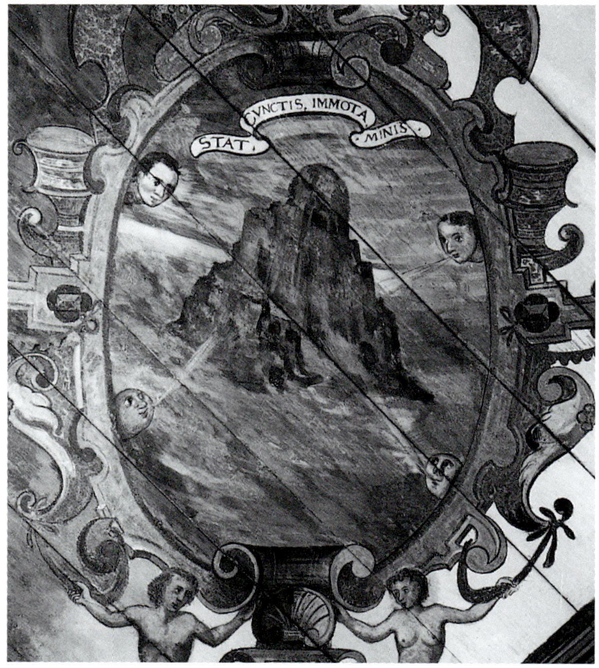

Left: *Pinkie House. Aeneas carries his father away from the burning city of Troy, a well-known emblem topic also found at Culross and at Cullen, though not here copied from any source that has yet been identified.* HS

Right: *Pinkie House. Emblem of fortitude in adversity, of which many versions can be found in emblem books, though no actual source has been found for this example.* HS

It is interesting to note that these same verses provided the inscription which Ben Jonson placed in the Temple of Janus in the highly emblematic triumphal arches which greeted King James on his procession into London in 1604, which Graham Parry rightly describes as 'a towering mass of classical scholarship to honour the scholar-king' (Parry 1981, p.18). The arch at Temple Bar in 1604 showed Irene, or Peace, triumphing over the 'groveling' figure of Mars, 'his armour scattered upon him in several pieces, and sundry sorts of weapons broken about him'. Her word to all was 'UNA TRIUMPHIS INNUMERIS POTIOR' (Jonson, *Works*, vol. vii, p.97). In 1604 this iconography, which had been designed for the king's English coronation procession of the previous year but which had to be postponed because of an outbreak of plague in London, centred on James's favoured persona of *rex pacificus*, and the Temple Bar arch with its gates of brass surmounted by the statue of Janus was at the symbolic heart of this programme – a British recreation of the famous Temple of Janus, which stood in the Forum, whose two doors were kept shut in times of peace but opened in time of war. It would be rash to claim that Alexander Seton's substitution of this motto, which is taken from Silius Italicus's poem on the traditional rivalry between Rome and Carthage, was a deliberate recall or reminiscence of its use in London. However, the emblems of peace are certainly meant to recall the situation of Seton's house, on the site of the last battle to be fought between the English and the Scots when, in 1547, Protector Somerset routed the Scots army in the Battle of Pinkie. These emblems thus confirm what various other inscriptions on Seton's house appear to be saying, namely that the Earl of Dunfermline built his *villa suburbana* on this site as a way of showing that the arts of peace and of humane studies had reached Scotland and that, with the accession of a Scottish king to the English throne in a union of the crowns, the ancient enmities between the two kingdoms had come to an end. And the fact that Alexander Seton had presided over the legal process which had effected that union would make it highly appropriate for him to adapt the emblem from Lebey de Batilly in such a way as to recall one of the

Pinkie House. The pilot of the Argonauts steers the ship propelled by goddess Fortuna's sails, 'Let Tiphys be Virtue'. HS

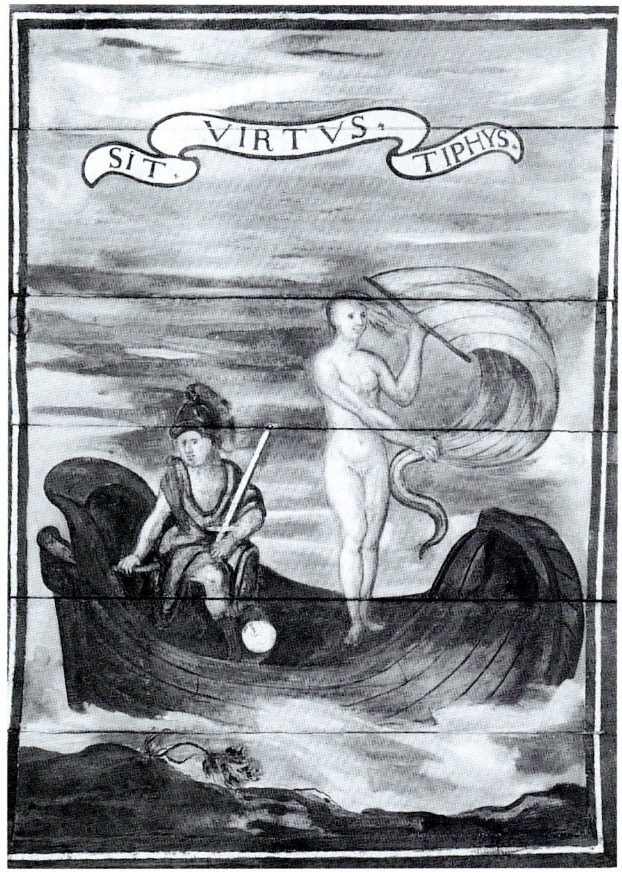

many inscriptions that had signalled James VI and I's role as *rex pacificus* in his delayed coronation entry of a dozen years earlier. Given his responsibilities and his scholarly interests, it is surely inconceivable that Seton would not have been familiar with the iconography and informing ideology of this celebrated entry. The iconography of the Stuart court has attracted an enormous amount of scholarly attention in recent years, but it is probably time to insist that this iconography had a Scottish dimension.

Printed emblem books have not been identified as sources for any of the remaining emblems on the ceiling, though analogues can be found for several of them. *Sat patriae Priamo datum* ('Enough has been done for country and for Priam') quotes Virgil, *Aeneid* 2.201, and shows Aeneas carrying his father Anchises away from the burning city of Troy, with his son Ascanius clinging to his coat-tails. This was a well-known emblem of filial piety which we have already encountered at Culross (*cf* Alciato, *Pietas filiorum in parentes*). The circular emblem at the foot of the central cupola showing a rock assailed by winds and waves is a widely used emblem of fortitude in adversity; the motto, *Stat cunctis immota minis,* means 'It stands unmoved amidst all that threatens'; and the second inscription in a separate cartouche, *Ad laeta et aspera pariter nati sumus nisi pari utraque animo excipiamus inutiles sumus,* means that we shan't achieve very much unless we can accept whatever life sends us, happiness and hardship alike. Whitney has a version of this emblem and it was later to be used in William Marshall's famous *Eikon Basilike* frontispiece, but the Pinkie image is closer to the way it is pictured in Luca Contile's *Ragionamento sopra la proprietà delle Imprese* (Padua: Bartoli 1574).

The emblem showing the naked figure of Fortuna, or Occasio, in the prow of a ship with a male figure dressed in red sitting at the tiller holding a sceptre, has an interesting relationship to various printed sources. The Pinkie motto *Sit virtus Tiphys* ('Let Tiphys be Virtue') identifies the man sitting in the boat as the famous pilot of the Argonauts who holds the rudder in one hand whilst the goddess Fortuna spreads her sail in the prow of the vessel. The moral is that virtuous men can control their own fortune, as the second motto explains: *Cuique mores fortunam fingunt sui* ('Each

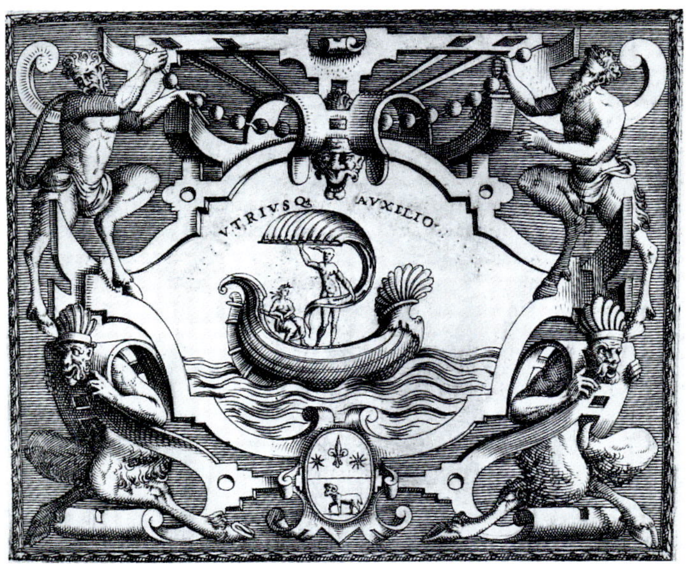

Girolamo Ruscelli, Imprese Illustri *(1566) p.517.* GUL

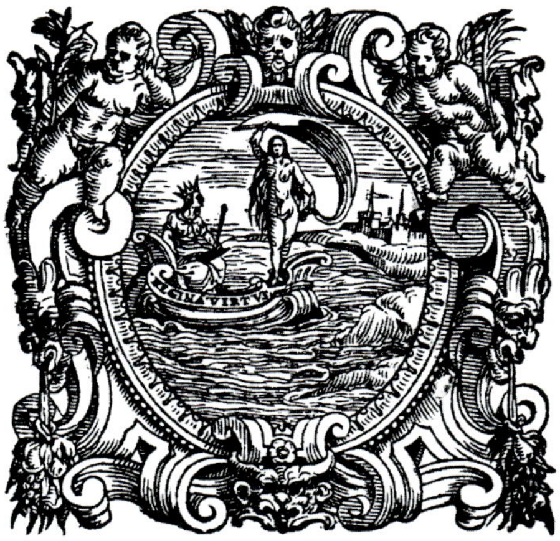

Printer's mark used in 1570s by the de'Franceschi printers in Venice. GUL

man's conduct shapes his own fortune'). This image goes back to an emblem Girolamo Ruscelli included in his *Imprese Illustri* (Venice 1566, p.517) as the *impresa* of Girolamo Giraldi, with the motto *Utriusque auxilio* ('In support of each other'). Ruscelli's picture shows a ship with two female figures; Virtus sits at the tiller in the same position as Pinkie's figure of Tiphys, and Fortuna stands at the prow with her sail, in exactly the same position as she is shown in the Pinkie emblem. The shape of the boat with curved prow and stern leaves little doubt that this was the source of the image at Pinkie. Ruscelli's commentary explains that the *impresa* illustrates the moral that Virtue cannot achieve its worthy ends unless the winds of fortune are favourable. The emblem was inspired by a number of Latin proverbs which suggest the control which a 'virtuous' man has over his own destiny, such as the Ciceronian adage, which Ruscelli cites, *Virtute duce comite Fortuna* ('Where Virtue leads, Fortune follows', from *Epist ad Fam* 10.3) or Ovid's adage, *Rara quidem virtus quam non fortuna gubernat* ('Rare indeed is the virtue that fortune does not steer'). Alciato had already used a version of this adage for his emblem under the motto *Virtute Fortuna comes* ('Fortune follows Virtue') though with a quite different picture – Mercury's caduceus entwined with two cornucopias (an image copied on the emblematic ceiling at Rossend).

Much closer to the *impresa* in Ruscelli is an Italian printer's mark used by Domenico and Pietro de'Franceschi in the 1570s. The motto which appears on some, though not all, versions of Pietro de'Francheschi's mark is *Ducibus his prospera quaeque* ('With these leaders all good fortune follows'); the printer's mark shows a crowned female personification of Virtus sitting at the tiller holding a sceptre; her identity is established by the label 'REGINA VIRTUS' inscribed along the gunwale of the ship. One version of the mark also has the motto 'VIRTUS ET/FORTUNA' on either side of the picture. The printer's mark copies Ruscelli's picture too closely for us to say which of the two might have been Seton's immediate source, though Pietro de'Franceschi printed books in the 1570s on subjects very likely to appeal to a man of Seton's tastes. In 1574, for instance, he issued an edition of Ariosto; in 1575 this mark appeared on his edition of *I Commentari di C Giulio Cesare* with illustrations by Andrea Palladio, and in 1570 he produced the first edition of one of the most famous works in the history of European architecture, Palladio's *I Quattro Libri dell'Architettura.* There is no way of knowing which of these books Seton might have owned, though his interest in architecture makes the possibility that the emblem might go back to the frontispiece to Palladio's *Architettura* somewhat attractive. That frontispiece uses a version of the printer's device without the 'REGINA VIRTUS' inscription on the hull of the ship; instead it promotes the figure of Virtus to a position of some prominence sitting on the recessed entablature between the broken pediments with her identifying label and an open book. This, and the device of Fortuna's ship, are no longer functioning as a simple printer's device, but rather as the title page of the book which follows, whose 'mind' they now express. Could it be that Seton, on recognising this device as an expression of Palladio's intentions for his book on architecture, determined to adapt it in order

Pinkie House. The lion of strength with the serpent of wisdom, 'How well they go together!'

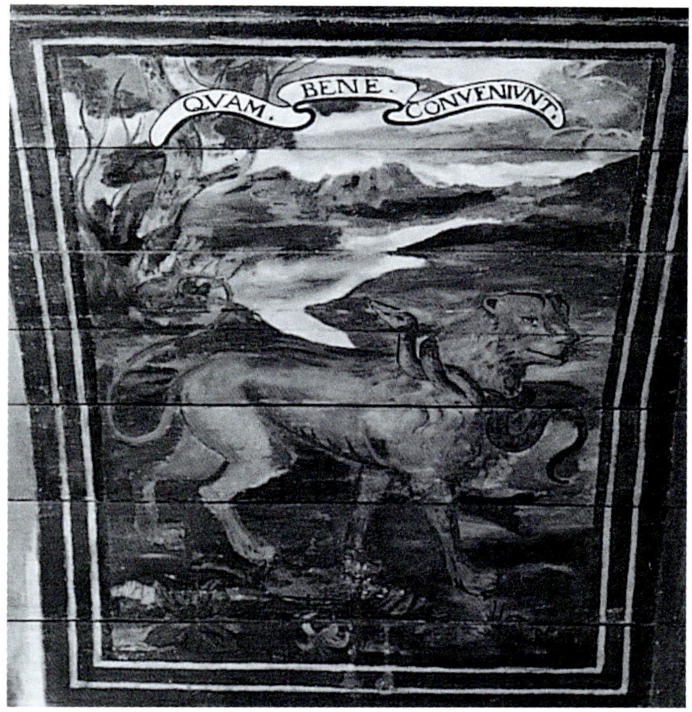

to serve as a declaration of his own architectural aspirations on his ceiling? Such an adaptation – in the interests of his own self-fashioning – would be entirely in keeping with the other adaptations of his sources on this ceiling.

Alexander Seton's substitution (and I think it probably was Seton and not any intermediate source) of the figure of Tiphys for that of Virtus also deserves some investigation. Perhaps the first thing to recognise is that the new motto, 'Let Tiphys be Virtue', refers to this very substitution. The new motto is notably self-reflexive; indeed it would only be intelligible to a reader who had prior knowledge of the source on which it is based. What motivated this substitution? Tiphys, as we have noted, was the pilot who steered the ship commanded by Jason on his heroic quest to recover the golden fleece. He does not figure in Renaissance iconologies and his presence in the Pinkie emblem would not carry any immediately recognisable meaning for viewers of the ceiling. It may be relevant, however, that the most celebrated Stoic long gallery to be decorated with emblems at this period apparently included an emblem of Tiphys, for John Aubrey tells us that there was an emblem of Tiphys in Francis Bacon's gallery at Gorhambury (1962, p.123).

Many of the emblems discussed above are what were known as 'historical emblems', emblems that expounded the moral of some famous story or action. In every case the appropriateness of the Latin inscriptions to the picture can only be accurately construed by a viewer who is familiar with the classical sources for the historical events depicted. These are functioning as illustrative historical commonplaces or *topoi*, which is why it makes sense to describe them as rhetorical. But conventionally emblems also found moral significance in objects from the natural world of plants and animals. This is what we see in the gallery at Pinkie with *Quam bene conveniunt* ('How well they go together!') – a lion in a landscape with a snake curled round its neck. This device is found in a number of emblem books; the lion signifies strength and the snake prudence or wisdom, and the moral is that a ruler should use his powers prudently (eg Camerarius 1595, no. 6; Ruscelli 1566, p.401).

Among the other animal emblems is the beautiful white stag with golden antlers and collar with the inscription *Libertas*. The collared stag usually recalls a

Girolamo Ruscelli, Imprese Illustri *(1566) p.401.* GUL

401

ALBERTO

BADOERO.

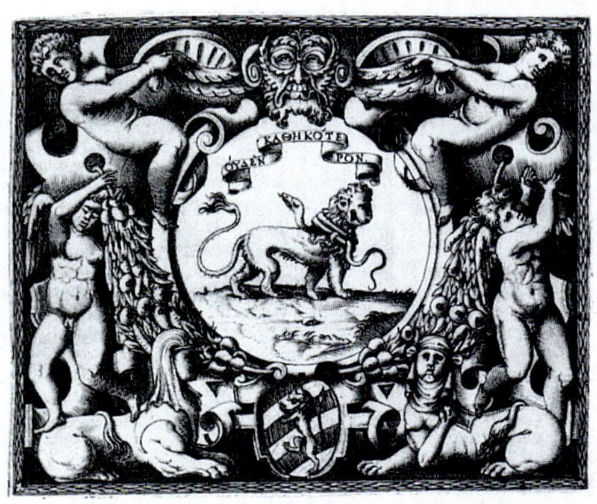

IL LEONE NON SOLAMENTE DAI Poeti, ma ancora nelle sacre lettere si truoua spesso posto per la fortezza, & il Serpe per la prudentia, com'è accaduto di ricordar'ancor nel precedẽte foglio all'Impresa di Sforza Pallauicino, & del Duca di Terra nuoua. Là onde per interpretatione di questa Impresa si potrebbe considerare, che l'Autor suo auendo posto il Serpe auolto al collo del Leone, voglia per auentura mostrare à qualche nemico suo, che se forse esso nemico procura, ò disegna d'usar contra di lui qual si voglia sorte di forza, ò di uiolenza, come sarebbe offenderlo, ò farlo offender con arme, ò per altra sì fatta uia, egli all'incontro con la prudentia sua era per auolgerlo, & legarlo in modo, che ne lo faria rimaner vinto senz'alcun dubbio, sì come col Motto dell'Impresa si fa intendere, dicendo,

ΟὙΔΈΝ ΚΑΘΗΚΌΤΕΡΟΝ. che in Latino direbbono,

EEE

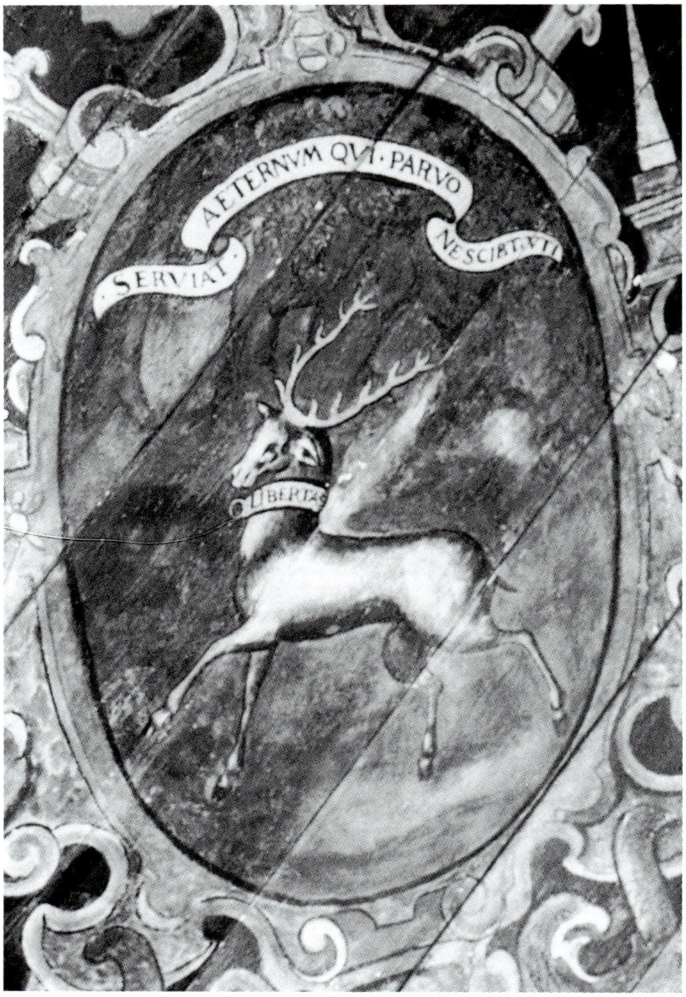

Pinkie House. Collared stag illustrating Aesop's fable of the horse and stag, with motto quoting Horace's version of the legend: 'Frugal freedom is better than affluent slavery.' Trevor Graham

legend of a famous king or emperor recapturing a miraculous stag whose collar recorded that it belonged to Caesar, and prohibited its killing (Bath 1992, pp.23-60). However the emblem at Pinkie goes back to other roots since the motto *Serviat eternum qui parvo nesciat uti* ('He will be a slave for ever, who doesn't know how to make do with little') again goes back to Horace (*Epist* 1.10.41). It is impossible for anyone to understand this emblem without knowing the rest of Horace's poem, which praises the simplicity of country life for which you have to be willing to give up the sophistications of town. It is in this context that Horace cites a fable from Aesop about the horse and the stag that the Pinkie emblem illustrates. Aesop tells how a stag struggled with a horse for the possession of some common pasture; the stag always got the better of it until the horse sought human help to drive the stag out of the pasture; but though the stag lost the pasture the horse lost its independence, since for ever after the man insisted on bridling it and riding it. Poverty with freedom is better than affluent slavery. Although this picture does not look like an illustration to the fable – it shows neither the horse, nor the man with the bridle – its motto is only intelligible to a viewer who recognises the Aesopic fable to which it alludes and, again, its emphasis is on the Stoic qualities of self-reliance and frugality.

The last of the animal emblems is in the oriel window bay dominating the end of the gallery. Both Greek inscriptions go back to a Homeric adage which means 'Do not sleep the whole night through' (*Iliad* 2.24) and they are here associated with an emblem of the vigilant crane, a widely used motif in emblem books where it moralised classical and bestiary descriptions of the crane, a sociable species that placed sentry-birds on duty at night to protect the sleeping flock. The sentry-bird kept itself awake by holding a stone in its outstretched claw; if it became drowsy the clatter of the falling stone would wake it up. This is what the picture shows. Vigilance was traditionally the leading quality required of kings and magistrates. The only place known to me where this Greek motto is associated with the vigilant crane is in a well-known emblem book by the Hungarian scholar Ioannes Sambucus, which shows Alexander the Great dozing on his imperial throne and holding a stone in his hand which he holds outstretched

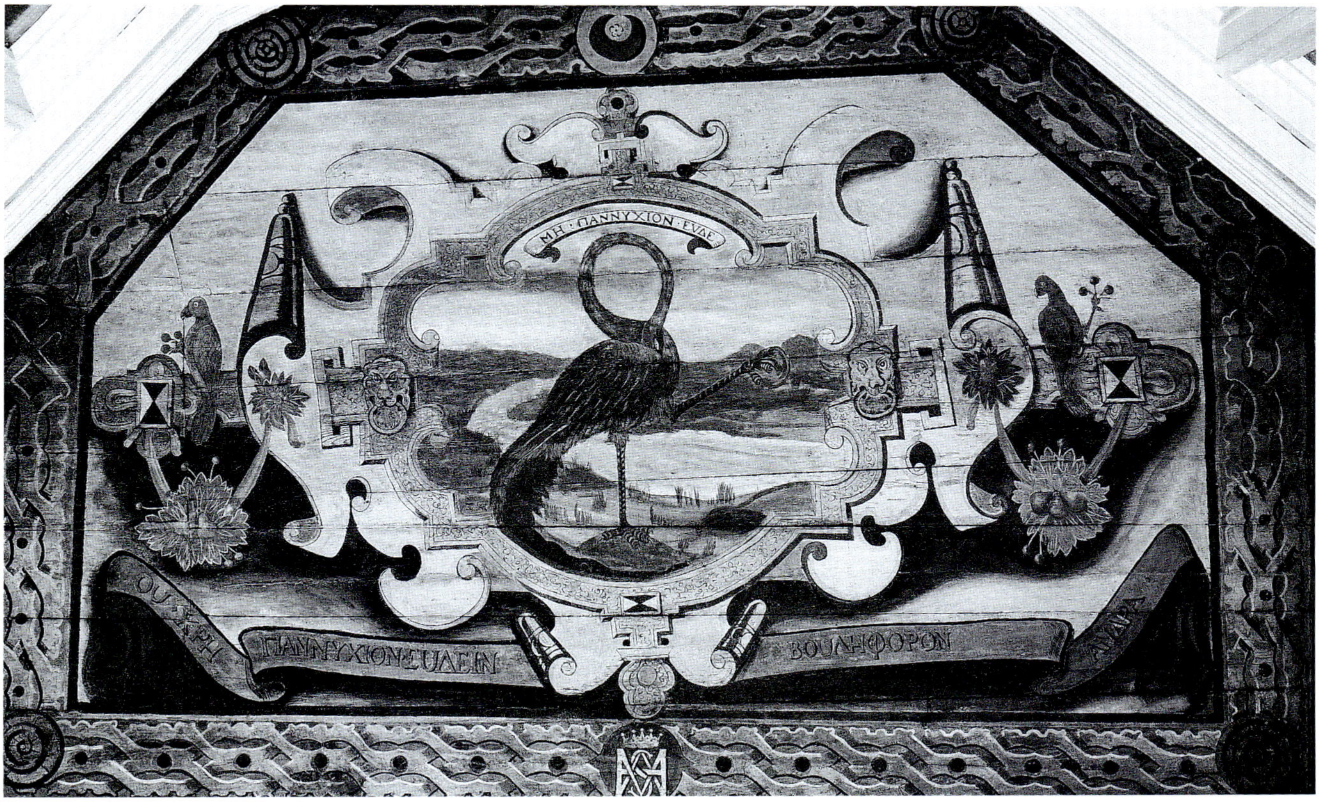

Pinkie House. Emblem making use of the commonplace image of the vigilant crane, with Homeric adage: 'Do not sleep the whole night through.' HS

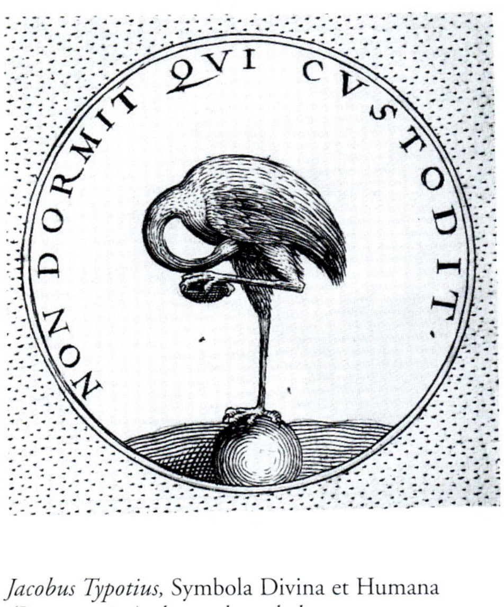

Jacobus Typotius, Symbola Divina et Humana *(Prague, 1600) pl. 47, the only known source showing the vigilant crane, as at Pinkie, with its head tucked under its wing.* GUL

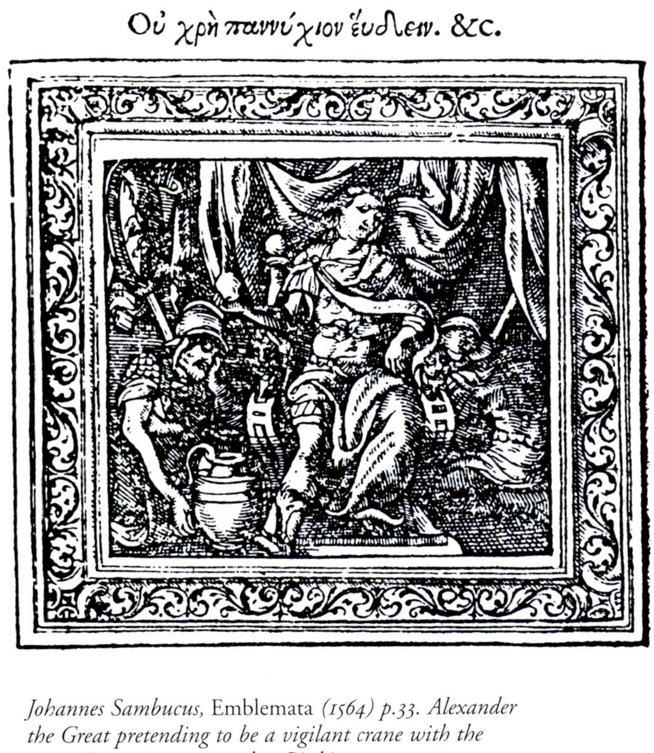

Johannes Sambucus, Emblemata *(1564) p.33. Alexander the Great pretending to be a vigilant crane with the same Homeric motto used at Pinkie.* GUL

over a brass urn; an emblem of civic vigilance whose moral was clearly appropriate to Seton's own public position and responsibilities.

The description above does not by any means exhaust the ways in which the emblems exploit the established semiotics of the Renaissance emblem format, but it should be clear enough that the classicism of such a ceiling is informed by a scholarly *humanitas* which is being used in the service of some kind of ideological self-fashioning. Why should Alexander Seton have sought to give such a strong neo-Stoic emphasis to his gallery of emblems? One reason may have been the need for some accommodation between his Catholicism and the outward profession of Protestant faith his public position required. He had, after all, been educated by the Jesuits but had witnessed the Protestant Reformation in Scotland. We also know that after his return from the continent his Protestantism had been questioned; indeed, his nineteenth-century biographer cites a letter written in 1605 to the General of the Jesuit order, which makes it plain that despite his outward conformity Seton remained a crypto-Catholic:

> He is a Catholic, as is also the Lord President and the Royal Advocate. In political wisdom, in learning, in high birth, wealth and authority, he possesses far more influence than the rest, and his power is universally acknowledged. But he publicly professes the state religion, rendering external obedience to the King and ministers, and goes occasionally, though rarely, to the sermons, sometimes to their heretical communion. (Quoted in Seton 1896, vol. ii, p.466).

Vaenius' emblems were intended to illustrate the major tenets of Stoic philosophy – the context for his book of Horatian emblems was the neo-Stoicism of Justus Lipsius, whose *Manductio ad Philosophiam Stoicam* (1604) is cited at the end of Vaenius' introduction. Leonard Forster has persuasively argued that the neo-Stoicism of Lipsius was addressed to humanist readers who desired a public code of ethics which, while generally compatible with Christian doctrine, remained untainted by the controversies which divided the warring Christian sects (1981, pp.117-28). Such a philosophy would well suit the public self-fashioning of a man like Seton, whose family had been strongly identified with Mary of Guise, Mary, Queen of Scots and was suspected of Catholicism throughout the latter half of the sixteenth century. Such a rigorous code of doctrinally neutral ethics, with its strongly classical bias, would be well adapted to define this Scottish nobleman's determination to show how his buildings, indeed his whole mentality, participated in a wider European Renaissance *humanitas.*

A different, though entirely compatible, way of accounting for the neo-Stoic emphasis of this gallery, however, would be to stress its architectural status as a Renaissance long gallery. In the 'Classical Postscript' to her authoritative study of the English long gallery, Rosalys Coope notes:

> In his description of Nonsuch written at the end of the seventeenth century Anthony Watson declared that the gallery was comparable with the best of the 'Greek galleries'. Evidently he was expressing the idea that galleries were

> continuing – or reviving – the tradition of the antique Stoa, ambulatory or *porticus*. (1986, p.57)

She ends: 'How far Watson's ideas about "Greek galleries" were prevalent in sixteenth-century England would be a question worth pursuing.' Alexander Seton's subject matter and choice of sources lends weight to the belief that at least one of the available models for the Renaissance long gallery was the Athenian *Stoa poikile* or 'painted gallery'. Stoicism had its origins in and took its name from this gallery attached to the Agora at Athens, where the philosopher Zeno did his teaching. He was assisted in teaching by the historical and moral paintings executed on the walls of the gallery by the artist Polygnotus, whom Aristotle describes as 'the ethic painter'. Any humanist of Seton's generation would have known of the origins of Stoicism in such a gallery, which is described in Pliny, *Hist Nat* 35.59; Pausanias 1.15; and Diogenes Laertius 7.5. The belief that the paintings in the gallery were panel paintings and not frescoes was encouraged by a reference in the letters of Synesius (fourth century AD) complaining that there was nothing left in Athens for tourists to admire, since the panels which decorated the Painted Gallery had been removed (Synesius 1926, p.229). This may be why Seton's emblems in the gallery at Pinkie are shown in *trompe l'oeil* frames. Synesius's letters were first printed by Aldus in 1499 with further editions, Paris 1553, 1605; by the time Seton built his gallery he could have found various modern descriptions of the *stoa poikile*, in Lipsius for instance.

That Watson's ideas about 'Greek galleries' were more widely prevalent is suggested by a claim made in the mid-seventeenth century about the classical provenance of these very Horatian emblems. In 1646 Marin le Roy, Sieur de Gomberville, published his plagiarised edition of Vaenius' Horatian emblems under the title *La Doctrine des Moeurs*. The book reproduces all of Vaenius' copperplates in newly engraved reverse copies by Pierre Daret with commentaries on each emblem by de Gomberville. However, in his preface de Gomberville claims that the copperplate engravings in his volume, which copy Vaenius' originals very closely and without acknowledgement, were produced from the actual bronze tablets which had decorated the original *Stoa*

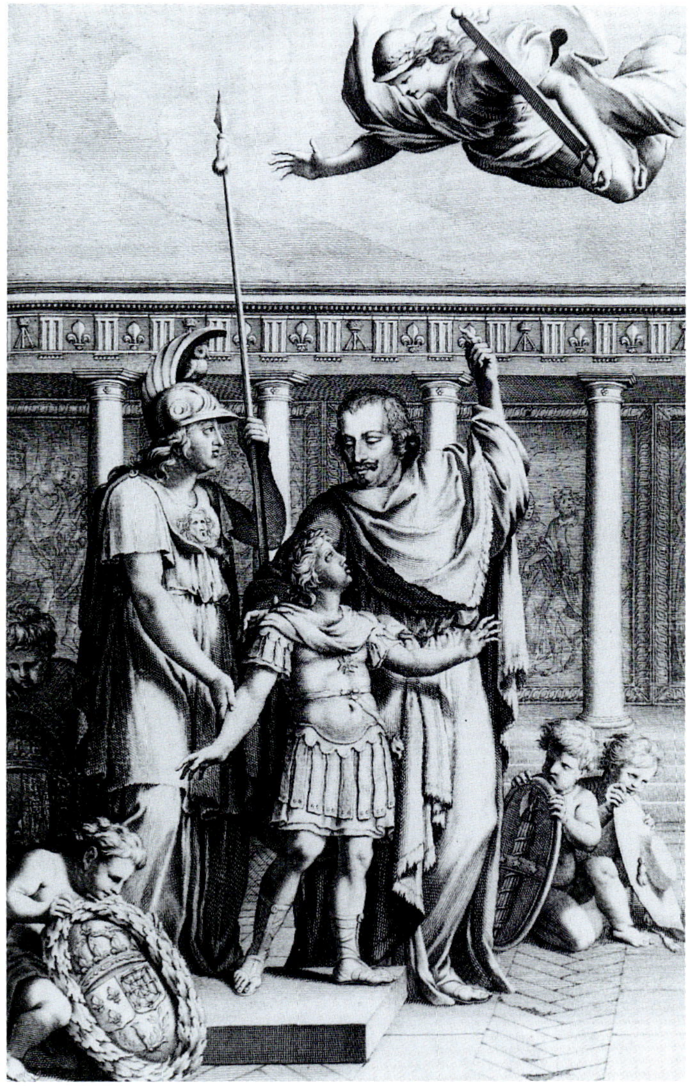

Marin le Roy, Sieur de Gomberville, La Doctrine des Moeurs *(1646) frontispiece showing Louis XIV being instructed in the Stoic painted gallery.* GUL

Poikile in Athens which, he says, an ingenious traveller had recently brought back as genuine antiquities from Greece. A frontispiece to the book shows the young prince Louis XIV being instructed by Wisdom and Virtue in front of a colonnaded gallery or loggia, in which hang pictures resembling those which make up the emblems in the book that follows. This is evidently Pierre Daret's rendering of the Athenian *Stoa*.

I have no evidence that either Vaenius or his earliest readers regarded these pictures as authentic copies of the antique *Stoa*; however the Athenian *Stoa* always seems to have been conceived as a colonnaded portico or loggia, and the arched, vaulted and corbelled partitions into which Seton's gallery is divided may have been meant to represent the series of vaulted recesses within which the antique images of a painted Stoic *moralitas* were traditionally hung. The fact that the emblematic *picturae* in the long gallery at Pinkie are shown in *trompe l'oeil* frames – complete with illusionist eye-hooks and nails – only reinforces this impression. De Gomberville presented his work as a book of instructions or *speculum principis* for the young Prince Louis, future Louis XIV of France. Seton's gallery was also the product of a court culture whose king himself wrote a conduct book, to which he gave a Greek name, *Basilicon Doron*, or 'The King's Gift', addressed to his infant son, Prince Henry. It is worth recalling that James' own education had been presided over for twelve years (1570-82) by George Buchanan who propagated the ideal of the Stoic King (*rex stoicus*) in his political writings and was himself dubbed 'a stoik philosopher' by his contemporaries. James' own advice to his son, which has been shown to reflect Buchanan's teaching, was itself turned into emblems in the early seventeenth century by the English emblematist and apologist for the visual arts, Henry Peacham. In a series of illuminated manuscripts to be found in the British Library the king's moralising instructions are fleshed out with vividly coloured allegorical and emblematic pictures, using Ripa and other sources, and are themselves translated into moralising Latin distichs (Peacham 1998). Seton had been entrusted with the upbringing of the infant Prince Charles in the early years of the century, and though there is no question that his long gallery was designed for the instruction of the prince, who had left Seton's charge long before 1613, the memory of his role as guardian of the future monarch might have influenced the conventions which led him to illustrate his gallery with Stoic emblems suitable for the education of kings and magistrates.

Seton's 'painted gallery' at Pinkie was not the only Renaissance long gallery to have been decorated with moral emblems and Stoic *sententiae*, for the famous gallery constructed by Sir Nicholas Bacon at Gorhambury, which Francis Bacon inherited, was also decorated with Latin *adagia* drawn from the writings of Seneca (see McCutcheon 1977). Though none of the manuscripts describing the gallery makes specific mention of the Athenian *Stoa* as its model, the inscriptions leave us in no doubt that the gallery was designed to illustrate the tenets of Stoic morality. Moreover we know from the short description in Aubrey's *Brief Lives* that the gallery also contained 'curious pictures, all Emblematicall, with Motto's under each' and animals and plants which might serve 'as Topiques for Locall memorie' (Aubrey 1962, p.123). It is not known whether Seton visited Gorhambury during his extended visit to London, 1604-5, but it was Bacon who drew up on the English side the proposals for the Union of the Crowns laid before the Commission over which Seton presided.

The combination of inscriptions and emblematic devices in the architectural vocabulary of Scottish builders at this period suggests that the context for the emblems as we find them on the long gallery ceiling also includes, as we shall see later, monumental carving on the external surfaces of buildings. Indeed the ceiling uses Roman majuscule lettering for all its inscriptions, and those functioning as *subscriptiones* to the actual emblems are indistinguishable in style or format from the further Latin inscriptions on the same ceiling – in the vaulted partitions at either end of the gallery and in the cartouches beneath the central cupola – which lack any accompanying *pictura*. The inscriptions in the two vaults nearest the oriel window, for instance, read: *Vir bonus patriam amat non quia dives aut opulenta sed quia sua. Sic Ulysses ad Ithacae saxa non minori studio contendit quam Agamemnon ad nobiles Mycaenarum muros* ('A good man loves his country not because it is rich or opulent, but because it is his own. Thus Ulysses hastened to the rocks of Ithaca with no less zeal than Agamemnon rushed to the mighty walls of Mycenae'); *Curandum magis ut laete quam ut late habitemus. Saepe in palatiis labor et dolor in tuguriis quies et gaudium habitant* ('We should care more about living in happy than in spacious dwellings; often travail and sorrow dwell in palaces, peace and joy in cottages'). The pretence that Seton's buildings are modest country dwellings is, of course, conventional, using the same modesty topos as Ben Jonson invokes in 'To Penshurst'.

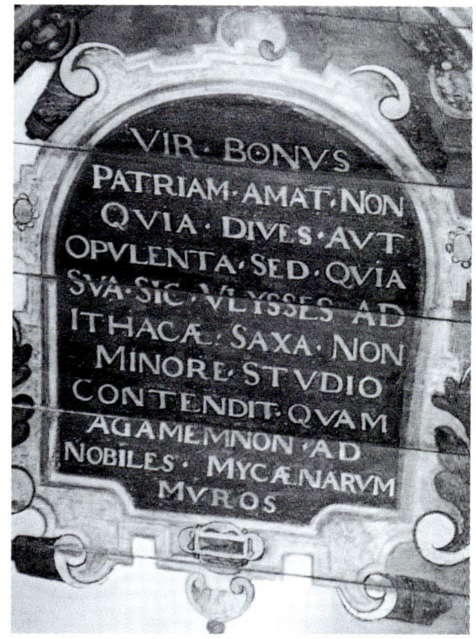

Classical epigraphy; the inscriptions in Seton's long gallery at Pinkie use Roman capitals that are stylistically of a piece with the carved inscriptions on the external face of the building. The relationship between epigraphy and emblem in the Renaissance was particularly close.

The conformity of the two kinds of device suggests that this decorative vocabulary made little distinction between *emblema* as a bimedial form of speaking picture, on the model of Alciato's *Emblematum liber*, and *emblema* in the older sense, which the term had in classical rhetoric, as the name for a sententious inscription or rhetorical commonplace inserted into a speech. The collection of antique inscriptions was a long-established preoccupation of humanist scholarship and its application to modern buildings has to be seen as one aspect of their neoclassicism, a sign of the owner's erudition and association with the ideals of humanist education. Indeed it is in precisely such a stone inscription that we find the clearest statement of the humanist ideals that informed all of Alexander Seton's buildings. It is preserved on what his biographer George Seton describes as 'two slabs, each about three by four feet, which lay detached at Pinkie for many years, and were built into the garden wall, by Sir John Hope, in 1884' (Seton 1896, p.822). Since this carving appears to record the motivation behind all of Seton's architectural activities, it will repay close attention. In translation it reads as follows:

> For his own pleasure, and that of his noble descendants and all men of cultivation and urbanity (*humanis urbanisque*), Alexander Seton, who above all loves every kind of culture and urbanity, has planted, raised and decorated a country-

> house, gardens and suburban buildings (*suburbana aedificia*). There is nothing here to do with warfare; not even a ditch or rampart to repel enemies, but in order to welcome guests with kindness and treat them with benevolence, a fountain of pure water, a grove, pools, and other things that may add to the pleasures of the place. He has brought everything together that might afford decent pleasures of heart and mind. But he declares that whoever shall destroy this by theft, sword or fire, or behaves in a hostile manner, is a man devoid of generosity and urbanity, indeed of all culture (*humanitas*), and is an enemy of the human race. The sacred stones will speak and proclaim it.
>
> To the greatest and best God, creator, dispenser and protector of all things, Jehovah Stator, whose will and benefits assure us in the possession of all gifts, honour and glory, praise and thanks.

Seton describes his building as *suburbanus*, which means 'close to the city' (in classical Latin, always Rome – Pinkie is about five miles from Edinburgh), and almost certainly alludes to Pliny the Younger's description in a letter to Caninus Rufus (I.3) of his house out-of-town (*suburbanum*) where it is always spring and where he retreats from the tiresome duties of the city. 'Create something,' Pliny writes, 'Perfect it to be yours for all time, for everything else you possess will fall to one or another master after you are dead, but this will never cease to be yours once it has come into being.' Pliny's identification of the building as an enduring expression of the mentality or intention of its owner could hardly be bettered as a definition of the process of architectural self-fashioning that I am identifying as the motive behind all of Seton's architectural activities. Seton's inscription establishes the two qualities of *humanitas* and *urbanitas* as what we might call the twin pillars of its edification. Neither term lends itself to exact translation, though *humanitas* doubtless includes not only the qualities which separate what the inscription calls 'the human race' (*humanique generis*) from the lower animals, but more specifically that skill in the *literae humaniores* of which the inscription itself, like so much of the decorative painting I have already discussed, would be an example. The concluding praise may reflect Seton's Catholicism; it certainly acknowledges divine sanction for the wealth which had enabled him to build so lavishly in all three of his Scottish dwellings. The expression *Jehovah Stator* is extraordinary, though it may suggest how closely Seton identified his neoclassicism with his paternal religion, for *Stator* is the epithet Livy provides for Jupiter in his role as supporter or protector. The inscription clearly associates the buildings with their garden, and suggests how closely the garden design was integrated into the overall statement these buildings are making. Indeed David Allen has argued, partly on the basis of this very inscription, that 'the development of gardening in Scotland is closely related to the acceptance, during the Jacobean period, of the substantially new philosophical principles enunciated by European neo-Stoicism' (1997, p.60, *cf* Allen 2000, *passim*).

Contemporary attitudes towards the use of inscriptions on buildings in Britain may be illustrated by what Henry Peacham has to say on the subject. In a passage 'On Inscriptions' which was added to the third edition of *The Complete Gentleman* in 1634, he writes:

> as for Inscriptions divers Authors have unfolded them. I will name you one for all, and that is *Lipsius*, who hath set forth the collections of another, and many of his owne besides. This booke of Inscriptions is in Folio, and printed at *Antwerp, ex officina Plantiniana Raphelengy*: where in the very beginning he bestoweth a leafe or two in decyphring unto us, and explaining the sence of old Characters, or short writing; as that D.M. stands for Dijs Manibus, which you usually find upon urnes .... [further examples follow]. (repr. 1906, p.111)

That Peacham should name Justus Lipsius, the writer whose neo-Stoicism inspired the emblems from Otto Vaenius that we have examined at Pinkie, as the latest exponent of such studies, is suggestive. Peacham goes on to identify Arundel House as 'the chief English scene of ancient Inscriptions':

> You shall finde all the walles of the house inlayde with them, and speaking Greeke and Latine to you. The Garden especially will affoord you the pleasure of a world of learned Lectures in this kinde. (p.112)

Peacham's testimony may suggest the spirit in which Seton's classical *emblemata* would already have been regarded some twenty years earlier in Scotland. Indeed, though there were no emblems in the Earl of Arundel's gallery, the literal meaning of the word *emblemata* is 'inlaid', the very term Peacham applies to Arundel's inscriptions.

The way Seton's false architecture reinterprets the architectural space of his long gallery raises a few questions. The false vaulting which divides the ceiling into a series of arcaded partitions certainly facilitates the identification of the ceiling with the painted Athenian gallery in which Stoic emblems were displayed which I have tried to make a case for. But it also introduces some curious ambiguities in its handling of space, for the emblem panels which are hung in their chamfered frames on illusional hooks and eyes in these partitions are not hanging at all vertically – to make sense of these eye-hooks the almost horizontal curve of the coved ceiling has to be interpreted as if it were a vertical plane. Is this a type of Mannerist illusionism, or is it pure naivety?

Similar questions are raised by the handling of space in the extraordinary *trompe l'oeil* cupola at the centre of the gallery. This octagonal lantern is by no means symmetrical – it assumes a viewer who is standing slightly to the north of centre. Are we to conclude that Alexander Seton, a man 'well-versed in the mathematics', could not secure the services of a painter who knew how to draw a regular octagon? We can defend him from such an accusation since it can now be shown that this eccentric cupola, far from being a Scottish naive painter's whim, is modelled on a design from one of the most advanced European pattern books devoted to the mathematics and theory of perspective, Jan Vredeman de Vries' book on *Perspective*, which first appeared in Leiden in 1604-5

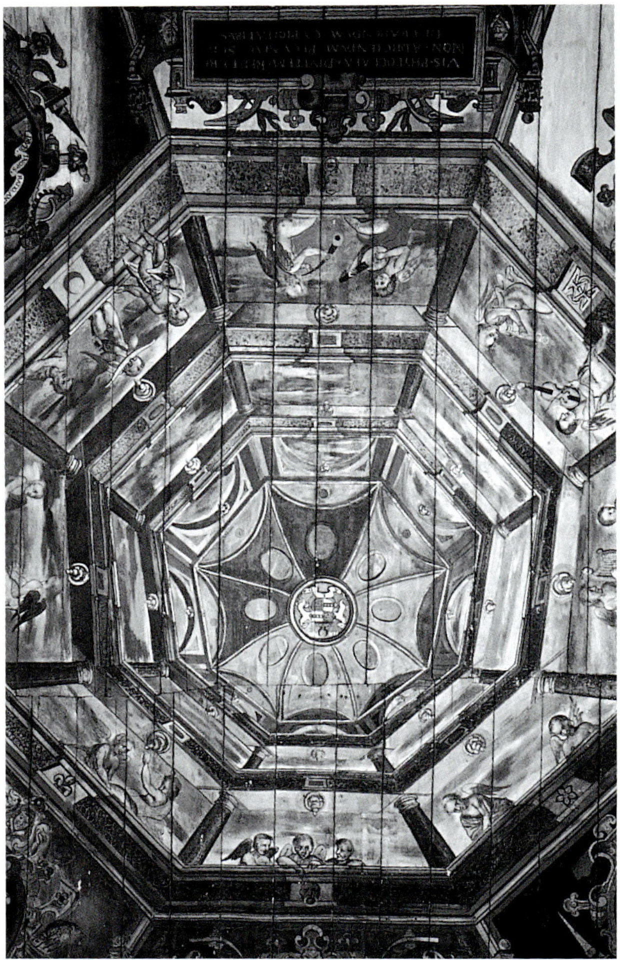

with numerous later editions. Vredeman's illustrations demonstrate the art of perspective through architectural forms, including a number of towers or lanterns seen from below. With a number of these images, as Martin Kemp puts it, 'architectural forms are portrayed at odd angles from such close viewpoints that the effects are those of anamorphic images which assume undistorted appearance only when viewed from a particular position' (Kemp 1990, p.110). It is probably a sign of his interest in the mathematical challenges of these images that Seton should have chosen as his pattern not one of the more fully realised and realistic engravings of architectural forms that fill Vredeman's book, but a design which is reduced to little more than a mathematical diagram. A patron who wanted to supply his artist with a labour-saving pattern for purely decorative purposes could easily have found a more useful model than this. Mathematics, however, was seen as fundamental to architectural proportion from Vitruvius onwards, and was particularly manifested in the technical virtuosity of the polyhedral sundials which proliferated in this period in Scottish gardens, whose calculations depended on Napier's invention of logarithms. Napier's Latin treatise of 1617 explaining the invention of the system of calculating rods known as 'Napier's Bones' – ancestor of the slide-rule – was, in fact, dedicated to Seton, though Napier declares his book to be 'unworthy of such a Maecenas'. Seton himself was described by his

Pinkie House. Long gallery, central trompe l'oeil *cupola.* HS

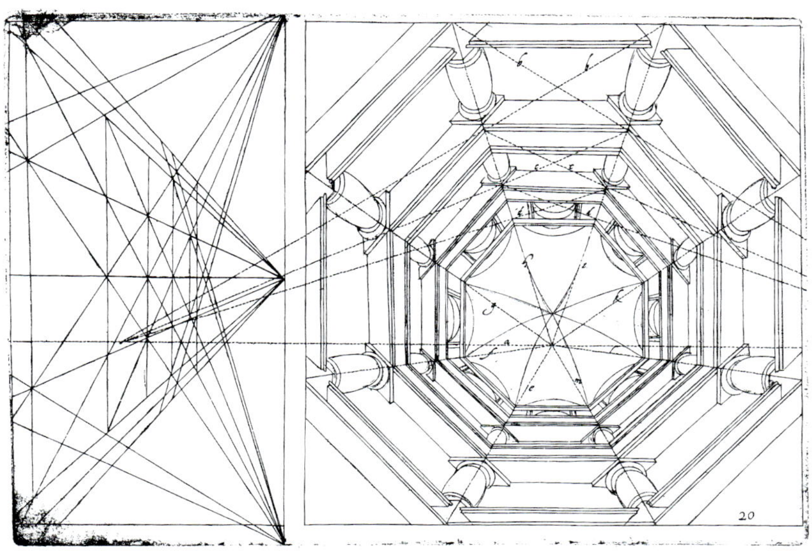

Hans Vredeman de Vries, Perspectiva *(Antwerp, 1604-5) p.20, design for octagonal cupola showing mathematics for achieving an eccentric viewing angle.* GUL

seventeenth-century biographer, we might recall, as not only well versed in mathematics but also as 'a great humanist in prose and in poecie, Greek and Latine … and had great skill in architecture and herauldrie'. The skills of mathematics, architecture and heraldry that Kingston identifies here have a greater interdependence than might be supposed. The relevance of heraldry to these arts is apparent not only in the profusion of coats of arms in the painted and sculptured decoration of Seton's houses, but in 'the self-conscious manipulation of personal and dynastic imagery' which Deborah Howard has identified as 'another aspect of their classicism' (Howard 1995b, p.60). These apparently, but only apparently, different aspirations – all of which, as we have seen, influenced the decorative vocabulary of his Stoic long gallery – have to be read as part of an extraordinary attempt to bring a Renaissance *humanitas* to early modern Scotland.

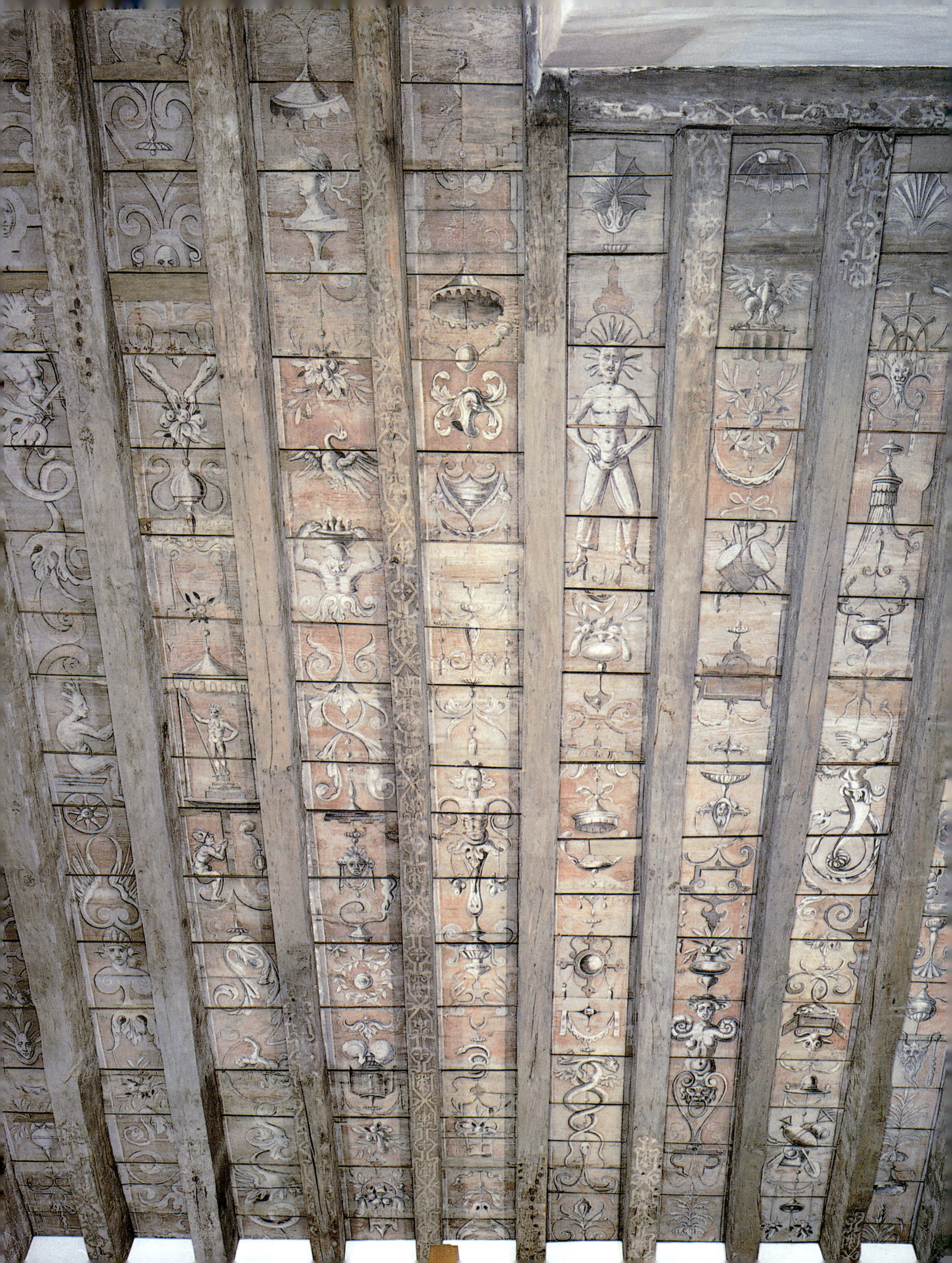

5

MARK KERR'S DREAMWORK

THE predominant style of decoration in English houses of the sixteenth and early seventeenth centuries was known as 'antique painting'. 'Antique work' was an English interpretation of Renaissance grotesque, and the best contemporary description is probably Henry Peacham's in his *Art of Drawing* (1606). Peacham makes it clear that the style 'was most auncient and in greatest request', but although it had good classical credentials it lacked the regularity of design that was coming to be seen as the index of a truly classical style.

> The forme of it is a generall, and (as I may say) an unnatural or unorderly composition for delight sake, of men, beasts, birds, fishes, flowers, etc. without (as wee say) Rime or reason, for the greater variety you show in your invention, the more you please .... You may, if you list, draw naked boyes riding or playing with their paper-mills or bubble-shels uppon Goates, Eagles, Dolphins etc: the bones of a Rammes head hung with strings of beads with Ribands, Satyres, Tritons, apes, Cornu-copias, Dogges yockt etc. drawing cowcumbers, cherries and any kind of wild trail or vinet after your owne invention, with a thousand more such idle toyes, so that herein you cannot be too fantastical. (pp.35-7)

By the mid-seventeenth century such painting had become so popular in England that it could be dismissed as 'ale-house painting'. Thus in 1658 Sir William Sanderson admits to a taste for 'Grotesco or (as we say) Antique-work' which uses 'forms of different Natures, or *Sexes, Sirenes, Centaures*, and such like', but he hesitates to recommend the style since 'it looks like an Ale-house; Citizen painting, being too common; and usually ... very ill wrought' (cited in Croft-Murray 1962, p.27). Its use of monstrous figures and hybrid or distorted forms eventually led to the accusation that it was a 'gothic', unregulated and essentially barbarous style – Vitruvius, after all, had no time for it.

And yet, as Peacham's description acknowledges, 'antique painting' was so called because it was an ancient and authentically classical style. It originated in the 1480s, when antiquarian collectors looking for buried statues in the rubble opposite the Colosseum in Rome rediscovered the wall paintings that had decorated Nero's huge palace. What they uncovered in its buried

Opposite: *General view of the ceiling of Prestongrange.* RCAHMS

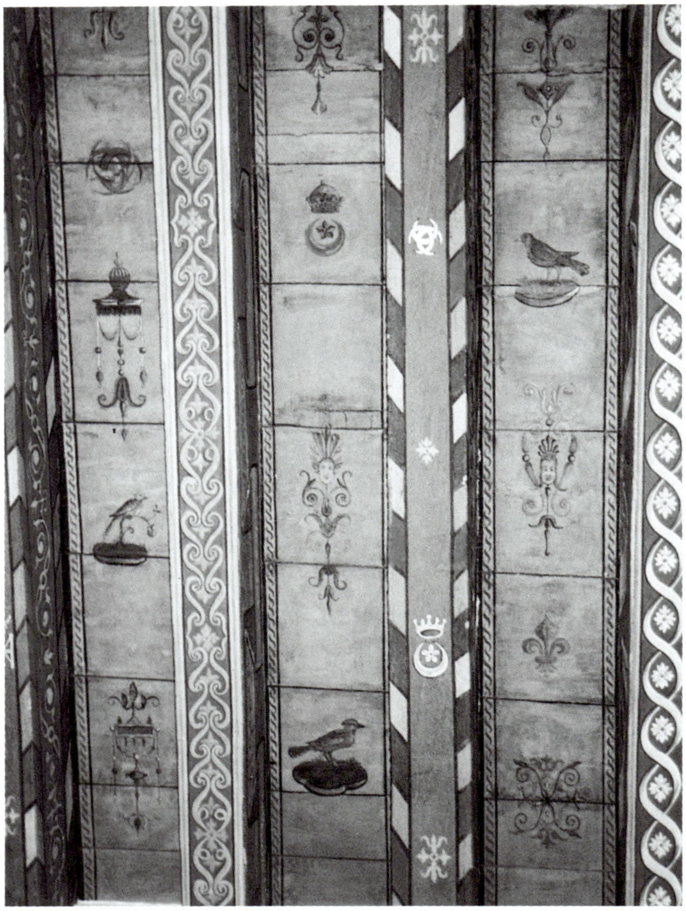

Decoration from east range first-floor 'Prefects' Room' at Pinkie House, now reinstalled in Huntly House Museum, Edinburgh; patterns on beam soffits are not original.

chambers or 'grottoes' (hence 'grotesque') were the most authentic examples of antique painting to have come to light at that date. This discovery excited the interest and emulation of Italian painters from Pinturiccio and Filippino Lippi to Perugino and Signorelli, who developed the *Domus Aurea* models into an extended vocabulary that became the recognised style for decorative painting *à l'antique*. Before Raphael decorated the Vatican *loggie* he first went down into the 'grottoes' and used them as his pattern books and it was from Raphael's authoritative Vatican model that artists went out to decorate in the new style the great houses and palaces of Europe – Fontainebleau, the Escorial, the Doge's Palace. As Geoffrey Harpham says, 'For decades after the initial discoveries, the appearance of the antique style was often the first sign that the Renaissance had arrived' (1982, p.43).

Over the next hundred years antique ornament evolved in ways which became increasingly independent of its antique sources. Grotesque ornament is characterised by a fertility of fantastic invention in which metamorphosis plays a major role – the transformation of animate into inanimate forms, of plants into strange beasts, of human into abstract or monstrous shapes. The essence of the style is transgression, violating the boundaries between different categories of things, creating distorted or hybrid forms that challenge doctrines of artistic verisimilitude, giving free rein instead to the unfettered invention of the artist. Accurate mimesis has no place in this type of representation; fantastic and copious invention is its guiding principle.

Some types of grotesque motif nevertheless rapidly became conventionalised in ways that make the identification of particular print sources hazardous, if not unnecessary. The decoration of the so-called 'Prefects Room' ceiling from Pinkie House, for instance, makes much use of a kind of elegantly foliated mask that can be found in some of the earliest ornament prints. Among the conventionalised figures characteristic of the latter is a female with diaphanous wings and, normally, transformed, foliated hips. We find a version of her in the exuberant grotesque-work of the painted ceiling in John Knox's House, Edinburgh, where we also find an example of another humanoid type long

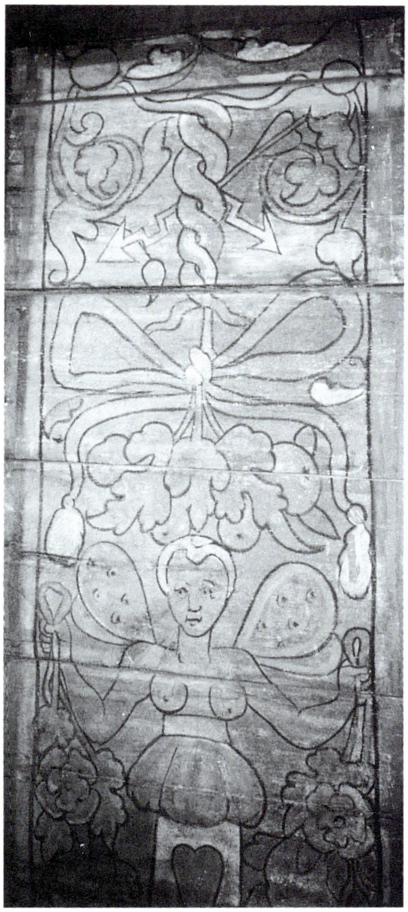

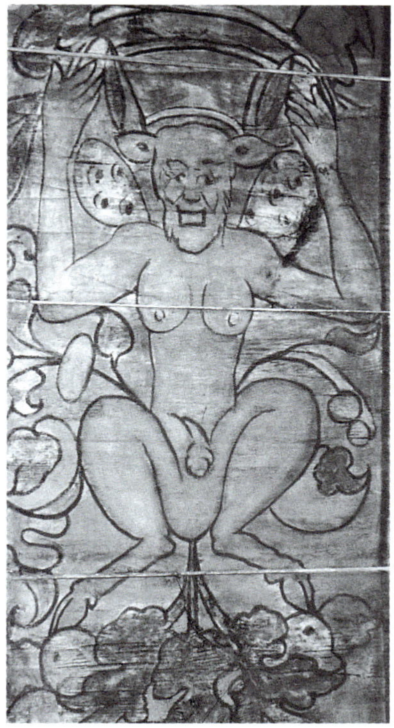

Types of grotesque include the diaphanous winged female and the squatting satyr, both from Edinburgh, John Knox's House.

conventionalised in the vocabulary of grotesque printmakers, the figure of the squatting satyr. Such images lent themselves to scatological treatment since the squatting figure was open to the suggestion that he might be defecating. In John Knox's House he is shown with a rich garland of leaves and fruit issuing from his backside, and though – like any satyr – he is manifestly male, he has the breasts and diaphanous wings of the female figure. No sources have yet been identified for any of these images, and though they may turn up eventually it is quite possible that such images were part of a vocabulary that could meet a growing taste for what Montaigne's translator called 'Boscage or Crotesko work; which are fantasticall pictures, having no grace, but in the variety and strangenesse of them' (Florio, cited in Fowler 1996, p.26). The fact that we find such work executed at a number of further sites, including Nunraw, Delgaty and Rossend, suggests that this particular style had become part of the acquired vocabulary of Scottish decorative artists.

Instrumental in its development were the engravings produced in large quantities from the mid-century onwards by French and Flemish designers of ornamental prints – Etienne Delaune, Jacques Androuet Ducerceau, Cornelis and Jacob Floris, Cornelis Bos and Hans Vredeman de Vries. Circulating widely, these prints were designed specifically to serve as patterns for decorative artists, and thus became instrumental in spreading a taste for the grotesque right across Europe. Grotesque patterns include a large number of designs for ornamental strapwork or cartouche frames holding inscriptions or subject paintings (Floris, Bos, Vredeman) and for caryatids or classical term-figures

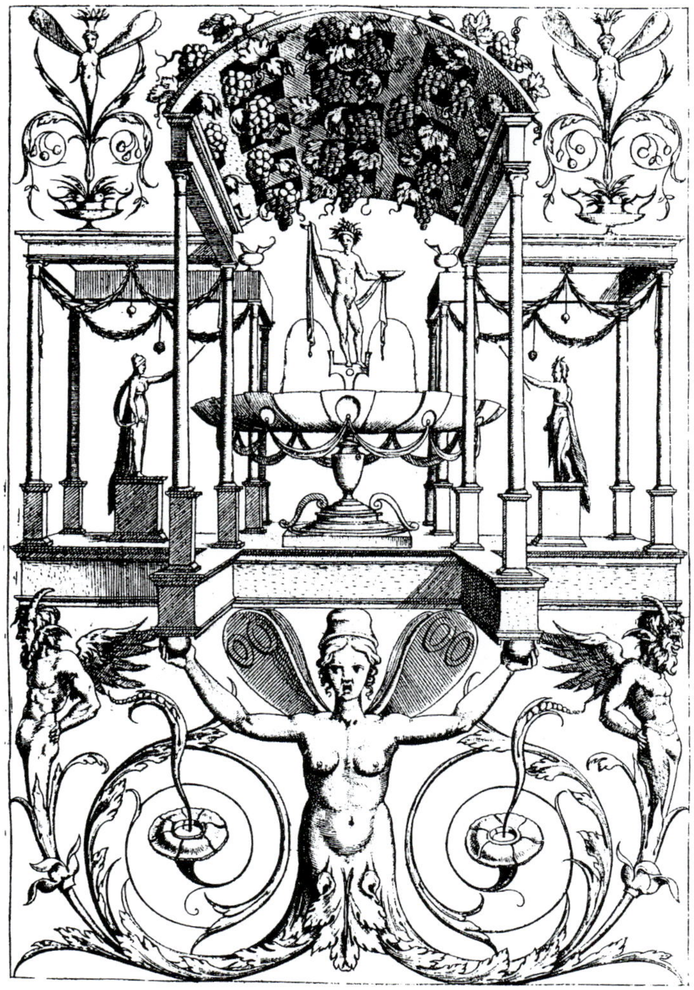

Grotesque design by Dutch engraver Cornelis Bos. GUL

(Ducerceau, Vredeman), but some of the same artists were also responsible for handbooks on architecture and perspective (Ducerceau, Vredeman), which suggests how close the identification was between the arts of design – and grotesque in particular – and the science of *architectura.*

We can see classical elements reflected in what is arguably the finest grotesque painting in Scotland, the ceiling from Prestongrange on the Firth of Forth, a few miles east of Edinburgh. The house was built for Mark Kerr (1517-84), Abbot and later Commendator of Newbattle Abbey, who married a daughter of the Earl of Rothes, became a Privy Counsellor, Lord of Session and supporter of Regent Morton. In 1578 he was chosen Governor of Scotland and became a supporter of Esmé Stewart, Lord Aubigny. He acquired great riches and his decorative painting probably has to be read as an expression of his wealth, status and advanced taste in a decorative style that was becoming increasingly fashionable throughout Europe, though it is both an early and an extremely accomplished example of such work in a British context.

The figures are painted in *grisaille* on a strikingly red ground, which might recall the *Stufetta* (bath room) constructed by Raphael for Cardinal Bibiena and decorated with grotesques by Giovanni da Udine, which also uses a bright red ground. As Nicole Dacos suggests, this was a deliberate attempt to give it the appearance of a Roman room, by imitating the 'Pompeian red' (Dacos 1969, p.102). Many of the Prestongrange details have an evidently classical register – its antique vocabulary includes a classical head in a medallion, a winged figure of *Fama* standing on a death's head above a winged hourglass, a dignified figure standing beneath a canopy supported on columns, and a mature and well-thewed Eros with bow and quiver. Other details, however, have a more fantastic and, indeed, carnivalesque register.

The iconography of this ceiling refers to at least four different sources. The major source for well over half of its details is Hans Vredeman de Vries's *Grottesco* (Antwerp: Gerard de Jode, c.1565-71), a set of sixteen engravings which, as we saw in Chapter 2, supplied the patterns for most of the non-emblematic detail on the ceiling from Rossend. Designed by one of the most prolific and influential of the Antwerp school of decorative artists,

Vredeman's architectural drawings circulated widely, and his print series on the art of perspective supplied the pattern, as we noted in the previous chapter, for Alexander Seton's *trompe l'oeil* cupola at Pinkie House. His grotesque designs were probably engraved by the Van Doetecum brothers.

The form of Vredeman's *Grottesco* engravings goes back to a type developed, also in the 1560s, by the Frenchman Jacques Androuet Ducerceau, in which a central motif in a frame is flanked by a wealth of seemingly random grotesque ornament on either side, consisting of a series of interlinked motifs rising one above the other. Each of these sequences is normally reduplicated on either side of the central cartouche or frame to provide a balanced and symmetrical composition. This was obviously well adapted to fill the type of narrow space between the joists of Scottish open board-and-beam ceilings, and the Prestongrange artist, like the Rossend painter, tends to copy a sequence of such interlinked motifs in the same order as they appear in the etching. He draws on all but one of the sixteen plates that make up the *Grottesco* series – Mark Kerr, or his artist, evidently owned the whole set. Five of the engravings portray identifiable subjects – Hercules slaying the centaur; Hercules with the Cretan Bull; Mercury and Pegasus; Venus on a chariot drawn by swans; Fame with trumpets and an hourglass – but others show subjects to which it is impossible to give a name and, in any case, these central cartouches are wholly overwhelmed by the mass of grotesque detail which surrounds them. It is this surrounding detail, in what would normally be the liminary space occupied by an ornamental frame or border, that is the essential *raison d'etre* of these prints and which, indeed, justifies their *Grottesco* title. As we noted in Chapter 2, the grotesque is almost by definition a style devoid of meaning, at least if we can accept Cotgrave's definition in his *Dictionarie of the French and English Tongues* (1611):

> Grotesques: Pictures wherein (as please the Painter) all kinds of odde things are represented without anie peculiar sence, or meaning, but only to feed the eye.

The same assumption lies behind Peacham's statement that antique painting is 'without Rime or reason', but the moment we introduce the issue of signification we are moving into questions of iconography and iconology. Clearly not all the images on the Prestongrange ceiling are devoid of allegorical significance; the figure of winged Fame, with her trumpets, triumphing over death and flying time, for instance, is not an image 'without anie peculiar sence, or meaning' but rather a detail which has moved some distance from its grotesque setting in the direction of allegory and emblem. The ceiling from Rossend, as we saw in Chapter 2, is dominated by emblematic images from Paradin and other emblem books, but it also uses a number of grotesque details from this same set of prints.

The way the Prestongrange ceiling uses its sources is well illustrated by its treatment of Vredeman's print showing a seated goddess on a wheeled throne in front of a burning censer, with two nude male worshippers (Hollstein, no. 246). Prestongrange ignores this somewhat puzzling central image; instead it

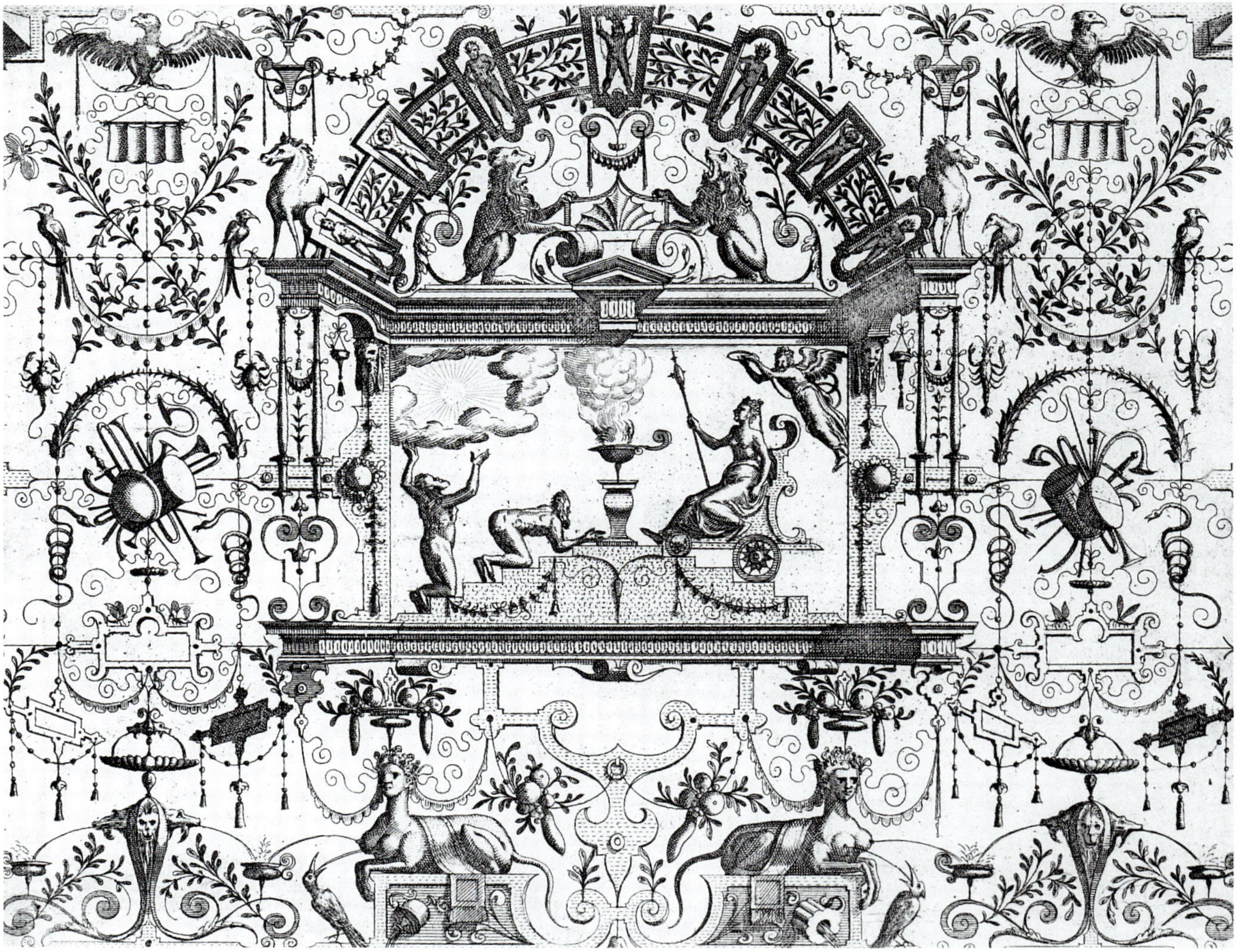

Hans Vredeman de Vries, engraving from the Grottesco *series (Antwerp, 1565–71).* BM

copies the whole sequence of diverse but interlinked images that rise up on either side of the central cartouche. At the base is a tricephalic animal head, above it a shallow basin supporting a smaller bicephalic version of the animal heads below, above this an empty ornamental cartouche, then a bunch of musical instruments below a wreath of foliage from which a drape of cloth hangs; at the very top is another cloth drape hung on a rail, with a spread eagle perched above it. The fact that the ceiling copies this whole sequence of images in exactly the same order as they appear on Vredeman's print leaves no doubt whatsoever that this was their source; moreover these are not the only details from this print which the ceiling makes use of, for a detail several sections away from this shows a rather splendid horse standing in an attitude suggesting attention or surprise. This is evidently copied from the horse that stands above the left-hand cornice surmounting the pillared trellis framing the central image in Vredeman's print. Just below this horse on the ceiling is a small cartouche with a curved branch of leaves on either side and a beaded ribbon hung with tassels below it. This evidently copies the tiny cartouche repeated four times on either side of the print, just above the tricephalic head. It is this blank cartouche the Prestongrange artist has chosen, most usefully for our purposes, to fill with the date 1581 when the ceiling was painted. Another section features the sequence of images copied also at Rossend from Vredeman's print showing two

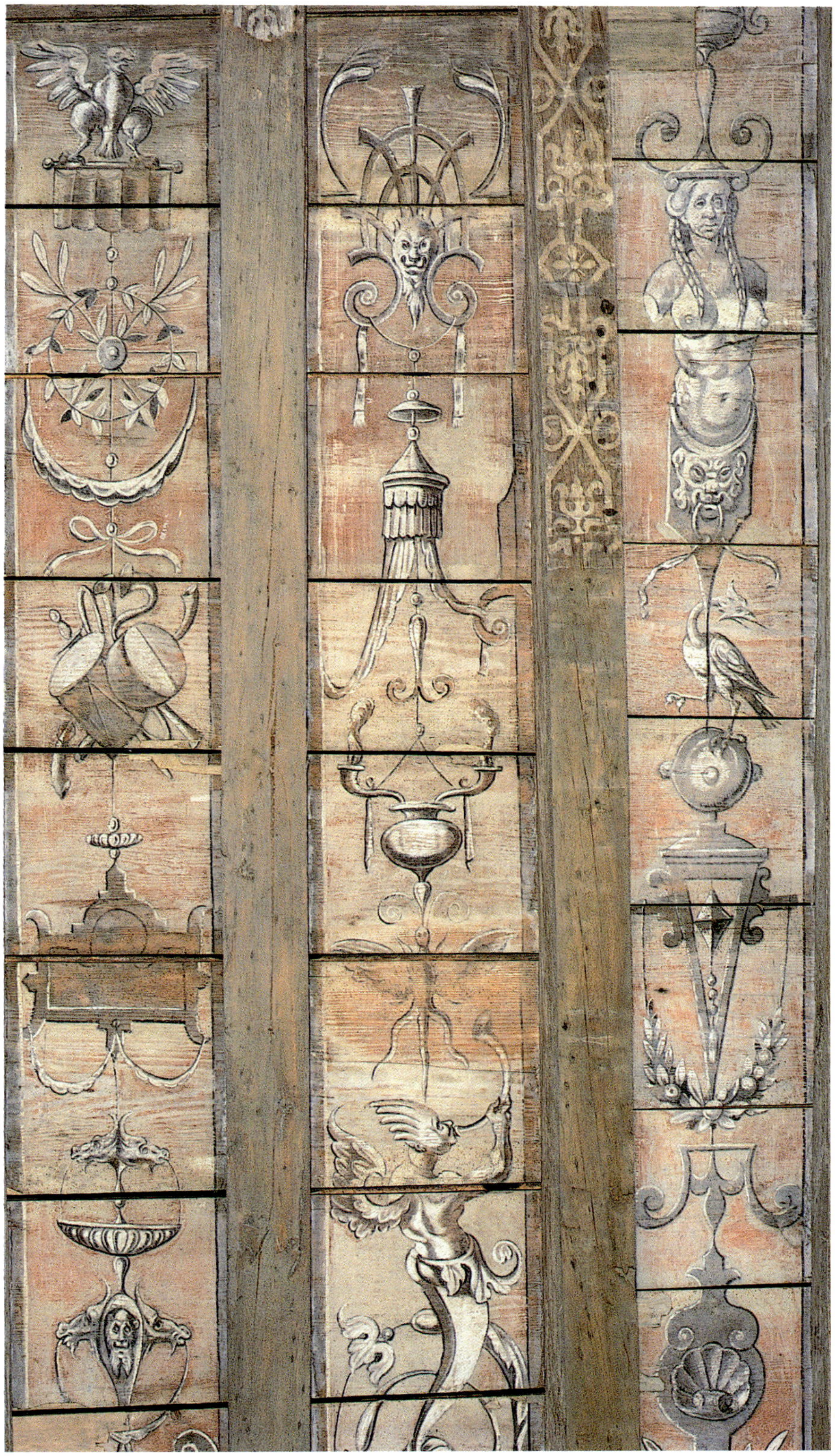

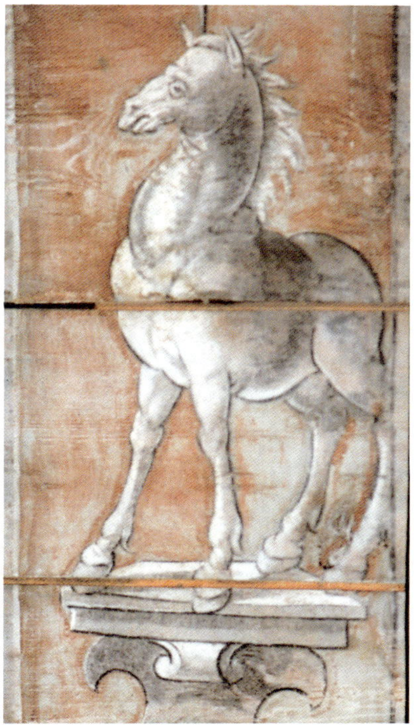

Prestongrange, hall ceiling, detail – the surprised horse copies that standing on the right-hand cornice of Vredeman's fantastic arch.

Above: *Prestongrange, hall ceiling, detail – the sequence of images in the left-hand compartment follows that in the right-hand border to Vredeman's print.* RCAHMS

Right: *The cartouche telling us when the ceiling was painted copies those in the bottom corners of Vredeman's print.* RCAHMS

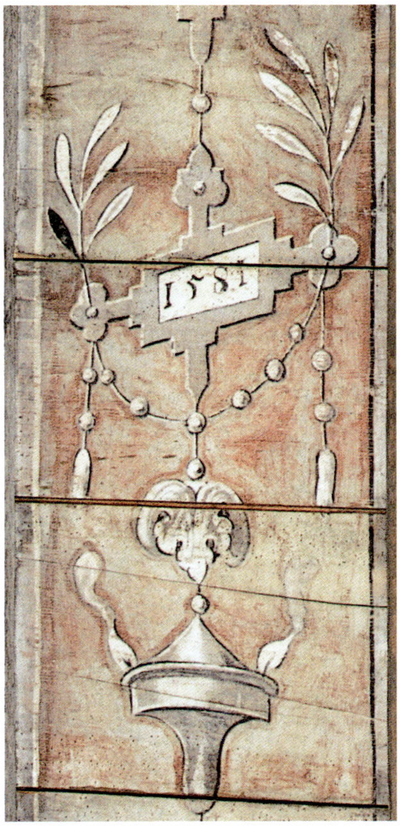

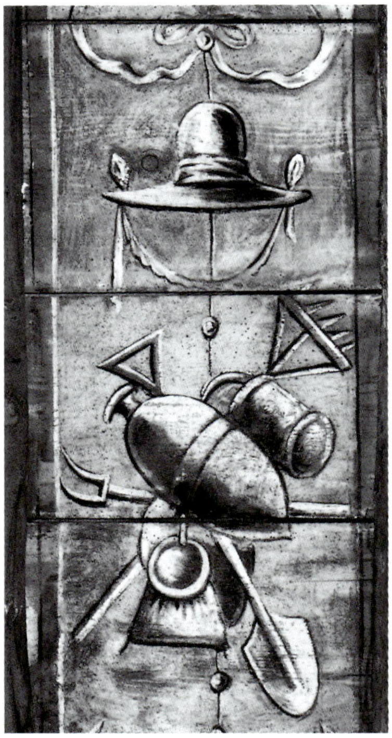

Prestongrange, hall ceiling, detail. The gardening tools and broad-brimmed hat are from a sequence of border details also copied at Rossend from the same engraving by Vredeman, see above p.47. RCAHMS

battling horsemen; the flanking decoration shows a collection of gardening implements beneath a broad-brimmed hat below an ox skull.

Details copied at Prestongrange are not wholly confined, however, to these liminary motifs. Among the principal subjects at the centre of the prints Prestongrange copies the image of winged Fame blowing two trumpets, each with a banner hanging from it, and standing on a skull which rests on a winged hourglass. This personification of *Fama* has moved decisively into allegory and emblematics. Winged Fame, we might interpret, triumphs over winged time and death, her trumpets declaring the immortal memory of those whose achievements will never be forgotten. Vredeman shifts this allegory towards the grotesque style by drawing puffs of smoke emerging from the trumpets, but Prestongrange ignores this detail and repositions the trumpets to point upwards. The ceiling decoration copies one further detail from this print, namely the nude bust who rises from an architectural bracket on each side of the central decorative arch and blows his curly trumpet; his truncated waist is transformed into a foliate scroll, and his hair elongated into leaves of grass, two of which transform into snakes' heads in the print. These are just a few of the images on this ceiling copied from Vredeman's *Grottesco* prints – I have set out the full list in the analysis of Prestongrange in the Inventory at the end of this book; this shows just how extensive Mark Kerr's use of this pattern book was.

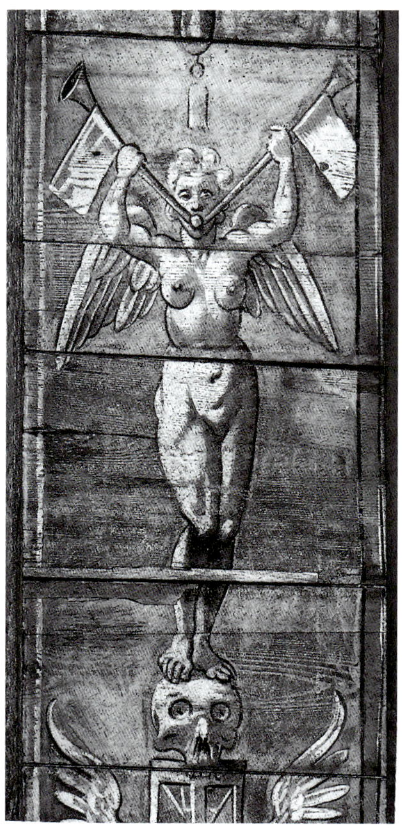

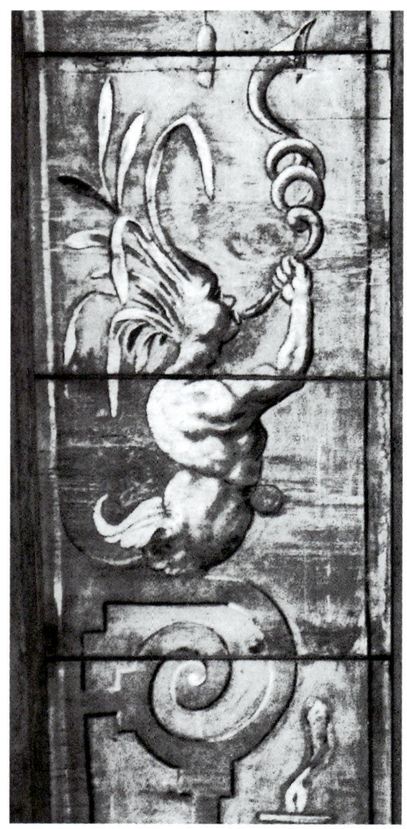

Left: *Prestongrange, detail based on Vredeman's image of Fame.* RCAHMS

Right: *Prestongrange, curly-trumpeter has a more fantastic appearance than his emblematic counterpart but is nonetheless copied from another detail in the same print.*

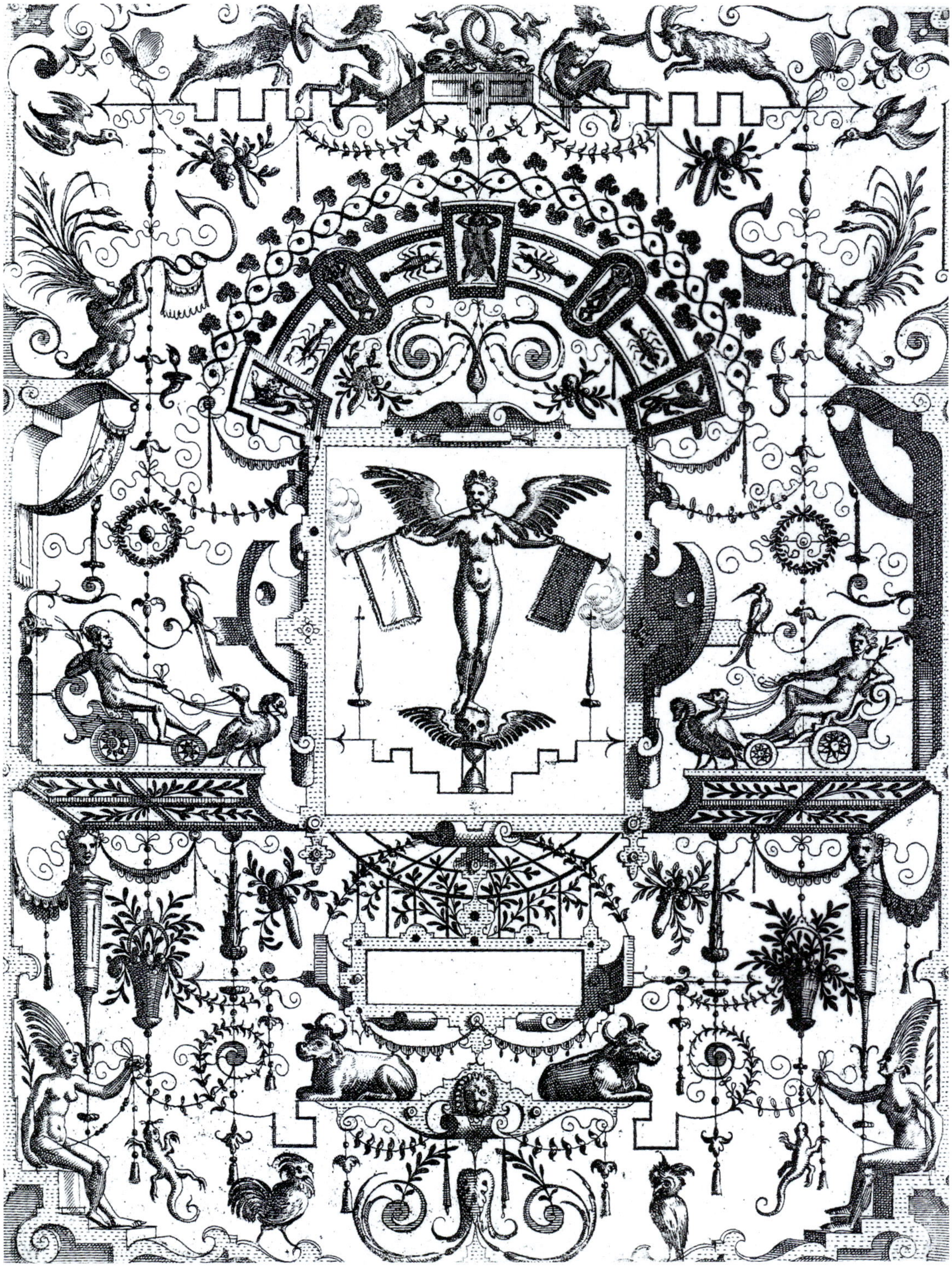

Hans Vredeman de Vries, engraving from Grottesco *series showing winged Fame triumphing over time.* V&A

Vredeman's engravings are known to have been widely used as patterns in England. Wells-Cole identifies details from *Das Erst Buech* and *Das Ander Buech* (1565), which illustrate the classical orders in architecture, on English tombstones of the 1580s and 1590s at Montacute, Quantoxhead, Bovey Tracy, Wollaton, Knole, Brereton, and elsewhere (Wells-Cole 1997, p.60). Vredeman's cartouche designs are copied at Bruton, Somerset, on overmantels in Worcestershire, Westmoreland and in Bristol (Wells-Cole 1997, pp.69-80).

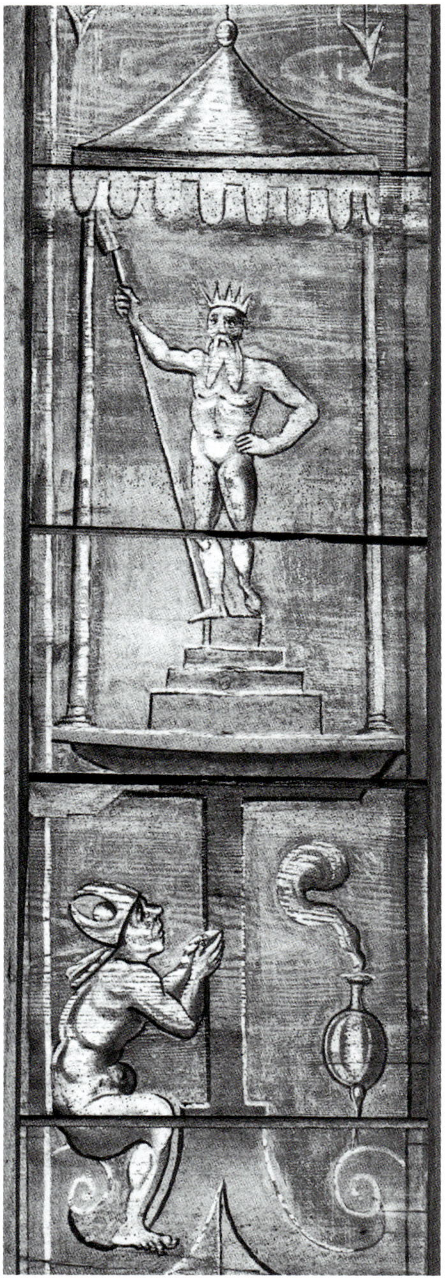

Prestongrange, crowned figure beneath his canopy with subjected worshipper complete with incense. RCAHMS

Vredeman's *Caryatidum* are copied in plasterwork in the West Country, the Midlands, and London, mural painting at Otley Hall, oak panelling in Ipswich. The *trompe l'oeil* cupola at Pinkie is copied, as we have seen, from Vredeman's *Perspectiva.* Though Vredeman represents a major source of patterns in Elizabethan and Jacobean England, the Prestongrange ceiling is unique in the extent of its exploitation of his *Grottesco.* In fact the *Grottesco* series is only known to have provided the pattern for one artefact, with strong Scottish connections: the border of the cushion cover at the centre of the Shrewsbury Hanging, executed by Bess of Hardwick, adapts one of the details also found on the Prestongrange ceiling. This cushion cover illustrates Paradin's emblem *Ingenij largitor* showing the thirsty crow who ingeniously raises the

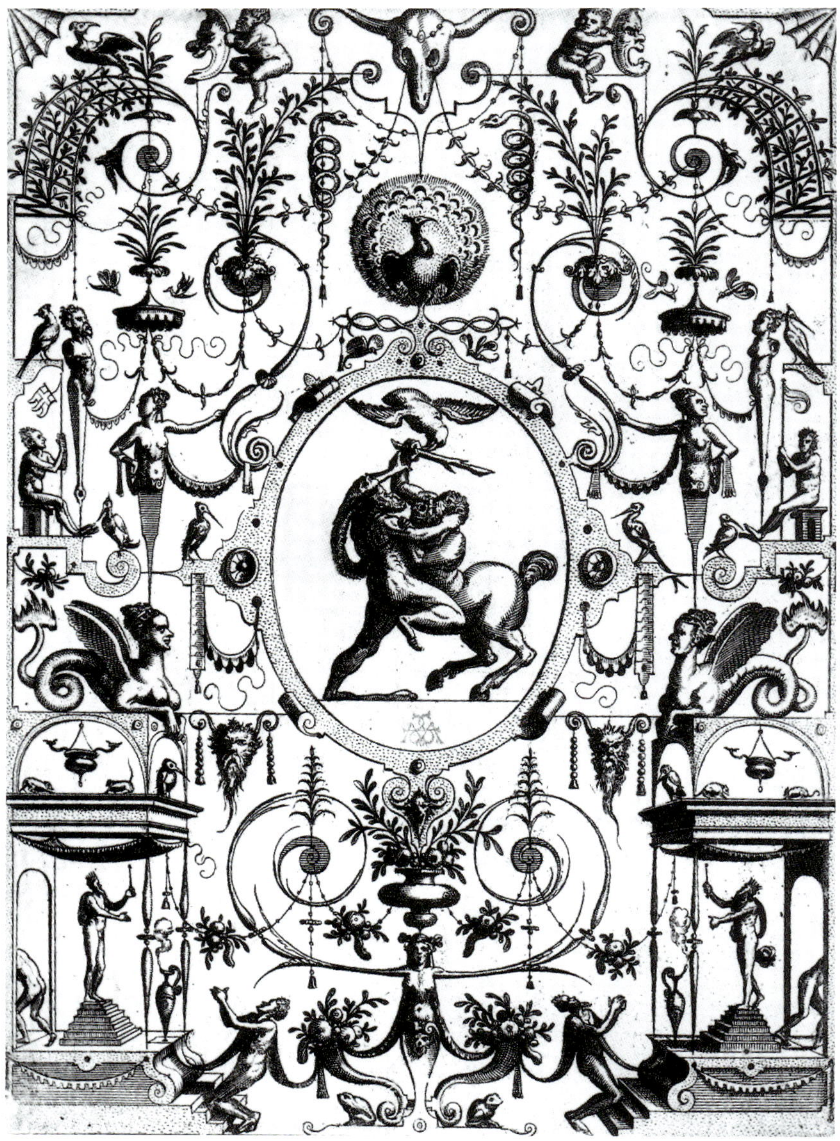

Hans Vredeman de Vries, 'Hercules slays the Centaur', engraving from the Grottesco *series. The detail in the bottom corners is copied both at Prestongrange and in the border to the Shrewsbury Hanging.* SP,A

Prestongrange, caryatid – a classical term-figure with both architectural and grotesque applications.

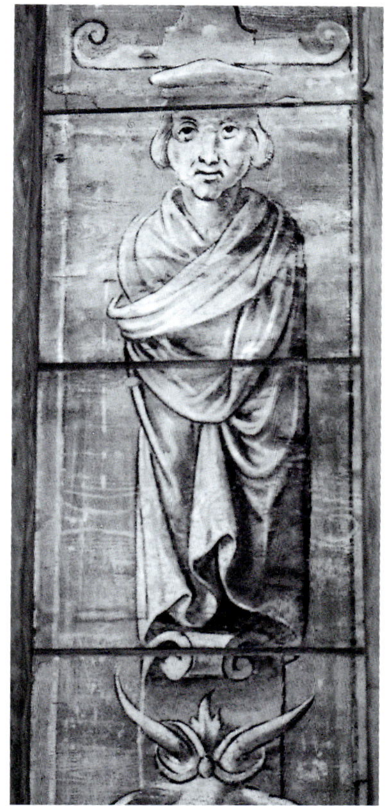

level of water in a vase by filling it with stones – an emblem also used on the painted ceiling from Rossend (see Chapter 2) – but its border shows a crowned nude standing on a stepped plinth beneath a canopy, with a praying figure in front and a third figure disappearing behind him. Prestongrange shows the crowned figure, still standing on his stepped plinth beneath a redesigned canopy, but facing full front and holding a long pole or lance. The differences might lead us to doubt whether the Vredeman print was, in fact, the source of this detail, at least until one notices the crouching figure and the smoking censer, which are now shown immediately beneath the canopy and plinth, as if quite unrelated to it. These are clearly modelled on the two details in Vredeman's print; essentially what the artist has done is to reposition the viewer to a frontal view of these details in relation to the main figure. The crouching figure whose hands are clasped in prayer has, rather wittily, been supplied with a mitre.

The human figures we have described so far may or may not show deliberate distortion, but there are a number of humanoid figures on the ceiling that are grotesquely transformed. Several of these are caryatids, or term figures – human busts rising out of sculpted pillars – a popular feature of pseudo-classical architecture at this period. Two of the caryatids at Prestongrange are copied from Vredeman's *Caryatidum* (Antwerp: de Jode c.1565). One takes the form of a capped figure wrapped in a shroud or winding-cloth; open-eyed, however: this is no corpse. The other is one of a series of 'foliate' term-figures, whose arms, hips and hair are transformed into leaf scrolls, giving the figure some of

Below: *Hans Vredeman de Vries, engraving from the* Caryatidum *series (Antwerp, c.1565); Bess of Hardwick used this print for a caryatid on the Shrewsbury Hanging.* V&A

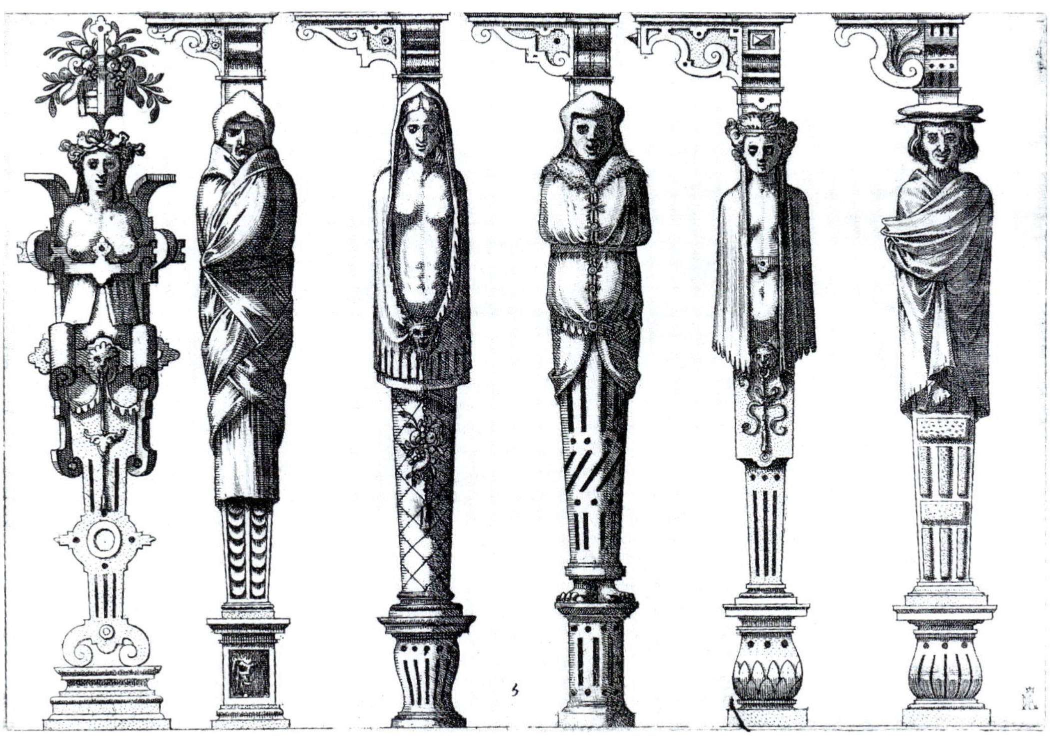

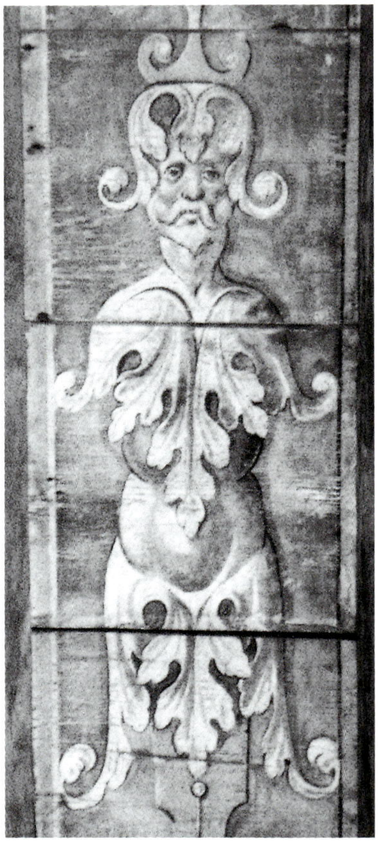

Prestongrange, caryatid copied from another print in the same series.

the characteristics of a traditional Wodwo or Green Man, though we should be cautious about ascribing such identities to these grotesque figures. The border to the Shrewsbury Hanging also uses two caryatid figures copied from Vredeman, one of them from the same print that supplied Prestongrange's shrouded male.

The grotesque context undoubtedly accounts, moreover, for the use the Prestongrange ceiling makes of a wholly unprecedented source for such grotesque figures. The sections at one end of the ceiling containing the two Vredeman caryatids also contain (or originally contained – the ceiling was rearranged to fit its new situation in Merchiston Tower in the 1960s) what are, perhaps, four of the most unexpected images to be found on any of these Scottish ceilings, grotesquely misshapen humanoid figures with exaggerated, ithyphallic codpieces. In the early 1970s F J Stopp recognised that these figures copy designs from a pattern-book published in Paris in 1565 by the Protestant printer Richard Breton, under the title *Les songes drolatiques de Pantagruel.* Stopp communicated this discovery to Michael Apted, who co-authored a Scottish *Antiquaries* article in 1975 illustrating these details and correcting the wholly erroneous thesis, argued by Ian Hodkinson in 1966, that the ceiling had some connection with Scottish witchcraft. In fact these figures represent a rather more surprising and, arguably, more interesting manifestation of Rabelaisian imagery in what, one would have thought, was the wholly unsympathetic context of Reformation Scotland. The printer Breton claims on his

Below: *Hans Vredeman de Vries, engraving from the* Caryatidum *series (Antwerp, c.1565).* V&A

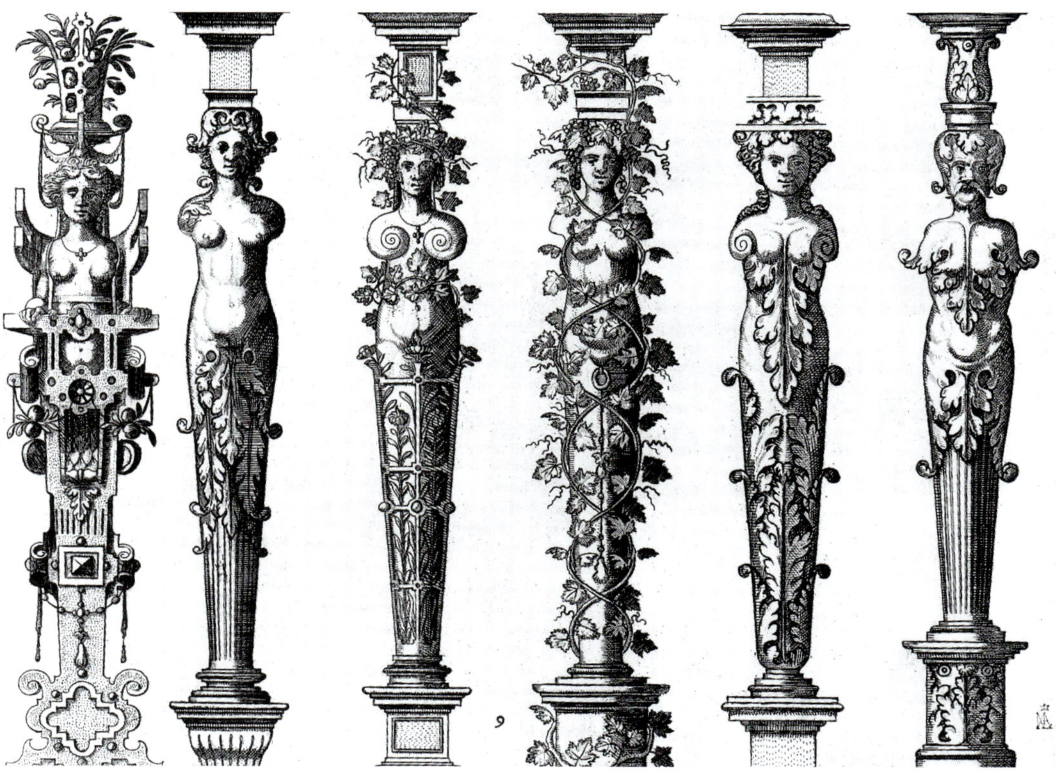

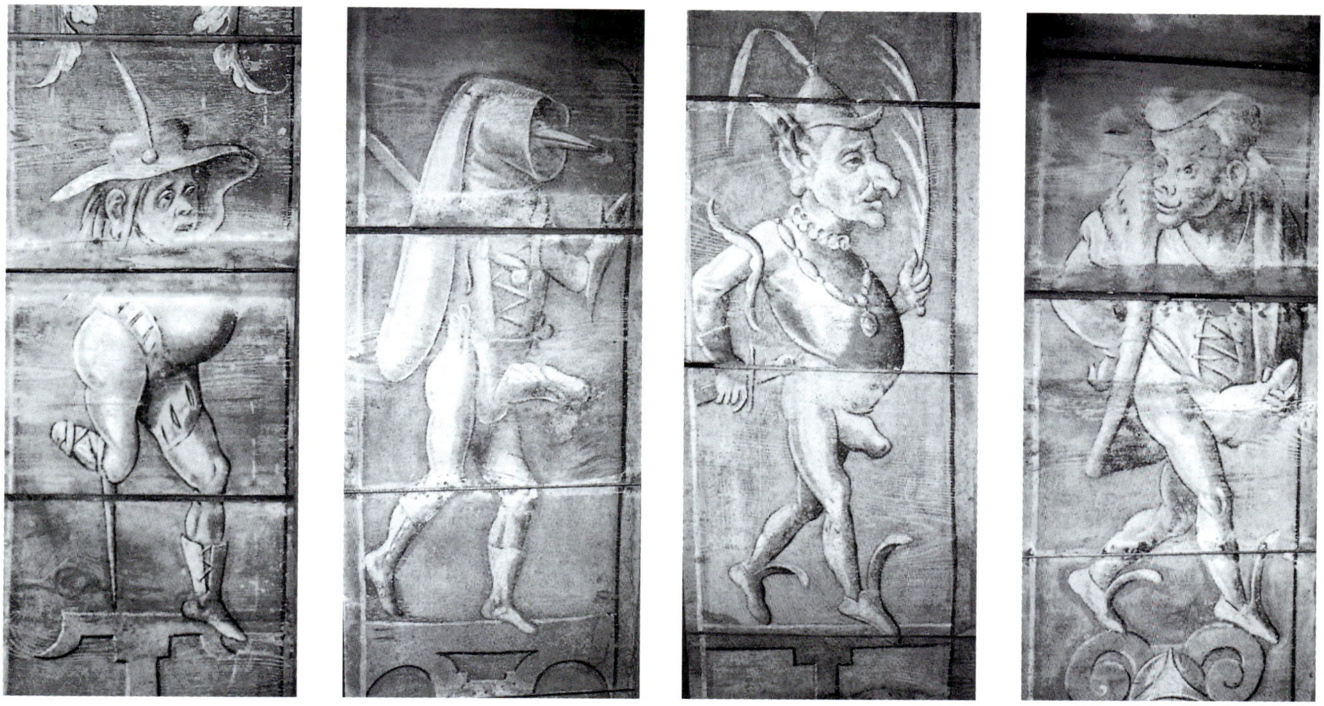

fol.106 *fol.31* *fol.80* *fol.112.*

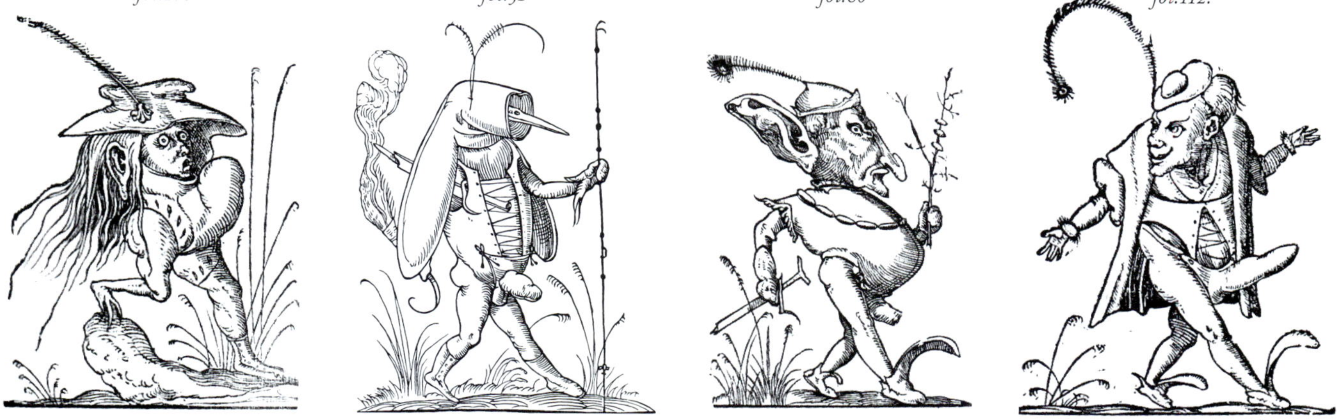

Top: *Four Rabelaisian dream-figures from Prestongrange.*

Bottom: *Four illustrations from a pattern book published by Richard Breton,* Les songes drolatiques de Pantagruel *(1565).*

title page and in his preface that *Les songes drolatiques* is an authentic posthumous work by Rabelais and it was generally received as such in the sixteenth century. The 120 engravings of fantastic humanoid figures that make up this book are almost certainly the work of an artist called François Desprez. We know of at least one copy of this work in a Scottish library at this period, for the extensive library of Adam Bothwell, Bishop of Orkney, is recorded as containing a copy of *Les songes drolatiques* along with Rabelais' *Oeuvres* (the contents of this library are described in detail by Duncan Shaw in Cowan and Shaw 1983, pp.141-69 – for Rabelais see p.161, and *cf* Cowan in the same volume, p.193).

The changes Prestongrange makes to its source serve, if anything, to heighten its Rabelaisian, scatological emphasis, providing one misshapen drollity, for instance, with a wooden leg, while another figure, evidently stepping out on an erotic quest, is provided with some handy support for his grossly extended codpiece. I cannot bring myself to believe that it was simply the narrowness of the pictorial space between these supporting beams which motivated this repositioning of Panurge's extended hand (if it is Panurge – none of these drollities is identified in the *Songes drolatiques*; indeed Breton jokes in his preface that he will leave to better-qualified readers the task of explicating '*le sens mistique ou allegorique, aussi pour leur imposer les noms, qui a chacun seroit convenable*' [fol. A1^{v}]).

The question of what values or associations motivated Kerr's choice of this particular design vocabulary at this moment in Scotland might seem difficult, if not impossible, to answer. There are one or two clues, however. Firstly, it is interesting, as always, to consider the common ground shared by the different sources used at a particular site. Secondly, it might help if we were to document a little more fully what is known about such designs in their immediate historical and geographical context. Contemporary attitudes towards the grotesque style are relatively well documented, and have been referred to in the present chapter. Its use of a pseudo-Rabelaisian source, however, raises the question of what the Prestongrange ceiling tells us about the reception of Rabelais at this date, and here there is an amount of fresh evidence to be considered. What do the *diversche manieren* of Vredeman de Vries's grotesques have in common with François Desprez' Rabelaisian fantasies?

Breton himself suggests that *Songes drolatiques* is suitable for use as a pattern book in the design of grotesques, or of *masquerades* ('*Plusieurs bons esprits y pourront tirer des inventions tant pour faire crotestes, que pour establir mascarades*'), and it is his term *crotestes* that clearly recognises their affinity with the type of humanoid figures found elsewhere on the ceiling, derived, as we have seen, from Vredeman's *Grottesco* and *Caryatidum*. Though these figures go back to a rather different source, we should be in no doubt that they nevertheless confirm the overall consistency of its design vocabulary, which is without exception characterised by what Vredeman's own title page aptly describes as the *diversche manieren*, or 'diverse styles' which go to make up the Renaissance grotesque.

The other term that Breton uses here, *masquerades*, alerts us to one of the other uses to which these drollities were put at this period, as designs for carnival and masque figures. The Prestongrange ceiling can be situated with a number of other documents that have attracted recent attention for what they tell us about the various ways in which Rabelais was received on this side of the channel, specifically in the process Anne Lake Prescott has called 'Imagining Rabelais in Renaissance England' (Prescott 1998). As a result, largely, of Prescott's work, we now know quite a lot about what Rabelais – indeed, about what these particular pseudo-Rabelaisian prints – meant to British readers and viewers at this period. Such documents offer us a context within which to 'read' the Prestongrange figures. The first thing to stress, perhaps, is that the Prestongrange ceiling is early – earlier than any of the other documents which Prescott has identified as showing the influence of *Les songes drolatiques*. The earliest of her sources is a work by the anonymous E D printed in 1585 called *Prayse of Nothing*, which refers to the 'slaepie phantasmata of Francois Rabilois', likely to be an allusion if only because the expression 'sleepy phantasms' is an exact translation of *Songes*. It is precisely the status of these images as phantasms, dreamwork, that establishes their most frequent association in the contemporary reception of Rabelais and also, as we shall see, their association with grotesque. In 1607 the poet Barnabe Barnes names Pantagruel in the context of 'subtill apparitions/Which no man can behold with mortall eyes' (Prescott 1998, p.148), and in 1612 the dying Bracciano in Webster's *The White Devil* sees a parting vision of a creature 'With a great codpiece stuck full of pins' which, Prescott shows, corresponds exactly to one of Desprez' drollities.

These are stage plays, not court masques, but in 1617 Ben Jonson's *Vision of Delight* initiated a succession of dramatic performances which were to bear out Richard Breton's suggestion that these drollities were suitable *pour establir mascarades*. Prescott shows that the succession of fantastic phantoms the character Fant'sy evokes in what Orgel and Strong call a 'verbal antimasque' in *Vision of Delight* includes at least ten images that have close parallels with figures from *Les songes drolatiques*. Thereafter these misshapen carnivalesque figures influence antimasque designs in Jonson's *Pleasure Reconciled to Virtue* (1618) and James Shirley's *Triumph of Peace* (1634), until finally, in 1640, William Davenant's *Salmacida Spolia* has an antimasque in which Discord unleashes four 'grotesques or drollities' including two of the four figures painted on the Prestongrange ceiling some sixty years previously. Inigo Jones' sketches for these costume designs have survived and have several times been reproduced in modern studies such as Orgel and Strong's *Inigo Jones. The Theatre of the Stuart Court* (1973, pp.732, 770-1). Davenant's was one of the last of the court masques to be produced before the English Civil Wars finally put an end to this genre of court entertainment, whose development had descended so directly from the accession to the English throne of the Stuart kings of Scotland. It appears that for Jonson and Jones these grotesques were associated with the antimasque forces of monstrous irregularity and disorder, which it was, conventionally, the function of the masque proper to overturn and set to rights. Whatever the distance in terms of application or decorum, however, between Mark Kerr's ceiling and Inigo Jones' masque, it is clear that the Scottish ceiling anticipates Jones in its use of this source and it is curious that two figures chosen by Jones from the 120 drollities of the *Songes drolatiques* should be two of the four painted at Prestongrange.

What these English applications of the Rabelaisian *Songes* repeatedly register is not so much the implication of carnivalesque disorder and trangression, however, as their status as products of the unregulated free play of imagination. These are 'slaepie phantasmata' (E D), and 'subtill apparitions' (Barnabe Barnes), 'chimera' (James Shirley), 'dreams of the maker and dreams of the teller' (Jonson). And this is probably what, finally, confirms their identity with the type of grotesques which Mark Kerr took over from the designs of Vredeman de Vries, since such grotesques are examples of what Dürer called *Traumwerk*, 'dreamwork'. Dürer uses this suggestive expression in his marginal notes to emperor Maximilian's prayer book: 'Whoever wants to do dreamwork, must mix all things together' (cited Gombrich 1979, p.251). We are surely justi-

Fantastic car, one of a series of impossible strapwork vehicles designed by Cornelis Bos and published by Hieronymus Cock in Antwerp, c.1552.

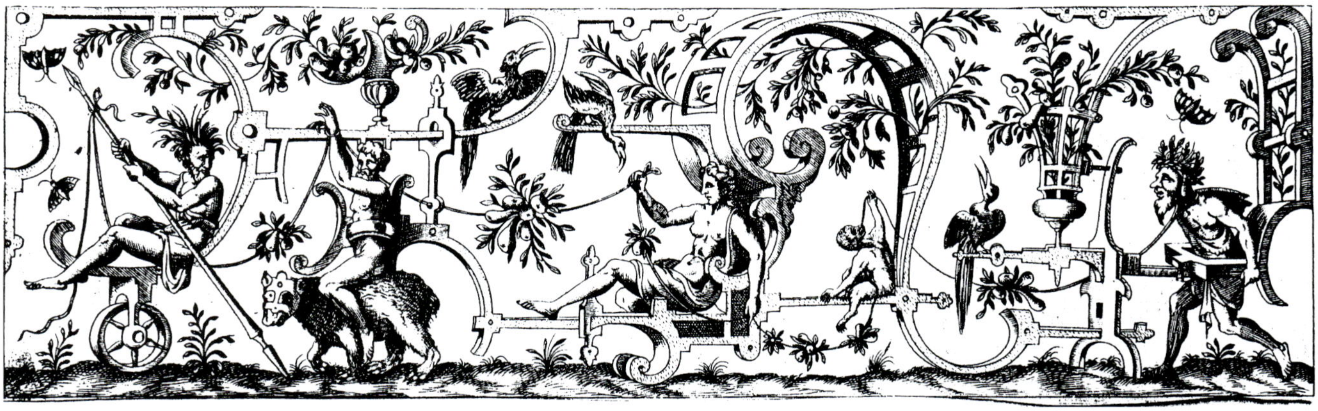

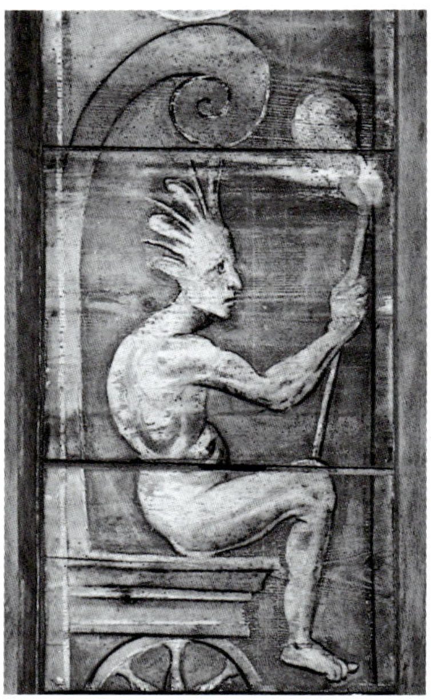

Feather-headed rider sits on the wagon, detail from Prestongrange (p.17).
RCAHMS

fied in concluding that both of the sources we have so far identified for Kerr's ceiling would confirm that what he thought he was producing on his ceiling in 1581 was a consistent piece of 'dreamwork'.

Moreover, another source for one of its motifs can only confirm this, since there is one detail that refers, directly or indirectly, to an engraving by the Dutch designer of grotesque subjects and patterns, Cornelis Bos. The naked figure with his feathered hair who sits on a wheeled cornice holding a spear, is almost certainly based on a detail from Bos's print of 1552. Bos's riders are engaged in a futile struggle to drive their impossible strapwork vehicle, which is firmly embedded in the ground – the type of impossibility one might regard as the hallmark of grotesque invention. Cornelis Bos was born in the town of Herzogenbosch, birthplace of his namesake Hieronymus Bosch, and his engravings are sometimes thought to take the art of grotesque ornament to similar extremes of fantastic or surrealistic exaggeration. If one wanted to identify the most obvious exemplar of Dürer's 'dreamwork' in decorative prints of this period, it is to the work of Cornelis Bos that one would probably turn.

Attempts to account for Mark Kerr's motivation in selecting such a style of dreamwork for his ceiling are likely to be highly speculative. The idea that these images have any connection with Scottish witchcraft, and specifically with the witchcraft trials that were to erupt ten years later in North Berwick, is entirely unfounded. Grotesque painting is a decorative style of European provenance and with antique (that is to say classical) pretensions. It has absolutely no association with witchcraft anywhere else throughout northern Europe, where it became so widely fashionable, and there is no reason why Scotland should be any different in this respect. The discovery that Mark Kerr had close connections with leading recusant families could be more relevant – Kerr had been educated in Italy and had spent time in Paris; his brother George was involved in the Spanish blanks episode. E J Cowan has also, apparently, discovered that he had (unspecified) connections with Alexander Dickson, Scottish exponent of the art of memory and associate of Giordano Bruno (Cowan 1983, p.139). The possibility that Kerr combined crypto-Catholic tendencies with an educated interest in Renaissance hermeticism is not unlikely. However, such interest in what we tend to think of as 'esoteric' philosophy in the Renaissance was by no means unusual or eccentric, and neither the engravings of François Desprez nor those of Vredeman de Vries were ever received as expressions of esoteric philosophy. These are not in any sense 'neoplatonic' or hermetic images – for that one would have to go to the diagrams of Robert Fludd or the alchemical engravings of Heinrich Khuhnrath and Michael Maier. Grotesque painting cannot have the slightest connection with such engravings precisely because it was thought to be, almost by definition, a style devoid of intellectual content, painting which is, as Peacham puts it, 'without Rime or reason'.

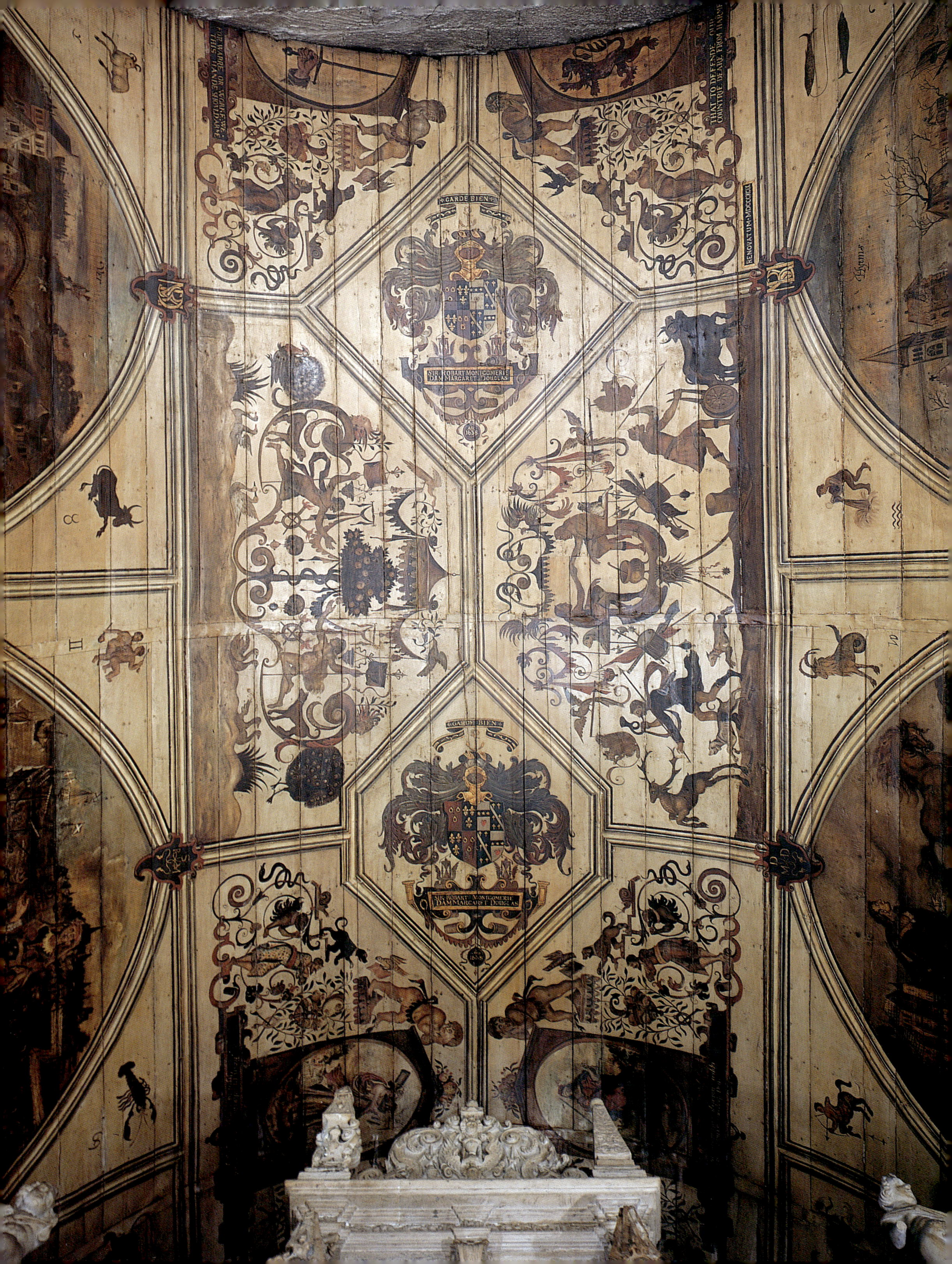
GARDE BIEN
SIR ROBART MONTGOMERIE
DAM MARGARET DOUGLAS
THAT TO DEFENDE
COUNTRIE DEARE FROM HARME
RENOVATUM·MDCCCXLI
GARDE BIEN
SIR ROBART MONTGOMERIE
DAM MARGARET DOUGLAS

6

'MONUMENTS OF IDOLATRIE'

THE Renaissance fashion for decorative painting arose at a time of Protestant iconoclasm, when the reformers' hatred of idolatrous images in churches led to the wholesale destruction of Scotland's rich heritage of medieval Christian art. It has, indeed, sometimes been suggested that the fashion was occasioned or encouraged by the very fact that journeymen artists who had always made their livelihood from religious painting were cut off from this source of income and patronage and therefore had to seek new, secular, outlets for their traditional skills. It is certainly surprising, if not paradoxical, that this explosion of a new style of decorative art should have come about at precisely the period when the Protestant reformers were fulminating against all kinds of graven images. Moreover the new style of painting was by no means restricted to purely secular subjects for, as we have seen, it includes religious painting, and that not only in 'private' domestic apartments but also in churches and chapels. The fact that new paintings were being commissioned for some Scottish churches at the very time when images of the Virgin and saints were being torn down in others should give us pause for thought.

We should, firstly, bear in mind that the Reformation was always patchy. Pockets of Catholicism remained, overt or covert, and even Protestant patrons might favour more lenient doctrines. The iconography of one of the outstanding examples of ecclesiastical painting, Grandtully Chapel, almost certainly reflects the adherence of Sir William Stewart to the liturgical reforms favoured by Charles I, who appointed him Sheriff Principal of Perth in 1630 and 1634. Sir William improved his chapel in 1636 at a time when the imposition of the Anglican prayer book on Scotland was leading up to the National Covenant in 1638; the eastern placement of the altar at Grandtully would certainly be sending a political signal at this date, which it seems reasonable to suppose the iconography of the ceiling would share. The zeal of the reformers varied from place to place and from time to time, and sometimes their image-breaking met with resistance. In 1640, for instance, the royalist Town Clerk of Aberdeen, Spalding, describes how a group of Covenanters – Gilbert Ross, Minister of Elgin,

Opposite: *Skelmorlie Aisle, Largs, painted ceiling, central panels showing Esau and Jacob, Adam and Eve, arms of Sir Robert Montgomery and Margaret Douglas, emblematic figures of Justice and Fortitude with texts; two half-panels with a hand holding a sword and a rampant lion with texts.* HS

the Laird of Innes, and the Laird of Bridie – broke down the choir screen:

> On the west syde wes painted in excellent cullouris illuminat with starres of bricht golde, the crucefixing of our blessed Saueour Jesus Christ. This piece wes so excellentlie done, that the culouris nor starris never faidit no evanishit bot keipit haul and sound as thay were at the beginning notwithstanding this college or channonrie Kirk wantit the roof sen the refourmatioun .... On the vther syde of this wall, towardis the east wes drawin the day of judgement. Aluayes all is throwne doun to the ground.

Spalding describes how the minister brought the timbers to his house to serve as firewood, but that it would not burn, 'whairat the servandis and vtheris mervallit and thairupone the Minister left and forboor to bring in or burne ony more of that tymber in his hous' (cited in Mackintosh 1914, pp.66-7). Minutes of the Synod of Fife in 1612 order the destruction of the paintings at Foulis Easter near Dundee: 'Item, it is statute and ordained that the paintrie quilk is upon the pulpitt and ruid-laft, being monuments of idolatrie, sal be obliterate be laying it over with grein colour. The minister with diligens to see the same exped' (cited Apted and Robertson 1964, p.273). Yet the fact that the painting at Foulis Easter was not destroyed suggests that opinions were divided.

Some images were held to be less offensive than others. Most Protestants had little objection to historical painting of Old Testament narrative: the Temptation of Eve, the Sacrifice of Abraham, the Judgement of Solomon, David and Bathsheba, Judith and Holofernes – these were all scriptural episodes which held important morals and messages for true believers. We find such subjects among the paintings Sir William Nisbet commissioned for his long gallery at The Dean in Edinburgh, possibly in 1627. He was Baillie and Lord Provost of the city at various times, so unlikely to fill his house with controversial images. Similar Old Testament subjects are included in the painting at Kinneil as early as the 1560s, along with a Good Samaritan sequence. Historians often make a distinction between Old and New Testament images in discussing Reformation iconoclasm – images from the Old Testament are less controversial, but if you must use the New Testament then parables probably offer the most appropriate subjects for Protestant painting.

What the reformers found most offensive, of course, were images of the Virgin, of the saints, and of the Godhead. These are likely to be idolatrous since they represent Christian mysteries, images of the divine. Yet we can find examples of all these in decorative painting of this period in Scotland. For instance, alongside images of the pagan Sibyls (which were not seen as controversial by Protestants) at his house in Burntisland ('Mary Somerville's House'), the burgess John Watson painted not only an image of the Agnus Dei – Christ as a lamb holding a Banner of the Resurrection – but also, apparently, an image of the Virgin Mary. The image has disappeared, but the boards that have survived include a fragment with the clear label 'MARIA'. We should be less surprised to find an image of the deity with the motto 'EGO SUM VIA VERETAS ET VITA' on the ceiling of Mary of Guise's palace in Edinburgh since the queen mother was a

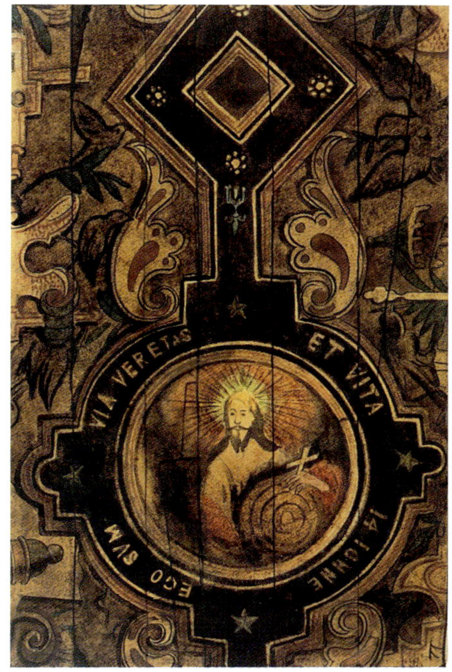

Thomas Bonnar's nineteenth-century sketch of the painting from 'Mary of Guise's House', Edinburgh; the palace and chapel occupied by Scotland's catholic queen regent, widow of James V, was pulled down in the nineteenth century. Such images of the Godhead were anathema to the Reformed Church. RCAHMS

Catholic, but the fact that the painting survived – seen or unseen – until the house was finally demolished in the nineteenth century is nevertheless notable.

More surprising is the painted gallery at Provost Skene's house in Aberdeen, for this was not the house of a Catholic queen regent but the home of a respectable burgess and sometime Provost of Aberdeen whose family had, at various times, been prosecuted and imprisoned in the same city for attending mass. It contains not only a cycle of panels illustrating the life of Christ – Annunciation, Adoration, Crucifixion, Entombment, Resurrection, Ascension – but also separate images illustrating the Instruments of the Passion. John Houston, who was in charge of the early stages of the restoration, reported that four of the panels which are now blank showed traces on exposure of Christ in the Temple, the Baptism of Christ, the Last Supper, and the Ascension. McRoberts (1954) suggests the sequence of pictures may have followed the threefold division of the Mysteries of the Rosary, and although the

Provost Skene's House, Aberdeen. Though painted for a prominent burgess and sometime Provost of the city, this gallery is painted with scenes from the life of Christ, images that were commonly seen as idolatrous by the Reformers. HS

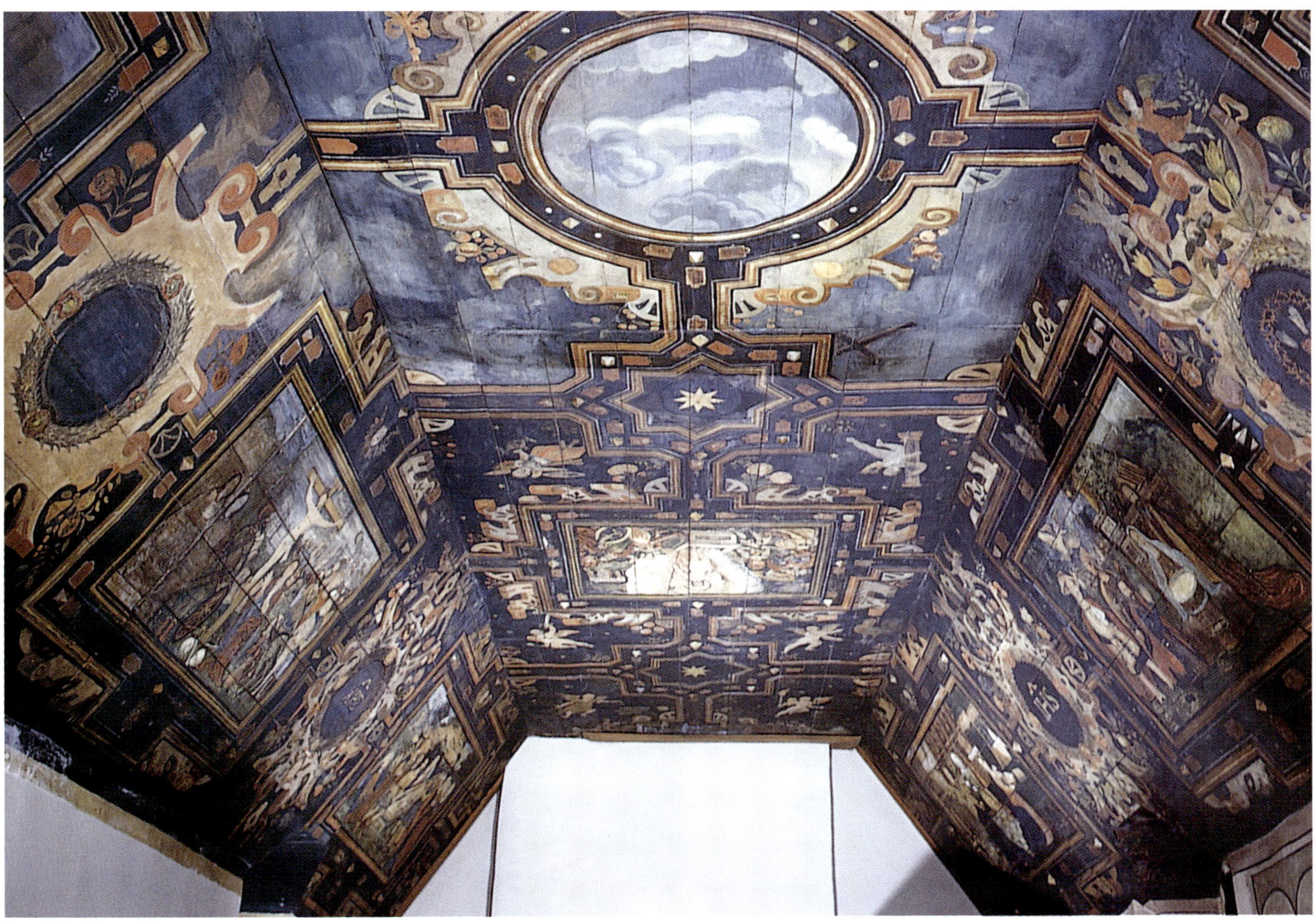

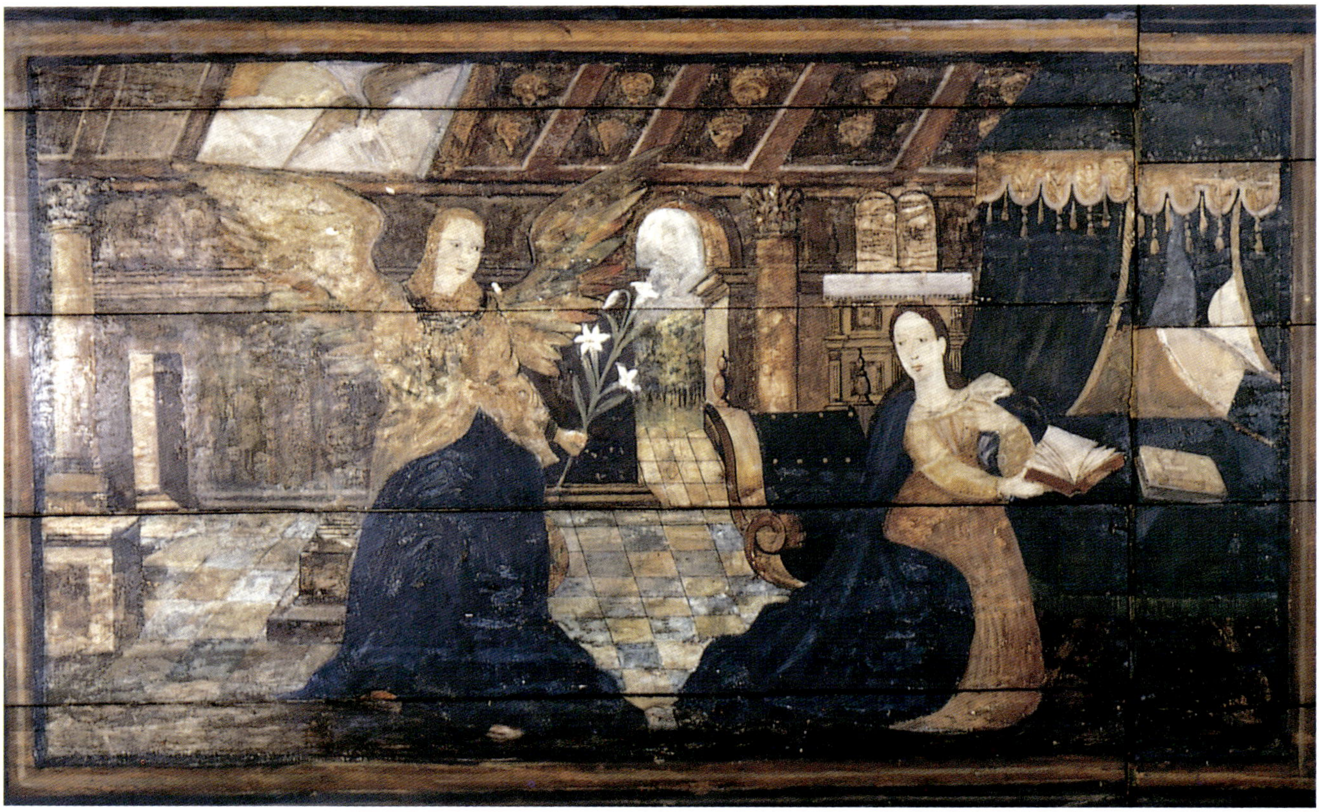

The Annunciation panel at Provost Skene's House, which almost certainly copies an engraving after a design by Maarten de Vos. HS

correspondence is not exact he is undoubtedly right to conclude that the gallery was designed as 'a secret chapel of the Old Faith' and that the north wall would originally have had an altar, behind which there is a small room which 'may have served the purpose of vestry and confessional' (p.122). Matthew Lumsden owned the house between 1622 and 1641, and a probable date of 1626 has been suggested for the painting. Although various members of his family were accused of recusancy, there is no independent evidence of his own Catholicism; indeed in 1634 he became a baillie of Aberdeen, and he fought on the Covenanting side during the Bishop's Wars of 1639-40. The iconography of the painted gallery or chapel is, however, enough on its own to justify the conclusion that Lumsden was 'in reality a crypto-Catholic, temporizing with the political and religious situation, in the hope that better days might come' (McRoberts 1954, p 122).

In practice it can be difficult to know just what doctrinal signals would be sent to contemporary viewers by the different types of imagery which these ceilings employ. One of the most interesting comments on their iconography comes from King James himself. In 1616-17 the king seems to have taken a close personal interest in the redecoration of the choir stalls in the Chapel Royal at Holyrood Palace in preparation for his return to his ancient capital. The carving was executed in London by the English sculptor, Nicholas Stone, under the direction of Inigo Jones, and the stalls were sent up to Scotland to be gilded and painted, along with paintings of the four Apostles and the biblical Virtues, Faith, Hope and Charity (Howard 1995, pp.38-9). Compared to the painting we have just been looking at this would seem a relatively uncontroversial choice of subjects, yet the Bishop of Galloway was active in voicing the iconoclastic misgivings of the Scottish Kirk at news of these preparations. James himself

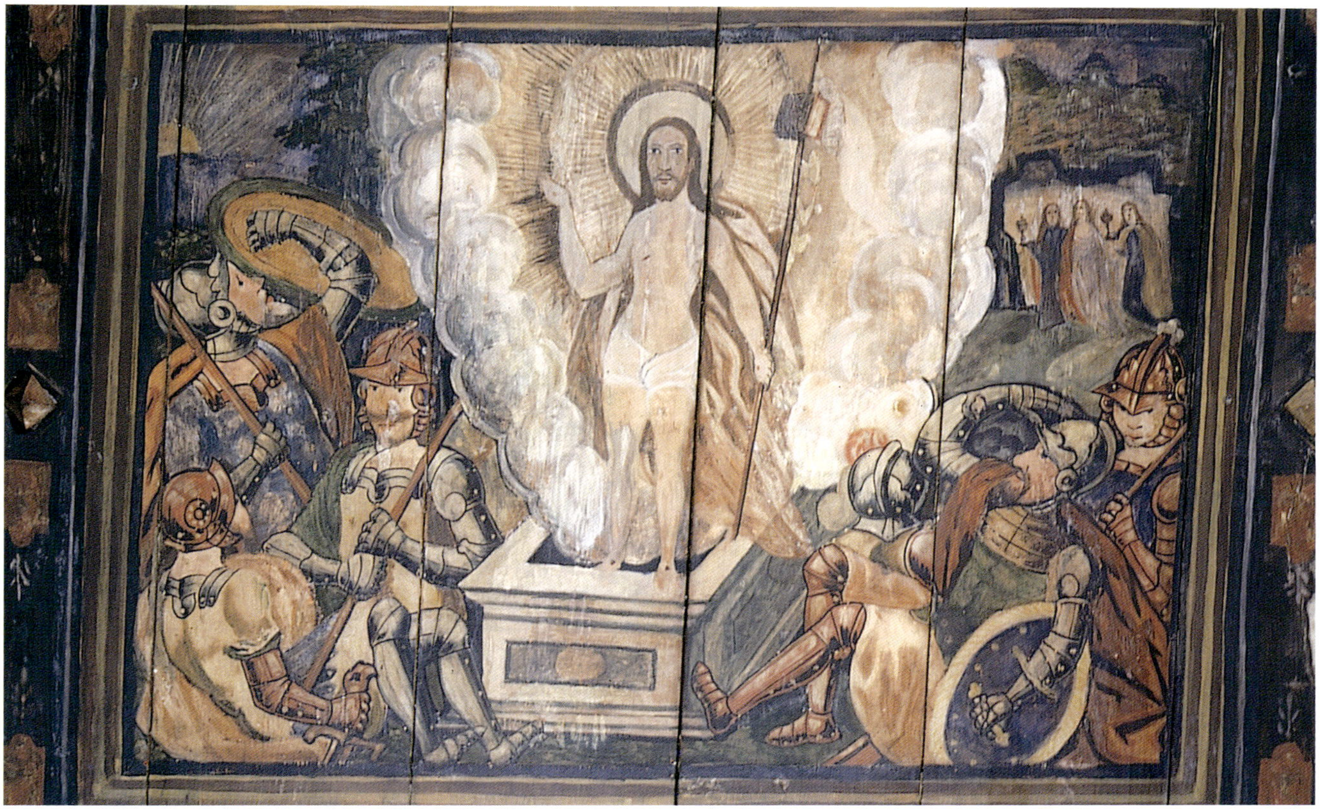

The Resurrection panel at Provost Skene's House. HS

attempted to allay such fears by writing a lengthy letter to the protestors in which he makes some interesting distinctions between the kinds of imagery which were iconographically permissible or not permissible on such an occasion.

> When we received and perused your letter of the 25th of February last, concerning the graven work of wood intended for decoring our seat in our chapel at Holyrood House, we were at first affraid that some of the directors or workmen had been Papists, and so without our knowledge had intended there to erect such idolatrous images and painted pictures as those of that profession had been in use to adore; but when we had better considered, and exactly tried what was done, we find but a false alarm, and that causeless fears have made you start at your own shadows .... And therefore do not deceive yourselves with a vain imagination of anything done therein for ease of your hearts or ratifying your error in your judgment of that graven work, which is not of an idolatrous kind like to images and painted pictures adored and worshipped by Papists, but merely intended for ornament and decoration of the place where we shall sit, and might have been wrought as well with figures of lions, dragons, and devils, as with those of patriarchs and apostles. But as we must wonder at your ignorance, and teach you thus to distinguish the one and the other, so are we persuaded that none of you would have been scandalised or offended if the said figures of lions, dragons, and devils had been carved and put up in lieu of those of the patriarchs and prophets. (cited in Burton 1905, vol. vi, pp.42-3.)

This royal reproof is as clear an indication as we could wish of the distinctions being drawn between legitimate and illegitimate subjects for painting at this time in Scotland, written at a date when the king's views on church rituals were already, shortly before the Five Articles of Perth (1619-21), arousing Calvinist fears. The royal reassurance makes a clear distinction between Old Testament subjects – patriarchs and prophets – and those unspecified 'images and painted pictures adored by the Papists which the King joins his opponents in rejecting'. It may be unclear whether purely secular subjects – 'lions, dragons and devils' – are to be included in such condemnation, since the motive for James's ironic inference that such ungodly images would not have provoked the same fears as Papist icons is largely rhetorical. Precisely such profane subjects were to be seen in secular buildings of this period, such as Prestongrange with its grotesques and Rabelaisian figures, but James's justification need not be read as passing judgement on the use of these secular images at such a location.

Among the most impressive examples of ecclesiastical painting in the new style is the Skelmorlie Aisle at Largs, Ayrshire. It shows particularly clearly just how difficult it can be to know what doctrinal signals religious painting of this period in Scotland was sending to its viewers. For this reason I shall spend the remainder of this chapter looking at this site in some detail in order to show how its iconography works. Perhaps the first thing to note is that, although it was added to the parish church, the aisle itself is a very personal commemorative space almost certainly adapted for the use of its patron. That is not to say that the parishioners of Largs were excluded – almost certainly they weren't – but this was clearly a space within which the local laird could express his own tastes and preferences. The aisle was built in 1636 onto the Old Church in Largs, Ayrshire, by Sir Robert Montgomery of Skelmorlie to house his own remains and those of his wife, Margaret Douglas. It is remarkable in a number of respects. It is the only example of decorative painting in Scotland of this period which its artist has signed – the panel showing a woman with a horse is signed 'J Stalker fecit 1638'. In 1632 James Stalker, son of David, was registered apprentice to John Sawers, painter, in the Edinburgh Register of Apprentices. Nothing further is known of Stalker himself but Sawers (fl.1617-d.1651) did work at Edinburgh Castle and at the new Parliament House; he had important connections with the Lyon Court, where he was appointed Snowdon Herald in 1643 and compiled a manuscript armorial which has survived (Nat Lib Scot Adv MS 31.4.4). Sawers' younger son, Henry, following in his father's footsteps, was appointed Carrick Pursuivant in 1650 (Apted and Hannabuss 1978, p.82). These connections with the Lyon Court are significant in view of the fine heraldic painting in three central panels of the aisle, and it seems likely that, although the ceiling bears the signature of his apprentice, Sawers himself may have had a hand in the painting at Largs, some parts of which are certainly more competently executed than others suggesting the work of more than one hand.

The Montgomery Aisle is also remarkable insofar as the patterns for several of its details have been identified in continental prints. Among the more distinctive and memorable are the two large central panels of Biblical subjects, the Temptation, and Esau and Jacob. What is most striking about these images is their treatment, for the figures of Adam and Eve are shown kneeling on 'antique' leaf scrolls which curve up to form grotesque heads; they hold banners

Opposite
Top: *Etienne Delaune, Adam and Eve, from a set of six Old Testament prints.* BM

Bottom: *Skelmorlie Aisle, Temptation of Adam and Eve copied from the goldsmith's pattern by Etienne Delaune.* HS

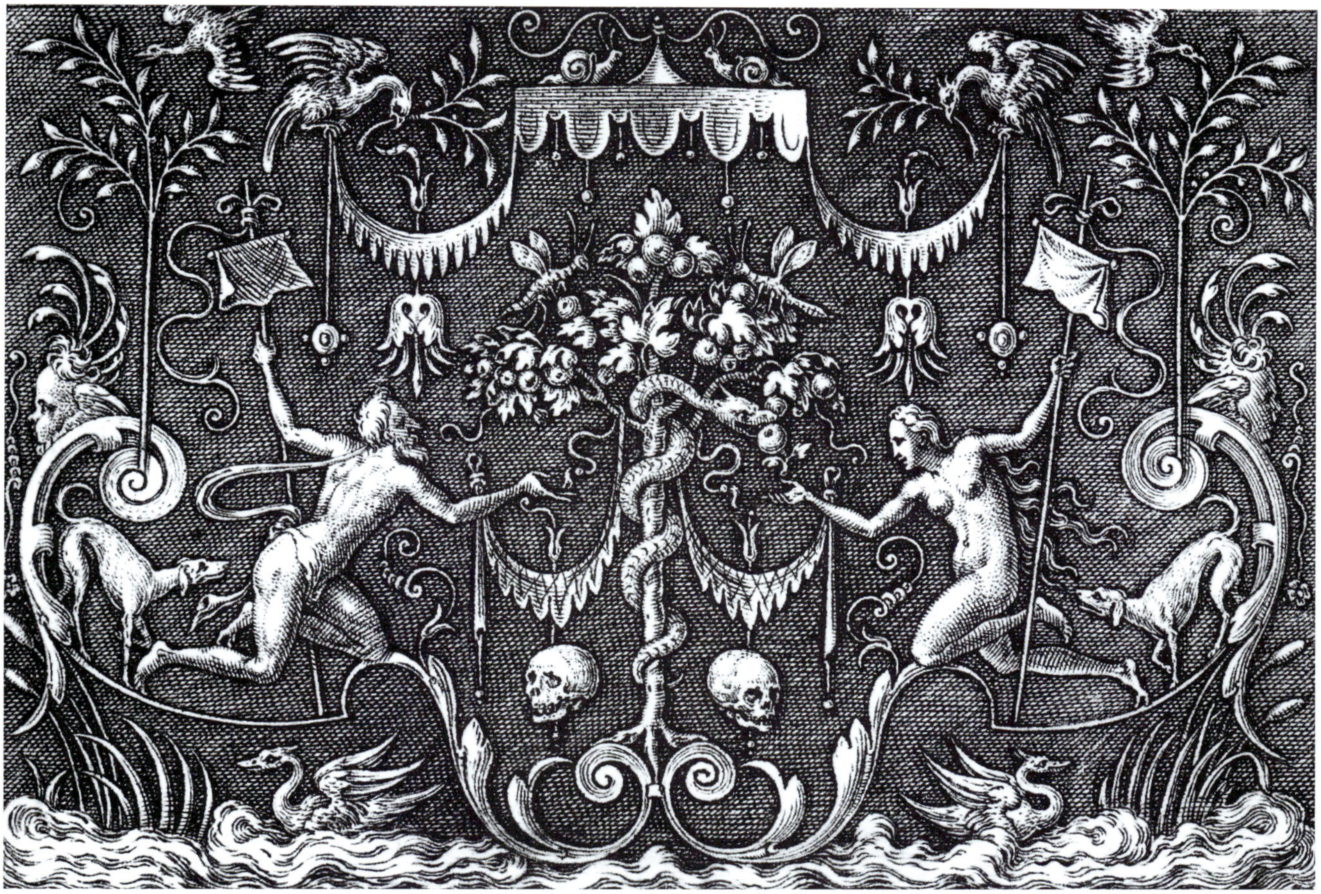

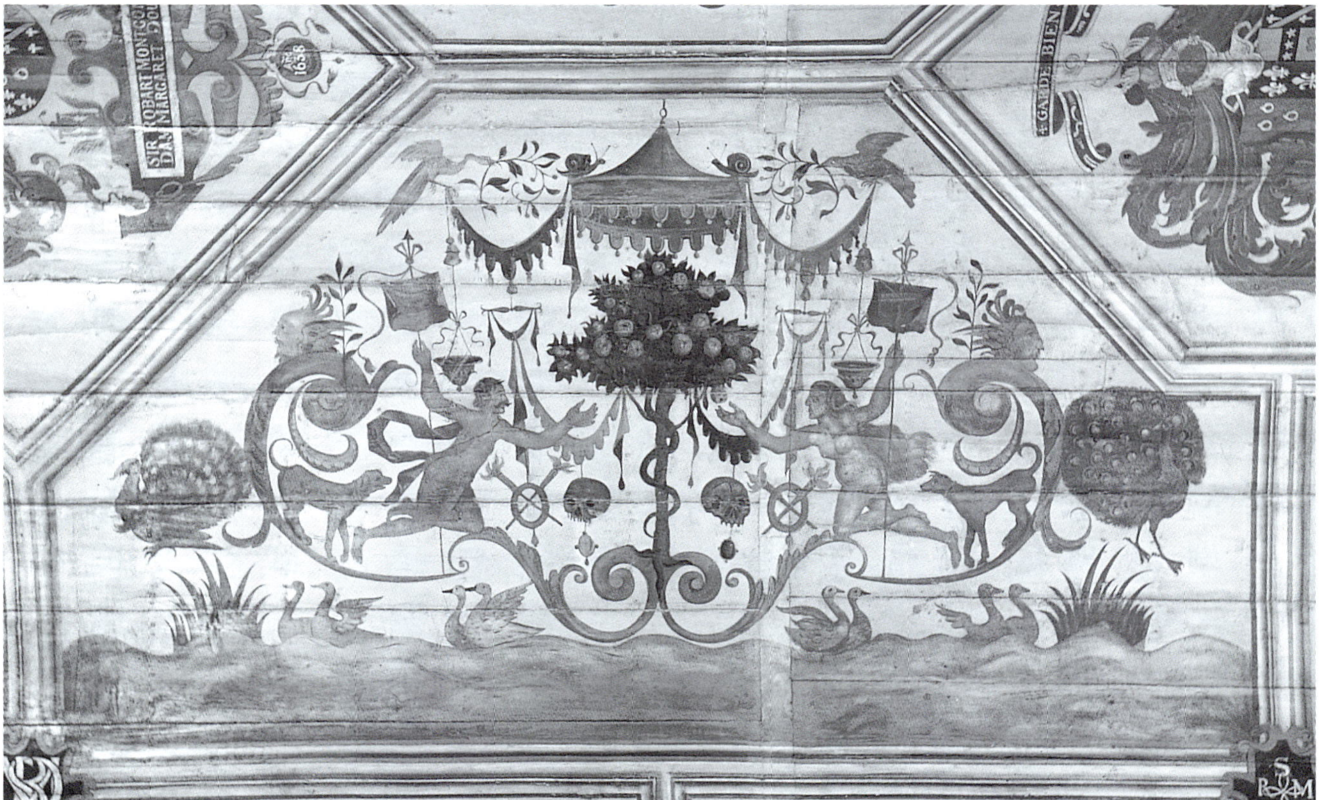
SIR ROBART MONT
DAM MARGARET
1638
GARDE BIEN

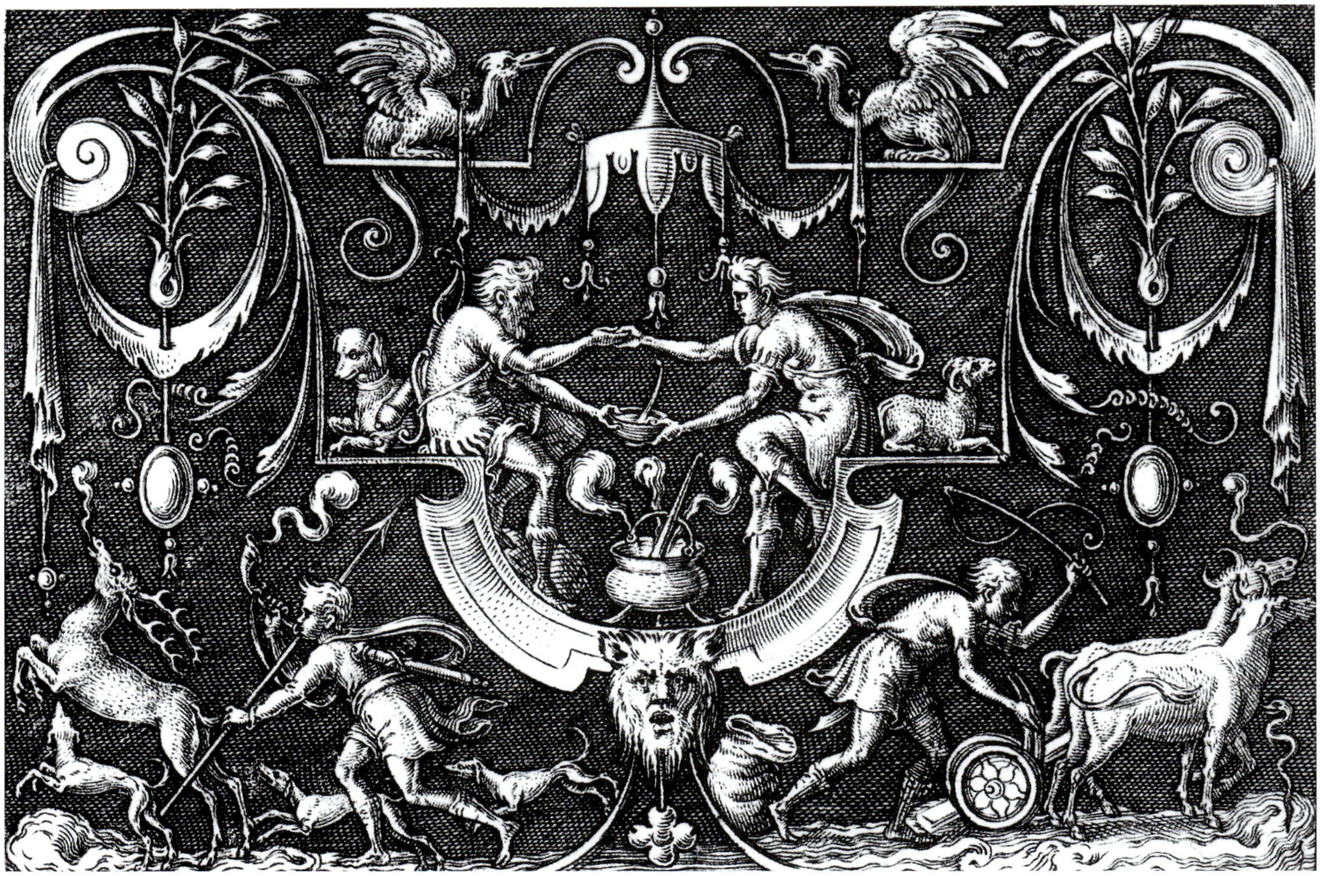

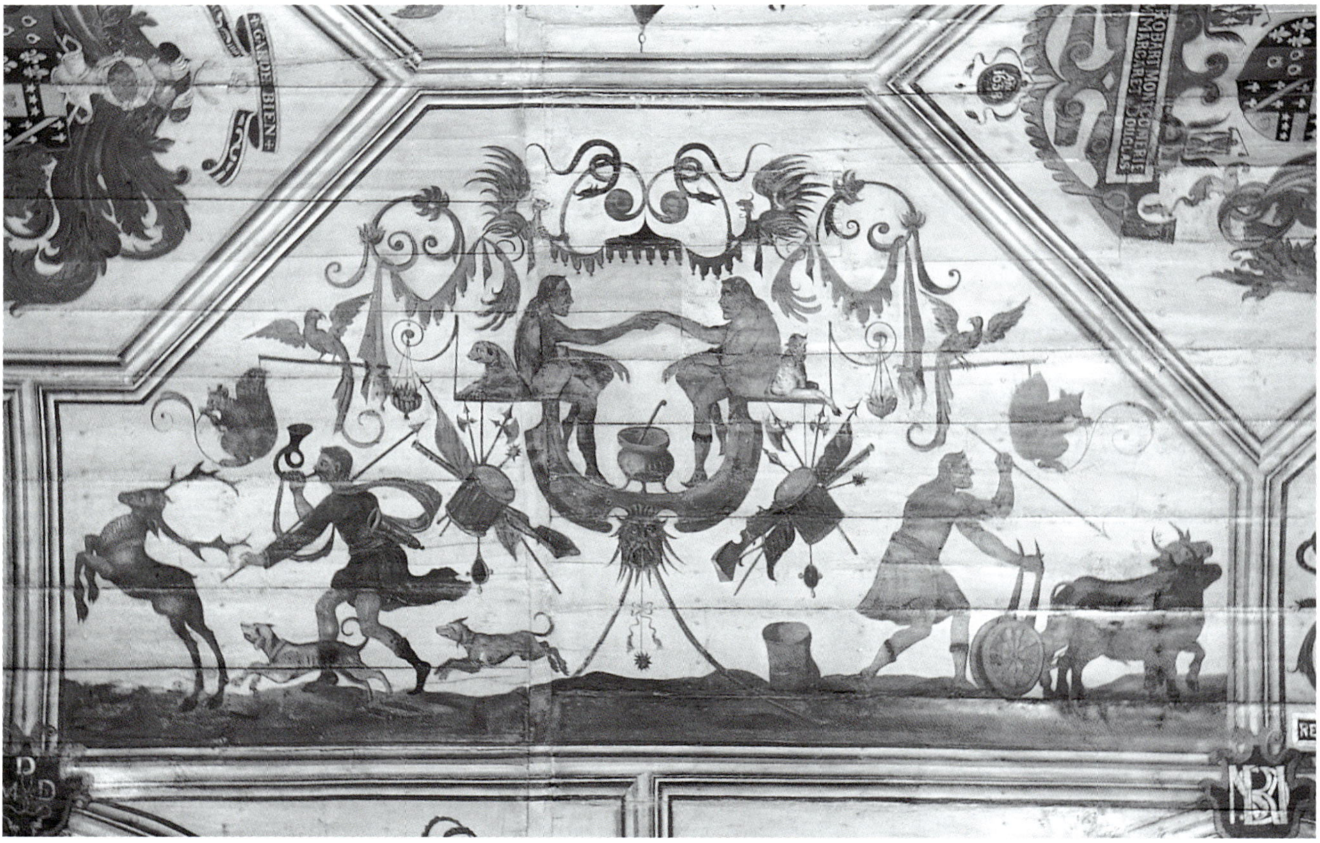

on poles, and the Tree of Knowledge with its serpent is surmounted by an elegant baldachino with birds; two peacocks display on either side, and water birds swim on waves beneath. Facing this is the panel showing Esau and Jacob. These were the twin brothers born to Rebecca and Isaac; Esau became a hunter, whereas Jacob became a farmer, a 'man of the field ... dwelling in tents' (Genesis 25.27). When Esau returned faint with hunger from the chase he sold his birthright to Jacob in return for a mess of pottage, and this is shown in the Largs panel where we see the two brothers seated on either side of a cooking pot sealing their agreement by joining hands. The brothers are shown again just below in a scene where Esau, with spear and curly hunting horn, chases a leaping stag with two hounds while prudent Jacob ploughs the land with two oxen which he is prodding with a spear; behind him is a sack of lentils which the Bible describes him as cultivating. Once again these biblical scenes are wholly contained within a pattern of elaborate decorative scrollwork with fanciful birds, squirrels and a trophy of arms. The ground on which Jacob's pot rests is transformed into a lion's mask from which hangs a ribbon.

There is no other example of biblical painting in Scotland which transforms Old Testament scenes into such Mannerist decoration. As Anthony Wells-Cole discovered, they are closely copied from ornament prints by Etienne Delaune, an engraver described by Arthur Hind (1923, p.103) as 'one of the finest of all ornament engravers'. Delaune's influence in Britain is extremely limited, the only known use of his prints in England being two textile designs at Hardwick Hall (Wells-Cole 1997, figs 441-2). His style of slender foliage and sinuous grotesques goes back directly to Raphael and Giovanni da Udine's decoration of the Vatican *loggie*. The two engravings copied at Ayr were executed around 1570 as goldsmith's patterns by Delaune, formerly engraver to the Paris mint and medallist to Henri II; after Henri's death he fled as a Protestant refugee to Strasbourg. As Wells-Cole remarks, 'Almost all [Delaune's engravings] are on a miniature scale and do not stray far from ornament associated with medals, jewellery or metalwork' (1997, p 40). This miniature scale accounts for the finesse of these designs, the original prints measuring a mere three by two inches, whereas on the ceiling they have been hugely magnified to fill panels measuring nine feet by five. How, we may ask, was this done? When Andrew Lyons, in 1897, made a scale drawing of the whole ceiling, he remarked that traces of pounce-work were discovered. Pounce-work is a method of marking out embroidery or other patterns – the pattern is marked out on paper and rows of holes are pricked out with a needle to mark the lines. A felt pad dipped in powdered chalk or charcoal is then rubbed over the pattern to leave a trace on the cloth. It is not easy to know what kind of traces Lyons could have found on the ceiling in 1897, but he was a leading Scottish antiquarian and a practising architect whose evidence is probably to be trusted. Pounce-work means, as he says, that 'the full-size design must have been very carefully drawn out and pounces prepared before proceeding with the painting' (p.111). Normally a grid was drawn across the engraving or cartoon and an enlarged grid drawn to scale on the pattern paper; the outline would then be copied into each rectangle.

Opposite
Top: *Etienne Delaune, Esau and Jacob, from a set of six Old Testament prints.* BM

Bottom: *Skelmorlie Aisle, Esau and Jacob, copied from a goldsmith's pattern by Etienne Delaune.* HS

The labour of preparing such full-sized patterns may explain why Stalker (or Sawers) should have reused one of them to fill some vacant space on the same ceiling. Two designs which abut onto the north-end wall above the window have only enough space for half-panels, but the left-hand panel repeats the figure of Jacob pursuing his plough, with all the surrounding decorative paraphernalia and to exactly the same scale as we find it on the central panel just described. The right-hand half-panel evidently re-used the other half of the same pounce-pattern since it shows us a repeat image of Esau with his hunting horn, spear, hounds and leaping stag, just as we see him on the central panel. I shall return to these truncated images when I examine the way space is articulated on the ceiling overall.

The whole ceiling is a notable exercise in false architecture, its barrel vault being intersected by *trompe l'oeil* 'stone' vaulting and rib-work rising up from fourteen Mannerist *trompe* corbels which pretend to project through the cornice. This false ribbing divides the whole ceiling into forty-one separate compartments, all of which are filled with decorative painting. The different types of subject and treatment with which these are filled can only be described as stylistically eclectic. Delaune's decorative Mannerism appears alongside landscapes that can only be described as pseudo-Dutch.

The painting is also iconographically complex. Starting from the bottom, we have firstly the ten false corbels, decorated with the badges of the tribes of Israel. The circular demi-vaulting that springs up from these encloses twelve texts from the Geneva Bible, each framed in an elaborate strapwork cartouche. Above these spring six vaults containing the Dutch-style landscapes, the four outermost representing the seasons of the year each with its occupations and labelled 'Ver', 'Aestas', 'Autumnus' and 'Hyems'. In the twelve spandrels formed by this vaulting are the signs of the zodiac, and the tops of the six vaults are marked with ornate shields containing monograms of Robert Montgomery and Margaret Douglas. This 'verticle' false vaulting supports a central section whose *trompe* stone ribs have to be seen as offering the illusion of 'horizontal' coffering, the rib-work creating three central lozenge-shaped compartments of coats of arms, flanked by irregular panels containing various subjects.

These include the 'Temptation' and the 'Esau and Jacob' already described. Next to these are two designs of a different character, depicting the allegorical figures of Justice and of Fortitude, each with her conventional attributes (Justice blindfolded with sword and scales; Fortitude bare-armed and carrying her pillar over her shoulder). The two well-drawn personifications are shown as if in painted ovals with a landscape background, on a wooden board or rebated panel looking rather like an inn sign, with a Latin inscription beneath. Justice has the motto, *Cuique suum iusto pensans libramine reddo/Concilioque homines concilioque Deos* ('I render to each man what is his due, weighing it with true balance, I find favour with men and with gods'). Fortitude has the motto, *Fortis in adversis animosaque pectora gestans/Infractis animis ardua queque fero* ('Strong in adversity and showing a brave heart, with unbroken spirit I shoulder every burden'). These two emblems are surrounded with identical finely drawn

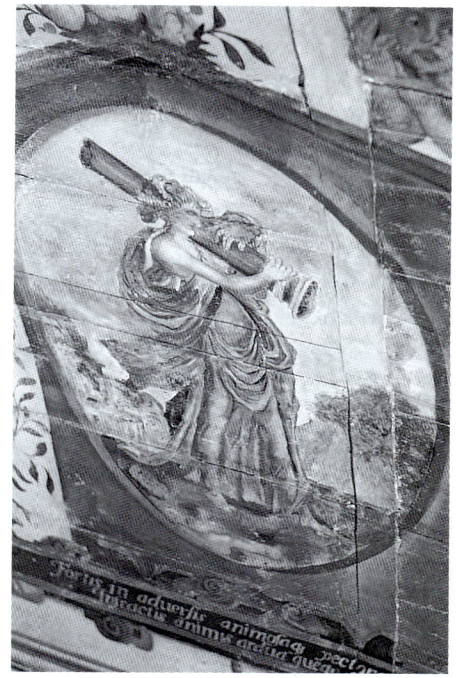

Skelmorlie Aisle, emblem of Fortitude holding her conventional pillar. HS

grotesque decoration featuring two large putti who lean their elbows on the signboard, a bird of prey, a collared dog, a snail and the torso of a bear, with two bearded male figures in loose-fitting costume, who lean nonchalantly amidst the scrollwork. These leaning figures are copied from another of Delaune's prints, where they feature amongst the decorative detail surrounding two of the allegorical figures, *Retorique* and *Aritmetique*, which go to make up Delaune's *Liberal Arts* series. This decorative ensemble is reproduced no less than six times, with no variation of detail, on the Skelmorlie ceiling and it must have been copied each time from a prepared pattern.

Though this decorative surround confirms the Mannerist *antique* style of the Old Testament scenes, the allegorical figures themselves, with their Latin mottoes, have an altogether more emblematic register. Justice and Fortitude are two of the traditional Cardinal Virtues. No source has yet been identified for the paintings or for the two Latin inscriptions, which are not quoted from any classical author I have been able to identify, and although this combination of speaking picture and moralising verse is clearly functioning as some kind of Renaissance emblem they do not appear to derive from any of the printed emblem books. It should be noted that the inscriptions are voiced – they do not simply moralise the image but are spoken in the first person by Virtue herself. That is uncharacteristic of the epigrams to Renaissance emblems, whose images are seldom given a voice, even though we may call them 'speaking pictures'.

We have seen that the two half-panels at the northern end reuse one of the Delaune patterns, which they evidently cut in half – Esau gets divided from Jacob (perhaps not inappropriately, in view of their brotherly rivalry). Something similar occurs at the southern end of this central coffered section of the ceiling, for it too joins the end wall very abruptly with no surviving cornice but with two further 'emblematic' devices which appear to have been cut in half. They have the same oval format, in the rebated wooden 'inn sign' panel, as the Justice and Fortitude panels, and they are surrounded by the same grotesque ornamentation – reclining putti, moustached attendants, bird, dog, bear and snail – clearly using the same pattern as the decorative surrounds to Justice and Fortitude. At first sight it looks as though these incomplete shields might have been brutally sliced off when, in 1802, the adjoining Old Church was demolished and the aisle entrance was walled up, but in fact it can be demonstrated that these were always designed as half-panels, or rather designed as halves which together constitute a whole panel in themselves. The first shows a rampant lion, with an inscription below which reads: 'THAT TO DEFENDE OUR/ COUNTRIE DEARE FROM HARME'. The second shows an arm holding an upraised sword and an inscription that has to be read as a follow-on from the previous panel, if only because it completes the rhyme: 'FOR WARRE OR WORKE; WE/ THIS HAND SHOVLD ARME'. Clearly this needs to be read as a single emblem, with the device a rampant lion, and the *subscriptio*: 'That to defend our country from all harm/For war or worke we this hand should arm'. It is a single inscription, a single emblem. Moreover it is an emblem which the motto now allows us to

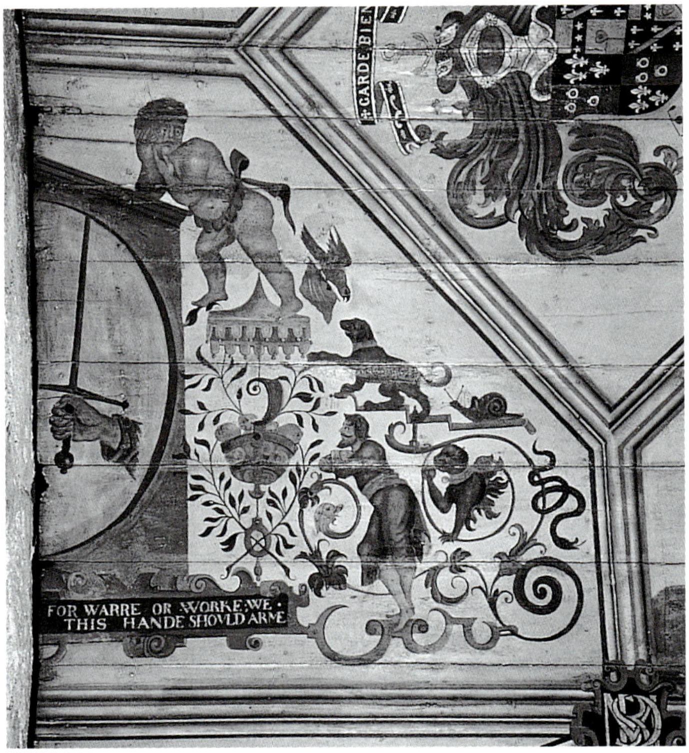

Skelmorlie Aisle, Largs, half-panel with decorative antique surround, the male figure leaning on a grotesque tendril is copied from either the Retorique *or* Aritmetique *engravings from Etienne Delaune's* Liberal Arts *series.* HS

Etienne Delaune, Retorique *from the* Liberal Arts *series.* BM

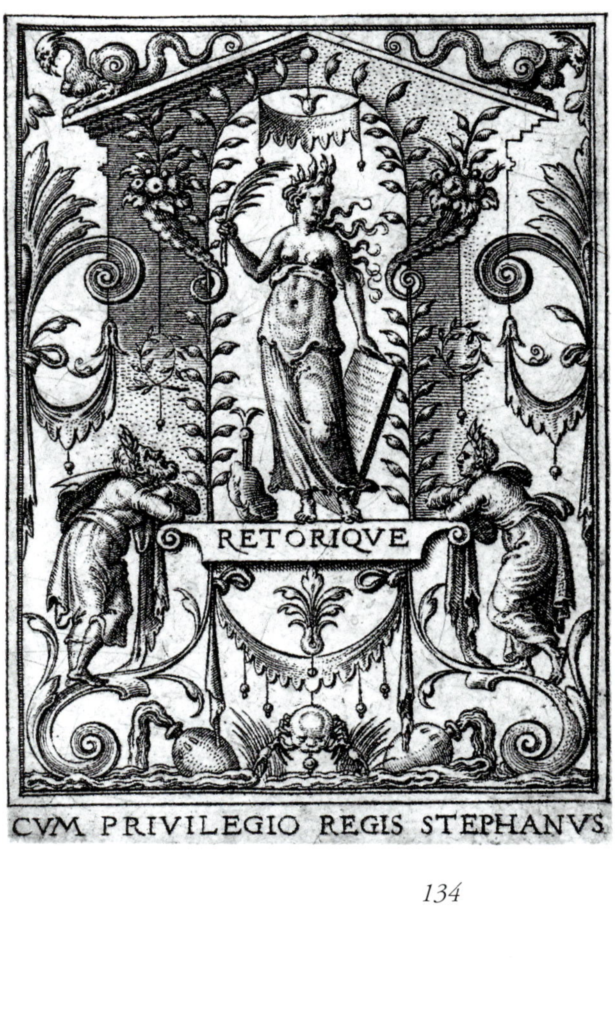

source, for H S Adams has shown in an unpublished Glasgow University dissertation that it uses the concluding couplet to Whitney's *In utrumque paratus* emblem (*Emblemes* 1586, p.66; Adams 1999, pp.47-8). Whitney's picture shows a right hand bearing a sword and a left hand waving a trowel, an image we have seen, along with other devices from Paradin, Whitney's source for this emblem (*Devises heroïques*, p.115), on the ceiling from Rossend. The Skelmorlie artist has substituted the rampant lion for the hand holding the trowel, evidently taking its hint from Whitney to transform this into an emblem of patriotic vigilance.

The way this emblem is carried round the end-of-section raises the question of how the space overall and the various images on this ceiling are articulated. There are some determinate sequences. The *trompe* corbels are decorated with ten of the twelve badges traditionally assigned to the tribes of Israel. These proceed in order of seniority of the twelve sons of Jacob, their progenitors (Genesis 49, Numbers 1.1) – Reuben, Simeon, Levi, Judah, Dan, Asher, Issacher, Zebulum, Joseph and Benjamin (Gad and Naphtali are omitted). This implies a sequence that would start at the north-east corner, and run round to the south east. The sequence of seasons and zodiac signs immediately above it, however, starts at the south-west corner, and runs round to the south east. The four seasons are, appropriately, at the four corners of the aisle, with the appropriate zodiac signs above them: Aries, Taurus and Gemini for spring; Cancer, Leo and Virgo for summer; Libra, Scorpio and Sagittarius for autumn; Capricorn, Aquarius and Pisces for winter. Each of the seasons is labelled in Latin and illustrated by a landscape showing the rural labours, with local buildings and scenery in some of the scenes. The central two landscapes of these six, however, are not seasonal, and do not seem to be part of this temporal sequence. They are in many respects the most puzzling panels on the ceiling.

The picture on the western wall shows a well-dressed woman in a seaside or marine landscape. She is kneeling in a rather awkward posture on the shore, facing the viewer. Her long hair is caught in a red headband, and her left hand holds up her overskirt as she kneels. Her head appears to be crowned with a small crescent moon, and in her right hand she holds a cup which contains a

Geffrey Whitney, Emblemes *(1586). The Skelmorlie verses quote the last two lines of Whitney's epigram; this emblem was also copied at Rossend, at Blyth's Close, Edinburgh, and at the Bay Horse Inn, Dysart.* GUL

In vtrumque paratus.
To IOHN PAYTON *Esquier.*

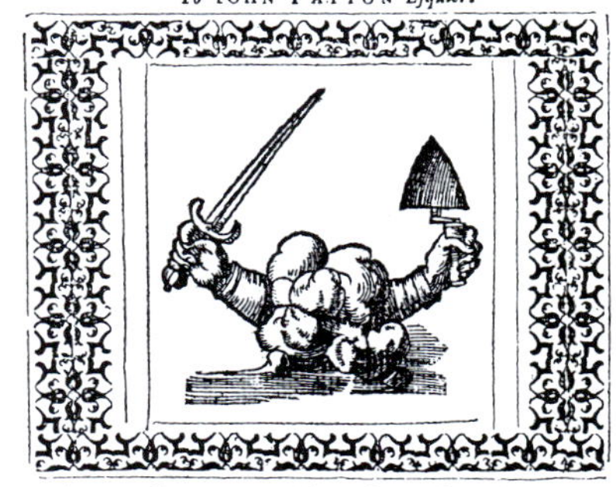

WHEN SANABAL Hierusalem distrest,
With sharpe assaultes, in NEHEMIAS tyme:
To warre, and worke, the Iewes them selues addrest,
And did repaire theire walles, with stone, and lime:
One hande the sworde, against the foe did shake,
The other hande, the trowell vp did take.

Of valiant mindes, loe here, a worthie parte,
That quailed not, with ruine of theire wall:
But Captaines boulde, did prooue the masons arte,
Which doth inferre, this lesson vnto all:
That to defende, our countrie deare from harme,
For warre, or worke, wee eyther hande should arme.

burning heart – these defining attributes ought to offer us an immediate key to her identification, but they do not appear to correspond to any of the allegorical figures in standard Renaissance mythologies such as Ripa, Cartari or Contile. On the ground beside her there is a large fish and two more monstrous ones are shown sporting in the waves behind her, where three and four-masted ships with saltire flags are shown. In the background we see a town on a hill and a long wooden pier with men working in boats. The burning heart in a chalice ought to supply our clearest clue as to the significance of this picture. In established Christian iconography the figure of Ecclesia is shown holding a chalice in which she catches the blood of Christ flowing from the cross, but Ecclesia is normally shown with the contrasting figure of Synagoga, pictured as a woman wearing a veil which Christ removes, symbolising the Old Testament whose veiled truths are 'done away in Christ' (2 Corinthians 3.13-16). It is just possible that the rather strange headgear worn by the kneeling figure at Skelmorlie Aisle represents such a veil, but it is unusual to find Ecclesia apparelled in the raised veil of Synagoga. There are few, if any, analogues for such an image of the heart resting in a chalice, though Protestant Georgette de Montenay has an emblem, *Beati mundo corde*, in which a man holds aloft a shallow cup in which a heart is being washed in the purifying water poured from Heaven (*Devises Chrestiennes*, 1571, no. 81). The chalice at Skelmorlie Aisle can hardly be anything but a eucharistic symbol and the burning heart must signify the

Skelmorlie Aisle, Largs, figure of Ecclesia(?) in a marine landscape; in her right hand she holds a chalice with a burning heart. HS

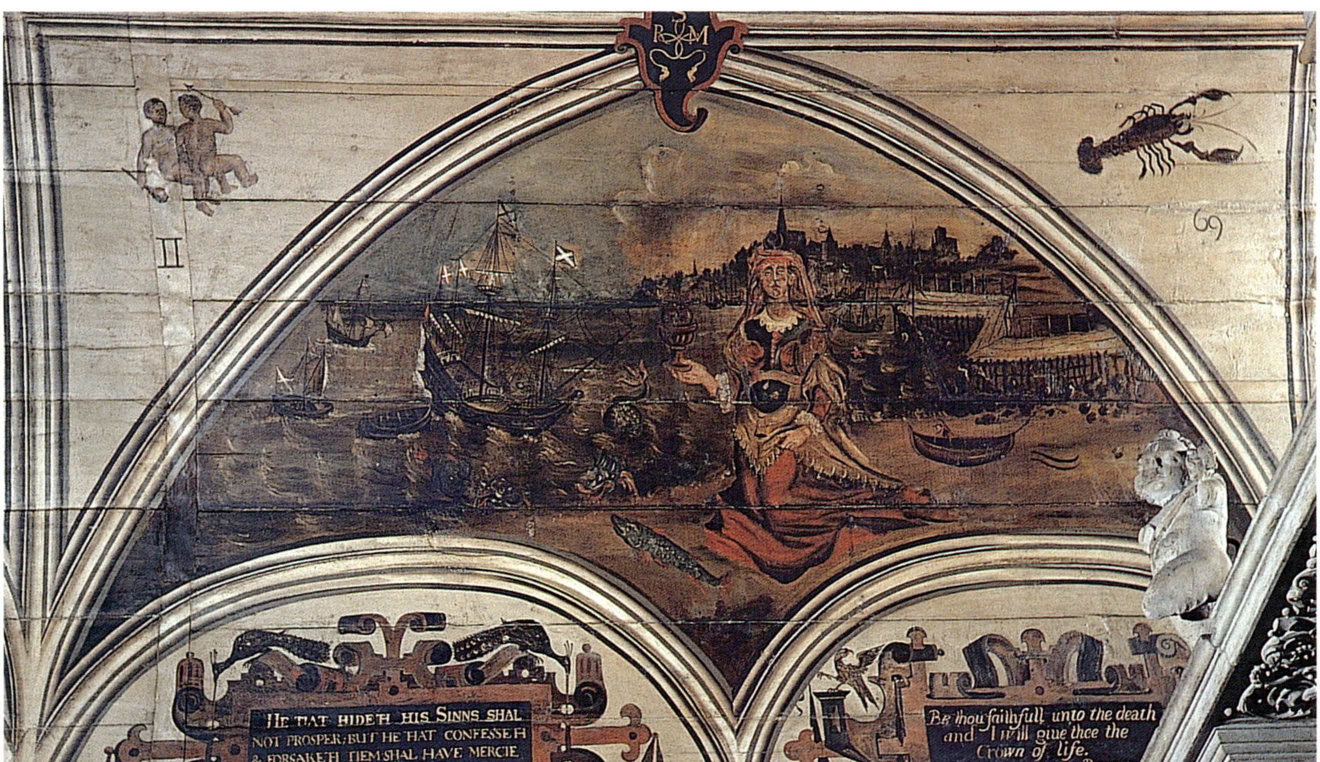

fervour of the pious soul. The fish on the shore can be accommodated to such symbolism readily enough as a familiar emblem of Christ, though the monstrous fishes sporting in the waves are more puzzling, unless they are meant to recall the story of Jonah, traditionally taken as a prefiguration of Christ's own death and resurrection on the authority of Matthew 12:40. One tiny detail amongst the various nautical activities in the background appears to show a small child lying in a boat. It should be clear that the panel includes a number of details that are moving towards a religious symbolism likely to be controversial in the context of Scottish Presbyterianism. As we shall see, there is good reason to believe that the aisle was designed primarily as a chapel of private devotion, in which the *sensus spiritualis* of the images need not be apparent to visitors as long as it was understood by Sir Robert himself. It could be significant that the gaze of the kneeling woman is directed towards the viewer, whom she is thus challenging to realise or understand her message in some kind of spiritual exercise.

The panel opposite shows a woman standing in long robes watching a spirited, prancing and unbridled horse with flowing mane and tail. In the background is a large house or castle and three people playing with a dog; an assortment of fruit and vegetables lies at the lady's feet and on a white label is the artist's signature: 'J Stalker fecit 1638'. In his 1964 Edinburgh thesis, M R Apted suggested that this copied another emblem from Whitney, with the motto *Pulchritudino vincit,* 'To the fairest' (1586, p.182), which shows a woman reclining in a landscape with various animals, including a prancing horse not unlike that in the Skelmorlie Aisle painting. The moral might be seen as an appropriate tribute to the memory of Montgomery's wife, since it explains that although nature gave all creatures the means to defend themselves from their enemies it gave women no defence except their beauty; nevertheless such beauty is enough to reduce the fiercest and boldest to submission. The fact that one further emblem on this ceiling can be shown to copy Whitney lends strength to this source identification. I do not believe, however, that Whitney's *Pulchritudino vincit* emblem was a source for this detail at Largs since the picture can now be shown to copy a quite different print. Though the iconography of the standing figure remains unsourced, the prancing horse refers to an engraving by Hendrik Golzius from a set of forty prints published in 1578 by Philips Galle in Antwerp illustrating *The Royal Stable of Don John of Austria.* The resemblance between Golzius' horse and the Skelmorlie painting is too close for it to be anything other than a direct copy, which means that the painting as a whole is reworking different details, possibly from various sources, into an original composition. The series illustrating horses from the famous stable of Don John was begun by Hieronymus Wierix and continued after 1578 by Golzius from designs by Stradanus (ie Jan van der Straet, *Illustrated Bartsch*, vol. 3, Hendrik Golzius, nos. 290-3). The print in question is entitled 'Equus Liber et Incompositus' ('Wild and untamed horse') and the verse *subscriptio* describes it as a warrior horse which charges high into the battlefield (*campo sese arduus insert* quotes Virgil, *Aen* 9.53, describing Turnus) even though it scorns the

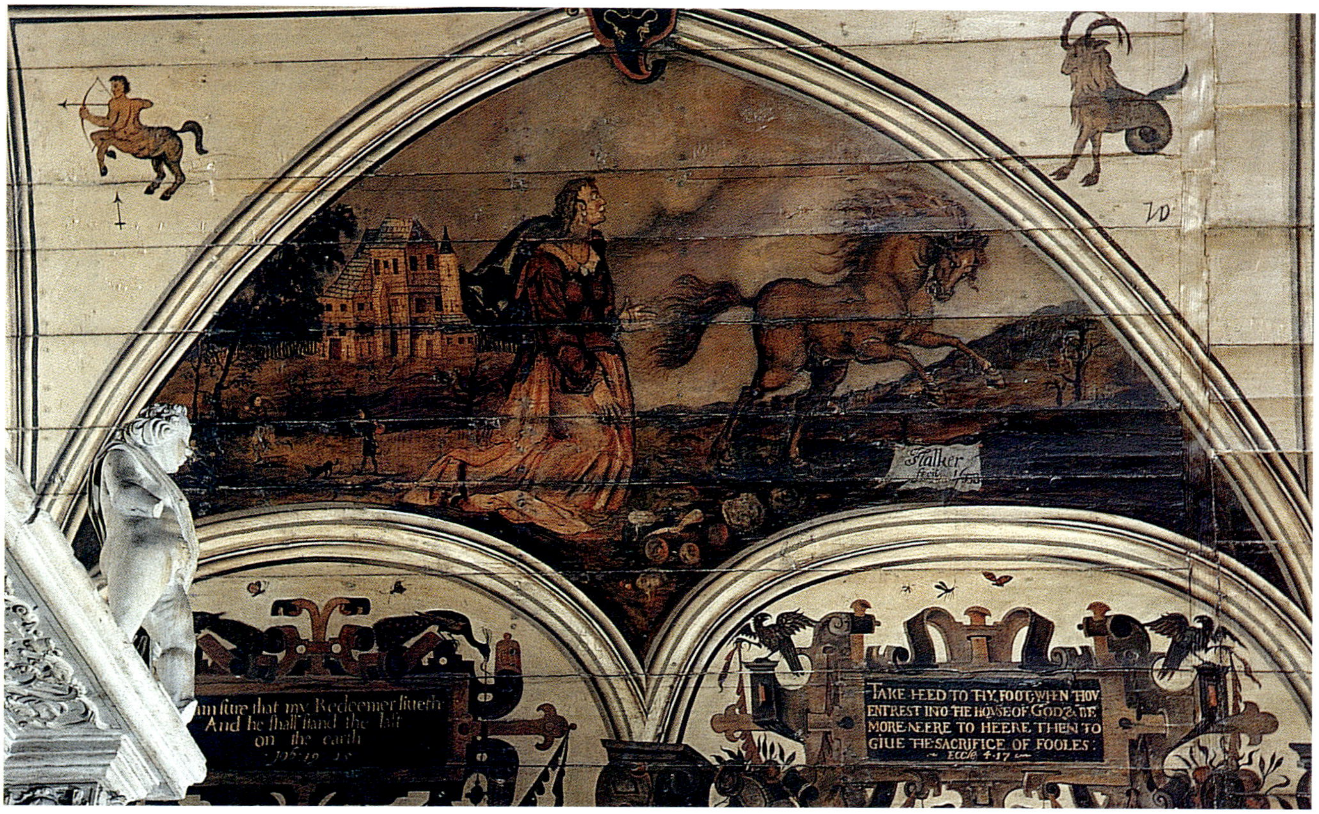

Skelmorlie Aisle, Largs, unidentified allegorical figure, the prancing horse is copied from an engraving by Hendrik Golzius. HS

bridle; in more peaceful times, however, it submits to being tamed. Although this quasi-emblematic picture is again difficult to interpret as a whole, it seems that this detail refers to wild military impulses that the woman is seeking to tame. A local tradition claiming that this panel refers to Sir Robert Montgomery's wife, alleged to have been killed when she fell off her horse, can certainly be dismissed as nonsense (see *Statistical Account of Scotland 1791–99*, repr. 1982, vol. vi, p 428), though the possibility remains that the panel has at least some reference to Montgomery and his wife, Margaret Douglas. This funerary aisle was almost certainly designed to serve as a place of private devotion for its patron, and it specifically commemorates Montgomery's wife.

The relation of these two paintings to the similar landscapes of the four seasons which surround them is unclear. The style is quite close to the kind of thing one finds in the *Four Seasons* engravings by Maarten de Vos, where we see figures labouring in fields with similar landscape details and buildings. Though the Skelmorlie pictures are certainly not copies of the de Vos prints, there are a number of details that suggest that the Skelmorlie artist must at least have known this set and modelled some of his details on it. For instance, the winter scene in both the engraving and the painting

Hendrik Golzius, Equus liber et Incompositus, *c.1579, from set of forty engravings by various artists illustrating* The Royal Stable of Don John of Austria. BM

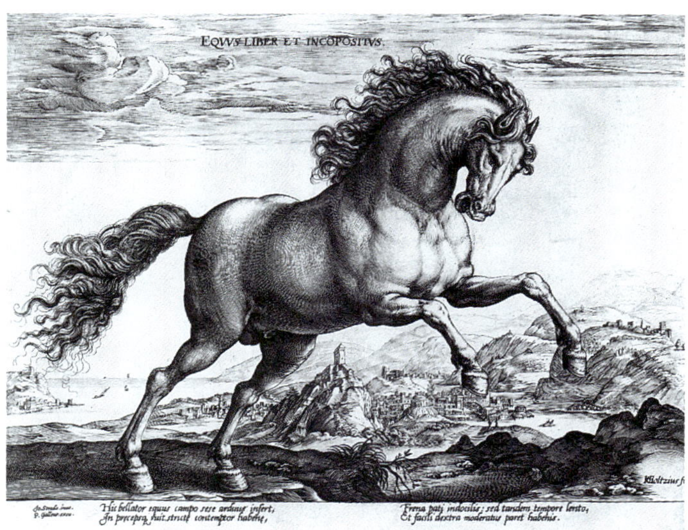

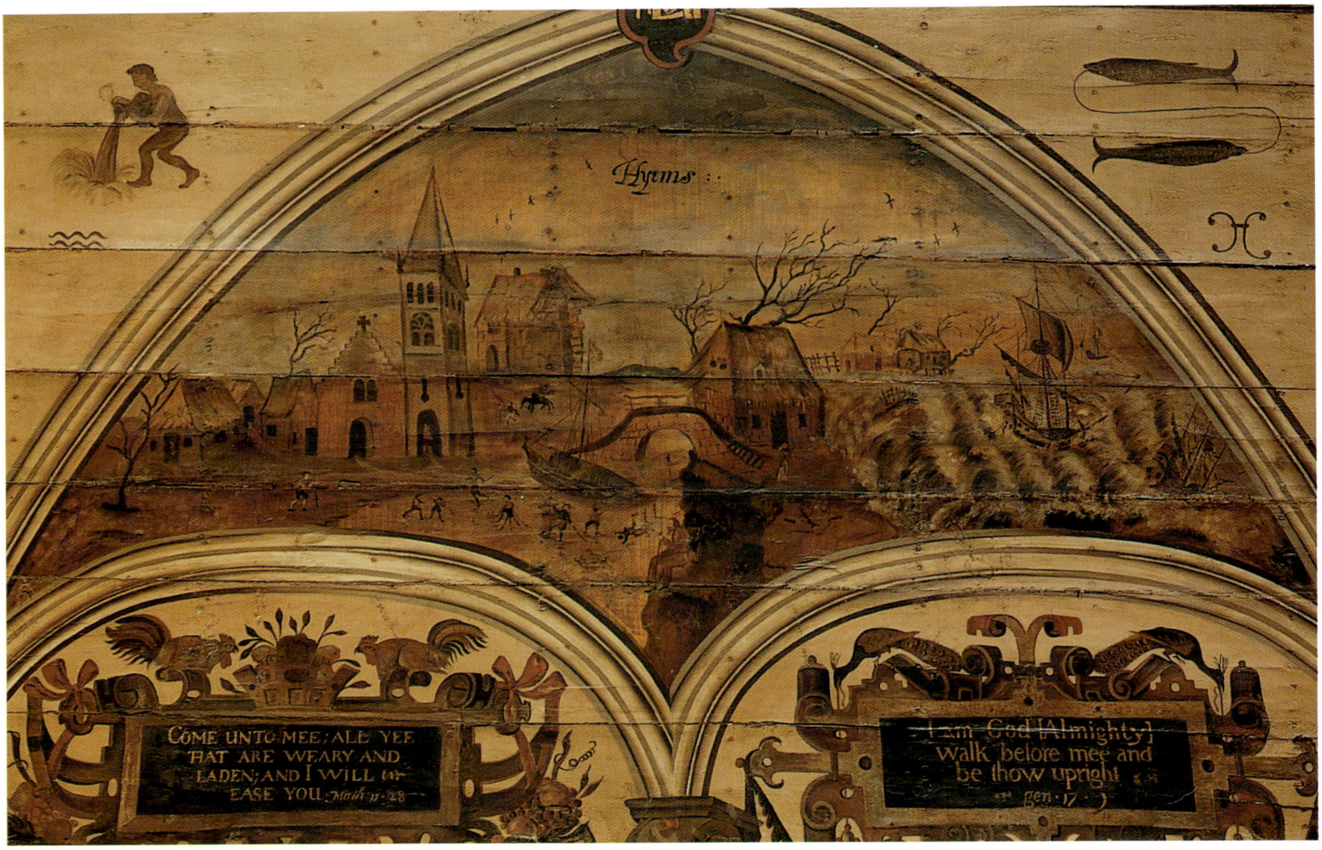

Skelmorlie Aisle, Largs, Winter panel. HS

Adriaen Collaert after Maarten de Vos. Winter from the set of Four Seasons *shown with their presiding gods.* PR,L

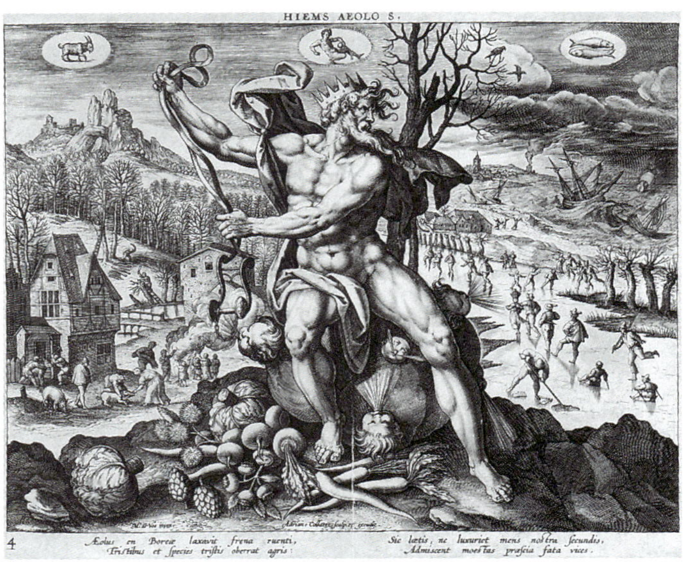

shows a seascape top right with two storm-wrecked ships – while the presence in both of small figures skating on the ice (one prodding it with a pole) could be pure coincidence, the details of the seascape and its position in the picture seem unlikely to be coincidental. The autumn landscape shows a wattle-fenced enclosure in the left foreground, in exactly the same position and the same proportions as the stakes enclosing the vineyard in de Vos's *Autumnus* engraving; again this could be pure coincidence, were it not for a detail in the middle of the Skelmorlie scene, just behind the fenced enclosure. This is very difficult to make out even in the original; however John Houston's unpublished typescript description of the painted ceiling, written in 1932 and now preserved in Historic Scotland files, seems accurate: 'There is a tent-like structure erected on wooden piles, while in the foreground of the tent there lies a number of barrels which are apparently filled from the tent .... One man is carrying away a full barrel .... Two oxen are dragging a sleigh with a large barrel upon it towards the buildings.' There can be little doubt, I think, that the detail Houston is describing in the Skelmorlie painting is a version of the very similar covered winepress in the de Vos print, beside which there are indeed two oxen ploughing. Though it is now

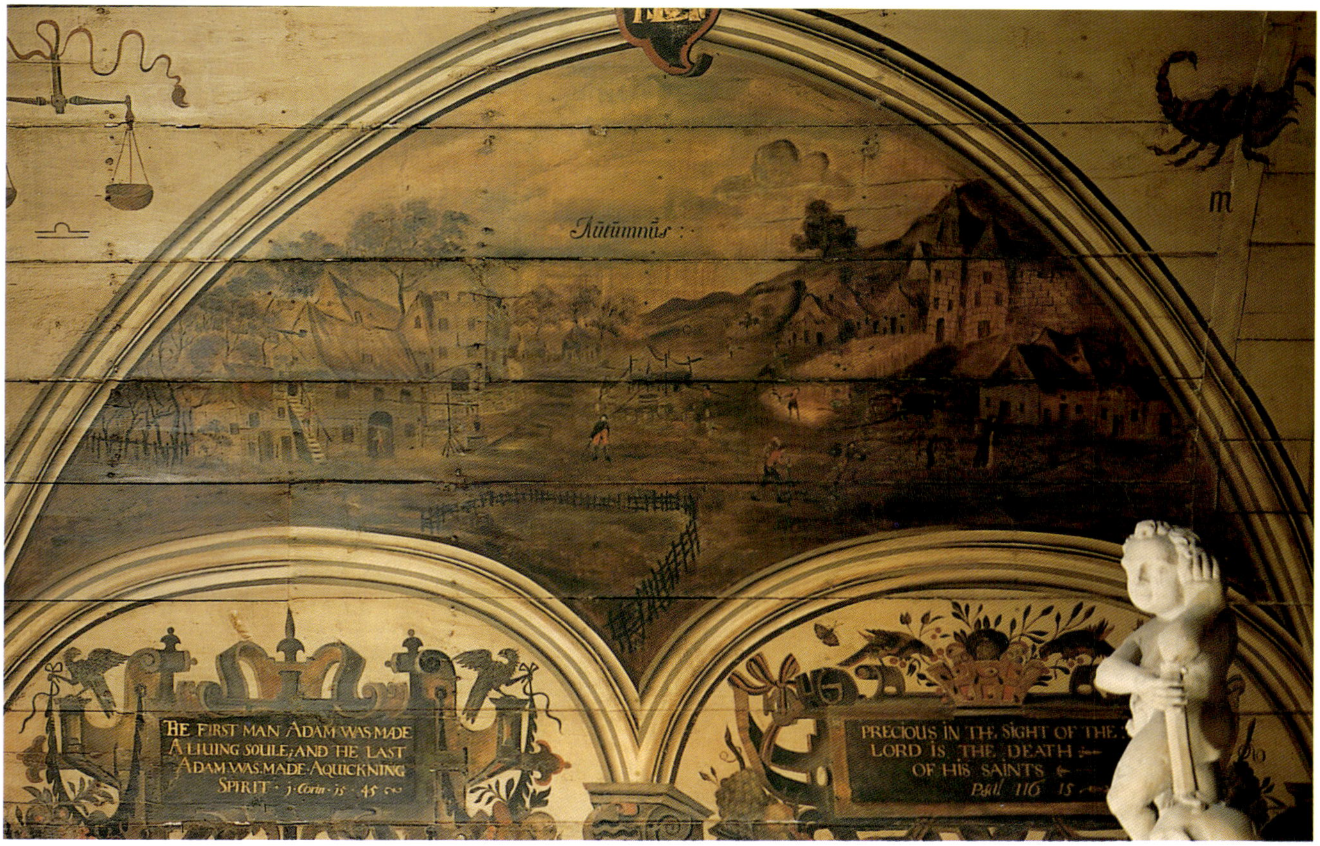

Skelmorlie Aisle, Largs, Autumn panel. HS

impossible to make out quite what is growing in the fenced-off field in the foreground of the Largs picture, one can still see what look like the remains of the close-packed vine poles that fill de Vos' similar field. These have a more immediate relevance to the subject insofar as the allegorical figure of Bacchus, god of wine, presides over de Vos' picture. The Skelmorlie painting ignores these allegorical figures, or presiding deities, though it may well have taken its hint for the zodiac signs from the similar signs that figure in de Vos' engravings. Although the engravings establish very precisely the iconographic type that Stalker is following in his four seasons paintings at Largs, he reinvents all these landscapes to his own design, including a church in the *Aestas* picture which is unmistakably a representation of the very church the viewer is standing in. For all *Autumnus*'s inclusion of de Vos' vineyard and winepress, we may recognise in such details an attempt to localise some of the landscapes and labours. Certainly, by comparison with the engravings, we have to say that Stalker's painting is amateurish and badly drawn – apprentice work, perhaps. As John Houston noted in 1932, it does not seem likely that it was executed by the same artist who carried out the other panels. Although Stalker has removed the allegorical figures (Venus for

Adriaen Collaert after Maarten de Vos. Autumn from the set of Four Seasons *shown with their presiding gods.* PR,L

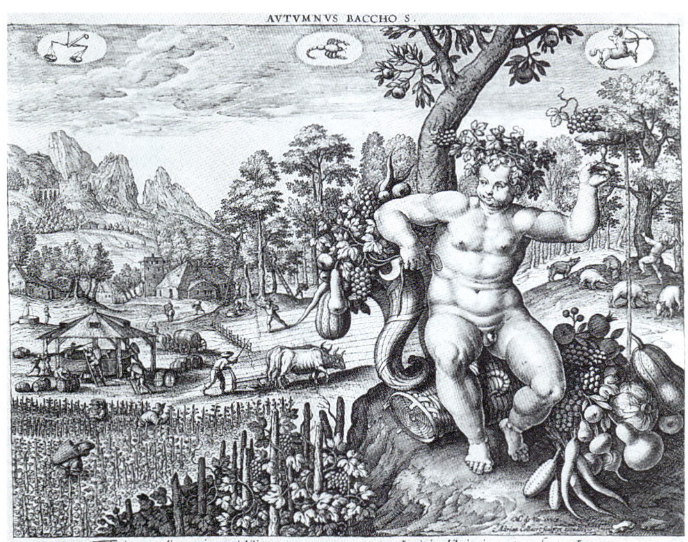

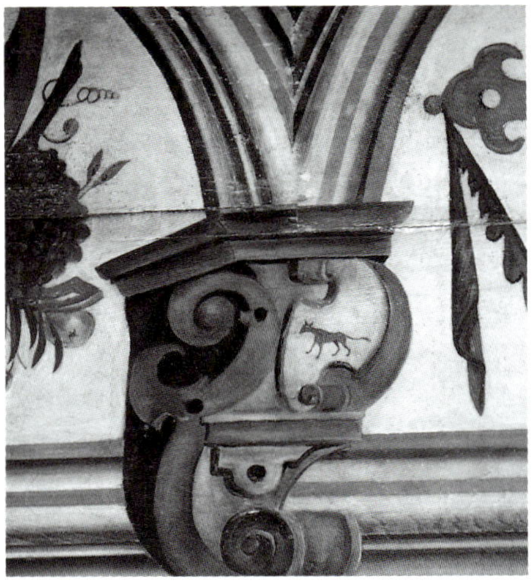

False architecture, the elaborate trompe-l'oeil *corbels in the Skelmorlie Aisle are decorated with the badges of the tribes of Israel, here the Wolf of Benjamin ('Benjamin shall ravin as a wolf....' Genesis 49.27).*

spring, Ceres for summer, Bacchus for autumn, Aeolus for winter) that dominate de Vos's engravings, there can be no doubt that his two females with their allegorical attributes in the two centre compartments were designed to function as emblematic figures whose significance, if identifiable, might provide a key to the symbolic programme of the ceiling as a whole. It should be clear that for all its decorative exuberance, this is a strongly sententious and emblematic programme of images.

That may account for its inclusion of the badges of the tribes of Israel, for these were often interpreted in the seventeenth century as biblical *imprese* or standards. That is because, in Numbers, God commands Moses and Aaron to order each of the tribes of Israel to 'pitch by his own standard, with the ensign of their father's house' (2.2). The actual 'ensigns' are not identified, but their iconography was traditionally supplied from Genesis (49), where Jacob on his deathbed calls together his sons, and associates each of them with a symbol or *impresa*: 'Judah is a lion's whelp ... he stooped down, he couched as a lion' (49.8); 'Zebulun ... shall be for an haven of ships' (13); 'Issachar is a strong ass couching down between two burdens' (14); 'Dan shall be a serpent by the way' (17); 'Naphtali is a hind let loose' (21); 'Benjamin shall ravin as a woolf' (27); 'All these are the twelve tribes of Israel' (28). The badges survive in church decoration elsewhere in Britain; in Burton Latimer, Northamptonshire, for instance, they are set in strapwork cartouches containing figures of the twelve patriarchs copied from a book printed in the Netherlands. Wells-Cole remarks, 'These are remarkable for having been painted in the first place, at a time when "ornaments of the church" were obnoxious to the opponents of imagery on the grounds that they served idolatry'. (p.210)

In 1646 Sir Thomas Browne includes received ideas 'Of the Scutcheons of the Tribes of Israel' among his 'Vulgar Errors'.

> We will not pass over the Scutcheons of the Tribes of Israel, as they are usually described in the Maps of Canaan and several other pieces; generally conceived to be the proper coats, and distinctive badges of their several Tribes. So Reuben is conceived to bear three Bars wave, Judah a Lyon Rampant, Dan a Serpent nowed [knotted], Simeon a sword impale the point erected, etc. The ground whereof is the last Benediction of Jacob, wherein he respectively draweth comparisons from things here represented. (1927, vol. ii, p.229)

Browne points out that there are inconsistencies and omissions in the biblical list, which commentators had traditionally overcome by making various questionable assumptions that he is intent on challenging. His concluding comment on some of the analogies 'Cabalists' traditionally made between the badges of Israel and the seasons of the year looks suggestive for the kind of assumptions that might have underpinned the iconographic programme at Largs.

> But more widely must we walk, if we follow the doctrine of the Cabalists, who in each of the four banners inscribe a letter of the Tetragramaton, or quadrilateral name of God: and mysterizing their ensigns, do make the particular ones of the twelve Tribes, accommodable unto the twelve signs in the Zodiack, and

> twelve moneths in the year: but the Tetrarchical or general banners, of Judah, Reuben, Ephraim, and Dan, unto the signs of Aries, Cancer, Libra and Capricornus: that is, the four cardinal parts of the Zodiack, and seasons of the year. (p.233)

Suggestive though this might be for some sort of correspondence between the seasonal iconography, the zodiac signs, and the badges of Israel, on the lower sections of the ceiling at Largs, the articulation of the programme in the Montgomery aisle would appear to frustrate this, since, as we have seen, the ceiling decoration reduces the twelve tribes to ten, thus negating any close links between the twelve signs of the zodiac and the twelve tribes. This is despite the fact there would have been ample room available (seven corbels on each side to support the six arched ribs). The sequencing of the badges does not permit any grouping into what Browne calls 'the four principal or Legionary standards' – the badges of Dan, Judah and Reuben are, indeed, all shown on the same wall, and the Ox badge of Ephraim (descendent of Joseph) is on the opposite wall. The articulation of this programme foils any attempt to signal the division of the twelve months/tribes/zodiac signs into the tetrads, the analogical system of correspondences that Browne is describing would require. That may be because the artist was not skilful enough to impose it, but it may be simply because it was unknown to him and irrelevant to his purposes. The association of different elements in this decorative programme may, after all, be merely arbitrary.

This question clearly relates to the way the aisle was used, the purposes its decoration was designed to serve, and here we do have some evidence. The aisle is dominated by the spectacular stone mausoleum, of a type inspired by the tombs King James erected in Westminster Abbey. In 1605 James became the first English monarch since Henry VIII to commission monuments for Westminster Abbey when he ordered tombs to be erected for his mother, Mary, Queen of Scots, and for her English rival and eventual executioner, Elizabeth I. The two tombs were of a similar and quite novel kind in the shape of a triumphal arch with two side canopies raised on Corinthian pillars; the central arch is barrel-vaulted with coffering, the side canopies flat with classical entablatures. Montgomery's tomb may not be copied directly from either of the Westminster Abbey originals, which were completed in 1606 (Elizabeth's) and in 1613 (Mary's), for Adam White has shown that both tombs were widely imitated in the years immediately following – he lists no fewer than nine monuments of this type built between 1613 and 1629 at locations as far apart as Devonshire and County Cork (White 1989, 19-29). Sir Robert Montgomery's tomb nevertheless belongs in this extraordinary efflorescence of a particular style of neoclassical funerary architecture inspired by the Westminster Abbey models. Clearly, those models were sending a political signal to do with the reconciliation of historic and religious rivalries and conflicts between the two realms and two women to whom James was immediate heir. How much, if any, of that symbolism was echoed or associated with their imitators is difficult to judge, but ideas of national peace, unity and reconciliation would not be out of

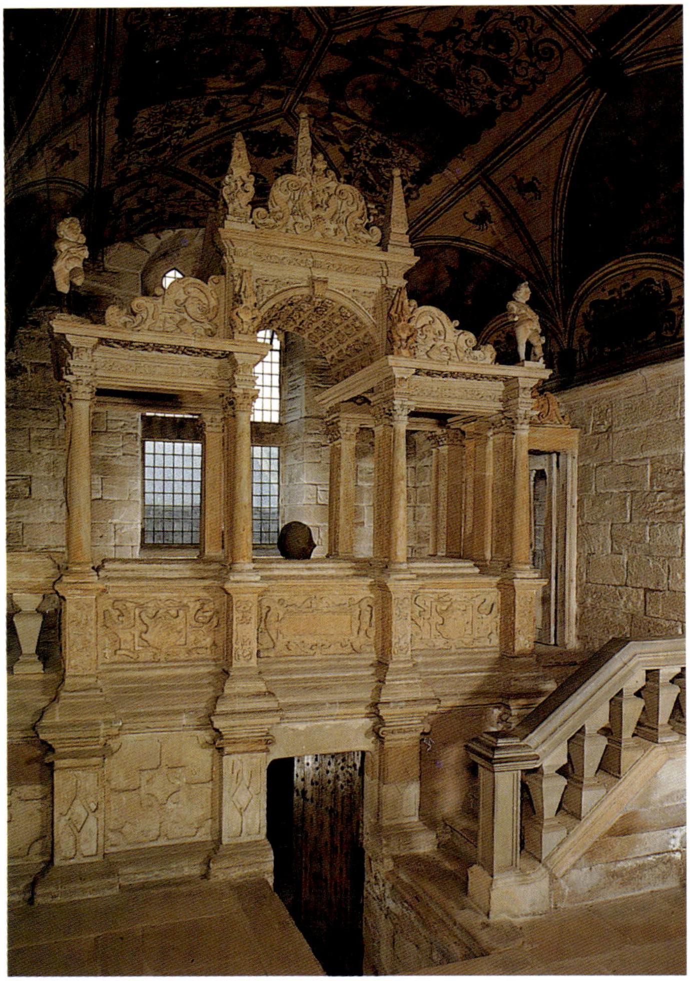

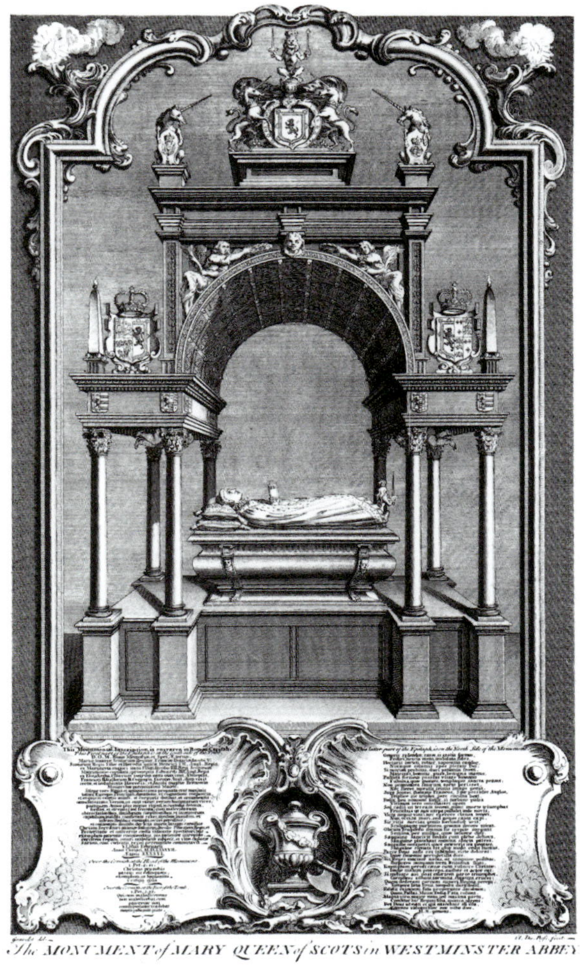

Left: *The Montgomery tomb, the classical arch raised on columns copies the design of the royal tombs erected by James VI in Westminster Abbey to commemorate his mother, Mary, Queen of Scots, and her executioner Elizabeth I of England.* HS

Right: *The tomb of Mary, Queen of Scots, executed by stonemasons Cornelius and William Cure in Westminster Abbey, 1607-12, as illustrated in a contemporary print.* SA,L

place on Montgomery's memorial, which stands above the sunken crypt containing the coffins of Sir Robert and his wife. Montgomery's inscription on his own coffin suggests the whole aisle was erected as a retreat for private devotion, to which much of its surrounding iconography would have served as a stimulus.

> *Ipse mihi praemortuus fui, fato funera*
> *Praeripui, unicum idque Caesareum,*
> *Exemplar, inter tot mortales secutus.*
> [I anticipated my death and forestalled my departure as I followed the unique example amongst men of Caesar.]

The reference here is to Emperor Charles V, who rehearsed his own funeral shortly before his death in 1558 in the last months of his retreat to the cloisters of Yuste. The inscription suggests a deliberate attempt on Montgomery's part to model himself and his funeral aisle on the pattern of piety represented by the emperor who had most famously abdicated in order to spend the closing years of his life in private prayer and contemplation. Montgomery had spent much of his early life in vindictive feuding with his neighbours, the Cunninghams, but afterwards, seized with remorse, he performed many acts of expiation, including the habit of coming to this tomb in Largs and spending the night in prayer – according to *Statistical Account of Scotland 1791-99* the vault beneath the tomb was 'built by Sir Robert Montgomery, who, becoming serious in the after part of his life, repaired hither at night for devotional exercises; by these means burying himself as it were alive' (repr. 1982, vol. vi, p.428). Although this record is late, we are probably justified in assuming that it represents a reliable tradition. If we are right in seeing this funerary aisle not so much as a commemorative monument to the deceased but rather as a place of private devotion designed for Sir Robert's own use following the death of his wife and some years before his own demise, then we may begin to make sense of the motivation behind much of its sententious iconography.

Most obviously relevant to such a programme of private devotion and mortification are the biblical texts, with their emphasis on penitence, faith, and judgement. The heraldic achievements represent those neighbouring families – Drumlanrig, Lochinvar, Eglinton, and Sempil – with whom the Montgomeries were most closely connected, while the central heraldic panel, of larger proportions than the rest, shows the arms of Sir Robert himself and his late wife. These heraldic achievements, of a kind one comes to expect of sepulchral decoration, serve as reminders of family and lineage which would undoubtedly have a bearing on the viewer's own sense of his duty to king and nation, which is what the evidently patriotic 'Warre or Worke' emblem refers to with its prompting to vigilance in both civil and military defence of one's country. The emblems of Justice and Fortitude can be read in the same spirit and it seems more than likely that their Latin inscriptions are the work of Montgomery himself, always supposing that it was he who was likewise responsible for the Latin verses we have quoted from his own tomb, or those on the central panel of the monument facing the north window:

Bis duo bisq decem transegi uirginis annos
Ter duo tres decem consociata viro
Et bis opem Lucina tulit [-] *mas patris imago*
Spesq domus superest f[*ae*]*mina iussa mori*
Clara genus generosa animi speciosa decore
Chara deo uixi nunc mihi cuncta deus.

For twice ten years and four a maid,
For thirty-six a wedded wife,
Twice did Lucina bring her aid,
And two fair children blest my life.

The image of his sire, my boy,
Survives, the hope of all our race,
But death, commissioned to destroy,
My daughter tore from mine embrace.

Of gentle soul and gentle birth,
And clad in beauty fair to see,
Loved by my God I lived on earth,
God now is all in all to me.

[Trans: J Houston 1932]

Any attempt to reconstruct the motivation behind the decorative programme as a whole in the Montgomery aisle has to be inconclusive at this stage. It does seem important, however, to see the decorative painting as part of an ambitious scheme that also includes the extraordinary mausoleum and its associated inscriptions. The painted decoration uses various topics which, conventional though they are, do not appear to have any clear interdependence or common grounding – heraldic, biblical, seasonal and moral subjects are brought together into a programme which has no very clear moral or doctrinal basis and which, for all the false architecture which serves to articulate it overall, has no clearly defined structure. Although the iconography of the two central facing panels – of a woman with an unbridled horse, and a woman in a marine landscape – is certainly obscure, it does include some suggestive details. The image of the flaming heart was the subject of some very specific developments in Catholic devotional literature at this period. It is the attribute specifically of Saint Augustine, signifying his devotional ardour, and of Venus, sometimes also shown with a flaming torch or a vase burning with the flame of divine love ('Celestial Venus', *cf* Hall, *Dictionary of Subjects and Symbols*, p.319). It may be relevant that the putti surmounting the mausoleum include one holding an inverted, extinguished torch, though the crescent moon, dimly visible above the woman's head, ought to be an attribute of Diana, not Venus.

The image of the flaming heart had been treated to some specifically emblematic interpretation in the eighteen engravings entitled *Le Coeur devot*, by Antoine Wierix, used to illustrate a treatise by the Jesuits Etienne Luzvic and Etienne Binet (Douai 1627). In 1634, four years before Montgomery built his aisle, its English translation, by Henry Hawkins, had been printed in Rouen. A burning heart supplies the frontispiece to this, and is also the illustration to emblem seventeen on 'The devout heart enflamed with love'. Neither of these engravings is the source of Sir Robert Montgomery's image, but they help to establish that one of the contexts for such imagery at this period was Catholic devotional literature.

However, no source identified to date shows the flaming heart in a chalice – a conjunction that can only be interpreted as eucharistic. In Boccaccio's *Decameron*, Tancred's daughter, Ghismonda, is sent her lover's heart in a cup, with the intention that she should eat it as punishment for disobeying her father's wishes. But we need not read the Skelmorlie Aisle image as an explicit reference to Boccaccio once we recognise how closely all such narratives participate in the sacramental symbolism surrounding the idea of eating the heart in both sacred and profane texts which, as Milad Doueihi has shown, leads up directly to some of the Catholic devotional traditions of the Sacred Heart in such writers as François de Sales and Etienne Binet.

> The theology of the sacred heart, invested and informed by the foundational dimension of the Eucharist, plays ... a determining role in the articulation and specificity of the literary and cultural dimensions of the narratives of the eaten heart from the Middle Ages to the early seventeenth century. The Devout and mystical tradition, represented by Jean-Pierre Camus and Saint François de

> Sales, defines and locates the symbolic heart as the locus of exchange between the human and the divine, between the infinite and the finite, between the miracle of incarnation and transfiguration and the work and possibility of salvation. The mystical and Devout heart thus names the central organ of the mystical body of Christ, of the *ecclesia* and the Church, and as such it figures, in terms of the corporeal representations of the Incarnation, the full potential of Christological meditations. (Doueihi 1997, pp.125-6)

If the raised chalice and raised veil at Skelmorlie retain anything of the inherited symbolism in Christian art as attributes of the rivalry of Ecclesia (or the new church of Christ) and Synagoga (the old, blinded faith of the Jews), then there might be some connection between this and the very different image of Jacob and Esau on the central panel, for the rivalry of these twin brothers for the patrimony of Isaac was also traditionally interpreted as a symbol of the conflict of Church and Synagogue (Hall, *Dictionary of Subjects and Symbols*, p.163). Is it possible that Montgomery might have seen this rivalry as somehow representing the conflict between the old faith and the new in Reformation Scotland? The date of this painting, 1638, is also the date of the signing of the National Covenant in Scotland – though such coincidence cannot in itself tell us anything about Montgomery's motives.

What this implies for our understanding of the emblematic functions of the Skelmorlie Aisle is that, however unprogrammatic the decoration as a whole, it seems to include details which could only have signalled to an initiate – namely Sir Robert Montgomery himself – a devotional context with specific, and specifically Catholic, applications. Since those applications would have been largely unrecognisable to the uninitiated, it was evidently quite safe to include them in the private aisle of what was a Protestant, indeed a Presbyterian, parish church. The obscurity of some of the surrounding iconography might well be seen as a protective screen, and the use of texts from the Geneva Bible and of uncontested and uncontroversial heraldic, seasonal and Old Testament images would help to allay any such suspicion. Once the devotional iconography is recognised, however, we begin to see a scheme centred on ideas of love and of mortality which seem to reflect what can only be seen as its patron's Catholic spirituality, using female images which somehow suggest the close connection between love of God and love of his wife, to whose memory the whole aisle is dedicated. The two central panels must have had some personal significance in this context, with their prominent use of a central female figure who can hardly not represent Margaret Douglas in some guise, whether as the wife who tamed the unbridled spirit of her husband, or as the figure whose smouldering heart is offered up in a chalice. If the meaning of such images remains tantalisingly obscure, that may be one of the consequences of cutting Christian iconography off from those sources of authority which had traditionally sanctioned their received meanings, one of the results of regarding all such images as 'monuments of idolatrie'.

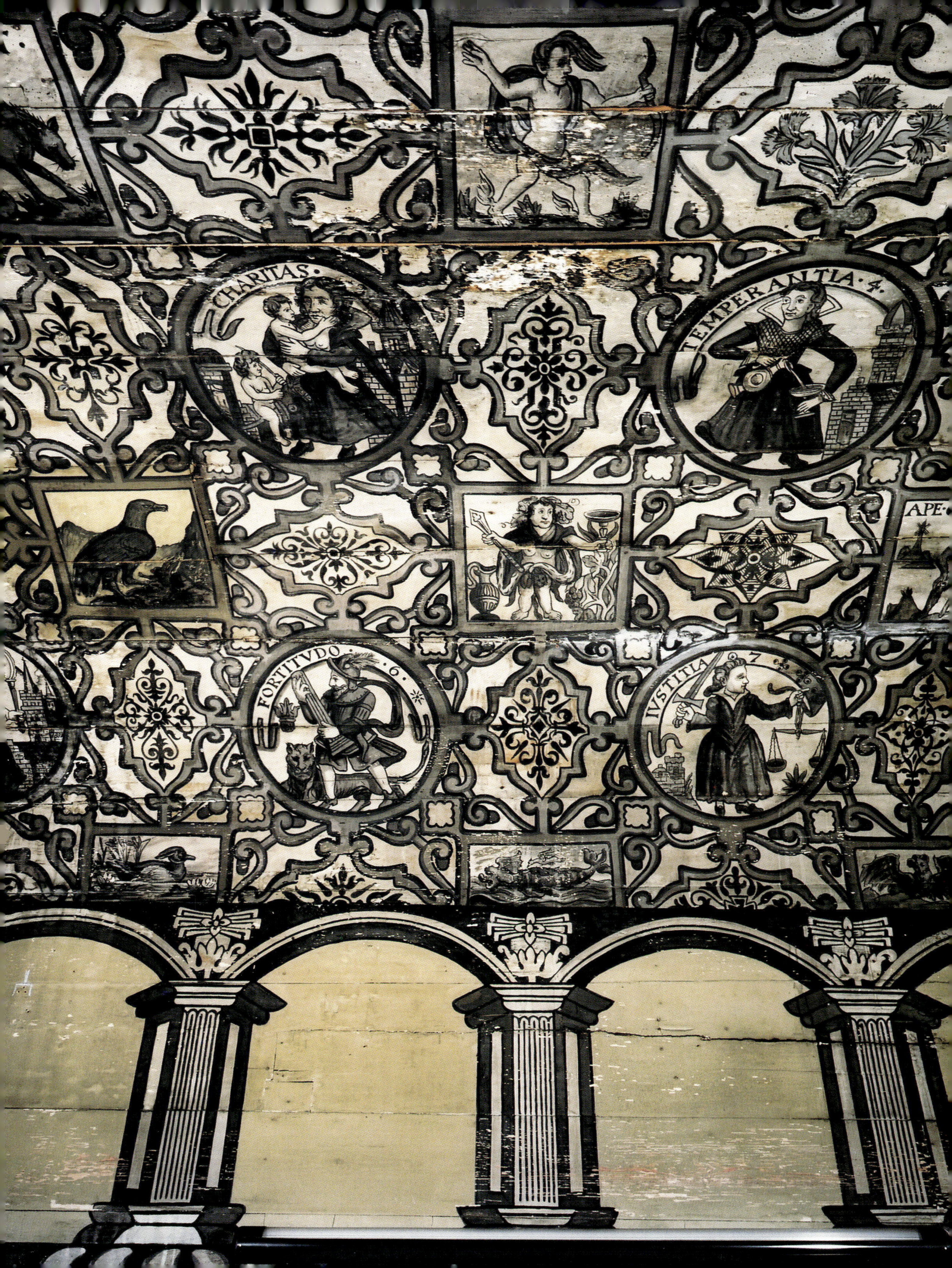
CHARITAS
TEMPERANTIA·4·
FORTITVDO·6·
IVSTITIA·7

7

EARLSHALL

THE long gallery on the second floor of Earlshall Castle near Leuchars, Fife, is remarkable for the sheer prolixity of its detail. Each of the thirteen longitudinal sections into which the ceiling is divided is decorated with up to fifteen different subjects. The extraordinary richness of this decorative scheme with its proliferation of heraldic and bestiary images is difficult to describe, and it is not easy to suggest any inclusive system of iconographic ordering that might account for the disposition of the various images in its overall programme. Yet there appear to be some local sequences with their own *syntaxis*; for instance several coats of arms of the Scottish nobility in the western half of the gallery are marked with arabic numerals and it seems likely that this numbering originally included all eighteen such shields in this half of the gallery. Elsewhere on the ceiling we find a similarly numbered sequence of the seven Cardinal Virtues shown as labelled allegorical figures. A central area is taken up with monograms and shields of various members of the Bruce family of Earlshall, while the coats of arms in the slightly larger group that fills the eastern end of the gallery are all historical and legendary rulers. These include the kings of England, France, Hungary, Castile, Denmark, Ireland, 'Greiland', 'Swadrick' and 'Bewme', the Prince of Orange, Duke of Lorraine and, at the east end of the gallery, the supposed arms of the nine Worthies and of the three Kings – 'Melchior of Araby', 'Balthasar King of Saba', 'Gaspar King of Tharse' – these clearly form intelligible sub-groups. It is surprising to find the authentic and familiar coats of arms of European royalty and Scottish nobility in a scheme which also includes the evidently fabricated and fictive heraldry of such legendary and biblical figures, and we might wonder what authority the ceiling could claim for ascribing these imaginary and retrospective coats of arms to such legendary characters.

Many of the sixty or more animals are labelled, and they include not only such familiar beasts as elephant, rhinoceros, camel, horse and cow but also such species as the 'genitha', 'mertrick', 'coatimondi', 'simiwlpa', the 'ape of Arabia' and the 'mouse of Arabia'. The ceiling thus offers us an extended bestiary, though the animals appear to be ranked in no particular order. The central compartments of the ceiling include eighteen monograms

Opposite: *Earlshall, Fife, long gallery, detail from the painted ceiling executed in 1620 and restored by Robert Lorimer in the 1890s.* RCAHMS

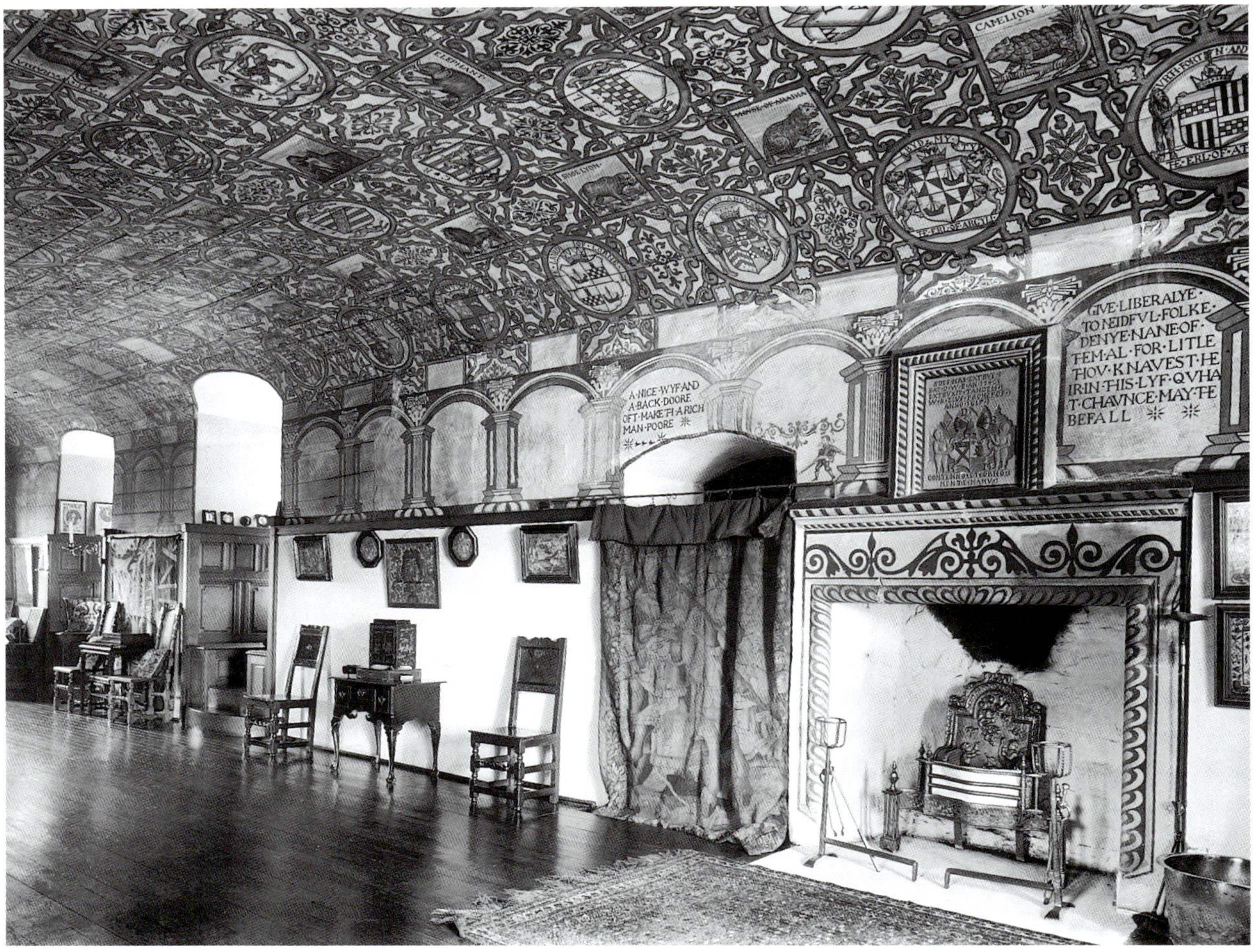

Earlshall, Fife, general view of long gallery. EH

or initials of the house's owners, some with accompanying coats of arms. Four of these use two interlocked hearts with a monogram of William Bruce, grandson of the founder, and his second wife Dame Agnes Lyndsay (d.1635). One of these supplies the date 1620 which we may take to be that of the ceiling as a whole (the same date is repeated in one of the adjacent compartments). Other initials refer to Margaret Meldrum, wife of William Bruce the elder, who began building the house in the 1540s, and Elizabeth Leslie, wife of Alexander Bruce.

This central part of the ceiling includes the only images in square panels that are not animals. One shows what looks like a Cupid figure with winged feet, holding what seems to be a bow, dressed only in a swirl of drapery and with a long forelock of unkempt hair. This detail offers some clue to the figure's real identity, for such a forelock is conventionally the attribute of Occasio (proverbially you have to seize Time by the forelock), and it is now possible to demonstrate that this is the figure of Occasio as depicted in the woodcut which illustrated an emblem in Guillaume de la Perrière's *Le Theatre des bons engins* (Paris, 1539). This important French emblem book was reprinted several times in the sixteenth century, but the last edition had appeared almost forty years before William Bruce painted his ceiling. In 1590, however, an English edition (of which no copy survives) is recorded in the Stationers' Register, and in 1593 Richard Field printed a translation by Thomas Combe under the title *The Theater of Fine Devices.* This edition had been reprinted in 1614, and it seems likely that the Earlshall artist used one of these English editions as his model.

Combe's translation of la Perrière is one of the rarest of English emblem books, surviving in only two known copies, but this may be not so much because it was rare in its day as because the copies got hard use – illustrated books used as pattern books were likely to be dismembered and worn to pieces.

Combe's pictures are close copies of the woodcuts that had illustrated the Lyons, de Tournes, editions and 'Embleme LXIII' shows us the figure of Occasio as we see her on the Earlshall ceiling. Combe's motto identifies the conventional moral invariably associated with this image, 'It is a point of no small cunning, / To catch Occasion at her coming', and his verse epigram explains her various attributes – her bald patch and forelock tell us that one has to seize an opportunity before it passes, her winged feet show that she cannot stay, and her knife is 'in hand to cut off long delay'. It is difficult to tell whether the transformation of this knife into the rather awkwardly curved Cupid's bow that we see on the Earlshall ceiling is a result of the original artist's misunderstanding of his pattern book, or of the mistaken guesses of its modern restorer, of which I shall have more to say later.

The square panel immediately below this on the ceiling also copies an emblem from the *Theater of Fine Devices*. It shows a rather plump figure of indeterminate gender, wearing a shapeless drape over the shoulders and some kind of foliage in his hair; he stands between a ewer and a vine holding a mace in one hand and a shallow bowl in the other. It would be difficult to know what to make of this figure without access to la Perrière's image of Bacchus (Combe's

Left: *Thomas Combe,* The Theater of Fine Devices, containing an hundred morall Emblemes *(repr. 1614) sig. E5v.* GUL

Right: *Emblem of Occasio copied from la Perrière,* Theatre des bons engins, *holding a knife in order, as English translator Thomas Combe explains, 'to cut off long delay'. The lower shaft of the bow has to be the modern restorer's attempt to make sense of an image he did not understand.*

EMBLEME LXIII.

It is a point of no ſmall cunning,
To catch Occaſion at her coming.

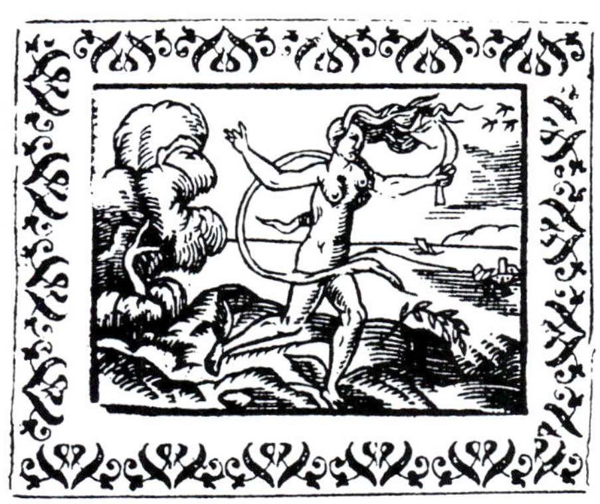

Behold Occaſion drawne before your eies,
As though ſhe ſtill were fleeting on her waies,
Which image ſo *Liſippus* did deuiſe,
With knife in hand to cut off long delaye.
Her locks before bids hold ere that ſhe flies,
Her wings do ſhew ſhe can abide no ſtaies:
And by her bald ſhe tels vs at the laſt,
There is no hold behind when ſhe is paſt.

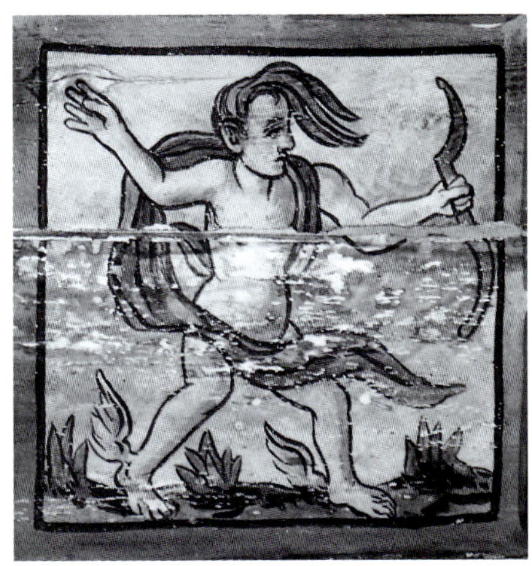

'Embleme LXIII'), which interprets it as an emblem of unconvincing disguise:

> *Bacchus* cannot himselfe so well disguise,
> By clapping on his backe a Lyons skin,
> But that his flagon and his bolle descries,
> It is no *Hercules* that is within.

In other words this is an image of Bacchus (hence the vine, the flagon and the ivy-crown) impersonating Hercules (hence the mace, or club, which he holds, and the loosely draped lion's skin over his shoulders).

Evidence that either the Earlshall artist, or the modern restorer, did not recognise the identity of these figures is suggested by their indeterminate, if not mistaken, gender. The figure of Occasio on the ceiling looks more like an adolescent Cupid than the female personification the emblem requires, while Bacchus is endowed with female breasts, not shown in la Perrière's (or Combe's) woodcut. This detail could be taken as indicating Bacchus's effeminacy, and the suggestion that the artist did not understand what he was painting certainly seems to be discounted by another change he evidently made to his source, for whereas Combe's woodcut shows the lion's skin with a cat's paw tied in front of Bacchus's groin the Earlshall painting makes the nature of the garment much clearer by changing this to a lion's head. Such a change of detail cannot have been unmotivated and has to be seen as clarifying the identity of Hercules by rendering the iconography less ambiguous. Such clarification may have appeared more necessary once the emblematic image was stripped of

Left: *Emblem copied from Guillaume de la Perrière, Bacchus posing as Hercules.*

Right: *Thomas Combe,* The Theater of Fine Devices *(repr. 1614) sig. D6r.* GUL

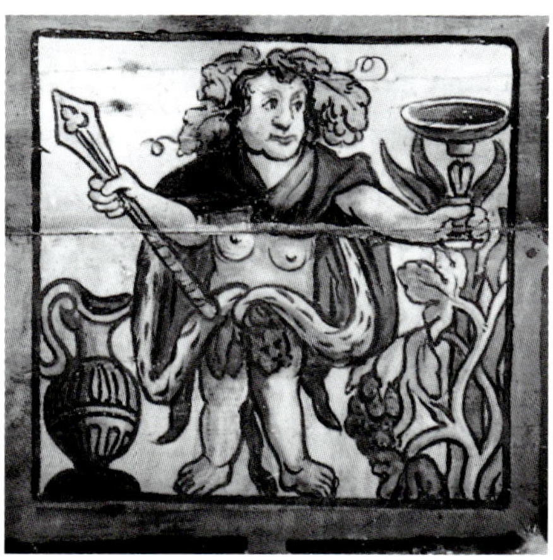

EMBLEME XLVIII.

Disguised things may seeme most strange,
But nature seeld is seene to change.

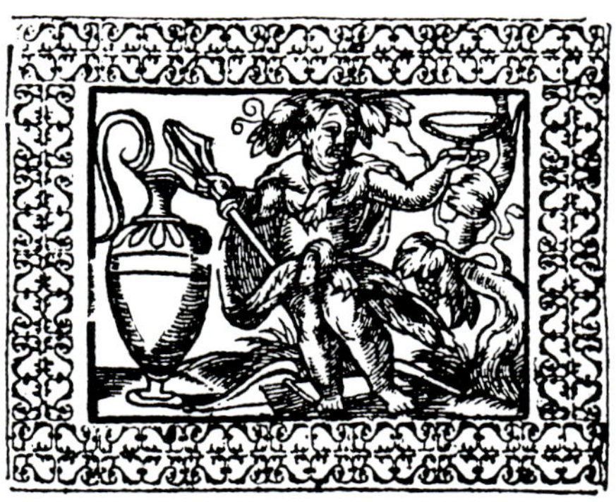

Bacchus cannot himselfe so well disguise,
By clapping on his backe a Lyons skin,
But that his flagon and his bolle descries,
It is no *Hercules* that is within.
So though a foole haue shew of being wise,
By hoarie head, or by a bearded chin:
Yet by his talke a man may quickly know,
Whether he be discreete indeed or no.

its accompanying verses, in which the 'Lyons skin' is specifically identified, but in any case the explicit rendering of this detail must surely be taken as confirming the artist's understanding of what he was depicting and his determination to communicate that meaning to the viewer. The only other place La Perrière is known to have been used in decorative painting in Britain at this period is on the plasterwork of a merchant's house in Bury St Edmunds, where two different emblems are used along with their mottoes and the emblem numbers that prove that the emblems were copied from Combe's translation and not from the French original (see Bath and Jones 1996).

The suggestion that these two emblems may retain an emblematic function, denuded though they are of any moralising texts, might be strengthened by the fact that they are immediately surrounded by images which, although wholly conventional and familiar, nevertheless have a moral significance. The Cardinal Virtues, numbered, labelled and disposed in two ranks appear to support the adjoining images of Occasio and Bacchus, leading the eye up to the interlinked hearts of the owner and his wife surrounded by the monograms of his immediate paternal and maternal relatives at the centre of the ceiling. Extending out from this nucleus of moral virtue and immediate kinship lie the extended ties of Scottish nobility on one side, and the images of earthly sovereignty on the other.

The *moralitas* with which these few allegorical images seemingly invest this programme (or parts of it) is reinforced by one further element in this complex decorative scheme, for the arcaded frieze on the surrounding walls, with its *trompe l'oeil* hexagonal pilasters, was once filled with moralising and proverbial inscriptions. We find a similar arcaded frieze on the first floor of Gladstone's Land in Edinburgh, also dated 1620, though there it has no inscriptions. Only a few of the moralising inscriptions now remain at Earlshall, over the entrance door and the main fireplace, for example: 'TRY AND THEN TRVST EFTER GVDE ASSVRANCE BOT TRVST NOT OR YE TRY FOR FEAR OF REPENTANCE'. The carved and painted stone panel over the fireplace itself, containing the impaled Bruce and Meldrum arms and initials, has an inscription recording that William Bruce built the house in 1546, and that his grandson enlarged it in 1617. A second inscription reads 'CONTEMNO ET ORNO MENTE ET MANV' ('I despise with the mind what I adorn with the hand'). All the painting in the gallery except this is executed in black paint on a white ground, not, as sometimes happens, because the original paint has faded to leave only black outlining. This ceiling was evidently always meant to be seen in black and white, rather like some prolix printed broadsheet.

Despite the diversity of its iconography the decorative programme is dominated by heraldry and any attempt to understand how the decoration was functioning as whole in this extraordinary gallery must start by trying to understand this heraldry. The ceiling unrolls its rows of shields like an extended armorial of a type that has survived in numerous examples, both from the English College of Arms and from the Scottish Court of the Lyon King. Indeed, such illuminated armorial manuscripts provide the closest analogues to the heraldic programme

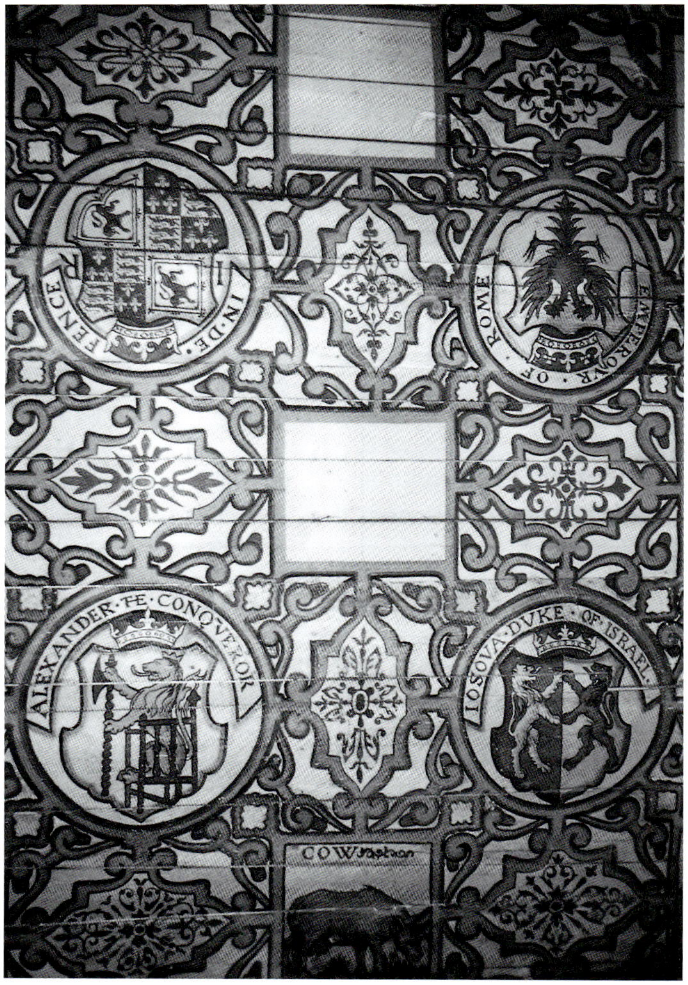

Earlshall ceiling, arms of two of the nine Worthies, Alexander the Great and Joshua, shown here with the royal arms of Scotland and those of the (Holy) Roman Emperor. The arms of Joshua are, however, incorrect.

on the ceiling and there are good reasons for thinking that it might have been the work of one or other of the herald painters who themselves compiled such manuscripts in the Lyon Court.

The habit of marshalling the arms of the Scottish nobility in a sequence headed by the arms of the established monarchies appears to preserve a tradition developed long before the sixteenth century and not confined to Scotland. The manuscript armorial known as Walford's Roll, for instance, compiled as early as c.1275 in England, marshals the arms of the kings of Germany, France, England, Spain, Cicily, Navarre, Castille, Aragon, Bohemia, Hungary, the Emperor of Constantinople, and the kings of Acre, Scotland, Cyprus, Norway, Denmark, and the Isle of Man, before settling to its sequence of arms of the nobility of France and England. A number of other English medieval rolls of arms repeat this pattern. In Scotland the same tradition is represented in the great manuscript armorial compiled in 1542 by Sir David Lindsay of the Mount, Lyon King of Arms and one of the most celebrated poets of the Scottish vernacular renaissance, author most notably of *Ane Satyre of the Three Estaitis*. This contains nearly all the coats of arms displayed on the Earlshall ceiling including the three Magi and the nine Worthies; indeed the manuscript has the same overall structure as Earlshall's heraldic scheme, for after two shields of the Royal Arms of Scotland and 'Ye rycht potent prince Preist Jhone, Emperiour off the Greit Ynde' it displays the arms of the Magi, 'quilkis maid the first offerent till our saluiour Crist Jesu', namely Balthasar, King of Saba, Gaspar [Caspar], King of Tharse [Thrace] and Melchior, King of Araby. These are followed by the arms of the nine Worthies divided into 'thre Jowis' [Jews], three 'Gentiles' and three 'crissynhed men'. This was the conventional ordering of the nine Worthies, but at first sight the way they are disposed on the ceiling appears to violate the familiar and commonplace grouping into three biblical, three classical, and three medieval heroes. Although Godfrey of Bouillon ('Boulogne', as the ceiling label has it) is ranged with Arthur and Charlemagne at the head of what I am identifying as section two of the ceiling, Section 4 offers us Judas Maccabeus, Hector and David, while Section 6 links Joshuah, Alexander and Julius Caesar. However, the

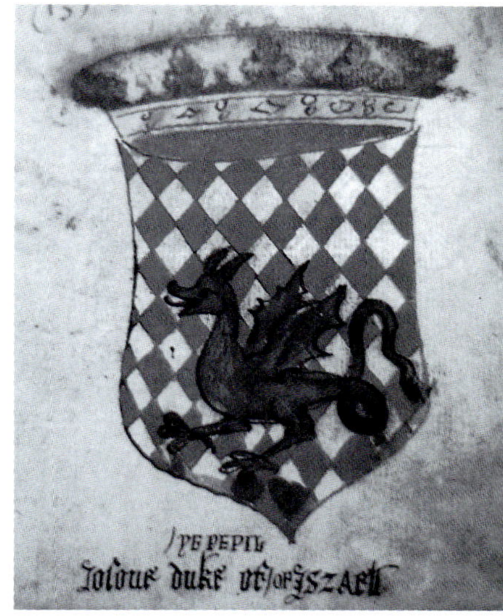

Arms of Joshua as depicted in the Forman Armorial, Lyon Court MS 17, fol. 62.

Earlshall artist appears to have assigned the arms of Hector of Troy (two confronting lions rampant) to Joshuah, and to have assigned Joshuah's arms (a winged dragon on a lozengy ground) to Hector. In other words the shields are in the correct order and in the right positions, but two of the labels have been switched. Sir David Lindsay's armorial may serve as our witness for the correct iconography of these shields. Thereafter both the manuscript, and the ceiling as we move from east to west, present us with what Lindsay's prefatory header calls the 'armys off certane crissynhed kyngis' including most of those displayed on the ceiling – for instance the Emperor of Rome and the kings of Denmark, Scotland, Hungary, Naples, and of 'Bewme' (Bohemia) and 'Swadric'. Of the twenty-eight arms of royalty on the Earlshall ceiling, nineteen correspond to all but three of the twenty-one 'crissynhed kyngis' illustrated in this section of the manuscript. After a further section of arms closely associated with the Scottish royal house, the manuscript settles to its prolonged catalogue of the arms of the Scottish nobility, which includes virtually all the shields in the western half of the gallery.

The correspondence between the Lindsay armorial and the Earlshall ceiling is thus close enough to suggest that both represent a common heraldic tradition. The armorial is not, however, the direct source of the heraldic scheme in the gallery, since a number of coats of arms on the ceiling are not found in the manuscript and the ceiling includes their heraldic supporters and mottoes whereas the manuscript shows only the shield. Both would appear to be informed, however, by the same national, dynastic and religious assumptions, which are summed up in Lindsay's prefatory verses:

Si spectari cupis praeclara insignia Regum
Illustre heroum semideumque genus
Et clarum exardens quos vexit ad ethera virtus
Et quibus hac vita gloria maior erat
Vt paucis sapias haec sunt insignia quorum
Defensa invicto Scotia marte fuit
Cum patrie fortes animam effudere superbam
Talia pro meritis sunt monimenta data
Nobilium ut moveant animos pro ingentibus actis
Premia quo exemplis postera turba colat
Mira arte et varijs ut cernis picta figuris
Ordine queque suo versa tabella dabit.

(If you wish to see the famous insignia of the illustrious line of kings, heroes and demigods, and the shining valour which thrust them zealously up to the skies, and by which this life was made more glorious, these few insignia will inform you of those by whom Scotland was defended from conquest in war when the strong poured out their proud spirits for their country. Such are the memorials awarded for their merits so that they might inspire the spirits of the nobility to great deeds, from which the throng of their successors may cherish their examples. So that you may see them painted in various figures and with wonderful art, the following list offers each in its proper order.)

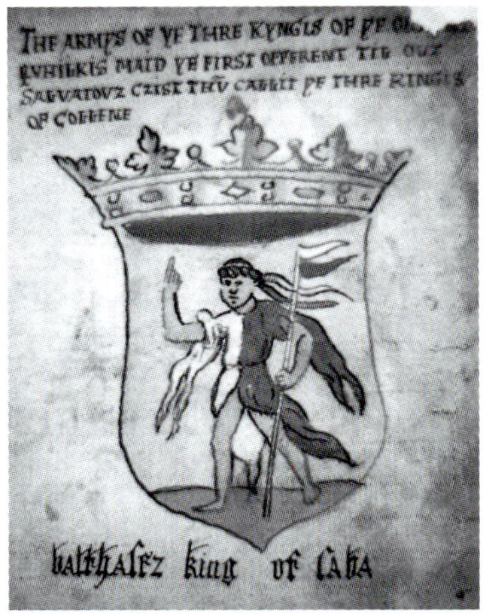

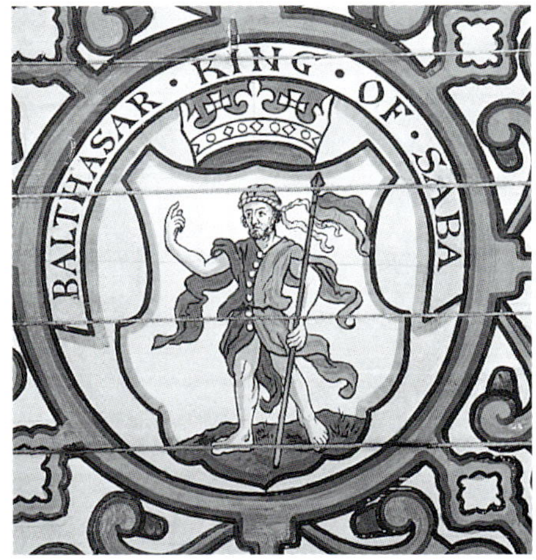

Left: *Arms of Balthasar, King of Saba, from section of Forman Armorial devoted to 'The armys of ye thre kyngis of ye Or[ient] quilkis maid ye first offerent til our salvatour Crist thv-callit ye thre kings of Collene', fol. 57.*

Right: *Arms of Balthasar on the Earlshall ceiling; if the resemblance to the Forman Armorial seems close it may be not because Workman painted the c eiling but because Robert Lorimer, who restored the ceiling, copied the Workman manuscript.* HS

There are a number of other Scottish heraldic manuscripts that marshal the arms of the Scottish nobility together with the established monarchies of the world, the three Magi and the nine Worthies. Perhaps the most interesting of these is the Lyon Court's Forman Armorial, MS 17, most of which is assigned on good authority to James Workman who became Marchmont Herald in 1597. This is evidently a compilation of materials of various dates in different hands and styles and is described in an early hand as 'ane authentick record' of the arms of Scotland 'in the reigns of Queen Mary and King James', and as having belonged to James Workman in 1623, very close to the date when the Earlshall ceiling was painted. Parts of the manuscript are undoubtedly earlier than this, and Workman is also known as the author of a quite different armorial (Nat Lib Scot Adv MS 31.3.5). Like most of these manuscripts it was compiled to serve as an official record of the coats of arms to which Scottish families held a legal title which it was the job of the Lyon Court to protect in law. A verbal blazon would certainly provide an accurate record for legal purposes, but the Lyon King and his officers seem periodically to have recognised the desirability of preparing illuminated armorials to show the authorised charges and tinctures (and sometimes also the supporters, helmets and mottoes) of Scottish royalty and nobility.

The Forman (Lyon Court) Armorial, moreover, was undoubtedly not just compiled as an official record for consultation by the Lyon King and his officers. Its pages are much worn, and they are interspersed with material of different kinds which tends to suggest it was used as an artist's pattern book. We know James Workman did armorial work at Edinburgh Castle in 1617, and his name has occasionally been associated with decorative painting elsewhere in Scotland. The Forman Armorial begins with the arms of the three Magi under a section heading which identifies them as 'Ye thre kyngis of ye Orient quhilkes maid ye first offerent til our salvatour Crist thu callit ye thre kingis of Collene' – the page and the header are identical with the corresponding page from the Lindsay armorial. The 'three kings of Collene' was one of the traditional titles of the Magi, though no one seems to have known quite where 'Collene' was – it might surprise us to find that it was normally taken to mean Cologne, from the medieval tradition that the relics of the three kings had been first preserved in Constantinople, whence they were removed to Milan, and reached their final resting place thanks to a certain Renatus, Bishop of Cologne. Sir Thomas Browne, however, in his *Pseudodoxia Epidemica*, Book 7 Chapter 8 'Of the

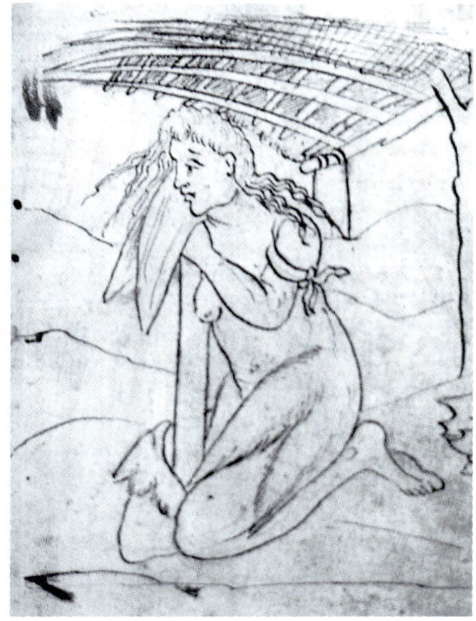

Penitent Magdalene, one of four sketches from the Workman Armorial which suggest that it was compiled as a decorative pattern book, Lyon Court MS 17, pp.247-8.

three Kings of Collein', points out that the Bible offers little authority for their number, their names, or their place of origin. It was the received opinion that they were kings, an idea that goes back to the second-century writer Tertullian, that had long influenced their representation in paintings of the Adoration, and it is this tradition that motivated their inclusion in armorials listing the arms of the established monarchies.

The Forman Armorial then proceeds to the arms of the nine Worthies, just as we find them on the Earlshall ceiling, before reaching a section illustrating what, as in Lindsay, is described as 'ye armys of certane crissynhed kyngis'. This is followed by the royal arms of Scotland as these had developed down to the time of Mary, Queen of Scots and then by the arms of the Scottish nobility. At one point, however, the manuscript breaks off from purely heraldic material to offer us two pages of moral and proverbial verses of exactly the type we find inscribed on the beams of such places as Crathes or Delgaty or on the walls of Earlshall itself. It follows this with five pages of line drawings of figures in architectural and landscape settings – undoubtedly part of an artist's sketchbook of moral or biblical subjects. They include the figure of a kneeling, penitent Magdalene, a crowned beggar, and a winnower with a fan. The inclusion of such sketches suggests that the whole of this much-stained and dog-eared manuscript was used as an artist's pattern book of the type which would have been employed at such a site as Earlshall. It is for this reason a document of the greatest interest for the history of decorative painting of this period, if only because it confirms that we should not make any distinction between what is sometimes known as 'herald' painting and what we tend to think of as 'ordinary' painting. Heraldry, as the Earlshall ceiling establishes beyond question, was an integral and essential part of the decorative artist's vocabulary and not something separate from the other types of iconography available for use in such a programme.

The Earlshall ceiling is not, moreover, the only place in Scotland where a series of arms of 'christened kings' was used to decorate a ceiling. As we noted in Chapter 1, a hundred years before, c.1520, Gavin Dunbar, bishop of Aberdeen, had erected a panelled ceiling of oak above the nave of St Machar's Cathedral whose intersections were decorated with forty-eight carved and painted shields in three rows. The central row represents the personal arms of the current bishops and archbishops of Scotland and the southern row the shields of a selection of Scottish nobility, but the northern row is taken up with the arms of European monarchs. As in the Lindsay and the Workman manuscripts, and as at Earlshall, they are all labelled. Moreover the painted ceiling at Nunraw, East Lothian, also includes, along with a variety of grotesque motifs and bestiary subjects, two rows each containing ten coats of arms with identifying labels. Fourteen of these twenty shields are drawn from the list of 'crissynhed kyngis'. Two of the shields at Nunraw – the King of Freisland, and the King of Sweden – though not found in Lindsay's armorial are nevertheless found at Earlshall, suggesting both ceilings were executed by an artist or artists who had access to a very similar armorial pattern book.

Royal coat of arms from the series painted at Nunraw: the King of Freisland.

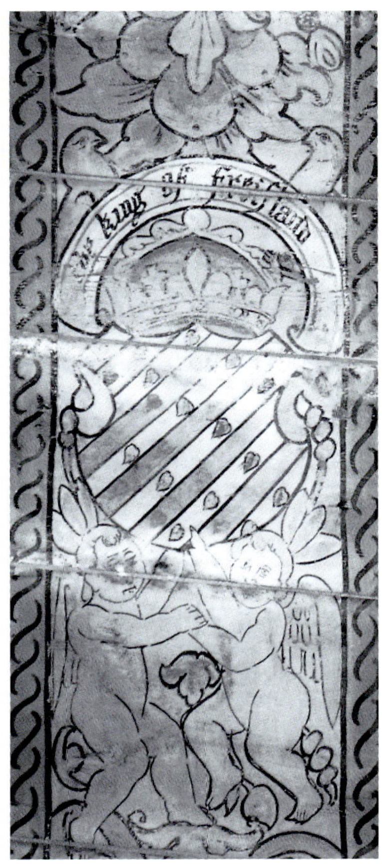

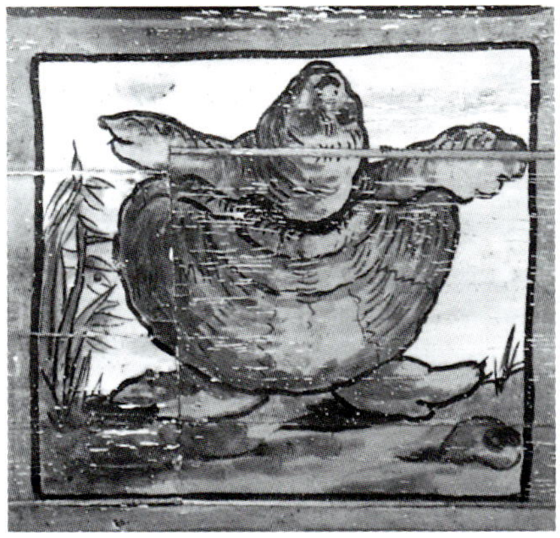

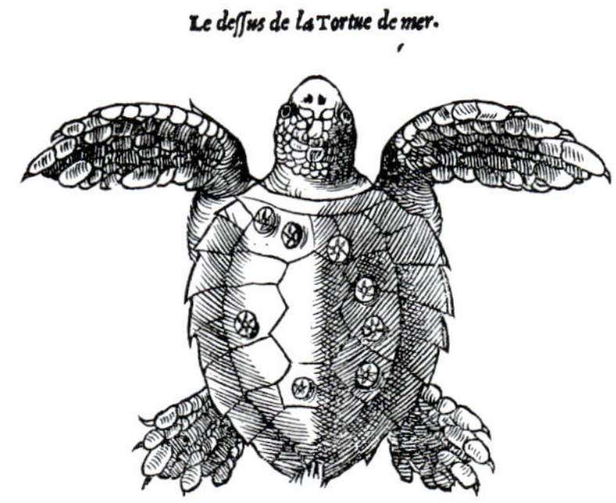

Left: *Fish or fowl? The upside-down tortoise at Earlshall owes its curious posture to Pierre Belon's illustration of the marine turtle viewed from above (he also illustrates its underside), but the Earlshall artist has rather perversely given it some ground to stand on.*

Right: *Peirre Belon,* La nature et diversité des poissons *(1555), p.46.* GUL

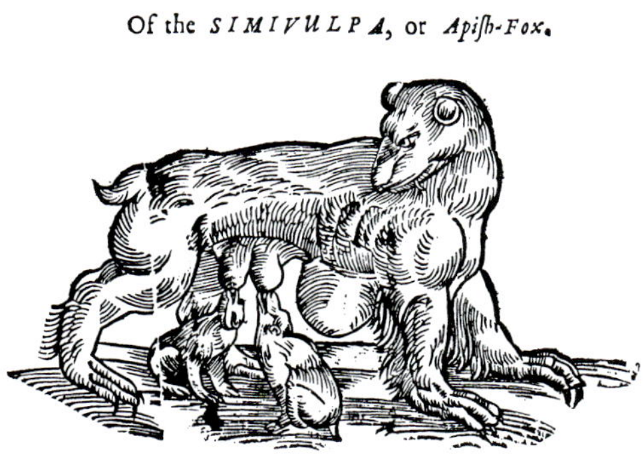

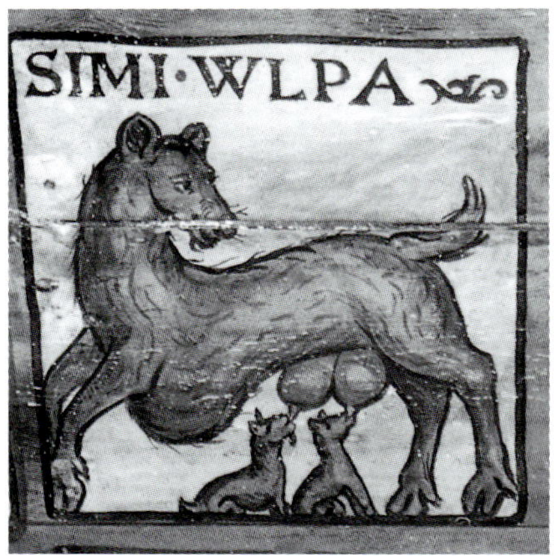

Left: *Edward Topsell,* Historie of Foure-Footed Beastes *(1607, p.16) engraving illustrating the 'Simivulpa, or Apish-Fox'.* GUL

Right: *Earlshall, long gallery detail, 'Simiwlpa'.*

The practice of marshalling the arms of the Scottish nobility alongside those of the established monarchies of the world was probably motivated by a desire to assert Scotland's place as an equal and sovereign nation within the economy of Christian kingdoms, and the prominence often given to the insignia of Rome, or Jerusalem, at the head of such lists suggests their overall inflection. Indeed the three rows at Aberdeen show a remarkable symmetry, with the monarchical sequence headed by 'Imperatorie Majestatis' (the arms of the Roman Emperor), its ecclesiastical sequence by the Pope, and its Scottish sequence headed by the royal arms of Scotland followed immediately by Saint Margaret, Queen of Malcolm Canmore. The Reformation would inevitably lead to some modifications of this scheme, but the hierarchical and universalising tendency to which this programmatic convention witnesses was evidently sufficiently robust to survive the Reformation.

The animals at Earlshall cannot be easily accommodated to any such symbolic programme, and there does not seem to be any *translatio* of signification between the heraldic scheme and the bestiary motifs. Fortunately for us most of the animals, like the coats of arms, are labelled and it is likely that all of them were originally named. Some of the named animals are familiar, others very strange. The identity of particular beasts is easier to establish once it is realised that many of them, though by no means all, are copied from Edward Topsell's *Historie of Foure-Footed Beastes* (1607). Topsell's illustrations not only supplied their images, but his commentary, in many instances, supplied their

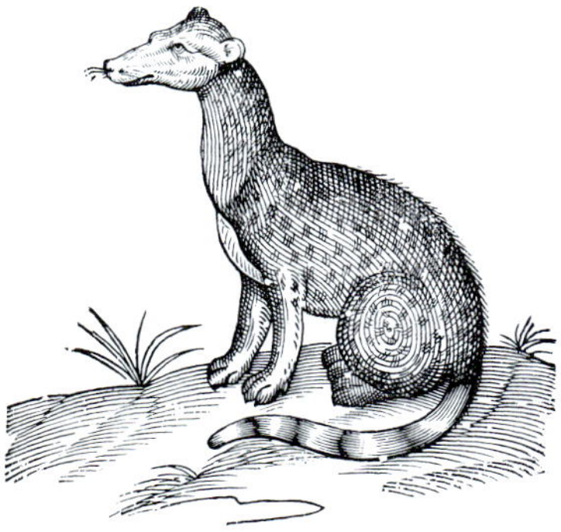

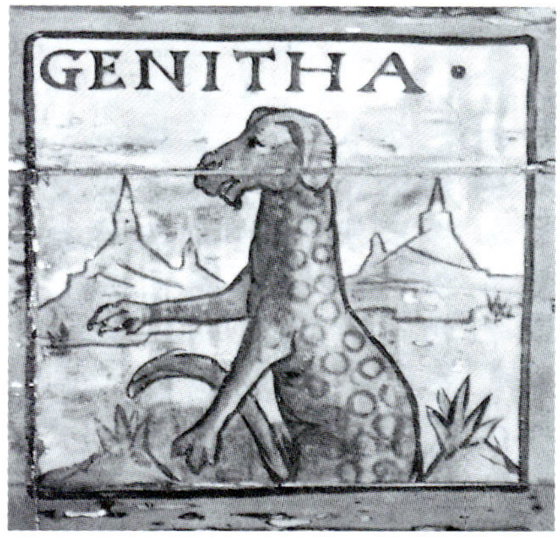

Edward Topsell, Historie of Foure-Footed Beastes *(1607, p.180) engraving illustrating the 'Gennet-cat, called Genetha'.* GUL

Earlshall, long gallery detail, 'Genitha' or gennet.

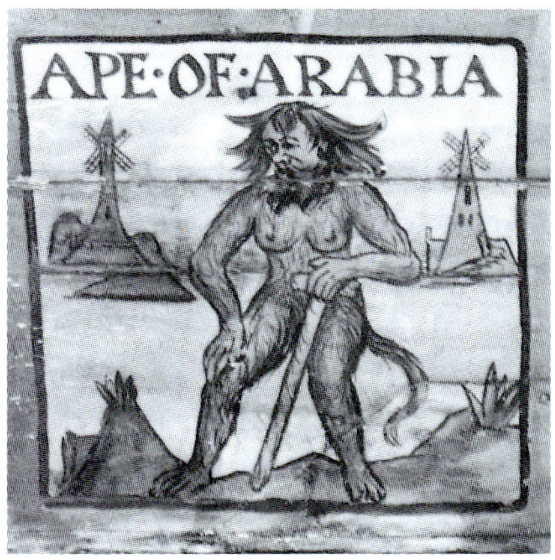

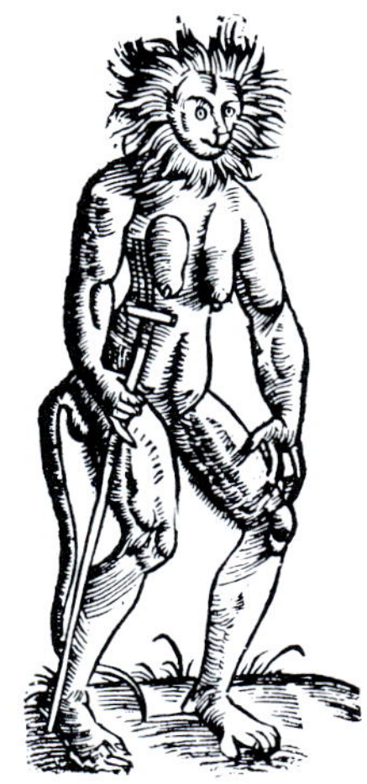

Left: *Earlshall, long gallery detail, 'Ape of Arabia'.*

Right: *Edward Topsell,* Historie of Foure-Footed Beastes *(1607, p.8) engraving illustrating the 'Prasyan Apes'.* GUL

names. The use of animals is commonplace in decorative schemes of this period; we find them at Stobhall and in houses in Edinburgh, and Mary, Queen of Scots copied numerous animals from this same set of engravings – which had previously appeared in Conrad Gesner's *Historia Animalium* (Zurich, 1551-8) – in her needlework (Swain 1973, pl.55-87). In the 1660s a decorative plasterer working in Devonshire, John Abbott, copied many of these same engravings from Topsell into his pattern book (Bath 1998). Animal pictures, and this set of engravings in particular, were clearly a standard resource for decorative artists of this period. The animals copied from Topsell at Earlshall are not confined to the long gallery, for there is a separate room off the eastern stair turret whose ceiling is decorated entirely with named animals from the same source – goat, tiger, chameleon, unicorn, wolf, dromedary, beaver, leopard.

To show the relationship between these animal paintings and their engraved sources we have only to look at the Earlshall panel that shows a quadruped with swollen breasts suckling two young, labelled 'SIMIWLPA'. This is a reverse copy of the animal Topsell calls 'Simivulpa, or Apish-Fox', which is described as having the foreparts of a fox, the hindparts of an ape, human feet and ears of a bat. The underpart of the belly forms a pouch in which the Simivulpa carries her young for protection and from which they only emerge in order to suckle, as we see them doing in the picture. Slightly less bizarre is the creature labelled 'Genitha', which copies Topsell's 'Gennet-cat, called Genetha' (p.179). This is evidently the southern European or Asian genet, or civet-cat, whose fur was valued for garments. Both Topsell's engraving and the Earlshall painting realise what Topsell describes as 'the abundance of spots' whose 'shining splendor and brightness, give place to no other party-coloured beast, as you may observe in the true figure therof here declared' (p.180). Earlshall's 'Ape of Arabia' is depicted as an upright, humanoid figure, with facial hair and breasts, holding a wooden crutch. This copies what Topsell describes as the apes of Prasia, 'a Region in *India*, which are no lesse than great Dogs, and five cubits high, having hair like a Man coming forth of their forehead and beards, being altogether white except their tails, which are two cubits and a half long, very like a Lions' (p.7). The wooden crutch seems to be the engraver's attempt to realise the anecdote which Conrad Gesner and, following him, Topsell quote from Peter Martyr, who tells of an archer on a sea voyage who captured one of these apes and cut off its arm; the wounded beast nevertheless became tame and was adopted by the sailors. Though the ape has not lost any of its limbs in this illustration, the crutch probably signals the artist's recognition that it was somehow disabled.

Topsell's *Historie of Foure-Footed Beastes* (1607) was followed in 1608 by his *Historie of Serpents.* The Earlshall artist almost certainly had access to the second of these volumes since the picture of the chameleon appears to copy the engraving from *Historie of Serpents* (p.673). Topsell's 'serpents' also include the many-headed Hydra (p.736) but the Earlshall artist depicts the Hydra as a quadruped and owes nothing to Topsell's illustration. Topsell similarly classifies the winged dragon as a serpent and shows it with two legs like the heraldic wyvern (p.705), whereas the Earlshall image gives it four legs and a barbed tail, like the heraldic dragon. These are not the only animals at Earlshall that evidently refer to different sources, for its painted bestiary includes a number of birds. Its fox goes back to Aesopic sources, since it is shown in full flight with a hen in its mouth, while the hedgehog is shown with grapes impaled on its spines, an image deriving from medieval bestiary iconography which follows Pliny's account of the hedgehog rolling on its back to collect fallen grapes on its spines. Neither of these images owes anything to Topsell.

There are signs that the long gallery ceiling has been heavily restored. In 1887 MacGibbon and Ross reported that it was badly decayed:

> It is most unfortunate that the beautiful ceiling of the gallery ... should be allowed to fall piecemeal into utter ruin. A good deal of it is entirely gone, and the remainder is in a very fragile condition. The wood-work of the ceiling and roof is rotting from the effects of damp, and the whole has been most rudely patched up with wooden straps nailed across the ceiling in the most unsightly fashion. (vol. ii, p.289)

Only a few years later the castle was purchased by a Perth bleach manufacturer, RWR McKenzie, who in 1892 commissioned the young Robert Lorimer (who was to become one of Scotland's most celebrated architects) to restore it, and it is undoubtedly this restoration that we have to thank for the fact that the

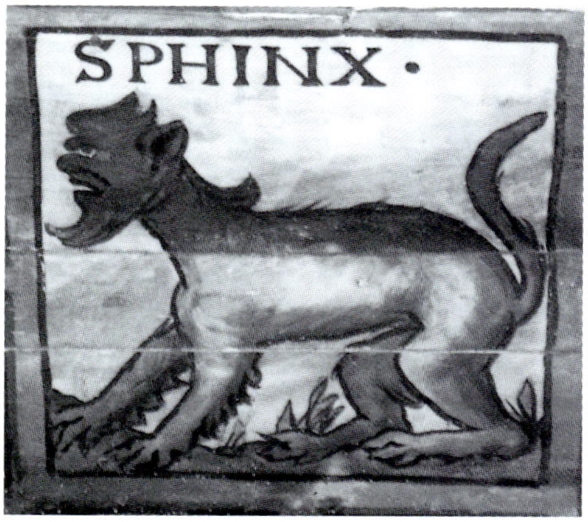

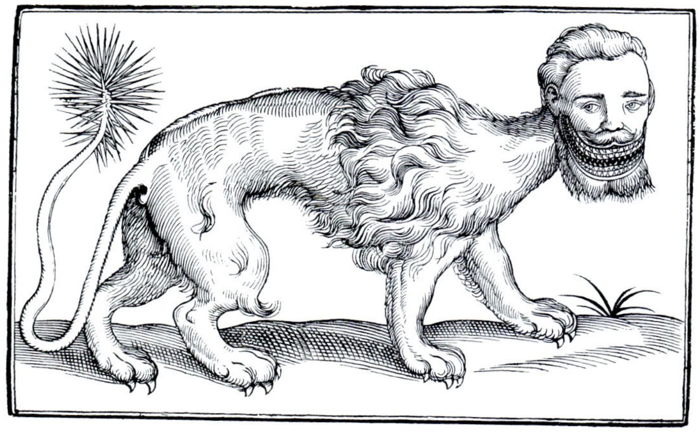

Left: *Earlshall, long gallery detail. Although labelled 'Sphinx' this is almost certainly a copy of Topsell's 'Mantichora'.*

Right: Edward Topsell, Historie of Foure-Footed Beastes *(1607, p.344) engraving illustrating the 'Mantichora'.* GUL

ceiling has survived at all (see Savage 1980, pp.9-14). It is evident, however, that the restoration did not scruple to supply missing detail where it was lacking, or to 'improve' on what it found remaining, though the panels that were beyond such restoration have simply been blanked out. The methods employed for this restoration are described in an article on Earlshall that appeared in *Country Life* in 1905, which states that 'The painting was all on timber, which the rain through the roof had made too rotten for a nail to stay in, and much had already fallen. Piece by piece the surface was sliced away, and glued like veneer to sound wood, which could then be secured as in former time to the upper couples of the roof. This achieved, the painting, still clearly to be seen, was slowly brought back to its original colours with distemper' (p.948). Some pre-restoration photographs taken about 1890 by Erskine Beveridge survive in the RCAHMS which suggest the extent and nature of Lorimer's repainting. In these the creature in Section 9, now labelled 'Sphinx', shows no sign of a name and does not resemble a sphinx but is almost certainly a reverse-copy of Topsell's 'Mantichora', a man-eating monster with a lion's body (hence the supposition that it must be a sphinx) and the face of a man showing a triple row of teeth. In the same photographs the arms of the Earl of Mar are shown with their label in the bottom right hand corner of the circular rim and the motto 'Sans plvs' at the top. As restored, the motto is omitted and the label repositioned at the top; this change was necessitated by Lorimer's decision to remove the boards that squared off the vaulted window recess which lay behind this section of panelling. Moreover, the attributes of the arms have been corrected, replacing the chevron which appears in the quarterings with a bend, suggesting that Lorimer restored these shields in the light of his own knowledge of Scottish heraldry, correcting their blazonry and charges wherever he thought necessary. It is probably worth noting that Sir Thomas Innes of Learney, a herald pursuivant, writing on Scottish Heraldry in 1934, expressed his satisfaction that 'Great architects, such as the late Sir Robert Lorimer, are continually in touch with the Lyon Office, and so are all our prominent craftsmen and designers, most of whom are known to H. M. Officers of Arms' (p.55).

It will be clear from this analysis of the detail that it would not be easy to suggest any controlling idea governing the different iconographic schemes at Earlshall. The fact that we have at least two long galleries in Scotland with much of their original decoration in place might suggest that we could draw some conclusions about the articulation of this most characteristic feature of Renaissance domestic architecture, yet the comparison with Seton's painted

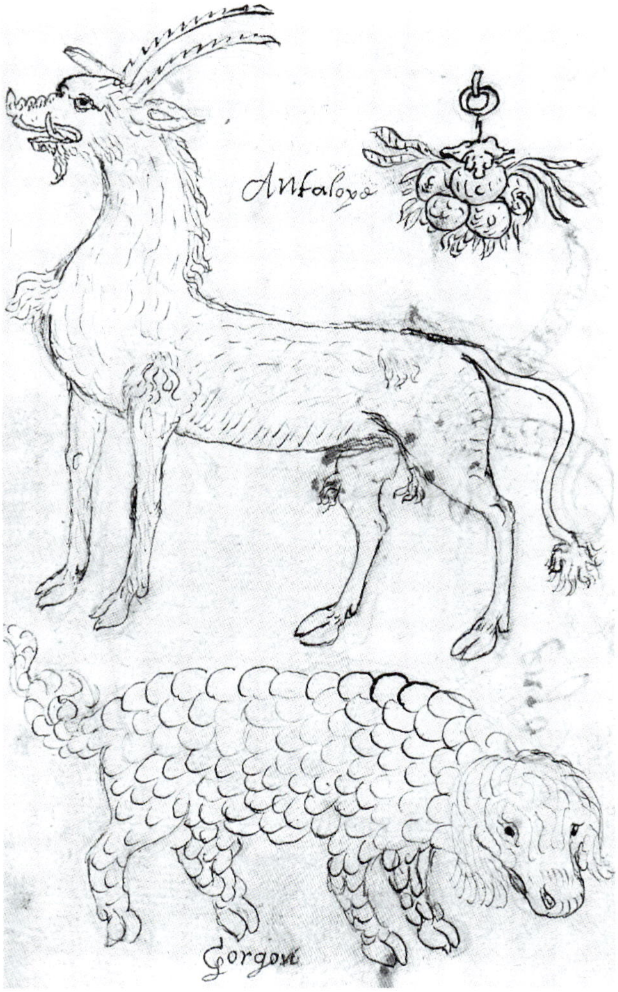

The continuing popularity of Topsell's animal illustrations as patterns for use by decorative artists is suggested by the notebook compiled by Devonshire plasterer John Abbott in the 1660s, which includes a dozen or more animals copied from Topsell's engravings, such as the Antelope and Gorgon shown here.
DRO

gallery at Pinkie seems to suggest as many differences as correspondences in their articulation of architectural space and iconographic schemes. Compared to the focused Stoic programme of emblems at Pinkie, the various schemes at Earlshall seem to follow no overall plan. Long galleries were rooms meant, as Christy Anderson puts it, 'not for static study but for walking back and forth, observing the gardens outdoors through large windows, or the taking of exercise in inclement weather' (1995, p.252). Pinkie's scheme seems to illustrate rather well the advice which one sixteenth-century account offers for the proper ornamentation of such galleries: 'histories, grave stories, and the best workes become galleries; where one may walk and exercise their senses in viewing, delighting, judging and censuring' (quoted in Coope 1984, p.449). Such perambulant reading was certainly 'spatial, constrained, or supported by the space where it occurred' (Anderson, p.252), but it was not necessarily constrained to follow a fixed overall syntax, and the assemblage of the various schemes at Earlshall may follow no overall sequence.

Its local, numbered and labelled schemes may nevertheless have been designed to function as memory schemes. The local sequencing of the imagery in the visual vocabulary of the ceiling certainly would not rule out such an application and may well reflect that movement which the random perambulation of the gallery seems to suggest for, as Anderson says, 'The advantage of the spatial formula in memory is the ability of the rememberer to move around, "forward and backwarde ... upwarde and downwarde", to recall information in a flexible order and not only in a linear, sequential structure' (p.252).

Pictures of animals and birds are, of course, not at all uncommon in decorative painting – we find various animals represented amidst the other types of subject at Stobhall, at Gladstone's Land, Traquair and elsewhere. As late as the 1660s the English decorative plasterer, John Abbott, was still copying animals from Topsell into his pattern book along with cartouche designs from continental prints or pattern books and emblems from George Wither (Bath 1998). But there is no such painting that includes quite such an extensive bestiary as that in the Earlshall gallery. It is just possible that this might owe something to the use memory treatises advocated for such sequences of animals. A little-known seventeenth-century manual on *The Art of Memory*, published in London and Edinburgh, explains:

> Others, instead of a House Palace or Building, have chosen such Beasts as answer to all the Alphabetical Letters in the Latin Tongue, and instead of Rooms have assigned their several Members for our fancy to fix our Ideas there, and place them for our better rememberance: These are the names of the Beasts, Asinus, Basilicus, Canis, Draco, Elephas, Faunus, Gryphus, Hircus, Juvencus, Leo, Mulus, Nectua, Ovis, Panthera, Qualea, Rhinoceros, Simia, Taurus, Ursus, Xystus, Hyaena, Zachus. Everyone of these they divide into five Parts or Places, into Head, Fore-feet, Belly, Hinderfeet, and Tail; for this is the Order that Nature it self directs, neither can our Imagination be disordered in reckoning or telling them over. So that by this means the Fancy may have one hundred and fifteen Places to imprint the Images of memorable things. (d'Assigny, p.99)

Any claim that the Earlshall animals, however, were designed to function as a memory sequence, would need to recognise that the animals named on the ceiling do not fall into such an alphabetical sequence, and also that there are far more of them than any alphabetical sequence requires – more than sixty on the original ceiling. Since the traditional memory arts were so closely associated with the articulation of both text and image in architectural spaces, however, it is probably worth considering more fully what we know about their practice in Scotland at this period.

The idea that some, if not all, of the painted ceilings in Scotland were designed to serve – among other things – as memory theatres may not appear at first sight very plausible. Claims that decorative schemes in particular buildings – the Scrovegni Chapel (Giotto's 'Arena Capella') in Padua, for instance – were designed primarily for such a use are notoriously difficult to prove, and have had to rely on evidence of their conformity with schemes for the numerological sequencing and placement of *loci*, or their use of particular types of imagery which were recommended in the standard artificial-memory treatises (Yates 1966, pp.92-4; Engel 1996, pp.12-21). The art of memory did not, after all, require its practitioners to actually build the architectural places

THE
HISTORIE
OF
FOVRE-FOOTED
BEASTES.

Deſcribing the true and liuely figure of euery Beaſt, with a diſcourſe *of their ſeuerall Names, Conditions, Kindes, Vertues (both naturall and* medicinall) Countries of their breed, their loue and hate to Mankinde, and the wonderfull worke of God in their Creation, Preſeruation, and Deſtruction.

Neceſſary for all Diuines and Students, becauſe the ſtory of euery Beaſt is amplified with Narrations out of Scriptures, Fathers, Phyloſophers, Phyſitians, and Poets: wherein are declared diuers Hyeroglyphicks, Emblems, Epigrams, and other good Hiſtories, Collected out of all the Volumes of CONRADVS GESNER, *and all other Writers to this preſent day.* By EDWARD TOPSELL.

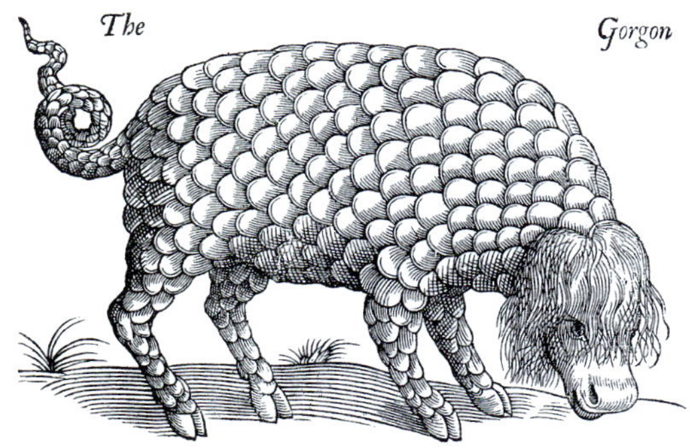

LONDON,
Printed by William Iaggard.
1607.

Title page of Topsell's bestiary, showing the mythical Gorgon. GUL

which they were advised to employ as the seats of ideographic images for their memory systems; almost any existing building would do and one's memory theatre might, indeed, consist of what were long known as *ficta loca*, 'imaginary places' (Yates, p.115). Yet, as Frances Yates suggests, it would be surprising if the art of memory, with its strong emphasis on the placing of suggestive icons in particular architectural settings, had not exercised some influence on the arts of painting and architecture. The art of memory always had at least two potential connections with our subject matter in this book. Firstly, as an art that encouraged its practitioners to locate their ideas in artificial *loci*, it associated the art of memory with buildings – it was an art with ancient connections with architecture. And secondly, by teaching its practitioners to associate ideas with striking visual images, it had potential connections with painting. It might therefore be particularly relevant to the fashion for decorating buildings with painted images, and there is strong *prima facie* evidence that the art of memory was cultivated and practised in Scotland within the circle of patrons and clients who were responsible for the remarkable efflorescence of this style of decorative painting in the reign of James VI.

Such evidence rests on two distinct (or perhaps not so distinct) historical facts. The first is the set of statutes drawn up by William Schaw, King James's Master of Works, in the closing years of the sixteenth century, in which Schaw attempted to reform the traditional organisation of the craft guilds of the Wrights and Masons. It has been shown that these statutes are the basis of modern freemasonry, with its system of lodges to which non-operative masons were, for the first time, admitted. As David Stevenson recognises, one of the most interesting of these statutes was the requirement that the Masters of the new masonic lodges should test every apprentice and fellow-craft in 'the art of memorie and science thairof' (Stevenson 1988a, p.45). This statute appears to mean that practising masons – both journeymen operatives and the new category of non-operative masons – were required to show proficiency in precisely those artificial memory systems explored in the classic studies by Frances Yates and Mary Carruthers. It is important to realise that the painters responsible for the walls and ceilings which decorate so many of these Scottish buildings did not, as in England, have their own separate guild (in England, the Painter Stainers Guild) but traditionally belonged to the Wrights and Masons (Apted and Hannabuss 1978, p.3) – the very guild which William Schaw's new statutes were intent on reforming.

That Schaw's new statutes are the basis of modern speculative freemasonry means that it could be important to investigate the connections this painting may have had with some of the esoteric traditions which freemasonry was to perpetuate and develop. Needless to say this evidence needs to be treated with some caution, but it is suggestive that so many of the families in Scotland who commissioned painted decoration in their houses were to have continuing connections with the development of freemasonry during the seventeenth century and later. Much of this evidence is necessarily retrospective because the new Masonic lodges which developed out of William Schaw's reforms were an essentially secret society whose actual constitution and membership only begins to emerge in the eighteenth century. Some, though by no means all, of its early practitioners were, moreover, crypto-Catholics who appear to have carried its rituals across to France with the exiled Stuart court, and in the eighteenth century what was known in France as the Masonic *ordre écossais* appears to have had particularly close connections with the Jacobite cause.

For instance George, fifth Earl of Winton – who played a prominent role in the rebellion of 1715, when he was captured and impeached but escaped from the Tower of London – went on to become 'Great Master' of the Roman Lodge before it was suppressed by the Pope in 1737 (Seton 1896, vol. i, pp.274-5). Winton was a Seton, descended from Alexander Seton's elder brother, Robert, first Earl of Winton, and his wife Margaret Montgomery. The Montgomery earls of Eglinton had themselves been closely associated with the Kilwinning Lodge in Ayrshire from its earliest beginnings – William Schaw's 1599 statutes were addressed specifically to the Lodge of Kilwinning since this lodge already claimed a peculiar supremacy over the other masonic lodges of Scotland, a claim which Schaw was called on to arbitrate (Stevenson 1988a, pp.44-51). Much later, in 1764, Karl Gottlieb von Hund was required to account for his claim that he had been initiated into a Masonic order of 'Strict Observance' which, he alleged, depended on a secret hierarchy of Jacobite Knights Templar. These unknown superiors, who were thought to manage the system behind the scenes, operated through a Masonic lodge of Scottish Jacobites in Paris that included a so-called 'Knight of the Red Feather' whom von Hund identified with Prince Charles Edward Stuart himself. However, Michael Baigent has recently claimed to have uncovered a letter in the archives of the Edinburgh Stella Templum Lodge in which the 'Knight of the Red Feather' is identified as Alexander Seton. Baigent identifies this individual not, as we might suppose, with the first Earl of Dunfermline, but rather with Alexander Montgomery, tenth Earl of Eglinton, 'who was, by virtue of his ancestry, also a Seton' (Baigent 1993, p.161). As George Seton stresses in his nineteenth-century *History of the House of Seton* (vol. ii, p.676), the earls of Eglinton, though nominally Montgomeries, descended through a cadet branch of the Setons and in the eighteenth century could claim headship of the historic house of Seton following the extinction of the Seton lines which had descended through successive earls of Winton and of Dunfermline. Similar connections are suggested by the fact that the noted Scottish alchemist and Rosicrucian Sir David Lindsay, Lord Balcarres, married Sophia Seton, daughter of Alexander, first Earl of Dunfermline. While it would be foolish to make exaggerated claims for the significance of these marital alliances between members of the Scottish nobility, it is nonetheless suggestive that so many of these names are the same responsible for some of the more remarkable examples of decorative painting and architecture in the early modern period in Scotland: it was a Montgomery who built the remarkable Skelmorlie Aisle at Largs; it was Alexander Seton who commissioned the painted gallery at Pinkie, who patronised William Schaw and who wrote the obituary inscription on his tomb in Dunfermline Abbey;

and it was Sir David Lindsay's uncle who built the garden, with its remarkable carvings of planets, Cardinal Virtues, and Liberal Arts, at Edzell.

The second piece of *prima facie* evidence which suggests that the art of memory might have some relevance to decorative painting in Scotland has to do with the career and connections of Alexander Dickson. Dickson was the St Andrews-educated disciple of Giordano Bruno who defended Bruno's art of memory against the Ramist attacks of William Perkins in what Frances Yates describes as 'one of the most basic of all Elizabethan controversies' (1966, p.266). In 1583-4 his *De umbra rationis* and in 1584 his *Defensio pro Alexandro Dicsono* were published by Thomas Vautrollier in London. Perhaps the most important thing to understand about this controversy is that it centred on the question of whether the art of memory ought to resort to images. The traditional memory arts aimed to strengthen the student's memory by associating the ideas and words that had to be recalled with striking, vivid, or unusual icons. Such images had traditionally included the Vices and Virtues, the Liberal Arts, or any of the other received schemes of *imagines agentes* (ie personifications); they might rely on biblical figures such as the Prophets or the Sibyls; they might use the signs of the zodiac or the planetary deities; or they might invent wholly original topics – grotesque or hybrid figures whose attributes should, ideally, have some metaphorical or punning association with the material to be recalled.

William Perkins, however, attacked all such imagery as 'Dunsical', arguing that logic alone – by which he means Ramist method – provided everything that one's memory required in order to fix ideas in the mind in a methodical order. Instead of images, memory should be trained, Perkins argued, in the purely abstract dichotomies of Petrus Ramus, through which ideas were linked together in a descending order of 'generals' and 'specials'. It is no accident that Perkins was a Puritan, whereas Dickson was a self-confessed 'papistical Papist', for this controversy about the use of images has an iconoclastic dimension, which is why, as Yates stresses, 'it is at bottom a religious controversy' (p.267). If we properly understood Dickson's role in this debate, and his Scottish connections, it might give us some purchase on the doctrinal context for this remarkable efflorescence of decorative painting in post-Reformation Scotland.

Both terms of the pseudonym 'Haius Scepsius' under which Alexander Dickson published his 1584 *Defensio* are suggestive for our argument, for 'Haius' reveals (or conceals) the fact that he was related through his mother to the Hay family, that is to say to the Earl of Errol who was, along with the Earl of Huntly, one of the two northern Catholic lords who led the final, futile resistance to Protestant hegemony in Scotland in the closing decades of the sixteenth century. It was, indeed, Dickson's kinsman, Alexander Hay, ninth Earl of Errol, who decorated his castle at Delgaty with painted ceilings and with a remarkable scheme of proverbial inscriptions. Alexander Dickson is known to have been in the service of the Earl of Errol in the 1590s, when he was described as Errol's secretary, a post from which he was dismissed in 1595, just two years before his kinsman painted one of the ceilings at Delgaty. Dickson, like his master the earl, was quickly restored to royal favour in the aftermath of the Catholic rebellion of 1695, and is known to have been active in the royal household in the closing years of the century. Indeed, there is good reason to believe he was teaching the traditional memory arts in Scotland at the very period when these ceilings, including those in the house of his noble kinsman, were being painted. Dickson was not alone in this for the poet William Fowler, secretary to Anne of Denmark, lists an 'art of memorye' treatise among his works, and records in a manuscript note that he had been employed in 'teaching your majestie the art of memorye' (Stevenson 1988, p.93, citing *The Works of William Fowler*, Edinburgh: Scottish Text Society 1914-40, vol. ii, p.3).

Dickson's pseudonym 'Scepsius' indicated his position as a follower of the memory system of Metrodorus of Scepsis, which Quintilian tells us was based on the twelve signs of the zodiac. Dickson's choice of this epithet reflects his commitment to the elaborate and esoteric cosmological system of his master, Giordano Bruno, and it may be this dimension of Dickson's teaching which we should recognise in the planetary deities and zodiacal schemes that find their way into the decorative vocabulary of at least a few of these painted ceilings. It is difficult to know, however, how deeply infused this teaching might have been with those hermetic traditions with which the memory arts were so closely identified during the Renaissance in the occult philosophy of such figures as Ramon Lull, Giulio Camillo, and Giordano Bruno, which attracted Frances Yates's interest. Dickson's status as Bruno's disciple might suggest that his teaching would have been heavily charged with such occult symbolism, and might account for some of the esoteric traditions which passed, via Scotland, into freemasonry. This also characterised some of the alchemical and Rosicrucian philosophies of the seventeenth century which had some notable Scottish adherents, for example Sir Robert Moray, whose connections with Elias Ashmole, alchemy, freemasonry, and Rosicrucianism are explored by Stevenson (1988a, chapter 7). But we shall not find on any of these Scottish ceilings the fantastic astral diagrams, with their complex systems of concentric circles and intersections, in the more elaborate systems of Fludd or Bruno. It is nonetheless possible that, on a day-to-day basis, Scottish practice preserved the more accessible and practical techniques of the classic teachers which had descended to the sixteenth century from the standard sources – Cicero, Quintilian and Aquinas. Indeed, as Frances Yates showed, Dickson's actual teaching seems to have been less ambitious and esoteric than that of his master. Hugh Platt, for instance, who received lessons from Dickson whilst the latter was in England in the 1680s, reported that the method was effective but 'hardly came up to the expectations raised by his teacher's descriptions of his "great and swelling art"'. As Yates comments: 'He seems to have been taught a simple form of the straight mnemotechnic which he did not know was a classical art but thought was "Maister Dickson's art". He was evidently not initiated into Hermetic mysteries' (Yates, p.285).

We shall, I think, look in vain for much evidence on these ceilings of hermetic symbolism, and it should not be assumed that in identifying the connections which some of their patrons and architects may have had with what Yates called 'The Occult Philosophy' I am intent on establishing an essentially esoteric basis for their symbolism. The art of memory was not, as some have assumed, a uniquely esoteric pursuit. For centuries it had been more routinely practised, among other things, as a means of committing to memory precisely the type of proverbial inscriptions and *loci communes* we find on ceilings such as those at Crathes and Delgaty. Combinations of emblematic image and sententious text are found on a remarkable number of these Scottish painted ceilings in a variety of formats where the relation of text to image varies considerably – ranging from the strictly emblematic to the disconnected and arbitrary. Though their formats do not appear to be controlled, however, by any shared set of generic or semiotic conventions, they may nevertheless all owe something to the art of memory. This is not, I believe, the esoteric branch of that art as it was elaborated in the occult and neo-Platonic philosophies which Frances Yates favoured, but the more routine rhetorical practices that were taught in the schools. Erasmus had little time for the former, but his *Adagia* and *Apophthegmata* were the standard resources for the latter. And their innumerable progeny – the printed collections of proverbial *sententiae* and moral commonplaces – can be shown to have provided source books for the inscriptions on at least some of these painted ceilings.

As Mary Carruthers has shown, many of the conventional topics and schemes we find represented in the visual arts went back to rhetorical *loci communes* whose original function had to do with defining the seats of an argument and assisting the memory. The names and attributes of the four Cardinal Virtues, for instance, were themselves taken from Cicero's First and Second Rhetoric (ie *De inventione* and *Ad Herennium*), though reference is also always made to *Wisdom* (ie the apocrypha's *Wisdom of Solomon*) 8.7, 'for [wisdom] teacheth temperance, and prudence, and justice, and fortitude, which are such things as men can have nothing more profitable in life' (Carruthers, p.65). The reason why the medieval Bestiary was also preserved in so many monastic libraries, she suggests, was because it was routinely recommended for such rhetorical purposes. As she says,

> Mnemonic writers such as Thomas Bradwardine and John of Garland assume their students have certain 'sets' of images already in their memories – in addition to the alphabet and numbers, these include the Zodiac and the 'characteristics of animals, [*voces animantium*]' a collection of attributes that derives from the various versions of the Bestiary .... Ordered lists of this sort, I propose, were deliberately memorized in order to serve as potential mnemonic heuristics, 'seats' into which one could place the variety of diverse material one would acquire in one's education and reading. (p.110)

A recognition of this traditional function, which certainly outlasted the medieval period, cannot resolve the problem of how to make sense of the decorative programme at Earlshall. It may nevertheless have some relevance to the way the whole programme is divided into various subsets of numbered schemes, all of which would have been well enough adapted to serve, in the phrase Aubrey uses to describe the decoration at Gorhambury, as 'Topiques for Locall memorie'. If we want to understand how some of the more elaborate schemes of moralising inscriptions and memorable images in Scottish buildings functioned, it may well be to the traditional arts of rhetoric and of memory that we should turn.

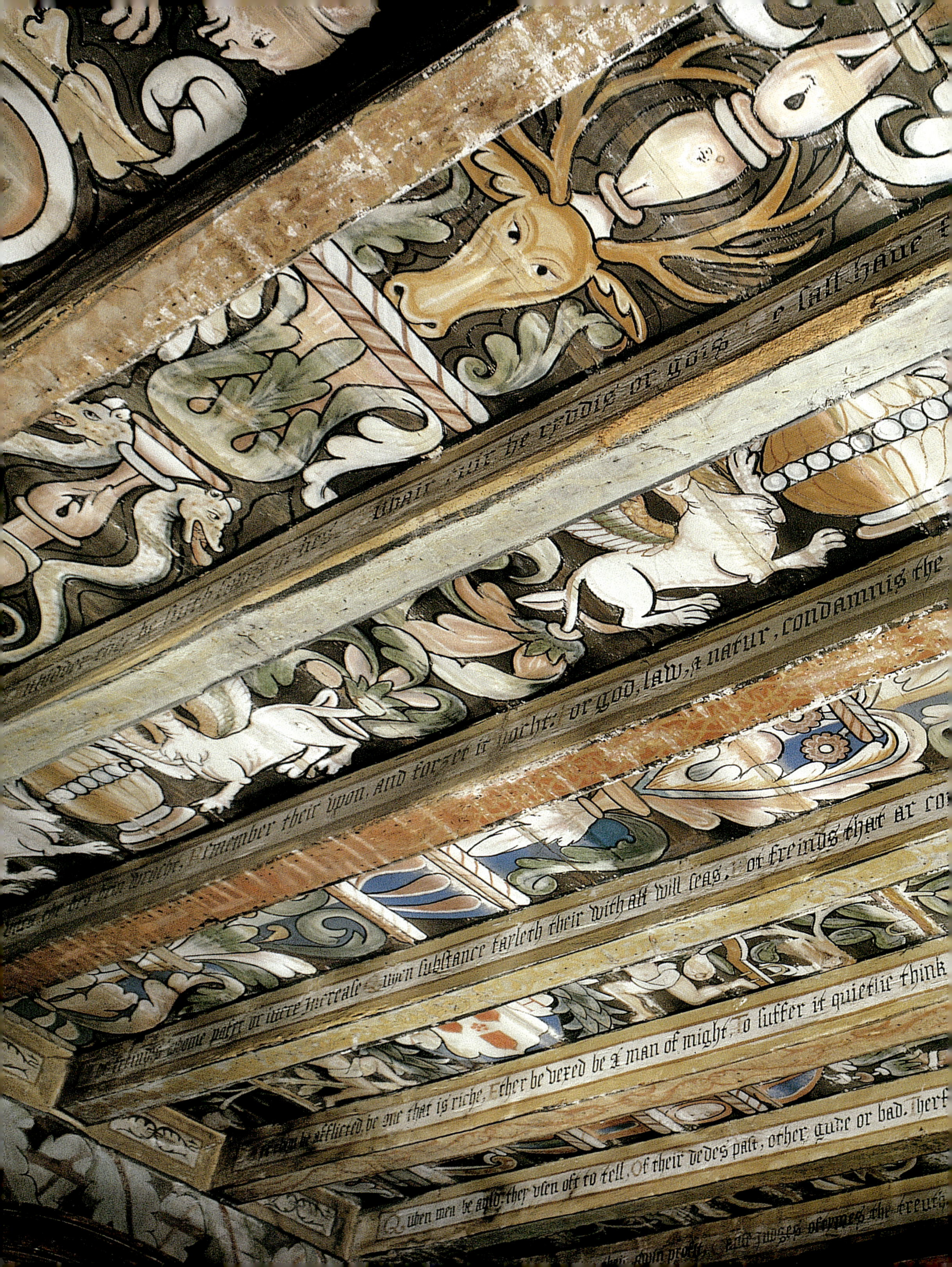

8

GRAVE SENTENCES

ONE of the most characteristic types of decoration found in Scottish houses during the sixteenth and seventeenth centuries is the extended anthology of moralising or biblical inscriptions. We find such inscriptions at Earlshall, at Crathes, at Delgaty and at Culross where, as we have seen, they are abstracted from Whitney's emblems. We also find biblical texts inscribed on beams at Traquair and at Sailor's Walk, Kirkcaldy. Such biblical texts are not uncommon in houses in England where most of the surviving examples date from the period c.1560-80. Their general function and motivation are perhaps best indicated by the passage from Deuteronomy, 6.4-10, inscribed on a chimneybreast at Feering House in Essex, which uses the Geneva Bible:

> And these wordes, which I command thee this day, shalbe in thine heart. And thou shalt rehearse them continually unto thy children, and shalt talke of them when thou tariest in thine house .... And thou shalt write them upon the postes of thine house, and upon thy gates. (Watt 1991, p.217)

It seems more than probable that both the biblical texts and the moralising and proverbial sayings were used in this spirit, as a carefully chosen anthology of appropriate teachings which were intended to be memorised ('these wordes ... shalbe in thine heart') in order to define the particular ethical and doctrinal principles of the household in an enduring form that passed down to offspring and descendants ('thou shalt rehearse them continually to thy children'). Such a function would not be out of keeping with the heraldic and dynastic significance the surrounding iconography often served to define, even though the immediate relationship between these inscriptions and the proximate decoration, dynastic or otherwise, is seldom very close. Although it could sometimes be instructive to investigate the particular values which seem to have influenced the choice of texts in the various anthologies at different locations (as with the Stoic maxims at Pinkie), most of this teaching seems to be doctrinally and ethically unspecific and it would normally be tendentious to suggest any particular connection between, say, the morality of the inscriptions and the particular circumstances of the individuals who selected them.

Opposite: *Delgaty Castle, 'Painted Chamber'.*

It is also unclear how far we would be justified in assuming, as some recent scholarship has done, that the very use of such texts signals a Protestant bias in favour of text over image, or that this fashion in Scotland necessarily represents what Tessa Watt has described, in England, as 'the new text-based aesthetic' (p.218). Watt notes that the English examples of such biblical quotations in domestic decoration echo the texts being inscribed in churches, where they were often used to cover the whitewashed spaces on walls whose idolatrous wall paintings had been effaced.

It is also likely, however, that these inscriptions, and sometimes the surrounding imagery, are functioning within the rhetorical systems I began to outline in the previous chapter. We can get some sense of this by looking at two of the more famous painted ceilings outside Scotland which have the advantage – unlike their more numerous Scottish counterparts – of having already been subject to scholarly investigation. The best known of these must be Montaigne's famous library, decorated with fifty or so moral sentences inscribed along its beams. Recent research has established that this room not only served as the powerhouse of Montaigne's writing, but that it did so because it was functioning, essentially, as a memory theatre. Perhaps the best account is William Engel's:

> Montaigne composed his *Essais* from within the space of a commonplace book writ large. The visible structure of the library indicates that Montaigne, quite literally, 'elevated' sententiae and physically 'raised' commonplaces above the books from which they had been taken .... He describes the virtues of this room in ways that are strikingly similar to the construction of an artificial memory system. (Engel 1996, p.101)

As Engel notes, Montaigne describes himself sitting in his library, from whose vantage point he could survey the different parts of his house in an implicitly fixed order, much as Quintilian had described the disposition of memory *loci* in ancient buildings:

> The first thought is placed, as it were in the forecourt; the second, let us say, in the living-room; the remainder are placed in due order all round the impluvium ... all these places are visited in turn and the various deposits are demanded of their custodians, as the sight of each recalls the respective details. (*Inst Or* 11.2.20)

The other famed example is Sir Nicholas Bacon's long gallery at Gorhambury, whose Senecan inscriptions so closely resemble the Stoic emblems in Alexander Seton's gallery at Pinkie, as we noted in Chapter 4. The *sententiae* which filled Bacon's gallery were not, apparently, attached to the emblematic pictures and there is no question of reading them as conventional tripartite Renaissance emblems, but we know from John Aubrey's description in his *Brief Lives* that the gallery also contained 'curious pictures, all emblematicall, with Motto's under each', together with animals and plants which might serve, Aubrey tells us, as 'Topiques for Locall memorie'. Usage of the term 'emblem' was not always as strictly regulated at this period as modern emblem studies tend to assume, and it could sometimes refer to detached *sententiae* or, indeed, to symbolic pictures rather than to the bimedial combination characteristic of printed emblem books. We should therefore agree with William Engel when he identifies both Montaigne's library and Bacon's gallery with 'other stately homes of the period decorated with *sententiae* as well as with emblems and *imprese* so that a visitor to such a room felt as if he had entered an emblem book', and we should wholly support his judgement that 'Such a design for the arrangement of *sententiae* (with or without accompanying emblems) is consonant with the decorum of artificial memory schemes of the period' (p.103).

What seems most suggestive about John Florio's prefatory commentary on the Frontispiece to his 1632 translation of Montaigne's *Essayes*, which Engel usefully reproduces at this point in his discussion, is how vividly it describes the way a contemporary visitor might have responded to the painting of such rooms.

> When first this portlike *Frontispiece* was wrought,
> To raise a *Pile* compleat, it was our thought,
> Whose *Roomes* and *Galleries* should have been trim'd
> With *Emblemes*, and with *Pictures* fairly lim'd,
> And drawn from those neat *Peeces*, which do lurke
> Within the *Closets* of this *Authors* worke:
> So placing them, and them contriving so,
> That ev'ry *Reader* (passing to and fro)
> By casting thereupon a glauncing eye,
> Might in that *Model* or *Epitome*,
> (E'en at the first Aspect) inform'd have beene,
> Of ev'ry *Raritie* contain'd within.
> But walking through that *Place* of *Invention*,
> (The better to accomplish our intention)
> We found unlookt for, scattered here and there,
> Such *Profits*, and such pleasures, ev'ry where,
> In such *Variety*, that, to but name
> Each one, would make a *Volume* of the same.
> ....
> Instead of *Emblemes* therefore, to explaine
> The Scope of this great *Volume*, we are faine
> To fixe the *Author's Title*, on the *Gate*,
> Annexed to his *Name*; presuming that
> Will give this following *Treatise* much more praise
> Then all the *Topiques* which our skill can raise.

What seems remarkable about this preface in the present context is not so much the way it confirms those familiar analogies between books and buildings, between frontispieces and title pages, which are commonplace in this period, as the support it offers for my assumption that buildings – particularly when they were decorated with emblems – were themselves regarded as 'places of invention', to borrow Florio's highly suggestive and not wholly figurative expression. A painted gallery or a decorated chamber, that is to say, was as much a rhetorical space as it was a living room. Hence it is only by reconstructing the way it functioned within the rhetorical systems of the day that we can account for some of its most distinctive characteristics, and we may not find it easy to separate its epistemological from its strictly architectural functions.

There can be no doubt that the collection of rhetorical commonplaces, and their organisation under topical headings in the manuscript and printed commonplace books which were such a feature of Renaissance rhetoric, had close connections both with emblematics and with the art of memory. Such connections were often spelled out in contemporary treatises and in the anthologies themselves. In his *Pandectae locorum communium* (1572), for instance, John Foxe stresses that the 'Index of Places' into which his book is organised is designed to function as 'a storeroom of memory' to which students 'may skillfully and diligently bring back what daily exercise furnishes to be noted down' (quoted in Rechtien 1978, p.85). Foxe acknowledges that educated men commonly use established topical schemes such as Virtues and Vices, Flattery, Adversity, or the Misery of Human Life as the headings under which particular quotations may be assembled and stored; and although this is not the system his own book proposes (he favours the use of *loci* drawn from logic), he makes it plain that it is the function of such places to serve as 'a storeroom of memory'. The connections between emblem books and commonplace books are suggested not only by the early grouping of Alciato's emblems under topical headings including: the Cardinal Virtues; the seven Deadly Sins; Love, Fortune, Honour and Friendship; but also by the fact that emblem books, including the work of Alciato, Whitney and Thomas Combe, were themselves plundered to provide material for some well-known printed collections of commonplaces (Bath 1994, pp.32-5). The habit of employing such established schemes as the Vices and Virtues, or the Heroes and the Prophets as suitable *loci* for remembering sententious commonplaces means that representations of such topics in the painted decoration that we are studying always had the potential to fulfil a function that was rhetorical as much as it was moral. Moreover it might fulfil such a function whether or not it was accompanied by the actual quotations – the proverbial inscriptions, apophthegms, adages – which it was designed to locate. Simply by being represented in graphic form, such images provided schemes that could readily supply the seats of arguments in the memory of the beholder. And, conversely, the apophthegms inscribed around one's chamber did not necessarily have to be located in their appropriate seats in the room itself, as long as one had internalised an appropriate scheme of *loci* which might, or might not, be derived from the same location. This may help us to recognise why the relation of text to image on these painted ceilings could be sometimes so exact, and yet sometimes so arbitrary.

One of the buildings containing an extended anthology of biblical quotations is Traquair, Peebleshire. This house is now best known for its history as a centre of Catholic recusancy and Jacobite loyalty, whose owners, from the fifteenth to the nineteenth century, have been noted for their continuing loyalty to the Stuart dynasty whose name they shared and to whom they were related. In the seventeenth century and later, the house accommodated its own Catholic priest who lived in isolation in a secret priest's room where mass was celebrated and the heirs of Traquair were educated in the religion of their forefathers. It is therefore somewhat surprising to discover that in both of the rooms where substantial painted decoration has been preserved the biblical texts which accompany the decorative painting are taken from the Geneva Bible, for that translation of holy scripture, first printed in 1557, had been prepared, as its name suggests, by English exiles from Marian persecution and its use at the date when these paintings were probably executed was likely to be signalling at least outward conformity with the reformed religion.

The first-floor ('Drawing Room') ceiling was exposed in 1954 to reveal painted beams and boards, with interlaced foliated grotesque and strapwork designs on the boards and six biblical quotations taken from the Geneva Bible on the sides of the beams. The texts are taken from Psalms, from the Epistle of Peter, and from the Epistle to the Romans. Their doctrinal characteristics are illustrated by the following example, which, in fact, conflates passages from three separate Psalms (119.1; 33.1; 25.4):

> BLESSED AR THOSE THAT AR UPRYCHRT IN THAIR WAY AND WALKE IN THE LAW OF YE LORD, REIOCE IN YE LORD O YE RICHTEOUS FOR IT BECOMETH UPRICHT MEN TO BE THANKFULL. SCH[E]W ME THE WAY O LORD & TEACHE ME THY PATHS. PLM CXIX

All but two of the inscriptions similarly conflate discrete passages from the chosen source, as with the following text from Romans 12. 4-5 and 12. 12:

> FOR AS VE HAVE MANY MEMBERS IN ONE BODIE, & ALL MEMBERS HAVE NOCHT ANE OFFICE, SO VE BEING MONY AR [O]NE BODIE IN CHRYST, AND EVERIE ONE, ONE [AN]OYERIS MEMBERS. REIOYCE IN HOPE, BE PATIENT IN TRIBU[L]ATIOUN, CONTINEW IN PRAYER. PAUL [TO] YE RO[MANS].

The painted decoration on the plaster of a room on the second storey (now the 'Museum Room') shows vine-scrolls with rich clusters of grapes, birds and animals – at least one of the animals is copied from the engravings illustrating Conrad Gesner's *Icones Animalium* (1560) reused in 1607 in Edward Topsell's *Historie of Foure-Footed Beastes* (which supplied many of the animals painted in 1620 on the long gallery ceiling at Earlshall). This decoration, which forms a frieze five feet wide and four feet from the floor, is bordered at top and bottom with a single line of black-letter text, in both cases using quotations from the Geneva Bible. These undated paintings were probably executed in the time of the fifth laird, Sir William Stuart, who inherited in 1591, was Gentleman of the King's Bedchamber and Privy Counsellor, and died in 1605. His brother and successor James died two years later, too soon to make many improvements to the house, and James's son John, who was to have a long career as Privy Counsellor, High Treasurer, Lord High Commissioner to the General Assembly of the Church of Scotland, and first Earl of Traquair, was only born

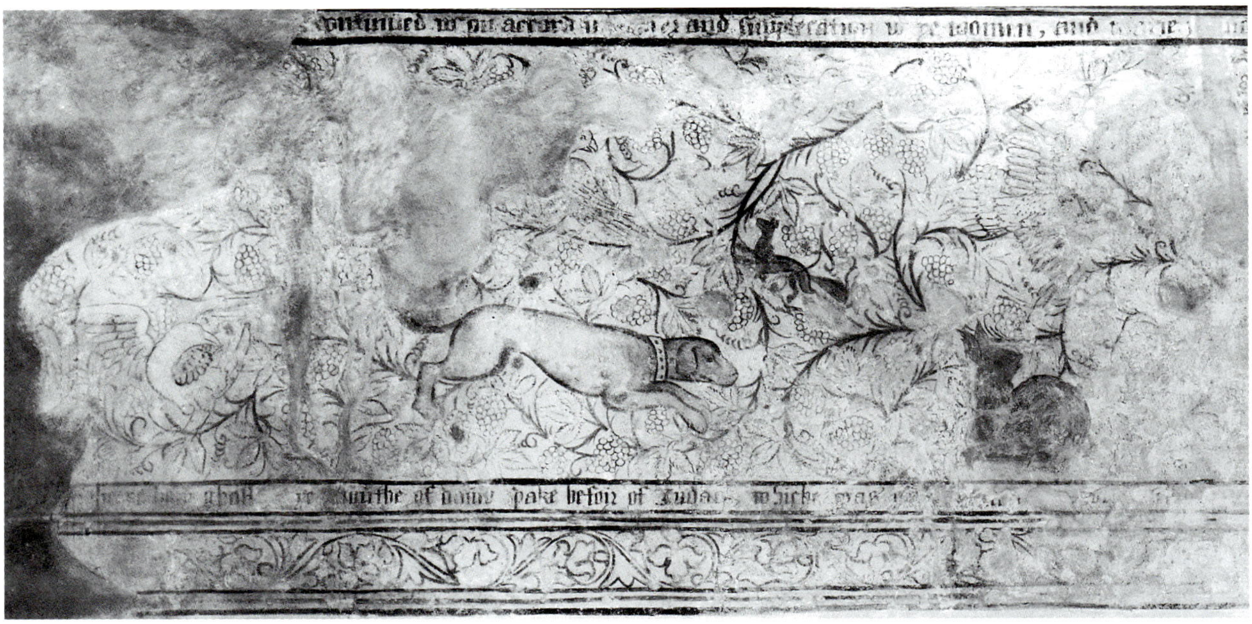

Traquair House, Peeblesshire, animals amidst vine scrolls, with biblical inscriptions extending right round the walls. RCAHMS

in 1600. A *terminus post quem* has to be 1557, the date of the first edition of the Geneva Bible, though the ceilings are probably later than this. Though the family had supported Mary, Queen of Scots earlier in the century, both Sir William Stuart and his nephew, the first Earl, occupied public offices which would have required their conformity with the reformed church in Scotland. The latter's attempts to steer a middle way between king and kirk in implementing King Charles's desire to impose the Laudian liturgy in Scotland got him into trouble with both sides. It was not the first earl, but his successors in the later seventeenth century, long after these paintings had been executed, who made the Traquair dynasty into one of the great bastions of Catholic faith in Scotland following the marriage of the second earl in 1654 to Lady Anne Seton, daughter of the Earl of Winton. The choice of the Geneva Bible at Traquair might be seen as conforming with the text-based Protestant aesthetic and several of the texts, such as the passage from Romans 12.4-5, are concerned with Pauline doctrines of righteousness and salvation which had the wholehearted approval of Scottish Presbyterianism.

The most extensive use of inscriptions in any house in Scotland is at Crathes Castle, Aberdeenshire, where four of the major rooms have beams painted on both sides with moralising texts. In two of these rooms most of the verse inscriptions relate to accompanying pictures of the nine Worthies, the nine Muses, or the Cardinal Virtues, and the way these appear to be functioning will be examined in our next chapter. However, several inscriptions even in these rooms appear to be freestanding and unillustrated, and in two further rooms – the stair chamber and the so-called 'Green Lady's Room' – the beams are covered in moralising texts with no evident connection with the surrounding images. The inscriptions throughout take two different forms, either biblical

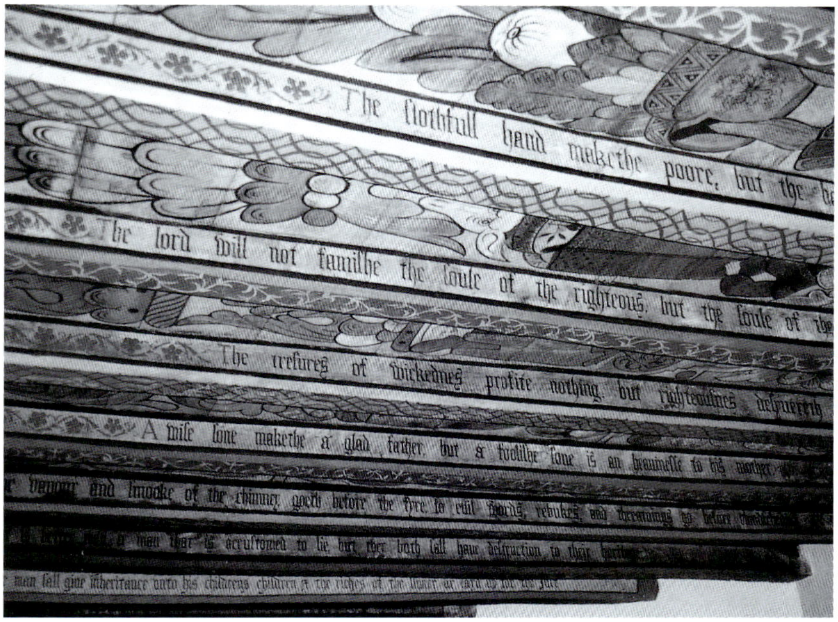

Crathes Castle, Aberdeenshire, inscribed beams from the 'Green Lady's Room'; verse proverbs and biblical texts having no apparent connection with the proximate images.

texts which quote exclusively from two Old Testament books, Proverbs and the apocryphal Ecclesiasticus, or versified proverbs for which no source has yet been identified. At least thirty biblical texts are still to be found among the beam inscriptions at Crathes, and more than a dozen versified proverbs, and it will be apparent that these two forms have much in common. The style of the verse-proverbs may be illustrated by such examples as the following from the 'Green Lady's Room':

> Flie sone all naughtie companie
> From fools no freindship crave
> Keep fellowschip with such as be
> Both wittie sage and grave.

More elegant and resonant is the following quatrain from the same room:

> A maidin but ['without'] modistie
> A clarke but courtesie
> A howsewyfe langinge fairleis ['wonders'] to see
> Wants all there seimliest propertie.

Clearly proverbs such as these ask to be read as family counselling, but their moral position is hardly distinguishable from the proverbial advice from biblical sources quoted on neighbouring beams: 'A wise sone makethe a glad father but a foolishe sone is an heavinesse to his mother' (Proverbs 10.1), or 'The curse of the Lord is in the house of the wicked but he blessed the habitatione of the righteus' (Proverbs 3.33).

Very similar inscriptions to these at Crathes are to be found some fifty miles away at Delgaty, near Turriff, where two rooms each contain fourteen or fifteen verse proverbs in rhymed quatrains painted on the sides of the beams. One of these rooms retains an interesting programme of heraldic and grotesque painting on the ceiling boards, but the other has lost any decorative painting it may once have had, and there is no sense that the images even in the 'Painted Chamber' have any connection with the accompanying inscriptions. Evidently painted (beams carry the dates 1592, 1593 and 1597) only a few years before Alexander Burnett had similar moralising inscriptions painted on his ceilings at Crathes (where the dates 1599 and 1602 are recorded), the Delgaty inscriptions are in exactly the same style.

The Scots verses have strong similarities with a rich tradition of native proverbial wisdom whose influence on Scottish literature of the early modern period has occasionally been recognised by students of Scottish literature (Whiting 1949, 1951). Printed and manuscript anthologies of such proverbial sayings were, in fact, produced in both England and Scotland at this period, anthologies which have many similarities with the rhetorical commonplace books and *florilegia* used from the later middle ages onwards by students of rhetoric (Moss 1996). One of the best known printed sources in Britain was Thomas Baldwin's *Moral Philosophy Containing the Sayings of the Wise* (1547). Part of Baldwin's anthology supplied a whole section of the Bannatyne manuscript, that great anthology of Scots Renaissance poetry compiled in 1568 when George Bannatyne retreated from Edinburgh, where the plague was raging, and passed his time in copying the Scottish makars, notably Dunbar, Henryson and Alexander Scott. The second of the five books into which Bannatyne divided his anthology is devoted to 'wisdome and moralitie' and this includes a section headed 'Certayne wyiss sentences draw furth the buik callit Morall philosophie' which is, in fact, copied directly from Baldwin (Bannatyne 1928, vol. ii, pp.218-20). Several of the proverbial formulae inscribed on the beams at Delgaty Castle are recorded in this part of the Bannatyne manuscript. It follows that these verse proverbs go back to a common (English) source. Both Baldwin and Bannatyne, moreover, ascribe these 'sayingis of wyiss philosapheris' to such eminent thinkers as Musonius, Plato, Socrates and Pythagoras. In this they are following a tradition which goes back to Caxton's *Dictes and Sayings of the Philosophers* – Anthony Woodville's translation of a French tradition that, in turn, refers to a thirteenth-century Spanish and Latin work known as the *Liber Philosophorum Moralium Antiquorum.* What we need to bear in mind, then, is that the proverbial sayings we find inscribed along the beams of these Scottish ceilings belong to a well-established European literary tradition which not only influenced major Scottish poets of this period but also ascribed at least some of these proverbs to the great philosophers of antiquity. For all their Scots spelling, the voices we are meant to hear enunciating this wisdom are those of the classical sages.

A good example might be the proverb we find on a beam at Delgaty: 'Be godlie & honest, both mirrie & vertous Gyf thou wald pleas god & angir ye enuous.' This is a version of the proverb which Bannatyne records as 'Be mirry and glaid honest and vertewous/ffor that sufissis to anger the Invyuous' (1928, vol. ii, p.259).

However, Bannatyne ascribes these verses, following Baldwin, to 'Hermes the philosopher' and he follows them by quoting the whole of a William Dunbar poem, 'Be miry man and tak not far in mind'. That several of these formulae can be identified in Scots poets such as Robert Henryson and Dunbar might lend weight to the claim that this storehouse of proverbial wisdom was an authentic, native Scots tradition; however, the fact that this whole section of the manuscript goes back to Baldwin suggests that the proverbial tradition on which such Scottish sources draw was by no means unique to Scotland and that such proverbial sayings easily crossed national and linguistic frontiers.

The following are among the verses at Delgaty that we find also recorded in Baldwin's *Moral Philosophy* (Arber edn 1907, p.171) and in the Bannatyne manuscript:

> The freindis whome posyt [Baldwin 'profit'] or lucre Increase,
> Quhen substance fayleth their withall will seas.
> Bot freindis that ar coupled with hart & with love,
> Nether feir nor force, nor fortune may remove.

Most of these verse quatrains cobble together proverbial formulae that are recorded elsewhere as proverbial phrases in their own right, thus the verses which end, 'Sen ['since'] word is thrall & thocht is fre Kepe well thy tongue I counsele thee' correspond to the proverb which Whiting records from other sources as 'Sen word is thrall, and thocht is only free' (1951, p.139), or which *The King's Quair* quotes as 'For word is thrall' (Whiting 1951, p.161). 'Ane Just man treu & Leill, His saw sud be his seill' is Whiting 1951, p.121, where it is cited from Henryson. 'He is wise that is war er he be wae' is the phrase Whiting quotes (1951, p.50) as 'be war, or ye be wa'. 'Abouf all thing, love God above, And as thy self, thy nybour love' is certainly biblical, as is 'Soft wordis slakes Ire' which quotes Proverbs 15.1, but such biblical quotations have been assimilated to proverbial sayings which are part of an undifferentiated corpus of 'grave sentences', as Ecclesiasticus itself defines them:

> He onely that applieth his minde to the Law of the most High, and is occupied with the meditations of the rest, seketh out the wisdom of all the ancients .... He kepeth the sayings of famous men, and entreth in also to the secrets of darke sentences. He seketh out the mysterie of grave sentences, and exerciseth him selfe in dark parables. (Ecclesiasticus 39.1-3, Geneva Bible).

That all these proverbial inscriptions were to be taken in such a spirit is perhaps indicated by the placement of the text 'Love God, and love thy neighbour as thyself' which stands at the head (or perhaps at the tail – it is certainly on an end-beam) of the series of non-biblical proverbs in the 'Painted Chamber' at Delgaty, for the quatrain which begins by citing this biblical text continues, 'So sall thou keip the teine commandis, Quilk god wryt with his awin handis'.

The question of how these anthologies are ordered, however, raises once again, the problem of how the whole decorative programme in particular rooms and buildings is articulated. As already noted, the relation of *scriptura* to *pictura* evidently varies from place to place and even, at Crathes, from room to room. Before we leave Delgaty, however, it is worth looking at the iconography of the 'Painted Chamber' even though, or perhaps precisely because, it appears to have no connection with the proverbial inscriptions on the supporting beams of the same room. At first sight, the ceiling looks to be quite a good example of grotesque painting, as we have seen, a style noted for its arbitrary and disordered composition. As Henry Peacham puts it,

> The forme of it is a generall, and (as I may say) an unnatural or unorderly composition for delight sake of men, beast, birds, fishes, flowers, etc. without (as wee say) Rime or reason, for the greater variety you show in your invention, the more you please, but remembering to observe a method of continuation of one and the same thing throughout your whole work without changing or altering.

Peacham's description is interesting, among other things, for the way it seems to be in two minds about the decorum of grotesque work, for this style is both 'most ancient and in greatest request', and yet not to be used too promiscuously ('you shall seldom have any great use of it'). The more varied and 'fantastical' the better, yet 'remembering to observe a method of continuation ... throughout'. It is not too difficult to apply Peacham's description to the ordering and detail of the Delgaty ceiling. This appears to be a collection of topics which is quite without 'Rime or reason', as Peacham puts it – certainly, its random assemblage of miscellaneous detail is what strikes the observer at first glance. And yet this ceiling may not be quite such an 'unorderly composition' of arbitrary icons as Peacham's definition of the 'Antique' style might lead us to expect, indeed it may have a more clearly focused political and historical message than appears at first sight.

We can begin to reconstruct that message if we start to look at some of the icons that are most obviously not 'Antique work' insofar as they are semantically loaded. The most obvious of these are the heraldic details that dominate the central (fifth) section of the nine into which the supporting beams divide the ceiling. Here we see the arms of Alexander Hay, Earl of Errol – argent a cinquefoil gules between three escutcheons gules, with the initials A H, surrounded by a laurel wreath, flanked by supporters, and the motto 'SVB IVGVM'. Balancing this, to its left in the same compartment, are the arms of Hay's wife, Barbara Forbes, similarly treated – the Hay arms of three escutcheons are impaled with the Forbes arms of three boar's heads, muzzled.

These heraldic arms might be seen as an isolated detail, functioning as an incidental signature of ownership, rather like the entwined Hay-Forbes monogram in the endmost section. They appear to commemorate a dynastic alliance at the date when the ceiling was commissioned – a date the ceiling itself confirms in the '1597' added to the inscription on one of its beams. Indeed, the naked, rustic figures who support the two coats of arms may seem stylistically indistinguishable from the other uncouth figures – the merman playing a viol,

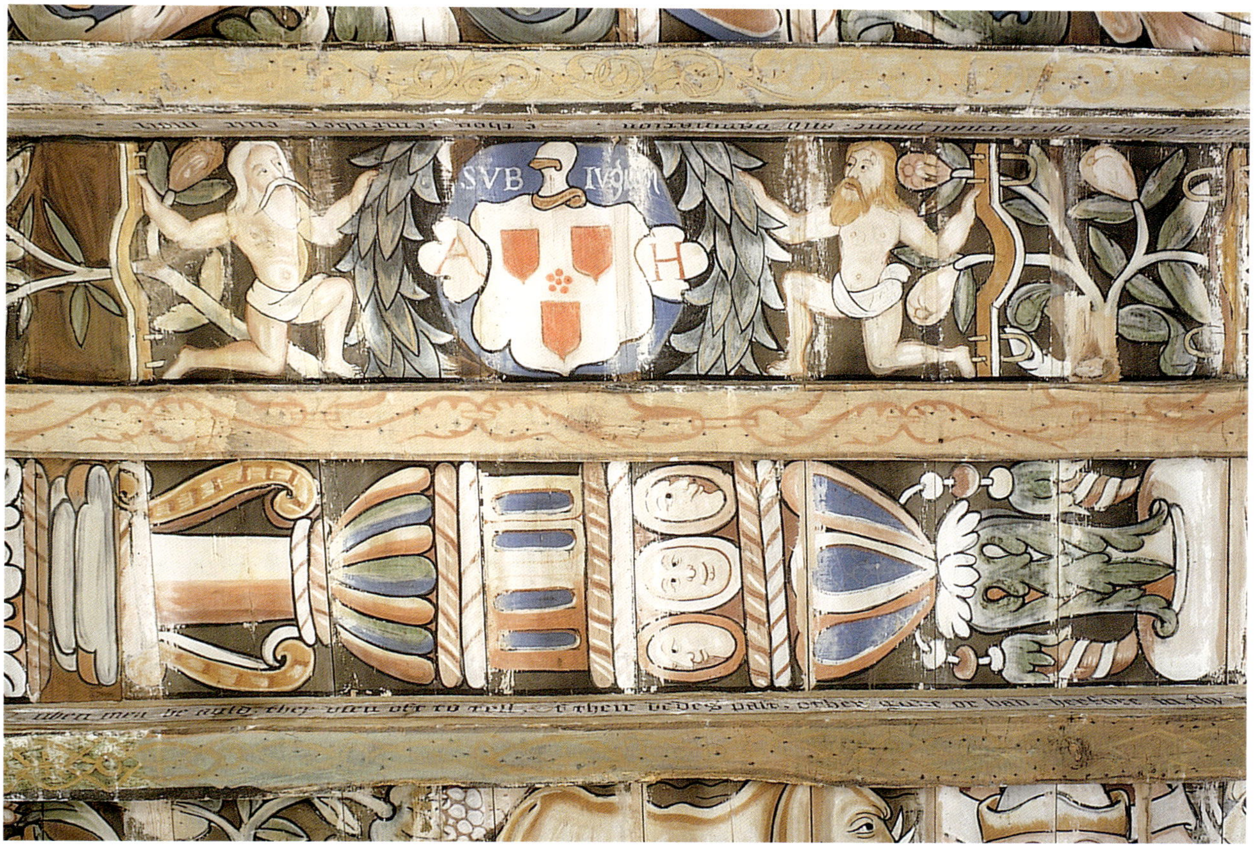

Delgaty Castle, 'Painted Chamber', the arms of Hay with 'candelabrum' and grotesque ornament.

the tricephalic heads, or the female sphinxes, which all help to define the grotesque vocabulary of the rest of the ceiling. In fact, however, these rustic Wodwos or wildmen, each holding an ox-yoke, are the most heraldically specific details on the whole ceiling and once their heraldic and dynastic significance is recognised they enable us to identify the unitary programme which controls the apparently arbitrary conjunction of imagery on the ceiling as a whole.

The arms of Hay were perhaps the most celebrated achievement in Scottish heraldry. Indeed when the chapter on 'The Practice of Blazonrie' was added to Henry Peacham's *Compleat Gentleman* in 1661 these were the only Scottish arms to be described in this English book (Peacham 1906, p.171). This is because they were associated with an anecdote from the legendary annals of Scotland according to which a ploughman and his two sons, named Hay, came to the rescue of the nation when its king, Kenneth III, and his army were put to ignominious flight at the hands of the invading Danes. On witnessing the Scots' retreat, Hay unyoked the oxen from his plough and with no other weapons confronted his fleeing countrymen in a narrow defile and turned them back to inflict a crushing defeat on the foreign invaders. The king offered to decorate Hay and his sons with gold and valuable ornaments but Hay 'na thing desyring thairof, come with his twa sonnes in thair old and rusty habitt, strynkillit with dust and swete of batall, in the samyn maner as thai faucht, reddy to do quhat chargis he mycht at the Kingis pleseir', or so Hector Boece tells us in his *Scoto chronicon.* Despite his modesty, Hay was granted all the lands between Tay and Errol and in order that none of his deeds should perish, 'bot ay remane as recent to his posterite', he was given three red shields in a field of silver, to signify that he was promoted from small and obscure lineage to great riches and lands, and the figure of the yoke with which he had helped the Scots in their hour of greatest need was added to his arms.

This legend is exceptional in the chronicles of Scotland in associating a heroic act of patriotism with the grant of arms. Not surprisingly it became extremely well known; George Buchanan repeats it, and it is in Holinshed, which may explain how it eventually found its way into Peacham's *Compleat Gentleman*, but the significance of this legend is not confined to the overtly heraldic details on the ceiling at Delgaty. The three shields were widely believed to refer to father Hay and his two sons and almost certainly account for a number of other tripartite motifs on the ceiling – details with no overtly dynastic or heraldic significance.

Perhaps the most interesting of these are the three linked faces which feature in two of the overtly 'grotesque' details of the painting. We can find such tricephalic figures in grotesque painting, but as A W Lyons noted, in a Scottish Antiquaries' article of 1910 that remains the only scholarly study of this ceiling, this detail bears a remarkable resemblance to a monumental carving on the gable wall of the Old Church at Turriff. Lyons was probably right to conclude that the three central, crowned figures in this piece of ecclesiastical sculpture represent the Magi, and thus have a primarily religious significance, but it is at least plausible that the six companions on the two trefoils to each side of them are a version of the three kinsfolk whose heroic deeds are commemorated in the three shields of the arms of the Earls of Errol. Other details on the ceiling which appear to be part of the arbitrary *bricolage* of the ornamental grotesque also turn out to have an unexpected dynastic symbolism, for the stag's head almost certainly alludes to the Forbes crest (a stag's head), while the two large elephants, 'with their fantastic trunks and floriated tails, seem to have some connecting link with the family of Oliphant' (Lyons 1910, p.252). As Lyons notes, 'Laurence, first Lord Oliphant, married Lady Isobel Hay, daughter of William, first Earl of Errol, so that there is every reason to believe that a family reference is meant to be conveyed' (p.151).

What we seem to have, then, is a species of decorative painting whose details move into significant heraldic and dynastic statements in unexpected ways. That is not to say that all the details on this ceiling have to be read as some kind of speaking picture – I am not suggesting that the confronting sphinxes, or the musical merman have any more significance than the floriated scroll-work, or the elaborate urns and acanthus leaves. We do seem, however, to have a decorative vocabulary which slips very easily into and out of signification, and a painted ceiling which, for all its arbitrary arabesque work, has for its unifying text or subtext some kind of central statement that extends through a number of its details. That is to say a design which for all its 'unnatural or unorderly composition' is not wholly without rhyme or reason, but rather 'remembering to observe (as Peacham puts it) a method of continuation of one and the same thing throughout [the] whole work without changing or altering'.

To bring that statement into historical focus one has only to note the date 1597 at the end of one of the inscribed beams. This was the date when the two

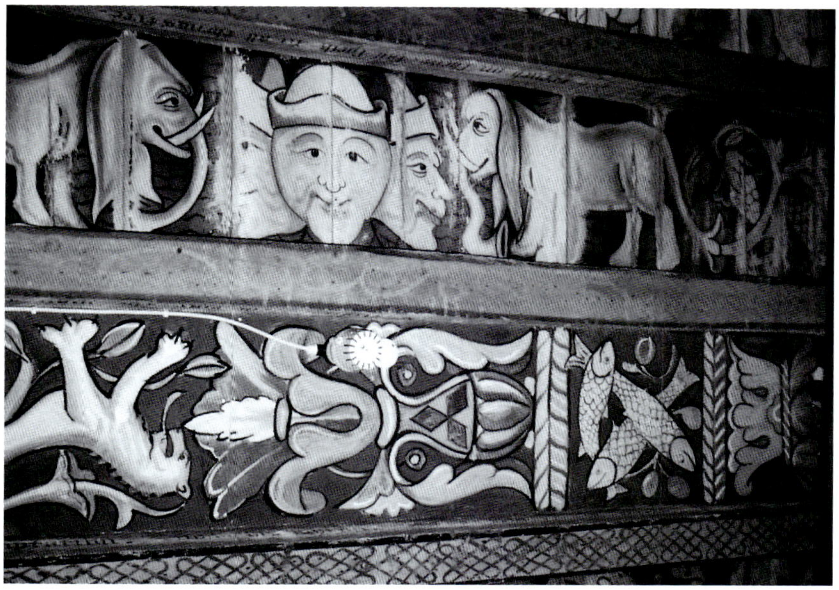

Delgaty Castle, 'Painted Chamber', tricephalic head; pure grotesque, or a reference to the three kinsfolk who helped defeat the Danes and were identified with the three shields on the arms of the earls of Errol?

most prominent of the northern Catholic earls, Huntly and Errol – who had led the last Popish rebellion in Scotland three years earlier – were pardoned and rehabilitated. Alexander Hay, Earl of Errol and Constable of Scotland, had been principal ally of the Catholic Earl of Huntly when, in 1592, Huntly had earned the hatred of the Protestants following his murder of the Earl of Murray and the discovery of the so-called 'Spanish blanks', letters which implied that the two earls had been conducting secret negotiations with Philip of Spain for the restoration of Catholicism in Scotland. In 1594 the Earl of Argyle raised troops to bring these 'Popish lords' to justice, only to be defeated at the Battle of Glenlivet, whereupon King James himself was obliged to march north and bring the earls to book.

So there were good reasons why Alexander Hay might have been disposed to include such reminders of the loyalty of his progenitors to the kings of Scotland in the iconography of a ceiling painted in his house in 1597, for although King James had been instrumental in his downfall three years earlier, the king's role and motivation in his dealings with the Popish lords was questioned both at the time and by later historians. James, it is generally thought, had been anxious to steer a *via media* between the opposed sectarian forces in his kingdom and although he was compelled by the growing power of the Protestant establishment to take strong action against the errant northern earls he was not intent on their annihilation. Though their defeat in 1594 resulted in the complete destruction of Errol's other castle – the Old Castle of Slains on the Buchan coast – and of a large part of Huntly's castle at Strathbogie, the leniency of the sentence passed on them and the speed with which they were pardoned and allowed to return from exile was a sign of James's moderating clemency.

In June 1597, immediately before the Delgaty ceiling was painted, the two earls were received in the church of St Nicholas, Aberdeen, before a packed

Kitchen wisdom? Proverbial sayings in the gallery at Earlshall use Roman capitals, signalling their continuity with classical epigraphy, and verse distichs which are conventional for classical epigrams and aphorisms.

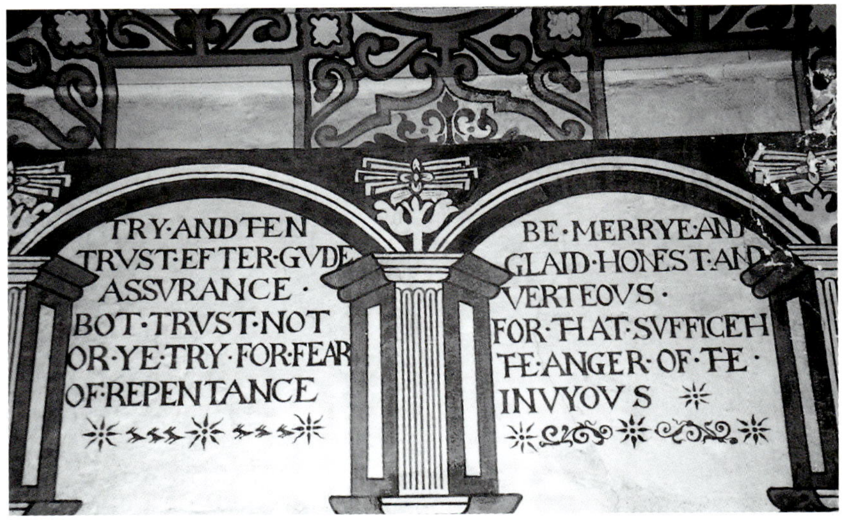

congregation, to hear a sermon preached by the bishop and to make a public confession of their defection and apostacy, before renouncing all Papistry and affirming Protestantism as the only true faith. To quote a contemporary account: 'The Earl of Huntly confessed his offence first to God, next to his majesty, to the Kirk and country.' The service was followed by public celebrations on the streets of Aberdeen at which wine was 'drunken in abundance'. Alexander Hay's foregrounding of the legendary loyalty of his family, and of its willingness to bear the yoke of adversity in Scotland's defence, would then make good sense in the painted decoration of his ceiling. One way of reading this ceiling, then, would be as a tacit acknowledgement of the terms on which the Earl of Errol's reinstatement within the kingdom of Scotland had been proposed and received in Aberdeen in the year of its painting. Thus although there may be no very clear overlap between the heraldic symbolism and the proverbial texts on this ceiling, the claims which the latter are making for moral probity and biblical righteousness would surely not be out of place, though their style and content are of a piece with the verses which Errol had inscribed in a neighbouring room five years earlier in 1592.

Such moralising verses as we have been examining in this chapter also circulated in other media – in trencher designs, in broadsheets, and on painted cloths, where they were often associated (or at least conjoined) with imagery of various kinds. Much of this proverbial philosophy seems to us like kitchen wisdom, part of a popular, oral or vernacular tradition. However it is important to recognise how extensively it also circulated in written or printed sources, and especially in the genre of commonplace book, or anthologised *loci communes*, which represent a vernacular equivalent to the *Adagia* of Erasmus. That connection might suggest a classical *gravitas* and elegance wholly inappropriate to the homespun wisdom and cracker-barrel philosophy of these vernacular verses. Erasmus, however, had no hesitation in identifying the homely, proverbial basis of his adages and apophthegms, and I want to suggest that many of our elitist assumptions about a radical break between educated and popular culture at this period are misleading and likely to prevent us from getting adequate theoretical or historical purchase on how these ceilings work. In Baldwin's book these verses are not presented as bits of homespun wisdom, which is how they read on the Delgaty ceiling. On the contrary, his *Treatise* is presented as an introduction to ancient philosophy and the bulk of it is taken up with accounts of the major propositions of classical philosophers from Pythagoras through Socrates and Aristotle to Epictetus, Diogenes, Seneca, and Marcus Aurelius. It follows that we should, perhaps, beware of imposing even the most elementary opposition of 'vernacular' versus 'classical' onto the type of inscriptions we find on these Scottish ceilings. What we are looking at are inscriptions of a type that a highly popular English book at this period circulated as though they were authentic gobbets of ancient wisdom.

As Tessa Watt stresses, 'it would be misleading to describe this as "popular" printed culture, if "popular" is taken to imply something exclusive to a specific social group' since, as she says, 'Pictorial themes which appeared in the crudest woodcuts were also painted on the walls of manor houses'. As she says, 'The model of a binary opposition of "popular" and "elite" has already been criticized, modified and sometimes disowned by recent social historians' (1991 p.2). Although Watt is preoccupied with English examples, her caveats are equally relevant to the Scottish context. The proverbial inscriptions owe at least something to the commonplace books in which Renaissance students were taught to store what Florio calls 'the place[s] of invention' – seats of arguments upon which rhetorical composition could be based. Similarly, the popular iconographic topics and schemes such as the Vices and Virtues, Sibyls, Prophets, Seasons, and Muses were precisely the kind of thing long recommended for use in what Aubrey calls 'topics for local memory'. If the 'grave sentences' examined in this chapter are fundamentally a written, textual medium, the iconographic schemes to be examined in our final chapter are primarily a visual medium. But though each can function without the other, it is important to recognise that both sententious sayings and visual icons belong to a system in which, through the arts of rhetoric and particularly of memory, image could always be used to locate text, and text was committed to memory through its association with significant images. The way this decorative painting handles some of those significant images is the subject of our concluding chapter.

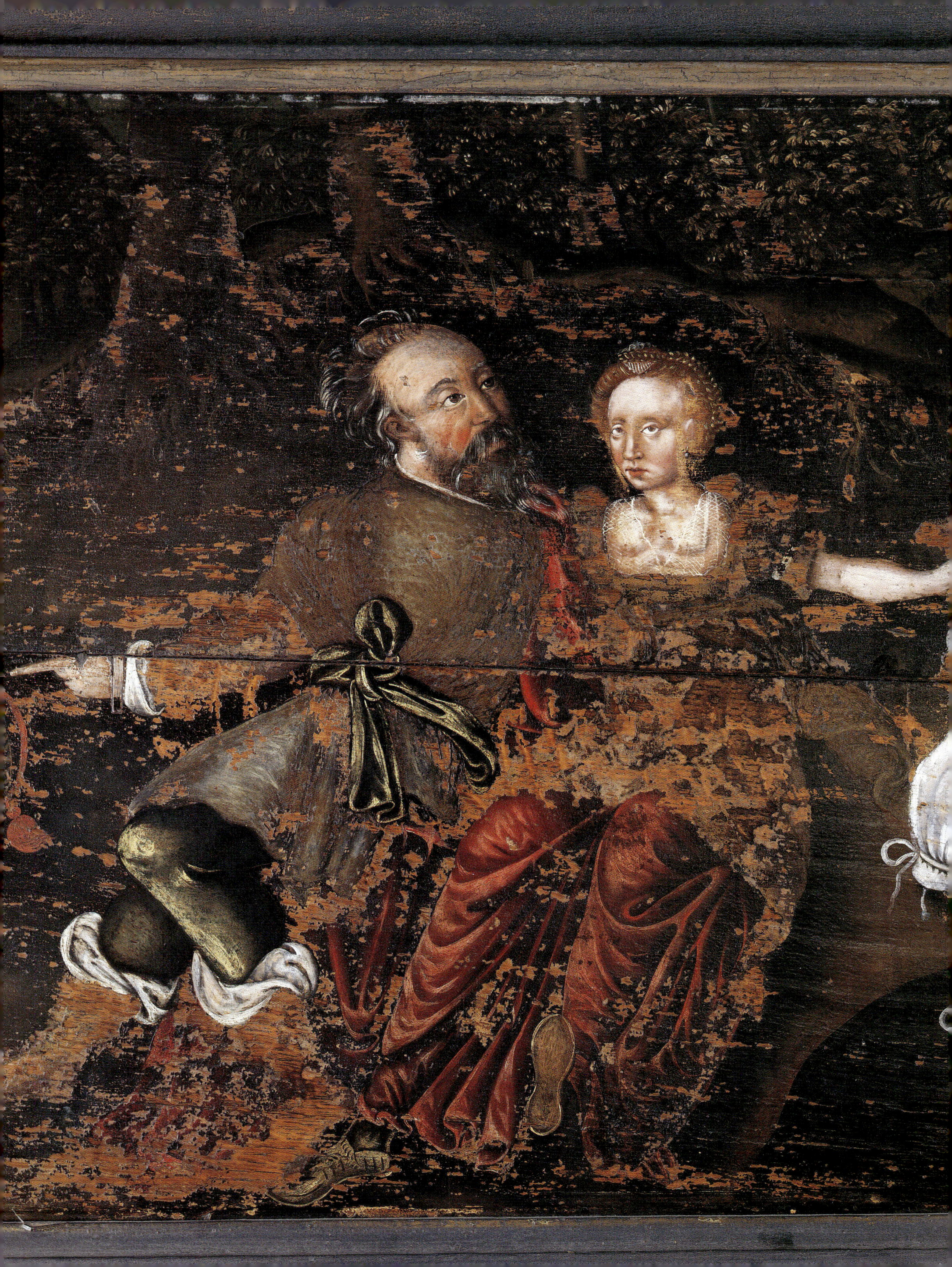

9

TOPICS AND SCHEMES

It should by now be apparent that much of this Renaissance decoration treats buildings as texts – not only when it covers them in inscriptions but also when it embellishes them with forms such as emblems and *imprese* which the Renaissance regarded as 'speaking pictures'. This is a style of decorative painting that refuses to be purely decorative, even when – as at Prestongrange – it uses a vocabulary that contemporaries claimed to be entirely without sense or meaning. Such a tendency to treat architecture as a kind of speech act accounts for the constant resort this painting makes to received topics and schemes. The schemes we shall be identifying in this final chapter may appear to be an odd assortment – the four seasons, the four evangelists, the five senses, the Cardinal Virtues, the planetary deities, the nine Muses, the nine Worthies, twelve signs of the zodiac, twelve Sibyls, and the labours of the months. Most of these are, however, such standard topics in the visual arts that it is easy to regard them as routine, but to dismiss them as 'merely' conventional is to miss the chance of interrogating one of the crucial differences between the decorative arts of this period and most of its successors. Such subjects require a modern viewer to research topics that would, presumably, have been immediately recognisable to earlier spectators. In rhetoric a topic is the seat or resting place of an argument, and a scheme is an order of words. The figures that make up such schemes in the visual arts are themselves figurative, and the primary task of their modern viewer has to be to reconstitute the aura of meaning and association that traditionally informed them. Hence our task in the concluding chapter of this book will largely be to re-establish some of the conventions and traditions surrounding some of the topics and schemes used – often more than once – in the decorative painting of this period in Scotland.

The Nine Worthies

Entirely characteristic of such schemes are the nine Worthies. In Chapter 7 we looked at the way their assigned coats of arms are incorporated into the heraldic painting at Earlshall, and their association with moralising inscriptions was mentioned in the previous chapter. At both Crathes and Earlshall they are disposed in their traditional sequence of three pagans

'Lot and his Daughters', detail of panel from Dean House, Edinburgh, now at John Knox's House. NMS

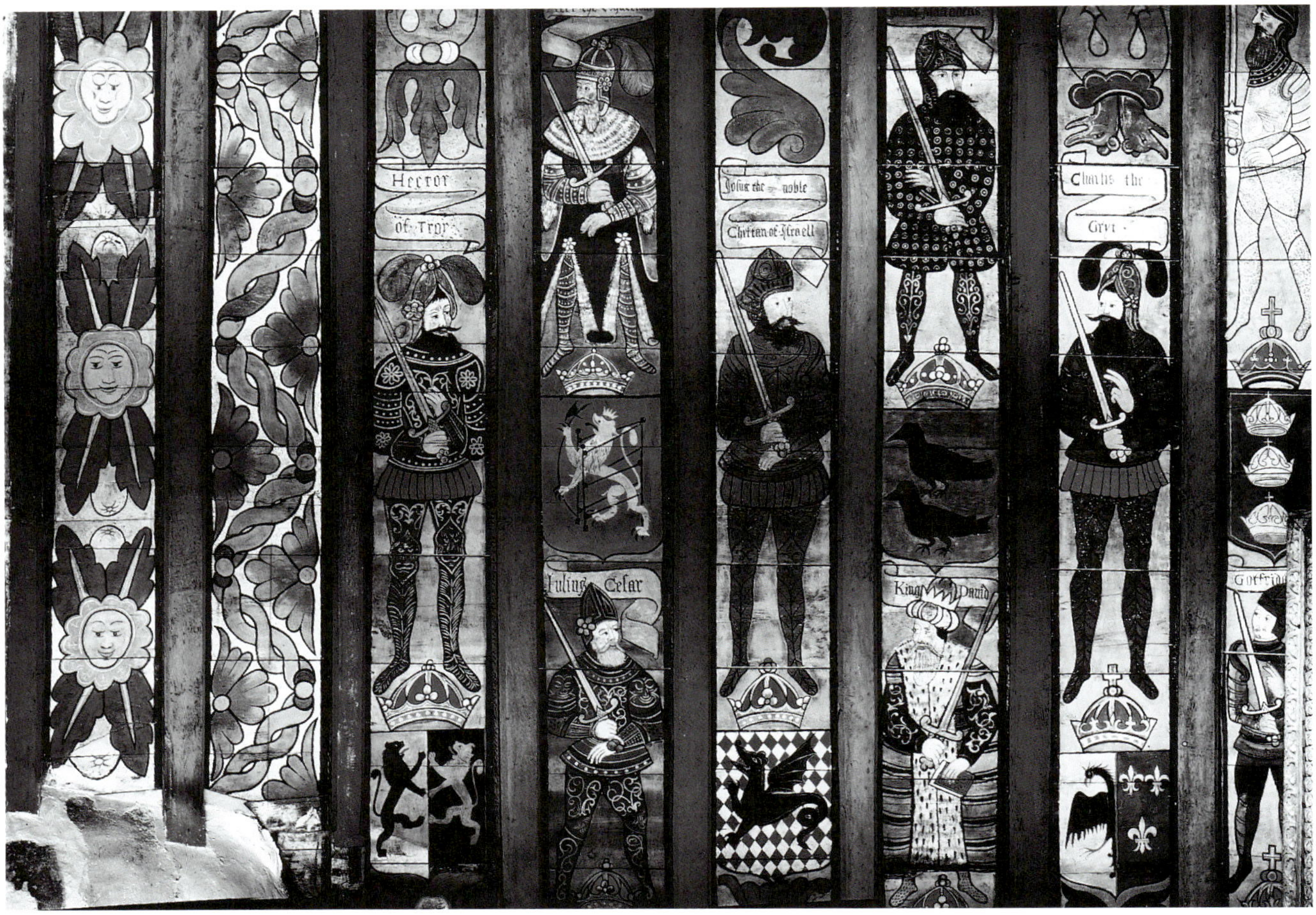

Crathes Castle, nine Worthies.
Alasdair Smith, NTS

(Hector, Alexander, Julius Caesar), three biblical heroes (Joshua, Judas Maccabeus, King David), and three moderns (Charlemagne, King Arthur, Godfrey of Bouillon). Each of the standing figures is shown with his fictive coat of arms, confirming the traditional function of these figures as archetypes of nobility. The nine Worthies topos goes back to the early thirteenth century *Les voeux de Paon* of Jacques de Longuyon, who divides them into the three groups of three that remained conventional thereafter. De Longuyon's influence had certainly reached Scotland by the mid-fifteenth century, when *The Buik of Alexander* uses a translation of it. This earliest treatment established details in the legends of each Worthy that were to become definitive and which the Crathes verses preserve. For instance, Hector is claimed to have killed 'nyntein kings' and his own death at the hands of Achilles is described as a work of treachery. The speed of Alexander's conquest of the world 'in short space' is emphasised in this tradition, and Caesar's conquest names the particular countries over which he ruled – 'Africk, egipt, france & Spain' are those that Crathes singles out. Joshua overcomes precisely thirty-one kings in both *The Buik of Alexander* and at Crathes, and he parts the waters of the river Jordan in two, alluding to the scriptural book of Joshua, 3.14-17. Judas Maccabeus's defeat of Antiochus, David's killing of Goliath, Charlemagne's defence of Christianity, Arthur's conquest of France and Spain, and Godfrey's slaying of Solyman are among the specific details which have been claimed to characterise this 'Scottish tradition as it existed a century before the [Crathes] inscriptions were written' (Hargreaves 1989, p.378).

However, long before Alexander Burnett had this ceiling painted in his castle at Crathes, the nine Worthies had spread beyond such chronicles, ballads and romances into a variety of other media, including theatrical performances, the heraldic armoury and, most notably, the decorative arts. The Crathes paintings are heir to all these traditions. By 1602 they had also found their way into a number of prints and engravings, and for this reason the likelihood that the Crathes paintings might copy a set of commercial prints needs to be carefully investigated. The Worthies appear in the theatre as early as 1455, when they delivered a speech of welcome on the entry of Queen Margaret into Coventry. Their most notorious theatrical appearance is, however, in Shakespeare's *Love's Labours Lost* when Holofernes responds to the request that he should devise 'some delightful ostentation, or show, or pageant, or antic' for the courtiers by resolving that there is 'none so fit to present as the Nine Worthies'. The way Shakespeare sends up the absurd pretensions of this amateur performance has commonly been taken as a sign of how far such traditional topics had sunk in esteem by the closing years of the sixteenth century; as William C Carroll puts it, 'For a sophisticated audience in the 1590s, such a pageant, however it was performed, would have been something of a joke' (1976, p.83). The way the actors identify themselves ('Judas am I, yclipped Maccabeus' as Holofernes declares, V.ii.594) doubtless helped to confirm this contempt of a popular form, though the use of the first person pronoun probably signals the debts which inscriptions such as those at Crathes owe to the conventions and discourse of dramatic performance. The first three Worthies at Crathes do indeed speak in their own voices: 'I Alexander conquest in short space\The world.' Their six successors' descriptions, however, revert to the third person: 'Joshuee of Jewes first wass frie\ Ane & threttie kingis conquerit he.'

Shakespeare's send-up identifies some of the other extra-literary contexts in which the nine nobles traditionally featured. The heraldic register is identified when Sir Nathaniel declares, 'My scutcheon plain declares that I am Alisander' (V.ii.562), to which Costard dismissively responds, 'your lion that holds his pole-axe sitting on a close stool, will be given to Ajax: he will be the ninth Worthy'. The joke depends on its audience's familiarity with the fictive arms of Alexander – gules a lion or, sejant in a chair, holding a battle-axe argent; and the pun on 'Ajax' and 'a jakes' recognises the way this wooden chair was conventionally represented in illustrated armorials – at Crathes it looks like a clothes-horse, at Earlshall it is raised with arm-rests, and in the Workman manuscript it looks very much like Costard's toilet-seat. We noted in Chapter 7 how the arms of the nine Worthies found their way into such Scottish armorials as the Seton Armorial, Sir David Lindsay of the Mount's famous armorial, and its successor, the Scottish armorial attributed to Sir David Lindsay II, Lyon King 1568-91 (Lyon Court, MS 20). The late fifteenth-century heraldic manual translated into Scots by Kintyre Puisuivant Adam Loutfut under the title *Deidis of Armourie* already argues that 'the eldast knawledge that men findis of armes that is the armes of Iosue, quilk wes the first Worthy that tuk armes, quhar-by may be knawyn and expoundyt the stait of him and of his dedis to

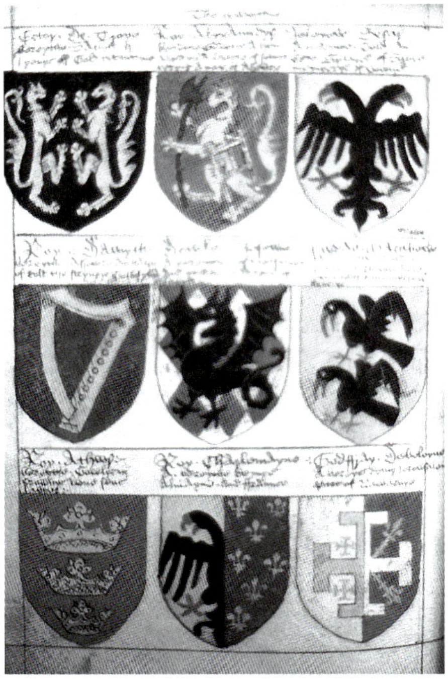

Arms of the nine Worthies from armorial attributed to Lyon King of Arms, Sir David Lindsay II of Rathillet, Lyon Court MS *20.*

memoir perpetuall' (Loutfut 1994, p.19). Costard's taunt that Ajax might become the ninth Worthy recognises the ease with which honorific pageantry and rhetoric tended to substitute or supplement the nine by including local or non-canonical figures in the list – the *Ballet of the Nine Nobles* which appears in manuscripts of Fordoun's *Chronicle*, for instance, adds Robert the Bruce to the list.

Costard's reference to the heraldic close-stool is the same speech – indeed the same sentence – in which he refers to the most notable medium in which the nine Worthies traditionally featured, as he argues that the penalty for having 'overthrown' Alexander is that 'You will be scraped out of the painted cloth'. The decorative arts were undoubtedly the place where most sixteenth or seventeenth-century people would have gained their familiarity with the nine Worthies. Painted cloths were wall hangings serving much the same function as more costly tapestries. Very few have survived, but it has recently been shown that one of John Balechouse's remarkably accomplished series at Hardwick Hall copies two of the biblical Worthies – Joshua and Judas Maccabeus – from the nine Worthies prints by Philips Galle; in the Hardwick painted cloth they are adapted to serve as guardsmen in the scene depicting St Paul's appearance before Agrippa (Wells-Cole 1997, figs 483-4, 487). In view of the close association which Shakespeare (and he is not alone) signals between the nine Worthies and painted cloths, we might see it as fitting that one of the rare survivals of this decorative medium should feature, however indirectly, two such figures. The nine Worthies had, of course, been appropriated for decorative uses long before this period – they feature in mural paintings-plus-inscriptions at the Castello della Manta in Piedmont in the early fifteenth century, and hangings of the nine Worthies are listed in Henry VII's extensive collection of tapestries; moreover 'the 9 worthies in roundels enealed' are listed among the works of art at Lumley Castle in the 1590 Lumley Inventory (Hearn 1995, p.158). There is plenty of further evidence that by the seventeenth century domestic decoration of this kind was the medium in which the Worthies were most commonly represented. A character called Martia, for instance, dismisses her unworthy champion in Beaumont and Fletcher's *The Double Marriage* (1620) with the reproof, 'Thou woven Worthy in a piece of arras,/ Fit only to enjoy a wall!' (cited in Carroll 1976, p.234).

The nine Worthies are, indeed, not uncommon as a subject for wall paintings in England. Examples survive, or are recorded, at Harvington Hall (Worcs), at Nether Hall, Roydon (Essex), and at North Mymms Park (Herts) where they copy engravings by Maerten Van Heemskerk. The example which has received most attention is at Amersham (Bucks) which Horst Schroeder (1981) showed used the same patterns as Thomas Trevilian's commonplace book of 1608; Wells-Cole has now identified the pattern book, namely the series of prints executed by Philips Galle which show the Worthies as single figures standing in pseudo-antique military costume and holding banners. The classical dress distinguishes these standing figures from those we see at Crathes, while the fact that they are not mounted distinguishes both these sets from the

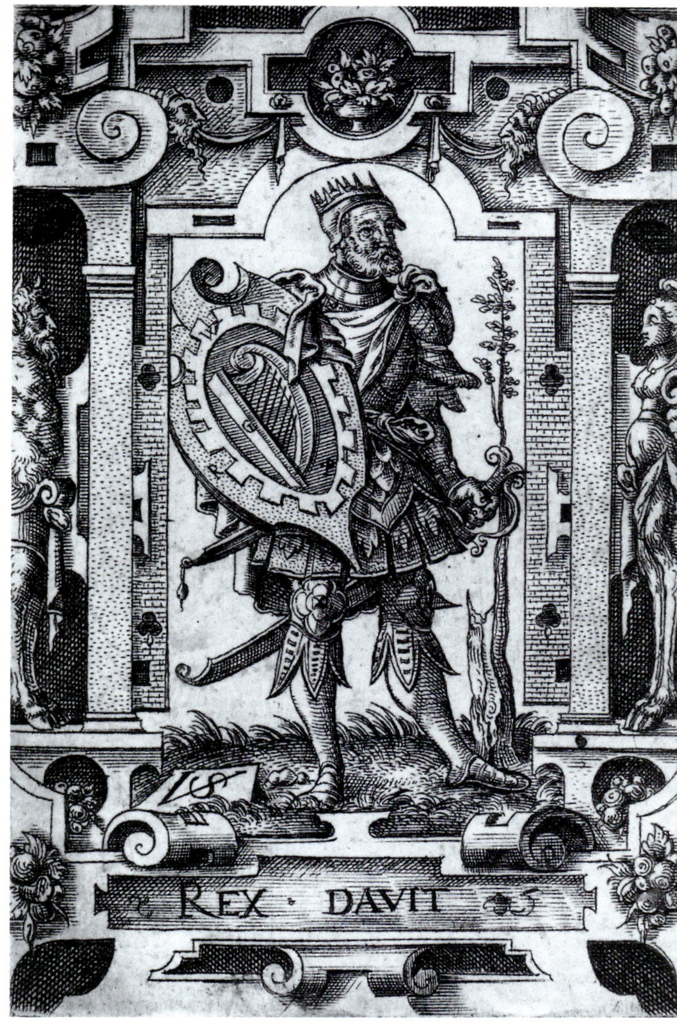

Virgil Solis, engraving, King David from his Nine Worthies *series.* V&A

Heemskerk figures copied at North Mymms. It was probably Heemskerk's series of mounted figures that provoked Sir Thomas Browne in that section of his *Pseudodoxia Epidemica* dealing with 'Many Things Questionable as they are Described in Pictures' to specify the major error 'Of the Pictures of the Nine Worthies' as their inappropriate use of mounted figures, for, as he says, Hector fought in a chariot, Caesar did not use a saddle and stirrups, and 'Some will enquire why Alexander the Great is described upon an elephant: for, we do not find he used that animal in his armies, much less in his own person' (Browne 1927, vol. ii, p.237). Heemskerk's print, indeed, shows Hector on a horse, Caesar with stirrups, and Alexander on an elephant. The Worthies also found their way into early seventeenth-century decorative plasterwork in the form of medallion-like roundels most of which go back, directly or indirectly, to a set of engravings by de Bruyn. Best known are those from the palace of Bromley-by-Bow in London whose matrices were reused in Scotland at Balcarres, Fife, and at Merchiston Tower, Edinburgh, with further examples in at least nine other houses in Scotland well researched by amateur historian John Touche in a file of unpublished notes and photographs now preserved in RCAHMS.

At Crathes the Worthies are shown in more or less modern dress or elaborately engraved plate-armour, each standing above his crowned heraldic shield. The print source that seems to come closest to the Crathes figures is the series by Virgil Solis, which also shows the Worthies as single figures standing full-length and wearing elaborate armour. Each is accompanied by his shield of arms, but neither the details of the armour nor, in some cases, the heraldry, correspond precisely to those of the Crathes figures. There is, indeed, reason to believe that the Crathes paintings, or at least the inscriptions, are not copied from any such print source. The reason has to do with Crathes' description of Charlemagne. Charlemagne is one of only two Worthies who are allowed a whole compartment to themselves at Crathes, the other being Hector of Troy. This pre-eminence is further accentuated by the fact that Charlemagne is the only one of the nine to whom two four-line stanzas are devoted on successive beams; all the others have a single stanza of verses. The first of these stanzas celebrates not so much Charlemagne's legendary achievements as his Scottish connections:

> A league wit Scottis of mutual amitie
> This Charlis maid to last eternalie
> Whais successors observis the same alway
> Inviolat unto this present day.

This 'league' is what is still known as the 'auld alliance' between Scotland and France, and mention of it here makes it hardly plausible that these verses can go back to anything other than a Scottish source.

Moreover, the prominence accorded to Charlemagne almost certainly offers a key, as Henry Hargreaves has argued, to the overall purpose (Hargreaves 1989, pp.380-1). Before we meet Hector, the first of the nine, some prefatory verses offer us the following invitation: 'Lerne gallant youthes to aeternise your name,/ As did thir nyn with deids of endless fame.' This imitation of virtue was the prime purpose which images of the Worthies traditionally served; as Franciscus Junius, seventeenth-century librarian to the Earl of Arundel, puts it in his *Painting of the Ancients*, 'So was it then a praise-worthy custome observed among the ancients ... because they could not endure that vehement longing they had after the virtues of the deceased Worthies, they did at once seeke to ... stirre up other noble spirits to the love of virtue' (cited by Margaret Aston in Gent 1995, p.201). However, in the concluding verses this parade of the Nobles is proposed to the reader as some kind of quiz game – as we leave the room we are asked: 'Gude reder tell me or thou pas/ Whilk of thir nyn maist Valiant was.' The pre-eminence accorded to Charlemagne in the verse inscriptions by reason of his Scottish alliance is almost certainly enough to supply the answer to this quiz; the scheme offers us the traditional nine Worthies with a precise application to the affairs of Scotland and its European connections, and the 'maist Valiant' of the nine Worthies at Crathes is surely Charlemagne.

The Sibyls

At two locations in Scotland the painted decoration includes figures of the pagan Sibyls, classical prophetesses who were thought to have foretold the birth of Christ and were consequently, in the later Middle Ages, drawn into the iconography of Christian Art (Mâle 1908, pp.267-96). Sibyl paintings, together with pertinent inscriptions, have been found at a house known as Mary Somerville's at Burntisland, and at Wester Livilands in Stirling.

The paintings at Mary Somerville's House were discovered in 1957 beneath plaster during renovation work, when they were removed for conservation and storage. The house is named after one of its later inhabitants, the nineteenth-century scientific writer whose name is also perpetuated in Somerville College, Oxford. In the seventeenth century, however, the house belonged to a family of Burntisland merchant shipowners called Watson. Traces of painted decoration

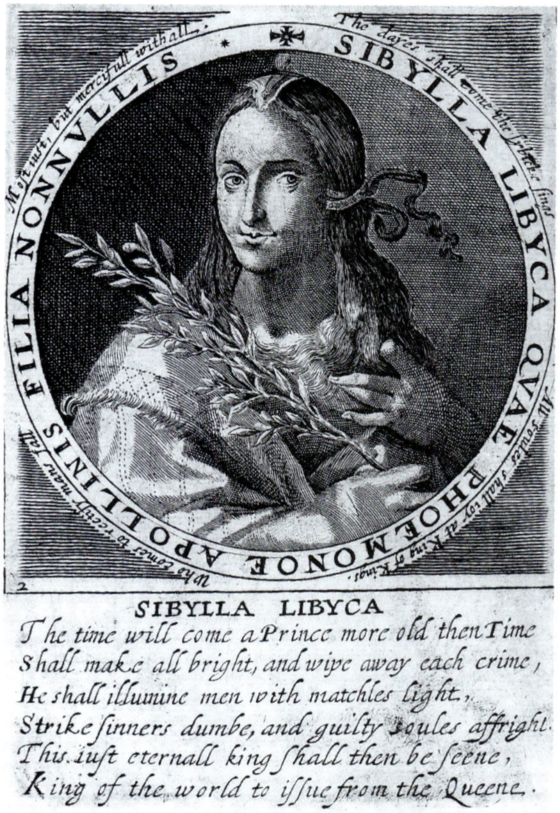

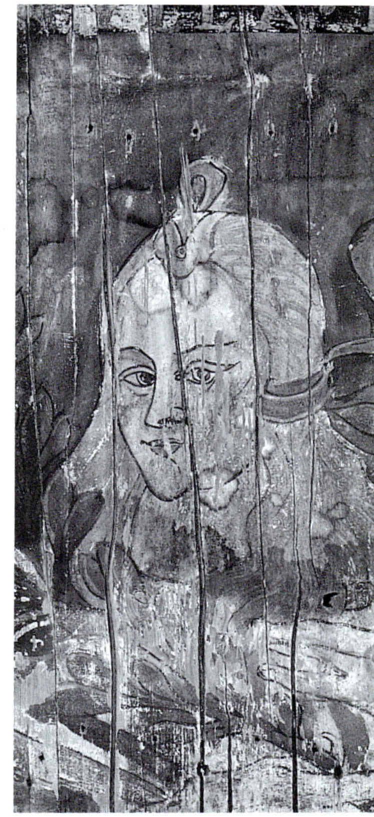

Left: *Martin Droeshout, 'Sibylla Libyca' from* XII Sibyllarum Icones *series, London: Thomas Johnson, before 1616, copied from the set by Crispijn de Passe the elder. This set was also copied into the manuscript of embroidery patterns compiled in 1616 by Thomas Trevilian, see page 191.* BM

Right: *Sibylla Libyca from painted ceiling, Mary Somerville's House; the painted boards were split for use as lathing for later lath-and-plasterwork and had to be patiently reassembled.*

were found in several rooms, including an astral ceiling with signs of the zodiac, and a coffered ceiling divided by means of *trompe l'oeil* mouldings into octagonal and cross-shaped compartments. The octagonal compartments contained not only religious images already discussed in Chapter 6 – Agnus Dei, Salvator Mundi, St Matthew, Mary – but also half-length portraits of ten Sibyls. The Sibylla Europaea, Sibylla Phrygia and Sibylla Libyca are the only ones whose images have survived (more or less), but the inclusion of the remainder can be inferred from the fact that fragments of decayed Latin text were preserved which M R Apted was able to show correspond to the Latin labels inscribed around the portraits of the Sibyls on a set of wooden trenchers, belonging to C F Cooksey, exhibited and described in an article in the *Proceedings of the Society of Antiquaries* (London) in 1888. Thus the letters 'SIBYLLA ... LLINIS FILIA ... NNULLIS' on the ceiling were shown to correspond to the label 'SIBYLLA LIBICA QUAE PHOEMONOE APOLLINIS FILIA NONNULLIS' on one of the trenchers, and other text fragments showed a similar correspondence, as a result of which most of the missing inscriptions could be reconstructed with some confidence.

The set of trenchers – circular wooden platters on which cheese or fruit was served, and which were regularly decorated with emblematic or decorative designs and sententious inscriptions in the sixteenth and seventeenth centuries – also included verse quatrains describing the spiritual prophecy of each of the Sibyls. That for the Sibylla Libyca reads:

> The dayes shall come the lybicke sings:
> All soules shall ioy at King of Kings.
> Who comes to rectify mans fall.
> Most iust, but mercifull with all.

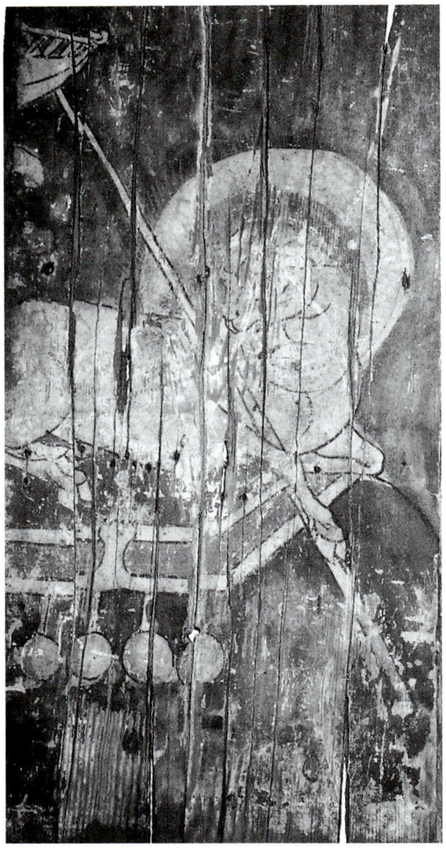

Agnus Dei resting on the book with seven seals of Revelation 5.6, from Mary Somerville's House.

These trencher verses, and the Latin labels which the ceiling decoration borrowed, can be shown to copy the verse quatrains and the Latin labels which encircle each of the portraits on a set of engravings executed by M Droeshout, entitled *XII Sibyllarum Icones.* In addition to the inscriptions framing the circular medallion portrait, Droeshout's engravings also supplied a verse *subscriptio*, of which that for the Sibylla Libyca offers a representative example:

> The time will come a Prince more old than Time
> Shall make all bright, and wipe away all crime,
> He shall illumine men with matchles light,
> Strike sinners dumbe, and guilty soules affright:
> This iust eternall king shall then be seene,
> King of the world to issue from the Queene.

These verses, which do not appear on either the trenchers or the ceiling, give voice to the particular prophecy of the Sibyl, shown as a young woman with flowing hair held in place by a snood and a ribbon, holding a branch of laurel or olive in her right hand. The surviving paintwork of this detail is sufficiently well preserved to leave no doubt that it too was copied from a version of this engrav-

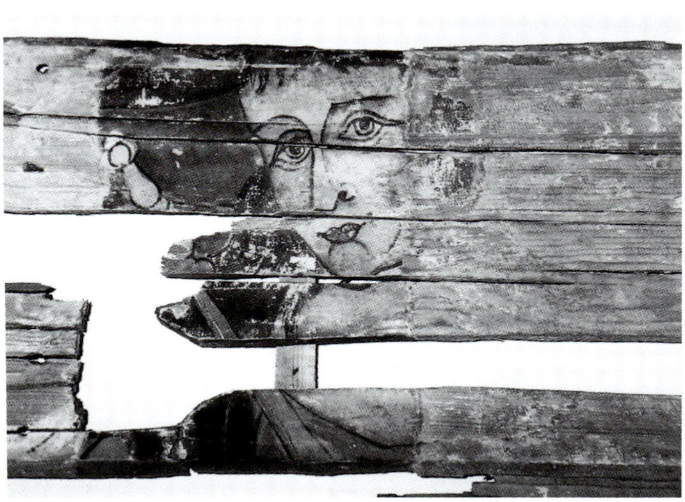

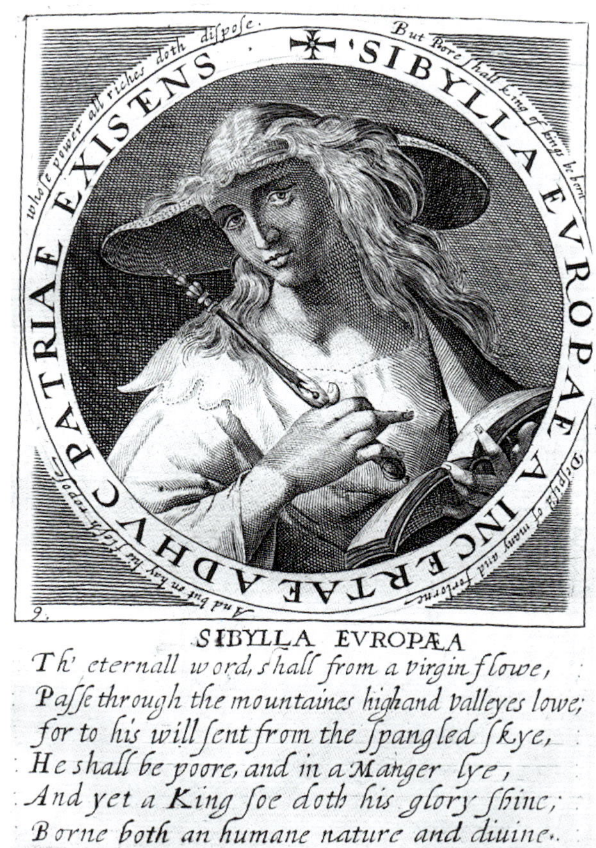

Left: *Sibylla Europaea from painted ceiling, Mary Somerville's House.*

Right: *Martin Droushout, 'Sibylla Europaea' from* XII Sibyllarum Icones *series.* BM

ing, as were the surviving fragments of the two other portraits of Sibyls – the Sibylla Europaea wearing a broad-brimmed hat and holding a wand or sceptre, and the Sibylla Phrygia holding a raised sword. Droeshout's set of engravings were themselves copied from a better known set of prints by the Dutch engraver, Crispijn de Passe, which include the Latin inscriptions around the medallion portrait which both the Cooksey trenchers and the Burntisland ceiling copied, but not the encircling English verses which the trenchers copied. It follows that the trenchers go back to the Droeshout set of prints, but that the Sybil portraits on the ceiling at Mary Somerville's House may go back to either.

That these classical figures are participating in a developed programme of Christian iconography is left in no doubt once the remaining details to have survived in the surrounding compartments of this *trompe l'oeil* coffered ceiling have been identified. They include a head of St Matthew and an image of Christ as Salvator Mundi with the Greek inscription 'IESOUS. CHREISTOS. THEOI. UIOS. EOTER. STAURUS', and an Agnus Dei with the damaged label 'DMNVS ES ... GVI'. Our surprise at finding such manifestly Catholic icons on the ceiling can only be confirmed by the image of the head of the Virgin which, indistinct though it now is, is identified by the accompanying label as 'MARIA'. For an image of the Virgin Mary to declare its identity so clearly in Reformation Scotland presents a challenge, as we noted in Chapter 6, to much of the received wisdom concerning the pervasive effects of Scottish iconoclasm at this period.

Ownership of the house by Andrew Watson I (d.1590), his son John (d.1626?), his younger son Andrew II (d.1650) and his grandsons, both John, is well documented throughout the seventeenth century (Apted 1960, pp.168-9). The Watsons were substantial shipowners and burgesses in Burntisland, but there is nothing to suggest they had Catholic leanings. It is not known who might have executed the painting in the house, though as Apted notes (1960, p.171), the painter James Workman owned property and resided in the town from 1606. This is the same herald painter who compiled armorial manuscripts which have a close affinity with the heraldic painting at Earlshall and at Collairnie, also in Fife, and whose brother John was described in his testament in 1606 as 'painter to His Majesty'. (For records of payments to Workman for other painting at Edinburgh, Holyrood and Linlithgow, see Apted and Hannabuss 1978, pp.108-11).

The six paintings of the Sybils at Wester Livilands were discovered in 1866, when the then owner of this seventeenth-century burgess's house in Stirling was making alterations to the interior. In removing a wooden staircase that led up to the garret, he uncovered a small passage on the first floor at the southern end, about six feet wide, which was divided from a larger adjoining chamber by a painted oak partition, lit by a narrow window opening at the far end. The surface facing the passage was divided into six panels by painted Corinthian pilasters supporting a cornice and frieze. Each of the six compartments of this frieze was decorated with a half-length portrait of one of the Sibyls, beneath which were six lines of rhymed verse couplets. The name of the Sibyl was inscribed on either side of her head in labels which identified the following

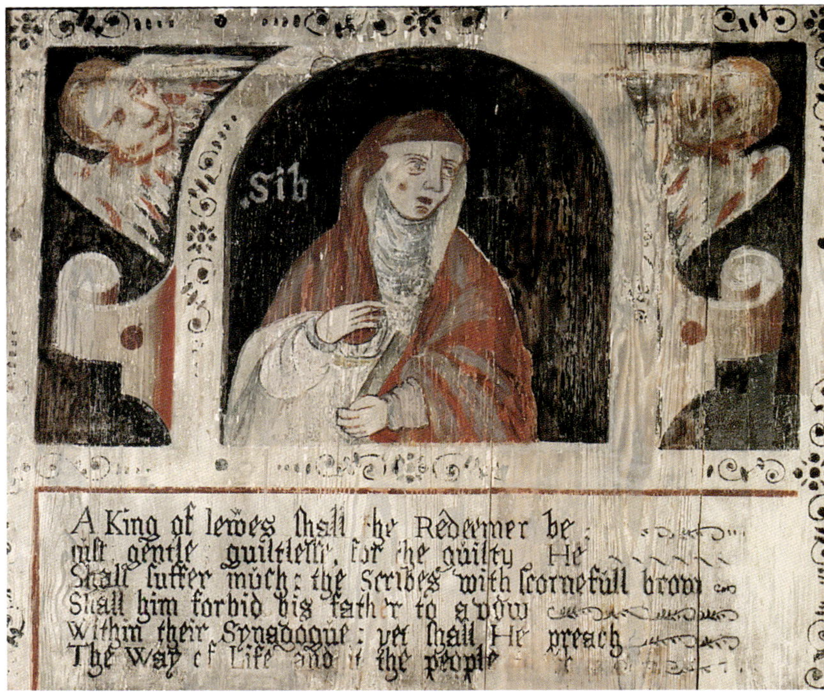

The Sibylla Delphica from Wester Livilands, Stirling. NMS

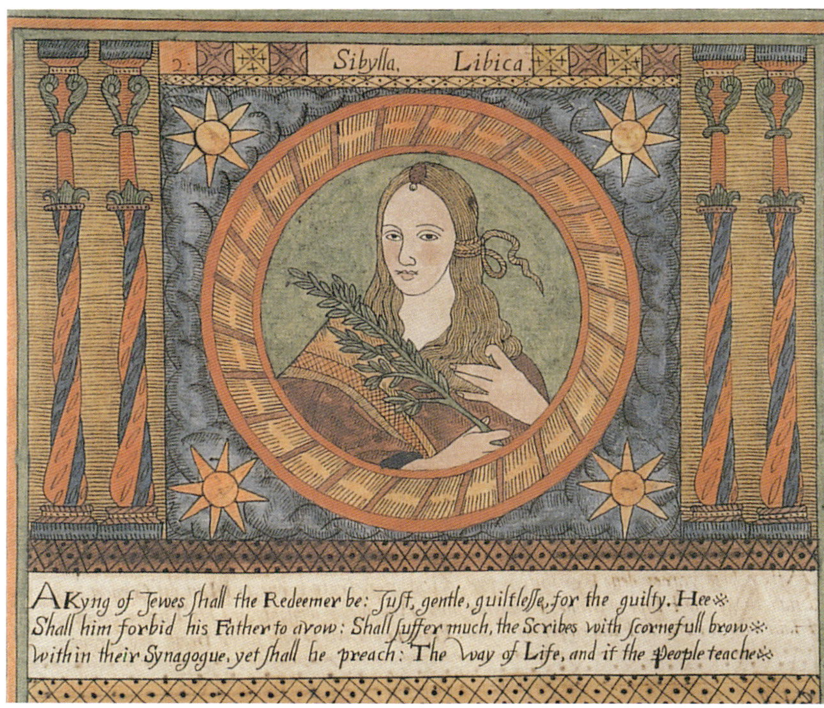

Mix and match: the Sibyl portraits in Thomas Trevilian's Great Book *(1616) copy the set of engravings by Martin Droeshout (after de Passe); however the appended verses below each portrait are not the same as Droeshout's verse inscriptions, but do correspond to the verses found on the Sibyl paintings from Wester Livilands, even though these do not copy Droeshout's pictures.* GUL

Sibyls: Persica, Libica, Delphica, Cumaea, Erythraea, Samia (in that order). The cornice carried the date 1629 and the monograms 'MRM' and 'CC', which have been identified as those of Robert Murray, a Stirling advocate at this period, and of Cristian Cowan his wife. The other side of the oak partition, facing the larger adjoining chamber, is decorated with flowers of different species on crossed stems enclosed in square *trompe l'oeil* frames.

In 1899 these painted boards were exhibited at a meeting of the Society of Antiquaries of Scotland, in Edinburgh, and discussed in an address by Thomas

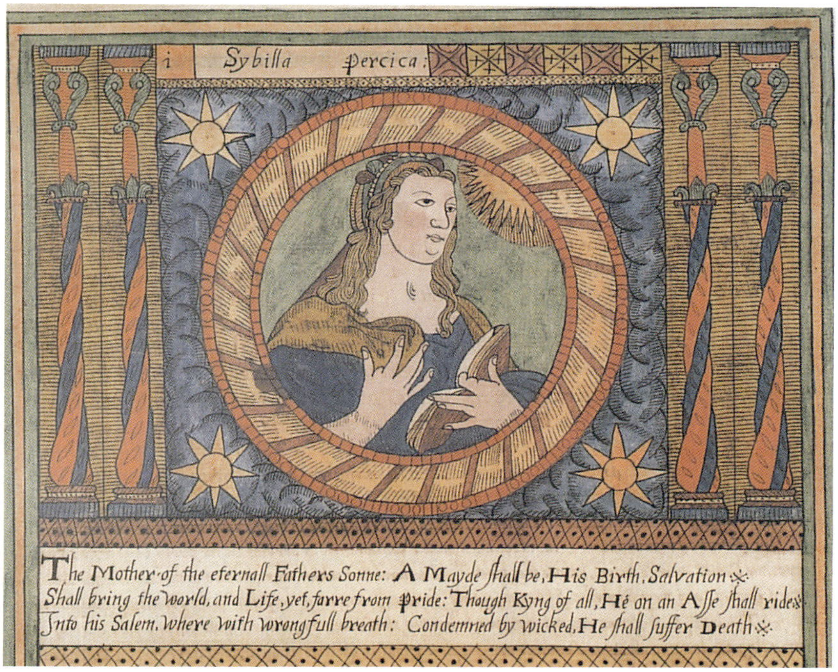

Thomas Trevilian's rendering of 'Sibylla Persica' from the Great Book *(1616).* GUL

Ross, who recognised that the Sibyls at Wester Livilands bore a striking resemblance to another series of Sibyls painted in mural decorations at a house, Cheyney Court, in the village of Bishop's Frome, Herefordshire. Ross had been alerted to the existence of these by a brief note that had appeared some years earlier in *Notes and Queries*, and he appears to have contacted a local informant in Herefordshire, who supplied him with a transcription of the verses accompanying the Cheyney Court series, which turned out to be identical with those at Wester Livilands. Since Cheyney Court burnt down a few years before he completed his researches, Ross's article in the Scottish Antiquaries' *Proceedings* remains our only record of the Herefordshire cycle of Sibyl paintings. Just as the Droeshout engravings allow us to supply some of the missing detail from Mary Somerville's House, so the Cheyney Court cycle enabled Ross to supply the inscriptions for the remaining six Sibyls of whom no trace remains at Wester Livilands. The replication of these verses at two such widely separated sites suggests that they must go back to a common print source, but if so it has yet to be identified.

Publication of the *Great Book* of Thomas Trevilian, however, now reveals a set of Sibyls that not only confirms the likelihood that there was some such ephemeral set of popular prints, but offers us a remarkably close model for the Wester Livilands Sibyl paintings themselves. Pages 443-55 of Trevilian's huge 1616 pattern book contain the twelve Sibyls, one per page, shown as half-length portraits which copy the Droeshout engravings. However, the six lines of English verse quoted beneath the Sibyl portrait do not – as one might expect – copy the verse *subscriptio* which Droeshout added to his reworking of de Passe's set of prints; instead they use verse inscriptions which correspond word-for-word to the otherwise unrecorded verses which we find on the Wester Livilands panels and on the Cheyney Court cycle. We must almost certainly, therefore, posit the existence of unknown sets of prints of this subject which pirated either the de Passe designs for the portraits, or one or other of the verse *subscriptiones* which we find appended to these pictures in the Droeshout prints and in various decorative applications, none of which uses exactly the same combination of sources for the different constituents of text and image. Unique to Trevilian's handling of the Sibyls is the long prose commentary, summarising the ancient, learned and classical sources on the prophecies, which fills two-thirds of each of his huge pages. These commentaries would surely repay the attention of anyone wishing to understand how received opinion on the Sibyls came down to the seventeenth century in England; though clearly such learned commentaries would not be suitable for copying in any decorative scheme, and their inclusion in Trevilian's manuscript suggests why it is unsafe to regard it simply as a 'pattern book'. Malcolm Jones, incidentally, points out to me that the 'M. D.' identified as engraver on the title page of the *XII Sibyllarum Icones* cannot be Martin Droeshout, famous as engraver of the portrait of Shakespeare that appears on the First Folio in 1623, since he was only born in 1601 (these engravings are not the work of a fifteen year-old apprentice), but must be his father Michael Droeshout, also an engraver (Griffiths 1998, p.106).

Sibylline prophecy goes back to classical times, when the Sibylline Books were deposited in the Capitol in Rome to be consulted as oracles at moments of national crisis. Virgil's Aeneas consults the Cumaean Sibyl before descending to the underworld to learn the future destiny of Rome, and other Sibyls were associated with this prophetic tradition in classical times before it was subjected to *interpretatio Christiana*. Throughout most of the Middle Ages, however, only two or three of the Sibyls were celebrated by name; the Tiburtine Sibyl was credited with having vouchsafed the emperor Augustus his *ara coeli* vision of the Virgin and Christ child, and the Erythraean was identified as the Sibyl who forecast the day of judgement in the *Dies Irae*. However, in the late fifteenth century ten Sibyls suddenly emerge into the iconographic light of day, associated with a set of prophecies and attributes which go back to two particular sources. The first of these is the *Divinae Institutiones* of Lactantius (c.304-13), which identifies ten Sibyls in the following sequence: Persian, Libyan, Delphic, Cimmerian, Erythraean, Samian, Cumaean, Hellespontic, Phrygian, and Tiburtine. According to Lactantius the Sybils had, between them, predicted the birth, the miracles, the Passion, death, resurrection, and the second coming of Christ. First printed in 1465, Lactantius's work went through eight further editions in the next fifteen years, and the Sybils soon found their way into ecclesiastical art, beginning with the choir stalls executed 1469-74 in Ulm Cathedral (Mâle 1908, p.270), followed by numerous cycles in Italian art which climax in Michelangelo's Sistine Chapel ceiling.

In 1481 a book appeared by an Italian Dominican, Filippo Barbieri, which has been shown to have influenced the representation of the various Sibyls in the visual arts, and the texts with which they are associated, into the sixteenth century and beyond. This scheme managed to identify each of the Sibyls with successive stages in the life of Christ and established a set of attributes which hardened into a received iconography; particular Sibyls carry a lantern, a lighted candle, a bowl, a drinking horn, a cradle, a raised sword, an amputated hand, a crown of thorns, a scourge, and a cross with a pennant attached. The scheme found its way into engravings by such printmakers as Baccio Baldini, Francesco Rosselli and Philips Galle. The transmission and transformation of many of these details in iconographic traditions which quickly established themselves in the late fifteenth and early sixteenth centuries throughout Europe will help to account for at least some of the otherwise incomprehensible details of the seventeenth-century paintings at Burntisland and Wester Livilands, even though their attributes and associated texts show very little stability. In Scotland the best known is probably a series of panel paintings in Aberdeen, Marischal College Museum, once erroneously attributed to George Jamesone.

Some details from the Latin inscriptions at Mary Somerville's or Wester Livilands, though not the inscriptions themselves, can be shown to go back to antique sources. Thus de Passe's description of Cumana characterises her as 'Quae et Amaltheae nuncupatur' ('Who was also known as Amalthea') – the phrase goes back to Lactantius, who tells us that this Sibyl 'went by the name of Amalthea'. Lactantius also gives the Tiburtine her cognomen 'Albunea', thus authorising the expression 'Quae et Albunea' which we find on de Passe's engraving and at Mary Somerville's House, and he tells us that she holds a book in her hand ('tenens in manu librum'), which is how she is described by Barbieri, though the Aberdeen panel and de Passe's engraving shows her holding a bowl and a palm branch. In Barbieri it is the Erythraean Sibyl who holds a sword, but in Mary Somerville's House, as we have seen, it is the Phrygian who has this attribute, as she does in the de Passe engraving and in the Aberdeen panels, where the Erythraean also holds the Lamb. In the iconography described by Mâle it is the Delphic Sibyl who holds the crown of thorns, but de Passe and the Aberdeen panels bestow this attribute on the Samian. Perhaps the most dramatic transformation in any of these Scottish exemplars is the Lybian Sibyl at Aberdeen, who is shown as a negress.

This uncertainty surrounding the exact number and the identity of the Sibyls made them another target for Sir Thomas Browne in his catalogue of the vulgar errors perpetrated by modern painters, which includes a chapter 'Of the Pictures of the *Sibyls*' in which he points out that although 'pictures of the *Sibyls* are very common, and for their Prophesies of Christ in high esteem with Christians', their number and their names vary considerably, both in the descriptions of classical writers and in the work of modern painters: 'And therefore not discovering a resolution of their number from pens of the best Writers, we have no reason to determine the same from the hand and pencil of Painters' (*Works* 1927, vol. ii, p.234). Browne also points out that modern portraits of the Sibyls generally show them as attractive young women – as they appear at both Wester Livilands and at Mary Somerville's House – whereas the testimony of such writers as Virgil and Livy stresses that they were aged crones. Browne's irritation concerning the instability of such established topics and schemes might be seen as a sign of a more fundamental epistemological shift at this period, for the desire to regulate the number of members in any such scheme was itself motivated by the traditional assumption that the world was a fixed, unchanging order. To confess to not knowing the exact number of the Sibyls was only

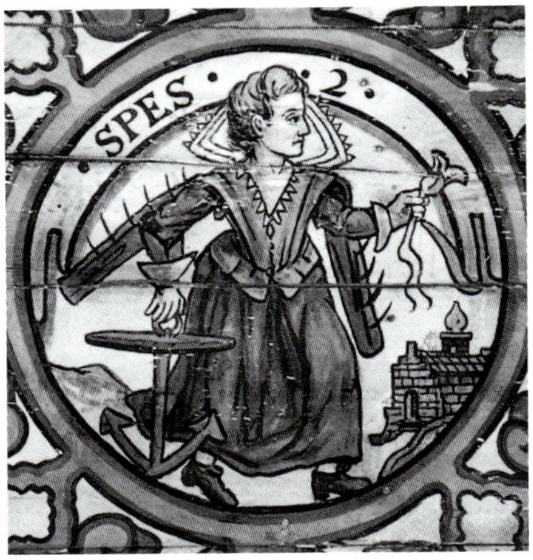

a)

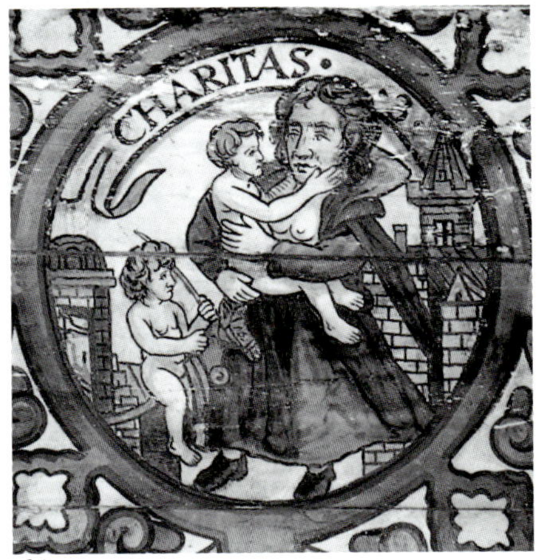

b)

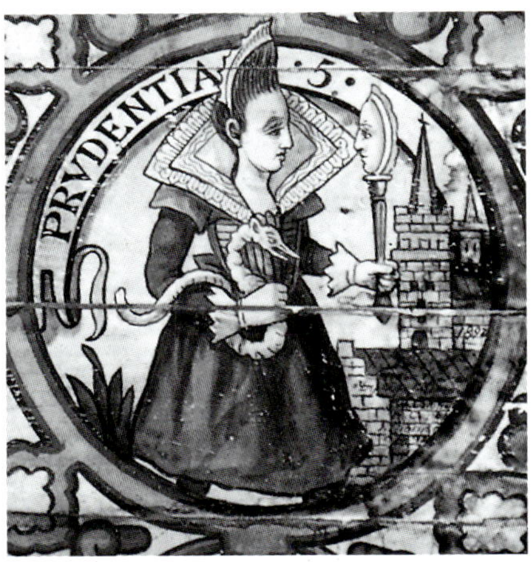

c)

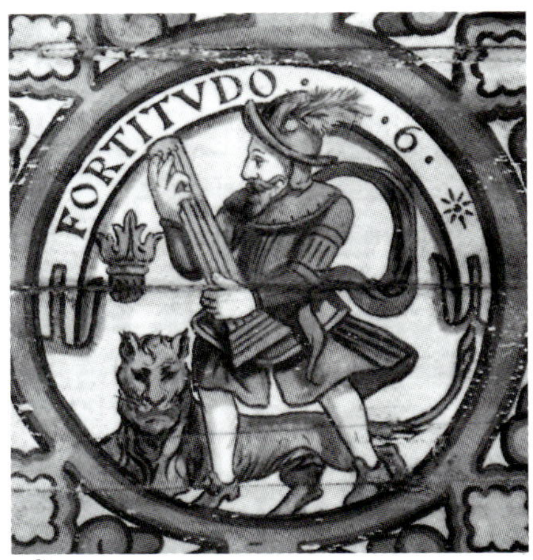

d)

Earlshall, long gallery,

a) Hope, second of the seven Virtues shown with her conventional anchor (Heb. 6.19) and flower implying the hope of fruit to come.

b) Charity, third of the three theological virtues, not only suckles her offspring at Earlshall but seats one of them on a hobby horse.

c) Prudence, one of the four Cardinal Virtues, shown with her conventional snake (Matt 10:16) and mirror; presumably it is the mirror that persuaded her to wear her widest collar and hat.

d) Fortitude shown, conventionally, seated on a lion and holding a pillar; it is unconventional to show this Cardinal Virtue as a bearded male.

slightly less disturbing than it would have been to admit that one did not know the exact number of the elements, the temperaments, the seasons, the signs of the zodiac, or the planets. The tendency of the visual arts to reproduce all such schemes in a fixed order has to be seen as a sign of their commitment to a conservative view of the creation as a mathematically ordered and unchanging cosmos. Just as there are five senses, four evangelists, twelve tribes of Israel, and twelve signs of the zodiac, so there are nine Worthies, nine Muses, seven Deadly Sins, seven Cardinal Virtues, and twelve Sibyls (or is it only ten?).

The Cardinal Virtues

A modern world view would be likely to make distinctions between those schemes which are grounded on the natural properties of things – four elements, four seasons, five senses, seven planets, nine spheres, for instance – and those which have only a biblical or, indeed, a rhetorical basis. The four Evangelists or the twelve tribes of Israel have at least biblical authority, whereas the idea that there were just seven Virtues and seven Vices lacks any clear natural or biblical basis; indeed, although the three 'theological' virtues of Faith, Hope and Charity take their cue from 1 Corinthians 13.13, the remaining four 'Cardinal' Virtues of Justice, Prudence, Fortitude and Temperance go back to a classical grouping expounded by such writers as Plato (*Republic*, 4.427 ff). However diverse their sources, the desire for an ordered symmetry influences

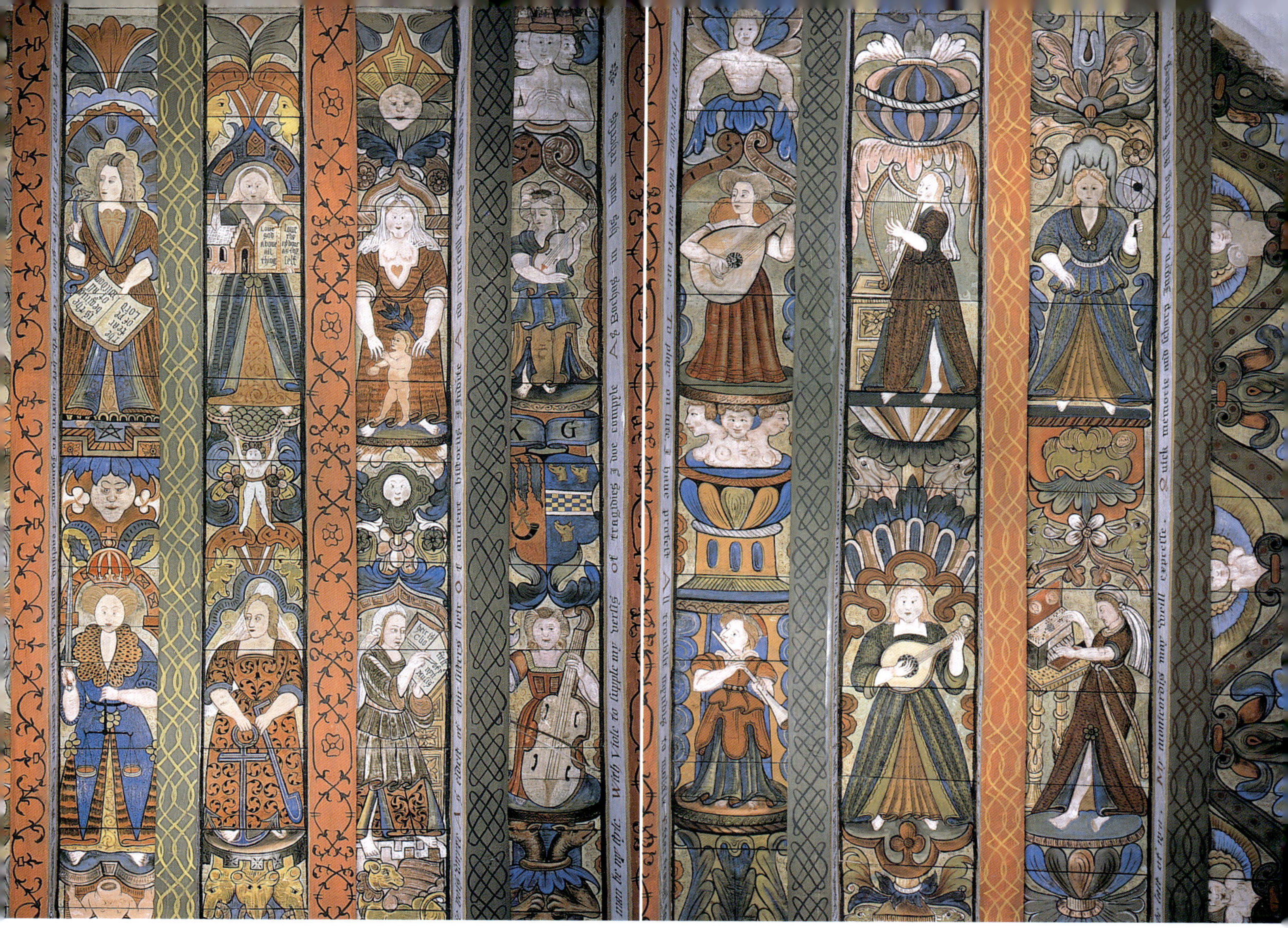

Crathes Castle, Muses Room, five of the Virtues: Wisdom and Justice, Faith, Hope and Charity, with the nine Muses: Clio, Thalia and Melpomene, Terpsichore and Euterpe, Calliope and Erato, Urania and Polyhymnia.
Alasdair Smith, NTS

the development of a fixed scheme and the older cosmology erects no boundaries between the natural and the moral and theological worlds; all are equally governed by order and number.

The seven Virtues at Earlshall are, indeed, numbered, with the three Theological followed by the four Cardinal Virtues, each in their conventional order. All are shown in seventeenth-century costume, with more-or-less conventional attributes – Faith holds a cross in one hand and the sacraments in the other; Hope holds her anchor (Hebrews 6.19) and a flower; Charity is a bare-breasted matron holding a child whilst a second infant rides a hobby-horse at her feet; Temperance pours water into a cup of wine; Prudence holds her usual mirror and a serpent; Fortitude strides over a lion holding his conventional pillar – and he alone of these figures is shown as a bearded male, presumably because Fortitude is the most masculine of the Virtues; Justice holds her familiar sword and scales. All these attributes are standard and conventional, though the figures are handled with a certain originality and vigour.

The Virtues at Crathes have a greater stiffness and formality. They are painted on the same ceiling that contains the nine Muses, each with an accompanying quatrain of verses inscribed on the supporting beams, expounding their qualities and attributes. The association of the Virtues with the Muses is certainly no accident, since it was conventionally the role of the Muses to eternalise the fame the Virtues deserved; indeed the opening inscription, at the south-east side of the room, applies to both sets of allegorical figures:

> Honour & grace is the dew recompence
> Of vertueus warkes done in this lyfe
> Quhilk maketh men to be haid in reuerence,
> And als their praise to be soundit most ryfe.

It may have been the need to balance the nine Muses with a more equal number of Virtues (or at least an equal number of inscriptions on the sides of the beams) that prompted the addition of an extra Virtue, namely Fame, who is non-canonical. Fame's role might, however, be seen as equally appropriate to both sets of figures; both an eighth Virtue in her own right and a figure for the immortal memory which it was the business of the Muses collectively to preserve. This is doubtless why she heads the sequence of Virtues that the introductory quatrain celebrates in the immediately preceding inscription. Crathes is also slightly unconventional in placing the four Cardinal Virtues ahead of the three biblical, and it substitutes Wisdom for the more conventional figure of Prudence:

> Wisdome is the ground of all praise & gloir
> Fe of the lyff contrar to Ignorance
> Teaching quhat will speake euermore
> [G]yid of all vertues quhilk men do aduance.

The variant is not a major innovation, however, since the affinity of Prudence with Wisdom was traditionally close – Prudence traditionally holds the serpent of wisdom, as she does both here and at Earlshall ('be therefore wise as serpents', Matthew 10.16).

Two of the Cardinal Virtues – Justice and Fortitude – are also depicted with emblematic inscriptions, along with the various schemes already discussed in Chapter 6, in the Montgomery Aisle at Skelmorlie. That ceiling is unique in Scotland in its inclusion of the badges of the tribes of Israel, but the signs of the zodiac is a feature which it shares with decorative painting from Ravelston, where they are recorded as accompanying the labours of the months; at Old Saughton, and at Mary Somerville's House, whilst we find the Four Seasons also illustrated at Monkton and at Old Craighall.

The Planetary Deities

Cullen House, Banff, contained a long gallery which included, before it was destroyed by fire in 1987, not only accomplished paintings of classical subjects along the angled sides of its pent roof – a panoramic Siege of Troy, Atalanta's Boar Hunt, and Diana and Actaeon – but also a more crudely executed stellar ceiling covering the soffit, with labelled figures of 'Mercurius', 'Neptunus', 'Flora', and 'Luna' shown seated amidst swirls of cloud, numerous winged putti and embossed stars. These figures belong in a tradition which goes back to a scheme of allegorical figures representing the sun, moon and planets, based on

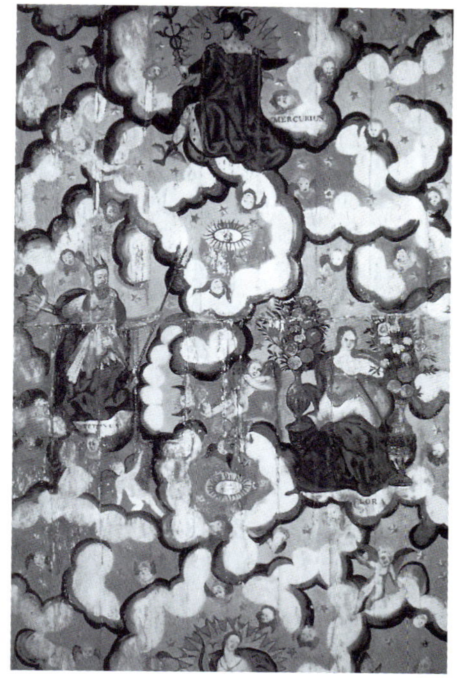

Cullen House, Banffshire, long gallery, astral ceiling. Kit Martin

an anonymous text known as the *Libellus de imaginibus deorum* of c.1400 whose iconography was borrowed from Petrarch's *Africa* (Levenson et al 1973, nos 54-66). The planetary gods – Saturn, Jupiter, Mars, Venus, Mercury, Sol, Luna – were commonly represented in sixteenth-century almanacs (Luborsky and Ingram 1998, nos 398.3, 432, 449, 463); they also figure in prints such as the *Planetary Gods* by Georg Pencz, which resembles the Cullen examples insofar as it shows the planetary deities sitting or riding their chariots on swirls of cloud (*Illustrated Bartsch*, vol. 16, nos 11-17); we find similar figures in the *Planets* cycle of Virgil Solis (Bartsch 1803-21, vol. ix, p.265, nos 163-9) which supplied the patterns for wall paintings at Stodmarsh Court (Kent), now in the Victoria and Albert Museum (Reader 1936, pl. xvi; Croft-Murray 1962, p.184).

The seven planets are not exactly what we see at Cullen, however, for Cullen's Flora and Neptune are earthly, not planetary, deities and do not belong on an astral ceiling. Nor do their attributes conform with the conventional representation of these figures; Mercury certainly has his winged hat and boots and he holds his winged caduceus, but Luna is shown with an anchor, presumably to indicate her control over the tides; and instead of her habitual crescent she is encircled by a sunburst, like that which encircles Mercury. Neptune rides on a whale holding his trident, and Flora holds two vases of flowers. If Flora and Neptune are anomalous in this scheme, the error is compounded by fragments of painting from the original ceiling recovered in the 1960s when, prior to conservation work, a partition was dismantled which separated the two rooms into which the original long gallery had later been divided. The plaster on the partition wall had used laths made up from some of the original painted boards, on which much of the original paint was preserved, including fragments of cloud and sky suggesting that they had formed part of the original ceiling. Among them is a fragment containing the label 'Pluto'. We may well wonder what motivated the promotion of the classical god of the underworld to sit amongst the planetary deities on this astral ceiling.

The Five Senses

The five senses were traditionally shown as female figures with conventional attributes: Hearing has a lute and a stag, since stags were reputedly keen of hearing and attracted by music; Sight holds a mirror in which she views herself and is shown with an eagle since the eagle is sharp-sighted and can look straight at the sun; Taste has a basket of fruit and a monkey with fruit in its mouth; Smell is shown with flowers and a dog; Touch with various tactile objects. Three such figures are among the panels removed in 1845 from a house known as The Dean in Edinburgh, now displayed in the Museum of Scotland. Other panels from the ceiling of a room described in 1735 as 'a fine long painted gallery' (Tayler, cited Thomson 1975, p.47), are Old Testament scenes. The house, and almost certainly the ceiling, was built for William Nisbet (1569-1639), who served as Provost of Edinburgh at various times and entertained dramatist Ben Jonson on the latter's famous visit to Drummond of Hawthornden in 1619; he was knighted during James VI's visit to Edinburgh in

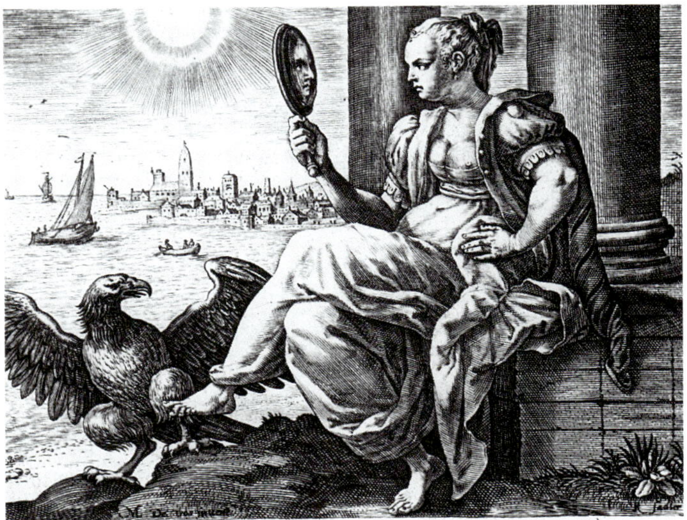

Above: 'The Sense of Sight' engraving by Johannes Sadeler after Maarten de Vos. SP,A

The sense of Sight panel from Dean House, Edinburgh, now NMS. HS

1617. Nearly all the panels owe at least something to published prints, though they handle such sources with a great deal of freedom. The three senses panels rework designs found in individual prints from various sets executed after designs by Maarten de Vos. The personification of the sense of Sight, for instance, shows a seated female figure, richly dressed in early seventeenth-century costume, who looks at herself in a hand-held mirror; beside her is the eagle and behind her a view of the sea with a three-masted ship and a distant landscape with features which have been identified as 'a rough representation of Edinburgh, with Arthur's Seat on the left, the sloping High Street in the centre, and the Castle on the right' (Thomson 1975, p.47). The seascape suggests that this panel is based on the print by Johannes Sadeler after Maarten de Vos (Hollstein, vol. xlv, fig. 1506), which shows the figure of Sight seated at the base of two classical columns on a sea shore, with a ship in sail and a distant townscape. The woman's

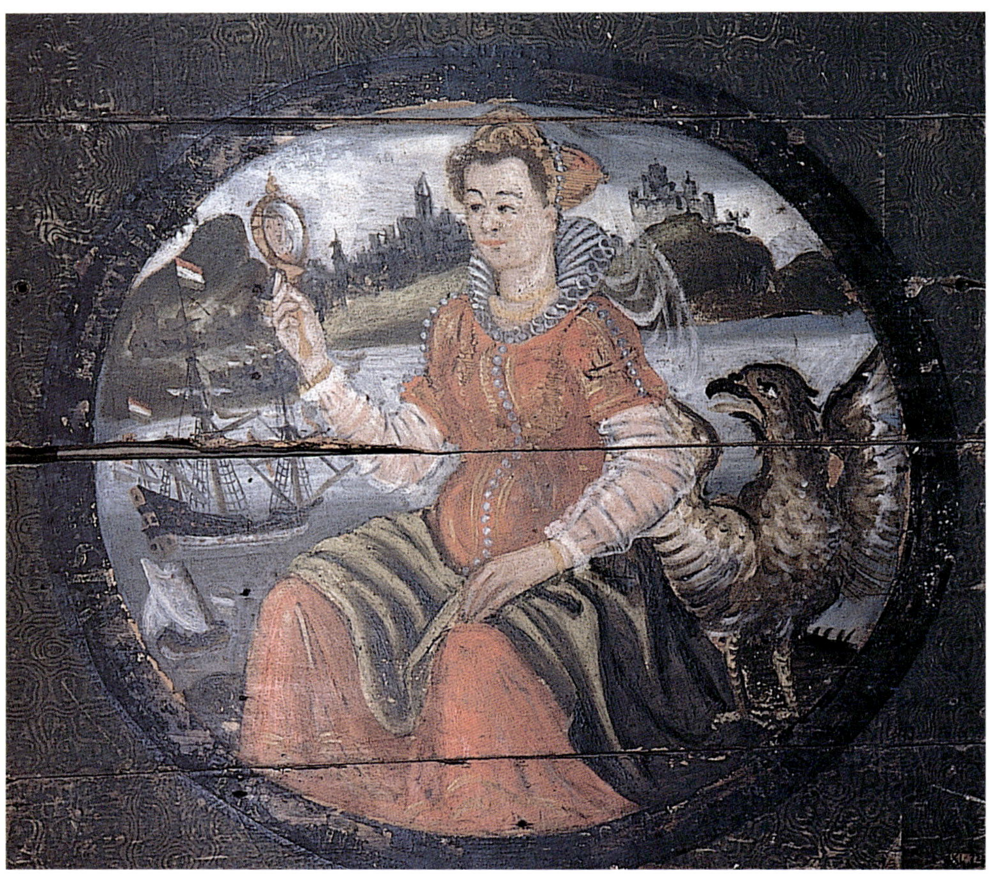

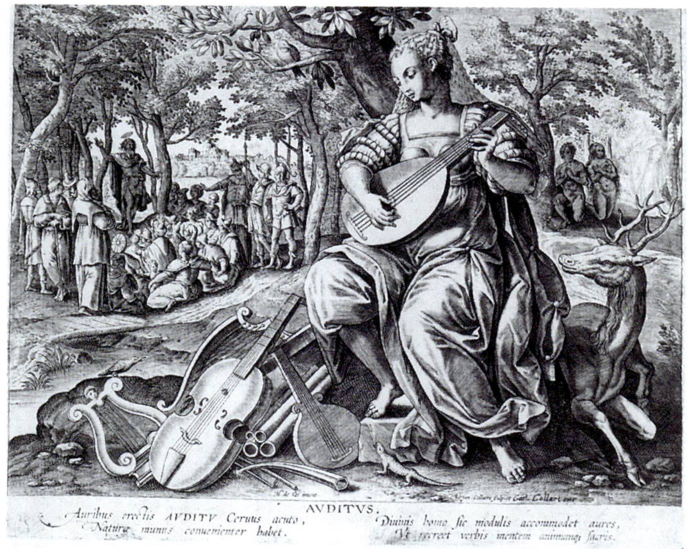

Above: 'Auditus', engraving by Adrien Collaert after Maarten de Vos. SP,A

costume is modernised in the Dean panel and the eagle repositioned, but the hand positions are identical and the short sleeve of her dress reveals her elbow with a prominent dimple which the Dean artist appears to have somewhat awkwardly copied from the print; the eagle's spread wings and turned head make the one a mirror image of the other. The Dean panel omits the prominent classical pillars and reinterprets the background townscape as mountainous. The oval panel is encircled by a damaged inscription in the border, not copied from the similar motto in de Vos's print.

The sense of Hearing is similarly shown as a seated female in a woodland landscape with swans on a lake and buildings in the distance. She plays a lute, and a trumpet and a harp lie on the ground beside her along with a stag (a traditional attribute of hearing, *cf* Bath 1992, pp.207-20, 288, 311). This panel almost certainly copies the *Auditus* engraving by Adriaen Collaert after Maarten de Vos, c.1682 (Hollstein, vol. xlv, no. 1494/II).

The sense of Hearing panel from Dean House, Edinburgh, now NMS. NMS

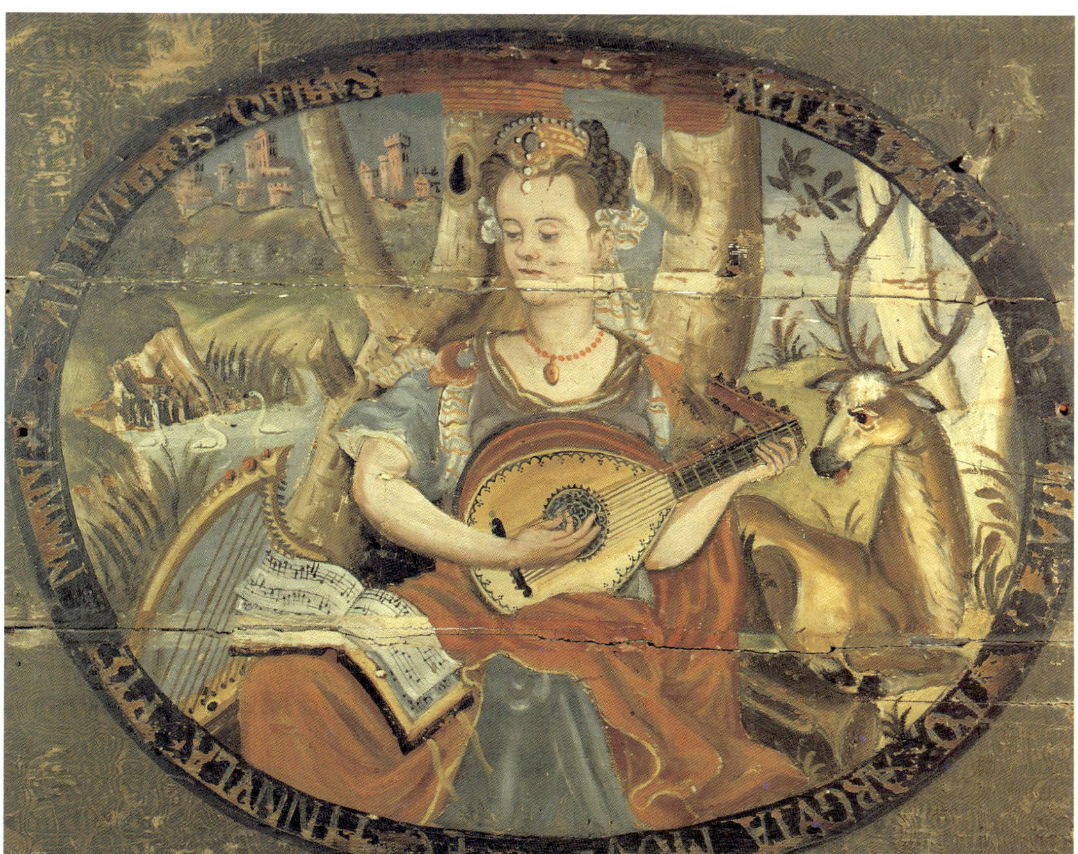

The position and attitude of the stag, and the direction of the lute-player's glance which the Dean's artist reinterprets as directed down upon a musical score, leave little doubt. Collaerts' set of prints was used for the five Senses plasterwork panels executed in 1623 at Boston Manor, Brentford, Middlesex. The Dean painting, again, finds a different border inscription from anything in the Latin verses appended to de Vos's print.

Entirely missing from the panels at The Dean are the background details that give de Vos's treatments of this subject a biblical dimension. The series executed by Collaert, for instance, associates Sight with God showing Adam and Eve the Tree of Knowledge and Christ healing the blind man by the pool of Siloam; Taste is illustrated by the Fall and by the miracle of the loaves and fishes; Hearing is Adam and Eve hiding from the sight of God, and John the Baptist preaching. The inclusion of such Old and New Testament details witnesses to a taste for typology in the Renaissance treatment and reception of this scheme, and a tendency to interpret the whole scheme in a biblical context. In some ways the omission of this biblical application of the five Senses at The Dean is surprising, since it would give these panels a greater conformity with the other subjects represented on the ceiling, which are all religious.

History Painting

Conventional topics in decorative painting of this period are not limited to allegorical schemes, and our remaining examples all handle subjects drawn from literature. These can usefully be divided into scenes illustrating episodes from the Bible on the one hand, and episodes from classical literature on the other. Both types of subject are examples of 'history painting', that is to say painting which illustrates a familiar (or perhaps not so familiar) story. Understanding what we are looking at in such cases will inevitably require some familiarity with the story being illustrated, but it may also require a recognition of how that story had traditionally been treated in the visual arts. Most of these examples illustrate subjects that, like the allegorical schemes we have been discussing so far, had already been widely used in painting and print sources. I shall therefore examine not only the way these paintings represent the literary texts they illustrate, but also the way they handle some of the received conventions that inform their topics in the visual arts.

The Old Testament scenes from The Dean are closer than much of the religious painting examined in Chapter 6 to the type of religious subject which conventional art history teaches us to expect in a Protestant tradition. At least some of these scenes appear to copy existing prints, though they show a great deal of independence of their source. The painting of Abraham and Isaac is the only one for which a print source has so far been suggested. The subject is so widely represented in the decorative arts of this period, however, and the way it is represented so conventionalised, that we may well hesitate before ascribing any one image to a particular source. Wells-Cole nevertheless observes that 'the position of the intended victim and the appearance of some of the background buildings' in the Dean panel relate closely to the version executed after the designs, once again, of Maarten de Vos, in the Old Testament series known as *Thesaurus veteris et novi Testamenti*, first published in Antwerp by Gerard de Iode in 1579 (Wells-Cole 1997, p.104). The Dean panel shows Abraham and Isaac in a landscape, Abraham glancing up to the monitory angel in the clouds, whilst Isaac kneels, arms crossed, by the sacrificial pyre of branches on a square stone slab. Beside them on their hillock is a smoking censer, and the ram which was destined to be sacrificed in place of Isaac is shown entwined in the leafy branches of the thicket in which, the Bible tells us, it was caught. At the foot of the hill we see the young men, whom Abraham ordered to abide with his ass, resting in a woodland setting where deer can be seen, and on the viewer's right the background landscape shows the city of Beersheba to which

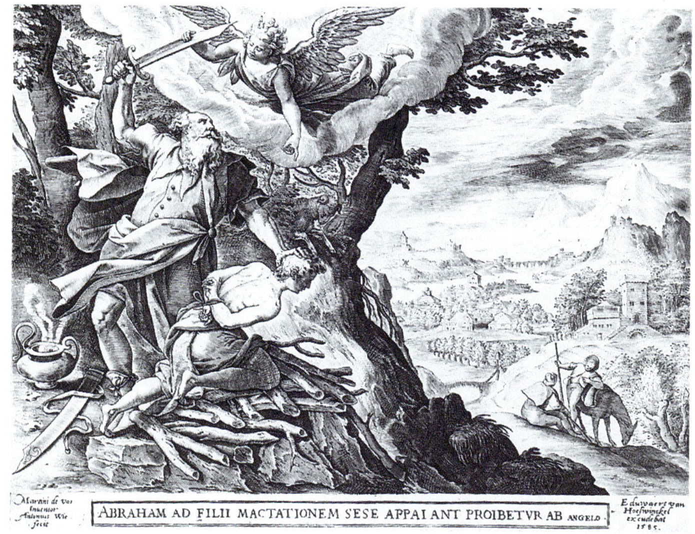

'Abraham and Isaac' engraving by A Wierix after de Vos, print dated 1585.
BR,B

Abraham and Isaac panel from Dean House, Edinburgh, now NMS.

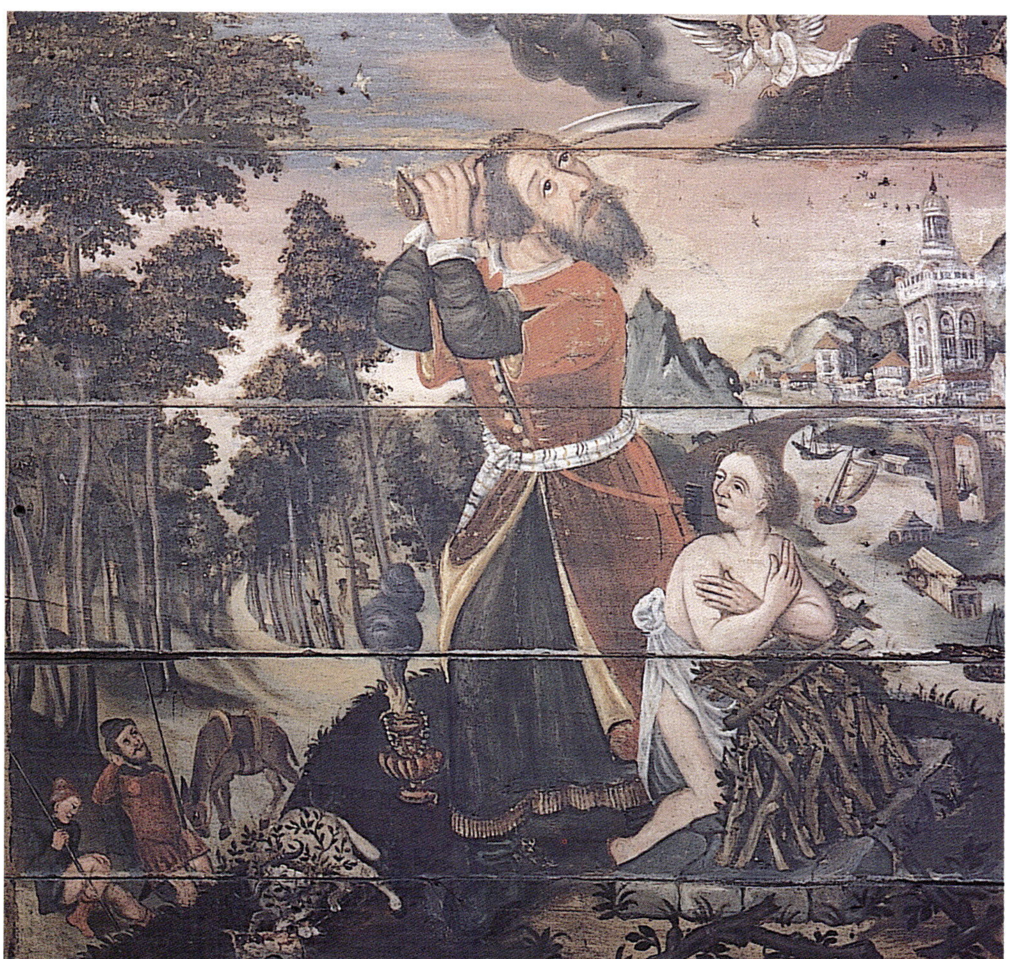

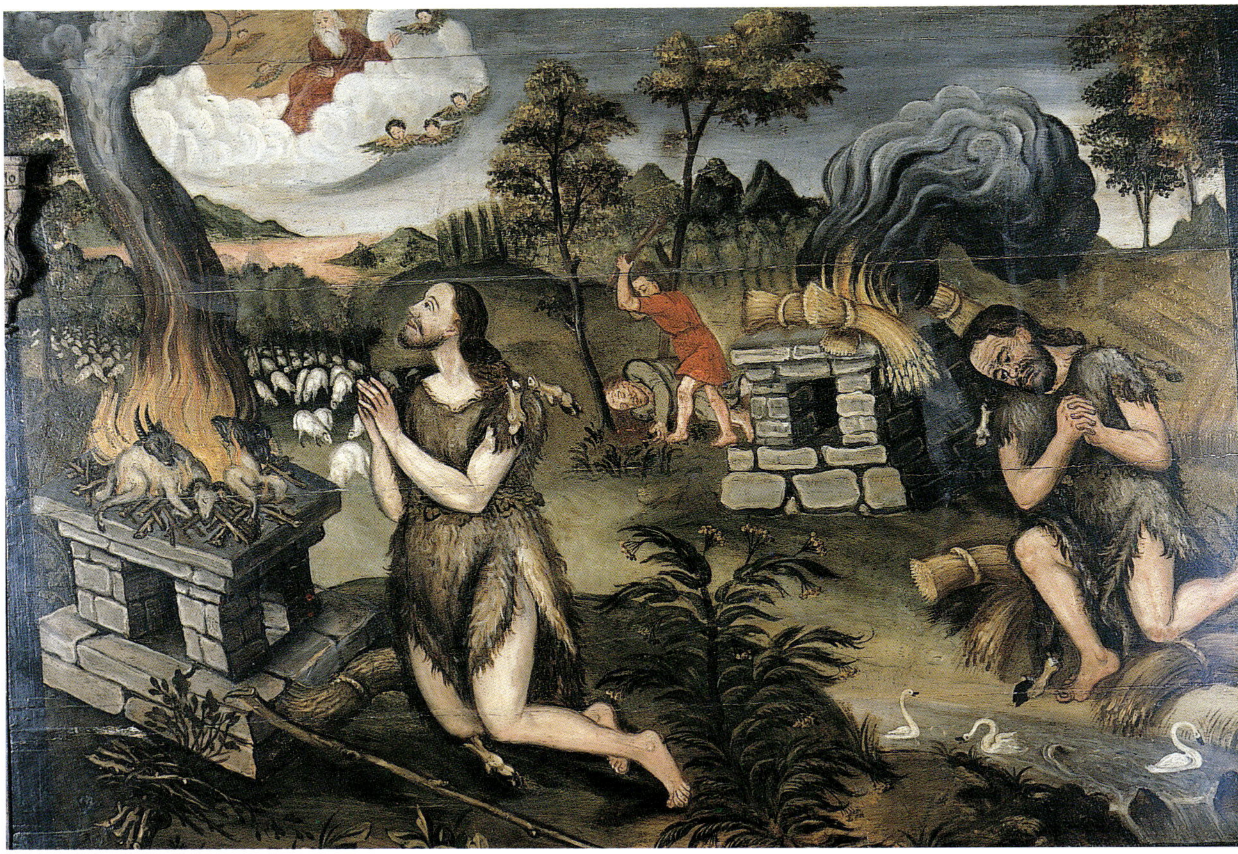

Cain and Abel panel from Dean House, Edinburgh, now displayed in John Knox's House, Canongate. NMS

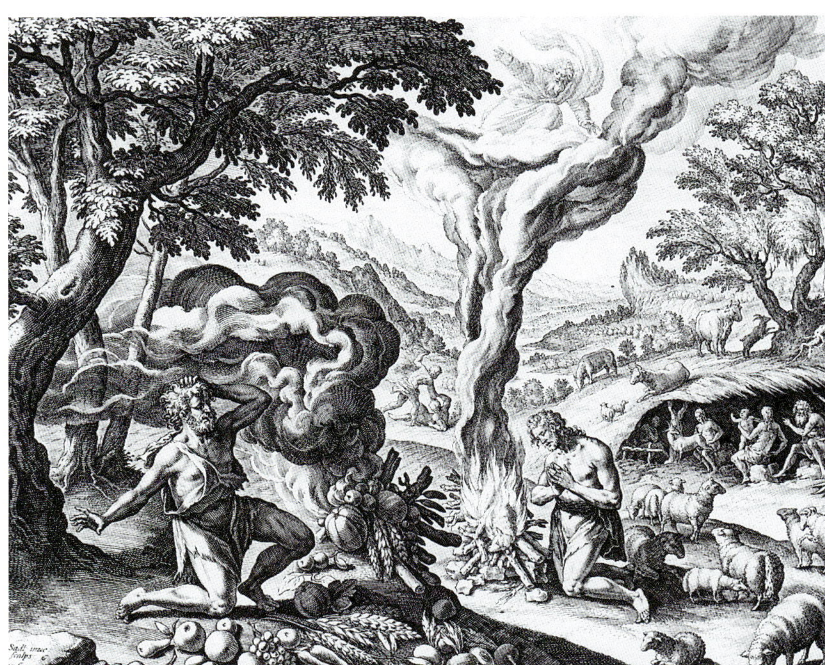

'Cain and Abel' engraving by Johannes Sadeler after de Vos. SP,A

they return after the sacrifice; it is shown on the opposite bank of a river with sailing ships and a water mill, and is spanned by a high bridge which leads to an elaborate temple. The Wierix engraving (Hollstein, vol. xlv, no 248/I) shows the sacrifice taking place on a rocky crag quite unlike the grassy knoll in the Dean painting and it does not include the left-hand woodland scene with its deer. Nevertheless the rather vaguely sketched bridge in this valley probably gave the painter his hint to reinterpret this whole left-hand scene as a river valley with a water mill and sailing ships, and the reclining postures of the two attendants and the appearance of the grazing ass are close enough to suggest that the painting took its cue for these details from the print.

A similar relationship between print and painting can be demonstrated in the Cain and Abel panel from The Dean. The foreground shows the two offerings the Bible tells us the two brothers made – Cain, on the right, kneels before a stone altar on which sheaves of corn are burning, on the left Abel kneels in prayer before a similar altar in which sheep are burning. As Genesis tells us, 'Abel was a keeper of sheep, but Cain was a tiller of the ground' (4.2). Abel's glance is upwards, to where God looks down with angels from a cloud, whereas Cain's glance is downwards, towards a small pool on which swim three diminutive swans. In the background Cain, who has changed his dress into a red tunic, slays his brother. In the border above the picture is an inscription, not now fully legible: '[...] AIN TVS ABEL OFERENTES'. The painting is certainly based on the print from the Old Testament Series by Johannes Sadeler after Maarten de Vos (Hollstein, no.30/II), though the details are treated with some freedom; de Vos shows Cain's sacrifice on the viewer's left, Abel with his sheep on the right and neither sacrifice is burnt on a stone altar, though the smoke which rises to the heavens from Abel's fire, where it encircles a figure of God the Father, and the smoke which curves back down to earth from Cain's unacceptable offering in both print and painting, leave little doubt that the print was The Dean's model. The posture of Cain in the print, kneeling with hands clasped in prayer, is particularly close to that of Cain in the painting, and the background detail of the slaying is also close. The pool with swans is unwarranted, but we find this detail on several of the other Dean panels (*cf* the *Taste* and *Hearing* panels described above), suggesting that it was a habitual signature of this painter. The Dean inscription is, once again, not copied from the engraving.

The panel showing Judith with the head of Holofernes also includes at least two episodes within a single frame, for although Judith stands with an upraised sword in one hand and the head of the decapitated Holofernes in the other, the right-hand side of the painting shows her slaying the disarmed Holofernes in his tent, while the left background shows the city of Bethulia and below it the army of mounted Assyrian warriors besieging it. The inclusion of the two episodes suggests that it may go back to one or other of the print series on this topic which depicted the separate episodes in sequence; there were at least three such series produced by Dutch engravers after designs by Maarten van Heemskirk, of which that executed by Philips Galle (*Illustrated Bartsch*, Supplement vol. 56 016:1-8) is closest to the Dean panel.

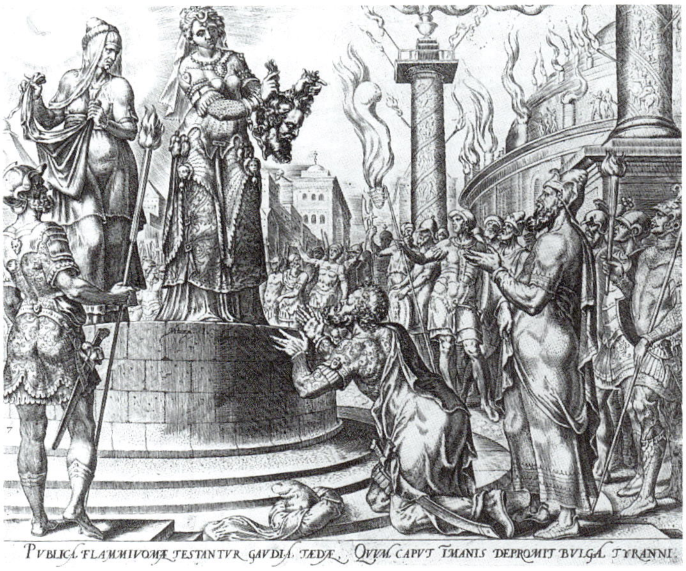

Though the two relevant prints are treated with some freedom, there are enough similarities in the treatment of Judith's costume to leave little doubt that the painting is based on Galle's engaving of 'Judith Displaying Holofernes' Head to the People'; in both, her overskirt is caught up on brooches at the hip, a similar brooch hangs from her beaded necklace, the headdress is similar, as is the way her tunic is elaborately cut at the waist. Though she holds a scimitar, which is not shown in the print, Holofernes' features are recognisably the same. The painting offers us a frontal view rather than a

'Judith Displaying Holofernes' Head to the People', engraving by Philips Galle after Maarten van Heemskerck.
BR,B

Judith and Holofernes panel from Dean House, Edinburgh, now NMS.

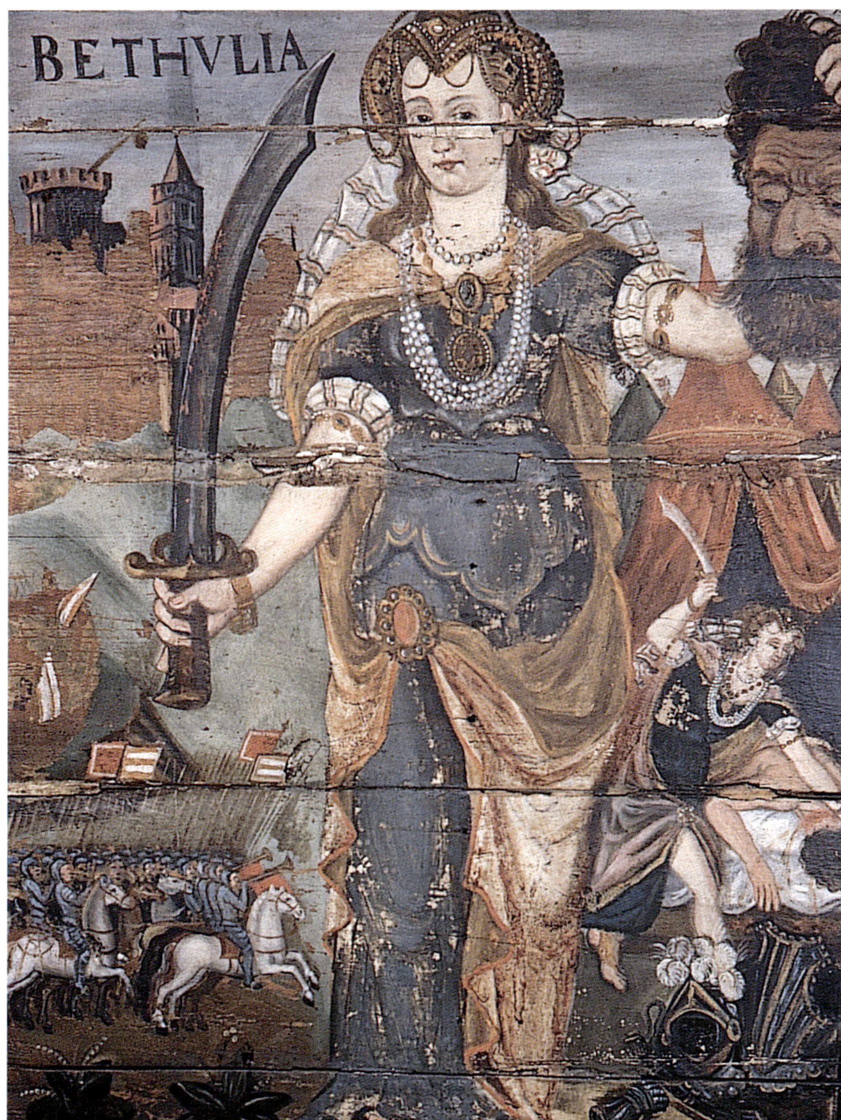

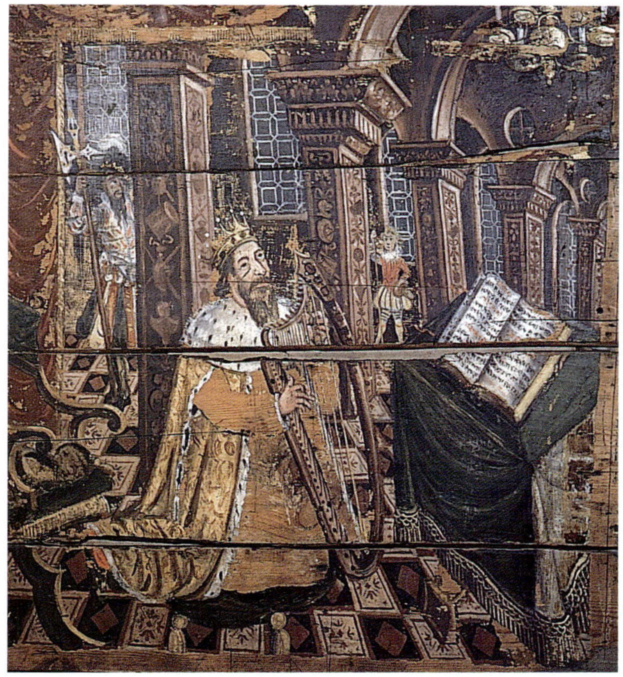

King David psalming, panel from Dean House, Edinburgh, now NMS. HS

Parable of the Good Samaritan, Kinneil House, Bo'ness. HS

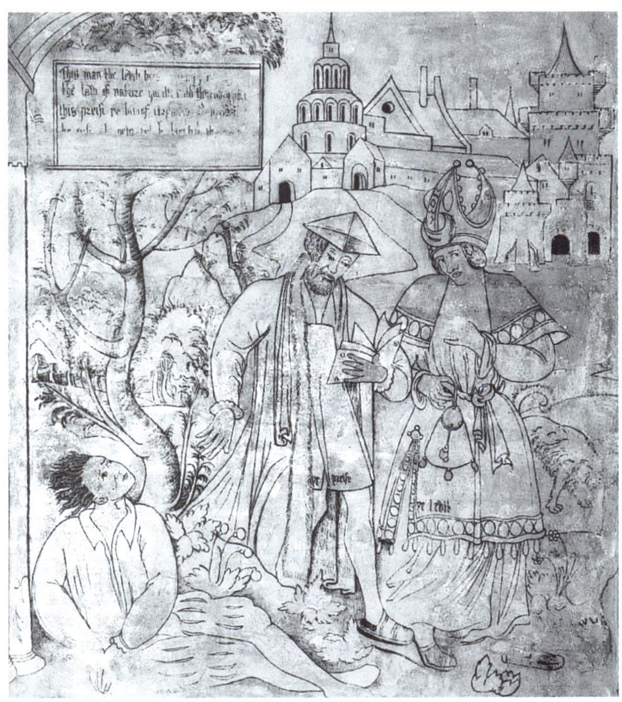

profile, boldly extending the decapitated head towards the viewer so that its hair and one ear overlap the surrounding picture frame. The inset decapitation scene takes only the merest hints from Galle's treatment in the previous print from this series.

No sources for the remaining biblical subjects from The Dean have as yet been identified, though it seems likely that they all rework such sources in similar ways. Among the remaining three panels King David playing the harp kneels in front of a lectern on which rests a book of psalms inscribed with what is evidently meant to suggest Hebrew script. The setting is a colonnaded gallery with square, decorated columns rising from a chequered floor, and what appear to be leaded window lights between them, but the proportions of the building and its perspective are very curious, not to say incompetent; two figures in Jacobean dress, one with a long beard, stand guard with pikes. Another panel shows Lot and his Daughters: on a rocky, mountainside Lot sits beside one daughter, who is in a loose gown that exposes her breasts. She points back towards the burning city of Gomorrah, where flames fill the sky; Lot points in the other direction. Beside them his second daughter lies asleep on the ground, cushioned by three white bags or bolsters; bottom right is the inscription: 'GENESIS.XIX'.

It will be clear that religious subjects were by no means restricted to religious sites. The painting at Kinneil, for instance, includes images of St Jerome in the Wilderness, Mary Magdalene and, in the so-called 'Arbour Room', Samson and Delilah, the Temptation of St Anthony, Abraham and Isaac, and David and Bathsheba. It is most notable, however, for its extended sequence of scenes illustrating the parable of the Good Samaritan. This is narrative painting in discrete episodes, suggesting that it might copy a set of prints such as Maarten van Heemskerk's series dated 1549, which is certainly early enough to serve as a source (this 'first period' painting at Kinneil is thought to date from the 1550s). However, Heemskerk's four numbered plates do not correspond to the six episodes represented at Kinneil; Heemskerk does not portray the initial scene of man falling among thieves, and he shows the two following scenes in which the Priest and Levite pass by and the Samaritan succours the wounded man as a single episode. Stylistically the painting is certainly

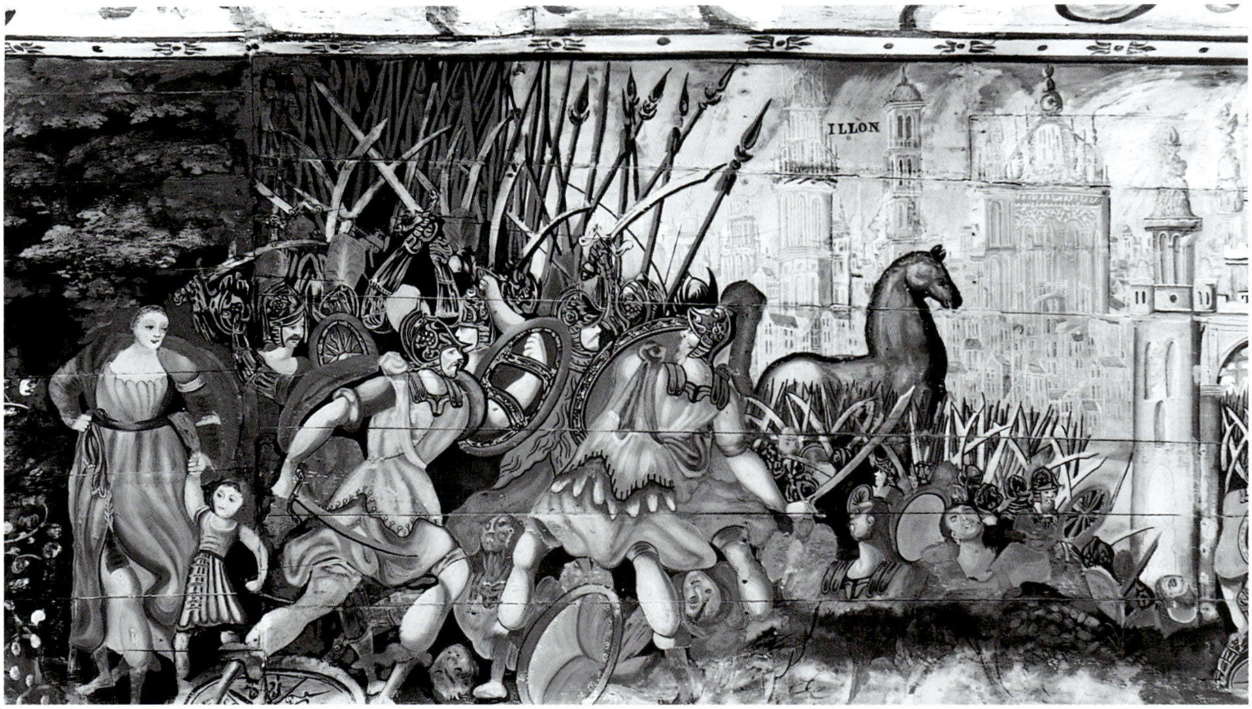

'The Siege of Troy' at Cullen House, Banffshire. HS

close to Heemskerk, particularly in its treatment of some of the background buildings, but it does not copy the engravings. It seems more than likely that the Old Testament subjects in the adjoining 'Arbour Room', which also belong to the 'first period' painting at Kinneil, copy print sources – the treatment of David spying on Bathsheba bathing, though too badly decayed to be certain, shows David on a projecting balcony of a building that resembles the engraving of this subject by Cornelis Massys (*Illustrated Bartsch*, vol. 18/1, no.7), and though the picture is reversed, the posture of Bathsheba sitting on the edge of her bath with a raised arm, and the approaching messenger with a similarly raised arm, are close enough to suggest that the Massys engraving was its source.

Such history painting in domestic buildings also includes classical subjects. One of the sloped sides to the long gallery ceiling at Cullen, for instance, shows the Sack of Troy. Drawn with considerable vigour, the city labelled 'ILION' above its multitude of towers rises behind a throng of warriors brandishing upraised swords and spears and with the Trojan Horse amongst them; to the right is a seascape with Greek ships moored, to the left a mother holding her child's hand in a wooded landscape as they flee the conflict. Further to the left there is a figure beneath a classical archway, who appears to be invoking the aid of the Gods. The painting combines in its single frame several discrete episodes from Book Two of the *Aeneid.* The female beneath the archway to the left can only be Cassandra, whom Virgil describes as 'uplifting her glowing eyes' in the temple of Minerva (II. 405), but the representation is inexact, since in Virgil she does this as she is being dragged out of the temple by the invading Greeks, and the reason she raises her eyes to heaven is that she cannot raise her hands, which have been bound by her captors. The Cullen picture evidently shows us Cassandra in the temple just before this capture, since there are no Greeks to be seen. The mother and child to the right of her amongst the bushes can only be Aeneas's wife Creüsa and their son Iulus (alias Ascanius). They appear to be fleeing the battle unassisted, whereas Virgil describes them escaping only with

Aeneas' help – Iulus should be shown holding his father's hand, whilst his mother follows after them ('*pone subit coniunx*', II. 725). Moreover, this is the passage in which Virgil describes Aeneas rescuing his family by carrying his father Anchises on his back, a subject represented in the emblems at Culross and at Pinkie House. If this is Creüsa and Iulus fleeing the city, then Aeneas ought to be fleeing with them carrying his aged father on his shoulders. Aeneas may be omitted from this part of the painting because he is meant to be identified with one of the two warriors who are fighting with upraised swords just to the right, though the identity of these two figures is in doubt since Virgil nowhere describes Aeneas as engaged in single combat; the closest he comes is when Aeneas first sallies out into the city with a group of companions and they encounter the Greek Androgeos – Virgil mentions his plumed helmet and finely decorated shield (II. 392), which may be what we can see in the painting. Whatever the accuracy of the painting in its representation of details of Virgil's description, there can be little doubt that this is offered as a synchronic representation of a sequence of events. Though it has some of the characteristics of a single landscape panorama, the shifts in the background detail – from Cassandra's temple archway, through Creüsa's flight into the wilderness of bushes, to the military turmoil in front of the towered city and the large Trojan Horse – should be read as signalling episodic shifts in the narration as much as shifts of location. This is history painting as narrative.

That may be because, for all its inaccuracies, this is painting which is illustrating a literary text. The same would be true of the facing side-panel, which shows two classical scenes. The first of these is interesting because it represents a subject which had come down to the Renaissance in one of the most famous ancient descriptions of classical paintings, the *Imagines* of Philostratus. These descriptions of the way classical artists had brought their paintings to life were models of ecphrastic description and they include an account of the Calydonian boar hunt, based on a myth from Ovid's *Metamorphoses* according to which the young man Meleager went with a band of fellow huntsmen in order to kill the monstrous wild boar which the goddess Diana had sent to ravage the land of Calydon. The relative skill or bravery of the various huntsmen in attacking the boar is described, but is outdone by that of the huntress Atalanta who surpasses them all with an arrow from her bow which strikes the boar. Both Ovid and Philostratus describe various huntsmen and their actions, which can be seen in the painting (*cf* Bracegirdle 1997). Atalanta herself is shown far left, with a female attendant, loosing her arrow; her appearance conforms quite closely to Philostratus' description:

> Atalanta – for we must recognize that the girl is she – having put to the bowstring the arrow she has ready, is about to let it fly. She wears a garment that does not reach the knee and boots fastened on her feet; her arms are bare to the shoulders for freedom of movement, and the garment is fastened there by brooches; her beauty, which is naturally of the masculine type, is made more so by the occasion, since her glance is not alluring, but she strains her eyes to observe what is going on. (Loeb edn, trans. Arthur Fairbanks, pp.358-9)

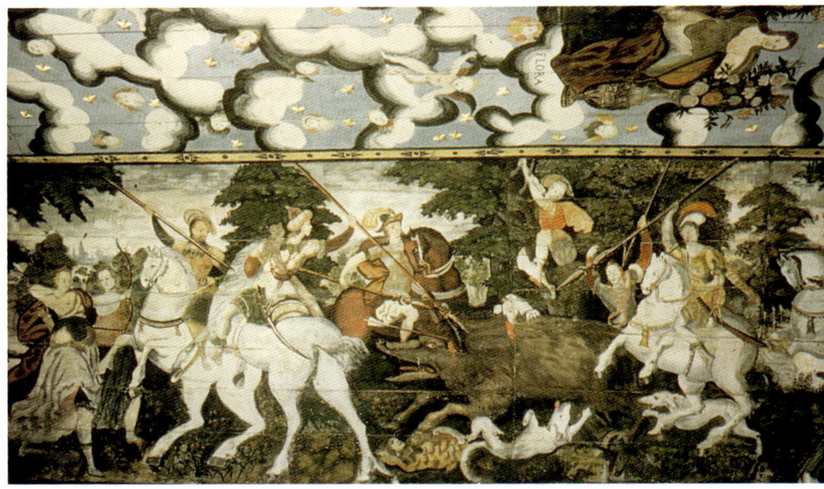

'The Calydonian Boar Hunt' at Cullen House, Banffshire. Kit Martin

As they assail it, mounted or on foot, with spears and arrows, the boar is shown trampling one of the hounds underfoot, together with a youth who lies disembowelled. Both Ovid and Philostratus identify him as Ancaeus. The man who has leaped up into a tree behind the boar is identified by Ovid as Nestor, who used his spear as a vaulting pole 'and leaped into the branches of a nearby tree, whence he looked down, from a safe height, on the foe he had escaped'. Philostratus makes no mention of this, and it follows that the iconography of the painting at Cullen must owe at least as much to Ovid's description as that of Philostratus. Meleager is shown riding a white horse, whereas Philostratus describes him as hunting on foot – indeed Philostratus spends some time describing Meleager's posture as he 'throws his weight on his left foot' to await the boar. This is not what we see in the Cullen painting, and although Ovid does not describe Meleager explicitly as mounted he says nothing that would rule this out. The two men with their spears who are shown on horseback on the other side of the boar are almost certainly Castor and Pollux as described by Ovid: 'Castor and Pollux, not yet raised to be stars in the heavens, rode up together, a striking pair on their horses whiter than snow, and both sent their javelins quivering through the air' – exactly what we see in the painting at Cullen.

In a sense it hardly matters which of the classical writers the Cullen painting follows most closely since it may be copying the received iconography of other paintings of these subjects in the Renaissance (if so, the immediate sources have yet to be identified). While it would be exciting to discover that such decorative painting had deliberately set out to realise one of the *Imagines* of Philostratus, we might bear in mind that Philostratus and Ovid were both regarded at this period as models of ecphrastic description – verbal pictures which suggested a painting even when (as with Ovid) they did not claim to be describing actual paintings. The Cullen pictures certainly represent a significant Scottish response to the pervasive *paragone* debates about the respective claims of word and image at this period. If Ovid and Philostratus are celebrated exponents of the received doctrine of *ut pictura poesis*, then we might say that Cullen's realisation of the various ecphrases of these classical authors has to be seen as a notable example of what one can only call *ut poesis pictura*. 'If Virgil can describe it, then I can paint it ....'

A very different treatment of a classical, Homeric, subject is at Monymusk, Aberdeenshire, where a window bay is painted to look like the open flaps of a tent. On one side sits Hector, on the other sits Achilles, while the heads of Greek onlookers peer over the tent flaps above them. An inscription between the two identifies the subject: 'When duryng a trewes of four monethes maist worthy & noble hector walked into the grekes host & of the talking betwyne him & ferce Achylles.' What we see represented on the Monymusk window recess is a topic that goes back to a medieval reworking of the Troy story that had been given pictorial treatment in late medieval manuscript illumination and in decorative art. Unlike the Sack of Troy, as depicted at Cullen, Hector's meeting with Achilles in his tent is an event one looks for in vain in classical authors; it goes back, rather, to the *Roman de Troie* written in the twelfth century by Benoît de Sainte Maure. This had inspired sets of late medieval tapestries on the history of the Trojan war, of which the most famous were commissioned as a present for Charles the Bold from master-weaver Pasquier Grenier, whose cartoons were also used for the 'ix peeces of clothes of Arras of th'istore of Troye' created in 1488 for Henry VII of England. This cycle lists subjects that coincide with late medieval miniature cycles illustrating various versions of Benoît's *Roman de Troie*, including the meeting of Hector and Achilles. At this meeting, according to medieval chronicles, Hector proposed during a truce that the war be decided by personal combat and in the late fifteenth-century Tournaisian tapestry the two heroes are shown inside their tent whilst Agamemnon and the Greeks look on. This is what we see in the Monymusk painting, whose iconography must go back to such earlier treatments of this subject. (This iconographic tradition is well documented in an unpublished doctoral thesis by Alison Thorne 1989, pp.157-185.)

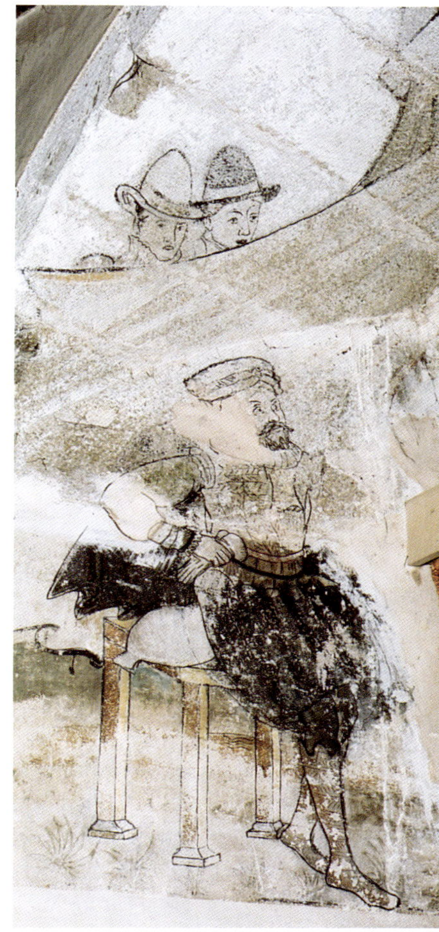

Monymusk, Aberdeenshire: Hector talks with Achilles; both in knee-breeches and with onlookers, the window bay is turned into a tent-opening. RCAHMS

Perhaps the most notable feature of this painting at Monymusk is its confident handling of pictorial space, notably its treatment of the onlookers shown peering over the tent flaps. What we see might well be regarded as a realisation of Philostratus' recommendation for the Thebes painting (I. 4, 'Menoeceus'), in which armed men would be shown 'some in full figure, others with the legs hidden, others from the waist up, then only the busts of some, heads only, helmets only, and finally just spearpoints' (Loeb edn, p.17). Monymusk certainly shows us the 'heads only, helmets only' detail. Philostratus makes his recommendation in the context of a discussion of illusionist painting, where that which is not shown stimulates the mind's eye to realise the hidden details – Philostratus's advice is that the artist should 'reveal what he obscures', that is to say reveal it by obscuring. Such an illusion might be thought to be particularly appropriate to a subject such as this because, as Philostratus points out, the illusion was greatest when the tongue created a vivid image of things which could only be seen by the eye and, conversely, when the eye created the illusion that it could see what could only be heard by the ear – the painting of the Siege of Thebes indeed includes Teresias uttering an oracle. What the Monymusk painting aims to show, and what the inscription appears to be insisting on, is the ability of a painting to represent two classical heroes who are talking. The realisation of this *paragone* topos is entirely in keeping with the notable attempt at illusionist architecture in this Monymusk painting, a painting which says: 'I am not a window-opening; I am a tent-opening' – a sort of visual pun.

These classical and biblical subjects in Scottish decorative painting represent episodes from written texts. Such history painting was the kind of thing which, in the Renaissance, was always likely to raise questions, so hotly debated by Italian *paragone* disputes, over the respective merits of poetry and painting in their ability to represent historical subjects. While it would be tendentious to suggest that Scottish decorative painting reflected any kind of serious intervention in these debates, it may well be that the choice of such subjects as 'The Calydonian Boar Hunt' at Cullen, which had been drawn into such a *paragone* context by Philostratus, or the depiction of the 'talking' between Hector and Achilles at Monymusk, reflects at least some awareness by educated Scots of these issues. Such painting should, at least, be seen as an attempt to bring to life biblical and classical subjects which were felt to have some importance in the culture of Renaissance Scotland, giving an immediate presence in the intimate surroundings of one's domestic life to images and episodes from remote biblical and classical narratives. While biblical topics were always likely to serve as reminders of doctrinal or ethical issues, classical subjects were also open to moralised readings – most clearly in contexts such as the neo-Stoic gallery at Pinkie, where they are accompanied by moralising texts that transform them into moral emblems or speaking pictures. Although it makes sense to distinguish the kind of history painting one finds at Cullen, or the biblical subjects one finds at The Dean or at Kinneil, from such overtly emblematic schemes and topics, it is quite possible that the subjects chosen always had a specific relevance to the situation, values and aspirations of the house's occupants. The whole relation of this distinctive Scottish tradition to similar decorative painting elsewhere in Europe – in France, Italy, Spain, the Netherlands, Scandinavia, and Eastern Europe, all places where Scots had close contacts – remains to be fully explored. If I have been able to show, however, what the various pictorial styles and iconographic traditions are which this painting draws on, particularly in its use of contemporary print sources and its frequently inventive rehandling of such sources, and if it is becoming a little clearer what such uses can tell us about the tastes and cultural aspirations of Scotland in the Renaissance period, then at least we may have a better groundwork for exploring some of the questions that still remain to be answered.

INVENTORY

EXAMPLES AND LOCATIONS

ABERDEENSHIRE	Beldorney House, nr. Huntly; Bishop's House, Elgin; Cairnbulg Castle, nr. Fraserburgh; Craigston Castle, nr. Turriff, Buchan; Crathes Castle, Deeside; Cullen House, Banffshire; Delgaty Castle, nr. Turriff; Druminor Castle, nr. Rhynie; Huntly Castle, Banffshire; Monymusk House; Provost Skene's House, Aberdeen; Ravenscraig Castle, nr. Peterhead; St Machar's Cathedral, Aberdeen; Tolquon Castle, nr. Old Meldrum
ANGUS	3-5 High Street, Arbroath; Auchterhouse, Forfar; Claypotts, Dundee; Craig Castle, Montrose; Gardyne's House, Dundee; Guthrie Aisle, nr. Arbroath
AYRSHIRE	Cassilis Castle, nr. Maybole; Cessnock Castle, nr. Galston; Garnock House; Newark Castle, Port Glasgow; Skelmorlie Aisle, Largs
BERWICKSHIRE	Old Bridge Tavern, Berwick on Tweed; Old Manor House ('Sparrow Castle'), Cockburnspath
DUMFRIES AND GALLOWAY	Amisfield Tower, nr. Dumfries; Lochnave Castle, nr. Stranraer
EAST LOTHIAN	Herdmanstone, nr. Haddington; Northfield House, Prestonpans; Nunraw House, Garvald; Pinkie House, Musselburgh; Prestongrange, nr. Prestonpans
EDINBURGH	Abbey Strand, Canongate; Advocates Close, 357 High Street; Blyth's Close, Castle Hill ('Mary of Guise's House'); Canongate Tolbooth; Caroline Park; Craigmillar Castle; Dean House; Edinburgh Castle; General Dalziel's House, Big Jack's Close; Gladstone's Land, Lawnmarket; Holyrood Palace; John Knox's House, 43-45 High Street; Johnstone's Close; Lawnmarket; Liberton House; Mahogany Land; Moubray House, 51 High Street; Nisbet of Dirleton's House; Old Saughton House, Corstorphine; Riddles Court, Castle Hill; Somerville's Land, Lawnmarket

FIFE	71 South Street, St Andrews; 119-23 High Street, Kirkcaldy; 225-229 High Street, Kirkcaldy; 339-43 High Street, Kirkcaldy; Abbot House, Dunfermline; Aberdour Castle; Bay Horse Inn, Dysart; Castlewynd House, St Andrews; Collairnie; Culross Palace; Dunfermline Abbey; Earlshall, Leuchars; Falkland Palace; Fisherman's Cottage, Dysart; The Giles, Pittenweem; Mary Somerville's House, Burntisland; The Merchant's House, 49 South Street, St Andrews; Queen Mary's House, St Andrews; Red Lion Inn, Culross; Rossend Castle, Burntisland; Sailor's Walk, 443-449 High Street, Kirkcaldy; Town House, Culross
INVERNESS-SHIRE	Dalcross Castle, nr. Inverness
KINCARDINE	Arbuthnott House; Balbegno, nr. Fettercairn; Inglismaldie, nr. Laurencekirk; Thornton Castle
LANARKSHIRE	Farme Castle, Rutherglen; Hamilton Palace
MIDLOTHIAN	Borthwick Castle, nr. Gorebridge; Elphinstone Castle, nr. Ormiston; 'Garden House', Polton; Monkton House, Newcraighall; Ravelston House; Roslin (Rosslyn) Castle
MORAY	Bishop's House, Elgin; Pluscarden Priory, nr. Elgin; Spynie Palace, nr. Elgin
ORKNEY	Kirkwall Palace
PERTH & KINROSS	Balmanno Castle, nr. Glenfarg; Church of St Mary, Grandtully, nr. Aberfeldy; Dunkeld Cathedral; Finlarg Chapel, nr. Killin; Foulis Easter, nr. Dundee; Huntingtower Castle, nr. Perth; Innerpeffray Chapel, nr. Crieff; Pitcairn Church; Scone Palace, nr. Perth; Stobhall, nr. Perth
SCOTTISH BORDERS	Neidpath Castle, Peebles; Old Gala House, Galashiels; Traquair, Innerleithen
STIRLING	Argyll's Lodging, Stirling; Stirling Castle; Wester Livilands
WEST LOTHIAN	Cafe Inn, Main Street, Linlithgow; Kinneil House, Bo'ness; Midhope Castle, nr. Abercorn; Robert Stewart's House, High Street, Linlithgow

ABERDEENSHIRE

Beldorney House, nr. Huntly

Built for George Gordon, who bought the land from the Earl of Huntly (d.1575) in 1545, succeeded by his son Alexander (d.1627). Traces of original painted decoration discovered in various parts of the house during modern removal of later panelling. A dozen supporting beams with a variety of patterns on sides and soffits were exposed on the first floor, though not now visible. South-east corner tower 'Priest's Room' has window recess with paint on plaster showing male figure, with flat hat and earring, playing a lute, which he plucks with his left hand. Exposed plaster on wall shows a band of decorative scrollwork on a dark ground below the fragment of a figure wearing armour, of which only the mailed leg remains. Fragment of painted decoration on the first floor shows a band of leaf scrolls on a dark ground with fragment of a robed figure above. Upper hall in the south gable has a *trompe l'oeil* pilaster with fragments of an inscription over the door-opening from the turret staircase. Wall plate on east wall of secret chamber above the hall has remains of texts, now illegible, and traces of paint on corbels; joists decorated in black and white scrollwork with fruits; fragment of original boards also decorated in black and white.

Literature
Gordon Slade 1972, 262-80.

Bishop's House, Elgin

Destroyed. Principal room on first floor described in 1914 as 'ornamented with fresco paintings, the remains of which were visible until the recent "preservation"' (Mackintosh 1914, p.29).

Cairnbulg Castle, nr. Fraserburgh

Destroyed. Tower house of the Frasers of Fraserburgh, extended around 1545 when the new wing contained a great hall, at whose east end was a private room in the new round tower, sixteen feet in diameter with four windows and a fireplace. MacGibbon and Ross report that, in 1887, 'The plaster still remaining on the walls of this room is covered in painted ornament' (vol. i, p.311).

Craigston Castle, nr. Turriff

Red stone and white harled house, built 1604-07 by John Urquhart. Painted ceiling. High-level arch joining wings supports corbelled stone balcony of carved grotesques, the soffit of the arch painted with *trompe l'oeil* corbels and ribs. Interior once covered with wall and ceiling paintings which may survive beneath later decoration; Apted (1964, p.263) records that hall ceiling has beams painted with inscriptions 'as at Delgatie', not normally visible due to plaster ceiling of later date suspended beneath it. Fragments of painted decoration, of which RCAHMS has 'conjectural reconstruction from fragments in stable' showing roses.

Literature
Apted 1966, pl. 16; McKean 1990, 63.

Crathes Castle, Deeside

L-shaped tower house with elaborate corbelling, turrets and heraldic carvings. Begun in 1553 and completed in 1596 by Sir Alexander Burnett of Leys, responsible for the painted decoration throughout the house, the most extensive programme to have survived in any building in Scotland. Burnett was one of six brothers educated, variously, to practise medicine in England; philosophy at Basle and Montaubon; and to the priesthood (a later descendant, Gilbert Burnet, became Bishop of Salisbury and author of *History of his Own Time*). Painting in several rooms was revealed in 1876 beneath later lath and plaster coverings and some restoration was carried out at that time; further 'retouching' was carried out in 1921, and in 1961 a more comprehensive restoration was undertaken involving the removal of whole ceilings for conservation treatment. This revealed some new painting in the stair chamber beneath the floor of the 'Nine Worthies Room'. The earlier restoration involved heavy overpainting with occasional guesswork; pre-restoration photographs do not appear to have been kept. Despite the prevalence of painted boards elsewhere in the building, the long gallery is, uniquely in Scotland, panelled in oak.

Owner: NTS.

Nine Worthies Room Painted figures of the nine Worthies, each labelled, on the underside of boards, between ten beams with verse inscriptions describing the legendary achievements of each. Four proverbial inscriptions in prose and verse with two verse inscriptions at either door, addressing the reader and inviting us to reflect on the heroic example of each of the Worthies, represented as full-length standing figures in elaborate armour, each holding a sword and with his identifying label and coat of arms surmounted by a crown. The end sections and blank spaces are decorated with scrollwork and grotesques. End beam bears date '1602'. The text of the beam inscriptions recorded below is based on Hargreaves (1989), who corrects some of the evident restoration errors.

Section 1 – Blue and ochre flower faces with gourds on white ground.

1a As a dog turneth to his owne vomit so the foole returneth to his owne foolishnes [Prov 26.11]

1b Blesed is the Riche, whiche is founde without blemishe
And hath not gone efter nor hoped in money & tresures [Ecclus 31.8]

Section 2 – Blue and ochre arabesques on white ground.

2a They that rejoyce at the fall of the righteus
Salbe taken in the snare & anguishe S
all consume them before they die [Ecclus 27.29]

2b Lerne gallant youthes to aternise your name
As did thir nyn with deids of endles fame
Whose martial actes nobilitates for ay
Their glourius names but deing or decay

Section 3 – 'Hector of Troy' standing above closed crown with shield or arms: per pale argent and sable two lions combatant counterchanged; grotesque animal with spread wings and tail.

3a I nyntein kings, but help of any slew
A thousand Greeks in on day I overthrew
Had not Achilles slayn me tressonablie
Troy yit had stand & lost no libertie

3b I Alexander conquest in short space,
The world & joyt this monarchie in peace,
Yet all this wealth fulfilled not my desire
Sick was my lust by mesure to Impyre

Section 4 – 'Alex^{r} the Conqueriour' standing above closed crown with a shield of arms: gules, a lion sejant or, in a chair holding a battle-axe; 'Iulius Cesar' standing above a closed crown and a double-headed eagle whose unrestored original paint casts doubt on the authenticity of the overpainted and restored details above it.

4a [...] was emperiour & wan
By armeis Africk, egipt, france & Spain
I past the rhyne & dantit Germanie
Brutus at hame syne slew me crewalie

4b Betymes I will destroy even
All the wicked of the land
that I may from Gods citie cut
The wicked workers hand

Section 5 – 'Josuae the noble Chiftan of Israell' standing above closed crown and shield or arms: lozengy gules and argent, a basilisk sable.

5a Joshuee of Jewes first wass frie
Ane & threttie kings conquerit he
And reft thame of there lands also
The floode Jordan he parted in tuo

5b This Judaes manheid all Israell maid frie
From servile yok of heathen tiranny
He Vincult Licias & Antiochus
After gryt weris slayn by Demetrius

Section 6 – 'Judas Maccabeus' standing over closed crown with shield of arms: argent two ravens sable; 'King David' holds sword and book, standing on closed crown with shield of arms: azure a harp argent.

6a For wit & manheid David was maid king
From schepirds ranke over all Israell to ring
He slew the gryt Goliath hand to hand
And did gryt damage to the heathen land

6b A league wit Scottis of mutual amitie
This Charlis maid to last eternalie
Whais successors observis the same alway
Inviolat unto this present day

Section 7 – 'Charlis the Gryt' standing over a closed crown surmounted with a cross above shield of ams; dexter or, half a double-headed eagle displayed sable, sinister azure, three fleurs de lys or.

7a This Charlis was for his Christian faith renownit,
And emperiour for deids of armis crounit
He be his micht & worthie chevalrie
Was cheif defence of Christianitie

7b King Arthur crounit was Emperiour & wan
Gryt bounds in France and all the lands of Spain
The knichts of the round table he ordained
Whais praise sall sound unto ye warldes end

Section 8 – 'King Arthur' shown in profile standing over closed crown surmounted with a cross above shield of arms: azure, three closed crowns palewise; 'Gotfrida' standing above closed crown with a cross and shield of arms: dexter, azure an escarbuncle or, sinister half an escarbuncle argent.

8a From rage of Turks this Godofried, maid frie
The holie land to Christian libertie
Gryt Soliman he slew & crounit was king
Over all the land of Jurie for to ring

8b Seaye not thy Harte on welth or earthlie gains
They perish suine but honor still remains

Section 9 – White arabesque work on red ground.

9a Gude reder tell me or thou pas
Whilk of thir nyn maist Valliant was 1602

Section 10 – White arabesque work on red ground.

10a [...] in earth has spent there deyes.

Green Lady's Room Underside of boards decorated with a row of ten full-length standing figures in exotic costumes between elaborate foliate grotesque work, scrolls and fruit swags. Undersides of beams have scrollwork in various patterns, sides of beams have on the one side biblical quotations from Proverbs (Geneva Bible), on the other side moralising verse quatrains in Scots.

1b A maidin but modistie
A clarke but courtesie
A howsewyfe langinge fairleis to see
Wants all there seimliest propertie

2a The beggining of wisdome is the feare of the Lord and the knawledge of holie things is understanding [Prov 9.10]

2b The mouthe of everie wicht
Defames that graceles man
Qua by his sloothe tynes onie richt
That his forbears wan

3a Say not to thy nightbour go & cum agayne & tomorrow will I give you if thou have it [Prov 3.28]

The curse of the Lord is in the house of the wicked but he blessed the habitatione of the righteus [Prov 3.33]

3b Praise be to him qhuoise verteus deids
Through payne and labor gr[awes]
Schame to the belliegod that feids
On sueat of others brawis

4a Thoughe the deceatfull speake favorable beleve him not for he hath seven abominations in his hart Intending hurt against his nighbour seing he doeth duell without feare by thee [Prov 26.25]

4b At vertues stoole lerne first thy grounds
Renounit if thou walde be
Insegnarie conteins all bounds
Of true nobilitie

5a The sluggard is wyser in his awen conceit then seven men that can render a reasone [Prov 26.16]

Stryve not with a man causelesle when he hath done the no harm [Prov 3.30]

5b Thryce happy is that man indeed
That weids ane vertues wyf
Sho is the blessing of his seid
And comfort of his lyff

6a The slothful hand makethe poore but the hand of the diligent maketh riche [Prov 10.4]

6b Blessed wil his house for ever be
Qua servis the lord alway.
Thais wallis his awin posteritie
Inherit sal for ay

7a The Lord will not famishe the soule of the righteous but the soule of the wicked sal be consumed [Prov 10.3]

7b Wine wemen taken insatiablie
Has brocht gryt kings to miserie
Therefor my god I pray to thie
Keep me from crimes and harlotrie

8a The tresures of wickednes profite nothing but righteousnes delyvereth from death [Prov 10.2]

8b Ane avarious mans plentie
[I]s to him selfe hydropolie
For quhy the mair in welth he flows
The thirst for riches gryter grows

9a A wise sone makethe a glad father but a foolishe sone is an heavinesse to his mother [Prov 10.1]

9b Contemne no man in miserie
Augment with spyt no poore mans sorow
For fortunes false inconstancie
May cause his case be thine tomorrow

10a As the vapour and smooke of the chimney gooth before the fyre so evil words rebukes and threatenings go before bloodscheding [Ecclus 22.24]

10b Flie sone all naughtie companie
From fools no freindship crave
Keep fellowschip with such as be
Both wittie sage and grave

11a A theif is better than a man that is accustomed to lie but they both sall have destruction to their heritage

11b [blank]

12a The goode man sall give inheritance unto his childrens children and the riches of the sinner ar layd up for the Just

12b [blank]

13a All that are proude in hart ar an abominatione to the Lord though hand joune hand he sall not go unpunished [Prov 16.5]

Muses Room Open board-and-beam ceiling, the boards decorated with full-length personifications of seven Cardinal Virtues plus Fame, and of the nine Muses in two rows, with grotesque work. Underside of beams decorated with scrollwork, sides with quatrain stanzas of Scots verse on each of the Virtues and Muses. Central compartment bears the initials 'KG' for Katherine Gordon of Lesmoir, wife of Alexander Burnett, with her heraldic achievement, confirming that this room with its host of female figures was for her use. Two beams bear date '1599'.

1b Honour & grace is the dew recompence
Of vertueus warkes done in this lyfe,
Quhilk maketh men to be haid in reverence,
And als their praise to be soundit most ryfe

2a I Fame, be my eies & wingis wondrous fair
Ane trumpet shyle through all the warlde wide
Am drawin thus my heid doth perce the air
Althocht my feit heir on the earth abyde

2b Temperence of things most doth refrain
The frailty of man as with strong bitt
Bridling ye affectis of lustis every one
Stryfing with reasone a reuler most fitt 1599

3a Fortitude is most power onto man,
A vertue recht and stillt in equitie
With curage balde doing quhat scho can
Wrong to repelle and despyse miserie

3b Wisdome is the ground of all praise & gloir
Fe of the lyff, contrar to Ignorance
Teaching quhat will speake evermore
[G]yid of all vertues quhilk men do advance

4a Justice is a vertue quhilk ane doth frame
All thingis in this lyff with ane juste ballance
Holding a suorde to execute the same
That no wrang bot right may have affiance

4b Faith is a truth and constancie of things
Spoken and promised be god or man
The gyft of god, quhilk onlie with it brings
Lyff for Christis saik to ilk Christian

5a Hop is a vertue of singular grace
Groundit on faith quhilk to the conscience
Expelling all dout brings Joy and peace
Awating still with a sure confidence

5b Charitie is a vertue principall
The chyld of faith accomplesing the law
With pitie bent to seik the weill of all
And as a nureis to babes young & raw

6a I Clio craftelie dois wryte
As eldest of thir sisters heir
Of ancient historiis I indite
And marciall featis of men of weir

6b And I dame Thalia may be sein
To loup and fling with firines
My fiddile furth shawis my yeris grein
As maistres of all mirrines

7a Melpomine man be my style
With viole to supply my versis
Of tragidies I doe compyle
As Bochas in his buke rehersis

7b Heir Tercichor take tent to me
To play on lute I have profest
All troublit myndis to molifie
Efter travel to take sum rest

8a Euterpe I am this arte did found
To play on quhissile first devysit
All melodie and plesand sound
Be me they be better prysit 1599

8b For cunning Caliope dois excell
With harp in hand ye may persave
In ballet royall I bear the bell
And prasit be poetis by the leave

9a Erato heir behalde and se
With seister set for galyardine
The law of love cum leir at me
Bot nocht veneriall palyardine

9b Urania behalde me heir
My globbe may travell testifie
I reule the planetis and the speir
As maistres of astronimie

10a Polymnia the last of nyn
My monicordis may weill expresse
Quick memorie and scharp ingyn
Abhoring still forgetfulnes

10b [blank]

11a Sum tyme be thou mirrie, & sum time be thou sad
As plaice & tyme requiris to be had
For in a wise man it is no maner of cryme
His manners to cheang[e ...]

11b [blank]

12a Ether with a mirrie hart ouircum all hevines
Or with a faithfull freind redd all cairfulnes

Stair Chamber Nine painted beams decorated with scrollwork and inscriptions, some remaining paint around frieze, but underside of boards now blank. The decoration in this room was only recently discovered, and has not therefore suffered overpainting. Much original paint has faded or come away, and remaining inscriptions are difficult to make out, though most can now be restored from the biblical texts which they take from the Geneva Bible.

1a [blank]

1b The descretione of a man defarrethe his anger [and his glorie] is to passe by an offence (Prov 19.11)

2a [blank]

2b The treasure[s of] wickednesse [profite] nothing, bot righteousnesse delivereth from death (Prov 10.2)

3a [blank]

3b Blessed is the man that hathe a verte[ous wife] for the number of his dayes [Geneva: 'yeeres'] salbe double (Ecclus 26.1)

4a A lie [is a] wicked schame in a man; yit [is] it [oft in the] mouth of the onwyse (Ecclus 20.23)

4b Give not over thy mynd to heavin[es] A[nd vex]e not thyselfe in thyn awin counsell (Ecclus 30.21)

5a He [that lov]eth pastyme salbe a poore man [and he that] loveth wyne & oyle sell not be riche (Prov 21.17)

5b My sone doe no thing without advisement s[o shall it not repent thee] efter the end (Ecclus 32.20)

6a [The yocke and] the whippe bow downe [the hard necke: s]o tame thine [evil] servant w^t^ the quhipps & correction (Ecclus 33.25)

6b He that passeth by & midleth with the [strife that belon]geth not into hym is lyk on yt taketh a dog by the eares (Prov 26.17)

7a The pryde of a man sall bring him [lowe: but th]e humble [in spirit shall] enioy glory (Prov 29.23)

7b He that hateth, will counterf[eit] w[ith his lips, but in his heart] he layeth op deceate (Prov 26.24)

8a As are the cold waters to a weary soule, so is gude newes from a farre countrie (Prov 25.25)

8b Confidence in an unfaithfull man in tym of trouble is lyke a broken toothe & a sliding foote (Prov 25.19)

9a It is [better to] duel in a corner [of] th[e] hu[se] top then [with a con]tentius [woman] in a wide [house] (Prov 25.24)

High Hall Paint on plaster, originally covering whole ceiling, of which only that on the soffits of three window alcoves has survived. The largest of these is divided into four compartments by elaborate strapwork in grey, red and green, decorated with the Burnett holly leaves, rising from ornate *trompe l'oeil* corbels with winged cherubs, and forming a central medallion containing the Burnett shield of arms with the initials 'AB'. Two smaller alcoves have circular ornamental cartouches with arms showing, firstly, the Burnett arms of three holly leaves and a horn impaled with the Gordon arms of three boars' heads and fess chequy for Janet Hamilton, wife of Alexander who commenced the building at Crathes, and secondly, the Burnett arms impaled with the Hamilton three cinquefoils for Katherine Gordon, wife of Alexander who completed the building.

Literature

Allardice 1901; Hussey 1937; Apted 1966, pl. 39, 40, 46; Scott 1971; Hargreaves 1989; Macmillan 1990, 53, pl. 38, 39.

Cullen House, Banffshire

Built in 1600 for Sir Walter Ogilvie, who became Lord Deskford in 1616 and Earl of Findlater in 1638. Painted ceiling restored in 1966, but destroyed in 1987 by fire. The room containing this ceiling, almost certainly designed as a long gallery, spanned two different parts of the building, half in the second-top floor of the main block and half in the top floor of the adjoining library wing. The room was evidently altered at a later date and the painting itself is of two different periods. The ceiling proper measures 9' x 20', and the side 'frieze' panels 8' x 20', but when being dismantled for restoration in the 1960s the lath forming the partition was found to have re-used timber with fragments of paint from the original ceiling. These boards are now in Historic Scotland Conservation Centre, and appear to include parts of a figure labelled 'Pluto', remains of an Adam and Eve, and a number of standing putti. Cordelia Oliver notes that it had been a long gallery before it became a library, described in 1780 as 'elegant and extensive, enriched with many thousand volumes, generally of the most expensive and splendid order' (Cordimer 1780, p.49).

Painted Chamber Coved ceiling with sloped sides forming a boarded frieze below central stellar ceiling showing swirls of white cloud on a blue ground scattered with winged *amorini* and appliqué gilded stars. Four classical or allegorical deities: Mercury, Neptune, Flora and Luna, each with an identifying label. Both Mercury and Luna are shown in a sun-like radiance, Luna holding the ring and crossbar of an anchor. 'Mercvrivs' rides on a cloud with his back to us, dressed in an ample red/brown cloak trimmed with ermine, holding caduceus, and a coiled object in his outstretched right. Flora sits between two vases of flowers, and 'Neptvnvs' sits in front of a fishtail, holding his trident.

End-wall pediment – Arms of Charles II with monogram 'CR2'

Opposite pediment – Royal arms of Scotland

Both coats of arms at opposite ends of the gallery are shown as if painted on framed panels behind flanking *trompe l'oeil* curtains which are being drawn back on either side.

Sloped frieze – Siege of Troy, labelled 'ILION', behind a throng of warriors with the Trojan Horse amongst them; to the right a seascape with the Argive ships moored, to the left a mother holding her child's hand in a wooded landscape as they flee the conflict; to the left of her a figure beneath a classical archway, framing the towers of Troy, appears to be invoking the aid of the gods with upraised arms.

Opposite frieze – Two classical scenes, divided by the window recess:

1 Atalanta and Meleager (left)

With their companions, traditionally Nestor, Telamon, Theseus and Ajax, the heroes whom Meleager called together to destroy the wild boar Diana had sent to lay waste the fields of Calydon. The boar is shown trampling one of their hounds underfoot as they assail it, mounted or on foot, with spears and arrows.

2 Actaeon Spying on Diana Bathing (right)

The disposition of the various parts is puzzling and they may have been repositioned when the gallery was divided by a partition wall. Parts of the original Diana and Actaeon scene remain on the frieze at the end, but other parts have been inserted into the boarding of the window recess. The end section of the frieze shows nude Diana bathing, with identifying crescent moon resting on her head, and two female attendants, one of whom, like Diana, wears a long necklace with a pendant. In the window recess one side shows two women dressed in long, loose robes standing in a wooded landscape, opposite stag-headed Actaeon standing holding a spear.

Window soffit has fragment of cloud and appliqué stars, and the end panel a monogram 'MSC'[?] in a circular frame with four fruit swags in the corners of the panel.

Literature

Hill 1953, figs 264-6; Oliver 1968; Macmillan 1990, 54, pl. 41, 42; Mackay 1995, 32; Bracegirdle 1997, 46-9.

Delgaty Castle, nr. Turriff

Five-storey tower with corbelled parapet, bartisans and crow-steps. Extended in early seventeenth century with crow-stepped wing. Two painted ceilings. 'Painted Chamber' has date '1597' on second beam, 'Inscribed Chamber' has date '1592' on one beam and '1593' in corner; end beam is signed 'JM', which may be the initials of John Melville (or Mellin) who did work in St Nicholas Kirk, Aberdeen (Apted and Hannabuss, p.64). Dates would ascribe the painting to the occupancy of Alexander Hay, ninth Earl of Errol, shortly before the rebellion of the northern earls Errol and Huntly.

Painted Chamber (18'4"x 14'2") Divided into nine compartments. Ceiling covered in lath and plaster until its discovery in 1885. Central section has arms of Alexander Hay, argent a cinquefoil azure [gules in current restoration], three inescutcheons gules with motto 'SVB IVGUM' encircled by laurel wreath, initials 'AH', and supported by two bearded nude men holding the ox-yokes to which the motto refers. To the right of this the arms of Hay impaled with those of Barbara Forbes: azure three boars' heads couped and muzzled, encircled by laurel wreath, with initials 'BF', and respective supporters of Hay (bearded male nude) and Forbes (white hound with red collar) to left and right. Combined 'AH/BF' monogram appears at centre of end panel. Inscriptions are in black-letter.

1b God resisteth the proud in everie plaice, Bot to the humill he gives his grace. Trust not therfore to ritches bewtie or strynth, As these be vaine & sall consume at length.

2a Flie covetousnes & also from prodigalitie, For nether of them agreeth with honestie. Quhen thou hes to doe with thy gryter ... eith with ....

2b Quhair that he heris or seis, quidder they be truth lawis or lies, Quhair evir he ryddis or gois he shall have few friendis & many fois.

3a Thou quhilk health of bodie do have, The best erthlie gyft, that evir god gave. Have pitie on them that suffer affliction, So sal thou enioye deathie ....

3b Gyf a gude turn into the hes bein wrocht. Remember their upon. And forget it nocht; For god, law, & natur, condamnis the Ingrate. The vilitie of that vice notang cand delat.

4a Do gude unto strangers evir be myn advice, For in so doying thy honestie sall arise; For qyhy it is a far better thyng, To have freindis, than be a king.

4b The freindis whome posyt [sic, *cf* Baldwin, 'profit'] or lucre Increase, Quhen substance fayleth their withall [Baldwin, 'therewithall'] will seas. Bot freindis that ar coupled with hart & with love, Nether feir nor force, nor fortune may remove. [*cf* Baldwin 1547, p.171]

5a Thy awin deith, and Christes passion, This fraudfull warld, and hevinlie gloir, The eternall paine, and damnation, Se thou remember evir moir.

5b Gyf thou be afflicted, be one that is riche, Ether be vexed be a man of mycht. To suffer it quietlie think it not muche, For oft be suffering, men cum to their richt.

6a Go labour in thy youth to conqueis sum rent To support the puir, the nedy and pacient Thou art more blest, to gyf, nor to take, The puir man's cause is aye put abake.

6b Quhen men be auld, they usen oft to tell, Of their dedes past, other gude or bad. Therfore in thy youth order thy self so weill, That of thy dedis to tell thou may be glade.

7a For tyme never was, nor never I thynk sall bee. That trueth on shent sall speik in all thyngs free. Ane Just man treu & leill, His saw sud be his seill.

7b Both hatred, love & their awin profit, Cause Judges oftymes the trueth to forget. Purge all these vices therfore from thy mynd. So sall ryt reule the, & thou the trueth find.

8a Weil war the man that wist in quhome that he main trust. Weil war the man that kneu the fals ... be the ....

8b God be his mercy dois preserve, His awin from temptation. And hi his judement dois reserve, The wicked to damnation. 1597

9a Abouf all thing, love God above, And as thy self, thy nybour love: So sall thou keip the teine commandis, Quilk god wryt with his awin handis.

Inscribed Chamber Beams inscribed on both sides, soffits decorated with scrollwork in various colours and designs.

1b Gyf thou wald live in rest & peace, Heir see suffer & seace, Soft wordis slakes Ire, Thole & thou sall have thy desyre. 1592 JM.

2a ... men talk in silence. Sen word is thrall & thocht is free. Kepe well thy tonge I counsele thee. 1593

2b Be war that thou engender no debait, Nor kendil no malice betwyxe thy friend & the, For wrath engendreth no thing, bot stryf & hait, And concord evir causeth love & charitie.

3a ... thou art wont to bicame, Be weill war that thou offend not in the same. For it is a very sheame, quhe[n] a man wil preache, Gif yt his dedes against his wordis do teache.

3b Forsie perrell, or it cum, For sudden chance is aye wilsum. Better it is to tary, & fortoun till abyd, Nor hastelie to climme, & suddantlie to slyde.

4a Be thou of mynd boith constant & strang, Thocht in thy cause the Judge do the wrang, For surelie thy adversarie sall not lang enioy, That qlk he winneth, be sik wickit way.

4b He is wise that is war er he be wae, He is wise that is weill, syn can hald him sae, He is wise that tholis & lattis ovir gae, He is wise that can make a ....

5a Doe no thing as thou art of power & micht, Bot let thy doyngs be of Justice & richt. Let thy Justice be indifferent, & the Judgement licht, Juge wrang to no man be power or micht.

5b Love betwyne wise men be efect may fall, Bot not betwyne foolis thought folie be equale, For wit goeth be order, & may agre in one, Bot folie laketh order so th ... ro ....

6a Loke quhat law thou doest make upon other, Be not agreved in thy self, the same to suffer: He that above the law hes micht Will borrow a litill mare then richt.

6b Those that to talk of wisdome ar bent, Not following the same, ar lyke ane Instrument Whose plesant sound the herers doth delyt, bot it self not hering hath therby no profyt.

7a I think mony matters wald cum to pas weill, Gyf first of thy self thou waldest tak counsell; Gyf thou waldest other mens counsel tak, Be sure to follow the best & evil forsak.

7b ... labour in honestie, Thy labour gois, the honor bydis with thee. Gyf thou dois ony vice also, The sheame remainis quhan pleasure is ago. 1592

8a Put hoipe in god & for no wraike take feir. For rwit of all evil is grediness of geir. Be godlie & honest, both mirrie & vertous Gyf thou wald pleas god & angir ye enuous.

8b Lose not thy soule for worldlie rent, He has eneuch that is content. Dust pleasure & warldlie vanities, Doe cause the saule all vertues to dispyse.

9a, 9b [blank]

Literature

Lyons 1910, 237-59.

Druminor Castle, nr. Rhynie

Traces of painting recorded on plaster of rooms on first and second storeys, recorded in Apted 1964.

Huntly Castle, Banffshire

Destroyed. Formerly known as the castle of Strathbogie. The *Statistical Account* (1794, vol. xi, pp.477-8) reports that most of the apartments were still 'in tolerable preservation', particularly the ceilings, which 'are ornamented with a great variety of paintings, in small divisions, containing many emblematical figures with verses, expressive of some moral sentiment, in doggerel rhyme'. Daniel Defoe reports that 'there are to be seen very ancient History-paintings on the ceiling' (*Tour of Great Britain*, 1769 edn, p.220). Cordimer, *Antiquities and Scenery of the North of Scotland* (1780, pp.9-10):

> there is a massy building of more modern date, in which some of the apartments, and in particular their curious ceilings, are still preserved pretty entire. They are painted with a great variety of subjects in small divisions; a few lines of poetry underneath each describe the subject of the piece. In these the virtues, vices, trades and pursuits of mankind are characterised by emblematical figures which though not the most elegant, are expressive. In the chamber which was appointed for a chapel or place of worship the parables and other sacred subjects are represented in the same style.

In 1617 we know that the painter John Anderson had to be summoned from Huntly to carry out work at Falkland Palace and Edinburgh Castle, where he painted the room in which James VI was born as part of the preparations for the royal visit, and it is reasonable to assume that he was occupied at Huntly in carrying out some or all of the painted decorations recorded by Cordimer.

Monymusk House

In 1554, property of Duncan Forbes. Died in 1587and was succeeded by his eldest son William, who married Margaret Douglas, daughter of the Earl of Angus. Alexander Hay of Delgaty married Margaret Forbes of Monymusk, and her initials appear on the ceiling at Delgaty Castle: arms three boars' heads, couped and muzzled. Great hall on ground floor contains extensive remains of painted decoration. Alterations to the house are recorded in 1618 when a new staircase was erected, and the decorative painting may date from this time. A photograph before restoration in the family album shows the Forbes arms to the left of the fireplace with a date which is either '1610' or '1618'. Painted plaster in a window bay interprets the window recess as a tent, in which two male full-length figures in seventeenth-century dress are shown seated on either side, whilst the faces of two onlookers on each side peer over the tent-flaps. The accompanying black-letter inscription identifies this scene as Hector talking to Achilles:

> When duryng a trewes of four monethes maist worthy
> & noble hector walked into the grekes host & of the
> talking betwyne him & ferce Achylles.

The overmantel painting is modern, but a single panel, evidently original, on the curved quoin in the corner of the room shows the arms of Margaret Forbes: azure three boars' heads muzzled and couped argent, the shield resting on and supported by three large bears, muzzled and chained, the motto 'Grace me guide', and the monogram 'DMF'. On either side of the fireplace, more Forbes arms with the monogram 'MF'. There are traces of lettering underneath parts of the modern plaster, but a patch that has been exposed is no longer legible. The exposed beams supporting the boarded ceiling are decorated on the vertical faces with a variety of decorative patterns on different beams – zig-zag bands, crouching and prancing animals, or vine scrolls – executed in light colours on a dark ground.

Owner: Private.

Provost Skene's House, Aberdeen

Painted Gallery (13'9" x 39') On second floor of west wing, exposed in 1951; coved ceiling is formed of lining boards with edges sloped under the pitched roof, supported on *trompe l'oeil* Corinthian pilasters painted on the plaster of the walls. Elaborate strapwork divides the ceiling into ten rectangular panels containing scenes from the Life of Christ, with a central circular panel now showing only clouds. Only five of the panels now retain their original painted scenes, the remaining six being blank. The surviving panels show the Annunciation, Nativity, Crucifixion and Entombment on the four sloping faces at the western end of the gallery, and the Resurrection in the central horizontal panel between them. Each of the spaces around the panels in the central section is painted with the figure of an angel, or *putto*, holding symbolic objects associated with the Passion: the pillar against which Christ was whipped; a flaming torch and a lantern by means of which the guards discovered Christ in the garden of Gethsemane; the sword with which Peter cut off the ear of Malchus; the cock symbolising Peter's denial; the purse and scattered pieces of silver which rewarded Judas's betrayal; the bowl and pitcher by means of which Pilate washed his hands; and the cross itself; all on a dark blue ground, spangled with stars. Roundel on sloping section shows the five wounds (disembodied hands, feet and heart) encircled by the crown of thorns, whilst the central roundels on either side of the Resurrection panel have the sacred monograms 'IHS' and 'XPS'. Boards in the south-west window recess are decorated with cloud shapes and stars, with the arms of Matthew Lumsden: azure two sheep's heads above a shell or within a laurel wreath. The same arms, with Lumsden's monogram, dated 1620, are on a carved stone on the outer gable of the house and they help us to date the decoration of the painted gallery to the period of Lumsden's occupancy. (The house takes its present name from Sir George Skene, Provost of Aberdeen from 1676-85, who made significant alterations to the building.) Specific sources for most of the paintings have not been identified, though the Annunciation panel must go back to one of the various New Testament prints after designs by Maarten de Vos; the engraving by Golzius has numerous similarities, including the position of the Virgin and the angel on either side of a door opening beneath sloping roof-beams, the reading desk with cabriole legs, the Virgin's turned head and hand gestures, the tablets of the law on the wall behind her, and the classical pillar to the left of the angel.

Owner: Aberdeen City Museums.

Literature

Apted 1966, pl. 31, 49, 85, 86; McRoberts 1954; Bracegirdle 1997, 44-6.

Ravenscraig Castle, nr. Peterhead

Destroyed. Fourteenth-century castle of the Keiths, now a ruin. MacGibbon and Ross (vol. iii, p.151) quote local historian William Boyd as reporting that 'an apartment still exists, constructed in the thickness of the western wall, which has been used as an oratory or small chapel, and, within my recollection, its ceiling still exhibited simple yet effective decorations in colours of red, black, and yellow'.

St Machar's Cathedral, Aberdeen

Nave Ceiling covered with oak boards. Intersections of the mouldings of the crossbeams are ornamented with forty-eight armorial shields, in three longitudinal rows of sixteen each, with raised carving, painted, with identifying labels. Executed c.1520 for Gavin Dunbar, Bishop of Aberdeen. Restored 1869-71.

Middle Row – Coats of arms of Scottish bishops, in each case showing the personal arms of the current incumbent rather than those assigned to the See, and thus allowing us to date the ceiling with some accuracy; the dates of their episcopate were recorded by P C Campbell, and are indicated in parentheses:

PONTIFICIS ROMANI	Pope Leo X
SANCTAND. ARCHIEP	Archbishop of St Andrews Andrew Foreman (1514-22) Glasguen Archiep Archbishop of Glasgow James Beaton (1509-22)
DUNKELDEN. EPISCOPI	Bishop of Dunkeld Gavin Douglas (the poet) (1516-22) Gavini Aberdonen. Bishop of Aberdeen Gavin Dunbar (1518-32)
MORAVIEN. EPISCOPI	Bishop of Moray James Hepburn (1514-24)
ROSSEN. EPI	Bishop of Ross Robert Cockburn (1507-22)
BRECHINEN. EPISCOPI	Bishop of Brechin John Hepburn
CATHENEM. EPISCOPI	Bishop of Caithness Andrew Stewart (1518-41) Candide Case Episcopi Bishop of Galloway David Arnot (1509-26) Dumblanen. Episcopi. Bishop of Dunblane James Chisholm (1496-1526) Lismoren. Episcopi. Bishop of Argyll, *alias* Lismore, David Hamilton (1504-22) Orchaden. Episcopi. Bishop of Orkney Edward Stewart (1513-152–)
SODOREN. EPISCOPI	Bishop of the Isles, unidentified arms
PRIORIS SANCIANDR	Prior of St Andrews John Hepburn
ALMAE HUJ'S UNIVERSITATIS	Arms of University of Aberdeen

South Row – Arms of Scottish royalty and nobility:

REGIE CELSITUDINENSIS	King of Scots
SANCTISSIME MARGARETE	Saint Margaret, Queen of Malcolm Canmore
ALBANIE DUCIS	John Duke of Albany
MARCHIAR. COMITIS	Earl of March
MORAVIE COMITIS RANDULPHI	Randolph Earl of Moray
DOUGLASIE COMITIS	
ANGUSIE COMITIS	
MARRIE COMITIS	Earl of Mar
SUTHERLAN. COMITIS	
CRAFURDIE COMITIS	
HUNTLIE COMITIS	
ARCHADIE COMITIS	Earl of Argyll
EROLIE COMITIS	Earl of Errol
MARISCHALLI COMITIS	Earl Marischal
BOCHTUILIE COMITIS	Earl of Bothwell
NOVAE ABERDONIE	New Aberdeen

North Row – Arms of royalty:

IMPERATORIE MAJESTATIS	Imperial eagle
FRANCORUM REGIS	
HISPANORUM REGIS	
REGIS ANGLORUM	
REGIS DANORUM	
REGIS UNGARIE	
REGIS PORTUGALIE	
REGIS ARAGONIE	
REGIS CYPRI	
REGIS NAVARRE	
REGIS SICILIE	
REGIS POLONIE	
REGIS BOHEMIE	
DUCIS BURBONIE	Charles Duke of Bourbon, Grandfather of Henry IV
DUCIS GILRIE	Duke of Gueldres
VETERIS ABERDONIE	Burgh of Old Aberdeen

Literature

Campbell 1867; McRoberts 1982; Shire 1996.

Tolquon Castle, nr. Old Meldrum

Destroyed. Built by William Forbes in 1584, extending old tower house to form a courtyard with round towers flanking the entrance. Carved figures on turrets have been compared to those at Fyvie and Balbegno, and a notable long gallery resembled those at Earlshall and Pinkie House. Fell into ruins in the late nineteenth century, but was evidently decorated with painted ceilings. John Stuart's note appended to an article on Culross in 1857 records beams covered with scriptural texts at Tolquon and elsewhere. W Douglas Simpson, in 1938, writes:

> One of the lamentable results of the delapidation that overtook Tolquhon Castle during the last century has been the disappearance of its painted ceilings. People still living remember their last mouldering traces. All that is known of them is that the joists of some of the chief rooms were covered with scripture texts.

Literature

Jervise 1854-7, 343; Simpson 1938.

ANGUS

3-5 High Street, Arbroath

Six boards decorated with black scrollwork and red fruit on a white ground, now in Historic Scotland Conservation Centre.

Auchterhouse, Forfar

The author of *Decorative Plasterwork* (Beard 1975, p.81) says that when the upper storey was refloored around 1930 the beams which carried the drawing-room ceiling showed traces of having formed part of a painted ceiling. House belonged to the Earl of Buchan in the sixteenth century, passing to James, Earl of Murray in 1619; modernised in nineteenth century.

Owner: Private.

Claypotts, Dundee

Traces of a painted dado-band on plaster of wall in first-floor solar.

Craig Castle, Montrose

Supposedly erected in 1637 by a cadet of the house of Southesk (MacGibbon and Ross, vol. iv, p.289). Portions of painted ceiling in Museum of Scotland. Surviving sections are boards, the spaces between the beams divided into roundels by ornamental scrollwork, each containing vigorously drawn images of animals, birds, grotesque heads, or ornamental lettering, in carefully shaded umber on a white ground. The confidence of the drawing and shading is exceptional. Each section is devoted to a single motif, the images reversed in an alternating sequence with variations of detail in adjacent compartments; a scheme quite unlike any other surviving example. One section shows a sequence of very lively stickle-backed pigs; another has heron-like birds; a third shows a series of dogs which bite the encircling scrollwork and embrace it with a raised foreleg – they have cloven hoofs. Another series consists of ornamental capital letters, and a separate fragment has two grotesque heads in fanciful headgear, reminiscent of the carved 'Stirling Heads' from the 'Presence Chamber' in Stirling Castle.

Dundee, various unlocated

A note in *Scottish Notes and Queries* (vol. 3, 1901-02, p.110) reports:

> During recent operations for the widening of the streets of Dundee ... many old buildings were removed in which it was discovered, when the plaster was taken down, that the joists, ceilings and in some cases the walls, had been decorated with the usual conventional festoons of fruit and flowers, and panels of scroll work.

Gardyne's House, Dundee

Destroyed. Merchant's house in Gray's Close, 70-73 High Street, a five-storey L-shaped block built 1600. Appears to have been owned in the earlier seventeenth century by a certain Patrick, son and heir of Alexander Kid; in 1657 it passed in an action raised at the Court of Appreizing to Alexander Bower, Merchant Burgess of Dundee. Painting came to light in 1886 during internal rebuilding. This was recorded in a contemporary newspaper report in the *Dundee Advertiser*, 21 February 1887, which describes how, when plaster was removed, tempera painting was revealed on the beams and boards of an unidentified room. The timbers were removed to facilitate a transcription of the texts which ran along the beams; photographs by local historian A C Lamb are now preserved in Dundee City Library. The beams were 'painted along the sides in panels with black lines, in right- or in curved angles, on a yellow ground – the field of the panels being shaded with purple ... Running or interlaced ornament of foliated description decorated the undersides of many of the beams'. The underside of the boards between the beams was 'richly painted in Jacobean panels and scrolls, with foliage, fruit, and flowers, in natural colours, but in a highly conventional manner. The most interesting part of the ceiling, however, was undoubtedly certain legends or writings painted on four of the joists nearest to the fireplace at the South end of the apartment'. These were 'in a very legible Italian letter, in some places much obliterated'. The writer of the *Dundee Advertiser* report recognised, however, that they were transcribed from Francis Quarles's *Emblemes* (1635), and he offered the following transcriptions. There is no evidence that the ceiling reproduced any part of the emblem picture upon which these verses comment or depend.

1a 'Tis but an apple, and it is as good
To do as to desire. Fruit's made for food;
I'le pull and taste and tempt my Adam too
To know the secrets of this dainty. Serp Doe.
... by this fall condemn'd us all.

Source: *Emblemes*, 1.1.55-8. The context is the conclusion of a Temptation-scene dialogue between Eve and the serpent; the last fragmentary line does not belong to this emblem.

1b Epigram. My soule if Ignorance puffe out this light
Sheell doe a favour that intends a spight
T'seems dark abroad but take this light away
Thy windows will discover break of day.

Source: *Emblemes*, 1.14, Epigram. The speaker comments on the soul's longing for spiritual illumination.

2a Lament, lament; look, look what thou hast done!
Lament the world's, lament thy own estate.
Look, look by doing how thou art undone;
Lament thy fall, lament thy change of State;
Thy faith is broken and thy freedome gone.

Source: *Emblemes*, 1.2.1-5. The context is the speaker regretting the consequences of Eve's fall, immediately following the dialogue recorded on Beam 1a.

2b Epigram. Unlucky Parliament, wherein at last
Both houses are agreed, and firmly past
An act of death confirm'd by higher powers
O had it had but such success as Ours.

Source: *Emblemes*, 1.1, Epigram. This is the epigram that concludes the Temptation dialogue recorded on Beam 1a, and its 'Parliament' refers to the dialogic mode of the emblem, though a political pun is clearly active in Quarles's wordplay.

3a No Key can lock the doore of my complaint.
Untill I smell this flower, or tast that fruit;
Go, Virgins, seek this tree, and search that bow'r.
O, how my soul shall blesse that happy houre.
That brings to me such fruit, that brings me such a flower.

Source: *Emblemes*, 5.2.41-5. The context is a meditation on Canticles 2.5, 'Stay me with flowers and comfort me with apples, for I am sick with love', in which the soul seeks spiritual refreshment, glossed from St Bernard: 'By flowers understand faith; by fruit, good works' (1635, 251).

3b Epigram. See how that fruitful kernels, being cast
Upon the earth, how thick they spring! how fast!
A full-ear'd crop and thriving, rank and proud
Prepost'rous man first sow'd and then he plou'd.

Source: *Emblemes*, 1.2, Epigram. Concluding epigram to the second emblem on the crop of sins generated out of the original sin dramatised in the opening emblem's Temptation dialogue; the opening lines to this emblem supplied the inscription on Beam 2a.

4a Epigram. Why, apples, O my soule? Can they remove
The pangs of grief or ease the flames of love?
It was that fruit which gave the first offence
That sent him hither, that removed him hence.

Source: *Emblemes*, 5.2, Epigram. Concluding epigram to the emblem whose closing *subscriptio*'s lines are quoted on Beam 3a.

Literature

Dundee Advertiser, Feb 21 1887, 2; Lamb 1895, xiv; Bath 2002.

Guthrie Aisle, nr. Arbroath

Like the Trinity painting and Crucifixion scenes at Foulis Easter, this is pre-Reformation ecclesiatical painting. Sir David Guthrie, Lord Treasurer and Lord Chief Justice to James II, obtained a royal warrant to build the castle of Guthrie, where he founded a college dedicated to the Virgin Mary and endowed for provost and three prebends, confirmed by papal bull dated 1479. Guthrie extended existing church and added the Guthrie burial aisle to the south. Paintings are first mentioned in 1790 and described in detail in 1817, when two scenes no longer visible are mentioned: a Nativity and a Flight into Egypt. Paintings form two distinct subjects on facing sides of barrel vault.

Side 1 – Judgement scene. Central figure of Christ, seated on rainbow, two swords, one on either side of his head, hands uplifted palms displayed to show wounds, feet likewise, and robe parted to reveal the wound in his side. John the Baptist below a rainbow on viewer's right, Virgin on left. On left are the walls of Heaven with angels looking over the parapet. On right the general Resurrection; demons with long claws pull damned to flaming jaws of Hell.

Side 2 – Passion scenes. Central Calvary; Longinus with spear resting on left arm; below this the Virgin, St Mary Cleophas and St John at foot of cross. Spaces on either side show, on right, part of a crucified figure, a kneeling female saint. Entombment with arcade tomb chest with recognisable traces of body of Christ; fragments below this evidently represent the Resurrection, with risen Christ stepping from tomb carrying banner of the cross, hand raised in blessing; next to this a similar figure with staff may be Christ descending into Hell. On left-hand side further scenes are now undecipherable, though they appear to include apostles and saints.

**Colours: black outline, red, yellow, umber and white. Paintings badly decayed, consisting of fifty-five boards out of a probable total of eighty-one. The aisle measures 21'6" x 14'6", and the boards were taken down during repair of the aisle in 1955. Apted and Robertson's plausible reconstructions of the complete paintings were obtained by tracing them onto polythene sheets after they had been removed and reassembling then on the floor in their original positions, and these brush drawings were then photographed (1961-2, no. 3, figs 4 and 6). Boards now displayed in Museum of Scotland.

Literature

Apted and Robertson 1964; Apted 1966, pl. 6.

AYRSHIRE

Cassilis Castle, nr. Maybole

Apted (1964, p.280) records the figure of a porter guarding the stair with an inscription behind his head.

Cessnock Castle, nr. Galston

(26' x 21') Destroyed. Dining room with open board-and-beam ceiling divided into eight sections decorated with abstract zig-zag patterns, medallions, scrollwork, or foliage in sections contained within guilloche borders; the beams were painted on all three sides with ornamental designs contained in oblong framed sections; reds and greens with black outlining.

Literature
Lyons 1904, 168; Lyons 1910, figs 6-7.

Garnock House

Nine boards decorated with flowers and fruit on a white ground, now conserved in Historic Scotland Conservation Centre.

Newark Castle, Port Glasgow

Fifteenth-century tower with important Renaissance extension added by Patrick Maxwell c.1597. Seven painted beams of first-floor ceiling in room of the east wing immediately adjoining the old tower house were revealed in 1941, the soffits decorated with trailing tassel, and the sides with *trompe l'oeil* square studs and arabesques in rectangular compartments; five beams in the adjacent ante-chamber are decorated with studs and compartments holding arabesque designs on all three sides.

Skelmorlie Aisle, Largs

Tempera painting executed in 1638 after the 1636 funerary aisle was added to the old church of Largs by Sir Robert Montgomery of Skelmorlie to house the remains of his wife, Lady Margaret Douglas. The aisle was preserved when the adjoining church was demolished in 1802 and the decorative painting was restored in 1899 and again in 1932. Dominated by the arched marble tomb based on those built in Westminster Abbey between 1605 and 1613 to commemorate Mary, Queen of Scots and Queen Elizabeth I (White 1989, pp.22-31).
Owner: Historic Scotland.

Aisle Barrel-vaulted ceiling (29' x 24') rising from a moulded string-course, consisting of painted boards built in three sections, the vertical jointing of the sections covered with a three-inch canvas strip nailed and glued to the boarding. The surface is divided by false vaulting and rib-work into forty-one panels, rising from fourteen *trompe l'oeil* corbels.

Corbel decoration – Ten of the corbels are marked with the traditional signs of the tribes of Israel: Reuben (three bars wavy vert), Simeon (two-edged sword), Levi (open book), Judah (lion rampant), Dan (serpent erect, torqued), Asher (covered cup), Issacher (ass), Zebulum (ship in full sail), Joseph (bull statant), Benjamin (wolf passant).

Compartment decoration – Compartments between corbels contain twelve texts, all but one quoted from the Geneva Bible, contained in ornamental cartouches.

1 Blessed are they that mourne for they shall be comforted. Matt 5.4

2 But the day of the Lord will come as a thiefe in the night in the which the heavens shall pass away with a noise. 2 Peter 3.10

3 He that hideth his sinns shal not prosper; but he that confesseth and forsaketh them shal have mercie. Prov 28.13

4 Be thou faithfull unto the death, and I shall give thee the crown of life. Rev 2.10

5 Trust in the Lord for euer; for in the Lord God is strength for euer more. Isai 26.4

6 Blessed are the children that inlargeth the kingdom of heauen and cursed are the children that inlargeth the kingdom of hell. [not biblical]

7 The first man Adam was made a liuing Soule; and the last Adam was made a quickning spirit. 1 Corin 15.45

8 Precious in the sight of the Lord is the death of his saints. Ps 116.15

9 I am sure that my redeemer liueth, and he shall stand last on the earth. Job 19.25

10 Take heed to thy foot; when thov entrest into the hoyse of God & be more neere to heere then to giue the sacrifice of fooles. Eccle 4.17

11 Come unto mee all yee that are weary and laden; and I will ease you. Matt 11.28

12 I am God (Almighty). Walk before mee and be thow upright. Gen 17.1

Three compartments each side enclosed by false vaulting contain landscape paintings, the outer four showing the labours of the seasons, two central compartments female figures in landscape (for descriptions see Chapter 6):

Seasons – Spring, labelled 'Ver'; Summer, labelled 'Aestas'; Autumn, labelled 'Autumnus'; Winter, labelled 'Hyems' and based on the 'Hiems' print by Maarten de Vos from his *Four Seasons* (Hollstein vol. xlvi, p.1411).

West wall – Kneeling woman in a seaside landscape holding a cup which contains a burning heart.

East wall – Standing woman watching a prancing unbridled horse with flowing mane and tail, copied from a print by Golzius, c.1579, 'Equus Liber et Incompositus' from the series *The Royal Stable of Don John of Austria* (Illust. Bartsch, vol. iii, p.292). On a white label the artist's signature: 'J Stalker fecit 1638'.

Spandrels – Six on each side of the vaulting contain the twelve signs of the zodiac, each with its conventional monogram or cipher. The groins are marked with ornamental shields bearing the monogram of Montgomery and his wife.

Centre panels – Two biblical subjects: Adam and Eve, and Esau and Jacob. They copy decorative engravings c.1570 by Etienne Delaune.

Two full panels –

1 Personification of Justice

Motto:

> *Cuique suum iusto pensans libramine reddo*
> *Concilioque homines concilioque Deos*

2 Fortitude

Motto:

> *Fortis in adversis animosaque pectora gestans*
> *Infractis animis ardua queque fero.*

North half-panels – Two at the end of the central section. They repeat the biblical subjects, just as they appear in the central panel: Esau and Jacob on the west side; Adam and Eve on the east.

South half-panels – Two more at the opposite end of the aisle, showing a lion rampant on one side and a hand holding an upraised sword on the other; each half-panel has an inscription beneath which together form the verse couplet:

> FOR WARRE OR WORKE; WE
> THIS HAND SHOVLD ARME.
> THAT TO DEFENDE OUR
> COUNTRIE DEARE FROM HARME

This quotes the last two lines of Whitney's epigram to the emblem *In utrumque paratus* (*Emblemes* 1586, p.66) which these panels are adapting (Adams 1999, pp.47-8).

Heraldic compartments – Three, highest up on the ceiling, depict the arms of the Montgomeries and of families related to them; the central and northern compartment bears the arms of Sir Robert and his wife (ie the two houses of Drumlanrig and Eglinton), complete with helmet, crest, mantling, the motto 'Garde bien', and a label beneath: 'Sir Robert Montgomerie/ Dame Margaret Douglas', with the date '1638'; between the label and the shield are two hourglasses with wings. The same heraldic achievement fills the compartment at the northern end, but the southern compartment shows the four coats of arms of the houses of Drumlanrig, Lochinvar, Eglinton and Sempil.

Literature

Dobie 1889; Lyons, *PSAS*, **35**, 1900-01, 109-11; Hay 1957, 226-7; Apted 1966, pl. 22-4; White 1989; Thomson 1990, 58, fig. 47; Wells-Cole 1997, 40-1, 47; Adams 1999, 42-9.

BERWICKSHIRE

Old Bridge Tavern, Berwick on Tweed

Mural painting on plaster above fireplace was conserved during demolition in 1963 and is now on view in Berwick Museum. Painted in white on a black ground, it shows eight or more Corinthian pilasters supporting a narrow crenellated cornice above and to either side of the fireplace. The spaces between the pilasters are filled with well-drawn foliate arabesques, some with small human figures, the space above being filled with similar decoration including full-length, winged, angel-like figures and small putti, surrounding two oblong panels containing inscriptions, only one of which is legible:

> wysedome & science, which are pure by kynde,
> shulde not be wryt in bookes, but in mynde

Old Manor House ('Sparrow Castle'), Cockburnspath

Two seventeenth-century houses, one abutting the other at an angle. Painted first-floor ceiling on south-east side of the building partly exposed in 1987; the uncovered portion revealed five sections of painted boards between beams; the first with a ribbon motif and a double-headed devil; the second showing a head in an aureole with a sword behind it; the third with a head, ribbon motif, crossed trumpets and fruit; the fourth and fifth with leaf scrolls.

Owner: Private.

DUMFRIES AND GALLOWAY

Amisfield Tower, nr. Dumfries

Traces of painted frieze in hall.

Lochnave Castle, nr. Stranraer

Apted 1964 records painted beams on first and second floors of the original tower and on ground floor of the adjacent extension.

EAST LOTHIAN

Herdmanstone, nr. Haddington

Nine painted boards displayed in Museum of Scotland show three sections between beams, each decorated with the same repeated decorative pattern of a spray of flowers in brown and green framed within a running green-ribbon ornament on a white ground.

Literature
PSAS, 90, 1956-7, 262.

Northfield House, Prestonpans

Decorative painting almost certainly executed for Joseph Marjoribanks, Edinburgh merchant, who bought the house in 1607, added the west wing and carved the inscription 'EXCEP THE LORD BVLD IN WANE BVLDS MAN' over the doorway with the date '1611', his initials and those of his wife, Marion Simpson. Painting revealed in 1950s when the owner, architect Schomberg Scott, removed later plasterwork to reveal a number of painted ceilings and boarded partitions.

First Floor –

Great Hall Partitioned around 1720 to form the present two rooms, has open board-and-beam ceiling. Underside of boards painted with repeated flowers, foliage and swags of fruit – gourds and grapes – in blue, brown and red on a black ground. Beam sides divided into framed sections with white arabesque leaf scrolls on alternating red, blue and black grounds. Soffits of beams painted with recurrent trailing tassel motif.

North Bedroom In new west wing beyond the hall. Section of timber wall divided into compartments by the exposed frame and decorated with bold sweeps of leaves and flowers, blue and brown on a white ground; running hound in upper compartment has been claimed to copy Gesner's Scottish water hound (Apted 1966, p.75); compartment below this shows a standing cock and those to the left show what looks like the rear leg and brush of a fox and the rear leg of a deer; the remainder of these compartments is boarded over and unexamined. Board-and-beam ceiling shows scrolled leaf forms, blue and brown on a white ground, and beams show a repeated tassel motif on all three sides.

South Bedroom In the same wing, board-and-beam ceiling decorated with fruits and flowers not unlike those in the great hall, though linked together by a scrolled stem; these compartments alternate with those in which gourds and stylised leaf forms with flowers and several small birds make up a symmetrical pattern. Brown, blue, green on a white ground; each compartment framed with a running guilloche pattern in red on a yellow ground. Soffits of beams show tassellated design and sides of beams show white unframed arabesque motifs on alternating blue or brown ground. The inside of a modern recess with no access, now holding a water-tank, has one boarded inner wall, originally part of this bedroom, decorated with a large strapwork cartouche containing an inscription, badly effaced by gouge marks to secure later plastering and not now fully legible, but transcribed by Forman (1961, p.26):

> Fear thy bed when thou lyest doune
> Thy bed presents the grave
> Remember Christ that thou dost ryse
> Thy soule from Hell to save.

Second Floor –

Gallery In the west wing. On removal of later boarding, a *trompe l'oeil* archway was revealed that interprets the corner of the room as a false ornamental arch with lion's mask keystone supported on square pilasters, and flanked on each side with Corinthian columns supporting the frieze, which is decorated with laurel leaves and flowers between guilloche borders. There is reason to believe that this archway is just one of a series of arcading that runs right round the room, though none of the rest has been exposed; Schomberg Scott (in an unpublished typescript) records that a tradition exists that the boarded ceiling was also originally painted, though the boards were removed when the ceiling was plastered in the early nineteenth century.

Literature
Forman 1961; Apted 1966, pl. 35-7, 73; Mackay, ed. 1978, 40-7; Macmillan 1990, 53, pl. 37; Mackay 1995, 41.

Nunraw House ('Whitecastle'), Garvald

Belonged before the Reformation to Haddington Nunnery, but was transferred by Elizabeth Hepburn, its last prioress, to John Hepburn. Estate passed in 1563 to his son Patrick, knighted 1574, and in 1583 to Patrick Hepburn II, who married Helen Cockburn. Initials 'PCH' on painted ceiling are theirs. Passed to his son, John, in 1617. Detail in middle of Section 7, which shows lion and unicorn as supporters to a thistle beneath a royal crown, indicates a date for the ceiling later than the Union of the Crowns in 1603. Building extensively altered and modernised in nineteenth century. Painting exposed in 1864 on removal of lath-and-plaster below it. House is now part of Cistercian Sancta Maria Abbey.

First Floor –

Sitting Room Painted ceiling with ten compartments between open beams, now measuring 20'3" x 17'6"; two sections removed during former alterations are now conserved in National Museums of Scotland. Each section is decorated with eight or nine separate motifs comprising, typically: (a) an armorial shield; (b) two confronting winged putti; (c), (d) and (e) animals, musical instruments or grotesques; (f) an armorial shield; (g) two confronting winged putti; (h) animals, fruit swags, or ornamental drapery. The motifs are outlined in black on a white ground, with infilling in red, green or blue. The spacing of the various types of motif in each section is irregular and they are not divided by borders into separate compartments, but the armorial and other sequences run in rows across the beam divisions and not between the beams. Each armorial device has an identifying label in a scroll above the shield. The supporting beams are painted with coloured bands interlacing each other at five or six points in differing ways on different beams, to divide all three faces of the beam into several oblong compartments bearing decorated centres in black or white on yellow or red grounds on alternate beams. Style and subject matter are close to the ceiling from Rossend; both use emblems from Paradin, *Devises heroïques* (1551) which had been reprinted in London, 1591, along with the *Heroical Devises* of Gabriel Simeoni. Since Section 7 uses the device of the wounded stag from Simeoni, the source references below are to the 1591 edition (London: William Kearney, repr. facsimile Toronto, *Index Emblematicus*, 1993, vol. 2). Rossend also drew on such a composite Paradin/Simeoni edition. The use of a cycle of labelled coats of arms of the European monarchies invites comparison with Earlshall and may well be indebted to armorial manuscripts of herald painters such as James Workman. A nineteenth-century colour sketch of the ceiling is preserved amongst the Bonnar drawings, RCAHMS: ELD/82/5.

Section 1 –
arms of King of Cyprus
two snakes intertwined in olive branch
device of Marguerite de France [Paradin, 291: *Rerum sapietia custos*]
goat with long curved horns bound by ribbon
crocodile
arms of King of Friesland [Frisia]
medallion head of crowned bearded man

Section 2 –
arms of King of Tole [Toledo]
two winged cherubs
pelican-in-her-piety
two grotesque confronting monsters shown as seated winged quadrupeds with human faces
seated fox facing vigilant crane
arms of King of Garnatye [Granada]
two winged cherubs
swag of fruits above grotesque animal heads

Section 3 –
arms of King of Hungary
two winged cherubs
bow and quiver of arrows behind cartouche containing monogram 'PCH' [Patrick Hepburn and Helen Cockburn]
vase of flowers resting on head of winged cherub with crossed hands
two confronting vigilant cranes each side of two entwined tails
arms of King of Cicilia
two winged cherubs
peacock displaying

Section 4 –
arms of King of Bewme [Bohemia]
two winged cherubs
knotted ribbon
'GRATVS EST' in scroll
a group of wind instruments
arms of King of Suadin [Sweden]
two winged cherubs
fruit and foliage

Section 5 –
arms of King of Naples
two winged cherubs
banner on pole with lion passant beside two crossed muskets
two crossed sabres
elephant and castle
arms of King of Naver [Navarre]
two winged cherubs
cock standing on trumpet [device copied from Paradin, *Pacis & armorum vigiles*, p.267]

Section 6 –
arms of King of Castille
two winged cherubs
two birds standing confronted on mound with heads turned back
bird perched between tied-back curtains
bird of prey eating fish
arms of King of Aragone
two winged cherubs
duck-like bird standing with object in its beak

Section 7 –
arms of King of Poland
two winged cherubs
bird of prey stands on rabbit
lion and unicorn supporting thistle
arms of King of Portingall
two winged cherub
seated stag pierced by arrrow with a medicinal herb (ditanny) in its mouth [*cf* Simeoni, *Esto tiene su remedio, y non yo*, p.354]

Section 8 –
arms of King of Spain
two winged cherubs
hand holding knot of ribbons from which is suspended a curved trumpet draped with banner showing an ox skull
arms of King of Denmark
two winged cherubs
seated dog confronting seated ape.

Section 9 –
arms of King of Scotland
two winged cherubs
foliage transformed into grotesque heads

lion sejant affronté holding sword and sceptre
arms of King of England
two winged cherubs
salamander in flames, device of François I [*cf* Paradin p.16]
stylised foliage ending in two grotesque heads

Section 10 –
arms of Emperor of Rome
two winged cherubs
ornate strapwork
two crossed muskets
pair of mailed gauntlets
arms of King of France
two winged cherubs
stylised foliage with grotesque heads
dove-like bird on perch

Literature
Lyons 1904; Apted 1966, pl. 55, 56.

Pinkie House, Musselburgh

L-plan tower house, belonging before the Reformation to the monks of Dunfermline. Became the property of Alexander Seton (1555?-1622), who had already built Fyvie Castle in Aberdeenshire, and was created Chancellor of Scotland in 1604 and Earl of Dunfermline in 1605. Following his third marriage to Margaret Hay in 1607, Seton added a regular, three-storey east range. Remains of painted decoration have been preserved, or are recorded, in various parts of the new range, which is also notable for important decorative plaster ceilings, several of which include Seton's monogram or his personal device.

Owner: Loretto School.

Long Gallery Boarded, coved ceiling (78' x 19', exclusive of the oriel), entirely covered with polychrome tempera decoration. Illusionist vaulting rises from decorated corbels immediately above the frieze to form sixteen pointed arches with circular lunettes in the spandrels. Each arch contains a picture panel, shown as if framed and suspended from a ring and a nail. The two panels at each end of the gallery contain Latin inscriptions whereas the panels in the twelve central arches contain emblems consisting of a picture with Latin *inscriptio* in a scroll at the top. A *trompe l'oeil* lunette at the foot of each arch contains a further Latin text, evidently functioning as a *subscriptio* to the emblem. At the centre of the ceiling is a remarkable *trompe l'oeil* octagonal lantern rising on columns in three tiers to a pierced dome, copied from a diagram in Vredeman de Vries's *Perspectiva* (1605); added details are the winged putti playing musical instruments who peer over the base, and the apex of the dome carrying the arms of Seton with coronet, horses-at-liberty as supporters and the initials 'AED' (Alexander, Earl of Dunfermline) on a label. The lantern is contained within a sixteen-foot square centre panel divided into eight compartments, of which the corner compartments contain four more emblem *picturae* in oval cartouches each with its *subscriptio* in a scroll; the four remaining compartments all contain Latin inscriptions in rectangular cartouches. The square central panel containing the lantern is enclosed in a border of floriated rib-work containing eight smaller oblong cartouches with Latin inscriptions; the same rib is carried along the centre of the soffit on either side of the central panel for the whole length of the ceiling to enclose two circular *trompe l'oeil* cupolae at either end of the gallery. The rib is decorated with arabesque work consisting of a variety of foliate scrolls terminating in grotesque heads and with eight armorial devices at various points. Thomas Bonnar's four sketches of the gallery decoration as it appeared in the mid-nineteenth century are preserved in RCAHMS. The boarded soffit above the oriel window at the south end of the ceiling contains one further emblem consisting of the picture of a vigilant crane in a landscape, with a Greek *inscriptio* on a scroll, and similar Greek *subscriptio* on a second scroll beneath the strapwork cartouche; the decorated frame displays Seton's device of cinquefoil and crescent, and the monogram 'ASMH' for Alexander Seton and Margaret Hay. Eight of the emblems can be shown to copy Otto van Veen, *Emblemata Horatiana* (Antwerp, 1607), and a further three copy Denis de Lebey de Batilly, *Emblemata* (Frankfurt, 1596). In the central panel beneath the lantern are four emblems consisting of pictures in oval strapwork cartouches, each with a motto on a scroll.

Emblems from central panel –

1 NESCIO AN ANTICYRAM RATIO ILLIS DESTINET OMNEM
('I know not whether reason should not consign all Anticyra to such men')

A man lies amongst barrels, eating. The emblem copies van Veen (1607, p.131), *Avarus quaesitis frui non audet*, though it does not use van Veen's motto and substitutes part of the Latin text which was inscribed on a scroll held by the physician in van Veen's emblem *Quo plus sunt potae, plus sitiuntur aquae* (p.111), an emblem used elsewhere on the Pinkie ceiling (no. 28).

2 A TENERIS ADSUESCE LABORI
('Accustom yourself to hard work from your earliest years')

The athlete Milo is shown twice, as a young man and as an adult, at both stages carrying an ox on his shoulders, in front of a house. Emblem copies Lebey de Batilly (1596, no. 38), *Adeo in teneris assuescire multum est*, which identifies its subject as the athlete Milo, who carried a calf in his youth so that he would be strong enough to lift an ox when he grew up.

3 SERVIAT AETERNUM QUI PARVO NESCIAT UTI
('May he be a slave forever, who does not know how to make do with little')

A white stag with golden antlers and a gold collar inscribed with the word 'LIBERTAS'. No printed source has been identified for this emblem, though the motto quotes Horace, *Epist* I.10.41, in which Horace cites the Aesopic fable of the stag and the horse who both shared a common pasture – the horse sought human aid to oust the stag, but found that the man bridled and saddled it for his own purposes; it thus sacrificed its liberty for the sake of increased wealth.

4 STAT CUNCTIS IMMOTA MINIS
('It stands unmoved by every threat')

A rock rises out of the sea, where it is blown by the four winds shown as disembodied heads. Commonplace emblem (*cf* Whitney 1586, p.96), but not used elsewhere with this motto, which quotes Statius, *Theb* 9.91.

Inscriptions from central panel –

1 NATURA NECESSARIA DOCUIT QUAE SUNT PAUCA ET PARABILIA STULTITIA SUPERFLUA EXCOGITAVIT QUAE INNUMERA ET DIFFICILIA
('Nature has taught us what things are necessary, which are both few and easily attained; folly has devised superfluities, which are countless and difficult to be acquired')

2 IN MAGNA FORTUNA UT ADMODUM DIFFICILE SIC ADMODUM PULCHRUM EST SEIPSUM CONTINERE
('As it is very difficult, in times of great prosperity, to show moderation, so it is very fine')

3 AD LAETA ET ASPERA PARITER NATI SUMUS NISI PARI UTRAQUE ANIMO EXCIPIAMUS INUTILES SUMUS
('We were born for joy and sorrow alike, and if we do not accept both in the same spirit we are worthless')

4 VIS PHYLOCLAEA DIVITEM REDDERE NON ADJICIENDUM PECUNIAE SED DETRAHENDUM CUPIDITATIBUS
('It is a Phyloclean violence to take away a rich man's wealth without removing his desires')

Alludes to Philocles, who ordered his Athenian countrymen to cut off the right hand of their captives in the Peloponnesian war.

There are eight further inscriptions in the rib-work border to the central section, of which only five remain legible.

Inscriptions from central border –

1 VIR BONUM NON ORDO SED MORES PRAESTANT
('Conduct, not status, shows the good man')

2 HOMINEM SE ESSE NON MEMINIT QUI INJURIARUM NON OBLIVISCITUR
('He who does not forget his injuries does not remember that he is a man')

3 UTILE EST AD USUM SECUNDORUM PER ADVERSA VENISSE
('It is valuable to have come into good fortune through adversity')

4 AEQUORA VENTIS TURBANTUR POPULUM ORATORES MOVENT
('The seas are agitated by the winds, orators sway the people')

5 CULPA EST MARITI SI UXOR EXCEDIT MODUM
('It is the husband's fault if his wife exceeds his income')

6 NEC TENERITAS O ... N ... ENTI .... [damaged]

7 R ... S PRA ... QESQU .... [damaged]

8 [damaged]

Emblems from northern panels –

1 FORTUNA NON MUTAT GENUS
('Fortune cannot change one's race')

Goddess Fortuna, with her conventional attributes of sail and rudder, stands beside an ape which is wearing a crown and holding a sceptre.

Subscriptio:

BONA MENS OMNIBUS PATET OMNES AD HOC NOBILES SUMUS
('A good mind is available to everyone, to that extent we are all noble')

Picture and motto both copy van Veen (1607, p.154), but the *subscriptio* is taken from Seneca, *Epist Moral* 44.2.

2 QUI SAPIT INNUMERIS MORIBUS APTUS ERIT
('He who is wise will adapt to countless fashions')

Diogenes in his tub argues with the sage Aristippus, whose robe is plucked by Alexander the Great.

Subscriptio:

VITA NOSTRA TEMPERANDA INTER BONOS MORES ET PUBLICOS
('Our life must steer between good customs and those that are generally accepted')

Picture copies van Veen (p.150), *In quocunque vitae genere philosophari licet*, but the motto is drawn from the additional adages quoted by van Veen, and goes back to Ovid, *Ars amat* 1.760. No source has been identified for the *subscriptio*. The emblem is based on Horace, *Epist* 1.17, in which Diogenes the Cynic claims that Epicurian Aristippus would abandon the tables of princes if only he could survive on herbs, to which Aristippus replies that Diogenes would come out of his tub if he really understood courtly life.

3 SAT PATRIAE PRIAMOQUE DATUM
('Enough has been rendered to our country and to Priam')

Aeneas in plate-armour carries his father Anchises away from the burning city of Troy; his son Ascanius clings to his coat tails.

Subscriptio:

CUIQUE SUUM REPENDIT POSTERITAS DECUS
('Posterity renders to every man the honour due to him')

A well-known emblem which goes back to Alciato's *Pietas filiorum in parentes*, also used at Culross. The picture at Pinkie is not a copy of any of the illustrations to this emblem in the various editions of Alciato, which do not show the child Ascanius and have an opposite orientation, though the treatment of some of the architectural details, in particular the curious triangular building in the foreground, look like a free interpretation of the ruined archway in the Lyons: Rouille/Bonhomme Alciato editions. The Pinkie motto, which quotes Virgil, *Aen* 2.291, is not known to be associated with this emblem in any printed emblem book.

4 NIL EGO CONTULERIM JUCUNDO SANUS AMICO

('In my saner moments, I know there's nothing better than a good friend')

In a city street a bearded man leads his friend, whose ear he is earnestly filling with good advice, away from a table on which are placed various objects and coins; the tradesman and his wife, whose table it is, look on disconsolately.

Subscriptio:

NEMO REGERE POTEST NISI QUI ET REGI

('No-one can govern unless he can also be governed')

Emblem copies van Veen (p.136), based on Horace, *Sat* 1.5.44, where the poet is glad to meet familiar friends whilst in a strange country; van Veen's picture, however, is based on a text from Ecclesiasticus, 29.13, which urges us to sacrifice wealth for friendship.

5 FIRMA AMICITIA

('Friendship is firm')

In a landscape with a river and a walled city a young man, Zethus, in red with a hat and carrying a spear holds a number of hounds on leashes; he leads by the hand his brother Amphion wearing a laurel wreath who is turning to throw a harp and sheet music down on the ground.

Subscriptio:

BENE FERRE MAGNAM DISCE FORTUNAM

('Learn to bear great fortune well')

The emblem copies van Veen (p.142), *Idem ferre atque idem nolle, ea demum firma amicitia est* ('To like and dislike the same things, that indeed is firm friendship'; Sallust, *Bellum Cat* 20.4), which shows us friendship in the guise of Zethus who loved hunting, and his twin brother Amphion who loved music. The emblem is based on Horace, *Epist* 1.18, who recalls that Amphion abandoned his harp in order to humour his brother and retain his friendship.

6 QUAM BENE CONVENIUNT

('How well they go together')

Landscape in which a lion stands with a snake encircling its neck.

Subscriptio:

VIS EXPERS CONSILII MOLE RUIT SUA

('Power without guidance falls by its own weight')

Based on an *impresa* found in Ruscelli (*Imprese Illustri*, Venice, 1566, p.401) and elsewhere, where the lion signifies strength and the snake prudence; their combination is an emblem of good government. The picture does not copy any known engraving for this emblem, however, and the motto appears to be original.

Inscriptions from northern panels –

1 VIR BONUS PATRIAM AMAT NON QUIA DIVES AUT OPULENTIA SED QUIA SUA SIC ULYSSES AD ITHACAE SAXA NON MINORI STUDIO CONTENDIT QUAM AGAMEMNON AD MYCENARUM MUROS

('A good man loves his country not because it is rich or opulent but because it is his own. Thus Ulysses hurried back to the rocks of Ithaca no less keenly than Agamemnon to the noble walls of Mycenae')

2 CURANDUM MAGIS UT LAETE QUAM UT LATE HABITEMUS SAEPE IN PALATIIS LABOR ET DOLOR IN TUGURIES QUIES ET GAUDIUM HABITANT

('We should care more about living in happy homes than in large houses; labour and sorrow often dwell in palaces, peace and joy in cottages')

Emblems from southern panels –

1 NYMPHARUMQUE LEVES CUM SATIRIS ME SECERNUNT POPULO

('The dancing nymphs and satyrs separate me from ordinary people')

A group of dancing nymphs, one waving a timbrel, are shown with a satyr and two other figures, at the foot of a classical circular tower-shaped temple, on the steps of which other figures are sitting or standing, and a naked baby lies on a pile of bedding; within the arched doorway of the tower sits a figure dressed in red.

Subscriptio:

DIGNUM LAUDE VIRUM MUSA VETAT MORI

('The muse forbids that the man worthy of praise should die')

Unsourced emblem, of which the picture poses numerous puzzles, though the motto is drawn from Horace, *Od* 1.1.32, where the poet rejoices in his ability to consort with the gods in rural retirement, and the *subscriptio* is also from Horace, *Od* 4.8.28, on the fame which poets bestow on praiseworthy people.

2 PAX OPTIMA RERUM

('Peace is the best of things')

Seated king Cecrops, founder of Athens, makes a crucial choice between Poseidon, shown as a naked man standing beside a white horse and holding a sceptre, and the goddess Athena, loosely robed but wearing her helmet, her shield on the ground at her feet, and standing beside an olive tree.

Subscriptio:

PAX UNA TRIUMPHIS INNUMERIS POTIOR

('One peace is worth a thousand victories')

Emblem copies Lebey de Batilly 1596, no. 28, *Paci studere praestat quam bello* ('Better to study peace than war'). Seton drew both Latin texts from de Batilly's prose commentary to the emblem (1596, sig. H3^{v}), where both expressions are cited from *Silius Italicus*. The emblem uses the legend recounting the foundation of Athens: the gods promised Attica to whichever god could give the most useful gifts to mankind; Poseidon struck the ground with his trident and a horse sprang up whereas Athena produced the peaceful olive tree.

3 NIHIL AMPLIUS OPTO

('I wish for nothing more')

In a landscape with a river a bearded man, loosely robed and bare-legged, fills the small flask he is holding at an ornamental fountain decorated with a Cupid figure which is set against the trunk of a tree. In the background a second man holding a larger flask falls into the river.

Subscriptio:

BENE EST CUI DEUS OBTULIT PARCA QUOD SATIS EST MANU
('It is well for him on whom God has conferred, with sparing hand, what is just enough')

Emblem copies van Veen (p.113), *Quod satis est cui contingit nihil amplius optet* ('He to whose lot sufficient falls, should covet nothing more'). Based on Horace, *Sat* 1.1.52-8, recommending moderation and expressing amazement at those who covet more than they need, as though a man needing only a modest drink should risk his life by drawing water from the River Aufidus, rather than going to a modest fountain. The picture copies van Veen closely except for the face of the man at the fountain which is changed into a portrait of Alexander Seton.

4 SIT VIRTUS TIPHYS
('Let virtue be the pilot')

Man in loose red robe sits in the stern of a wooden boat which has no mast, holding the tiller; in the bows stands the naked figure of Occasio, bald with her long forelock and holding her usual sail, taking place of the mast.

Subscriptio:

CUIQUE MORES FORTUNAM FINGUNT SUI
('A man's character decides his fortune')

Tiphys was pilot of the Argonauts. Emblem adapts the *impresa* of Girolamo Girardi as illustrated in Ruscelli, *Le imprese illustri* (Venice, 1566, p.571) showing two female figures, Virtus and Fortuna, in a ship with the motto 'Utriusq. Auxilio'; the same device was used as a printers mark by the de'Franceschi, printers in Venice in the 1570s. All these emblems go back to Cicero's saying to the effect that Fortune helps the brave, 'Virtute duce, comite Fortuna' (*Fam Epist* 10.3). Pinkie's identification of the ship in which Jason voyaged to bring back the golden fleece appears to be original, although the identification of this ship with the Argonauts appears to have become conventional since a version of this emblem, 'Duce Vitute, Comite fortuna' in the *Emblemata politica* of Peter Isselberg and Georg Rem (Nuremberg, 1617, no. 9) identifies the hero as Jason and the ship as the *Argo*.

5 SEMPER AVARUS EGET
('The greedy man is always hungry')

A man sits in a bed chamber before a fireplace, his gouty leg is bandaged and he is drinking from a flask; a larger urn is on the floor beside him. His physician is in attendance, examining a glass phial.

Subscriptio:

SCILICET IMPROBAE CRESCUNT DIVITIAE TAMEN CURTAE NESCIO QUID SEMPER ADEST REI
('It happens that unearned riches do indeed grow but I do not know what ever gets added to straightened circumstances')

Emblem copies van Veen (p.111), *Quo plus sunt potae, plus sitiuntur aquae* ('The more there is to drink, the more he thirsts'), where the man with dropsy signifies irrational avarice. Seton's motto was supplied from the additional adagia cited by van Veen, (p.110), and the only change to the picture is the omission of a scroll held by the physician in van Veen's engraving, which carried a motto quoting Horace, *Sat* 2.3: 'Danda est hellebori multo pars maxima avaris/ Nescio an Anticyram ratio illis destinet omnem.' Though he omitted this scroll Seton used it to supply the new motto to the first emblem above which, though it copies a different emblem from van Veen, is also about avarice.

6 NULLUM NUMEN ABEST SI SIT PRUDENTIA
('If prudence is shown then no divine power is lacking')

Roman general Fabius Maximus with a spear-carrying companion stands before the altar of Bacchus where the god is shown holding a cornucopia, and a golden pole with a circular mirror on top is entwined with a laurel branch and a snake.

Subscriptio:

SAEPE ACRI POTIOR PRUDENTIA DEXTRA
('Prudence is often better than a strong right arm')

Emblem copies Lebey de Batilly (1596, no. 32), which shows Fabius Maximus being offered the fruits of wisdom, peace and plenty at the altar of Bacchus: he was known as 'the delayer' since he preferred to weaken Hannibal by delaying tactics; prudence rather than impetuous courage. The *subscriptio* is adapted from de Batilly's epigram: *Saepe animis etiam in bello Prudentia, saepe/ Acri etiam dextra est, viribus & potior* ('Often, indeed, in war prudence is skilful and often better than courage and strength').

Inscriptions from southern panels –

1 PLACEANT HOMINI QUICQUID DEO PLACUIT HOC SUADET RATIO QUAM QUI AMAT CONTRA DURISSIMA ARMATUS EST
('Whatever pleases God should also be pleasing to man; reason argues thus, and whoever loves reason is armed against the hardest things')

2 REGIAE AMPLISSIMAEQUE OPES SI IN MALUM ET IMPROVIDUM INCIDERENT MOMENTO DISSIPANTUR AT QUAMVIS MODICAE BONO CUSTODI TRADITAE USU IPSO CRESCUNT ET AUGENTUR
('If regal and ample wealth falls into the hands of a wicked and improvident owner it is immediately squandered but riches, however modest, bestowed on a good trustee grow even in use and are increased')

Emblem in soffit of oriel window –

MH PANNUCION EUDE
('Don't sleep all night long')

In a landscape with a river a vigilant crane stands on one leg with its other leg upraised and holding a stone; its head is tucked under its wing, as though roosting.

Subscriptio (in ribbon-scroll beneath the cartouche frame):

OU CRH PANNUCION EUDEIN BOULHFORON ANDRA
('A counsellor ought not to sleep all night')

Though not copied from any known source the emblem uses the commonplace motif of the vigilant crane, a bird which symbolises vigilance because of its supposed habit of posting sentinel birds around the sleeping flock who stay awake by holding stones in one foot – if the sentinel becomes drowsy, the stone falls and wakes it up. The Greek motto and *subscriptio* are both based on Homer, *Iliad* 2.24. This Greek motto is associated with the vigilant crane motif in Sambucus, *Emblemata* (Antwerp, 1569, p.29); it is unusual to find the vigilant crane depicted as though it were not vigilant but sleeping *cf* Typotius, *Symbola* (Prague, 1600, pl. 47, *Non dormit qui custodit*). Sketch of this detail in RCAHMS, Bonnar drawings, FID/78/14.

Heraldic devices from central border –

In addition to the arms of Alexander Seton at the apex of the central lantern, there are eight further coats of arms displayed in the decorative rib-work which frames the central panel. Each is displayed complete with supporters, crest, motto and identifying label.

1 The Earle of Winton

Shield quartered with three interlinked crescents (Seton) and three sheaves of corn (Buchan) and surtout a star of twelve points in a double tressure flory and counter-flory for the title of Winton. The supporters two foxes; crest a dragon vert spouting fire, charged with a star; motto 'Hazard yit fordward'.

2 The Lorde Yester

Shield quartered with three cinquefoils argent (Fraser) and thee bars ermine (Gifford of Yester), surtout three shields azure (Hay, normally gules). The supporters two stags; crest and motto were described as 'effaced' in the 1960s but have now been restored to show a goat's head and the motto 'Spare nocht'.

3 The Earle of Cassilis

Chevron between three cross-crosslets within a double tressure flory and counter-flory. Supporters two swans; crest a dolphin; motto 'Avise la fine' (sic).

4 The Earle of Bothvell

Shield quartered with a bend azure (Vass, Lord Dirleton), gules on a chevron argent, two lions (Hepburn), surtout the arms of Scotland. Supporters two lions; crest a horse in front of a tree; motto 'Keip traist'.

5 Ferquhard of Gilmerscroft

Shield quartered with first, a lion rampant. second, three hands. third, a galley. fourth, a chevron cheque between three water bougets. No supporters; crest a dexter hand; motto 'A tout'.

6 The Lorde Borthwick

Argent three cinquefoils sable. Supporters two angels, winged; crest a savage's head; motto 'Qui conduit'.

7 The Earle of Angus

Shield quartered with first, lion rampant gules (Earl of Galloway); second, lion gules surmounted on a ribbon sable (Lordship of Abernethy); third, argent three piles azure (Wishart of Brechin); fourth, fess chequy surmounted on a bend sable, charged with three buckles (Stewart of Bonkill). Surtout argent, a man's heart gules ensigned with a crown proper and on a chief azure, three stars (Douglas). Supporters dexter a savage holding a baton and sinister a stag – the achievement is placed within a pale of wood; crest a salamander amidst flames; motto 'Jamais arriere'.

8 The Marqueis of Hamilton

Shield described as 'entirely effaced' in the 1960s now shows the Hamilton cinquefoils quartered with the Arran galley with crest an oak tree and frame-saw, and motto 'Jamais arriere' evidently repeated from the arms of Angus (the Hamilton motto should be 'Saw through').

First Floor –

'Prefects Room' (12' x 8') In the east range. Open board-and-beam ceiling with polychrome tempera decoration discovered in 1953 beneath plaster. In 1954 part was restored and partly repainted *in situ*, and part was removed to make way for new access stairs to the rooms above. The section removed is now on display in Edinburgh, Huntly House Museum. Supporting beams appear to have divided this ceiling into nine sections, the beams decorated with a variety of different patterns including chevrons, leaf scrolls, folded ribbon, and a long ribbon-encirled branch with leaf buds. The undersides of the beams had been adzed, and the present decoration was added as part of modern restoration. The boarded sections are decorated with a random selection of isolated motifs on a light grey ground, some of which are heraldic whilst others are purely decorative. Seton's personal device of the cinquefoil and crescent surmounted by a coronet is used, as is the device of three interlinked crescents which Seton also used, better known as that of Henry II of France. The monogram of Alexander Seton and Margaret Hay, surmounted by a coronet, appears more than once; the Hamilton cinquefoil appears on its own several times as does a fleur-de-lis. The decorative detail shows a number of repeated motifs, notably a bird standing on a small patch of ground, shown in various guises. The remaining motifs show a variety of well-drawn grotesque and arabesque ornamental devices. Fragments of one board from this room with antique ornament preserved in Historic Scotland Conservation Centre.

Library In the course of alterations to the present library in 1953 workmen took down a section of the panelling and it was discovered that 'a whole wall surface, ceiling and beams of this and the adjoining two rooms had been painted in a most elaborate manner' (unpublished 1954 conservation report by W R Adams, Technical Officer to the Ministry of Works). No photographs seem to have been taken, at least none appear to have survived, and the painting was all then covered up. The only record of its subject matter appears to be Adams's description of some of the mural painting in the library: 'The subject revealed was an Eastern dancer and behind him a pagoda, the whole being framed by pillars on either side and an arch above.' The description is historically implausible, if suggestive. Adams reports that fragments of painted work were found in many places during the course of these alterations. Beam from unlocated room, preserved in Historic Scotland Conservation Centre, is decorated along its length with a grey ribbon encircling a branch with leaves and stubs on a blue ground.

Literature

Seton 1888; Lyons 1904, 170-3, fig. 11; Apted 1966, pl. 30, 53, 58, 59; Macmillan 1990, 54; Bath 1993, 259-305; Bath 1995, 79-108; RCAHMS, *Midlothian and West Lothian*, 81-6.

Prestongrange, nr. Prestonpans

Lands at Prestongrange were owned before the Reformation by the monks of Newbattle Abbey who worked the coal on the site and exported it from the harbour on the estate. At the Reformation the lands passed to Mark Kerr, second son of Sir Andrew Kerr of Cessford, who became Abbot in 1547 and later Commendator of Newbattle. From about 1560, when he publicly professed the Protestant faith, to his death in 1584, he played a role in the affairs of Scotland as Extraordinary Lord of Session and member of the Privy Council 1569-82, when his opposition to the Ruthven Raid lost him this favour. The estate and the house passed to Mark Kerr the younger who became Earl of Lothian in 1606 (d.1609). Prestongrange was then sold to John Morison whose heirs held it until the mid-eighteenth century. In 1962 during alterations a painted ceiling was discovered in the first-floor hall, further traces of a painted ceiling in a room to the east of the hall and remains of wall painting on plaster in a second-floor bedroom.

Hall (42' x 20') Dated 1581, the earliest dated ceiling known in Scotland; it was completely removed for conservation work in the 1960s and reinstalled in Merchiston Tower, Edinburgh, now part of Napier University. This involved some restructuring and not all the compartments of the open board-and-beam ceiling are now visible or in their original positions. Before removal it consisted of twenty-three compartments between the open beams filled with grotesque paintings executed in grisaille on a red background. Ian Hodkinson notes that the beam decoration is stencil work of later date, 'examination revealed that it is later and overlies a simple band and chevron decoration, apparently the original since it is carried out ... in the same three pigments as the board painting' (Apted *et al* 1966, p.127). The chevrons alternate in white and orange, outlined in black, about a grey band. The grotesques copy at least four different print sources, by far the larger number from Jan Vredeman de Vries's *Grottesco*, comprising seventeen etchings executed by the van Doetecum brothers and published by Gerard de Jode in Antwerp, c.1565-71. Two term-figures are copied from Vredeman's *Caryatidum*, also published by de Jode, c.1565, whilst four more grotesque figures on the ceiling are copied from the 120 pseudo-Rabelaisian prints published in Paris, 1565, by Richard Breton under the title *Les songes drolatiques de Pantagruel*. One further detail is copied from an ornament print by Cornelis Bos. Sections 1, 2, 12, 13 and 23 were on sections of planking which had to be cut off when the ceiling was reassembled at Merchiston Tower; they are now in storage with Historic Scotland conservation. Each section fills one compartment of painted boards. In the following analysis the Vredeman prints are identified by their numbers in Hollstein, *Dutch & Flemish Etchings, Engravings and Woodcuts*, vol. 67.

Section 1 –
ornate scrollwork
bird with spread wings rising from flames (phoenix)
tent with trailing flaps
leaf scrolls
[damaged section]
foliage with interlaced bands

Section 2 –
ornate scrollwork
military breastplate
leaf scrolls
grotesque figure with serpent tail, holding candle
medallion with ?animal face
side view of bird standing with downturned head
[damaged section]
?strapwork cartouche with suspended head of figure with leaves for hair

Section 3 –
male classical profile in medallion transformed into trailing acanthus scrollwork
military helmet below tent with trailing flaps (244)
ornamental scrollwork
umbrella-shaped object encircled with laurel wreath (247)
bunch of foliage
eagle rising above thunderbolt

Section 4 –
scrollwork
urn with plants
human head sprouting leaves
curled band-work
ox skull with beaded drape suspended from horns
hybrid figure consisting of nude male torso with legs transformed into interwoven serpentine shapes ending in acanthus leaves and upraised arms holds leaf scrolls above his head
human mask suspended from leaf scrolls

Section 5 –
foliate scrollwork with bunches of fruit
humanoid bust with shoulders transformed into curled scrolls and trunk into acanthus leaves
spread bird's wings
nude male with feathered hair seated on an architectural cornice supported by a wheel and holding a rod (copied from print by Cornelis Bos)

grotesque male torso holding sword and pointed shield whose trunk transforms into serpentine shape ending in acanthus scroll
band-work enclosing male face

Section 6 –
grotesque face in profile transformed into wing-shaped acanthus and serpentine tail
winged Cupid emerging from stem of leaf scroll (253)
crouching male nude wearing bishop's mitre and with hands clasped in prayer opposite an urn or censer from which a puff of smoke emerges; above these a nude male crowned and with double beard stands on a stepped plinth beneath a fringed canopy raised on pillars (248)
two arms reaching down through holes in strapwork to pluck a bunch of fruit
face peering through hole in strapwork above

Section 7 –
swag of fruit enclosed in ornamental frame (249);
open lantern above fruit swag; above this a drape, an ornamental wreath with fillets, a curled pipe from which smoke puffs, a face with a cloth draped under the chin, and a canopy (253)
acanthus trail hanging from male torso who holds a nest of young birds on his head above which a parent bird flies up
swag of fruit and foliage hangs on beaded cord from classical bust with laurel crown, above which a fringed canopy is suspended

Section 8 –
acanthus scrolls above ornamental cartouche
open-work vase or basket of foliage hanging from a cord which is encircled by a coiled snake (245)
ornate urn supports torso of term-figure with scrolled arms and two swags of fruit suspended from his leafy hips
slender leaf scrolls and a rectangular cartouche hang by beaded cords from a heart-shaped shield whose sides are transformed into animal faces, above which is a helmet surrounded with heraldic mantling and hanging by a cord from a fringed canopy; a large bead in the middle of this cord sends out two puffs of smoke (251)
decorative strapwork

Section 9 –
urn enclosed in acanthus scrolls
two intertwined winged snakes with human faces coil around a beaded cord hanging from a rod on which a fringed cloth is draped (254)
oval strapwork cartouche hanging, with fringed canopy and other objects, on beaded cord suspended from vase containing fruits and leaves
male with feathered hair, wearing loose-fitting pyjama trousers and standing with hands on hips (242)
fan-shaped, umbrella-like object rises from an architectural bracket (242)

Section 10 –
urn or censer with handle sends out puff of smoke (248)
swag of fruits and foliage
female term-figure on metalwork plinth with lion mask has coiled-up arms, a vase of fruits and flowers rises from her head below an ornamental bracket from which two beaded cords hang (248)
tricephalic monster supporting a fountain, strapwork cartouche, bunch of musical instruments, wreath of foliage with branches from which a swag of cloth is suspended, bird with spread wings perched on pennant (246)
fluted and inverted fan-shaped object (256)

Section 11 –
stem of leaves
bell-shaped pendant hung from double-headed arrow with drape, bunch of gardening tools below wide-brimmed hat, ox skull, hinged triptych panel, entwined foliate scrolls with animal heads (241)
grotesque figure of a feather-haired and winged trumpeter emerging from a coiled leaf scroll beneath a winged lizard, two smoking trumpets emerging from a circular urn hanging below a raised canopy with falling drapes (243)
human face, from which a lattice of curved bars emerges, below two symmetrical scrolls leading up to a fluted fan (254)

Section 12 –
basket of foliage (245)
oval mirror in cross-shaped frame (243)
perched peacock below bucranium with tassels hanging from horns (248)
shield-like cartouche with hangings below human face
bird with spread wings on canopy supported by ornamental stem with two trumpet-shaped branches (249)
child's face with suspended drape below ornamental shield (249)

Section 13 –
ornate scrollwork
lobster (246)
basket of leaves and fruit
assorted scrollwork
term-figure with scrolled arms, feathered hair and acanthus leaves at waist
vase with hanging drape and supporting scrollwork (251)

Section 14 –
stem of leaves rising from urn beneath canopy
bearded face with horns hung with tassels
acanthus fan
slender pedestal festooned with a garland supports globe on which bird stands with raised foot above which rises a female term-figure with two plaits; above her a long stemmed vase, holding a single branch of symmetrical leaves (241)

Section 15 –
fretwork with foliage and fruit swag (246)
tall branch of leaves and fruit rises on single stem from narrow vase (250)
semicircle of foliage hangs from mouths of two symmetrical

animal masks, winged thunderbolt, male mask with cloth drape, double-headed arrow, symmetrical foliate scrollwork (250)
scrollwork

Section 16 –
panoply of arms around upright spear with pennant at point (249)
scrolled achitectural bracket with hanging tassel and torch supporting humanoid term-figure blowing long, coiled trumpet and hair elogated into grassy leaves (253)
panoply of arms with flag and battle-axe beneath flaming mortar, above which is another panoply of arms consisting of classical breastplate with spears, hanging by beaded thread from visored helmet, with large crest hanging from canopy with trailing flaps (244)
owl perched on cockle shell beneath acanthus fan (244)

Section 17 –
ornamental fretwork with bunch of fruit and foliage; fretwork with fruit swags and trailing tassel
winged nude figure of Fame with two trumpets standing on a skull above a winged hourglass (255)
small cartouche hung with tassels on beaded cords and with two branches of leaves rising at each side containing date '1581' (246)
ornamental architectural bracket (246) supporting horse with raised head standing beneath vase with cloth drapes holding branches (246)
ornamental scrollwork

Section 18 –
large foliate scroll (250) rises from slender vase with curved handles (244)
a thunderbolt in the shape of a winged sphere pierced by a double-headed arrow, above which stands a nude archer with bow and quiver, his upraised hand pointing to a bird above his head (250)
strapwork and scrolls with leaf stems and fruit swags rising up to a female bust enclosed in strapwork

Section 19 –
basket of fruits and leaves below leaf scrolls rising to enclose or support floral motif (252)
leaf stem (252) rising to strapwork designs hung with beaded threads below bucranium
male term-figure with flat cap and wrapped in a winding sheet (Hollstein, *Caryatidum*, p. 228)
basket of fruits below scrolls and fan

Section 20–
long-stemmed vase bearing spray of leaves with bloom (252)
cartouche
male term-figure with hair, shoulders and hips transformed into acanthus scrolls (*Caryatidum*, p. 232)
male figure, pot-bellied and wearing wide-brimmed hat with feather, with amputated right leg and supported by a wooden prosthesis (*Songes drolatiques*, p. 112)
two ancanthus leaves hang from a fruit swag hanging from a bust whose shoulders form strapwork volutes

Section 21 –
vase with leaf stems
rhomboidal cartouche below circular wreath with two intersecting branches beneath canopy suspended on beaded cord from slender arch, upon which stands a perching bird with long upturned beak (251)
ornate fretwork rising to fan shape beneath human mask with cloth drape around chin and volute scrolls on head, standing male figure in doublet, hose and loose jacket, head turned, one arm akimbo, the other hand holding his grossly enlarged codpiece (*Songes drolatiques*, p.31)
various objects suspended on a tasselled thread, including a shallow lamp from which two puffs of smoke emerge (242)

Section 22 –
ornamental fretwork enclosing bearded mask with horns
figure in doublet, hose and projecting codpiece, with sword through his shoulder (or under his arm), no face visible, but long beak projecting from a large hood (*Songes drolatiques*, 80)
fretwork containing mask
male figure with pointed cap and large upward-pointing ears, wearing beaded necklace, and codpiece, holding sword in right hand, grass-frond in left (*Songes drolatiques*, 106)

Section 23 –
various strapwork and scrolls, some with fruit swags

First Floor –

Painted beams in room on first floor have repeating foliate compartments in white, green, red and black, of which only fragments remained in 1962.

Second Floor –

Wall painting in small room in the east end. On plaster, it shows decorative strapwork forming two elaborate shields with inscriptions and a separate monogram. Inscriptions are two verse proverbs, recorded in William Baldwin, *Treatise of Moral Philosophy* (1555, enlarged Palfreyman 1610):

> He that to wraithe & anger is thrall
> Over his wit sall have no power at all.
>
> The having of riches is not so commod[ious]
> As the departing frome thaime is dolorous.

Hodkinson says that the design was higher than the 1962 ceiling level and the top of the painting was hidden from sight, possibly 'part of a much larger architectural development to the east which has since been altered' (Apted *et al* 1966, p.30). The painting was on a thin layer, below which was older, thicker plaster showing signs of black, yellow and red pigment from an earlier mural.

Literature

Apted, Hodkinson and Murray, 1966; Apted 1966, pl. 41, 42; Apted and Robertson 1975; Sanderson 1987, ch.7; Howard 1995a, 86;

EDINBURGH

302 Lawnmarket

One of a row of five-storey tenements, with two open board-and-beam ceilings painted in a style closely resembling that in Gladstone's Land on the opposite side of the street. Now part of an Edinburgh City Council office complex.

Second Floor –

Beams decorated on all three faces, sides divided into rectangular compartments containing rinceau leaf scrolls in white on alternating red and blue ground, very similar to beam decoration on first floor of Gladstone's Land; undersides with trailing tassel. Boards decorated with swags of fruit – pears, gourds, grapes – and flowers or acanthus leaves in various shades of brown, red, yellow and blue, on a black ground, with heavy outlining. Interspersed amongst this vegetation are five animals – a rabbit, a standing bird of prey in profile, a bird with a long neck and bill, a lion, and a fox – together with a single grotesque male head resembling a Green Man. The two end sections are decorated in a different style with red arabesque scrolling on a white ground.

Fourth Floor –

Beams decorated on all three sides with trailing tassel. Boards have carefully drawn and regular scrollwork in red, yellow, blue, green and white, of acanthus leaves with quatrefoil flower heads and densely petalled roses, all heavily outlined. End-section boards decorated with the same red arabesque leaf scroll on white ground as in first-floor room. Historic Scotland Conservation Centre has thirty-eight loose boards from an unlocated room or rooms in this building comprising a whole ceiling divided into two parts, with different patterns indicating the likelihood that the boards spanned two rooms separated by a dividing wall. Three sections are decorated with continuous arabesque scrollwork in red on a white ground, whilst a further nine sections show leaf scrolls with fruit and flowers in blue, red and brown on a white ground.

Literature

Apted 1966, pl. 20, 52, 95, 96.

Abbey Strand, Canongate

Ground Floor –

Beams built into this room were removed from Edinburgh, Caroline Park (qv).

First Floor –

Board-and-beam ceiling. Sides of beams divided into rectagular or lozenge-shaped sections on alternate beams, similar to those at 302 Lawnmarket and at Gladstone's Land, each section with arabesque leaf scrolls, crescent moons, radiant suns or crosses in white, on blue, red or brown background. Only two fragments of original decoration now remain on underside of boards, showing red arabesque scrollwork with green leaf forms on a white ground. Remains of a monogram in medallion, of which only a portion of the letter 'H' now survives. A number of beams from this site, decorated with fruit and flowers, scrollwork, geometric strapwork and stars, are in Historic Scotland Conservation Centre.

Literature

RCAHMS, *Edinburgh*, 156-7.

Advocates Close, 357 High Street

First-floor board-and-beam ceiling in building which dates from 1590. Beams with white arabesque leaf scrolls in rectangular compartments with alternating red or blue/black backgrounds. Only two portions of original decoration remain on underside of boards, showing leaf scrolls. Fragment of painted plaster on wall above door also shows elaborate ornamental leaf scrolls in red on white.

Owner: Edinburgh Old Town Renewal Trust.

Blyth's Close, Castle Hill ('Mary of Guise's House')

Destroyed. A complex of buildings off the Lawnmarket, displaying a rich variety of carved and painted decoration recorded by local historians prior to, or shortly after, their demolition in 1845. Some of these houses were connected by closes and by a gallery along the north front: the buildings known as 'Mary of Guise's House' are from the tradition that they had been occupied by the widow of James V during her regency (ie between 1551, when she returned from France, and 1559, when she broke with the Lords of Congregation and moved to Leith). William Drummond, *Old Edinburgh*, says that a spiral stair led to a series of large apartments, 'well-lighted and having beautifully designed ceilings', stone mantelpieces, carved oak door panels, hooks for hanging tapestry, and elaborately carved stone gothic niches. The arms and initials of James Hamilton as Duke of Châtelhérault (Regent immediately prior to Mary's return in 1551) are recorded, together with the arms of Guise, so some of the decoration must go back to the period of Mary's regency, although other decoration may well be later. Other parts of the close were built for and occupied by Edinburgh burgesses; one property belonged to Edward Hope, prominent citizen and Commissioner for the city of Edinburgh in the 1560s, and another was improved in 1591 by Edinburgh merchants, Robert McNaught and James Rynd.

Paradin Chamber Wilson (1848, vol. i, pp.149-51) describes two apartments from a house in Todd's Close, 'on the west side of Blyth's Close'. One had a coved ceiling which Wilson describes as 'adorned with a variety of emblematic designs'. He recognised three of these as copied from Paradin's *Devises heroïques* (1551) but also claims that some of the emblems are from an otherwise unidentified work which he calls the *Traicté des devises royales,* and Wilson describes three further emblems which 'are not to be found in either of these works' (p. 150). In fact, however, all six of the devices he describes are to be found in Paradin. Wilson describes the following details from this ceiling. (My page references, below, are to the Paris: de Tournes edition of Paradin [1557, repr. Scolar Press 1989, ed. Saunders].)

1 an ape crushing her offspring in the fervour of her embrace, with the motto '*Caecus amor prolis*'
('Blind love of offspring') (p.226; *cf* Rossend 3f)

2 a serpent among strawberry plants, '*Latet anguis in Herba*'
('The snake lurks in the grass') (p.70)

3 a porcupine with apples on its spikes, '*Magnum vectigal parsimonia*'
('Thrift is a great revenue') (p.140)

The word 'parsimonia' is added, and the animal is a hedgehog, not a porcupine, since the provident hedgehog was traditionally thought to collect fruits by rolling on them and impaling them on its spines, *cf* Earlshall, long gallery, Section 1.

4 two hands out of a cloud, one holding a sword, and the other a trowel, '*In utrumque paratus*'
('Ready for either') (p.115, *cf* Rossend, 4d; Bay Horse Inn mural Panel 1; Skelmorlie Aisle.)

5 a hand amid flames, holding up a dagger, with the motto '*Agere et pati fortia*'
('To do and suffer great things') (p.120)

6 a branch covered with apples, '*Ab insomni non custodita dragoni*'
('Not guarded by the vigilant dragon') (p.57, the device refers to the golden apples of the Hesperides, guarded by a dragon, which Hercules stole as the last of his labours).

Inscribed Chamber Wilson (1848, vol. i, pp.149-50) describes this room as adjoining the previous chamber, 'immediately above what was called the Queen' bed-room' and 'lighted by windows ranged along each side of the arched roof'. The wooden ceiling

> was painted in rich arabesques and graceful designs of flowers, fruit, leaves, &c., surrounding panels with inscriptions in gothic letters. On one portion, all that could be made out was, 'Ye trubilis of ye Richtious'. On another, was perfectly defined the following metrical legend:
>
> Gif yow wt. syn affleitit be,
> Och yan say Chryst cum yow to me.
> Swith ye way, walk yow thairin,
> Embrace ye truth, abandon —
>
> The last word, obviously 'Sin', had been curiously omitted, and a dash substituted for it, as though for a guess or puzzle.

Wilson (pp. 150-1) also describes heraldic blazonry which featured in 'some of the rooms'. The vestibule or lobby to the large first-floor room reached by the turnpike stair, and containing a gothic niche or piscina, had a ceiling with a central entablature of carved oak, painted with the arms of the Duke of Châtelhérault, with his initials, 'IH' (ie James Hamilton, Earl of Arran, whose Châtelhérault title was confirmed in 1551). The similarly carved and painted arms of France, with the initials 'HR', are carved in the same position on the second floor. Wilson also records the arms of Guise impaled with the Scottish lion and the initials of Mary as Queen Regent, 'MR'.

Mary of Guise's Chapel Wilson describes this as halfway down the close, on the east side, where a turnpike stair gave access to a vestibule on the first floor 'which formed only a small portion of what had originally been a large and magnificant apartment', with a doorway giving access to the gallery which led across to the palace on the opposite side of the close. Wilson identifies this with the room William Maitland had described as the 'chapel or private oratory' of Mary of Guise. The identification rests wholly on the few relics of apparently Catholic decoration that were recovered from this site, among which are fragments of painting from a room above, on the top floor of the building. These included:

1 An alcove in one wall, filled with painting and divided into two compartments by ornamental borders. On the left,

> a young man was kneeling before an altar, on which was standing an open vessel amid flames, while from a dark cloud overhead, a hand issued, holding a ladle, just about to dip it into the vessel. A castellated mansion, with turrets and gables in the style of the sixteenth century, appeared in the distance; and at the top was inscribed on a scroll, the words *Demum pur gabiter* ['It will be made clean']. In the other compartment, a man of aged and venerable aspect was seen, who held in his hands a heart, which he appeared to be offering to a figure like a bird, with huge black wings. Above this were the words ... *impossibile est.* (Wilson, 1848, vol. i, p. 155)

Wilson comments that the whole apartment appeared to have been decorated in the same style, though only slight traces remained.

2 Board-and-beam decorations in lower rooms, which were revealed on removal of lath and plaster; the beams 'and the under sides of the flooring above, were all covered with ornamental devices; those on the main beams being painted on three sides, and divided at short distances by fillets or bands of various patterns running round them' (p.155). Wilson illustrates one of these beam patterns 'from one of the oak beams in our Publisher's possession'.

McNaught and Rynd's House At the head of the close, built on land assigned in 1590 to Robert McNaught and James Rynd, merchant burgesses. Ashlar frontage carried inscription in iron letters 'LAVS DEO', and the date '1591'. Wilson (vol. i, p.156) describes six or seven paintings on a coved ceiling on the second floor 'accidentally discovered some years since'. The ceiling was divided into compartments by broad borders 'richly decorated with every variety of flowers, fruit, harpies, birds, and fancy devices' which 'divide the ceiling into irregular square and round compartments, with raised and gilded stars at their intersections' (p. 157). These included:

1 Large circular compartment at centre of ceiling showed Christ encircled by a radiance, his left hand resting on a globe, in a foliated strapwork frame and encircling inscription 'EGO SUM VIA VERITAS ET VITA *14* IOHNE'. This detail was seen by the Edinburgh architect, Thomas Bonnar, when he was collecting designs from historic Scottish buildings for possible use or imitation in his own practice, and his impression of it is among the Bonnar Drawings in RCAHMS. This portion was also among the ceiling boards which passed to C K Sharpe in the 1850s, now preserved in the Museum of Scotland.

2 Four 'larger compartments' identified by Wilson as Jacob's Dream, Christ Asleep in the Storm, the Baptism of Christ, and the Apocalypse, each with one of the symbols of four evangelists above it. Christ Sleeping by the Sea of Galilee used a contemporary landscape which Wilson recognised as a view of Edinburgh from the north with the castle on the extreme right and Salisbury Crags on the left; since it also included the steeple of Netherbow Port, erected in 1606, we can assign a date in the early seventeenth century for this ceiling. The section showing Christ Sleeping was preserved by C K Sharpe, and is now in the Museum of Scotland. Very little of the detail that was visible to Wilson in 1848 can now be made out.

3 Allegorical painting, described by Wilson thus:

> A ship, of antique form, is seen in full sail, and bearing on its pennon and stern the common symbol, IHS. A crowned figure stands on the deck, looking towards a burning city in the distance, and above him the word VÆ [ie *vita aeterna*]. On the mainsail is inscribed *Caritas*, and over the stern, which is in the fashion of an ancient galley, [Sa]*piencia*. Death appears as a skeleton, riding on a dark horse, amid the waves immediately in front of the vessel, armed with a bow and arrow, which he is pointing at the figure in the ship, while a figure, similarly armed and mounted on a huge dragon, follows in its wake, entitled *Persecutio*, and above it a winged demon, over whom is the word *Diabolus*. In the midst of these perils, there is seen in the sky a radiance surrounding יהוה; and from this symbol of the Deity, a hand issues, taking hold of a line attached to the stern of the vessel. (p.157)

Wall painting from same room, found on boards forming back of a cupboard recess. Group of musicians, including lutanist and horn player, with music books in front of them. Wilson states that these boards were in the collection of C K Sharpe, and that 'fragments of a much larger, but much ruder copy of the same design' were found at Dean House.

Literature

Wilson 1848, vol. i, 146-58; Brydal 1889, 54-6; RCAHMS, *Edinburgh*, 126.

Canongate Tolbooth

Open timber ceiling in room on first floor decorated with flowers and fruit. Tolbooth also now holds small section of ceiling removed from Edinburgh, Nisbet of Dirleton's House (qv).

Caroline Park

Beams found during demolition of this house are now built into ground-floor room of Abbey Strand. Fragments of painted decoration, including leaf scrolls, fruit or gourd and leaf decoration alternating with sections of zig-zag lozenge patterning, little colour remaining.

Craigmillar Castle

Destroyed. Billings (vol. i, pp.93-8) records that 'In several portions of the vaulting there may be traced the remains of old paintings, chiefly of an heraldic character, a feature which it enjoys in common with Borthwick. On the lower part of the side there are some paintings much more distinct, which are evidently, however, modern attempts'. Billings's illustration of the 'Interior of the Keep Tower' shows indistinct details of some of this painting, together with a carved keystone showing the date '1510'.

Dean House

Owned by Sir William Nisbet of the Dean (1569-1639), baillie and Lord Provost of Edinburgh, who bought the estate in 1609. Wilson (1848) states that one of the panels bore the date 1627, but this is not now visible. Destroyed in 1845 to make way for a cemetery, when painted panels on boards from its barrel-vaulted long gallery ceiling were acquired by C K Sharpe; now in the National Museums of Scotland, with two further panels – Cain and Abel, and Lot and his Daughters – on display in John Knox's House. The surviving panels show Old Testament scenes and personifications of the senses. A colour sketch of the King David panel is among the Thomas Bonnar drawings in RCAHMS.

1 Abraham and Isaac in a Landscape

Wells-Cole (1997, p.104) notes that 'the position of the intended victim, and the appearance of some of the background buildings' relates closely to an engraving by Wierix after Maarten de Vos (Hollstein, vol. xlv, no. 248/I).

2 King David Playing the Harp

3 Judith with the Head of Holofernes

Inscription in top border: 'HOLOFERNES DECOLLATVS', and top left: 'BETHVLIA'; picture adapts engraving 'Judith Displaying Holofernes' Head to the People' by Philips Galle after Maarten van Heemskerck.

4 Cain and Abel

Now in John Knox's House; in the border above the picture an inscription, not now fully legible: '[...] AIN TVS ABEL OFERENTES'; picture copies engraving by Johannes Sadeler after de Vos.

5 Lot and his Daughters

Bottom right is the inscription 'GENESIS.XIX'.

6 St Luke

The patron saint of painters, seated and reading open book on a desk with a palette of paints and brushes, in room with two classical fluted pilasters, open window and onlooking ox.

7 Personification of the Sense of Sight

Inscription in the border: 'SOLE ... SPE ... AVIS ... BLANDVLA'. Oval panel appears to be based on the print by Johannes Sadeler after Maarten de Vos (Hollstein, vol. xlv, no. 1506) though Latin motto is not copied from de Vos's print.

8 Personification of the Sense of Hearing

Inscription in the border: 'ALTA DEA PI ... O ... HAC ... TO ARGVTA MOVEO ... NNVLLA VI ... MANV AD NVMENIS QVIBVS'. Oval panel almost certainly copies the *Auditus* engraving by Adriaen Collaert after Maarten de Vos, c.1682 (Hollstein, vol. xlv, no. 1494/II).

9 Personificaton of the Sense of Taste

Inscription in border, of which the words 'ANIMOS PVLSA ... C ... ARVM NVBE SE ....' can be made out. Oval panel.

10 Musicians

Wilson (1848, vol. i, p.157) affirms that the Dean panels also included a larger and cruder version of the group of musicians, including lutanist and horn player with music books in front of them, which he describes at McNaught and Rhynd's House, Blyth's Close, Edinburgh.

Literature

PSAS, 1, 1852, 10; Apted 1966, 46-8, 67; Anon 1959, Item 89; RCAHMS, *City of Edinburgh* 1951, 241-2; Apted 1966, pl. 46-8, 67; Thomson 1975, 46-7, figs 40-6; Macmillan 1990, 54. pl. 40.

Edinburgh Castle

Queen Mary's Room In south-east corner of Crown Square, small room off the Queen's chamber, in which James VI was born in 1566. Decorative painting on boarded ceiling and frieze painted by James Anderson in 1617 to commemorate James's visit to Scotland. Ceiling divided into four rectangular compartments with thistles in each corner and the initials 'IR' in first and fourth compartment, 'MR' in second and third. Wall has royal arms of Scotland painted on boards above a metrical prayer:

> Lord Jesu Chryst that Crounit was with Thornse
> Preserve the Birth quhais Badgie heir is borne
> And send Hir Sonee Successione to Reigne still
> Lang in this Realme. If that it be Thy will
> Als Grant O Lord quhat ever of Hir proceed
> Be to Thy Glorie Honer and Prais sobied.

Frieze on other two walls has strapwork cartouches containing James's birthdate '19: IVNII' and '1566'.

Owner: Historic Scotland.

Literature

RCAHMS, *Edinburgh*, pl. 27, figs 79 and 81.

General Dalziel's House, Big Jack's Close

Destroyed. Among the examples of decorative painting recorded by Wilson, *Memorials of Edinburgh*, 1848, is a barrel-vaulted ceiling in the remains of the town house of General Thomas Dalziel, commander of the forces of Charles II, persecutor of the Covenanters, and victor in the Battle of Pentland, 1666. According to Wilson, 'The chief apartment was a hall of unusually large dimensions, with an arched or waggon-shaped ceiling adorned with a painting of the sun in the centre, surrounded by gilded rays on an azure ground. The remainder of the ceiling was painted to represent sky and clouds and spangled over with a series of silvered stars in relief'.

Literature

Wilson 1848, vol. ii, 95.

Gladstone's Land, Lawnmarket

Six-storey tenement building, bought in 1617 by Thomas Gledstane, a merchant from Kirkcudbright, who extended it by building new rooms on the frontage extending into the High Street, adding his own and his wife's carved initials to the skewputts. Painted decoration in three rooms on three floors dates from his occupancy.

Owner: NTS.

First Floor –

Painted Chamber Board-and-beam ceiling divided by a massive crossbeam, which marks the point at which Gledstane broke through the old outer wall to construct his new extension. Beams decorated on each side with arabesque leaf scrolls in white rectangular or lozenge-shaped compartments of alternating red and dark blue backgrounds. Underside of beams has repeated trailing tassel pattern in opposite directions on alternate beams. Underside of boards painted with fruit and flowers – apples, red and blue grapes, red and blue roses – and with white leaf forms including large, doubled acanthus-style leaves. Ceiling rests on a painted frieze of *trompe l'oeil* arcading, not unlike that in the Earlshall long gallery, with classical pilasters and semicircular arches, outlined in black on white plaster with red infilling, and containing ornate vases filled with flowers.

Second Floor –

Lecture Room Board-and-beam ceiling. Beams have arabesque motifs, black on white, white on black, or black/white on red;

on the underside of the beams these are enclosed in rectangular compartments separated by square chamfered studs. Board sections alternate between fruit and flowers similar to those on first-floor ceiling, though with heavier swags of fruit including pears and gourds, and pseudo-architectural designs including a stacked box column flanked by leaf scrolls, and a diagonally striped column between acanthus leaves. At two places the date '1620' is painted. Similar chamfered bosses to those on the cross-beams decorate the supporting beam on the end wall, into which the crossbeams are mortised, whilst a similar beam in the opposite wall is painted with false arcading similar to that on the first floor, though no sign of the continuation of this arcading is now visible on the surrounding plaster.

Third Floor –

Office Board-and-beam ceiling. Beams similar to those on second floor, divided again by a massive crossbeam, and including a row of six oval medallions featuring birds and animals. These include a phoenix, an ape, a standing hawk, a standing crested bird, a duck, and a crested eagle(?) with outspread wings. There are fragments of painted decoration on the plaster of the walls, notably another arcaded frieze above the present window recess.

Literature
Apted 1966, pl. 69, 75; Hill 1953, figs 254-5; RCAHMS, *Edinburgh*, 74, figs 209 and 211-15.

HOLYROOD PALACE

Queen Mary's Outer Chamber Second floor, north-west corner of palace. Boarded ceiling with wooden mouldings dividing it into sixteen rectangular compartments, each of which has a raised plaquette, carved and painted with monograms 'MR' for Mary and 'IR' for James V of Scotland, 'FD' for her husband François, Dauphin of France, and 'HR' for her father-in-law, Henri II; each monogram surmounted by a crown, and the four central compartments with the arms of Henry, James, François and the royal arms of Scotland. Executed in 1558-9 to celebrate the royal marriage.

Queen Mary's Bedroom Leading off Queen Mary's outer chamber. Erected for James VI and painted for Charles I; monograms 'MR', 'IR' and 'CR' for Mary, James and Charles. Ceiling divided into alternating rows of lozenge-shaped and hexagonal compartments by wooden mouldings, with national emblems of Britain in cartouches painted on the flat underside of the boards in the hexagonal compartments, and royal monograms carved on raised wooden plaquettes at centres of lozenge-shaped compartments. First row of national emblems has a crowned portcullis, crowned fleur-de-lis, crowned harp, and crowned thistle. Central row has crowned thistle and crowned rose on either side of the monograms 'CR' (Carolus Rex) and 'CP' (Carolus Princeps). End row has crosses of St Andrew and St George, both crowned. Elaborate frieze in this room, painted in grisaille on plaster, is quite unique in Scotland, and is undoubtedly earlier work than the painted ceiling, with cornucopias and plant stems between running borders of guilloche. Though these two rooms are all that now remains of early painted decoration at Holyrood, there are records of painting elsewhere in the palace. Preparations for James's 1617 visit, for instance, included the redecoration of Holyrood, but since the work could not be satisfactorily carried out in Scotland the Privy Council commissioned Matthew Goodrick, 'Citienair and paynter in London', to paint and gild the chapel, and Nicolas Stone, 'carver', to carry out wood-carving. A letter from the chamberlain to Sir Dudley Carleton says that Inigo Jones was in overall charge, and that there were 'pictures of the Aposteles, Faith, Hope, and Charity and such other religious representations, which, how welcome they will be thither God knows' (cited Ross 1899, p.397). In 1611 Alexander Seton was made keeper 'of the palice, park and yairds of Halyrood-house', an office he held for life at a fee of £33.6s.8d, though it is not possible to say what role he might have played in the plans for redecoration. On Matthew Goodrich, see Croft-Murray, pp.202-4.

Literature
Apted 1966, pl. 27.

JOHN KNOX'S HOUSE, 43-45 HIGH STREET

House constructed at two different periods, an inner structure and outer shell. Burgh Register records it as property of John Arres in 1525, and in 1573 it is registered as the property of James Mossman, goldsmith, and his wife, Mariota Arres, whose initials and coat of arms are carved on the west front and who were almost certainly responsible for extending the building, constructing the outer shell which gives it its present distinctive shape. It has ashlar facing to the west front, a Renaissance-style window with pilasters, frieze and cornice, and a unique sundial on the south-west angle which is surmounted by the figure of Moses pointing upwards towards a sculptured radiance containing the inscription 'ΘEOS/DEVS/GOD'. Inscription along the frieze over the ground-floor windows reads, 'LVFE GOD ABVFE AL AND YI NYGHBOVR AS YI SELFE'. The house owes its present name to the wholly erroneous tradition that the great Scottish reformer lived there and in the nineteenth century the corner sundial was obscured by a wooden canopy with the figure of Knox preaching. Painted board-and-beam ceiling with grotesque decoration was revealed on first floor during restoration work in 1958.

Owner: Netherbow Theatre and Museum.

First Floor –

L-shaped ceiling with six beams running east to west in the larger southern end, and seven beams running north to south in the northern part of the room. These end in a massive double crossbeam, beyond which are four short beams running east to west to create a further four short compartments. Overall dimensions

21'6" x 20'. The irregular construction of this ceiling was dictated by the need to pierce through the original walls to the southern and western extensions of the outer walls, most probably during James Mossman's ownership, sometime after 1573. Though impossible to ascribe a precise date to the painting it would seem likely that it was executed during this major reconstruction of the building – the new beams and boards must have been installed at this time. The construction divides the ceiling into three discrete sections, with six compartments in the first, six in the second, and four in the third, all filled with the same style of grotesque ornament. The beam decoration is characterised by a repetitive pattern of gourd-shaped fruits, often carried over the corners to unite all three surfaces, and sometimes with oblique banding dividing the beam into discrete sections; one of the beams has a repeated chevron pattern. The boards show grotesque ornament consisting of ribbon-work, foliage and fruit swags interspersed with humanoid and animal figures, monsters, pieces of armour and a winged cherub's head. One or two of the boards are misaligned and evidently not in their original positions, but in the analysis that follows no attempt is made to reposition these details. In umber, yellow, white and green with black outlining.

Section 1 –

1a Small fragment of foliate ornament.

1b Foliate scrollwork.

1c Ornate foliage with ribbon-work.

1d Foliage with fruit swag; confronting dog and lion sejant; ribbon-work; bird perched beneath circular awning with tied-back drapes; foliate ornament.

1e Two confronting birds supporting a knot of ribbon-work; human face with large segmented collar; leaf scrolls ending in two grotesque animal heads above fruit swag; bust of nude female figure wearing laurel crown and ending in column below waist, shoulders transformed into grotesque heads; two grotesque figures supporting entwined serpent tails or plant stems.

1f Foliate ornament incorporating two grotesque equine heads; helmet; foliate strapwork; breastplate armour with crossed pike and spear; knot of ribbon-work.

Section 2 –

2a Knot of ribbon-work; winged cherub's head; bucranium (reversed and board misplaced).

2b Fruit swag with scrollwork; drum encircled with ribbon tied in bow; bird of prey with head turned to peer down over its tail; ornate foliage (misplaced).

2c Knot of ribbon-work; frontal view of grotesque humanoid figure with animal legs, diaphanous wings, four ears, upraised arms, female breasts and stalk of foliage with fruits emerging from its backside; foliate scrollwork.

2d Classical thunderbolt above knot of ribbon-work tied round bunch of leaves and fruit; frontal view of bust of female figure with diaphanous wings and upraised hands holding ribbons, from which hang leaves and flowers; acanthus leaf scroll with fruit and foliage.

2e Two birds of prey perched on top of canopy from which tied-back drapes hang; scorpion; knotted ribbon; bird of prey on back of crouching rabbit.

2f Foliate scrollwork closely resembling that in Section 1b.

Section 3 –

3a No detail now visible.

3b Large spray of leaves and flowers springing symmetrically from single stem.

3c Domed canopy with tied-back drapes above parrot-beaked bird perched on fish above acanthus scroll.

3d Fragments of leaf scrolls (misplaced).

Literature

MacGibbon and Ross 1892, vol. iv, 424-32; Apted 1966, pl. 19, 68; Smith 1996; RCAHMS, *Edinburgh*, 96, figs 250 and 252, 258.

Johnstone's Close

Destroyed. Ceiling painted with flowers and geometric shapes reported in Grant 1880-3, vol. i, p.314, and in *The Scotsman*, 8 Feb 1878.

Lawnmarket

Unlocated. Eight sections comprising seventeen loose boards decorated with leaf scrolls, roses and pansies in brown and red on a white ground, removed c.1997 from a house in Lawnmarket and now stored in Historic Scotland Conservation Centre.

Liberton House

Destroyed. Mansion house owned by the successors of burgess William Little (1587), including a Lord Provost of Edinburgh and the co-founder (1580) of Edinburgh University Library. External carvings bear the dates '1675' and '1683', with the initials of William Little. According to MacGibbon and Ross, 'The original plaster of the dining hall exhibited considerable traces of painting in distemper. The panels into which the surface was divided were separated by dark lines ... Traces of more elaborate decoration exist in other parts of the house, as, for example, in the present dining-room, and on the modern ceiling of one of the upper apartments' (vol. v, pp.320-1). Sketch by Thomas Bonnar (RCAHMS, EDD/144/3) shows details, including a stag and a shield of arms above a fireplace.

Mahogany Land

Destroyed. Ceilings reported to have been decorated with paintings 'precisely similar to those found in the Palace of Mary of Guise', ie Blyth's Close.

Literature
Grant 1880-3, vol. i, 319.

Moubray House, 51 High Street

Adjoining John Knox's House, and built in 1477 by Robert Moubray, one of a family of wealthy merchants and burgesses. In 1999 an open board-and-beam ceiling was exposed in the ground-floor apartment to the rear of the building. With windows all along one wall, the apartment may have been a gallery, though there are signs of a partition dividing it into two chambers. Thirteen compartments on beams in the south end showing ornate symmetrical scrollwork and human heads, possibly grotesques, of exceptional quality, and beam decoration on sides and soffits show arabesques in rectangular frames separated by *trompe l'oeil* studs, black on white, black on red, white on black, white on red. Five compartments at the north end have boards showing traces of arabesque leaves, though cleaning and conservation are needed before the design will emerge. From 1633-44 painter George Jamesone lived in the top two storeys of the house, though these would have been separate lodgings at that date.

Owner: Cockburn Conservation Trust.

Literature
Norris 2000.

Nisbet of Dirleton's House

Section of ceiling with floral and architectural motifs and a draped head was rescued from this site and installed in Canongate Tolbooth.

Old Saughton House, Corstorphine

Destroyed. Seventeenth-century, three-storey, L-plan manor house, home of Watson family from its beginnings up until early nineteenth century. According to MacGibbon and Ross, 'The ground floor is vaulted throughout, and is now divided by partitions ... The room marked "Parlour" on the Plan is interesting, having quaintly panelled walls, and a recessed cupboard at one end. The arched ceiling is painted, and is probably one of the best preserved of any painted stone ceiling in Scotland ... The vault at Saughton shows in the centre, on a blue ground, the sun surrounded by the signs of the zodiac, and along the walls at the springing of the arch there runs a series of garden scenes, with rudely-executed figures. At intervals, above this band, a row of ships on a wavy sea completes the design. The painting contains the initials S.V., with the date 1694.' According to local historian G Upton Selway, the spring of the arch on one side showed a line of ships in full sail, and faint traces of a similar design could be made out on the opposite wall: 'Beneath the waves through which the ships are sailing runs a grotesque design, which is repeated with much variation on the other side of the room ... On a castle in the corner of the grotesque work next the door are two flags, one bearing the letters S.V. and the other the date 1694.'

Literature
MacGibbon and Ross, vol. v, 337-8.

Ravelston House

Destroyed. Built by George Fowlis, 1603. Ceiling of principal chamber painted with labours of the months in twelve compartments, each accompanied by corresponding sign of the zodiac. Centre showed group of angels in a circle playing musical instruments, including a bagpipe.

Literature
Brydall 1889, 65, citing Cunningham's *Lives of the Most Eminent British Painters, Sculptors and Architects* 1832, vol. v, 15-16.

Riddles Court, Castle Hill

First floor, north-west corner. Board-and-beam ceiling, thirteen beams decorated with arabesque patterns carried over from soffits to both sides of each beam; green on white, white on umber on alternate beams. The twelve sections between the beams are copiously filled with just two frequently repeated motifs – a crowned imperial eagle and a winged cherub – in a sequence of foliated strapwork, green and brown on white.

Owner: Edinburgh City Council.

Somerville's Land, Lawnmarket

Three-storey house abutting entry to Milne's Court, with two spiral stairs in stone-built south and east walls, the remainder built of timber. Owned in early seventeenth century by Bartholomew Somerville. Demolished in 1882/3, when its construction and contents were recorded in a paper for the Society of Antiquaries (Scotland) by J M Dick Peddie, who includes a description and drawing of the painted ceiling on the second floor, discovered during demolition beneath later plaster. The boards were removed and reassembled to allow partial reconstruction of the painting. It was an open board-and-beam ceiling (18'6" x 14'6"). Peddie states: 'The beams were painted white with running ornaments on both soffits and sides, reminding strongly of Pompeian decoration' (p.476). The beams divided the ceiling into seven sections, painted with birds and beasts surrounded by fruit and foliage with ribbon ornaments, in a style closely resembling that in John Knox's House and at Nunraw, with some of the same motifs. The colours were restricted to black, brown, green and yellow. Motifs are:

Section 1 –
fragment of foliage

Section 2 –
foliage with fish

Section 3 –
foliage
knots of ribbon-work
animal with ? fox's brush
bird

Section 4 –
cock
lion rampant
bird of prey on back of water bird
scrolls of foliage

Section 5 –
bird with spread wings descending
knot of ribbon-work
bird of prey on back of rabbit
foliage scrolls

Section 6 –
lion sejant affronte with thistle
knot of ribbon
standing pigeon
couched unicorn
leaf scrolls

Section 7 –
rinceau leaf scrolls

Literature
Peddie 1884.

FIFE

71 South Street, St Andrews

Painted ceiling recorded but removed: Apted (1964) reports that part was said to be stored in St Salvator's College, part in the National Museum of Antiquities, Edinburgh, but these have not been traced.

119-23 High Street, Kirkcaldy

Two sections of board-and-beam ceiling removed for storage to Historic Scotland Conservation Centre: seventeen boards decorated in black and white with leaf scrolls, flowers and fruit; eight boards with black scrollwork and fruit.

225-229 High Street, Kirkcaldy

Painted boards exposed in 1969 in ceiling of first floor, extending over parts of west and south apartments and passageway; taken to Historic Scotland Conservation Centre. Three compartments of board-and-beam ceiling decorated with: (1) intertwined plant stems; (2) fruit swags; (3) flowers.

339-43 High Street, Kirkcaldy

House of a merchant ship-owner, overlooking the harbour, the earliest owner has been identified as David Law in 1590. In the mid-seventeenth century it belonged to James Coalzier; by the turn of the century it had passed to sea captain and ship-owner John Boswell. Decorative painting of open-beam ceilings and on plaster of walls found in 1989 on two floors. Since plaster ceiling could not be removed some of the painted floorboards were raised for conservation in 1992 and loosely relaid in their original positions; other painting *in situ* remains to be fully revealed. First storey comprised a large central hall with smaller chambers at each end and a large central fireplace; over east chamber ceiling boards have painted strapwork linking round, square, or lozenge-shaped frames holding a nail-head stud motif and fruit swags filling gaps between these frames; beams, where visible, show signs of a painted geometric pattern. Ceiling above centre room has boards with fruit swags and flowers in Gladstone's Land style on a dark ground, whilst those over the west chamber have red and blue arabesque work on a white ground. Second-storey central area has a remarkable and unparalleled wall painting on plaster showing a two-masted ship in full sail with guns, a lion figurehead and flags; also behind later panelling on west-wall fireplace is painting on plaster that has been identified as a lion. Later partition walls dividing the main first-floor apartment have recently had vertical and horizontal rails exposed to reveal a painted wave pattern, suggesting they had re-used painted timber from another part of the house. Tests made on the wall painting of both first and second floors revealed early marbling and graining paint-finishes. The present owner, Scottish Historic Buildings Trust, is managing a comprehensive programme of restoration.

Literature
Robert Scrimgeour, unpublished record and report for Scottish Historic Buildings Trust; Rougvie 1999.

Abbot House, Dunfermline

Remains of painting on plaster on wall of first-floor room was uncovered during restoration work on this building within the abbey precincts. Everything except the façade of the house was rebuilt in 1571 by James Murray, whose brother William was Comptroller General for Mary, Queen of Scots. Badly damaged painting surrounds the filled-in semicircular arch of what appears to have been a later doorway between two rooms, and shows, on the left, a Corinthian pillar rising above a nude female torso with draped hips, beside her a damaged figure wearing a buttoned doublet or breastplate with skirts. On her other side is a nude bust of a bearded figure who points to the right, labelled 'Vulcan'. Above him sits a semi-nude female with a child on her knee and holding a lance or trident(?), and a very indistinct figure reaches towards her below a label which reads 'neptune'. Above the arch is an inscription of which only the fragments, 'If he g ... /Wannis ... also ....' can be made out. To the right of the arch is a picture of a two-storey house with chimney, windows and doorway above further damaged figures, including one in armour holding a shield, and a semi-nude female with a cloak clasped around the neck and angel's wings; the head of a male bearded figure looks towards her from the left. Though the two labelled figures of classical gods ought to supply a clue, it has not so far proved possible to identify the subject of this painting.

Aberdour Castle

Previously owned by 'Regent Morton', murderer of Darnley (d.1581). Painting probably carried out for William Douglas, eighth Earl of Morton (d.1648). 'Gallery Chamber' decorated with open board-and-beam painted ceiling, on first floor of east-range stair tower, adjoining the gallery (itself recorded in 1647 as containing forty-six pictures). Underside of boards: eight compartments decorated with swags of fruit, flowers, cherubs, antique work, mouldings, grotesques on black ground. Traces of paint on beams, but little detail now visible, though Lyons recorded in 1904 that 'each has its sides and face subdivided by yellow painted bands into several oblong blue panels bearing in their centres a small light-coloured ornament with a red heart – the charge of the Douglas family – introduced at either end of the design, enclosed by square and bevelled ends alternately' (1904, p.154). Lyons also records a tempera-painted door (from another part of the castle) which was divided into *trompe l'oeil* panelling.

Owner: Historic Sfcotland.

Literature

Lyons 1904, 153-4, fig. 1; Apted 1966, I 15.

Bay Horse Inn, Dysart

Part of a complex of buildings close to St Serf's Tower, Dysart, overlooking the River Forth estuary, almost certainly the 'new biggit house' which Patrick Sinclair, son of Henry, fifth Lord Sinclair, conveyed to his wife, Katherine Nisbet in 1585; initials 'PS' are carved over a dormer pediment, and both 'PS' and 'KN' are recorded on the first-floor painted ceiling. House remained the property of the earls of Rosslin, though by the mid-nineteenth century it is identified in the Ordnance Survey as the 'Bay Horse Inn'. Painted ceilings were revealed in the 1960s during a general scheme for restoring historic buildings in Dysart under the supervision of NTS. Painted boards and beams were discovered above a later plaster ceiling in first-floor apartments in the east and west gables; there were also remains of mural panels on boards. The painted boards and beams are now in storage with Historic Scotland Conservation.

East-gable Apartment (15'x 12') Fourteen boards in five sections and a smaller area divided into three sections, all supported on six beams. All sections are decorated with leaf scrolls, two musical instruments – a pipe and drum – and the initials 'PS', interlaced, for Patrick Sinclair and 'KN' for his wife Katherine Nisbet in roundels. Colours are blue, yellow and orange.

West-gable Apartment (15'x 12'9") Seventeen boards, most of which are divided into five sections except for those abutting on a corner recess which have four. Each section contains symmetrically interlaced strapwork of a different geometrical design, with foliate scrollwork also in two of the sections. The supporting beams for both ceilings showed remains of a pattern of fruit and flowers, scrolls, or blue and red panels lined in black.

Remaining boards are from two different unlocated mural panels, though further fragments of re-used timber were found beneath a later fireplace, with traces of paint suggesting that the original decoration may have been extensive; traces of decorative paint were also found on some early plaster.

Panel 1 – Four boards, evidently from a wall beneath a sloped gable-end, 3' 4" in width and rising from 4' 7" on the left to nearly eight inches on the right. Although the surviving paint is patchy and badly decayed, the gable-end appears to have been treated as false architecture, interpreted as a classical exterior with Ionic pillars supporting an entablature, above which rises a sloped, scallop-tiled roof, through which there projects a dormer window whose pediment shows an anthemion decoration. To the side of this classical building is a landscape background showing a castle on a rocky outcrop. At the foot of the panel are the remains of a heraldic motif which is of the greatest interest, described as follows in the 1969 conservation report: 'Within the archway of the classical motif a ribbon which encloses a virtually indecipherable crest contains the motto 'IN VTRVMQUE PARA ...' The ribbon itself is surmounted by detached arms, dexter bearing a sword and sinister a spade-like object, possibly a mason's trowel [...] The shield appears to be charged with three mullets in chief; of the motto only the letters '... PACE ...' can be distinguished.' The description is sufficient to leave no doubt that this armorial device reworked the *In utrumque paratus* emblem from Claude Paradin which is also copied at Rossend, at Blyth's Close, Edinburgh, and (adapted from Whitney's version) at Skelmorlie Aisle. The reverse of these boards contains arabesque ornament of scrolled foliage outlined in black on a white ground forming a frieze fifteen feet high. A fragmentary board bears part of a coat of arms: a griffin supporting a shield charged with three mullets in chief and fess chequy of three tracts.

Panel 2 – Three boards and a fragment decorated with a regular pattern of stars and alternate roundels.

Castlewynd House, St Andrews

Fragment of tempera painted ceiling, now in National Museums of Scotland. Pine board, two by one inches, showing female bust with foliage designs in black and white.

Literature
PSAS, 60 1926, 301.

Collairnie

Originally L-shaped tower house with courtyard, now forming part of a farmsteading, from which turnpike stair in tower leads to a single room on each successive floor; those on second and third floors have painted board-and-beam ceilings filled with coats of arms. MacGibbon and Ross remarked in 1887, 'They are in a very neglected state, and will doubtless soon disappear' (vol. ii, p.172). Building has suffered further deterioration, and recent structural damage to these floors has destroyed most of the ceilings; the colour sketches in RCAHMS, which include Thomas Bonnar's (FID/67/4-5) and drawings reproduced in Lyons (1904, figs 3-4) must now be regarded as our major witnesses to their appearance. House belonged to the Barclay family in unbroken succession from the fourteenth to the eighteenth century; carvings over the entrance lintel have initials of David Barclay with the date '1581', and initials and arms of Hugh Barclay with the date '1607'.

Owner: Private.

Second Floor –

Board-and-beam ceiling (14'2" x 13'10") divided into seven compartments by joists, all three sides of which are subdivided into three long sections by yellow and red bands, scrolled at the section divisions, each section of the underside of the beam decorated with delicate scrollwork on alternating red or black grounds; the circles formed by the scrolling filled with the initials 'HB' (for Hugh Barclay) and 'DB' (for David Barclay). The three sections on the sides of the beams were filled with black-letter inscriptions which MacGibbon and Ross describe as 'after the manner of the ceilings at Earl's Hall, Pinkie, and other places' (vol. ii). Lyons describes these as 'scarcely readable', and they appear never to have been recorded or transcribed, though Nigel Tranter records one as: 'FLIE YE COMPANY OF A LIER.BUT THOW NEIDES KEIP COMPENY WT HIM.BEWAR YAT IN NA WAYES THOW TROW HIM'. Each of the seven compartments between the beams contains four labelled coats of arms, without crests, supporters or mottoes. These were identified by Leighton (1890) as follows:

BARCLAY OF COLLAIRNIE
BARCLAY OF TOUCH
BARCLAY OF TOWIE
BARCLAY OF MATHERS
BALFOUR OF GRANGE
BALFOUR OF BALGARVY
BALFOUR OF BALFOUR
BALFOUR OF DENMILN
BETHUNE OF CREICH
BETHUNE OF BALFOUR
BETHUNE OF NETHERTARVIT
MELVILLE OF BALGARVIE
COLVILLE OF CLEISH
FERNIE OF THAT ILK
FORRESTER OF CARDEN
HENDERSON OF [UNIDENTIFIED SEPT]
HENDERSON OF FORDELL
INGLIS OF TARVIT
INNAIRD OF THE CARSE
MONCRIEF OF THAT ILK
MONYPENNY OF PITMILLIE
MELVILLE OF CAIRNIE
LEARMOUTH OF DAIRSIE
RAMSAY OF COLLUTHIE
WEMYSS OF THAT ILK
SANDISLANDS OF ST MONANCE
TRAIL OF BLEBBO

Third Floor –

Board-and-beam ceiling (14'9" x 14'), divided into seven compartments by the joists, which are here decorated with abstract and geometrical decorative scrollwork, and with four shields of arms in each of the compartments. Leighton in 1890 transcribed the following labels identifying the coats of arms:

SCOTT OF ABBOTSHALL
MELVILLE OF RAITH
STEWART OF ROSYTH
SETON OF [UNIDENTIFIED SEPT]
MURRAY OF GLENDOICK
SCOTT OF BALWEARY
SIBBALD OF BALGONIE
EATON OF PITMEDDEN
COLVILLE OF EASTER WEMYSS
LUNDY OF THAT ILK
RAMSAY OF CRACKNESTOUN
LUNDY OF BALGONIE
STRANG OF BALCASKY
KINCRAIGY OF THAT ILK
STEWART OF MINTO
TOWERS OF INNERLEITH
LORD INNERMEATH

Several further coats of arms were indecipherable.

Literature

Leighton 1890, vol. ii, 93; Lyons 1904, 154-8, figs 2 -3; Innes of Learney 1956, pl. 37; Tranter 1962, vol. ii, 31.

Culross Palace

The south block of the palace dates from 1597; the north block from 1611, the year its owner, George Bruce, was knighted. The property passed to the National Trust for Scotland in 1932, when restoration work was carried out on painted decoration in a number of rooms. Inappropriate conservation methods at that time resulted in the destruction of much of the painted decoration throughout the house. Accurate colour sketches of the decoration in several rooms had been made, however, in the 1930s by John Houston for the Office of Works in Edinburgh, and in the 1990s an extensive programme of restoration was carried out by Historic Scotland Conservation. The Houston drawings, and the more recent restoration work, now permit us to arrive at a fairly comprehensive analysis of the decorative painting throughout the house.

Owner: NTS.

South Block

First Floor –

South Gable Boarded eastern and western end walls are divided into matching square panels by *trompe l'oeil* frames; central panel of each contains a red circle in a white ring, fringed with black spikes (a radiant sun?); panels on either side contain square strapwork cartouches.

'Laird's Room' Open board-and-beam ceiling now boarded over, but when exposed shows sides of beams decorated with repetitive arabesque ornament in rectangular frames, white on black, black on white, white on red. Soffits have winged cherubs' heads. Undersides of boards now blank. Walls of the room painted in pale green *trompe l'oeil* panelling.

Second Floor –

Emblem Chamber (20'8" x 14'10") Coved ceiling painted in tempera, covered with sixteen allegorical paintings separated by a broad black line with traces of arabesque decoration, each panel framed with a band of yellow, and shaded to give the effect of a moulded gilt frame. The paintings were first noticed in a paper by A Jervise to the Society of Antiquaries (Scotland) in 1867. In 1885 they were described in greater detail, and with some corrections to Jervise, in an unpublished manuscript by T Etherington Cooke, deposited with RCAHMS in 1990. Thomas Bonnar's sketches show nine of the panels as they appeared in the mid-nineteenth century (RCAHMS, FID/78/10-11). These sources record a number of details no longer visible, and I have therefore drawn on them in the following analysis. Each of the ceiling panels adapts an emblem from Geffrey Whitney's *A Choice of Emblemes* (1586) to create a new tripartite emblem, consisting in each case of:

1) a Latin motto, drawn in every case but one from Whitney;
2) a picture which uses motifs from Whitney's woodcut but adds further details, notably a large allegorical figure;
3) a verse couplet *subscriptio* which adapts lines or phrases from Whitney's verse epigram to suggest the moral significance of the emblem.

In nearly every case the picture has two parts: a dominant allegorical figure, usually female; and a number of further details drawn to a smaller scale. It is these secondary details that most often copy the emblematic motif from Whitney's woodcut. Several additional fragments of painting are visible in the arched, boarded window recesses, and on the upper part of the wall at the boarded east end of the room. The following analysis attempts to show how each of the emblems adapts its source. Words or details in square brackets are those described by Etherington Cooke in 1885 but which are no longer visible.

– Culross –	**– Whitney, 1586 –**
Panel 1 –	Whitney, 1586, p.166a
[MANET] INVICTA VERITAS	*Veritas invicta*
Damaged; outspread wings bearing open book: VERITAS RESTITUA. [background of clouds and glory, wings issue from open eye, below are rocks]	Hand of God holds pair of outspread wings bearing up open book: ET VSQVE AD NUBES VERITAS TVA. Satan has encircled book with chain and attempts to pull it down to hell-mouth.
Vnto his word, the lord doth give such light and secret power devine; That in despyt of menns micht [his glorie still doth] schyne	Yet to his worde, the Lorde doth give such lighte, That to the East, and West, the same doth shine: [ll.3-4]

Motto: 'Invincible truth', goes back to Georgette de Montenay, Whitney's source.

Panel 2 –	Whitney, 1586, p.208
SECVRITAS	*Tunc tua res agitur, paries cum proximus ardet.*
Seated woman, head resting on left hand, asleep; crow-stepped building encircled by flames	Two men playing chess in burning room
Awake from sleip secure when perrell doth apeir For if beginnings we withstand, the les we neid to feir	Awake from sleepe secure, when perrill doth appeare: [l.1] For if beginnings wee withstande, the conquest sooner wonne.[l.10] ...and not the worst to feare [l.2]

Motto: [Culross] 'Safety'; [Whitney] 'It concerns you, when your neighbour's wall is on fire' (Horace, *Epist* 1.18.84, from la Perrière). This is the only emblem at Culross which does not use Whitney's motto, and it seems likely that the motto (or label) 'Securitas' derives from Valeriano, *Hieroglyphica* (1556, fol.319 v.)

who describes Securitas as a goddess seated in a chair supporting her head, as here, on her hand.

Panel 3 –	Whitney, 1586, p.23
MIHI PONDERA LVXVS	*Mihi pondera, luxus.*
Female figure holds golden cup in right hand and bunch of grapes left. A sheaf of corn in a lakeland scene	Sheaf of corn, stalks bent and broken by weight of full ears
Then sen exces, procuris oure spoile and paine, The meane prefer before immoderat gaine	Then since Excesse procures our spoile and paine, The meane preferre, before immoderate gaine. [ll.11-12]

Motto: 'Excess is a burden to me' goes back to Paradin.

Panel 4 –	Whitney, 1586, p.180
Verbum emissum non est revocabile	*Verbum emissum non est reuocabile.*
Seated female figure personifying Silence holds finger to lips, closed book on her knee	Man in peasant's dress releases a bird.
And he whose tonge before his witt doth runne, Oft speikis too soone, and grevis when he hes doon	But hee, whose tonge before his witte, dothe runne Ofte speakes to soone, and greeues when he hathe done. [ll.5-6]

Motto: 'A word once spoken cannot be called back' from la Perrière.

Panel 5 –	Whitney, 1586, p.67
MVRVS ÆNEUS. SANA CONSCIENTIA	*Murus Æneus, sana conscientia.*
Female figure grasps trunk of tree with right arm, holds laurel branch in left hand; swan swims in pool [white cloud floats over distant mountains]	Man grasps trunk of laurel tree in storm, Jupiter *tonans* astride eagle in clouds; swan with collar of laurel swims in pool
The richteous, ar lyk unto the laurell tree The wicked lyk the blasted boughis that dee	Suche men are like vnto the Laurell tree, The others, like the blasted boughes that die. [ll.9-10]

Motto: 'A clear conscience is a wall of brass' Horace Epist 1.1.60 via Sambucus.

Panel 6 –	Whitney, 1586, p.219
IN AMORE TORMENTVM	*In amore tormentum.*
Seated allegorical figure holds scourge in left hand, and [three pronged fork] in right [which she is dipping into golden dish filled with flames on a table covered with a white cloth], lighted candle on table surrounded by flies	Lighted candle surrounded by flies standing on table in landscape; in background two women fan flames of separate bonfires
Then leave to love or love as reasone will; For lovers lewde do vainlie languische still.	Then leaue to love, or loue as reason will, For, louers lewde doe vainlie languishe still. [p 183, ll.5-6]

Motto: 'Torment in love' from Junius. Culross epigram is drawn from Whitney's emblem: *Qui me alit me extinguit*, p.183, which is similarly concerned with the fires of passion and evidently offered a more easily abstracted summary of the moral point. The attributes of this figure are now very indistinct, but can be supplied from Etherington Cooke's description.

Panel 7 –	Whitney, 1586, p.217
OMNIS CARO FOENVM	*Omnis caro foenum.*
Allegorical female figure seated holding golden vase of flowers held on her knee, on her left another tall vase of flowers, on her right what looks like a tree, but is in fact a version of Whitney's hay hanging from staff.	Bundle of hay hanging from staff, representing the Latin manipulus or badge of the Roman legions.
All flesche is grasse and withereth lyk the haye, And warneth ws how weill to live, bot not how long to waye.	All fleshe, is grasse; and withereth like the haie:[l.1] Howe, well to liue: but not how longe to waie. [l.10]

Motto: 'All flesh is grass' *Isaiah* 40.6 via Paradin. The picture is reinterpreted.

Panel 8 –	Whitney, 1586, p.222
[no motto now visible]	*Neglecta virescunt.*
Seated female holding lance and shield, wearing breastplate. [At the edge of the picture is the corner of a golden tabernacle or temple, indicating the future habitation of the righteous]	Seated helmeted figure (?Pallas) holding lance and ?mace. Ivy and snakes climb wall of building behind her.
Althoghe the world, the verteous still despyse, Yet up aloft in spyte of them they ryse	So, thoughe the worlde the vertuous men dispise, Yet vp alofte in spite of the they rise. [l.5-6]

Motto [Whitney]: 'Despised things flourish' from Sambucus. One of the few examples where Whitney's picture also shows a seated female figure; Culross replaces her mace (?) with a shield, but though much is changed, the position of the right arm holding the upright lance appears to be modelled on that of Whitney's figure, in which case, as with Panel 5, we should probably not look for an independent source for the allegorical figure. The Culross figure does not represent the conventional figure of armed Pallas, however. Whitney's ivy symbolises the virtuous who flourish, though neglected by the world. It is no longer possible to say whether Culross showed the ivy-covered wall, though what Etherington Cooke describes as the 'tabernacle of the righteous' may go back to this detail.

Panel 9 –	Whitney, 1586, p.11
Res humanæ in summo declinant	*Res humanæ in summo declinant.*
Ship founders in storm; seated Fortuna with her wheel looks on	Ship foundering in storm; sun melts patch of snow
This warneth all, on fortunes whele that clime To beare in mynd, how schort thay have there tyme.	Which warneth all, on Fortunes wheele that clime To beare in minde how they haue but a time. (ll.11-12)

Motto: 'Mortal things decline when at their height' from Sambucus. Though not represented in Whitney's picture, the allegorical figure is clearly prompted in this instance by the motto, which goes back to Ovid, and by the mention of Fortune in Whitney's epigram.

Panel 10 –	Whitney, 1586, p.216
Sol non occidat super iracundiam	*Sol non occidat super iracundiam vestram vestram.*
Seated woman with hands on lap, on far side of river two figures struggle or embrace [large two-handed sword lies at their feet], sun [with human features] in top left-hand corner	Two men who have thrown down their swords embrace
Win foes with love, subdueing zoure rasche desyirs; Let not the sunne go doune upon zour yir	Let not the Sonne goe downe vppon your ire. [l.2] And frendshippes force subdue your rashe desire. [l.4]

Motto: 'Let not the sun set on your anger' Ephesians 4.26, from de Montenay. The allegorical figure is not from Whitney, whose motif is consigned to the far side of the picture.

Panel 11 –	Whitney, 1586, p.10
SIRENES	*Sirenes.*
Woman seated at foot of tree holds lyre in right hand, [bunch of withered grapes] in left; a ship sails to rocky shore [Four Sirens, one of whom is blowing a long trumpet, are wading out towards the vessel, and luring the sailors to destruction]	Fish-tailed sirens with various musical instruments entice Ulysses and his companions in ship and luring the sailors to destruction]
Mens pleasures fond, do promeis only Joyes Bot he that yeldes, at lengthe him self destroyes.	Suche Mairemaids liue, that promise onelie ioyes: But hee that yeldes, at lengthe him selffe distroies.

Motto: 'The Sirens' from Alciato. The Culross artist transfers the Sirens' lyre to his favourite seated allegorical figure.

Panel 12 –	Whitney, 1586, p.137
Constantia comes victoriæ	*Constantia comes victoriæ.*
Seated female figure holds pillar in right hand, palm branch in left [Rest of picture filled with large oak tree, typifying Endurance]	Ship in full sail
He that doth kepe, his constant course he winnis, That wisched porte, where lasting Joyes beginnis.	And if he keepe his course directe he winnes That wished porte, where lastinge ioye beginnes. [ll.11-12]

Motto: 'Perseverance the companion of victory'. The column and the palm branch are commonplace attributes of Constancy and Victory. The allegorical figure recalls Valeriano's description of 'Securitas' (1556, fol. 367) in his chapter 'Columnæ' on the significance of columns. Securitas is described as a woman leaning on a pillar, holding a palm branch in her left hand; the Culross artist shows these attributes, rather than in his own 'Securitas' emblem, Panel 2.

Panel 13 –	Whitney, 1586, p.228
SOLI DEO GLORIA	*Soli Deo gloria.*
Allegorical figure of a crowned ?woman to whom Hand of God reaches down sceptre in top right-hand corner of picture; man stands to her right [picture badly damaged; Etherington Cooke describes main figure as a king who grasps handle of proffered sceptre, man on right walks out of the sea bearing sheaf of corn to lay at the king's feet, emblematic of tribute from distant lands]	Man takes axe to bole of tree
Man of him self most weake to good doeth live Bot god gives grace to whome all glorie give.	[God] with his grace, to good, doth make him ronne: And of him self, hee weake theretoo, doth liue; And god giues power, to whome all glorie giue. [ll.9-12]

Motto: 'To God alone be the glory' from de Montenay. The man on the left is only distinguishable as an outline, all other traces of paint having disappeared, but he stands beside the tree in the centre of the picture and the angle of his legs and the skirts of his tunic are clearly copied from Whitney's woodcutter – Etherington Cooke's interpretation may be mistaken. Whitney explains that the axe can achieve nothing of itself, just as the Christian can do nothing without the grace of God.

Panel 14 –	Whitney, 1586, p.163
PIETAS FILIORUM IN PARENT[ES]	*Pietas filiorum in parentes.*
Seated female figure reading an open book; Aeneas carries Anchises on his shoulders [across a river]	Aeneas carrying his father Anchises on his shoulders away from burning city of Troy
Thair children shall with god- lines and pietie procede: To reverence thair parents, and help them if they nede	Which showes, that sonnes must carefull bee, and kinde, For to releeue their parentes in distresse: And duringe life, that dutie shoulde them binde, To reuerence them, that God their daies may blesse: [ll.7-10]

Motto: 'The love of sons towards their parents' from Alciato. The Culross verses take only the merest hints from their source.

Panel 15 –	Whitney, 1586, p.220
PATIENTIA OMNIA VINCIT	*Vincit qui patitur.*
Seated female figure in land-scape; tree and reeds bent by wind blown by Zephyrus figure in top left-hand corner	Oak tree bent over in blast of wind breaks its trunk; reeds at side bend but do not break; Zephyrus figure in top left-hand corner
With patience suffer still, and then we sall in fine; Oure foes subdue, when they with shame sall pyne	But suffer still, and then wee shall in fine, Our foes subdue, when they with shame sall pyne shame shall pine. [ll.11-12]

Motto [Culross]: 'Suffering conquers all things', [Whitney]: 'He who endures conquers' from Junius.

Panel 16 –	Whitney, 1586, p.230
[TEMPUS OMNIA] TERMINAT	*Tempus omnia terminat*
Seated male bearded figure holds globe on which '[EUR]RO[PA]' is marked and measures its circum-ference with a pair of compasses	Three oak trees, one flourishing, one dying, one dead and fallen; seascape with setting sun

[No epigram now visible]

Motto [Whitney]: 'Time brings all things to an end'.

Fragments of an inscription can still be seen on two of the recessed window bays. That on the north wall beside the door shows a scroll which, unlike those on the ceiling, is doubled into several folds suggesting that it is still in its intended position. The only letters remaining read, 'PAUPERTATEM [...] HANTUR'. This must be Whitney's *Paupertatem summis ingeniis obesse ne provehantur* (p.152), 'Poverty obstructs the progress of the most gifted of minds'. Etherington Cooke quotes the complete motto and accurately describes the picture, which evidently copied Whitney, who shows a man with winged hand who aspires to the heavens, weighed down by the stone of poverty to which his other hand is bound.

Etherington Cooke records that the window recess opposite the centre window showed several flowers on one stem with a label, '*Vitae arbor*' ('Tree of Life'). This has no source in Whitney. On the south-east corner of the ceiling, in a square line, were the words 'CONTRA OMNIA [S]PEM VIR REPELLIT', and on the east wall, on labels surrounded by foliage, the words 'ANGUSTA ... HERBA'. This seems most likely to be a version of the emblem that Whitney gives as *Latet anguis in herba* ('The snake lurks in the grass') which goes back to Paradin, and shows a snake climbing a branch of foliage towards fruit at the top (Whitney p.24).

Substantial portions remain of the painting on boards at the east end of the room. These show no Latin mottoes, and little or nothing of their original inscriptions now remains. There are two distinct subjects, one showing what Etherington Cooke describes as two hogs at the base of a large tree, one about to attack the other, a verse couplet pointing the moral: 'Which warneth ws in peace o[ur] mynds for weir to frame,/ Wherby we aye sall subdue, or wine ye field with fame.' This was evidently based on Whitney's *In pace de bello*, showing a boar which has sharpened its tusks on the bark of a tree, facing a fox which peers around the tree-trunk. One of the two animals which Etherington Cooke describes as hogs was evidently a fox, as can still be seen. The Culross *subscriptio* adapts the last two lines of Whitney's epigram: 'Which teacheth vs, in peace, our force for warres to frame: / Whereby, we either shall subdue, or loose the field with fame' (p.153). The second of these subjects is described as a lion and squirrel, again on either side of the base of a large tree, with only a few words of the moralising couplet legible: 'This schawes ye ... airts at feld .../ with ....' This copies Whitney's *Dura usu molliora* (p.156); a fox confronting a lion with an epigram explaining that though a fox is afraid of the fierce lion on their first encounter, increasing familiarity makes it less fearful: 'Which shewes, that artes at first moste harde to see,/ With triall oft, both playne, and easie bee' (ll.5-6).

North Block

First Floor –

Two rooms on either side of central stairwell.

East Room Six compartments of open board-and-beam ceiling decorated with fruits and flowers; the west wall is recorded in Houston's sketch as decorated in 1932 with vertical stripes, each in a different colour including umber, black, red, green, and blue, below a decorative frieze of repetitive cartouches containing tree shapes; the skirting below stripes has two rows of alternating red and brown tile shapes. Remains of paint on other walls.

Connecting Passage Boarded walls painted with geometric patterning in black and brown.

West Room Board-and-beam ceiling with ten compartments filled with fruit swags and flowers; remains of paint on all four walls now too indistinct to describe, though colour sketch by

John Houston records Judgement of Solomon on east wall in 1930s: King Solomon sits enthroned on a dais of seven steps which rise from a black and white chequered floor, above him a canopy supported on four pillars; on the bottom step lies a child, and on the second a dog; on either side at the foot of the dais are soldiers and a supplicating woman.

Second Floor –

East Room Barrel-vaulted boarded ceiling painted with false mouldings in blue-black to suggest coffering in a pattern of lozenges and hexagonal stars. Alternate stars have at their centres either a swag of fruits – grapes or pomegranates and pears, with leaves, and roses at their centre – or a white circle with four loops. Each of the lozenges has a star at its centre. This decoration – in black, brown, blue and white – is carried down onto the walls to form a deep frieze. Houston's colour sketch of 1935 and an earlier sketch by Thomas Bonnar (RCAHMS, FID/78/13) show that the dado on the end wall was decorated with *trompe l'oeil* curtains, with deep gatherings and valances in a rich creamy brown, with valance-tassels and bottom border in red. In the centre a corniced recess had its white curtains tied back to reveal what looks like a bed recess, though it is shown as quite empty; none of this curtain-painting is now visible.

West Room Barrel-vaulted boarded ceiling painted with false mouldings in red and white to suggest coffering in a pattern of linked circular and rectangular panels, filled with arabesque leaf scrolls, coils of strapwork, and a curious irregular white patch resembling a stretched animal skin, decorated with finely drawn blue arabesque work. As in the adjoining room, this pattern is carried down onto the walls to create a deep frieze, but the dado of all four walls is divided into rectangular panels. The central blue-black band of the moulding that frames these panels is ornamented with delicately drawn white plant forms, and the panels are filled with alternate designs, either a plain-framed lozenge without further decoration, or a dark blue double oval containing stylised floral or seed-like shapes in white. The decoration is in black, brown, blue, red and white. RCAHMS Bonnar Collection has colour sketches made in the mid-nineteenth century of this emblem ceiling, and of the second-floor east room.

Literature

Jervise 1854-57, 339-44; Apted 1966, pl. 28, 54, 97-101; Bath 1993, 259-305.

Dunfermline Abbey

Vaulting divides a section of north aisle into four compartments, each of which is decorated with a labelled image of one of the apostles, painted on plaster, each shown with a closed book, and the names 'Peter' and 'Paul' inscribed on scrolls, the other two labels now effaced – though evidently including St Andrew, who holds his cross, and St Paul holding a sword. The lower corner to two of the vaults shows a helmeted male head whilst a third shows a female head with a coif; all these are separated off from the apostle portraits by an inner painted frame and all four vaults are framed by zig-zag, fleur-de-lis or other decorative borders carried over onto the supporting ribs. In 1590 William Schaw was paid to restore and modernise the adjoining palace block for the queen's use and any post-Reformation painting within the abbey probably dates from this period; he was ordered to carry out repairs to the abbey church by the General Assembly of the Kirk of Scotland in 1588 (Howard 1995, p.29). Alexander Seton's monument to Schaw is situated beneath the north tower (Howard 1995, fig. 5.22).

Owner: Historic Scotland.

Literature

Apted 1966, pl. 7.

Earlshall, Leuchars

In 1504 Sir William Bruce succeeded his father Alexander, who had been granted the lands of Earlshall in 1497. Favoured by successive monarchs from James IV to James VI, he began building the castle in 1546, work which was completed by his grandson William Bruce, following his succession to the title c.1588. He married firstly Elizabeth Wood of Largo, by whom he had four sons, and secondly Agnes Lyndsay of Kirkforthar, by whom he had no family. Their elaborate sculptured tombs can be seen in Leuchars parish church. The painted decoration in the house was reported by MacGibbon and Ross (vol. ii, p.289) as being badly decayed due to rain penetration, but in 1891 the new owner commissioned the young architect, Robert Lorimer, to restore it. Some painting elsewhere in the house recorded by A H Millar in 1895 had evidently already been destroyed, and Lorimer's restoration blanked out some details in the long gallery which were beyond recovery.

Owner: Private.

First Floor –

Sitting Room On the west front, the ceiling is painted in full colour with the arms of Bruce impaled with Lyndsay, including supporters, crest and mantling, all contained in a large, circular strapwork cartouche on a dark ground which covers the whole of this flat boarded ceiling. The appropriate sides of the impaled arms are flanked by the monograms 'WB' and 'AL', with the date '1636'. This has to be a posthumous tribute, since Dame Agnes died in 1635. Sketch of this ceiling by Thomas Bonnar is preserved in RCAHMS, FID/95/86.

Second Floor –

Long Gallery (51' x 24') Divided into thirteen sections running east to west, with up to fifteen different subjects in each. Alternate sections depict either animals and birds in square frames or coats of arms in round frames, each separated from its neighbour by ornamental spaces of arabesque work and floral motifs. Many, though by no means all, of the animals are copied from Topsell's *Historie of Foure-Footed Beastes* (1607) or from Pierre Belon's *La nature et diversité des poissons* (1555) and his *L'histoire de la nature des oyseaux* (1555). However, two emblematic figures are copied from Guillaume de la Perrière, *Theatre des bons engins* (1539). The sections identified below are numbered from north to south, the series of motifs in each section listed from east to west; a dash indicates a blanked-out panel; brackets round the name indicate an unnamed or conjectural image. Some of the images are grouped in local, numbered sequences as indicated below.

Section 1 – Rectangular panels of unnamed animals.

(hound running)
(deer fleeing arrow)
(deer fleeing pursuing hound)
(hedgehog with grapes on spines)
(fox with stolen hen)
(bird with outspread wings)
(sea monster with bird on its back)
(duck)
(crocodile)
(swan)
(fish)
(fish)

Section 2 – Circular panels of coats of arms and three numbered Virtues.

Godfrey Duke of Boulogne
Arthur King of Brityne
Charles ye Maigne
King of Ierusalem
King of Norway
King of Silitia
Duke of Lennox
Iustitia (7)
Fortitudo (6)
Prudentia (5)
Ye Erl of Pearth
Erl of Mar
The Erl of Mortoun
Liord Carleil (15)

Section 3 – Rectangular panels of named animals.

Asse (Topsell p.17)
Alce (Topsell p.166)
Panther (Topsell p.447)
Hyena (Topsell p.340)
Mertrick
Genitha (Topsell p.180)
Ape of Arabia (Topsell p.8)
(Bacchus dressed as Hercules) (from la Perrière no. xlviii)
(bird of prey standing with dead rabbit in its claws, *cf* Belon, *Oiseaux*, p.14, buzzard)
(animal)
Ram
Otter (Topsell p.445)
Porcapine (Topsell p.456)
(weasel) (Topsell p.562)

Section 4 – Circular panels of coats of arms and four numbered Virtues.

Iudas Maccabeus
Hector Prince of Troy
David King of Israel
King of Portingal
King of Denmark
King of Yreland
Earl of Marche
Temperantia (4)
Charitas (3)
Spes (2)
Fides (1)
Liord Carcart (14)
Arms of Lord Ross, 'God Send Graice' (13)
Erl of Montrose, (boar)

Section 5 – Rectangular panels of named animals.

Cow (Topsell p.56)
Horse
Nylghav
Camel (Topsell p.73)
The Knev Mare
Boar
Simiwlpa (Topsell p.16)
(Occasio) (from la Perrière no. lxiii)
Must Ket (Topsell p.?427)
(?heron)
(stag)
(ape)
(bird)
(animal)

Section 6 – Circular panels of coats of arms and monograms.

Iosoua Duke of Israel
Alexander the Conqueror
Julius Caesar
King of Pole
King of Freisland
Emperiour of Iudea
The Duk of Sprussi
ADL
ED
MD
DL
WB/DAL
Erl of Cassellis (11)
Erl of Cravfurd (10)
(deer)

Section 7 – Rectangular panels of monograms and animals.

[three blank]
(unident. heraldic crest)
(unident. coat of arms)
[blank]
WB/DAL
WB/DAL 1620
Ram of Arabia (Topsell p.185, 'Syrian goats')
Ostrag
(animal)
Hydra
(animal)
(turtle, copied from Belon, *Poissona,* p.46, 'Le dessus de la Tortue de mer')

Section 8 – Circular panels of coats of arms and monograms.

Emperour of Rome
(arms of James VI and I) IR
King of France
King of Hungary
Prince of Oragnge
King of Greiland
(carbuncle with motto 'Hed Lave')
WB (1620)
ER
AS
DMM
DES
Lord Borthick (8)
Liord Lindesay
(animal)

Section 9 – Rectangular panels of named animals.

[two blank]
Dromedarie (Topsell p.77)
Wolf
Sphinx (?Topsell p.344 'Mantichora')
(animal)
Greyhund
(animal with another on its back)
(swine) (Topsell p.512)
Elephant
Rhinoceros (Topsell p.461)
(dragon)
(Topsell p.119)
(English bloodhound)
(crab)

Section 10 – Circular panels of coats of arms and monograms.

Melchior King of Araby
Balthasar King of Saba
Gaspar King of Tharse
King of Swadrick
King of Castile
King of Neapolis
The King of Bewme
EW
EL
SR
EL
CR
EL
WB/DAL
Erl of Arrane
Ye Earl of Buchovhann
(animal)

Section 11 – Rectangular panels of animals.

(animal)
(animal)
[three blank]
Coatimon
(crocodile) (Belon, *Poissons,* p.36, 'Crocodil du Nil')
(tiger) (Topsell p.547)
(lion), Shoe Lyon
Mowse of Arabia (ibid., 406: 'Alpine Mouse')
Camelion (Topsell 1608, p.673)
(wild boar) (?Topsell p.537)
Cuning (Topsell p.86)

Section 12 – Circular panels of coats of arms.

King of Svaden
King of England
King of Navern
King of Aragon
King of Cyprus
King of Spain
The Que of Loraine
The Duk of Loraine
The Erl of Sutherland
The Liord of Lorne
The Erl of Angus
The Erl of Argyll
The Erl of Athole
The Erl of Earoll (4)

Section 13 – Rectangular panels, all blank.

The frieze on the two longer walls is divided into arcaded partitions by *trompe l'oeil* hexagonal pilasters with segmented vaulting painted in black on white plaster. All the partitions are now blank except four, which contain the following verse apophthegms, executed in Roman capitals:

> A NICE WIFE AND A BACK DOORE OFT MAKETH A RICH MAN POORE.
>
> GIVE LIBERALYE TO NEIDFVL FOLKE DENY NANE OF THEM AL FOR LITLE THOV KNAVEST HEIR IN THIS LYF QVHAT CHAVNCE MAY THE BEFALL.

TRY AND THEN TRVST EFTER GVDE ASSVRANCE BOT TRVST NOT OR YE TRY FOR FEAR OF REPENTANCE.

BE MERRYE AND GLAID HONEST AND VERTEOVS FOR THAT SVFFICETH THE ANGER OF THE INVYOVS.

Jervise (1860-2) records the following further inscriptions on the walls, now no longer visible:

... MAKE FEAST, AND BIGE, LENE AND CRAVE,
... SO SHALT THOV NEVER HAVE.

Near this inscription is the figure of a soldier, in the costume of the period, who points a gun towards the entrance-door of the hall. About nine and a half inches high, it is described as bearded, bare-headed, wearing a ruffle round the neck, and a coat with epaulettes and striped breast and sleeves, and wide knee-breeches, below which is a garter round the leg, tied with a knot. Jervise records two fragmentary biblical inscriptions on the walls: 'Prayer to God is the only ... meanes ... to prepare ... a man for ... a wicket ane ...' and: '... yeldeth ... e: bvt the .... destroieth ... er ovne hand' (p.391). Portion of plaster over fireplace has raised rectangular frame enclosing the arms of William Bruce the Elder with the initials 'WB' and 'MM' (ie Margaret Meldrum) and Latin inscriptions – above:

ÆDES HAS EXTRUEBAT D.W.B. AN. 1546 EXTRUXIT TANDEM W.B. EIVS PRONEPOS ANNO 1617

('D W B raised this building in the year 1546; his great grandson W B extended it in 1617')

and below:

CONTEMNO ET ORNO MENTE MANV
('I despise with the mind what I adorn with the hand')

Second fireplace at eastern end of gallery and adjoining door-surround are decorated with black guilloche or arabesque designs on white stonework. Bonnar drawings (RCAHMS, FID/95/85) include sketch of part of this ceiling.

Ante-room Destroyed. Millar (1895, vol. i, p.348) says that the walls of a small ante-room near the long gallery were decorated with 'fresco paintings of armorial bearings on a gigantic scale'. Millar records these as having been hidden by wooden panelling in the mid-eighteenth century and, when uncovered at the time he was writing, to have lost most of their colours. The ceiling of the ante-room 'was originally of the same height as the great hall' and was 'similarly decorated', but is now 'entirely destroyed' since the eighteenth-century owner lowered the ceiling and plundered the painted roof-timbers to make laths for the new plasterwork. Millar's 'great hall' is evidently the long gallery, and this 'ante-room' was presumably on the second floor adjoining it. No sign of this painting now remains.

Third Floor –

Bedroom Off the eastern stair turret, with board-and-beam ceiling, similarly painted in black on a white ground, with twelve named animals in its six compartments between the decorated beams. Each compartment is divided, like the sections of the long gallery, into alternating rectangular panels of bestiary images and of arabesque work, with two animals in each compartment. These are all copied from Topsell's illustrations, and all but one of them (the 'ICHNEVMON', *cf* Topsell p.350) also appear on the long gallery ceiling. The only notable departure appears to be the 'CAMEL', which names what is evidently Topsell's dromedary, whereas the 'DRUMADARIE' names the camel.

DRUMADARIE, WOLFE

CAMEL, GOAT

MULET, UNICORN

RAM OF ARABIA, ICHNEVMON

BEVER, CAMELION

TIGRE, LEOPARD

Mezzanine Room Off the stair turret, containing two wooden panels incorporated into the otherwise plain panelling of the walls, one painted with the arms of William Bruce and his initials, the other with the arms of Agnes Lyndsay and her initials, both with the date '1622' painted under the shield. This may not be the original location.

Literature

Jervise 1860-2; McGibbon and Ross, vol. ii, 282-90; Millar 1895, vol. i, 347-8; Lyons 1904, 160, fig. 5; Hill 1905; Hill 1953, figs 256-7; Innes of Learney 1956, pl. 36; Apted 1966, pl. 33, 34, 61. RCAHMS has pre-restoration photos taken c.1890 by Erskine Beveridge.

Falkland Palace

Chapel Royal Ceiling painted for Charles I's stay at Falkland in 1633, divided into compartments with royal monograms and devices, 'CR' (Carolus Rex), Henrietta Maria, 'CP' (Carolus Princeps), roses and thistles, badge of Charles as Prince of Wales (harp and crown), portcullis, lion rampant gardant, St George's and St Andrew's crosses. Date '1633' on cartouche panel, part of frieze above royal pew, which is decorated with ornamental *trompe l'oeil* brackets, and curved *trompe l'oeil* lintels and window lights to match and balance the actual windows on the facing wall of the chapel. A colour sketch of the ceiling is preserved in the Bonnar drawings at RCAHMS. Painted decoration was restored by the third Marquis of Bute (alias Crichton Stuart, keeper of the palace) in 1896.

Owner: NTS.

Literature

Lyons 1904, 158-60, fig. 4; *PSAS* 44 1909-10, figs 3-5; Apted 1966, 8-10, pl. 12, 13.

Fisherman's Cottage, Dysart

Painted boards with black-scroll decoration on white ground, similar to that in Kirkcaldy, Sailor's Walk; moved to Historic Scotland Conservation Centre for storage.

The Giles, Pittenweem

Group of seventeenth-century buildings known as 'The Giles' (or 'Gyles') at eastern end of Pittenweem harbour, restored in the 1960s under NTS Little Houses Improvement Scheme, when painted beams were discovered in a first-floor room decorated on both sides and soffits with a cable or ropework motif consisting of two intertwined and unbroken strands in red and white extending the length of the beam.

Mary Somerville's House, Burntisland

Built during first quarter of seventeenth century, when it was occupied by merchant ship-owners called Watson, of whom John died c.1626 and his son Andrew c.1650. Named after its early nineteenth-century occupant Mary Somerville, after whom Somerville College, Oxford, is named. Second storey contained two rooms with painted ceilings and fragments of painted plaster, discovered in 1957 when about eighty of the painted boards, overplastered and not all in their original locations, were laid out and rearranged to establish the overall design. The photographs and drawings made then to illustrate M R Apted's 1958 *PSAS* article provide a key to their overall content and iconography. Boards now held at Historic Scotland Conservation Centre.

East Chamber Astral ceiling – centre showed a resplendent sun with rays extending to the encircling labelled signs of the zodiac, painted in red in an oval red-framed cartouche. Only six of the twelve signs survive since the boards on either side were missing; reading clockwise they are: Gemini, Aries, Cancer (all labelled, though 'Cancer' shows the image of Scorpio), [three signs missing], Capricorn (named), Pisces (fragment only), ?Aquarius (fragment of draped figure), [three signs missing]. Fragments of the Taurus sign were also found, though not possible to position. This central sun-plus-zodiac detail was surrounded with figures of the planetary deities, mostly surviving as fragments. In the western end of the ceiling was Jupiter, shown full face, with a surrounding nimbus, seated on an eagle and holding a flaming thunderbolt in his upraised right hand, a sceptre in his left; the label 'IVPEITAR' appears to the left of his head. Fragments were recovered of a figure whose label, 'VENVS', was legible. On the south side of the ceiling was the figure of 'SOL', a man with a solar nimbus and playing a lyre, which identifies him as Apollo. A second figure at this end of the ceiling was too damaged to be identified. Traces of two figures, which Apted identifies as Saturn and Luna, appeared on the north side, both surviving only as shadowy outlines in which, however, Saturn's scythe is visible, and the name 'LOVNA' can be read.

West Chamber Ceiling with *trompe l'oeil* coffering forming a geometrical pattern of alternating crosses and octagons on a white ground. All but one of the crosses have a winged cherub's head in the centre, encircled in a laurel wreath, and the arms of the cross are filled with red triangular shapes on a yellow ground, perhaps to suggest chamfered supports for the raised cherub's head. The twenty-three octagons evidently contained labelled portraits of the twelve Sibyls, and of other biblical figures such as Christ, Mary, St Matthew, and an Agnus Dei. The figures are labelled in the black inch-wide border with an explanatory text in Latin or (in one case) Greek. The fragmentary remaining lettering to the Sibyls has been shown to correspond to that recorded on a set of decorated fruit trenchers owned by C F Cooksey (now in the British Museum); however both the Cooksey trenchers and the ceiling copy this Latin inscription from the set of engravings of *The Twelve Sibyls* by Crispijn de Passe (STC 22527a.7), issued c.1630 in London; reworked a few years later by Martin Droeshout for a series entitled *XII Sibyllarum Icones: The Prophecies of the Twelve Sybills, Plainely Foretelling the Incarnation, Birth, Life, Death, and Comming againe to Judgement of Our Lord and Saviour Iesus Christ.* These prints have now been shown to be the source of the Sibyl portraits in Thomas Trevilian's manuscripts (Barker 2000, vol. ii, pp.444-5).The four Sibyl portraits of which anything recognisable survives – Libyca, Erythræa, Phrygia, Europea – copy the engravings closely. The following analysis of the ceiling is based on Apted, and the full titles for the Sybil paintings are quoted as they appear on the de Passe engravings, with missing text supplied in square brackets.

Row 1 –
three octagons; only top of framing survives

Row 2 –
overpainted
portrait of St Matthew, title: S.MATTHAIVS
bearded figure
[…]BYLLA

Row 3 –
text fragment: [SIBYLLA DELPHICA QVAE ET DA]PHNE [TYRESIAE FILIA]

text fragment: [SIBYLLA TIBVRTINA QVAE]ET ALBVNEA [ET ITALICA ALIAS DICTA]

Row 4 –
portrait of Mary, title: MARIA

portrait of Christ as Salvator Mundi with defective title which Apted reconstructs: IESOUS CHREISTOS THEOI UIOS EOTER STAURUS

Agnus Dei, shown as Lamb seated on the book sealed with the seven seals of the Apocalypse, with aureoled head turned back and holding a tall pennant in right forehoof which rests on its shoulder; title: DMINVS ES …GVI

portrait of Libycan Sibyl, shown full-face, hair parted in middle with comb-like ornament holding the parting, and ribbon round left tress of hair; hands hold branch of leaves to her breast; title: [SI]BYLLA [LIBYCA QVAE PHOEMONOE APO]LLINIS FILIA [NO]NNULLIS

Row 5 –

portrait of Erythræan Sibyl, very indistinct, text fragments: SIBYLLA [ERYTHRAEA EX ASSYRIORVM BABY]LONE [ORIVNDA BEROSI FIL]

text fragments: [SIBYLLA CVMAEA QVAE ET CIMMERIA] APOLL[INIS IN CVMIS SACERDOS] (but *cf* Row 4 no. 4)

Row 6 –

fragments: SIBYLLA CVM[ANA QVAE ET AMALTHEA NVNCVPATVR]

fragments: SIBYLLA HELLES[PONTICA MARINESSENSIS EX AGRO THIRANO]

portrait of Phrygian Sibyl, indistinct, with text fragments: [SIBYLLA PHRYGIA] ANCYRAE V[ATES CASSANDRA NONNVLLIS]CRED[ITA]

portrait of European Sibyl, shown wearing a large hat and carrying sceptre, with sharply defined eyes and nose, text fragments: [SIBYLLA EVROPEA INCERTAE] ADHVC PATRIAE EX[ISTEN]S

Row 7 –

fragments only

Literature

Apted 1960; Apted 1966, pl. 8, 47, 48, 93, 94.

The Merchant's House, 49 South Street, St Andrews

Seventeenth-century town house. Painted open board-and-beam ceilings on ground and first floors revealed during alterations in 1932, when they were removed and reinstated in their present locations in the house (now a restaurant). Boards between the joists are decorated with fruit swags and flowers very similar to those at Gladstone's Land and at Northfield House. Initials 'CML' may refer to a member of the Lindsey family, or to Catherine Montgomery, second wife of Rev. Robert Blair, who purchased the property from John Lindsay in 1653.

Queen Mary's House, St Andrews

Painted ceiling recorded in Apted 1964, the boards missing but beams painted.

Red Lion Inn, Culross

Painted beams, with leaf-scroll decoration, were discovered in the ground-floor public bar in 1983.

Rossend Castle, Burntisland

Formerly known as the Tower and Fortalice of Burntisland, the lands belonged to Dunfermline Abbey and on dissolution were granted by Abbot Dury to his legitimised son. Mary, Queen of Scots conferred the property on Robert Melville and herself resided at Rossend in 1563. Melville forfeited it during Morton's regency and returned it to the Duries. James VI restored it to Melville in 1587 and it remained with Melvilles until the Civil Wars when captured by Cromwell. Four-storey L-shaped tower with staircase in re-entrant angle and arms of George Dury carved on north wall above main entrance with inscription 'XXII MAII 1554', the year Dury was appointed Keeper of the Privy Seal of Scotland. Initials 'SRM' on painted ceiling indicate a date between 1581 and 1621 for later decorative painting, Melville was knighted 1581 and his son, also Robert, became Lord Melville on the death of his father in 1621. Royal visit to Burntisland 1617 orders him 'to mak his house of Burntyland patent for His Majesties ressett' (Apted and Robertson 1971-2, p.228), and decorative painting may have been occasioned by this visit. Herald painter James Workman lived at Burntisland at this period. Open board-and-beam ceiling decorated with emblems, animals and arabesques discovered 1957 in first-floor great chamber, now displayed in Museum of Scotland; loose boards comprising Section A and Section L now conserved in Historic Scotland Conservation Centre. Second ceiling, coved and boarded, survived only as pieces of painted board which had been split and re-used for later lathing, surviving details indicate geometric *trompe l'oeil* coffering forming quatrefoil compartments, each containing a coat of arms.

First Floor –

Great Chamber (29' x 17') Twelve sections of painted ceiling divided by oak beams, each painted with decorative devices including animals, emblems, musical instruments, and grotesques, linked by arabesque work, outlined in black with brown, blue, green, red and yellow infilling on a white ground. Beams decorated with strapwork. Apted and Robertson identify sources for most of the emblem motifs in the *Devises heroïques* of Claude Paradin. Paradin's emblems were translated by the unidentified 'PS' in an edition which appeared in London in 1591 with all the original woodcuts and including the *Imprese heroiche et morali* (1559) of Gabriel Simeoni. References to Paradin/Simeoni in the following analysis are to the 1591 edition (London: William Kearney, repr. Toronto, *Index Emblematicus*, 1993, vol. 2). Two details copy Paris: Wechel editions of the *Emblematum libellus* of Alciato. The ceiling also draws on Vredeman de Vries's *Grottesco* (Antwerp, c.1565-71) for much of its ornamental detail; the following analysis identifies these prints according to their reference number in Hollstein 1997, vol. 47. Apted and Robertson suggest sources or analogues for several of the emblematic devices in the engravings executed by Crispijn de Passe for the *Nucleus Emblematum Selectissimorum* of Gabriel Rollenhagen (Utrecht, [1611]-1613), a set of engravings which was later used by George Wither for his *Collection of Emblems* in 1635, almost certainly too late to serve as a pattern book at Rossend. Nearly all these details, however, have more direct sources in Paradin/Simeoni, and I do not believe the ceiling owes anything to Rollenhagen's emblems. Some of the animals may be copied from Gesner or Topsell but the resemblances are not very close. All sections assume a consistent viewing angle and are numbered left to right in the following analysis.

Section 1 –
ornamental scrolled arabesque

Section 2 –
basket of fruits and foliage
covered cup (Paradin p.90: *Inter eclipses exorior*)
orb surmounted by cross
three interlocking crescents (Paradin p.21: *Donec impleat orbem*)
unidentified feline animal

Section 3 –
winged cherub's head (*cf* Vredeman, Hollstein p.254)
star encircled by snake biting its tail (Simeoni p.329: *Fato prudentia maior*, device of Catherine de' Medici)
crowned lion rampant with sword upraised between forefeet (Paradin, 105: *Celsa potestatis species*, crown added)
bird with spread wings in encircling cloud
ram standing on patch of ground from which four leafy plants arise, one of which it bites (*cf* Topsell p.489)
clasped hands holding posy of flowers
ape embracing young (Paradin p.282: *Caecus amor prolix*)

Section 4 –
rabbit (*cf* Topsell p.86)
beehive with poppies
knife cutting into anvil (Paradin p.68: *Non quam diu, sed quam bene*)
hands holding sword and trowel (Paradin p.145: *In utrumque paratus*)
ostrich shown in profile and wings folded, with horseshoe in beak

Section 5 –
two clusters of musical instruments, including drum, shawm, viol
four-legged animal with tusk, horn on head and another rising from square, scaly saddle on back (Apted and Robertson compare Gesner's rhinoceros, Topsell p.461)
helmet and lance above shield, containing monogram 'SRM', which rests on a crocodile (*cf* Paradin p.77: *Ultorem ulciscitur ultor*, though the lance is repositioned)
stalks of grain sprouting from patch of earth on which lie three crossed bones (Paradin p.320: *Spes altera vitae*)
bird perched with outspread wings

Section 6 –
unidentified crouching animal
basilisk, a cock-like bird with serpent's tail
goat suckling wolf cub (Alciato, Paris: Wechel, 1534, p.96: *In eum qui sibi ipsi damnum apparat*)
raven drinking from jar full of stones (Paradin p.179: *Ingenii largitor*)
bird with spread wings standing on rabbit

Section 7 –
two griffins combatant
three fishes interlaced (*cf* Delgaty painted chamber)
two nude *putti*, each holding base of large ornamental plant stem
unicorn
basket of fruits
hand shaking snake into fire (Paradin p.242: *Quis contra nos*)
a caduceus of two entwined snakes crowned by Mercury's winged hat, with two cornucopiae (Alciato, Paris: Wechel, 1534, p.22: *Virtuti fortuna comes*)

Section 8 –
dog
purse
caged bird
castle with central door, windows and turrets
display of arms, banner, gauntlets and helmet
blindfold horse (Paradin p.176: *Premitur, non opprimitur*)
hands clasping cornucopia (Simeoni p.352: *Ditat servata fides*)

Section 9 –
two facing masks
bagpipe crossing shepherd's crook (Paradin p.224: *Attendite verbis*)
pig (*cf* Gesner's Swine, Topsell p.512)
two entwined cornucopiae
goshawk shedding feathers beneath sunburst (Paradin p.220: *Renovata iuventus*)
bunch of thistles
antlered stag's head

Section 10 –
elephant and castle (Vredeman, Hollstein p.254)
ox skull; broad-brimmed hat; display of agricultural implements (Vredeman, Hollstein p.241)
goblet (Apted and Robertson *cf* Paradin p.119: *Quid non mortalia pectora cogis*, but the resemblance is not close)
two grotesque male figures with serpent tails embracing
panoply of classical body armour, banner, bow and part of a quiver of arrows (Vredeman, Hollstein p.254)
winged wreath from which two lizards are suspended above burning candle in open lantern (Vredeman, Hollstein p.253)

Section 11 –
two birds on ornamental perch, with two fishes beneath them
female figure holding a swag of drapery above two birds perched on scrolled stem of foliage (Vredeman, Hollstein p.245)
sphinx (Paradin p.37: *Inextrabilis error*)
double-headed eagle displayed (*cf* Paradin p.222: *Praepete penna*)
wreath encircled by two snakes, on two crossed arrows above bird of prey perched on canopy, below this a cloth drape hung on a crossbar above two entwined serpentine grotesques with dragon heads (Vredeman, Hollstein p.254);
camel and castle (Vredeman, Hollstein p.254)

Section 12 –
arabesques
turtle

[damaged section]
flaming torches and hourglass
two entwined serpentine grotesques with pair of spread wings
bonnet on staff with flag showing crescent moon
ox
scrolled arabesques

Upper Chamber Heraldic ceiling – all that remains are nine boards of various sizes from which Apted and Robertson were able to reconstruct the overall pattern as 'a geometric arrangement of quatrefoils and cross-shaped interstices painted to simulate the coffering of a timber ceiling' (1971-2, p.227). The original location of these boards, which had been split and re-used for the lathing of later plasterwork, has not been established. Each of the quatrefoils contained an armorial shield and each cross-shaped interstice appears to have had a roundel or boss encircled with dolphins and thistles in yellow and black. The twelve armorial shields, all fragmentary, which have survived from the eighteen or so original compartments suggest that this decoration was dominated by a heraldic scheme of the type we find at Earlshall, Nunraw and Collairnie, though it has not so far been possible to ascribe any of the charges on the surviving details to particular coats of arms. Apted and Robertson identify the following charges on the surviving fragments:

Gules two lions passant gardant or
Per pale sable and or two lions combatant countercharged
Sable fleur de lys between fretty or
Argent a lion rampant gules
Sable two lions passant gardant or
Or a cross gules over all a bend sable
Ermine over all (only three tails in base survive)
Gules an escarbuncle or
Argent five torteaux gules
Quarterly first and fourth argent a lion rampant, second and third azure a bend gules fimbriated argent
Quarterly first and fourth gules three garbs proper, second and third ermine

Literature

Apted and Robertson 1972; Apted 1966, pl. 64-6, 79-82, 90-2; Thomson 1975, 42-5.

SAILOR'S WALK, 443-449 HIGH STREET, KIRKCALDY

First-floor room in the south-east gable of a large merchant's house overlooking the harbour. Board-and-beam painted ceiling discovered in 1938 consisting of eleven sections, the underside of the boards decorated with a boldly executed continuous scrollwork elaborated into grotesque heads of animals and birds in black on a white ground. The sides of the eleven beams are inscribed with biblical texts in black-letter.
Owner: NTS (access by arrangement).

1 [illegible]
2a The Lord is my shepherd I sall not want PSAL XXIII VERS I
2b In my distresse I Cried unto the Lord and he heard me, PSAL CXX 31
3a Examine me O Lord and prove me, try my reins and my heart PSA CCVI
3b Delever my soul O Lord from lying lips, and from a deceitful tounge; PSA CXX 2
4a Hear, O Lord & have mercy upon me, Lord, be thou my helper PSA XXX 10
4b The Lord shall preserve thy going out and thy coming in: from this time forth,and even for ever more, PSA CXXI 8
5a [Who can find a virtuous woman] for her price is far above rubies ROVP XXXI.VERS 10
5b [illegible]
6a Blessed is he that considereth, the poor the Lord will delever him in time of trouble, PSAL XLI
6b [The Lord] giveth and the Lord taketh away; blessed be the name of the Lord IOB VERS 21
7a Remember thy creatour in the days of thy youth, ECCL
7b Come unto me all ye that labour and are heavy leaden and I will give you rest, to your souls MAT II 38
8a God is our refuge & strength, a very present help in trouble, PSAL XLVI VERS.I
8b Take my yoke upon you and learn of me for I am meek and lowly in heart, and ye shall finde rest unto your souls [Matt.11.29]
9a For I know that my redeemer liveth and that he shall stand at the latter day upon the earth. IOB XIX 25
9b For my yoke is easy an my burden is light MATTHEW CHAP XI VERS 30
10a These be the works of the Lord, and his wonders in the deep, PSALM CVII VERS 24
10b As the hart panteth after the water brooks: so panteth my soul after the; O God, PSAL XLII VERS I
11a They that go down to the sea in ships. that do businesse in great waters: PSALM CVII, VERS 23.
11b I will pay my vows unto the Lord; now in the presence of all his people PSALM CXVI VERSE 14

Literature

Apted 1966, pl. 62.

TOWN HOUSE, CULROSS

Tolbooth built in 1626.
Owner: NTS.

Town Clerk's Room East room on the first floor, open board-and-beam ceiling. Nine sections of boards decorated with repeated patterns of: (1) winged cherubs, white on red, in oval cartouche; (2) *trompe l'oeil* square chamfered studs in black, blue, red, white; (3) white star on blue ground in oval cartouche. Beams with arabesque scrollwork.

Green Room So-called because of its green-painted walls, ceiling exposed during modern conservation when both boards and beams were removed and reinstalled in entrance hall. Boards decorated with stylised foliage in large, flowing, uninterrupted pattern along each of four sections, brown on white. Beams with arabesque foliage in rectangular panels on sides, trailing tassel on soffits.

INVERNESS-SHIRE

Dalcross Castle, nr. Inverness

Built in 1621 for the eighth Lord Lovat. Nineteenth-century sketch by Bonnar (RCAHMS, IND/122/3) of 'Decoration of Banqueting Hall Dalcross Castle 1620' shows the end section of a board-and-beam ceiling; boards bare but three beam soffits decorated with knotwork enclosing alternating roses and thistles on one beam and winged dragons, alternating in red and blue, on another. Beams abut onto what appears to be an end section or frieze divided into two pilastered arches containing a Temptation scene and an Expulsion in lozenge-shaped frames.

KINCARDINE

Arbuthnott House

Painted decoration, including cherubs, on boards of closet at top of stair, recorded in Apted 1964.

Balbegno, nr. Fettercairn

L-shaped tower on the Howe of the Mearns, with the date '1569' carved on a battlement, built for a cadet branch of the house of Bonnington, namely John Wood, hereditary Thane of Fettercairn. One of the few castles in Scotland which, like Towie Barclay, have a great hall with ribbed and groined vaulting (29'6" x 19'6") dividing the ceiling into sixteen triangular compartments. The vigorous external stone carving extends to the carved corbels and bosses of the great hall, which include the arms of Scotland and a grotesque wildman carrying an uprooted oak tree, alluding to the family name of Wood. The sixteen vaults are painted with the arms of particular earldoms of Scotland, including in each case supporters, mantling, helm, crest and motto, above an identifying label and sinuous scrollwork. MacGibbon and Ross describe them as 'armorial bearings of some of the principal families in Scotland' (vol. ii, p.81), but Joseph Sutherland notes that they reflect the political junta which assumed power following the ousting of Regent Morton in 1580/81. Morton was charged with the murder of James's father, Darnley, by a faction dominated by the Stewarts, led by James Stewart, son of the Earl of Ochiltree. In the general share-out of perquisites that followed this coup d'état, Stewart assumed the title of Earl of Arran and acquired many of the Hamilton estates, including Kinneil (qv). The most persuasive reason for believing that the Balbegno ceiling was painted at this time, to celebrate the accession to power of this group of families to which Wood of Balbegno was connected by marriage, has to do with the heraldic achievement of the Earl of Arran as displayed on the ceiling, which are not the hereditary arms of Hamilton but rather the arms of James Stewart himself. Though this includes the Hamilton motto ('Saw through') and crest (an oak tree penetrated by a frame-saw), its supporters include dexter: the Hamilton antelope, and sinister: the Ochiltree wyvern (it was through his Ochiltree inheritance that James had claim to the Arran title and estates). The bordure compony surrounding the shield also hints at this sideways inheritance, since this is a heraldic sign of illegitimacy (Innes of Learney 1934, p.103). The one member of the Stewart faction whom one might expect to see included at Balbegno, but who is missing, is the Earl of Gowrie. The reason for this is almost certainly, Sutherland argues, because in August 1582 it was Gowrie who betrayed his former confederates when he captured the young king in the famous Raid of Ruthven, driving Arran from power and forcing Lennox into exile. The inclusion of turncoat Gowrie's arms on the ceiling in 1583 would have been embarrassing to the laird of Balbegno (Sutherland p.271). It has therefore been suggested that the one blank compartment on the ceiling is not a result of recent decay or damage, but rather because originally it contained the arms of Ruthven, created Earl of Gowrie in June 1581, but which had to be erased when he betrayed the common cause in 1582. These circumstances suggest that Wood of Balbegno must have painted the hall in the winter of 1581-2, erasing the Gowrie arms sometime between 1583 and 1585 when Arran himself was deposed; traces of paint remain visible in the blank compartment, though the heraldry has vanished. The following are the coats of arms and mottoes:

Owner: Private.

ERLE OF ATHOLE	FVRTH FORT[UNE] AND FILL THY FETTERS
ERLE OF LENNOX	AVAND DARNLY
ERLE OF ARANE	SAW THROUGH
ERLE OF MURRAY	SALUS PER CHRISTUM REDEMPTOREM
ERLE OF BOTHWELL	KEEP TRAIST
ERLE OF HUNTLEY	BVIDAND
ERLE OF ÆRGYL	I BUID MY TYM
ERLE OF ORKNAY	SIC FVIT EST ET ERIT
ERLE OF CRAFURD	IN POVIRE FORD
ERLE OF MARISCHAL	VERITAS VINCIT
ERLE OF ERROL	SERVA IVGVM
ERLE OF MONTROSE	NON OUBLIET

ERLE OF MARISCHAL	VERITAS VINCIT
ERLE OF ERROL	SERVA IVGVM
ERLE OF MONTROSE	NON OUBLIET
ERLE OF EGLINTOUN	[...] GARDE BIEN
ERLE OF CASSILIS	AVICE LA FINE
	[compartment now blank]
ERLE OF ROTHES	GRAIP FAST

Colour sketch of the ceiling in the nineteenth century by Thomas Bonnar is in the RCAHMS.

Literature
MacGibbon and Ross, vol. ii, 79-82; Lyons 1904, 166-8, fig. 9; Sutherland 1976.

INGLISMALDIE, NR. LAURENCEKIRK

Destroyed. Seventeenth-century residence of the Lords Falconer of Halkerton. John Stuart's note appended to an article on Culross Palace by Jervise records scriptural quotations: 'Some of the beams of the old castle of Inglismaldie, in Kincardineshire (built during the seventeenth century), were also inscribed with scriptural quotations. Until recently, when the house was put into a state of repair as a residence for the Earl of Kintore, these inscriptions were unknown, but unfortunately they were again covered up.'

Literature
Jervise 1854-7, 343.

THORNTON CASTLE

Royal arms reported to be concealed by panelling above a fireplace, female portrait behind window panel, according to Apted 1964.

LANARKSHIRE

FARME CASTLE, RUTHERGLEN

Destroyed. Fifteenth-century castle inhabited at various times by Stewarts, Crawfords and others. A late eighteenth-century local history written by David Ure records proverbial inscriptions:

> In May, 1792, one of the principal rooms in the old castle, at the Farme, was ordered to be repaired. The workmen, having torn down an old stucco ceiling, discovered above it another of wood. It was painted with water colours; but the figures were so much effaced, that excepting a few waved lines and stripes, it was impossible to form any distinct idea of what they consisted. Several lines of writing, in the old English characters, were observed on the sides of the great beams that lay across the house. The letters were black upon a white ground. Some of the lines were so greatly obliterated that they could not be read. The following, however, which were legible, are here offered to the public, as a literary curiosity; and as an example of the way the inhabitants of Scotland anciently used to inculcate the principles of morality and good breeding.
>
> > Faire speeche In presence, with guid report in absence; And manners In to fellowschep, obtain grait revrence.
> >
> > ... thou heinousness dois or Vice also; for scheme remainis quen pleisour is ago.
> >
> > He that sitis doun to ye hean for to eite forgetting to gyf god thankis for his meite; Syne rysis upe and his grace oure pass, Sitis doun lyk an oxe, and rysis upe lyk an ass. Thir armes that is heir, that ar abuive pented; Ar the nobill howses that the lard of this hows is descendit. J.C.A.H. written 1325 [sic ?1525]
>
> Each of the above stanzas is, in the painting, comprehended in a single line ... From the last it appears probably that all of them were written when the family of Crawford dwelt in the Farme.

Literature
Ure 1793, 134-5; Jervise 1854-7, 343.

HAMILTON PALACE

Destroyed. In 1627 the Marchioness of Hamilton paid £266 13s 4d Scots 'to Valentine Jenkin, painter, for his work in the Palace', evidently for the room later known as 'the Duchess's Painted Chamber'. In 1634 Jenkin was also paid for executing the new series of paintings in the Hamiltons' house at Kinneil.

Literature
Ross 1899, 396; Apted and Hannabuss 1978, 52; Marshall 1973, 38.

MIDLOTHIAN

BORTHWICK CASTLE, NR. GOREBRIDGE

Fifteenth-century tower house. Billings (vol. i, p.47) records that 'in the large and stately stone hall, there can still be traced the remains of some old fresco painting, evidently of a Gothic character' and, in his description of Craigmillar, he notes the 'remains of old paintings, chiefly of an heraldic character, a feature it enjoys in common with Borthwick' (p.94). Historic Scotland has photo (Y150/13) of an unascribed and unlocated (nineteenth-century?) sketch of the 'Ceiling of Hall Borthwick Castle' showing boarded surface with paint badly decayed but traces of what looks like a townscape with buildings and part of an illegible inscription.

ELPHINSTONE CASTLE, NR. ORMISTON

Destroyed. MacGibbon and Ross (vol. i, p.237) say, 'Traces of painting can be seen throughout the great hall, but in too fragmentary a state to admit of description'.

'GARDEN HOUSE', POLTON

A small two-storey rectangular building in the walled garden of Polton. Upper storey, reached by external stone stair, was discovered c.1980. *Trompe l'oeil* rectangular panelling with shading to suggest rebated panels; at centre of each is a large oval boss similar to *trompe l'oeil* panelling on ground floor of Argyll's Lodging, Stirling. Panelling was rescued and removed for conservation by the Earl of Perth, who has carefully installed it in a specially designed garden house at Stobhall, Perthshire.

MONKTON HOUSE, NEWCRAIGHALL

Situated between Musselburgh and Dalkeith at village of Newcraighall; older part of the house belonged to a branch of the Hays of Yester (MacGibbon and Ross, vol. iv, p.182). Painted ceiling discovered 1995 beneath plaster in an outbuilding where boards had been used to strengthen flooring; twenty-one boards now in Historic Scotland Conservation Centre, where they await conservation to reveal the full design; the only features so far revealed are a radiant sun with labels identifying the four seasons, of which 'Winter' is visible in yellow on a blue ground. These are evidently the same as those described in a report of 'Donations to the Library and Museum' printed in *PSAS*, vol. 7, 1866-8, which details 'Sketch of a painted Ceiling of the time of Charles II, at Old Craighall, near Musselburgh' by J Sands, who describes it as 'the painted ceiling of an old room of the cottage in which I reside'. He says, 'The painting is done in tempera, upon boards nailed to the underside of the joists. Although effaced in parts, it is on the whole in tolerable preservation. The sun is represented in the centre of the ceiling, which is divided into four triangular compartments, containing pictures of the Seasons.' The seasons are labelled, and dimensions of the ceiling are given as 15'x 15', with two boards for each length, scarfed together in the middle. The room had panelled walls and the royal arms 'CR II' painted and gilded above the chimneypiece.

Literature

Sands 1866-8.

ROSLIN (ROSSLYN) CASTLE

Thomas Bonnar RCAHMS drawings include a mid-nineteenth century sketch of 'Ceiling of Dining Room Roslin Castle' showing the ceiling divided by square coffering into compartments, each of which is subdivided by *trompe l'oeil* moulded rib-work into four sections with branches of foliage, centered on a circular boss decorated with a mermaid. The central compartment shows the arms of Sir William Sinclair with the monogram 'SWS' and date '1622'. The same ceiling is illustrated in MacGibbon and Ross 1887-92, vol. i, p.376.

MORAY

BISHOP'S HOUSE, ELGIN

Destroyed. Principal room on first floor was described in 1914 as 'ornamented with fresco paintings, the remains of which were visible until the recent "preservation"' (Mackintosh 1914, p.29).

PLUSCARDEN PRIORY, NR. ELGIN

Destroyed. In 1788 Charles Cordiner, minister of St Andrews Chapel, Banff, described 'fresco paintings' with 'mysterious and complicated designs ... elaborately executed':

> The most plain and obvious of these is on the loft arch of the entrance to the sanctuary of the great altar; there St John, about to write, in an attitude expressive of attention to the objects before him, is seated under a canopy, and accompanied by his well-known eagle, lifts his eyes to the concave of the arch above, where the glowing colours of 'that splendid bow, which is seen in the cloud in the day of rain' (Ezek I.28) attracts our notice ... Within the lofty arch, the sun and moon, an arrangement of constellations, and some other splendid characters are painted ...
>
> In the sacristy more complicated designs, and more wonderful schemes of theology seem to have been pursued ... It is a long vaulted gallery, the roof and walls of which has been wholly covered with emblematical paintings. Considerable traces of these remain, exhibiting evangelists and apostles nearly as large as life, accompanied with their several characterstic attributes, and many allegorical representations thronged around. In the midst of them, the august symbol of the Church 'a woman clothed with the sun and the moon under her feet and on her head a crown of twelve stars' (Rev XII.1) attracts our attention. But there is a yet more striking and awful figure above ... the Messiah seated on a throne, in the attitude of benediction, is mysteriously veiled, his head encircled with solar rays ... On the four angles of the square which contains the figure, there are symbols of the elements; a crescent is placed before the throne, and an expressive Alpha and Omega indicate

> the sacred reference of the whole; while St John and the Holy Virgin are bending with veneration towards these sacred insignia. (Cordiner 1788, unpag.)

Spynie Palace, nr. Elgin

Destroyed. Large fifteenth-century, six-storey tower and enceinte, now ruined, palace of the bishops of Moray, whose cathedral was at Elgin. *The Statistical Account of Scotland* 1794, pp.625-7, records, 'The remains of paintings, on a part of the walls, were so distinct a few years ago, as to shew that a landscape with trees, and several representations of scriptural history, had been the design'.

ORKNEY

Kirkwall Palace

Destroyed. Defoe describes the Renaissance palace built for the Earl of Orkney as 'curiously painted with Scripture Stories', *Tour of Great Britain*, 1769 edn, p.329.

PERTH AND KINROSS

Balmanno Castle, nr. Glenfarg

Destroyed. L-plan castle built 1570-80 for George Auchinleck, whose descendants owned it for the next hundred years. East attic contained 'considerable remains of decorative painting on the raftered ceiling and wooden partition, dating from the early seventeenth century' (Hussey 1931, p.31).

Church of St Mary, Grandtully, nr. Aberfeldy

Barrel-vaulted ceiling, twenty-five feet long with total breadth of about twenty feet. Earliest record of the chapel appears to be in 1533, but the painted ceiling was almost certainly added in 1636, the date carved on lintels which were part of a reconstruction by Sir William Stewart, eleventh laird of Grandtully, born 1566/7, died c.1646. His monogram and that of his wife Agnes Moncrieff fill two of the painted panels on the ceiling. The decoration consists of one large central panel and twenty-eight smaller ones, in ornate strapwork cartouches connected by strapwork banding. The spaces between the panels are filled with finely executed decorative arabesque work consisting of fruit swags, vases of flowers, birds (including peacocks and turkeys) and nude winged figures holding trumpets and palm fronds. Colours include red, pink, yellow, green and brown, with black outlining, however some parts are so badly decayed that their subject matter cannot now be made out, and modern restoration (1944) has supplied some details that were invisible to earlier viewers and may not be wholly trustworthy. The numbering and sequence of the panels follows that in Graham 1943, who notes that 'the ceiling as a whole, and likewise the central panel as an isolated unit, is intended to be looked at from the East' (p.148).

Owner: Historic Scotland.

Central Panel – Framed by a classical doorway with a moulded pediment supported upon columns wreathed with vine tendrils, is a Last Judgement scene in which a bearded dying man lies in a canopied bed resting on a chequered floor; the skeleton figure of Death probes him with his dart beside a grieving wife or attendant. Above the deathbed, angels of the Resurrection are shown on clouds at either side of a radiant sun, blowing their trumpets in order to summon a dozen corpses on the right-hand side of the panel to the general Resurrection which we see taking place as they rise from their graves up into the heavens.

Panels 14 and 15 – Above and below the central Resurrection panel, both panels show the monogram 'SWS' and 'DAM' for Sir William Stewart and Dame Agnes Moncrieff.

Panels 13 and 16 – Complete the central line of the design, at the furthest eastern and western ends of the ceiling respectively; Panel 13 shows the sun in slendour, and Panel 16 a crescent moon enclosed in two circles, the inner consisting of stars, the outer circle of clouds.

Panels 7, 8, 17 and 18 – These panels, all heraldic, form a base to the central panels at the eastern end of the chapel. Panels 7 and 17 both show the royal arms of Britain, enclosed in the garter, with lion and unicorn supporters holding standards of the saltire and cross of St George, behind them Panel 17 shows a rose and thistle, and below them a fleur-de-lis and a portcullis; above the mantling and crest is a lion displayed, and the motto 'IN MY DEFENCE'. Panels 8 and 18, both badly decayed, show unidentified shields of arms, each flanked by two encircling monsters; 8 shows two coats impaled: dexter, three fleurs-de-lis, and sinister, what looks like an escarbuncle; 18 shows the remains of a lion passant gardant, on either side of the shield are the unidentified initials 'AR'.

Panels 9, 10, 19 and 20 – All heraldic and to either side, north and south, of the central Resurrection panel, these oval panels show the labelled arms of 'THE EARLE OF ATHOIL' (9) opposite those of 'THE DVIK OF LENNOX' (19), and 'DAME AGNES MONCRIEF' (10) opposite those of her husband 'THE LAIRD OF GRAINTVILIE' (20).

Panels 11, 12, 21 and 22 – These form a balancing group at the west end of the chapel, representing the four Evangelists, each labelled and shown seated in front of architectural details featuring columns and arches, holding their books. Matthew is shown with his attendant angel; Mark has a pen and inkpot; Luke appears with his ox; John gestures with his right hand. All are dressed in loose, flowing robes, with long hair making them seem curiously effeminate.

Panels 1 to 6 – Above the south wall-head, and *Panels 23 to 8,* above the north wall-head, form two rows of allegorical figures with what have been taken to be biblical inscriptions in the cartouche borders above them. Many of the figures and the inscriptions are now too badly decayed to identify. The eight panels (four each side) at the western end are niche-shaped, but the four panels at the eastern end (two each side) are circular or oval. The panels at this end contain what might be described as emblematic subjects. Panel 1 shows a bearded male figure standing beneath an architectural canopy supported on four classical pillars; he is pouring liquid from a flask down onto a smouldering heart which lies at his feet, and from which smoke(?) billows; a stream of what look like ears of corn rise up(?) from the heart to his upraised right hand, suggesting, perhaps, a eucharistic symbolism. The upper cartouche border contains the letters 'NOVN[?E]', all that remains of the inscription. Panel 2 shows a male, bearded figure holding a three-stemmed branch with leaves, standing before a stone altar, on which rests an hourglass and a flaming heart and towards which he gestures. The only remaining part of the inscription in the cartouche border reads 'LIVES VNTO'. The two panels opposite these, 23 and 24, in the north-east corner of the ceiling, show female figures. One, in bodice and skirt, stands before a large domed structure and holds an anchor in one hand and a palm branch(?) in the other; her motto reads 'HOPE IN THE LORD'. The figure to her right, Panel 24, stands before a classical pillar holding an upraised sword, her other hand pressed to her shoulder. In 1943 Graham deciphered her inscription as including the words 'FEARE WA[LK C]IRCVMSPECTLIE THEY AR...', which appears to be correct, and may echo Ephesians 5.15. If the anchor clearly identifies Panel 23 as an allegory of Hope, the sword held by her adjoining companion ought to identify Justice, but there are no scales, and the relevance of this to the inscription is far from clear, unless the Ephesians verse, which continues by advising us to 'redeem the time, because the days are evil', can be taken as a call for justice. The remaining figures in this series, running along the lowest parts of the ceiling on both sides, are less clearly emblematic and little can now be made of their attributes or associated texts.

Panel 4 – Appears to be an allegory of Humility, for it shows a female figure in a dark dress and white headdress standing in front of a table, on which rest two open books, beneath parted curtains. The inscription '[LEARN] OF ME FOR I AM LOVLY AND HVMBL[E]' is based quite closely on Matthew 11.29.

Panel 5 – Shows a female figure standing beneath a curious arch resting on Ionic pillars, with decorative scrolls above it and to the sides, but only the outlining can now be seen (modern restoration has made this more distinct than it was previously). The left-hand part of the inscription, however, quotes 1 Peter 1.16, 'BE YE HOLIE FOR I AM HOLIE', though the right-hand part of this upper border has only the word 'LINES ...' remaining, which does not belong to this source.

Panel 6 – Badly decayed, shows a female figure beneath parted curtains pointing to a book. The words 'RIN ... REMEMBER THE TEN' do not correspond to any biblical text.

Panel 25 – Shows a kneeling female, and an inscription of which Graham, in 1943, could read the letters 'THE[?S]CRVE[?H] ... A ... TO THE END' but which, after more recent restoration, appear to show 'GOA ... THE CRVEL ... A ... O'. Restoration has evidently revealed (supplied?) some details on this ceiling that were invisible to Graham, as with Panel 26, of which Graham noted 'Nothing can be made of either painting or inscription' (p.154), but which now clearly shows a crowned woman holding a child on her lap; the child reaches up to her neck and has long and wavy fair hair behind its back, and the woman wears a red-sleeved garment and a long cape – her hair looks like a judge's wig and her right hand rests on what looks like the head of a lamb – only its ears are now visible. The picture might remind us of a crowned Virgin and Child, though the iconography is not correct for such a subject; nothing remains of the inscription.

Panel 28 – This, which Graham also says he could make nothing of, now shows a female figure whose right hand rests on an object on her lap and whose raised left hand points heavenwards.

Literature

Lyons 1904, 164-6, fig. 8; Graham 1943; Hay 1957, 225-6; Apted 1966, pl. 25-26; Macmillan 1990, 57, pl. 43.

Dunkeld Cathedral

North-west bell tower, paintings of Judgement of Solomon, Woman Taken in Adultery. Completed 1476-83.

Literature

Apted 1966, 2-3.

Finlarg Chapel, nr. Killin

Destroyed. According to the *Black Book of Taymouth,* when Sir Duncan Campbell, seventh laird of Glenurquay (1545-1631) built the castle of Finlarg he also repaired the chapel, 'and decored the same inwardlie with pavement and paintrie, for the bigging and warkmanship quairof he gaiff ten thowsand pundis anno 15' (ed. Bannatyne Club, 1855, p.35).

Foulis Easter, nr. Dundee

Collegiate church founded by the Gray family, probably in 1453. Polychrome oil on boards. James IV visited the church in 1497 and was presented with 'ane painted table' by the dean, James Gray. As Duncan Macmillan says, 'There may be some connection between these two events as this would be an appropriate date for the paintings' (1990, p.31).

Crucifixion – Originally formed boarded rood screen showing Christ on cross flanked by the two robbers on their crosses above a crowded group of eighteen figures, five of them mounted on horseback and five of them haloed. Landscape background with hills and trees. The figures include Longinus, carrying his long spear, and pointing with his left hand to his own eye; the Centurion, with upraised hand indicating the scroll, inscribed 'Ecce filius dei. erat iste'; Herod and Caiaphas (with a figure wearing a fool's cap behind them); and a figure behind left-hand robber holding a pike, with banner decorated with the device of a crab. Hand of God stretches from Heaven above this robber to grasp his dying soul, which emerges in the shape of a small embryo or homunculus from his mouth; on opposite side of Christ, a dragon-like creature snatches the similarly depicted soul of the other robber. Several loose boards showing other figures were evidently part of this rood-screen.

Christ in Majesty – Originally formed reredos on east wall. Aureoled figure of God the Father, with St Catherine holding wheel and sword to his right, John the Baptist and Virgin and Child to his right; six unidentified saints below. Panel originally mounted at foot of rood screen shows eleven figures of Christ, apostles and martyrs with identifying symbols, including St Peter, and St Ninian, the latter's alb embroidered with the arms of the Graham family, who acquired the right to use the choir as their burial place. A long painted lath, now mounted under Crucifixion scene, records that the church was founded in 1453.

Literature
Apted and Robertson 1964; Apted 1966, pl. 4-5; Macmillan 1990, 31-2, pl. 18.

Huntingtower Castle, nr. Perth

Formerly known as Castle Ruthven. Tower containing painted decoration dates from about 1500; Sir William Ruthven was created first Lord Ruthven in 1487. Patrick, third Lord Ruthven, was chief actor in murder of Rizzio; his son, William, was created Earl of Gowrie in 1581. In 1582 the 'Raid of Ruthven' happened here when Gowrie, with other Protestant nobles, kidnapped the boy-king James VI and held him prisoner for a year, for which Gowrie was beheaded in 1584. As a result of the 'Gowrie Conspiracy' in 1600, James had the young Earl of Gowrie and his brother put to death; the castle was forfeited to the Crown and renamed Huntingtower. Given by Charles I to William Murray, it passed thence to the dukes of Athole. Hall ceiling, undated, consists of three cross-joists supporting the beams of an open board-and-beam ceiling running the length of the hall. Underside of boards decorated with knotwork, black on white; large cross-joists decorated on three sides with monsters and arabesques, white on red, heavily outlined; beams decorated with a repeat pattern, white on red, black on red, white on black on adjacent beams. According to Hume of Godscroft, when the Earl of Gowrie was pressed to join the second conspiracy, 'Looking very pitifully upon his gallerie where wee were walking at that time, which he had but newly built and decorated with pictures, he brake out into these words, having first fetched a deep sigh, "Cousin" says he "Is there no remedie? Et impius haec tam culta novalia miles habebit? Barbarus has segetes" [And shall a wicked soldier have such fine plantations as these? The savage will acquire these fields]'.

Owner: Historic Scotland.

Literature
Lyons 1910, 244-7; Apted 1966, pl. 14, 34; Mackay 1995, 42.

Innerpeffray Chapel, nr. Crieff

Burial chapel of the Drummonds, earls of Perth, founded 1508 as collegiate church. Fragments of painted decoration on plaster were uncovered in 1980s, chiefly an astral ceiling in the west end consisting of a radiant sun with face, and cloud-swirls outlined in black, yellow and red, with yellow stars. Fragments of outlined quatrefoil in circle at several places on north wall of chapel. Attic of chapel later housed Scotland's oldest public library, founded in 1692 by David Drummond and, together with the chapel, still open to public.

Literature
MacGibbon & Ross 1896-7, iii, 506-9; Hay 1957, 227.

Pitcairn Church

Watercolour sketches in RCAHMS Bonnar collection include one entitled 'Old Tempera Ceiling Pitcairn Church' (ref. PTD/159/1). Sketch shows a boarded ceiling, divided up by painted ribs which extend from three central roundels to frame three strapwork oval frames on either side, each containing a figurative subject. Spaces between the roundels are decorated with winged, seated putti. Beyond these at either end of the ceiling are three round arches with elaborate cornicing, the spaces between these and the oval cartouches filled with confronting pelicans. Each of the six oval frames contains an unidentified standing figure holding a musical instrument or other object.

Scone Palace, nr. Perth

Painted Gallery Destroyed. Defoe, in his *Tour*, records that the gallery at Scone was the longest in Scotland and 'the ceiling is painted, but the painting is very old' (1769 edn, p.201). A fuller description is offered by Cunningham, *Lives of the most Eminent British Painters* (1832, vol. v, pp.15-16), who says that the gallery

Pitcairn Church, Perthshire, as recorded in Thomas Bonnar's nineteenth-century sketch. HS

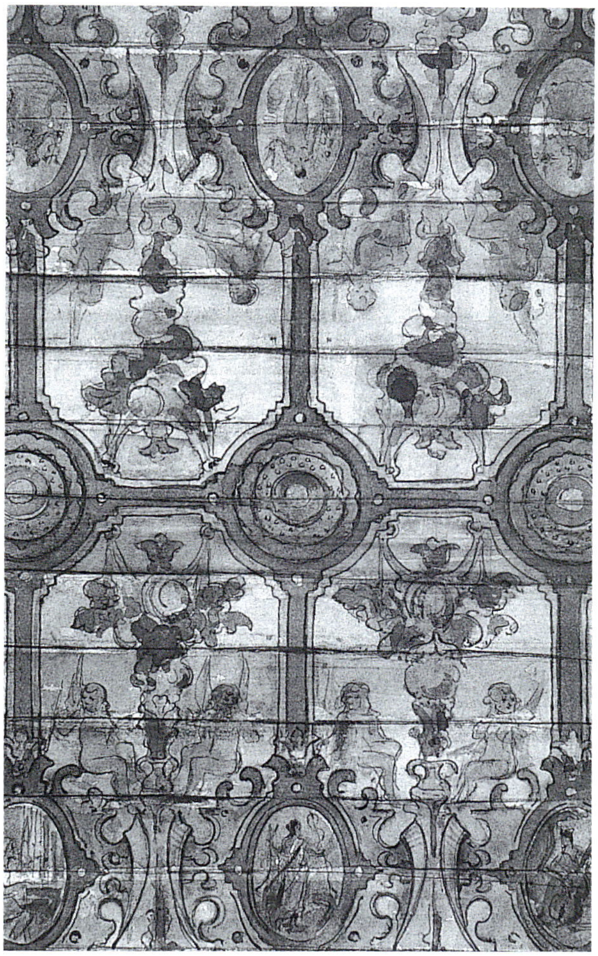

Mounted monarchs from Stobhall, Perthshire.

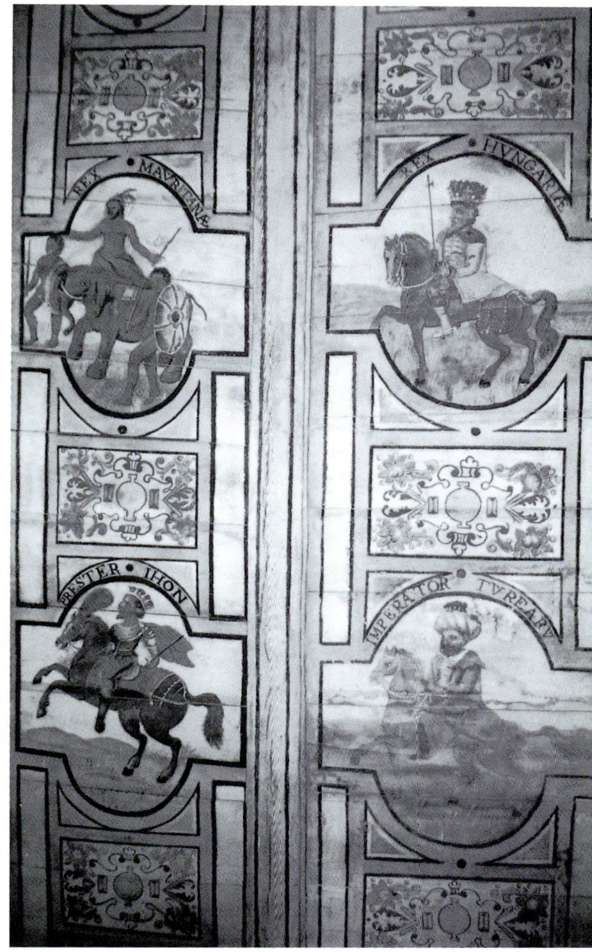

was built by the same Earl of Gowrie who decorated his house at Huntingtower with painting. The wooden, barrel-vaulted ceiling was painted in tempera; on a white ground groups of figures were painted in oval frames. Cunningham cites an unnamed 'antiquary', who had evidently seen the painting: 'In every one that I remember was King James, the principal figure, on horseback surrounded by his courtiers, mounted also; he had always his high-crowned hat and yellow beard, and his face much larger than those of his attendents. I remember no ovals on any other subject but that of the King's sports. The roof around these representations was daubed over with heads and harpies etc., the whole very ill done and much spoilt when I saw the house.' Thomas Garnett gives a similar description in his *Observations on a Tour of the Highands* (1800, vol. ii, p.199, quoted in McKean 2001, p.209). The gallery measured 140 feet in length, and was situated on the east side immediately above the old Coronation Hall (the kings of Scotland were traditionally crowned at Scone). The paintings represented successive stages of a stag hunt, with James VI appearing in every scene. The ceiling was destroyed when the house was reconstructed in 1802.

Stobhall, nr. Perth

Four buildings around central courtyard with painted decoration in several rooms of the oldest part, a building erected in 1578 by David, second Lord Drummond.

Owner: The Earl of Perth.

Chapel Ground floor, board-and-beam ceiling below vaults; the suspended ceiling is lower than the pointed arch of the end window. Crossbeams divide the ceiling into five sections, each containing two labelled portraits of reigning monarchs mounted on horseback or, in one case, on an elephant. Framed compartments containing these portraits are separated by arabesque ornament in blue, red and yellow, and both ends of each section are filled with an animal or bird in a semicircular frame, all on a white ground. This painting is now carried down onto the frieze of the end wall over the entrance where the two mounted monarchs are on either side of the heraldic achievement of the Earl of Perth, but this section originally belonged at the eastern end over the altar where the ceiling originally cut across the

The King of Cochin China, engraving by Jan Doetecum from Linschot's Icones, Habitusque, Indorum ac Lusinatorum ... *(Amsterdam: Nicolai, 1604).* J-M Massing

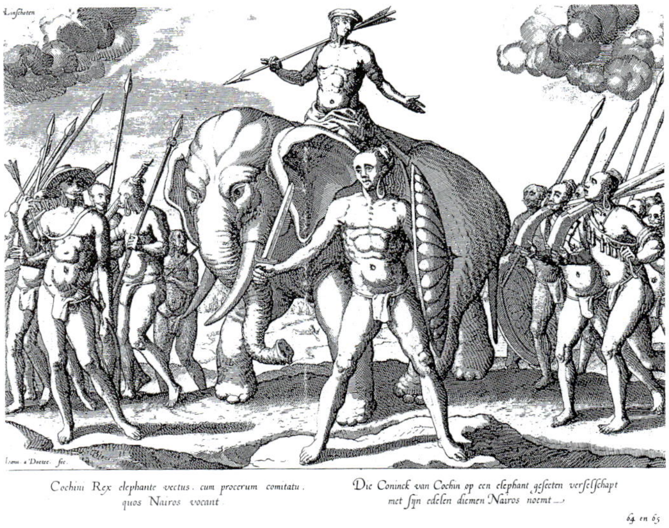

gable window; these panels were removed when the present mid-Victorian windows were installed. The subjects, from west to east, were, in their original order, as follows:

Panel 1 –
[brown horse upreared]
Rex Mauritaniae
Prester Ihon
[hawk standing beside small tree]

Panel 2 –
[bird perched on hillock]
Rex Hungariae
Imperator Turearu[m]
[couched stag]

Panel 3 –
[hawk standing with turned head and spread wings]
Rex Sveviae
Rex Hispaniae
[boar running]

Panel 4 –
[lion rampant]
Rex Magnae Britanniae
Rex Poloniae
[hawk standing with spread wings]

Panel 5 –
[peacock displaying]
Imperator Germaniae
[arms of Earl of Perth]
Rex Galliae
[rabbit]

The pictures of several of the monarchs resemble contemporary equestrian portraits of Charles I, Gustavus Adolphus and so on, but the King of Mauretania, who rides an elephant with naked attendants holding swords and shields, is modelled on a print by Jan Doetechem of 'Cochini Rex' in J H van Linschoten's *Itinerario Voyage Ofte Schipvaert ... naar Oost* (Amsterdam, 1596, English trans. 1598). Plaque in chapel records: 'This Chapel Ceiling was Repaired by John Johnson, Wright, Burrelton and Repainted or Restored in April 1858 by James Robertson, Painter ... 120. Hight Street PERTH. upon the old painting suposed to be don in 1642.' Since the 'Rex Magnae Britanniae' is unmistakably a portrait of Charles I the painting must date from his reign, 1625-48. Mid-nineteenth century colour sketches of the ceiling by Thomas Bonnar preserved in RCAHMS.

Rex Mauretanae from chapel ceiling at Stobhall.

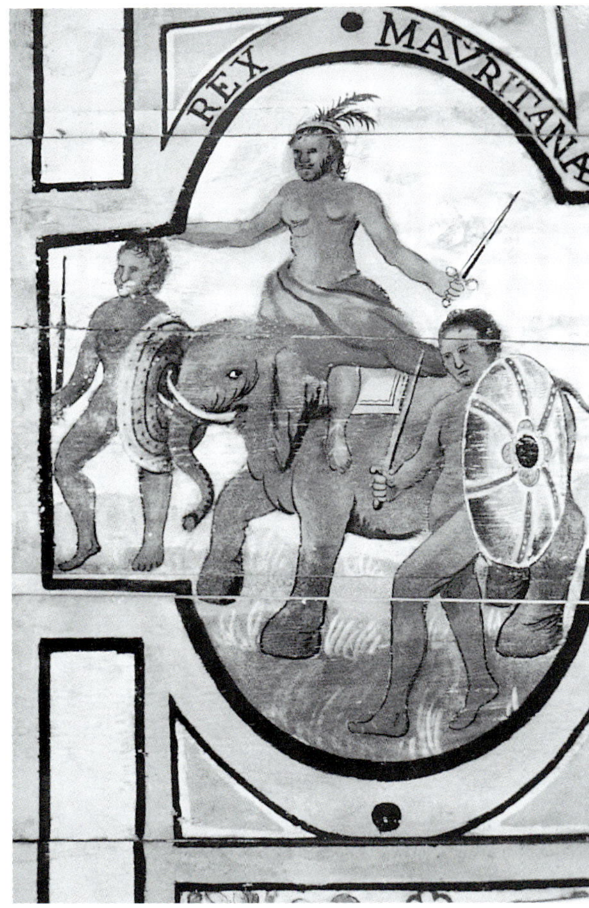

Chapel Vestibule Fragments of painting showing vine scrolls with bunches of grapes on sides and a row of stars on soffits of beams.

Tower Bedroom Beams painted on three sides with bunches of grapes, red and white roses and carnations on a black ground; other beams show green and brown gourds on a black ground.

'Priest's Room' Ground floor. Painted beams with green acanthus scrolling and bunches of grapes on a black ground.

Literature

Lyons 1904, 162-3, fig. 7; MacGibbon and Ross, vol. ii, 358-69; Hay 1957, 225; Apted 1966, pl. 77-8.

SCOTTISH BORDERS

Neidpath Castle, Peebles

Traces of painted decoration on beams of two top-floor garrets with a floriated pattern on the end wall.

Old Gala House, Galashiels

Small tower house built in 1583 by Andrew Hoppringill with later additions, the first made by his son James Pringle, a favourite of James VI, knighted 1610 and who erected the village of Galashiels into a Burgh of Barony. Marriage of his eldest daughter, Jean Pringle, to Hugh Scott of Deuchar in 1621 meant that Gala House passed into the possession of the Scotts on the death of Sir James in 1635. Painted ceiling on first floor has initials of Jean Pringle and Hugh Scott repeated several times, with the date '1635', which must be taken as signalling this event, whilst continuing a decorative tradition begun by the Pringles, as represented by the stone panel carved with the arms and initials of Andrew Pringle and his wife, Marion Borthwick, with the date '1583', and the impressive 9'5" fireplace lintel with the arms and initials of Sir James Pringle and his wife, Jean Ker. This is carved with the date '1611', a rose and thistle, and Latin mottoes 'NISI DOMINVS FRVSTRA, DEVS FACIT OMNIA, VIRTVS SUB VMBRA, SPES VITAE ALTERA' (MacGibbon and Ross, vol. v, p.279). Open board-and-beam ceiling forming eleven compartments, the beams divided into rectangular painted sections decorated with arabesque pattern (as at Gladstone's Land and elsewhere): red on white, white on red, black on white, white on black; these sections separated by square *trompe l'oeil* studs. The beam compartments are decorated with recurrent swags of fruit – apples, pears, gourds, grapes – and winged cherubs strongly resembling the type of decoration found at Gladstone's Land, in red, blue, orange and green, with heavy outlining. Ceiling heavily overpainted during modern restoration.

Owner: Ettrick and Lauderdale District Council (it is now a museum).

Traquair, Innerleithen

Thirteenth-century fortified house, came into ownership of James Stuart, Earl of Buchan, whose second son, James, became the first laird of Traquair. In 1566 Mary, Queen of Scots and Darnley were entertained at Traquair by the fourth laird, John Stuart, succeeded in 1591 by his brother William who was responsible for extending the house. Painted decoration almost certainly executed at this time. In first half of seventeenth century the house was further improved by John Stuart II, who became Lord High Treasurer and was made Earl of Traquair by Charles I on his State visit to Scotland in 1636. His successors made Traquair one of the great bastions of Catholic faith in Scotland following the marriage of second earl in 1654 to Lady Anne Seton. First-floor (drawing room) ceiling was exposed in 1954 to reveal painted beams and boards with grotesque figures, garlands, and biblical quotations from Geneva Bible on sides of beams. The ceiling was photographed and the texts transcribed by J G Dunbar of RCAHMS before it was re-covered, only two sections left exposed.

Drawing Room The numbering refers to inscriptions, recorded in sequence from north to south. Two beams at the north end of the room were blank.

1a Blessed ar those that ar uprycht in thair way and walke in the law of ye Lord, reioce in ye Lord o ye richteous for it becometh upricht men to be thankfull. Sch[e]w me the way o lord & teache me thy paths. Plm cxix [xxxiii, xxv]. (Ps 119.1; 33.1; 25.4)

1b God is our hope and strength & helpe in troubles, rea[d]y to be found, therefore wil not we [f]ear [thogh] the earth be moved and thogh ye mountaines fall [i]nto ye middes of ye seass. Unto ye o Lord do I crye. Psalms xl[vi] and xxviii. (Ps 46.1-2; 28.1)

2a Give eare Lord unto my prayer and hearken to ye voyce of my supplication. In ye day of my trubill, I will call on [ye] for thou hearest me. The Lord is ful of compassion and mercy, slow to anger and of grit kyndnes. Psal. lxxxvi [ciii]. (Ps 86.6-7; 103.8)

2a Save thy people and blesse thyne inheritance fede [thaim also &] exalt thaim for ever. Blessed is he qu[ose wickedness is forgiven and] quose sin is covered. Give us help God agains trouble. For vaine is ye help of man. Psal. Xxviii. Xxxiii xl. (Ps 28.9; 32.1; 60.11)

3a For as ve have many members in one bodie, & all members have nocht ane office, so we being mony ar [o]ne bodie in Chryst, and everie one, one [an]uyeris members. Reioyce in hope, be patient in tribu[l]atioun, continew in prayer. Paul [to] ye Ro[mans]. (Rom 12.4-5; 12.12)

3a Blessed is he yat fearest god & walkis in his wayes. Rychgteous art you lord, just ar thy iudgmentis. Glorie be to ye Lord for ever, lat ye Lord reioyce i[n] his vorks. Salvatioun is of ye Lord. Psal. cxx [viii cxix c] iiii [iii]. (Ps 128.1; 119.137; 104.31; 3.8)

4a Try m[e o god & k]naw myne hart. Prove [me &] knaw my thochtis, and considder gif thair by ony vickednes in me: and lead me in thy way fo ever. I knaw yat ye Lord God will avenge the afflicted and judge the poore. Psalm cxxxix cx[l]. (Ps 139.23-4; 140.12)

4b [Then faith] is be hearing and hearing be ye word of God. Quhosoever sall call upone the na[m]e of the lord sall be saved. Recompence upon no man evil for evil. Procure thy[ngis h]onest in the sy[cht] of God. Paull to ye [Romans]. (Rom 10.17; 10.13; 12.17)

5a [Now then there is no condem]na[tio]un to tha[im that are in Chri]st Jesus, qu[iche] walk [not after] ye flesch [but after ye spirit. Avenge not] yoursel[ves] bot gif place unto vrath, vengence is myne [i w]ill repay sayth [ye] Lord. [Pa]ul Cor 8.

5b Th[ey] that traist in ye Lord sall be as Mont Sion, quilk can nocht be [re]moved bot remaineth for ever. Quhosoever comm[itt]eth sinne tr[an]sgresseth also ye law: for sinne is ye transgression of ye law. P[sa]lm. [Cx]x[v]. (Ps 125.1; Joh 3.4)

6a [Blessed be God, even the father of] our Lord Jesus Christ qu[hic]he according to his abundant mercy has [begotte]n [us] againe [unto a] ly[ve]ly hope be ye resu[r]re[ctioun] of Jesus Christ [from ye] died in ye Epis[tl]e [of Peter]. (1 Pet 1.3)

6b Reioyce vith thaim yat reioyce and weep [with] th[aim] yat [we]ep Be of lyk affectioun ane toward ane oth[er], be not hie[mynded] mak you[rselves] equall to thaim of ye lower sort [Paul to ye Romans]. (Rom 12, 15-16)

Museum Room Painting on south-east wall of this second-floor room on plaster, four feet from the floor, 5'2" in height and 19'9" long. Central portion is decayed and only portions at its two ends survive, part of a frieze which originally ran right round the walls. Decoration shows vine scrolls with rich clusters of grapes, birds and animals, in red and black outline with some red infilling on a white ground, between ruled borders above and below containing extended black-letter inscriptions, the lower border above a separate border of scrollwork. Animals in the left-hand portion include a dog that can with some confidence be identified as the Scottish 'Rache' ('*Schottisches Wasserhund*') from Gesner's *Icones Animalium* (Zürich, 1551-8). The single line of black-letter text above and below the decoration uses texts from Acts, 1.14-18 in the Geneva Bible. The upper inscription (Acts 1.14-15) reads:

> [these all] continued wth on[e] accord in [pray]er and supplication wth ye women, and Marie ye mother of Jesus and wth his brethren. vers:14. and in thos dayes [Peter stood up in the midst of the disciples and said ...].

The lower inscription (Acts 1.16-18) reads:

> [Men and brethren this scripture must needs have been fulfilled] which ye Holy Ghost [by] ye mouthe of david spake befoir of Judas whiche was g[uide to them that took Jesus. For he was numbered with u]s a[n]d o[btain]ed pa[rt of this] ministr[y. Now this man purchased a field with the reward of inquity ...].

Thomas Bonnar's sketch of a detail of the painted gallery showing the hound is preserved in RCAHMS.

Old Library Portraits of historians and philosophers, not unlike Bodleian Library frieze although this is eighteenth-century decoration, the library having been created by the fourth and fifth earls between 1700 and 1740.

Literature

Watson and Graham 1942; Apted 1966, pl. 72, 84; Mackay 1995, 18-19.

STIRLING

Argyll's Lodging, Stirling

Built 1632 by Sir William Alexander, created Earl of Stirling, who made a fortune out of the scheme for colonising Nova Scotia. Widely regarded as the finest Scottish example of a French *hôtel* or town house, the building work was executed by Sir William's son Anthony, one of the king's Masters of Work, and enlarged by the Earl of Argyll in the 1670s when a contract is recorded (7 April 1675) to Edinburgh painter David McBeath for the decorative painting. Its richly carved pediments and classical pilasters flanking the courtyard entrance and on the projecting porch to the main doorway suggest a restrained classicism confirmed by the painted decoration which came to light in 1996, when restoration of the first-floor 'dining room' revealed remains of *trompe l'oeil* white Corinthian pilasters painted on the wooden hall-screen to form a series of columns running right round the room and supporting a painted frieze whose scrollwork, like that of the Corinthian capitals, is picked out with gilding. The scrollwork copies that on the carved stone lintel to the fireplace, and the tall pilasters divide the wall surface into the illusion of a series of recessed compartments, whose depth is suggested by *trompe l'oeil* shading.

Owner: Historic Scotland.

Stirling Castle

Chapel Royal Rebuilt for baptism of Prince Henry, 30 Aug 1594, to a design of William Schaw. Surviving painted work inside at frieze level fills polygonal lunettes over windows at each end, showing royal arms and crowns, bunches of fruit hanging from tasselled ropes, strapwork and illusionistic egg-and-dart mouldings. In 1628-9 the accounts of the king's Master of Work, James Murray, record the various expenses incurred in the repairs to Stirling Castle, including a large number of payments to painter Valentine Jenkins, and his assistant Andrew Home. These include the arches of the outer and inner gates 'To be weill done with oyle cullour', redecoration of the 'King's bed chamber', the 'law galerie', the 'Queen's chamber', 'Buckingham's two chambers which are above the King's bed chamber', Sir William Alexander's rooms, and two chambers above the 'King's hall'. The instructions are quite detailed, specifying 'an border round about the wallis whyte abone and gray under with the chimnayis marbillit', borders to be 'maid fair and perfyte' and window boards to be 'layit over without with oyle cullour and within in Temper cullour and the articles well set af'. It is not always clear from these descriptions how much of this involved decorative details, as opposed to plain colouring, though in the king's bed chamber the window boards were to be 'layit over and set af and the armes and letters to be set af in thair awin cullouris with gold and aisser and the borderis to be helpit and the dores and chymnayis to be marbllit and the pend of the windows and skonschionis to be weill layit over with ane blew gray', whilst the royal arms above the outer and inner gates were to be painted in gold and 'oyle cullouris'. By far the most detailed instructions are, however, for the Chapel Royal, where the Master of Works' instructions specify that the whole ceiling was to be painted 'in the forme it wes before', suggesting that Jenkins's work here involved conservation of the existing designs rather than the substitution of any new decorative scheme. The mural designs are described as a course of panels with arms and badges, conforming to the decoration on the ceiling, 'and ane border under all these'. For the joists of the Chapel Royal 'the field thairof blew with flouris going all along thame and antikis'. This reference to antique work echoes the detail of the queen's chamber, where the panels 'above the hangings' were to be 'fair wroucht with armes, antikis, and thair af-sets', conforming to those on the ceiling above and on the windows 'without and within' (Anon 1843, p.369, *cf* Apted and Hannabuss 1978, s.v. Jenkins).

Owner: Historic Scotland.

Literature

Hay 1957, 224-5; Apted 1966, pl. 88.

Wester Livilands

Wooden partition (17'3" x 9'1") painted on both sides, discovered in 1866 dividing a small passage on the first floor from a larger adjoining chamber. On the side facing the passage, painted Corinthian pilasters separate six panels, each decorated with a half-length portrait of a classical Sibyl above a verse inscription. Labels identify the following Sibyls: Persica, Libica, Delphica, Cumaea, Erythræa, Samia; and the cornice carries the date '1629' and the monograms 'MRM' and 'CC', ie Robert Murray and his wife, Christian Cowan. The side of this partition facing the larger chamber is decorated with flowers of different species on crossed stems enclosed in square *trompe l'oeil* frames. In a paper to the Scottish Society of Antiquaries in 1899 Thomas Ross described Sibyl paintings from a house called Cheyney Court, Herefordshire, which were remarkably close to the Livilands paintings: twelve panels divided, as at Wester Livilands, by columns with 'verses below them which almost agree word for word with those of the six verses at Livilands' (1899, p.398). Although the Cheyney Court paintings were destroyed by fire before Ross completed his article, he appears to have obtained a transcription of the verses in private correspondence with D J Vallance. The same verses are also recorded beneath the Sibyls portraits that appear in Thomas Trevilian's manuscript picture books of 1606 (in the Folger Shakespeare Library) and of 1616 (Wormsley Library, property of Sir Paul Getty, ed. Nicolas Barker 2000, vol. ii, pp.444-5). Panels now displayed in Museum of Scotland.

Sibyl Persica – Elderly woman, in profile, with short curly hair, dressed in a red tunic, holds book under her right arm and gestures with her raised right hand.

> The Mother of th'eternall Father's Sonne,
> [Gran]de shalbe. His Birth, Salvation
> Shall bring the World, and life; yet farre from pride
> Though king of all, He on an Asse shall ride
> Into his Relem; where with wrongfull breath
> Condemn'd by wicked, He shall suffer Death.

Sibyl Libica – Full face, dressed in hooded cloak and very long blue-green neckpiece above white dress with puffed sleeves. Holds book against her chest with her left hand.

> A King of Jewes shall the Redeemer be;
> Just gentle, guiltless, for the guilty, He
> Shall suffer much; the Scribes with scornefull brow
> Shall him forbid his father to avow
> Within their Synagogue; yet shall he preach
> The Way of life, and it the people [teach.]

Sibyl Delphica – In profile, full-busted woman with a short-sleeved green dress and bare neck, wearing pointed white hat with a long gauze-like train hanging down from its point.

> After long yeares due Revolution past,
> GOD, of a virgin borne, to Man dis-Grac't
> Shall make the Hope of Sinnes Remission shine;
> And, though Almighty (and his throne devine
> Have him for Ay in Heaven) yet His to save
> From Death, will He both suffer Death and Grave.

Sibyl Cumæa – In profile, wearing blue dress with narrow red edging and a yellow cloak; holds book under left arm, gestures with upraised right hand.

> An age shal shortly bring about the Day,
> When the great king of kings shal lodge in clay
> Three kings conducted by a glorious starre
> Vnto his Cradle, that from Eastward farre
> Come to adore Him; and tight humble Sould,
> To Him shal offer Incense, Mirrh, and Gold.

Sibyl Erythræa – Angled view, bare-headed, with necklace of red beads and inclined head; holds book against her breast.

> I see the Sonne of GOD come downe from Heaven,
> Held in an Hebrew Virgins armes; and even
> Sucking the milke of her pure mayden brests,
> He, in his Man-age, manifold distrests
> Shal beare for those Whom His he dained to mak
> Shewing to them a Fathers [care to take.]

Sibyl Samia – Picture too badly decayed for any features of the Sibyl to be described. Verse inscription badly decayed, but missing parts supplied by Ross from the Cheyney Court version.

> Heavens [sac]r[ed] Ordin[ance] is [now compleat]
> Of brighte[st] D[ayes this is t[he mos]t [repleat.]
> With good[ly rays, which shining] g[lorious]
> Dispell all [darkness. God sends down to us]
> His Sonne [to clear our sight. Behold th Immortal]
> Co[verd with thornes, for us becommeth Mortal.]

Literature

Maidment 1866; Ross 1899.

WEST LOTHIAN

Cafe Inn, Main Street, Linlithgow

Boards painted in oils on a blue ground with radiant sun showing a human face, crescent moon likewise, a scattering of stars and full-length winged putti blowing trumpets. Now at Historic Scotland Conservation Centre.

Kinneil House, Bo'ness

House of James Hamilton, second Earl of Arran, and Governor of Scotland during the minority of Mary, Queen of Scots, 1542-54, when he built both Hamilton Palace and Kinneil. House in two parts: a five-storey tower (1546-50); and three-storey east ('palace') wing built a few years later (1553-4). Painted decoration was discovered in two rooms on the first floor of this wing in 1936, when the local council sold to a house-breaker the right to demolish the whole building, which was unroofed and partly destroyed before word reached the Ancient Monuments Department that painted decoration had been discovered. Surviving traces suggested that the whole house had once been extensively decorated, but the two rooms in the east 'palace' wing contain the most complete schemes of decoration. The earliest decoration in both rooms almost certainly dates from the 1550s since, as Richardson points out, Arran's building work was largely paid for out of the national treasury, where frequent payments are recorded for painting and building work at Hamilton Palace in the early 1550s. Arran would have been unlikely to carry out such work any later than 1570 when he was out of office and out of favour (he died in 1575). Early work in the north room has been overpainted with quite different subjects at a later date, almost certainly by Valentine Jenkin in the summer of 1634 when the Hamilton account books record payment 'To Valentine the painter upon his task £20.6s' in August, and 'Given to Valentine Jenkein for painting the galleys £100' (Marshall 1976, p.58). 'Galleys' refers to the two ships in the Hamilton arms. Modern restoration has skilfully exposed as much as possible of the painting of both periods, though clearly both cannot be made fully visible simultaneously.

Owner: Historic Scotland (access by arrangement).

South or 'Parable' Room (20'6" x 17'6") On the east wing, first floor. Coffered oak ceiling with some rib mouldings painted black to imitate ebony, and boards outlined with red paint to give the effect of *trompe l'oeil* chamfering. All four walls decorated with line drawings painted on plaster with colour wash infilling some details. Richardson suggests that the paint was applied whilst the plaster was still damp, and notes the presence of 'incised hair lines on the plaster to coincide with the major outlines' (p.190). The painted areas are divided into four zones – frieze, picture panel, dado band and dado – except for the east wall where there is no frieze. The scheme is dominated by the large picture panels between frieze and dado band which illustrate biblical and classical subjects with lifesize figures. The panels are divided by *trompe l'oeil* classical columns with stiff-leaf capitals supporting arches. The spandrels are painted as though filled with ashlar masonry and containing recessed roundels framing a human head. The subjects consist of a series of six panels illustrating the parable of the Good Samaritan; a panel of St Jerome in the wilderness; a panel of Mary Magdalene; and a panel of Lucretia.

1 The Man Falling amongst Thieves
(east wall, above fireplace)

The traveller is shown behind a tree being attacked by three men whose swords pierce his body as he falls backwards; a fourth attacker approaches with a spear from the far side of a second tree. Above the trees are two circular floriated wreaths containing, viewer's left, the arms of Arran collared with the insignia of the Order of St Michael, conferred on the Earl in 1548 when he was granted the Duchy of Châtelhérault by Henry II of France and, viewer's right, the arms of Arran impaled with those of Morton (his wife Margaret Douglas) encircled with a love-knot. To the right of this shield, in the top right-hand corner of the wall, an angel with outspread wings plays a lute.

2 The Levite and the Priest
(south wall, west of window)

The victim, in shirt and slashed knee-breeches, is seated at the foot of a tree, face upturned in supplication towards 'The Levite' and 'The Priest', who are thus labelled, though their identities, as Richardson noted, are transposed. The bearded Levite is shown with a scholar's square cap and a furred robe, studying a book he holds in his left hand. The priest wears a jewelled mitre and priestly vestments; to his left is a dog. In the background is a group of towered and gabled buildings represents the city of Jerusalem with roadways leading from two gateways towards the foreground. In the top left of the panel a label contains a four-line black-letter inscription, of which the following words can be made out:

> This man the Levite b....
> The law of nature quilk [to]ld the....
> This priest ye law of....

3 The Samaritan Attending the Wounded Man
(west wall, south section)

Now badly defaced, though Richardson was able to decipher the figure of the victim in slashed knee-breeches lying on his back, and two others kneeling before him. The background shows a rocky landscape with a road leading over a bridge towards a distant city including a dominant building with a steeple.

4 The Wounded Man being Mounted on the Samaritan's Horse
(west wall, middle section)

Remaining detail of badly damaged panel shows the victim being helped onto the saddle of the Samaritan's horse. Background shows a walled city and a craggy hill, and an illegible label. Another blank label hangs by a fillet suspended from a ring on the *trompe l'oeil* pilaster which separates this from the previous panel.

5 The Arrival at the Inn
(north wall, middle section)

Much defaced, but the head of the Samaritan is clearly shown, bearded and wearing a tall hat; his left hand gestures towards the entrance porch of a nearby building, evidently the inn to which they are proceeding, its doorway flanked by columns supporting a pediment and tympanum which is pierced by a small circular window. Behind him is the head of his horse, facing downwards and away from the inn. The background shows the arched gate to a walled city. Richardson was able to make out a second man ascending the flight of steps to the inn and helping to carry the victim inside.

6 The Samaritan Paying the Two Pence to the Host
(north wall, east section)

Separated from the previous panel by a tricolumnar *trompe l'oeil* pilaster supporting a stiff-leaf capital, with a medallion head in the spandrel. The Samaritan places two pence on a tablet for receiving money, in front of the innkeeper, who looks down at it; horse behind Samaritan.

7 St Jerome in the Wilderness
(south wall, east of window)

A bearded St Jerome shown kneeling on left knee, barefoot in a loose robe, looking up at a crucifix with the 'INRI' monogram. His left hand passes behind the shaft of the crucifix and rests on a skull, and his right is against his breast. The top of the picture is framed by an arch with the label 'Sancte Jeronemus' in black-letter.

8 The Penitent Magdalene
(west wall, north section)

Only the upper part, barely a quarter, of this panel remains, showing the head and torso of a woman who supports her head on her right hand, the elbow resting on a round table with an hourglass and a human skull. Her left hand holds a heart-shaped object (the alabaster box of ointment?) against her waist. A bunch of leafed flowers can be seen behind her left elbow.

9 The Death of Lucretia
(north wall, west section)

Full-length female figure, facing the viewer, her head tilted sideways and her long curled hair flowing down over her shoulder. Her right arm is raised above her left shoulder, holding a sword with which she is stabbing herself in the breast.

Frieze –
Continuous pattern formed of wreathed portrait medallions in profile, three on each wall, the intervening spaces filled with arabesque *amorini* figures with interlinked acanthus leaf-tails.

Dado band – Foliate scrollwork, similar to that on frieze, with medallion roundels at various points including male heads in profile with laurel crowns, floral sprays and fruit swags, with foliate *amorini*. The dado zone is painted to represent an arcade supported on square pillars.

North or 'Arbour' Room (20' x 15') East wing, first floor. Decorative painting of two different periods, on plaster, covering all four walls and the barrel vaulted ceiling. Modern restoration opted to reveal representative painting of both periods by floating off the later paint on certain parts of the surface in order to make the underlying first-period decoration show through.

First Period –

The work of this period is dominated by large-scale scrollwork which curves its stems, leaves and blossoms up to cover all four walls and ceiling. Outlined in black, with red and ochre infilling in places, the coiling foliage contains birds and animals, distributed at random, together with ribbons bearing black-letter inscriptions, few of which are now fully legible. Animals include, on the south wall, a greyhound coursing a stag which stands with its head turned away; a rabbit, a pheasant, a bird perching on a stem, and a squirrel; a dove flies in front of a human face issuing from a flower. On the ceiling, just below the Arran arms, the collared antelope appears in the lodged position. Close to it are an owl and a galloping unicorn, and below them a rabbit faces a small dog, both emerging from the heads of flowers. The inscriptions on scrolls record moral commonplaces, of which only the following can be deciphered:

WT FAICHT VARALIE YS THAIR NA HONESTY
PRY TH LORD DOETH
AND HIM ONLYE SARVE WT ALL THY STYNCHT AND MY^{T}
BELIEVE [UPON] ME
DO SO I SAY I
HAVE MERCY OF ME
DAY AND NYCHT I

Six roundels contain history painting or heraldic arms:

1 Samson and Delilah
(south wall)

Delilah seated, wearing a reticulated coif, with Samson asleep at her feet, his head lolling to the right, and an arm stretched out below it; his legs are doubled back beneath him. A flight of steps leads up to a doorway where two armed Philistian soldiers stand.

2 The Temptation of St Anthony
(west wall)

Damaged, but the lower-left portion shows naked saint reclining with his hands upraised in prayer; in front of him are two chests filled with coins. Richardson describes a devil figure standing behind Anthony, and the legs of a nude female behind the chests, but these are no longer visible.

3 Abraham and Isaac
(north wall, west of window)

Abraham stands with upraised sword beside the kneeling Isaac, on whose shoulder he rests his left hand; an angel in clouds grasps the point of the sword; cartouche below the roundel bears a four-line inscription, of which the words 'to mak',

'Soune Isaak', 'Lordis Com[and]' and 'thy hand' are legible. The sky is tinted red.

4 David and Bathsheba
(north wall, east of window)

Damaged, but David with his harp is just visible standing on the roof of the king's house, above the naked Bathsheba, who is bathing and holding a towel in both hands stretched across her thighs. The king's messenger is shown approaching Bathsheba with outstretched arm below the house where David stands; he is dressed in a slashed doublet. The sky is tinted red. A cartouche below the roundel contained an inscription, none of which is now legible.

5 Arms of James, second Earl of Arran
(ceiling)

Quarterly first and third three cinquefoils, second and fourth a galley, surrounded by collar of cockle with the jewel of St Michael, the whole encircled by a decorative band.

6 Arms of Margaret Douglas, Countess of Arran
(ceiling)

Outer circle includes the Arran cinquefoil and the Douglas mullet.

Second Period –

During the seventeenth century, probably in 1634 when payments are recorded to Valentine Jenkin for painting at Kinneil, the walls were overpainted to represent wainscot panelling, three panels in height. The ceiling and arched upper portions of the end walls were covered with plaster which was then painted to divide the ceiling into false coffering with thick rib-work painted in yellow and brown forming an oval in the middle of the ceiling and smaller roundels on each side filled with armorial devices relating to the Arran family. The central oval has the arms of James, second Marquess of Hamilton, set on a dark grey ground. The oval shield of arms has the Hamilton cinquefoil and the Arran galley, encircled with the Garter; the crest shows the Hamilton device of an oak tree penetrated transversely by a frame saw with the Hamilton motto 'Saw through' above the monogram 'IMH' for James, Marquis of Hamilton. The smaller roundels on the ceiling are decorated alternately with heraldic devices of either the Hamilton galley or the Y-shaped Cunningham device known as the 'shake-fork' in respect of Anne, second Marchioness, who was daughter of James Cunningham, Earl of Glencairn. The rebus-like wordplay involved in both coats of arms is extended to the large panel in the soffit of the east window which displays Anne's arms (the shake-fork) in a strapwork cartouche, supported by two rabbits (heraldic 'cunnings' – hence Cunningham), with the motto 'Fork over'. The earlier iconography of this ceiling with its exuberant decorative and assured pictorial vocabulary appears to have been entirely replaced in the seventeenth century by a single-minded concentration on such heraldic word-games. The white spaces between the rib-work on the ceiling are decorated with naked Italian-style *amorini*, scattering flowers and fruit. An isolated sketch in the buffet recess of the west wall shows a small nude female figure spinning thread from a distaff and spindle, drawn with some skill in red line and coloured flesh tints on a light grey rectangular panel.

Literature

Richardson 1941; Apted 1966, pl. 29, 50, 51, 70, 71, 102-5.

Midhope Castle, nr. Abercorn

Tower built in late sixteenth century by Alexander Drummond; inscribed lintel has Drummond's initials and date '1582'. Remains of painting on supporting beams of ceiling; sides of beams painted with rectangular compartments framing arabesque ornament; soffits of beams decorated with unframed arabesques, stars and comets. Boards between beams show symmetrical scrollwork and swags of fruit and flowers with hanging tassels, only two such sections now remaining. A photograph in the National Monuments Record (RCAHMS) from an unlocated room shows a substantial fragment of elaborate wall painting on plaster of an interior scene featuring a long colonnaded gallery with receding perspective and a tiled floor. Beams and boards preserved in Historic Scotland Conservation Centre.

Robert Stewart's House, High Street, Linlithgow

Destroyed. On the south side of the High Street, with lintel bearing initials of Robert Stewart and Janet Forrest. Two oak ceilings consisting almost entirely of coats of arms discovered during the demolition of the house in 1867, when they were recorded in an article by T Etherington Cooke for *PSAS* with useful monochrome illustrations. The ceilings are also recorded in Thomas Bonnar's colour sketches in RCAHMS showing a section with grotesque and foliage ornamentation and heraldic arms of the Scottish nobility with identifying labels.

East Room (19' x 14') Open board-and-beam ceiling on the first floor, formed of eight sections, each containing five shields of the arms of Scottish nobility with labels but without the crest, supporters, mottoes or mantling; coronets above arms of earls, demi-cherubs above some barons.

Section 1 –
Lord Elfinston
Lord Rihven [ie Ruthven]
Lord Setoun
Lord Drummond
Lord Ros

Section 2 –
Lord Inermeath
Lord Zester
Lord Glammes
Lord Creithioun
Lord Boyd

Section 3 –
Lord Bortvyck
Lord Levyngstoun
Lord Houme
Lord Flemeng
Lord Synklar

Section 4 –
Erll of Orknay
Erll of Murray
Erll of Mortoun
Erll of Maz [ie Mar]
Eerll of Ros

Section 5 –
[Earl of Sutherland]
Erll of Manrois [ie Montrose]
Eerll of Ergyle
Erll of Eglintoun
Erll of Menteith

Section 6 –
Erll of Glencairn
Erll of Craufurd
Erll of Huntli
Erll of Arrel
Erll of Buchqha

Section 7 –
Erll of Rothes
Erll of Athol
Erll of Angus
Erll of Merchel
Erll of Cassilis

Section 8 –
Erll of Lennux
Erll of Arran

West Room (14' x 14') Open board-and-beam ceiling forming seven sections of foliate scrollwork with grotesques, and five shields of arms:

Gules, a lion rampant, or [label missing]
Lord Lyndsay
Erll of Ergyll
Lord Setoun
Lord Levyngston

There is also a scroll bearing the label 'Crafurd', but no shield.

Literature
Etherington Cooke 1868.

BIBLIOGRAPHY

[PSAS = *Proceedings of the Society of Antiquaries of Scotland*]

[ANON] 1843. 'Extracts from the Compt of James Murray, Master of Work'. *Miscellany of the Maitland Club*, 3, 369-77.

[ANON] 1959. *Renaissance Decorative Arts in Scotland 1480-1650* (Catalogue of Exhibition, Scottish National Portrait Gallery). Edinburgh: National Museum of Antiquities/Scottish National Portrait Gallery.

ADAMS, H S 1999. *The Construction and Form, Sources and Importance of the Early Scottish Ceilings 1550-1650*. University of Glasgow M Phil dissertation.

ALCIATO, Andrea 1534. *Emblematum libellus*. Paris: Christian Wechel, repr 1860, Holbein Society Reprints, ed Henry Green.

ALCIATO, Andrea 1551. *Emblemata*. Lyon: Mathieu Bonhomme, repr 1861, Holbein Society Reprints, ed Henry Green.

ALLAN, DAVID 1997. ' "A Commendation of the Private Countrey Life": Philosophy and the Garden in Seventeenth-century Scotland', *Garden History*, *25*, 59-80.

ALLAN, DAVID 2000. *Philosophy and Politics in later Stuart Scotland : Neo-Stoicism, Culture and Ideology in an Age of Crisis, 1540-1690*. East Linton : Tuckwell.

ALLARDICE, James 1901. *The Family of Burnett of Leys*. Aberdeen: New Spalding Club.

ANDERSON, Christy 1995. 'Learning to Read Architecture in the English Renaissance'. In Gent, ed, 1995, 239-86.

APTED, M R 1960. 'Two painted ceilings from Mary Somerville's House, Burntisland'. PSAS, 91,144-75.

APTED, M R 1964. *Painting in Scotland from the Fourteenth to the Seventeenth Centuries, with Particular Reference to Painted Domestic Decoration 1550-1560*. University of Edinburgh PhD thesis.

APTED, M R 1966. *The Painted Ceilings of Scotland*. Edinburgh: Her Majesty's Stationery Office.

APTED, M R and Hannabuss 1978. *Painters in Scotland 1301-1700: A Biographical Dictionary*. Edinburgh: Edina Press.

APTED, M R and Robertson 1964. 'Late Fifteenth Century Church Paintings from Guthrie and Foulis Easter'. PSAS, 95, 262-79, figs 18-29.

APTED, M R and Robertson 1972. 'Two Painted Ceilings from Rossend Castle, Burntisland, Fife'. PSAS, 104, 222-35.

APTED, M R and Robertson 1975. 'Four "drollities" from the painted ceiling formerly at Prestongrange, East Lothian'. PSAS, 106, 158-160, figs 16-21.

APTED, M R, Hodkinson and Murray 1996. 'Prestongrange and its Painted Ceiling'. *Transactions East Lothian Antiquarian and Field Naturalist Society*, 10, 92-132, pl I-VII, figs 1-8.

AUBREY, John 1962. *Aubrey's Brief Lives*, ed Oliver Dick. Harmondsworth: Penguin.

BAIGENT, Michael 1993. 'The Painting of the "Judgement of Solomon" at Culross "Palace", Fife'. *Ars Quatuor Coronatum: Transactions of the Quatuor Coronati Lodge No 2076*, 106, 154-71.

BALDWIN, William 1547. *Treatise of Moral Philosophy Containing the Sayings of the Wise*. London: Edward Whitchurche, repr E Arber 1907.

BANNATYNE, George 1928. *The Bannatyne Manuscript Writtin in Tyme of Pest 1568*. Edinburgh: Blackwood for Scottish Text Society, 4 vols.

BARTSCH, Adam, Ritter von 1978-. *The Illustrated Bartsch*, general ed Walter L Strauss. New York: Abaris Books, 77 vols.

BATH, Michael 1992. *The Image of the Stag: Iconographic Themes in Western Art*. Baden-Baden: Valentin Koerner.

BATH, Michael 1993. 'Applied Emblematics in Scotland: Painted Ceilings, 1550-1650'. *Emblematica*, 7, 259-305.

BATH, Michael 1994. *Speaking Pictures: English Emblem Books and Renaissance Culture*. London: Longman.

BATH, Michael 1995. 'Alexander Seton's Painted Gallery' in Gent, ed, 1995, 79-108.

BATH, Michael 1997. 'Vaenius Abroad: English and Scottish Reception of the *Emblemata Horatiana*'. In Bart Westerweel, ed, *Anglo-Dutch Relations in the Field of the Emblem*, Leiden: Brill, 87-106.

BATH, Michael 1998. 'The Sources of John Abbott's Pattern Book'. *Architectural History*, 41, 49-66.

BATH, Michael 2000. 'Quarles Goes North: Scottish Applications of the *Emblemes* (1635)'. In Harms, W and Peil, eds, *Multivalenz und Multifunktionalität in der Emblematik*, Bern: Peter Lang, 987-1004.

BATH, Michael and Jones 1996. 'Emblems from Thomas Combe on Wall Paintings at Bury St Edmunds'. *Emblematica*, 10, 195-203.

BEARD, Geoffrey 1975. *Decorative Plasterwork in Great Britain.* London: Phaidon.

BELON, PIERRE 1555. *La nature et diversité des poissons.* Paris: Charles Estienne.

BERLINER, Rudolf and Egger 1981. *Ornamentale Vorlageblätter des 15. bis 19. Jahrhunderts.* München: Klinkhardt & Biermann, 3 vols.

BEVERIDGE, David 1885. *Culross and Tulliallan or Perthshire on Forth, Its History and Antiquities.* Edinburgh: Blackwood, 2 vols.

BILLINGS, R W 1847-52. *Baronial and Ecclesiastical Antiquities of Scotland*, 4 vols, Edinburgh.

BOISSARD, Jean-Jacques, see Lebey de Batilly

BÖKER, Hans J and Daly, eds 1999. *The Emblem and Architecture: Studies in Applied Emblematics from the Sixteenth to the Eighteenth Centuries.* Turnhout: Brepols.

BRACEGIRDLE, Elizabeth 1997. 'Ornamented Dwellings: Studies in Scottish Painted Decoration, ca. 1570-1640'. *Inferno: St Andrews Journal of Art History*, 4, 37-52.

[BRETON, Richard] 1565. *Les songes drolatiques de Pantagruel.* Paris: Richard Breton, repr 1989, La Chaux-de-Fonds, Switzerland: Editions VWA, ed Jeanneret.

BRISTOW, Ian C 1996. *Architectural Colour in British Interiors 1615-1840.* New Haven: Yale.

BROWNE, Thomas 1927. *The Works of Sir Thomas Browne*, ed Sayle. Edinburgh: John Grant, 3 vols.

BRYDALL, Robert 1889. *Art in Scotland: Its Origin and Progress.* Edinburgh: Blackwood.

BULLOCH, John 1885. *George Jamesone: The Scottish Vandyke.* Edinburgh: David Douglas.

BURTON, John H 1905. *History of Scotland.* Edinburgh: Blackwood, 8 vols.

CAMERARIUS, Joachim 1595. *Symbolorum & Emblematum ex Animalibus Quadrupedibus ... centuria.* Nuremberg: Paul Kauffmann.

CAMPBELL, P C 1867. *Heraldic Ceiling of the Cathedral Church of St Machar, Aberdeen.* University of Aberdeen: Spalding Club.

CARROLL, William C 1976. *The Great Feast of Languages in* Love's Labour's Lost. Princeton: Princeton University Press.

CARRUTHERS, Mary 1990. *The Book of Memory: A study of memory in medieval culture.* Cambridge: Cambridge University Press.

CHAMBERS, Robert 1868. *Traditions of Edinburgh.* Edinburgh: W and R Chambers.

COMBE, Thomas 1990. *The Theater of Fine Devices*, ed Mary Silcox. London: Scolar Press.

COOPE, Rosalys 1986. 'The "Long Gallery": Its Origins, Development, Use and Decoration.' *Architectural History*, 29, 43-78.

CORDIMER, R C 1780 *Antiquities and Scenery of the North of Scotland.* London: privately printed.

CORDINER, Charles 1788. *Remarkable Ruins and Romantic Prospects of North Britain.* Vol I, London: I & J Taylor (Vol II, 1795)

COWAN, Edward J 1983. 'The Darker Vision of the Scottish Renaissance'. In Cowan and Shaw 1983,125-40.

COWAN, Ian B and Shaw 1983. *The Renaissance and Reformation in Scotland.* Edinburgh: Scottish Academic Press.

CROFT-MURRAY, Edward 1962. *Decorative Painting in England, 1537-1837.* 2 vols. London: Country Life.

DACOS, Nicole 1969. *La découverte de la Domus Aurea et la formation des grotesques à la renaissance.* London: Warburg Institute.

D'ASSIGNY, Marius [no date] *The Art of Memory.* London and Edinburgh: John Reid.

DICK PEDDIE, J M 1883-84. 'Description of an Old Timber Building in the Lawnmarket, Edinburgh'. PSAS, 18, 465-76.

DOBIE, W 1889. 'The Skelmorlie Aisle'. *Archaeological and Historical Collections Relating to Ayrshire and Galloway*, 6, 58-76

DOUEIHI, Milad 1997. *A Perverse History of the Human Heart.* Cambridge: Harvard University Press.

DUNBAR, J G and Imrie 1982. *Accounts of the Master of Works for Repairing Royal Palaces and Castles*, vol 2, 1616-1649. Edinburgh: HMSO.

DURKAN, John 1962. 'Alexander Dickson and STC6823'. *The Bibliothek*, 3, 183-90.

ENGEL, William E 1995. *Mapping Mortality: The Persistence of Memory and Melancholy in Early Modern England.* Amherst: University of Massachusetts Press.

ETHERINGTON COOKE, T 1868. 'Notice of the Heraldic Painted Ceilings in a House at Linlithgow', PSAS, 7, 409-12, Pl 50, 51.

EVANS, Joan 1931. *Pattern: A study of ornament in western Europe from 1180-1900.* Oxford: Clarendon Press, 2 vols.

EVANS, John 1888. ' Ornamental Fruit Trenchers'. *Proceedings of the Society of Antiquaries* London, 12, 201-223.

FORMAN, Sheila 1961. 'Northfield House'. *Scotland's Magazine*, 57 no 5, May 1961, 23-6.

FORSTER, Leonard 1981. 'Die *Emblemata Horatiana* des Otho Vaenius', *Wolfenbütteler Forschungen*, 12, 117-28.

FOWLER, Alastair 1996. *Time's Purple Masquers: Stars and the Afterlife in Renaissance English Literature.* Oxford: Clarendon Press.

GALLOWAY, Bruce 1986. *The Union of England and Scotland 1603-1608.* Edinburgh: John Donald.

GENT, Lucy, ed 1995. *Albion's Classicism: The Visual Arts in Britain, 1550-1660.* New Haven: Yale University Press.

GLENDINNING, Miles, MacInnes and MacKechnie 1996. *A History of Scottish Architecture.* Edinburgh: Edinburgh University Press.

GOMBERVILLE, Marin le Roy, Sieur de 1646. *La Doctrine des Moeurs.* Paris: Louis Sevestre.

GOMBRICH, E H 1979. *The Sense of Order.* London: Phaidon

GOW, Ian and Rowan, eds 1995. *Scottish Country Houses 1600-1914.* Edinburgh: Edinburgh University Press.

GRAHAM, A 1943. 'The Painted Ceiling in the Church of St Mary, Grandtully'. PSAS, 77, 147-54.

GRANT, James 1880-3. *Old and New Edinburgh.* London: Cassell.

GRIFFITHS, Antony 1998. *The Print in Stuart Britain, 1603-1689.* London: British Museum Press.

HARGREAVES, Henry 1989. 'The Crathes Castle Inscriptions'. In McClure and Spiller, eds, *Bryght Lanternis: Essays on Language and Literature of Medieval and Renaissance Scotland.* Aberdeen: Aberdeen University Press, 373-86.

HARPHAM, Geoffrey 1982. *On the Grotesque: Strategies of contradiction in art and literature.* Princeton: Princeton University Press.

HAWKINS, Henry 1634. *The Devout Heart.* Rouen: Jean Cousturier, repr 1975, Ilkley: Scolar Press.

HAY, George 1957. *The Architecture of Scottish Post-Reformation Churches 1560-1843.* Oxford: Clarendon Press.

HEARN, Karen, ed 1995. *Dynasties: Painting in Tudor and Jacobean England 1530-1630.* London: Tate Publishing.

HILL, Oliver 1905. 'Earlshall'. *Country Life*, 17, 1 July, 942-52.

HILL, Oliver 1953. *Scottish Castles of the Sixteenth and Seventeenth Centuries.* London: Country Life Publications.

HOLLSTEIN, Friedrich W H 1949-. *Dutch and Flemish Etchings, Engravings and Woodcuts 1450-1700.* 54 vols, Amsterdam: van Gendt.

HOLLSTEIN, Friedrich W H 1954-. *German Etchings, Engravings and Woodcuts 1400-1700.* 57 vols, Amsterdam: Henno Hertzberger.

HOWARD, Deborah 1995a. *Scottish Architecture, Reformation to Restoration 1560-1660.* Edinburgh: Edinburgh University Press.

HOWARD, Deborah 1995b. 'Scotland's "Thrie Estates"'. In Gent, ed 1995, 51-78.

HOWARD, Maurice 1987. *The Early Tudor Country House: Architecture and Politics 1490-1550.* London: George Philip.

HOWARD, Maurice and Snodin 1996. *Ornament: A Social History.* New Haven: Yale University Press.

HUNWICKE, John 1993. 'Robert Maxwell of Caerlaverock and his Fashionable Windows'. *Transactions of the Dumfriesshire and Galloway Natural History and Antiquarian Society*, 68, 107-21

HUSSEY, Christopher 1931. 'The Work of Sir Robert Lorimer'. *Country Life*, 70, 24 Oct, 456-60.

HUSSEY, Christopher 1937. 'Crathes Castle'. *Country Life*, 76, 18 Sept, 147-50. *Illustrated Bartsch*, see Bartsch.

INNES OF LEARNEY, Thomas 1934. *Scots Heraldry: A Practical Handbook.* Edinburgh: Oliver and Boyd.

ISSELBURG, Peter and Georg Rem 1617. *Emblemata Politica.* Repr 1982, ed Harms. Frankfurt am Main: Peter Lang.

JERVISE, A 1854-7. 'Poetical Maxims from a Painted Room in the Old House at Culross'. PSAS, 2, 343.

JERVISE, A 1860-62. 'Notices of the Castle and Painted Room or Hall of Earlshall'. PSAS, 4, 387-91

KEMP, Martin 1990. *The Science of Art: Optical Themes in Western Art.* New Haven: Yale University Press.

KEMP, Martin and Farrow 1990. 'Humanism in the Visual Arts, *c.*1530-*c.*1630', in MacQueen, ed, *Humanism in Renaissance Scotland.* Edinburgh: Edinburgh University Press.

LAMB A C 1895. *Dundee - Its Quaint and Historic Buildings.* Dundee: privately printed.

LA PERRIÈRE, Guillaume de 1539. *Le Theatre des bons engins.* Paris: Denis Janot, see also Combe, Thomas 1990.

LEBEY DE BATILLY, Denis 1596. *Emblemata.* Frankfurt am Main: Theodore de Bry.

LEE, Maurice 1983. 'King James's Popish Chancellor'. In Cowan and Shaw 1983, 170-182.

LEIGHTON, John 1890. *History of the County of Fife.* Glasgow: Joseph Swan, 3 vols.

LEITH HAY, Andrew 1887. *Castles of Aberdeenshire.* Aberdeen: D Wylie.

LEVACK, Brian P 1987. *The Formation of the British State: England, Scotland, and the Union 1603-1707.* Oxford: Clarendon Press.

LEVENSON, J A, Oberhuber and Sheehan 1973. *Early Italian Engravings from the National Gallery of Art.* Washington DC: National Gallery of Art.

LOUTFUT, Adam 1994. *The Deidis of Armourie: A Heraldic Treatise and Bestiary*, ed Houwen. Edinburgh: Scottish Text Society.

LUBORSKY, Ruth L and Ingram 1998. *A Guide to English Illustrated Books 1536-1603.* Tempe, Arizona: Medieval and Renaissance Texts and Studies, 2 vols.

LYNDSAY OF THE MOUNT, Sir David 1878. *Fac-Simile of an Ancient Heraldic Manuscript Emblazoned by Sir David Lyndsay of the Mount, Lyon King of Arms 1542*, ed David Laing. Edinburgh: William Paterson.

LYONS, Andrew W 1901. 'The Painted Ceiling in the Montgomerie Aisle of the Old Church at Largs, Ayrshire'. PSAS, 35, 109-11.

LYONS, Andrew W 1904. 'Tempera-painting in Scotland during the Early Part of the Seventeenth Century'. PSAS, 38, 151-173.

LYONS, Andrew W 1910. 'Further Notes on Tempera-painting in Scotland, and other Discoveries at Delgaty Castle'. PSAS, 44, 237-59.

McCUTCHEON, Elizabeth 1977. *Sir Nicholas Bacon's Great House Sententiae.* ELR Supplements, no 3.

MACGIBBON, David and Thomas Ross 1887-92. *The Castellated and Domestic Architecture of Scotland.* 5 vols, Edinburgh: David Douglas.

MACGIBBON, David and Thomas Ross 1896-7. *The Ecclesiastical Architecture of Scotland.* 3 vols, Edinburgh: David Douglas.

MACKAY, Sheila, ed 1978. *Scottish Renaissance Interiors.* Edinburgh: Moubray House Press.

MACKAY, Sheila 1995. *Behind the Façade: Four Centuries of Scottish Interiors.* Edinburgh: RCAHMS and HMSO.

MACMILLAN, Duncan 1990. *Scottish Art 1460-1990.* Edinburgh: Mainstream Publishing.

McKEAN, Charles 1987. *The District of Moray: An Illustrated Architectural Guide.* Edinburgh: Scottish Academic Press.

McKEAN, Charles 1990. *Banff and Buchan: An Illustrated Architectural Guide.* Edinburgh: Scottish Academic Press.

McKEAN, CHARLES 2001. *The Scottish Chateau: The Country House of Renaissance Scotland.* Stroud, Glos: Sutton Publishing.

MACKINTOSH, H B 1914. *Elgin Past and Present.* Elgin, privately printed.

McROBERTS, David 1954. 'Provost Skene's House, in Aberdeen, and its Catholic Chapel'. *Innes Review,* 5, 119-124.

McROBERTS, David 1982. 'The Heraldic Ceiling of St Machar's Cathedral Aberdeen'. Aberdeen: Friends of St Machar's Cathedral Occasional Papers.

McWILLIAM, Colin 1978. *Lothian.* Harmondsworth: Penguin (Buildings of Scotland Series).

MAIDMENT, J 1866. 'The Sibyls in Scotland: Livelands'. *Notes and Queries,* 3rd ser 10, 467-9.

MAITLAND, Richard 1829. *The History of the House of Seytoun to the Year 1559, with the Continuation by Alexander Viscount Kingston to 1687.* Glasgow: Maitland Club Proceedings.

MÂLE, Emile 1908. *L'art religieux de la fin du moyen âge en France.* Paris: Armand Colin.

MARSHALL, Rosalind K 1976. *The Days of Duchess Anne: Life in the Household of the Duchess of Hamilton 1656-1716.* London: Collins.

MASON, Roger A 1982. 'George Buchanan, James VI and the Scottish Polity'. In John Dwyer et al, eds, *New Perspectives on the Politics and Culture of Early Modern Scotland.* Edinburgh: John Donald, 9-33.

MILLAR, A H 1895. *Fife: Pictorial and Historical.* 2 vols, Cupar, Fife: A Westwood & Son.

MOSS, Ann 1996. *Printed Commonplace-Books and the Structuring of Renaissance Thought.* Oxford: Clarendon Press.

MOWL, Timothy 1993. *Elizabethan and Jacobean Style.* London: Phaidon Press.

NORRIS, Laura 2000. 'The Continuing Mystery of Moubray House'. *Architectural Heritage Society of Scotland Magazine,* 10, Summer 2000, 21.

OLIVER, Cordelia 1968. 'A Scottish Painted Ceiling Restored: The Second Salon, Cullen House, Banffshire'. *Country Life,* 21 Mar, 660-1.

ONG, W J 1974. 'Commonplace rhapsody: Ravisius Textor, Zwingler and Shakespeare'. In Bolgar, ed, *Classical Influences on European Culture AD 1500-1700.* Cambridge: Cambridge University Press, 91-126.

ORGEL, Stephen and Strong 1973. *Inigo Jones. The Theatre of the Stuart Court.* Berkeley: University of California Press.

PARADIN, Claude 1557. *Devises heroïques.* Lyon: de Tournes. Repr 1989, Aldershot: Scolar Press, ed Saunders.

PARRY, Graham 1981. *The Golden Age Restor'd: The Culture of the Stuart Court, 1603-42.* Manchester: Manchester University Press.

PEACHAM, Henry 1906. *Peacham's Compleat Gentleman 1634,* ed Gordon. Oxford: Clarendon Press.

PEACHAM, Henry 1998. *Henry Peacham's Manuscript Emblem Books,* ed Young. Toronto: University of Toronto Press.

PEDDIE, J M D 1884. 'Description of an Old Timber Building in the Lawnmarket, Edinburgh'. PSAS, 18, 465-76, pl.1-2.

PRESCOTT, Anne Lake 1984. 'The Stuart Masque and Pantagruel's Dreams'. *English Literary History,* 51, 407-30.

PRESCOTT, Anne Lake 1998. *Imagining Rabelais in Renaissance England.* New Haven: Yale University Press.

QUARLES, Francis 1635. *Emblemes.* London: John Marriot. Repr 1993, Hildesheim: Georg Olms Verlag, ed Höltgen.

READER, Francis W 1930. 'Wall Paintings of the Sixteenth and Early Seventeenth Centiries Recently Discovered in Bosworth House, Wendover, Bucks'. *Archaeological Journal,* 87, 71-97.

READER, Francis W 1932. 'Tudor Mural Paintings in the Lesser Houses in Bucks'. *Archaeological Journal,* 89, 116-173.

READER, Francis W 1935. 'Tudor Domestic Wall Paintings: Part I'. *Archaeological Journal,* 92, 243-279.

READER, Francis W 1936. 'Tudor Domestic Wall Paintings: Part II'. *Archaeological Journal,* 93, 220-262.

READER, Francis W 1941. 'A Classification of Tudor Domestic Wall Paintings'. *Archaeological Journal,* 98, 181-211.

RECHTIEN, John G 1978. 'John Foxe's *Comprehensive Collection of Commonplaces:* A Renaissance Memory System for Students and Theologians'. *Sixteenth Century Journal,* 6, 83-89.

RICHARDSON, James S 1941. 'Sixteenth and Seventeenth Century Mural Decorations at the House of Kinneil, Bo'ness, West Lothian'. PSAS, 75, 184-204, Pl 25-47.

RIPA, Cesare 1618. *Iconologia.* Padua: Tozzi.

ROSS, Thomas 1899. 'Notice of six paintings on wood, representing the Sybils, recently found at Wester Livilands, Stirling'. PSAS, 33, 387-403.

ROUGVIE, J 1999. 'The Merchant's House'. *The Scots Magazine*, March 1999, 276-9.

RUSCELLI, Girolamo 1566. *Le Imprese Illustri*. Venice: Francesco Rampazetto.

SAMBUCUS, Joannes 1564. *Emblemata*. Antwerp: Plantin. Repr. 1982, Budapest: Akademiai Kiado.

SANDERSON, Margaret H B 1970. 'Catholic Recusancy in Scotland in the Sixteenth Century'. *The Innes Review*, 21, 87-107.

SANDERSON, Margaret H B 1978. *Mary Stewart's People*. Edinburgh: James Thin.

SANDS, J 1866-68. 'Sketch of a painted Ceiling of the time of Charles II, at Old Craighall, near Musselburgh'. *PSAS*, 7, 479.

SAVAGE, Peter 1980. *Lorimer and the Edinburgh Craft Designers*. Edinburgh: Paul Harris Publishing.

SCHÉLE, Sune 1965. *Cornelis Bos, A Study in the Origins of the Nethelandish Grotesque*. Stockholm: Almqvist & Wiksell.

SCHILLER, Gertrud 1976. *Ikonographie der christlichen Kunst*. Gütersloh.

SCHRECKENBERG, Heinz 1996. *The Jews in Christian Art: An Illustrated History*. London: SCM Press.

SCHROEDER, Horst 1981. 'The Mural Paintings of the Nine Worthies at Amersham'. *Archaeological Journal*, 138, 241-7, Pl 17-24.

SCOTT, H Schomberg 1971. *Crathes Castle: An Illustrated Account*. Edinburgh: National Trust for Scotland.

SETON, Bruce Gordon 1939. *The House of Seton: A Study in Lost Causes*. Edinburgh: Lindsay and Macleod, 2 vols.

SETON, George 1882. *Memoir of Alexander Seton, Earl of Dunfermline*. Edinburgh: William Blackwood and Sons.

SETON, George 1888. 'Notice of the Ceiling of the "Painted Gallery" at Pinkie House'. PSAS, 22, 10-22.

SHAW, Duncan 1983. 'Adam Bothwell: A conserver of the Renaissance in Scotland'. In Cowan and Shaw 1983, 140-69.

SHIRE, Helena M 1996. 'The Heraldic Ceiling of St Machar's Cathedral, Old Aberdeen, c. 1520'. In J H Williams (ed.), *Stewart Style 1513-1542: Essays on the Court of James V*. East Linton: Tuckwell, pp.63-72.

SIMEONI, Gabriele 1559. *Le imprese heroiche et morali*. Lyon: Roville. English translation by PS, London 1591, repr 1993, Toronto University Press, 'Index Emblematicus: The English Emblem Tradition', ed Daly.

SIMPSON, Percy and Bell 1924. *Designs by Inigo Jones for Masques and Plays at Court: A Descriptive Catalogue*. Oxford: Oxford University Press for The Walpole Society.

SIMPSON, W Douglas 1931. 'Edzell Castle'. PSAS, 65, 115-78.

SIMPSON, W Douglas 1938. 'Tolquhon Castle and its Builder'. PSAS, 72, 248-72.

SINCLAIR, Sir John 1791-99. *Statistical Account of Scotland 1791-99*. Repr Wakefield: E P Publishing, 1982.

SLADE, H Gordon 1972. 'Beldorney Castle, Aberdeenshire: an Early Z-plan tower house'. PSAS, 106, 262-80.

SMITH, Donald 1996. *John Knox House: Gateway to Edinburgh's Old Town*. Edinburgh: John Donald.

Statistical Account of Scotland 1791-99, see Sinclair, Sir John.

STEVENSON, David 1988a. *The Origins of Freemasonry: Scotland's Century, 1590-1710*. Cambridge: Cambridge University Press.

STEVENSON, David 1988b. *The First Freemasons: Scotland's Early Lodges and their Members*. Aberdeen: Aberdeen University Press.

STIRLING, A M W 1928. *Fyvie Castle: Its Lairds and their Times*. London: John Murray.

SWAIN, Margaret 1986. *The Needlework of Mary Queen of Scots*. Carlton, Beds: Ruth Bean Publishers, first edn 1973, Van Nostrand Reinhold Inc.

SYNESIUS 1926. *The Letters of Synesius of Cyrene*, trans A Fitzgerald. Oxford: Oxford University Press.

THOMSON, Duncan 1974. *The Life and Art of George Jamesone*. Oxford: Clarendon Press.

THOMSON, Duncan 1975. *Painting in Scotland 1570-1650* (catalogue of Scottish National Portrait Gallery exhibition Aug-Sept 1975). Edinburgh: Trustees of the National Galleries of Scotland.

THORNE, Alison 1989. *Problems of Perspective in Shakespeare's 'Troilus and Cressida'*. London University PhD dissertation.

TOPSELL, Edward 1607. *The Historie of Foure-Footed Beastes*. London: William Jaggard; edition cited London: E.Cotes, 1658, repr New York: Da Capo Press, 1967.

TRANTER, Nigel 1962. *The Fortified House in Scotland*. 5 vols, Edinburgh: Oliver and Boyd.

URE, David 1793. *History of Rutherglen and East-Kilbride*. Privately printed.

VEEN, Otto van 1607. *Q. Horatii Flaccii Emblemata*. Antwerp: Jerome Verdussen. Repr (1612 edn) 1979, New York: Garland, ed Orgel.

WALLACE, Joyce M 1987. *Historic Houses of Edinburgh*. Edinburgh: John Donald.

WATSON, G P H and Graham 1942. 'A mural painting and a carved door at Traquair House, Innerleithen'. PSAS, 76, 5-7.

WATT, Tessa 1991. *Cheap Print and Popular Piety*. Cambridge: Cambridge University Press.

WAY, Albert 1846. 'Illustrations of domestic customs during the Middle Ages: Ornamental Fruit-trenchers inscribed with posies'. *Archaeological Journal*, 3, 333-9.

WELLS-COLE, Anthony 1997. *Art and Decoration in Elizabethan and Jacobean England: The Influence of Continental Prints, 1558-1625*. New Haven: Yale University Press.

WHITE, Adam 1989. 'Westminster Abbey in the Early Seventeenth Century: A Powerhouse of Ideas'. *Church Monuments*, 4, 22-31.

WHITING, B J 1949. 'Proverbs and Proverbial Sayings from Scottish Writings before 1600. Part One A-L'. *Medieval Studies*, 11, 123-205.

WHITING, B J 1951. 'Proverbs and Proverbial Sayings from Scottish Writings before 1600. Part Two M-Y'. *Medieval Studies*, 13, 87-164.

WHITNEY, Geffrey 1586. *A Choice of Emblemes*. Leiden: Francis Raphelengius. Repr 1969, Menston: Scolar Press, ed Horden.

WILSON, D 1848. *Memorials of Edinburgh in the Olden Time*, 2 vols. Edinburgh, Hugh Paton.

YATES, Frances A 1966. *The Art of Memory*. Chicago: Chicago University Press.

ZUCKER, Martin 1993. 'Baccio Baldini: "The Prophets and the Sibyls"'. In *The Illustrated Bartsch*, 24: *Early Italian Masters*. New York: Arabis Books, 159-164.

SELECT INDEX

(Page nos. in bold indicate illustrations)

All illustrations are courtesy of the author unless otherwise credited with permission:

BM:	© Copyright The British Museum
BR,B:	Bibliothéque Royale Albert ler, Brussels
DRO:	Devonshire Record Office
EH:	English Heritage.NMR
GUL	Glasgow University Library, Department of Special Collections
HS:	Historic Scotland
MP-M:	Museum Plantin-Moretus/Stedelijk Prentenkabinet Antwerpen
SNPG:	Scottish National Portrait Gallery
NMS:	Trustees of the National Museums of Scotland
NTS:	The National Trust for Scotland
RCAHMS:	Crown Copyright: Royal Commission for the Ancient and Historical Monuments of Scotland
SP,A:	Stedelijk Prentenkabintet, Antwerpen
V&A:	V&A Picture Library
PR,L:	Prentenkabinet der Rijksuniversiteit, Leiden
SA,L:	Society of Antiquaries, London

We acknowledge David Hamilton and the John Knox House Museum with thanks for permission to photograph the Dean Panels illustrated on pages 184 and 206.